Huebner School Series

FUNDAMENTALS OF INSURANCE PLANNING
Fourth Edition

Kevin M. Lynch
Glenn E. Stevick, Jr.

THE
AMERICAN
COLLEGE PRESS

HS311-4

This publication is designed to provide accurate and authoritative information about the subject covered. While every precaution has been taken in the preparation of this material, the authors, and The American College assume no liability for damages resulting from the use of the information contained in this publication. The American College is not engaged in rendering legal, accounting, or other professional advice. If legal or other expert advice is required, the services of an appropriate professional should be sought.

© 2011 The American College Press
270 S. Bryn Mawr Avenue
Bryn Mawr, PA 19010
(888) AMERCOL (263-7265)
theamericancollege.edu
All rights reserved
Congress Control Number: 2011909344
ISBN 10: 1-58293-056-2
ISSN 13: 978-1-58293-056-5
Printed in the United States of America

Individual Health Insurance Planning
Thomas P. O'Hare and Burton T. Beam, Jr.

Financial Planning: Process and Environment
Craig W. Lemoine

Fundamentals of Insurance Planning
Kevin M. Lynch, and Glenn E. Stevick, Jr.

Fundamentals of Financial Planning
David M. Cordell (ed.)

Fundamentals of Income Taxation
Christopher P. Woehrle and Thomas M. Brinker, Jr. (eds.)

McGill's Life Insurance
Edward E. Graves (ed.)

McGill's Legal Aspects of Life Insurance
Edward E. Graves and Burke A. Christensen (eds.)

Group Benefits: Basic Concepts and Alternatives
Burton T. Beam, Jr.

Planning for Retirement Needs
David A. Littell and Kenn Beam Tacchino

Fundamentals of Investments for Financial Planning
Walt J. Woerheide

Fundamentals of Estate Planning
Constance J. Fontaine

Estate Planning Applications
Ted Kurlowicz

Planning for Business Owners and Professionals
Ted Kurlowicz

Financial Planning Applications
Craig W. Lemoine

Advanced Topics in Group Benefits
Juliana York (ed.)

Executive Compensation
Paul J. Schneider

Health and Long-Term Care Financing for Seniors
Burton T. Beam, Jr., Nancy P. Morith, and Thomas P. O'Hare

Financial Decisions for Retirement
David A. Littell (ed.)

The American College® is an independent, nonprofit, accredited institution founded in 1927 that offers professional certification and graduate-degree distance education to men and women seeking career growth in financial services.

The Center for Financial Advisor Education at The American College offers both the LUTCF and the Financial Services Specialist (FSS) professional designations to introduce students in a classroom environment to the technical side of financial services, while at the same time providing them with the requisite sales-training skills.

The Solomon S. Huebner School® of The American College administers the Chartered Life Underwriter (CLU®); the Chartered Financial Consultant (ChFC®); the Chartered Advisor for Senior Living (CASL®); the Registered Health Underwriter (RHU®); the Registered Employee Benefits Consultant (REBC®); and the Chartered Leadership Fellow® (CLF®) professional designation programs. In addition, the Huebner School also administers The College's CFP Board—registered education program for those individuals interested in pursuing CFP® certification, the CFP® Certification Curriculum.

The Richard D. Irwin Graduate School® of The American College offers the master of science in financial services (MSFS) degree, the Graduate Financial Planning Track (another CFP Board-registered education program), and several graduate-level certificates that concentrate on specific subject areas. It also offers the Chartered Advisor in Philanthropy (CAP®) and the master of science in management (MSM), a one-year program with an emphasis in leadership. The National Association of Estate Planners & Councils has named The College as the provider of the education required to earn its prestigious AEP designation.

The American College is accredited by **The Middle States Commission on Higher Education**, 3624 Market Street, Philadelphia, PA 19104 at telephone number 267.284.5000.

The Middle States Commission on Higher Education is a regional accrediting agency recognized by the U.S. Secretary of Education and the Commission on Recognition of Postsecondary Accreditation. Middle States accreditation is an expression of confidence in an institution's mission and goals, performance, and resources. It attests that in the judgment of the Commission on Higher Education, based on the results of an internal institutional self-study and an evaluation by a team of outside peer observers assigned by the Commission, an institution is guided by well-defined and appropriate goals; that it has established conditions and procedures under which its goals can be realized; that it is accomplishing them substantially; that it is so organized, staffed, and supported that it can be expected to continue to do so; and that it meets the standards of the Middle States Association. The American College has been accredited since 1978.

The American College does not discriminate on the basis of race, religion, sex, handicap, or national and ethnic origin in its admissions policies, educational programs and activities, or employment policies.

The American College is located at 270 S. Bryn Mawr Avenue, Bryn Mawr, PA 19010. The toll-free number of the Office of Professional Education is (888) AMERCOL (263-7265); the fax number is (610) 526-1465; and the home page address is theamericancollege.edu.

CONTENTS

This book is a basic text in insurance. Like most other "fundamentals" or "principles" books, it covers risk and insurance theory as well as current products and practices. Many basic insurance books are written for college students who will become insurance consumers, risk managers, or insurance company employees. We took a different approach and emphasized what we feel a financial services professional must know about insurance in order to serve clients most effectively. Client service can involve either product sales or the analysis and evaluation of existing insurance programs. We set out to cover all the insurance topics a financial planner must master to become a Certified Financial Planner (CFP™) or a Chartered Financial Consultant (ChFC®). We also designed this text to provide a solid foundation for a life insurance professional who will pursue further insurance studies to become a Chartered Life Underwriter (CLU®).

Following introductory chapters on risk, insurance, the insurance business, and basic legal principles and contract analysis, the book describes Social Security, Medicare, and other government programs. For most clients, these social insurance programs and employer-provided benefits form the foundation on which an individual insurance program is built. The foundation topics are followed by an in-depth discussion of life insurance, annuities, medical expense insurance, disability income insurance, long-term care insurance, homeowners insurance, auto insurance, and other property and liability insurance coverages. Both the personal and business needs of clients are addressed.

This book had its beginnings as an American College publication in 2000. That publication was written by Burton T. Beam, Jr., and the late Robert M. Crowe. Portions of it were based on material from *General Insurance,* a textbook by David L. Bickelhaupt, CLU, ChFC, CPCU, ARM, currently professor emeritus of insurance and finance, College of Business, Ohio State University. After four editions, Eric A. Wiening became a coauthor. The title of the book was also changed, and this revision is the fourth edition under the current title, the first edition under the authorship of Lynch and Stevick.

Students in American College courses are provided with a supplement and additional online resources.

In creating this edition, the authors have striven to improve the technical content of the previous edition and bring it up to date. This revision was finalized in 2011, following a period of serious stress in the U.S. economy and a transition in political leadership. These and other environmental factors have the potential to produce substantial changes in insurance regulation, health insurance, or other areas discussed in this edition. Consult The American College's online resources for relevant updates.

The authors wish to thank Virginia Webb, librarian at The American College, and her staff for their support in finding all the information we have requested.

Kevin M. Lynch

Kevin M. Lynch, CFP®, ChFC®, CLU®, RHU®, REBC®, CASL®, CAP®, LUTCF, FSS is assistant professor of insurance at The American College. His primary course responsibilities include being author/editor for FA 200 Techniques for Prospecting, FA 211 Essentials of Disability Income Insurance, FA 255 Essentials of Long Term Care Insurance, and FA 256 Essentials of Annuities. He also teaches courses for The College's Huebner School, including HS 311 Essentials of Insurance Planning, for which he is author/editor.

Before joining The College, Professor Lynch worked in the lending, insurance and financial services industry. First licensed in life insurance in 1981, Professor Lynch has been licensed in property and casualty insurance since 1984. From 1998 through 2004, he built a "scratch" property and casualty agency, as an agency owner with Nationwide Insurance. From October 2004 until October 2005, Professor Lynch served The American College as associate vice-president of advancement. Most recently, Professor Lynch was affiliated with Thrivent Financial for Lutherans, where he served as a financial consultant and regional management associate. In 2010, Professor Lynch was recognized by NAIFA with the National Quality Award (NQA) for his dedication to the insurance industry and his clients.

Professor Lynch has been quoted in a number of industry publications, including *Financial Planning Magazine,* nationally recognized newspapers, including the *Fort Worth Star-Telegram,* and has contributed to online publications including *Insurance News Net, Bank Rate Monitor, Investor's Business Daily* and *Forbes.* In addition, Professor Lynch is the host of *Wealth Today,* a feature presentation of The Wealth Channel. (www.thewealthchannel.com)

Professor Lynch earned a bachelor's degree from The University of the State of New York in Albany, NY, and he holds a master of business administration degree from Central State University in Edmond, OK. He is currently enrolled in Wilmington University, New Castle, DE, completing requirements to earn his doctor of business administration degree.

Glenn E. Stevick, Jr.

Glenn E. Stevick, Jr., LUTCF, CLU, ChFC, is an author/editor and assistant professor of insurance at The American College. His responsibilities at The College include writing and preparing text materials for the LUTCF and FSS programs. He also teaches insurance and financial planning courses at The College.

Mr. Stevick is co-author of *Essentials of Long-Term Care Insurance, Techniques for Exploring Personal Markets, Essentials of Life Insurance Products*, and *Foundations of Financial Planning: The Process*; he is author of *Techniques for Meeting Client Needs, Essentials of Business Insurance, and Essential of Estate Planning*. All of these books are published by The American College. Mr. Stevick also writes articles for *Advisor Today*, the national magazine distributed to members of NAIFA.

Before joining The College, Mr. Stevick worked for New York Life as a training supervisor for 15 years in its South Jersey office. He also served as an agent with New York Life for more than 2 years. Prior to his insurance industry experience, Mr. Stevick taught psychology at the college level and worked in various educational and mental health programs.

Mr. Stevick earned his BA degree from Villanova University and his MA degree from Duquesne University.

Learning Objectives

An understanding of the material in this chapter should enable the student to

1. Define risk, loss, uncertainty, and other risk-related terms.
2. Describe ways to measure and classify risks.
3. Compare insurable and uninsurable risks.
4. Describe how individuals may respond to risk.
5. Explain the costs of pure risks.
6. Explain how insurance can treat pure risks.
7. Describe the benefits and costs of insurance.
8. List and describe the major categories of insurance.
9. Define key terms in insurance terminology.

Financial planning involves several coordinated components:

- insurance planning
- investment planning
- tax planning
- retirement planning
- estate planning

As its name implies, this text, *Fundamentals of Insurance Planning,* deals with the first of these components. Because appropriate insurance planning should precede investment planning and tax planning, the Chartered Life Underwriter (CLU)®, Chartered Financial Consultant (ChFC)®, and Certified Financial Planner (CFP)® programs all recommend an early course that focuses on the subject of insurance.

Both single purpose financial planners who specialize in insurance and comprehensive financial planners recognize that insurance provides an important tool to deal with many of the risks their clients face. In order to discuss risk exposures with their clients, financial planners need to have a sound understanding of risk and related concepts. Accordingly, we begin this book with a review of basic concepts associated with risk and risk management.

RISK AND RELATED TERMS

Risk

risk

possibility

probability

Risk can be defined as the possibility of loss. Note that this definition of risk refers to the possibility, not the probability or chance, of loss. *Possibility* means that something could occur, whether or not the chances of the occurrence can be measured or estimated. Possibility either exists or does not exist; it cannot be measured. *Probability* is the proportion of times that events will occur in the long run. The probability of an occurrence can be expressed numerically as a number between 0 and 1 or as a percentage from 0 to 100 percent. Insurance is concerned primarily with risks that can be measured, at least in a rudimentary fashion.

Risks are everywhere, ranging from unavoidable risks to those assumed by choice. Examples of risks often assumed by choice include crossing the street when the light is red, starting a family, or buying a house. Anyone who owns property faces risks from such perils as fire, windstorm, or theft, as well as the possibility of liability lawsuits from persons who might be injured on the property.

Insurance practitioners often use the word "risk" to describe the object of potential loss or the person or object insured. An applicant for auto insurance may be referred to as a "risk." Likewise, the building to be covered by fire insurance may be referred to as "the risk." A life insurance applicant who belongs to a class with a higher-than-average probability of premature death could be referred to as a "substandard risk." A healthy applicant or an auto insurance policyowner with a good driving record might be a "preferred risk."

Loss

loss

The undesirable end result of risk is *loss*—a decline in value, usually in an unexpected or relatively unpredictable manner. However, losses are not always related to risk. A person giving property to a friend or a relative as a gift no longer owns that property, but this planned and intentional loss is not the result of a risk. Likewise, declines in value are often predictable. Examples include the depreciation of property or the depletion of resources as they are consumed.

loss exposure   A client's cost of risk includes not only the cost of actual losses but also the cost of dealing with losses that might occur. Losses that might occur are often called *loss exposures* and include, for example, financial losses that would arise if a fire or a death were to occur. Because only some loss exposures result in loss, loss exposures are much more numerous than actual losses.

direct loss   Losses may be direct or indirect. *Direct losses* are the first or immediate losses that arise from an event. An
indirect loss   *indirect loss* is a loss that occurs only as a secondary result following the occurrence of a peril. For example, if a client's home is severely damaged by a fire due to defective wiring, the direct loss is the cost to repair the damage to the home. The client and his or her family will also experience an indirect loss if they must incur extra living expenses to stay in a motel and eat meals in restaurants while their home is being repaired. As another example, if a client's child is hospitalized in a specialized medical center several hundred miles from home, the medical expenses would be considered a direct loss for the client. When the client and family incur travel expenses, hotel bills, restaurant bills, and a loss of income in order to visit the hospitalized child, these would be considered an indirect loss.

Indirect loss may result for a client even when there is no direct loss for that client. For example, many residents of lower Manhattan whose apartments escaped direct damage were not permitted to return to them for some period of time following the September 11, 2001, terrorist attack on the World Trade Center.

Uncertainty

uncertainty   Risk and uncertainty are separate but often related concepts. *Uncertainty* is a state of mind, typified by lack of sureness about something. Uncertainty is subjective and experienced differently by each individual, despite the same set of facts, objective reality, or risk. For example, one client may refuse to ride in a glass-enclosed elevator on the outside of a high-rise hotel, while another may be perfectly comfortable doing so. The risk—the possibility of loss in the form of bodily injury—is the same for both clients, but the two clients' uncertainty (doubt, worry, fear) differs greatly.

Uncertainty is often the result of risk. For example, a client may be highly uncertain because of the risk that his or her dependent parent may someday have to be confined to a nursing home for an extended period. On the other hand, uncertainty is also often unrelated to risk. One may be present while the other is absent, and one may be great while the other is small. An ill-mannered client may be oblivious (no uncertainty) to the possibility (a very real risk) that a lewd remark to a colleague will lead to a suit for sexual harassment. Conversely, a timid client may be terrified (highly uncertain) of flying commercially because of the possibility (but low probability) of a crash. Uncertainty is not necessarily bad. An effective financial planner can play a very important role in helping his or her client develop a healthy sense of uncertainty by pointing out risks that the client has not recognized or cannot realistically evaluate. One important function of a financial planner is to achieve some balance between a client's risks and uncertainties. Although irrational phobias are hard to overcome, a planner can do a great deal to address the client's financial risks, thereby reducing the client's uncertainty.

EXAMPLE
A client with an irrational fear of contracting cancer expresses an interest in specified disease insurance. A financial planner can help the client recognize that he or she also faces an exposure to other health risks. The planner can then explain how adequate insurance against all health risks, not only those involving a specific disease, will address the client's uncertainties.

Perils and Hazards

peril

The word "peril" refers to a cause of loss. Perils are commonplace and include unemployment, illness, old age, death, forgery, theft, fire, earthquake, windstorm, flood, and hundreds of other causes of loss.

hazard

A *hazard* is an act or condition that increases the likelihood of the occurrence of a loss and/or increases the severity of a loss if a peril does occur. Ordinarily, any particular person or object is exposed to many separate hazards. Hazards fall into three major categories:

- physical hazards

- moral hazards
- attitudinal hazards

Physical Hazards

physical hazards   The first category of hazards is *physical hazards*. These are physical conditions relating to location, structure, occupancy, exposure, and the like. Insurance underwriting requires an evaluation of all physical hazards. The following are a few examples of physical hazards: high blood pressure, a dangerous hobby, newspapers piled on a staircase, gasoline stored on the premises, weak construction that may fail in a heavy wind, unsafe brakes on a car, holes in a sidewalk, and improper water drainage systems. Each of these conditions—as well as many others—increases the chance of a loss occurring or the magnitude of the loss if one does occur, in regard to a specific peril, such as illness, accident, fire, windstorm, or theft.

Moral Hazards

moral hazards   The second category of hazards consists of *moral hazards*. These are dishonest tendencies, often due to an insured's weakened financial condition, that are likely to increase loss frequency and/or severity. Examples include tendencies to cause deliberate damage in order to collect insurance proceeds or to intentionally inflate claims for insurance proceeds beyond the actual size of the sustained loss. A recent example of moral hazard involves the subprime mortgage crisis. When the monthly payments under adjustable mortgages adjusted upward, thousands of homeowners faced increased mortgage payments they could no longer afford. Combined with falling home values, many overextended homeowners found themselves in a difficult financial situation. Because of the moral hazard created by these conditions, insurance companies expected an increase in arsons by homeowners seeking to avoid a foreclosure.

Recognizing moral hazard requires studying the client's character and reputation. Evidence that an applicant ever defrauded another person, has a bankruptcy record, or has a poor credit reputation can indicate possible moral hazard with regard to insurance. Investigators also scrutinize insurance applicants' reputations in trade, their ratings with banks, their standings with competitors, and the regard in which they are held by those with whom they transact business. Individuals who have a reputation for taking unfair advantage of legal technicalities or people who have repudiated contracts in the face of possible financial loss are generally regarded as likely to resort to other unethical actions.

Financial planners need to understand the concept of moral hazard, a technical term well understood and often used among insurance professionals. This technical term is best avoided, however, when dealing with clients who understand "moral" in a different sense. A client whose financial condition is questionable is not likely to welcome any implication that someone is questioning his or her morality.

Attitudinal Hazards

attitudinal hazards

The third category of hazards consists of *attitudinal hazards*, evidenced by carelessness or indifference as to whether a loss occurs or the size of a loss if it does occur. For example, laziness, disorderliness, poor dental hygiene, and lack of concern for others are termed attitudinal hazards rather than moral hazards, which are more likely to involve dishonesty. Leaving car doors unlocked increases auto thefts, and heavy smoking increases health risks. Underwriting and rating of applicants based on apparent attitudinal hazards are important to the successful operation of the insurance mechanism, as is consideration of physical and moral hazards.

EXAMPLE

A client, Mr. Rich, is purchasing a large yacht. Mr. Rich faces loss exposures because various perils could damage or destroy the yacht or result in a liability claim as a result of the yacht's use. Mr. Rich therefore applies for yacht insurance. In evaluating Mr. Rich's application, the insurer will assess the physical, moral, and attitudinal hazards associated with this particular yacht. For example, the insurance underwriter will consider the yacht's age and condition (physical hazard), any indications of negligence in the care of the boat (attitudinal hazard), and Mr. Rich's financial stability or lack of stability (moral hazard). Financial stability is relevant because a policyowner who finds himself or herself in financial difficulty might be tempted to sink the boat and file an insurance claim to raise cash. Financial instability might result from high-stakes gambling or other questionable practices, or it might involve speculative and risky business ventures.

MEASUREMENT OF RISKS

In some cases, the probability of a loss can be measured, often precisely. In these cases, we can refer to the chance of loss, or the probability of loss, rather than merely to the possibility of loss. For example, if you enter a wager that, on the first draw from a fair deck of playing cards, you will not draw the ace of clubs, you know that the probability or chance of loss is 1 in 52.

In other cases, it is not possible to measure the probability of a loss. This is particularly true of unique or highly unusual risks. Consider the case of a healthy 42-year-old male client. Is it possible that he will die this year? Of course. Can we measure the probability in any meaningful way? No. Although we may learn from statistical studies that the probability of death within 1 year for a 42-year-old male is, say, 1.8 in 1,000, that is no help in measuring this particular client's likelihood of dying this year. He is one person, not a group of statistical persons. Either he will die or he won't die in the coming year, but statistical probabilities cannot be meaningfully applied in this case.

In what ways can some risks be measured? Basically, there are two ways: through deductive reasoning, sometimes called a priori reasoning, and through inductive reasoning, which is reasoning based on statistical analysis.

Measurement of Risks

- Deductive (a priori) reasoning: With a priori reasoning, risk is measured by physical examination before any losses occur.
- Inductive reasoning: With inductive reasoning, risk is measured by statistical analysis of past loss experience.

In the deductive reasoning approach to risk measurement, we can physically examine in advance all the possible outcomes associated with a risk and calculate the chance of loss. For example, we can examine a fresh and shuffled deck of playing cards and note that it contains fifty-two different cards, of which only one is the ace of clubs. We can thus deduce that, in the absence of cheating, the probability of selecting the ace of clubs on the first draw from the deck is 1 in 52. Similarly, we can measure the odds of heads being the result in a coin flip, the odds of rolling a seven with a pair of dice, or the odds of losing in Russian roulette.

It is important to remember that, in a small number of trials, the actual results may differ from the underlying probability. For example, ten flips of a coin may produce seven heads and three tails. As the number of trials increases, however, the actual results will gradually come closer to the underlying 50–50 probability.

In the insurance business, the probabilities of loss cannot be derived *a priori*, or deductively. For example, it would be fallacious to conclude that because a 42-year-old male client will either die or not die in the coming year, the probability of his death is 50 percent. Insurers measure risk through inductive reasoning based on statistical analysis. To illustrate, assume that an insurance company observes the loss experience on 10,000 single-family brick homes in a particular city for 1 year. Assume that 9 of these homes experience a fire during that period. The insurer could then conclude, at least tentatively, that the probability of fire loss for single-family brick homes in that city during a 1-year period is 9 per 10,000, or .9 per 1,000 homes. The insurer could then develop a premium for fire insurance based on, among other things, that probability of loss.[1]

Law of Large Numbers

law of large numbers

The statistical analysis that insurers use is based on the *law of large numbers,* which simply states that as the size of the sample or insured population (such as houses exposed to fire loss) increases, the actual loss experience will more closely approximate the true underlying loss probability. To function effectively, the law of large numbers requires mass, homogeneity, and independence among exposure units.

Mass

mass

As its name suggests, the law of large numbers requires a large sample size (mass). The statistical group that is observed for purposes of measuring the probability must have *mass*—that is, the sample must be large enough to allow the true underlying probability to emerge. This means not only that the insurer's statistical group must be large enough to produce reliable results, but also that the group actually insured must be large enough to produce results that are consistent with the underlying probability.

---

1. Among the other factors on which the premium would be based are the average size of the losses experienced, a margin for contingencies, a loading to cover the insurer's expenses, a margin for profit or addition to the insurer's surplus, and perhaps the investment earnings the insurer could realize from the time the premiums are collected until the losses must be paid.

Homogeneity

homogeneity   The statistical group that is observed for purposes of
                measuring loss probability must have *homogeneity*—that
is, it must include exposure units that have similar characteristics
(homogeneity) in order for the true underlying probability to emerge. Note
that the probability of .9 fire losses per 1,000 homes referred to earlier
emerged from a fairly homogeneous group of exposure units: single-family
brick homes in a particular city. A different probability would have emerged if
apartment buildings, motels, frame-constructed homes, and homes in rural
locations had been included.

The characteristics of the homogeneous group actually insured must be
similar to those of the homogeneous statistical group used in projecting loss
probability. Otherwise, actual loss experience may depart substantially from
expected experience. To take an extreme case, the loss probability derived
from a statistical study of single-family brick homes in a particular city is
unlikely to be the same as the loss probability for a homogeneous group of
oil refineries in Texas.

Independence

independence   For loss projections to be accurate, the insured
                exposure units must be independently exposed to loss.
Independence means, in this case, that the occurrence of a loss to one
exposure unit should not affect the likelihood of loss to another exposure
unit. In other words, there should be no correlation among exposure units
(independence). Statistical inference is based on the assumption that the
various possible outcomes occur more or less at random. To illustrate, each
home in a given geographic area faces an independent exposure to lightning.
Lightning strikes are essentially random, and the possibility of a lightning
strike to one home during a given time period is therefore independent of the
possibility that lightning will strike another home. Floods, on the other hand,
can cause widespread damage to all homes in a given area. Even if there
are a large number of similar homes in a flood-prone area, the houses are
not independently exposed to flood losses.

CLASSIFICATIONS OF RISKS

Risks can be classified in several ways. At least five of these classifications are all-inclusive and overlapping in the sense that any single risk fits into all five classifications. These classifications are as follows:

- financial versus nonfinancial
- particular versus fundamental
- static versus dynamic
- pure versus speculative
- insurable versus uninsurable

Financial versus Nonfinancial Risks

financial risk

nonfinancial risks

Risks can be *financial risks* in the sense that they involve a loss of money, or they can be nonfinancial risks. Clearly, the possibility that a client may be faced with mountainous medical bills and lost earnings following a severe stroke is a financial risk. Various *nonfinancial risks* also involve losses associated with a severe stroke: pain and suffering, paralysis, and loss of memory for the stroke victim; loss of consortium for the victim and his or her spouse; worry and distress on the part of the stroke victim's loved ones; and so on.

Insurance is primarily designed to treat financial risks through the payment of money as compensation in some way for monetary loss. However, insurance also frequently "compensates" for nonmonetary loss. For example, liability insurance often provides the funds to pay damages to individuals who have endured pain and suffering, emotional distress, or some other nonmonetary loss because of a policyowner's negligence. Although the insurer's payment provides compensation for a nonfinancial loss, the possibility of such a liability claim against a client involves a financial risk the client faces.

Particular versus Fundamental Risks

particular risks

Risks can also be classified as particular or fundamental. *Particular risks* are loss possibilities that affect only individuals or small groups of individuals at the same time, rather than a large segment of society. Losses from such events as embezzlement, lightning, disability, and retirement are examples that result from particular risks.

fundamental risks

Fundamental risks, in contrast, are loss possibilities that can affect large segments of a society at the same time. Examples include possibilities of widespread unemployment in an economic downturn, lost purchasing power due to runaway inflation, massive destruction due to a nuclear accident, or massive deaths as a result of a pandemic, such as avian flu.

Dealing with particular risks is generally thought to be the responsibility of the individuals who are exposed to them. Some social insurance programs, however, also deal with particular risks. Fundamental risks, on the other hand, are not directly related to any specific individual; dealing with them is generally thought to be the responsibility of society as a whole through government action.

Static versus Dynamic Risks

static risk

Static risk exist apart from changes in society or the economy and include such risks as death or fire damage to a client's home.

dynamic risk

Dynamic risks are possibilities of loss resulting directly from changes in society or in the economy. Changes in consumer tastes can cause losses to some businesses. For example, the low-carbohydrate diet fad caused a noteworthy drop in income for some business firms that produce high-carbohydrate food. Changes in technology cause losses to other businesses that fail to adapt as their technology becomes obsolete. In recent years, for example, traditional film-based photography has given way to digital photography for most purposes. These changes also affect the risks of individual clients. Dietary changes, for example, affect individuals' health, and changes in photographic equipment create changes in the types of equipment various clients own and insure. Although they tend to be unpredictable, dynamic risks often involve scientific advances that improve our society. Static risks generally do not benefit society over the long run. However, because static risks are usually fairly predictable, insurance can readily treat many of them.

Pure versus Speculative Risks

Risks can be pure or speculative. Pure risks involve only the chance of loss or no loss, whereas speculative risks involve the chance of loss, no loss/no gain, or gain.

pure risk

speculative risk

Pure risks are "pure" in the sense that they do not mix both profits and losses. Insurance is concerned mainly with the economic problems created by pure risks. Risk aversion applies to pure risks, in which the prospect of loss only is the cause of concern. The ownership of property involves a pure risk. In regard to a peril such as a windstorm, the owner may either suffer a loss or not suffer a loss. There cannot be a gain from having the loss as long as it is assumed that an insurance payment is not for more than the actual loss. On the other hand, risk seeking—for example, by businesspersons whose purpose is the realization of gain if the business venture is successful—applies to speculative risks. *Speculative risks* involve three possible outcomes: loss, no loss/no gain, and gain.

Pure vs. Speculative Risks

- Pure—possibility of loss or no loss
- Speculative—possibility of loss, no loss/no gain, or gain

Many activities involve both pure risks and speculative risks. For example, a client who purchases a house faces pure risks because a fire or other peril could damage the house, reducing its value. The client also faces speculative risks, because the market value of the house might either increase or decrease depending on the general real estate market or other local factors. Most of the pure risks can be insured, but the speculative risks are not insurable.

gambling

Gambling is deliberately creating a speculative risk by betting on an uncertain outcome. Gambling shares many of the attributes of insurance. Perhaps this is the reason so many uninformed persons think of insurance as gambling and sometimes even feel that they have "lost the bet" if they fail to have a loss equal to the cost of insurance. The methods of operation may appear similar, but insurance is concerned with an existing risk. Insurance does not create risk; it transfers and reduces a risk that already exists. Contrast this to a bet: No risk exists before the bet is made, but one is created at the time of the gambling transaction, thereby putting values in jeopardy that were not in jeopardy before the bet.

Personal, Property, and Liability Risks

personal risk

The pure risks confronting individuals and businesses are ordinarily divided into three categories. The first of these categories of risks is ordinarily termed *personal risks*. Personal risks are concerned with death, injury, illness, old age, and unemployment.

property risk   The second category of risks arises from the destruction or loss of property and is referred to as *property risks*. For example, one of the property risks Tom faces is the possibility that his own auto might be damaged in an auto accident. Direct losses from fire, lightning, windstorm, flood, and other forces of nature, and from man-made perils like vandalism, theft, collision, and terrorism offer a constant threat of loss to real estate, as well as to all kinds of personal property. Indirect losses also may occur as a result of property risks, including the loss of profits, rents, or favorable leases.

liability risk   Finally, *liability risks* involve the operation of the law of liability. An individual may become legally liable for injury to another person or damage to another party's property. For example, one of the liability risks Tom faces is the possibility that Tom's negligent driving might cause an auto accident in which another driver is injured or somebody else's vehicle is damaged. The damage to Tom's own auto is a first-party property loss, but his legal responsibility for damage to the other driver's vehicle is a third-party liability loss. Liability risks are termed third-party risks because, when insurance is used to shift the burden of responsibility, the insurer and the policyowner have agreed that a third party, the injured person, will be paid for injuries for which an insured is legally liable.[2] The liability risk includes the potential for causing bodily injury as well as various other types of risks. For example, an employer faces the liability risk of claims by employees alleging that the employer committed certain errors or omissions in administering an employee benefit plan.

Personal, property, and liability risks are sometimes collectively referred to as hazard risks. This term is then used to distinguish hazard risks from investment risks and other speculative risks.

Insurable versus Uninsurable Risks

insurable risk   An *insurable risk* has certain characteristics that can effectively be addressed with private insurance—that

---

2.   If the first party is the insured policyowner and the third party is the claimant, readers might be wondering, "Who is the second party?" The second party to the insurance contract is the insurer. However, the term "second party" is rarely used in practice.

is, insurance from privately owned insurance companies. Government insurance programs and other forms of social insurance do not necessarily meet the same criteria. Insurable risks are usually financial, particular, static, and pure risks involving losses that meet these five requirements:

- The amount of the loss must be important.
- The loss must be of an accidental nature.
- Future losses must be calculable.
- The loss must be definite.
- The loss cannot be excessively catastrophic.

Many insured risks do not meet each of the requirements perfectly, but when considered as a whole, they must meet the requisites to the satisfaction of an insurer.

Importance

Insurance functions most efficiently and effectively to treat substantial risks for which the major component in the insurer's premium is expected claims rather than the insurer's administrative expenses. An insurer's expense of selling and administering insurance for small claims is too high to make insurance efficient for small claims. Risks that involve a threat of no great consequence are best handled by other means.

For example, a client's favorite pen might be lost or eyeglasses broken. These are loss exposures. But the financial, particular, static, and pure risks they involve are not significant enough to warrant the use of insurance. The client can treat these losses as current expenses, to be paid out of pocket.

Some commonly insured losses violate the principle that insurance should be used for important losses. For example, many auto insurance policies cover towing costs for nominal amounts such as $25. This practice apparently developed years ago because a benefit offered by the American Automobile Association or other auto clubs prompted a demand for a similar benefit from auto insurers. Similarly, group health insurance often covers relatively minor medical expenses, partly because the costs are subsidized by the client's employer. The financial planning process often involves identifying unimportant insurance coverages that might represent an inefficient use of the client's financial resources.

Accidental Nature

Insurable risks normally must be of an accidental nature. Insurance is intended to cover fortuitous or unexpected losses. The loss need be accidental only from the insured's standpoint. The loss could, for example, be intentionally caused by someone else, such as a thief or a vandal. Intentional losses caused by the insured are usually uninsurable because the insurer cannot reasonably predict them, and payment for them would violate public policy by encouraging such actions as fraud or arson. Other losses are so common as to be expected rather than unexpected. Wear and tear and physical depreciation are examples of expected losses that normally are not insurable.

Calculability

A third requisite of an insurable risk is that the probability, size, and variability of future losses should be reasonably calculable. Losses may be unpredictable for any one individual, but an insurer should be able to obtain reasonable projections of future losses if it covers a sufficiently large number of homogeneous (similar) loss exposures.

Insurers occasionally cover isolated loss exposures for which there is no previous experience. For example, aviation insurers must provide insurance that will keep pace with the rapid advances in the industry. The advent of space travel created a need for large amounts of insurance in a field where statistical data once were entirely lacking. Most insurance is written, however, to cover risks where losses may reasonably be expected and where mathematical treatment or judgment based on experience permits a sufficiently exact estimate of losses to project the aggregate probable cost. When experience extends over a period of years, the number of exposure units is great enough, and underlying conditions have not changed, a premium can be computed that will reasonably ensure a sum sufficient to pay losses, compensate the insurer, and provide stability and permanence in the business. When new insurance forms are instituted, it becomes necessary to make rates that depend on underwriting judgment. In some instances, this is nothing more than an approximation or guess that is adjusted with the accumulation of experience. A good example is long-term care insurance, a relatively new product that began to appear in the early 1980s. Insurance rates were initially based on underwriters' judgment, but rates have been refined over the years as premium and loss experience accumulates.

The need for large numbers applies not only to the total business an insurer accepts but also to each class of business. In addition, the exposures must be independent of one another so that reasonable estimates of loss can be made.

Definiteness of Loss

Losses should be definite; otherwise estimates of possible loss are difficult. Many insurance contract provisions have the objective of making the determination and measurement of insured losses as clear and definite as possible. The contract must clarify the perils as well as the losses. Whether or not the loss actually occurred and, if so, when, where, and why it occurred, as well as how many dollars of loss are involved, all usually must be discernible. A loss due to lightning meets the definiteness criterion rather well, whereas a loss due to sickness may not meet it as well.

EXAMPLE
Ted is a salesman of beachfront homes in Florida. His income is entirely in the form of commissions, almost all of which he earns during the spring and fall months. In December, Ted becomes ill with a case of the flu and is unable to work for 7 weeks. Ted's loss is not very definite. Was he really ill or just taking a vacation from work? When did the illness begin and end; was he really laid up for the full 7 weeks? How much income would he have earned during the period of his illness?

No Excessively Catastrophic Loss

Ordinarily, no excessive catastrophic possibility of loss should be associated with an insurable risk. A single large loss or the simultaneous occurrence of many smaller ones could destroy an insurer's financial stability. A geographic concentration of many small loss possibilities, such as insuring most of the houses in the same small town, can be potentially catastrophic for an insurer. The size of loss deemed catastrophic depends on the financial resources available to the insurer.

Summary

The requirements for an insurable risk are not absolute. Insurability is best described as a relative matter in which the insurable quality of the risk is determined by evaluating all the requirements together. The size and ability of the insurer are also important. Many common kinds of insurance do not meet each of the requirements perfectly. Consider, for example, the following: Is a theft loss definite (that is, was the item really stolen or just lost)? Are all drivers similar in regard to the risk of auto accidents? Obviously not, although they may be relatively similar within age, type of car, and other classifications. Is a fire caused by carelessness always accidental? Aren't windstorms, such as hurricanes and tornadoes, catastrophic in nature?

Careful analysis in applying each of the requirements for an insurable risk to a particular peril shows that few, if any, are perfect insurable risks. Most are only relatively good ones, and some are fine examples of bad ones. Many insurance contract and insurer underwriting restrictions deal with this problem, trying to improve the insurability of a risk by such methods as limitations on the amount of coverage and locations, prohibited types of activities, specific contract definitions, deductibles, and reinsurance. What is insurable may change over time and with the use of such limitations. Long-term care, for example, was considered uninsurable for many years, but the costs of long-term care are now commonly insured.

EXAMPLE

Shem is a client who owns a vacation home on the lakeshore. In addition to such perils as fire and vandalism, Shem is concerned about the possibility of flood damage to this property. Is flood damage to a lakeshore home an insurable risk? Consider the criteria:

- Unless Shem's vacation home is a shack, the amount of the loss appears to be important.

- Unless the water level in Shem's lake is controlled by a dam, a flood loss would almost always be of an accidental nature.

- Unless conditions have changed, the frequency of flood losses on Shem's lake can probably be calculated based on historical records and a flood map available from the Federal Emergency Management Agency (FEMA) (see www.fema.gov). Unless Shem's land washes away or is permanently buried under rising water, the value of any flood loss should readily be calculable.

- Any flood loss will be definite. Nobody is likely to question whether a flood has occurred.

- The loss might, however, be excessively catastrophic from the viewpoint of any private insurer. A localized flood will probably affect many homes on the same lake. A widespread flood will result in losses not only at Shem's lake but also throughout the region.

Flood damage to real property meets most of the requirements to qualify as an insurable risk. However, the catastrophic loss potential is so great that private insurers are generally not willing to bear the risks associated with flood insurance. A government insurance program enables private insurers to offer this coverage.

DIFFERENT REACTIONS TO RISK

Risk may result in substantial losses, worry, and inefficiency. It can also lead to great reward and satisfaction.

Linus, in the famous *Peanuts* comic strip, enters the risky world reluctantly. He drags his security blanket around continually in order to have the comfort of familiarity to buffer the unknown. His friend Charlie Brown deals with unpredictable risk as he attempts to kick off the new football season, because he never knows whether Lucy will pull the ball away from him. This example illustrates the undesirable features of risk: unpredictability or not knowing, insecurity, and some resulting discomfort.

Risk is desirable to those who believe "nothing ventured, nothing gained." Entrepreneurs invest time, effort, and money for the uncertain profits that may result. Businesspersons conduct their operations with the hope of profit and the threat of loss in mind. The skydiver, the astronaut, and the drag racer also are risk takers. Sir Walter Scott valued risk taking, too, when he said, "One hour of life . . . filled with noble risks is worth whole years of paltry decorum."[3]

risk-tolerance
level

Each person's reaction to risks depends on his or her *risk-tolerance level*. A person's risk-tolerance level is the degree to which that individual is attracted to or averse to the possibility of loss. Risk tolerance clearly differs widely from person to person, situation to situation, and risk to risk. Although it is extremely difficult to measure risk tolerance accurately, it is also extremely important that a financial planner recognize each client's risk-tolerance level in order to tailor a financial plan that includes appropriate levels of risk.

In investment planning, much is made of the relationship between a client's risk tolerance and various types of investments. Higher risk investments are accompanied with the potential for higher returns, but many clients are not willing to accept a high level of risk in their investment portfolios. Risk tolerance also plays an important role in insurance planning. For example, a

---

3.   Sir Walter Scott, *Count Robert of Paris*, chapter 25.

client's risk tolerance plays an important role in deciding between fixed and variable life insurance and annuity products. Risk tolerance is also relevant when deciding whether to purchase some types of insurance or to "go bare" and face the possibility of an uninsured loss. Even when coverage is offered, many people make a conscious decision to forgo the purchase of disability income insurance or flood insurance. When various types of insurance are purchased, risk tolerance also plays a role in deciding whether to accept a higher deductible or a longer waiting period in exchange for a reduced premium.

Behavioral psychologists who examine individuals' risk tolerance have reached the following conclusions:

- Most people are more risk averse than they are risk tolerant.
- Risk taking in physical or social activities (for example, race car driving or marital infidelity) is not correlated with financial risk taking.
- The way in which questions about a risk are worded or posed to a person can influence the person's expressed attitude toward that risk.
- Emotions can severely limit a person's ability to make rational decisions about a risk.
- People tend to overestimate low-probability risks (for example, the risk of having one's child kidnapped) and to underestimate higher-probability risks (for example, disability).
- People are more likely to be risk averse if the major effect of a possible loss will fall on them or their loved ones, rather than mainly on strangers.
- Most people have a greater fear about risks with which they are inexperienced (for example, skydiving) than about risks with which they are experienced (for example, driving on an interstate highway).

COSTS OF PURE RISKS

Because pure risks produce either losses or no losses, they represent potential costs with few or no offsetting benefits. The costs of pure risks include not only actual losses that occur and associated expenses, but also worry and fear, less-than-optimal use of resources, and the expense of managing risks.

Costs of Pure Risks
• Actual losses that occur • Worry and fear about possible losses • Less-than-optimal use of resources • Costs of managing the risks

Actual Losses

Actual losses may be serious, crippling a business or causing an individual or family great financial hardship. Direct physical loss, such as fire damage, causes several billion dollars of property loss each year in the United States. The cost of indirect loss, such as lost profits following a direct loss, is also considerable. Billions of dollars are lost, too, because of the loss of human life values due to such perils as death and disability. It is no wonder that most people prefer to do something about pure risks rather than merely accept them.

Fear and Worry

Fear and worry are costly. Valuable time is spent thinking about real or imagined chances of loss. The opportunity cost of worry, time, and effort is probably staggering when we consider the many other things that we could do if there were no fear of loss. "If only we could work as hard as we worry" expresses the cost of lost peace of mind.

Less-than-Optimal Use of Resources

Pure risk leads to a less-than-optimal use of resources, the third factor that contributes to the cost of pure risks. Most people do not predict the chance of loss correctly. Some are pessimistic and overestimate; others are optimistic and underestimate. The result is either wasteful preparation for losses that are not as likely as expected or lack of preparation for unexpected losses that may have serious financial consequences.

Investments are frequently influenced by the exposures to loss with which they are associated. Sometimes activities or investments are completely avoided because the exposure to loss is high in spite of excellent earnings potential. Too much money "put away for a rainy day" may be in very safe liquid investments to be readily available if some loss occurs. Without such risk and uncertainty, the money could be invested in a much more productive capacity with potential for greater return. Returns in relation to true loss exposures are often less than optimal, and these reduced earnings are an additional cost of risk.

Because of loss exposures, there is also a tendency to concentrate planning on the near future, thereby missing out on the significant benefits of long-range planning. The cost of risk increases to the extent that exposures to loss cause this error in planning.

Cost of Managing Risks

The fourth type of cost that society experiences because of the presence of pure risks is the cost of managing pure risks. There are numerous ways to treat pure risks. For example, a sprinkler system can be installed in a factory to minimize the size of a loss if a fire occurs. An alarm system can be installed in a jewelry store to reduce the likelihood of a burglary loss. An annual mammogram or PSA test can help in the early detection of cancer. Insurance can be purchased to cover the possible legal liability for negligently driving an auto. However, all of these ways cost money, and these expenditures thus represent an added burden for society directly resulting from the presence of pure risks.

RISK EXAMPLE

Don and Andrea Green, a married couple in their early 30s, own a small home in a suburban community that borders on a large lake. They park their two cars in the driveway when they are not at work. Don, who has a masters degree, works as a bank loan officer. Andrea, who has a high school diploma, works as a supervisor in a local pet shop. The Greens have no children yet, but they have two dogs and many other pets. Both Don and Andrea are covered by the group medical expense plan available through Don's employer. Andrea has no employee benefits other than a 1-week annual vacation.

Risk is the possibility of *loss*. Don and Andrea face many risks. To name just three of them, their home could be damaged by the *peril* of flood, resulting in a loss of value of this asset; one of the dogs could bite a neighbor's child, resulting in a liability lawsuit against the Greens; and Don could lose his job, resulting in a loss of income. They address the *uncertainty* associated with these risks, at least in part, by purchasing homeowners insurance that provides both property coverage and liability coverage, purchasing flood insurance, and establishing a small emergency fund. For Don and Andrea, the insurance and the emergency fund are some of the *costs of risk*—costs they must incur because of the risks they face.

The *physical hazards* Don and Andrea face include the potential of flood damage because they live near a lake, plus any conditions that might cause one of their dogs to leave the yard and attack a child, such as a defective fence or leash. Because they are careful with the dogs, the situation does not present an *attitudinal hazard* that would be of special concern to an underwriter, and the Greens' sound financial and personal situation does not suggest a *moral hazard.*

Death and sickness rates can be computed for people their age, but general statistics do little good in evaluating the likelihood that either Don or Andrea will die or face a serious health problem in the coming year. The *law of large numbers* simply does not apply to only two people. This is true even though Andrea has a minor heart condition that puts her in a slightly higher-than-average risk category that might cause an insurer, applying the law of large numbers to its entire insured population, to charge a higher premium for any individual life or health insurance she might purchase.

Don and Andrea face *financial risks*, including the possibility of medical bills and a loss of income resulting from disability. They also face *nonfinancial risks*, such as the pain and suffering that could result from an auto accident.

The possibility that Don, the primary breadwinner, could lose his job because the bank that employs him is acquired by another bank presents a *particular risk*. The possibility that the bank could reduce its workforce due to a general decline in the overall economy presents a *fundamental risk.*

The risk that fire might damage their big-screen TV is a *static risk*. The risk that the TV becomes worthless because new home theater technology makes it obsolete presents a *dynamic risk*. In any case, the TV presents a *pure risk* rather than a *speculative risk*; the TV might lose value if it is damaged or becomes obsolete, or its value might hold fairly constant, subject only to depreciation. (It is not likely the TV will increase in value.)

Don and Andrea's *personal risks* include the risks of unemployment, injury, illness, disability, and death. Their *property risks* include the risks of damage to their home, cars, big-screen TV, or pets. Their *liability risks* include not only the possibility of a dog-bite claim against them, but also the possibility of an auto accident or other incident that might result in a claim for damages.

Insurance can address many of Don and Andrea's risks. Auto liability risks, for example, can be insured because the amount of a potential loss is important, any insured loss would be accidental, future losses are calculable, any loss would be definite, and the loss is not excessively catastrophic.

INSURANCE AS A TECHNIQUE TO TREAT PURE RISKS

In this section, we will examine insurance as a means of treating pure risks. For now, we will consider only what insurance is, the benefits and costs it creates for society, and the major categories of insurance.

What Insurance Is

Insurance, like risk, is difficult to define succinctly, and different definitions are used when insurance is examined from different viewpoints. For example, insurance may be viewed as

- an economic system that reduces financial risks through a transfer and combination (pooling) of losses
- a binding legal contract that transfers risks to an insurer
- a contract that meets specific legal or regulatory definitions
- a business institution that provides many jobs in a free enterprise economy
- a social device through which the losses of few are paid by many
- an actuarial system of applied mathematics
- a risk management technique for financing insurable risks

Defined As an Economic System

insurance   *Insurance* has been defined as an economic system that reduces financial risks when policyowners transfer their risk to an insurer that combines their potential losses. This is not the only definition in use, and it is far from perfect. For example, insurers sometimes cover unique situations that do not combine the losses of similar policyowners. And various loss-financing techniques, such as pooling (various parties agree to share their losses), can combine potential losses without transferring them to an insurer.

The insurance system responds to the economic law of supply and demand. Ideally, insurance increases value for the insured by reducing the insured's cost of risk while, at the same time, enabling the insurer to earn a profit. This win-win situation occurs when the cost of insurance is both low enough to appeal to insurance buyers and high enough to produce a profit for the insurer.

Defined As a Legal Contract

An insurance policy, also known as a contract, is a legal document used to transfer financial risk for a premium (price) from one party, known as the *insured* or the *policyowner*, to another party, known as the *insurer*. Through a legally binding contract, the possibility of an unknown large financial loss is exchanged for the certainty of a comparatively small premium payment. The insurance contract does not guarantee losses will not occur, but it provides a method of insuring repayment, or indemnity, if any loss occurs that is within the scope of the contract.

Legal or Regulatory Definitions

Because many types of regulation and taxation apply specifically to insurance, it is often critical to determine whether a given plan or contract qualifies as insurance under the relevant definition. Various state and federal laws and regulations define insurance for regulatory purposes, and the definitions are not necessarily concise or consistent. The National Association of Insurance Commissioners, for example, has drafted a 12-page definition of insurance.[4] Readers might be grateful that we will not attempt to summarize it here.

Insurance is not defined in the Internal Revenue Code, but court cases indicate that two elements must be present for a loss-financing arrangement to qualify as insurance for tax purposes:

- the transfer of risk to an entity that qualifies, for tax purposes, as an insurance company
- the pooling of a number of separate risks[5]

Situations in which a legal or regulatory definition of insurance can be critical include the following:

- Product warranties on new homes, autos, tires, and appliances are sometimes referred to as insurance, but they are not generally

---

4. National Association of Insurance Commissioners, *Definition of Insurance* (draft), Kansas City: NAIC, August 4, 2000.

5. Friedman, Lawrence M., and Hirsh, Bobbe, "Client Alert: What Is Insurance For The Taxman?" Chicago: Lord, Bissell & Brook, July 13, 2005 (www.lordbissell.com).

recognized by law as insurance. The companies that offer these products need not therefore organize an insurance company, hold reserves, or pay state insurance premium taxes.

- Variable annuity contracts, which are not defined by the courts as exclusively insurance contracts, are subject to state insurance laws and also to the federal regulation of the Securities and Exchange Commission.
- Employee benefit plans, including hospital and medical benefit plans, have been subject to many legal decisions that affect their status as insurance contracts.
- Tax planning may include determining whether premiums that are paid qualify as a tax-deductible business expense.

Business Institution

Insurance companies are financial institutions—often very large financial institutions—that specialize in the treatment of risks. As a business, an insurance company performs various functions that include marketing, underwriting, and claims.

Social Device

Insurance has also been defined as a social device by which the risks of many individuals are transferred to a group of persons who, in effect, agree to pool their losses. All members of the group contribute to a common fund, administered by an insurer, and payments are made from this fund to those who have a loss. Contributions to a fund are not essential. Groups may rely instead on assessments collected from the various participants after each loss.

Actuarial System

In a mathematical sense, insurance merely applies certain actuarial principles, such as laws of probability and statistical techniques, to achieve predictable results.

Risk Management Technique

Insurance can be viewed as one of many techniques used to manage risks. Specifically, insurance can be viewed as a risk-financing technique that transfers the financial consequences of covered losses to an insurance company. Losses can be transferred to other individuals or organizations, but unless an insurance company is involved, the technique does not qualify as insurance.

Benefits and Costs of Insurance

In a society without insurance, would banks lend money on homes or businesses if they were uncertain as to whether the collateral value could be lost due to fire, windstorm, or other perils? Would finance companies approve installment loans for autos or other household goods? Would anyone want to drive an auto if liability for losses caused to others could not be insured? Would anyone want to own a home that could be destroyed in a few hours without any way to recover the loss? Would workers choose hazardous but important occupations if they were uncertain whether employers would pay for work-related injuries? How would a young family man or woman ensure an income for dependent children without life insurance? How would a person provide for payment of large medical bills? Insurance provides protection regarded as essential throughout the economic and business environment.

Clearly, insurance provides many benefits. But these benefits are not cost free.

Benefits of Insurance

The most obvious benefit of insurance is that it pays claims when losses occur. Additional benefits, some of them more subtle, include that insurance

- encourages peace of mind
- provides a basis for credit
- stimulates saving
- provides investment capital
- offers advantages of specialization
- fosters loss prevention

We will briefly examine each of these benefits.

Pays Claims. Insurance supplies the financial resources that often permit a family or an organization to continue despite serious losses. The death or disability of a breadwinner can bring financial disaster to a family. With family income stopped, the spouse and/or children might have to give up their home and accept an undesirable alternative, such as a foster home, living with relatives, or relief payments. A fire or a liability suit can wipe out a family's assets. These perils can be met through insurance, which provides indemnification or repayment at the time of need in order to keep a family or business intact.

Encourages Peace of Mind. Uncertainty is a state of mind that leads to anxiety. To the extent that insurance improves policyowners' ability to predict their financial futures, it reduces uncertainty and improves peace of mind. Although this psychological benefit is hard to measure, peace of mind adds to the quality of everyday life.

Provides a Basis for Credit. Commercial lenders naturally want assurances that their loans will be repaid. Loans are available—often at a favorable interest rate—when insurance provides these assurances. Money is often borrowed to finance the purchase of property, such as an auto or a home, that could be destroyed or seriously damaged before the loan is paid off. Lenders routinely require debtors to purchase auto physical damage insurance, homeowners insurance, or other appropriate insurance to protect the lenders' interests in property used as collateral for a loan. Similarly, life insurance is used to guarantee that a loan will be repaid despite the borrower's death. Other forms of insurance may protect the lender in the event the borrower's disability reduces his or her ability to make payments on a loan.

Stimulates Saving. Many kinds of insurance encourage thrift. An insurance premium, although small in relation to the possible loss it protects against, is basically a prepayment of a potential loss. All the payments are combined in a fund from which those few who do suffer losses are paid. In essence, insurance encourages all to save so that the few who are unfortunate can be repaid for their losses. In addition, life insurance has special advantages in stimulating savings. Often lasting many years, life insurance contracts can build substantial loan, emergency, or retirement values. Policyowners treat their regular premium payments as an obligation to their families or beneficiaries; greater savings result than with other well-intentioned but less-regular savings programs.

Provides Investment Capital. Insurers are required to hold huge amounts of money in reserve to pay future losses and expenses. This money is invested in government and corporate bonds, stocks, and other assets. Because insurers' assets are huge, their investments provide a gigantic source of capital for the economy—hundreds of billions of dollars to governments and business organizations.

Offers Advantages of Specialization. Insurers specialize in handling risk, and they can often handle risks more efficiently than individuals or businesses can. By transferring financial risks to an insurer, insurance buyers say, in effect, "Here, you take care of these bothersome, unpredictable risks for us, and we will concentrate on our primary goals." Insurance can help a married couple, for example, to focus their retirement planning on positive lifestyle goals rather than on building a large emergency fund to deal with unpredictable health care expenses.

Fosters Loss Prevention. Insurance benefits society by fostering considerable effort to prevent losses. Loss prevention is a secondary goal for most kinds of insurance, but undoubtedly more loss prevention work occurs because of insurance than would occur without it. The net effect is advantageous, as lives are saved and property values preserved. Examples are fire-prevention campaigns, motor vehicle safety research, education by health insurers, and elevator and boiler inspections. Also important in this work are associations, such as Underwriters Laboratories Inc. and the Insurance Institute for Highway Safety.

Costs of Insurance

The costs of insurance include

- operating costs
- profits
- opportunity costs
- increased losses
- adverse selection

Policyowners fund these costs by paying premiums.

Operating Costs. Operating expenses that enable insurers to do business account for approximately one-fourth of each dollar that insurers take in. The proportion varies by type of insurance. Operating expenses include agents' commissions, home office and field administrative expenses, loss adjustment expenses, and taxes. The operating costs of insurers, their agency systems, and other services must be balanced against the benefits of insurance, enumerated earlier.

Profits. Insurers must earn profits to increase their surplus positions and reward investors. Profit margins are small, perhaps less than 5 percent on average, in relation to the total premium dollar. Profits are necessary, however, because insurers would not otherwise attract the necessary operating capital.

Opportunity Costs. Opportunity cost is defined as the cost of pursuing one alternative versus another. The insurance business requires financial capital, personnel, and materials that could make other valuable contributions to the economy and to society if they were not devoted to the insurance business. For example, people not employed in the insurance business, a service business, might instead work in a factory and produce tangible products. These opportunity costs represent one of the costs of insurance.

Increased Losses. Increased losses result because insurance sometimes stimulates moral and attitudinal hazards. The existence of insurance can encourage fraud—for example, the collection of losses that insureds cause intentionally and the exaggeration of claims beyond actual losses. The greater carelessness that occurs when people feel completely insured also increases the cost of insurance. These effects tend to be relatively minor and rare, but some, such as fires caused by arson, are a major and growing problem. Although the costs are difficult to measure precisely, constant effort to control these possible costs is necessary.

adverse selection   **Adverse Selection.** *Adverse selection* is the natural tendency for those who know they are highly vulnerable to loss from a specific risk to be most inclined to acquire and retain insurance to cover related losses. It also includes situations in which individuals tend to select insurance options that reflect their particular situation. A family with a 16-year-old son who has just acquired a driver's license will probably want full-coverage auto insurance on the car. And a homeowner living in some parts of California will be especially interested in obtaining earthquake coverage.

Adverse selection simply reflects a rational emphasis on the applicant's own self-interest. In any case, however, adverse selection leads to poorer loss experience among those who are insured than among those who are not insured.

The following table summarizes the benefits and costs associated with insurance.

Table 1-1 Benefits and Costs of Insurance	
Benefits of Insurance	**Costs of Insurance**
Pays claims	Operating costs
Encourages peace of mind	Insurer profits
Provides a basis for credit	Opportunity costs
Stimulates saving	Increased losses
Provides investment capital	Adverse selection
Offers the advantages of specialization	
Fosters loss prevention	

Major Categories of Insurance

Many types of insurance are available to households and organizations. Several overlapping ways of grouping these types are as follows:

- life and health insurance versus property and liability insurance
- personal insurance versus business insurance
- private insurance versus government insurance
- individual insurance versus group insurance

Each of these pairs is described below.

Life and Health versus Property and Liability

The life and health category of insurance includes various types of insurance that deal with personal risks related to death, medical care costs, disability, and old age. Examples in this category are life insurance, medical expense insurance, disability income insurance, and long-term care insurance.

The property and liability category of insurance includes coverages that provide reimbursement for direct and indirect losses to property. It also includes types of insurance that cover the possibility of being held legally responsible to someone else for damages. Examples in the property and liability category include auto insurance, homeowners insurance, aviation insurance, marine insurance, and surety bonds.

Personal versus Business

Personal insurance is the category of insurance used by individuals and families. Examples in this category are homeowners insurance, personal auto insurance, life insurance, and disability income insurance.

Business insurance is the category of insurance used by businesses and other organizations. Examples include key employee life insurance, commercial liability insurance, business overhead expense insurance, workers' compensation and employers liability insurance, commercial auto insurance, commercial property insurance, business income insurance, and disability income insurance to fund a disability buy-sell agreement.

Private versus Government

private insurance

government insurance

Private insurance includes all forms of insurance that privately owned insurers provide. *Government insurance* consists of various types of insurance programs that the state or federal governments operate. Government insurance programs include social insurance programs, such as Medicare, and other programs, such as flood insurance and crop insurance.

social insurance

Social insurance consists of various government programs in which the elements of the insurance technique are present. These programs are designed to help solve the major social problems that affect a large portion of society. Our country's social insurance programs are of several types: Social Security, Medicare, unemployment insurance, temporary disability insurance, and workers' compensation insurance.

Even though there are variations in social insurance programs, and exceptions to the rule always exist, social insurance programs tend to have the following distinguishing characteristics:

- compulsory employment-related coverage
- partial or total employer financing
- benefits prescribed by law
- benefits as a right
- emphasis on social adequacy

Compulsory Employment-Related Coverage. Most social insurance programs are compulsory and require that the persons covered be attached—either presently or by past service—to the labor force.

Partial or Total Employer Financing. Although there are significant variations in social insurance programs, most require that the employers of the covered persons fully or at least partially bear the cost of the program. The remaining cost of most social insurance programs is paid primarily by the persons covered under programs. With the exception of Medicare and certain unemployment benefits, the general revenues of the federal government and state governments finance only a small portion of social insurance benefits.

Benefits Prescribed by Law. Although benefit amounts and the eligibility requirements for social insurance benefits are prescribed by law, benefits are not necessarily uniform for everyone. Benefits may vary by such factors as wage level, length of covered employment, or family status. However, these factors are incorporated into the benefit formulas specified by law, and covered persons cannot choose an increased or decreased level of benefits.

Benefits As a Right. Social insurance benefits are paid as a right. The need for benefits is presumed. This feature distinguishes social insurance programs from public assistance or welfare programs under which applicants, in order to qualify for benefits, must meet a needs test by demonstrating that their income or assets are below some specified level.

social adequacy **Emphasis on Social Adequacy.** Benefits under social insurance programs are based more on social adequacy than on individual equity. Under the principle of *social adequacy,* benefits are designed to provide a minimum floor of benefits to all beneficiaries under the program, regardless of their economic status. Above this floor of benefits, persons are expected to provide additional resources from their own savings, employment, or private insurance programs. Within certain maximum and minimum amounts, benefits are a function of a person's covered earnings under social insurance programs. The main emphasis, however, is on social adequacy. An emphasis on social adequacy results in disproportionately large benefits in relation to contributions for some groups of beneficiaries. For some programs, high-income persons, single persons, small families, and the young are subsidizing low-income persons, large families, and the retired.

individual equity   In contrast, private insurance programs are based primarily on *individual equity*. Each individual's contributions to the program, in the form of insurance premium payments, are based on an actuarial analysis that reflects the insurer's cost of providing insurance benefits for the risks that individual faces.

Individual versus Group

Private insurance can be written on either a group basis or an individual basis. Most auto and homeowners insurance is individual insurance, whereas most medical expense insurance is group insurance provided through an employer. More persons have life insurance through group plans than under individual policies, but the premium volume and amount of coverage in force are greater for individual policies. People who buy individual life insurance often purchase substantial amounts of insurance as part of a financial plan that reflects the extent of their life insurance needs, while group life insurance usually covers most or all employees for more nominal amounts set by the employer.

individual insurance   *Individual insurance* is usually owned by the person or entity who is the insured or who owns the insured property, but there are some cases where the policy may be owned by a third party. Examples include life and health insurance purchased by individuals on their family members and by businesses on key employees. The acceptability for coverage and the premium charged are usually determined by the characteristics of the person, entity, or property insured.

group insurance

master contract   In contrast to most individual insurance contracts, *group insurance* provides coverage to more than one person under a single contract issued to someone other than the persons insured. The contract, referred to as a *master contract*, provides benefits to a group of individuals who have a specific relationship to the policyowner. Group contracts usually cover full-time employees, and the policyowner is either their employer or a trust established to provide benefits for the employees. However, the master contract policyowner can also be a union, association, fraternal group, or other organization.

EXAMPLE
Darrel and Sally Lewis, a married couple in their late 50s, are covered by both individual insurance and group insurance. Darrel's employer provides group health insurance that covers both Darrel and Sally, as well as group long-term and short-term disability and group term life insurance on Darrel's life amounting to two times his salary. Darrel pays part of the cost of his life insurance, which is deducted from his paycheck; his employer pays the other costs of his group insurance. Sally's employer provides $25,000 of group term life insurance covering Sally's life, which is paid entirely by her employer.
Their individual insurance includes auto insurance, homeowners insurance, and long-term care insurance policies. In addition, Darrel and Sally have both purchased individual whole life insurance policies.

certificate of insurance

Employees covered under the group insurance contract receive *certificates of insurance* as evidence of their coverage. A certificate is merely a description of the coverage provided and is not part of the master contract. In general, a certificate of insurance is not even considered to be a contract and usually contains a disclaimer to that effect. However, some courts have treated it as a contract when the provisions of the certificate or even of the explanatory booklet of a group insurance plan vary materially from the master contract.

Individual vs. Group Coverage	
Individual	Group
• Mostly property and liability insurance	• Mainly life and health insurance
• Policyowner is usually the insured	• Policyowner is usually the sponsor of the group
• Only one or a few people are insured under one contract	• Many people are insured under one master contract
• Insured is usually the policyowner and receives the policy	• Insured is usually not the policyowner and receives a certificate of insurance
• Coverage begins at the inception of the policy	• Many people's coverage begins long after inception of the policy
• Individual evidence of insurability required	• Usually no individual evidence of insurability required
• Class rating often used to set rates	• Experience rating often used to set rates

In individual insurance, the coverage of the insured normally begins with the inception of the insurance contract and ceases with its termination. However, in group insurance, individual members of the group may become eligible for coverage long after the inception of the group contract, or they may lose their eligibility status long before the contract terminates.

evidence of insurability

For group insurance, individual members of the group are usually not required to show *evidence of insurability* when initially eligible for coverage. Evidence of insurability is the documentation or other evidence submitted to the insurance company regarding the physical condition, financial condition, driving records, or other attributes of the applicant for insurance coverage. This evidence will be taken into account when the insurer determines whether or not to accept the risk.

This is not to say that group insurers neglect to underwrite group members, but rather that they focus on the characteristics of the group (such as its prior claims experience, size, composition, geographic location, and stability) instead of the insurability of individual members of the group. As with individual insurance, the underwriter must appraise the risk, decide on the conditions of the group's acceptability, and establish a rating basis.

A final characteristic of group insurance is the use of experience rating. If a group is sufficiently large, the past loss experience of that particular group will be a factor in determining the current premium the policyowner is charged.

OTHER INSURANCE TERMINOLOGY

applicant

policyowner

Insurance is a large and diverse business, and its discussion requires the use of many terms that have specific insurance meanings. An *applicant* is a person or organization that applies for insurance coverage. If an insurance contract comes into effect, the applicant becomes a *policyowner* or policyholder. Traditionally, the common insurance usage was policyholder. However, over time and for many types of insurance, the term policyowner has become increasingly common, and for the sake of consistency, this is the term the authors of this book have decided to use.

insured

An *insured* under a policy can be, but is not necessarily, the policyowner. In individual life insurance, for example, the person on whose life a policy is issued is always the insured and is often but not necessarily the policyowner. A policyowner may own a policy on the life of another person, the insured. Typically, the policyowner determines the beneficiary of the coverage for future death claims and has the rights to change, renew, or cancel the policy and the obligations to comply with policy conditions, such as the payment of premiums.

In most types of individual insurance other than life insurance, an insured can best be defined as a party to whom, or on whose behalf, benefits may be payable. The policyowner (often referred to as the named insured) is usually an insured, but many others—such as family members or employees of the policyowner, or other drivers of a covered auto—can also be insureds.

In group insurance, the policyowner is usually a business or some other type of organization. The insureds are the persons who have coverage under the group, and in most cases, the policyowner is not an insured.

EXAMPLE

Nathan purchases a life insurance policy that will pay $100,000 to his wife, Jane, if Nathan dies. Nathan is the policyowner and the insured; Jane is the beneficiary.

Nathan also purchases a life insurance policy that will pay Nathan $50,000 upon Jane's death. In this case, Nathan is the policyowner and the beneficiary, but Jane is the insured.

Nathan's father, Walter, purchased a $200,000 life insurance policy on Nathan's life to provide funding for the college education of Nathan's daughter, Lauren. In this policy, Walter is the policyowner, Nathan is the insured, and Lauren is the beneficiary.

Nathan also owns an auto insurance policy that covers the liability of family members and others using his car with permission. Nathan is the policyowner; Nathan, Jane, Lauren, and other drivers are insureds. No beneficiary is involved in an auto insurance policy.

---

line of insurance

In insurance terminology, *line of insurance* usually means a type of insurance. Regulators are specific about what constitutes a line from a regulatory standpoint because detailed statistics must be reported by line. For example, some lines of insurance for property and liability insurance companies include homeowners, ocean marine, workers' compensation, private passenger auto liability, and surety bonds. Lines of life and health insurance companies include ordinary life, credit life, individual annuities, and group accident and health. The functional operations of a specific insurer may or may not be broken down along these same regulatory lines, and an insurer may use the term "line" for nonregulatory purposes to describe its business from a functional standpoint. For example, all private passenger auto insurance may be handled by one department and be referred to as a line, while regulators consider this insurance two lines—private passenger auto liability and private passenger auto physical damage. Types of insurance for individuals and businesses are often referred to as personal lines and commercial lines, respectively.

CHAPTER REVIEW

Key Terms and Concepts

risk	speculative risk
possibility	gambling
probability	personal risk
loss	property risk
loss exposure	liability risk
direct loss	insurable risk
indirect loss	risk-tolerance level
uncertainty	insurance
peril	adverse selection
hazard	private insurance
physical hazards	government insurance
moral hazards	social insurance
attitudinal hazards	social adequacy
law of large numbers	individual equity
mass	individual insurance
homogeneity	group insurance
independence	master contract
financial risk	certificate of insurance
nonfinancial risks	evidence of insurability
particular risks	applicant
fundamental risks	policyowner
static risk	insured
dynamic risk	line of insurance
pure risk	

Review Questions

Review questions are based on the learning objectives in this chapter. Thus, a [3] at the end of a question means that the question is based on learning objective 3. If there are multiple objectives, they are all listed.

1. What is the difference between risk and uncertainty? [1]

2. Your client Jim owns a printing business but rents the premises where the business is conducted. What direct and indirect losses might a fire cause to Jim's business? [1]

3. Sally, a single working mother with two young children, recently learned that her stress at work is giving her high blood pressure. Sally is concerned that if she were to die, her children would no longer have her income to support them until they are grown. In Sally's case, what is an example of each of the following?
 a. risk [1]
 b. peril [1]
 c. hazard [1]

4. Your client Al is applying for auto insurance to cover Al and his wife, Anne. For each of the following conditions identified in the underwriting process, what type of hazard is involved?
 a. Anne is blind in one eye and has had two heart attacks recently. [1]
 b. Al recently received two speeding tickets. [1]
 c. There have been several instances in the past where Al submitted inflated claims for property damage under his homeowners insurance coverage. [1]

5. Your client Janet Jones is 29 years old and works full-time to support her two small children and her husband, who was disabled in an auto accident last year. Although money is tight, you suggest that she consider the purchase of life insurance to provide support for the children and her disabled husband if she were to die. How would you respond to the following questions posed by Janet?
 a. She first asks, "With the probability of death so small for a woman aged 29, there's very little chance that I'll die in the near future. So why do I really need to buy life insurance?" [2]
 b. After you respond, she asks, "If life insurance companies can use probabilities to determine the likelihood that a woman aged 29 will die, why can't I use them to determine the likelihood that I will die?" [2]

6. What is the difference between fundamental and particular risks with respect to
 a. whom they affect? [2]
 b. who is generally thought to be responsible for dealing with them? [2]

7. How can ownership of a home provide a client with each of the following?
 a. pure risk [2]
 b. speculative risk [2]

8. Insurance commonly deals with what types of risks? [3]

9. Your client believes that insurance is just a form of gambling and would prefer to gamble her money in Las Vegas rather than make bets with an insurance company. Why is insurance not a form of gambling? [3]

10. What requirements must be met substantially in order for a risk to be considered insurable? [3]

11. Why do various clients react to risk differently? [4]

12. What costs are experienced by society as a result of pure risks? [5]

13. How is insurance defined from the following viewpoints?
    a. economic [6]
    b. legal [6]
    c. business [6]
    d. social [6]
    e. actuarial [6]

14. What six elements are often included in a definition of insurance? [6]

15. What are the benefits and costs of insurance? [7]

16. What are the distinguishing characteristics of social insurance programs? [8]

17. How does group insurance differ from individual insurance? [9]

Learning Objectives

An understanding of the material in this chapter should enable the student to

1. Describe risk management and the role of the risk manager.

2. Describe the basic methods of treating risks.

3. Explain how insurance works.

4. List and describe each of the four steps in the risk management process.

risk management

Pure risks are accompanied by costs. Those costs include (1) the actual losses that occur from various perils, (2) fear and worry because of possible losses from those perils, and (3) the less-than-optimal use of resources because of the difficulty of estimating the probability of loss. Because these costs are not accompanied by corresponding benefits, most people want to do something about the pure risks they confront. *Risk management* is the term commonly used to describe a systematic process for dealing with these risks. The need for risk management, in turn, gives rise to a fourth cost of pure risks—the expenses that must be incurred to treat them.

enterprise risk management

Traditionally, risk management has focused on personal risks, property risks, and liability risks, collectively referred to as hazard risks. These are pure risks that present the possibility of loss or no loss, but no possibility of gain. Through the use of insurance, the financial consequences of these pure risks are commonly transferred to an insurer. However, it is becoming increasingly popular for businesses to take a broader view of risk management that encompasses both pure hazard risks and speculative business risks. This broader view, commonly referred to as *enterprise risk management*, is an approach to managing all an organization's risks and opportunities in order to maximize the organization's value. Risk management then takes place at the enterprise level.

Usually, risk management is departmentalized with hazard risks managed in a risk management department, financial risks managed in a finance department, and so forth. Organizations that follow this traditional approach rarely make relative comparisons among the various types of risks to determine the aggregate effect of any interaction among the risks. The broader view of enterprise risk management is designed to address these issues. The broad enterprise risk management philosophy of managing and coordinating various types of risks and opportunities is inherent in a comprehensive personal financial plan.

Financial planners must help their clients identify risks and alternatives for managing those risks. This involves understanding the basic methods of treating risks, because the major goal of risk management is the coordination of these various alternatives.

NATURE AND SCOPE OF RISK MANAGEMENT

The key steps in the risk management process are[6]

- **identification.** The process begins with the recognition and classification of various risks.
- **measurement.** The next step is the analysis and evaluation of risks in terms of frequency, severity, and variability.
- **choice and use of methods to treat each identified risk**. Some risks can be avoided, some controlled, some retained under planned programs, and some transferred by a method such as insurance.
- **administration**. Once the methods of treatment are chosen, plans for administration of the program must be instituted. This last step includes both implementing the methods selected and monitoring the choices to see that they are effective.

---

6. Some textbooks break the risk management process into six steps: identifying loss exposures, analyzing loss exposures, examining the feasibility of risk management alternatives, selecting the best risk management techniques, implementing risk management techniques, and monitoring results. See, for example, Wiening, Eric A., *Foundations of Risk Management and Insurance,* 1st ed., chapter 1, Malvern, PA: The American Institute for Chartered Property Casualty Underwriters, 2002, p. 3.7. Others combine identification and analysis for a total of five steps.

Insurance is the principal method of treating the pure risks of many businesses and households. But without careful study of all the risk management alternatives in a coordinated decision-making process, insurance may be used inappropriately, or not used where it is appropriate.

OBJECTIVES OF RISK MANAGEMENT

The objective of risk management is to preserve the assets and income of the organization or household against the possibility of accidental loss. Implicit is the idea that preservation concerns all assets—those of property and of people. Also, the idea of protection encompasses many different methods of treating pure risks.

More specific risk management goals might include the following:

- survival
- peace of mind
- lower costs or higher net income
- stable earnings
- minimal interruption of business operations or personal life
- continued growth
- satisfaction of social responsibility with a good public image

Some of these are pre-loss objectives, meaningful before a loss has occurred. Some are post-loss objectives, and several are significant both before and after a loss.

EXAMPLE
Karen and Joel Wolf are empty nesters in their late 50s who are considering an early retirement. They are not yet eligible to receive Social Security benefits, and retirement will eliminate the flow of earned income. However, Karen and Joel believe they can support themselves on income from their investments and their employers' retirement benefits. Karen and Joel's risk management goals are likely to focus on survival, peace of mind, reduced costs, stable cash flows from their retirement plans and investments, minimal interruption of their personal life, and maintaining their public image. Meeting these goals requires attention to preserving their assets and their retirement income, using insurance and other risk management techniques.

ROLE OF THE RISK MANAGER

Many business firms and other organizations employ a full-time risk manager. The risk manager of a larger firm has, in a majority of cases, full responsibility in the property and liability area for (1) identifying and evaluating risks, (2) selecting insurers, (3) approving insurance renewals and amounts, (4) negotiating insurance rates, (5) seeking competitive insurance bids, (6) keeping insurance records, (7) choosing deductibles, and (8) handling insurance claims. The risk manager usually shares authority for (1) deciding whether to insure or retain (including self-insuring) financial risks, (2) selecting insurance agents and brokers, (3) instituting safety programs, and (4) reviewing contracts other than insurance. In some organizations, the risk manager also has some responsibility for life and health insurance programs, while in others these programs fall within the scope of the human resources or personnel department.

Sometimes, particularly in small- and medium-sized firms, an insurance agent, broker, or consultant serves as the risk manager, because the organization has no one person assigned to these responsibilities. Larger agencies and brokerages, especially, offer to serve in this capacity. Care must be taken to see (1) that the services are much broader than mere insurance coverages and include loss prevention and other risk treatment alternatives, and (2) that the insurance agency or brokerage representative or consultant knows the firm's special individual needs.

Risk management is not only a business concept. Individuals and families can apply the same risk management principles a business uses, usually on a smaller scale. Like a business, almost every individual or household uses various techniques, including insurance, for treating pure risks. Few, if any, families employ a full-time risk manager. Like small- or medium-sized businesses, individuals and families often draw on the advice and services of an insurance agent or broker in addressing some of their risk management needs. Many also benefit from the services of a financial planner.

BASIC METHODS OF TREATING RISKS

risk control

risk financing

It is said that, if the only tool in your toolbox is a hammer, then every problem will look like a nail. The point, of course, is that no single tool adequately addresses all needs. By the same token, any single risk management tool does not provide an adequate solution to deal with all pure risks. In practice, usually all, or at least several, techniques are used together to provide the best answers for meeting the financial problems of risk. Two basic methods of treating risks are risk control and risk financing. *Risk control* refers to risk management techniques used to minimize the frequency and severity of losses; *risk financing* refers to techniques used to pay for any losses that do occur.

Risk Control Methods

The major methods of risk control that a client might use can be classified in various ways. Each of the following risk control methods aims to minimize losses to assets and income:

- risk avoidance
- loss prevention
- loss reduction
- noninsurance transfers

Risk Avoidance

risk avoidance   *Risk avoidance,* the most extreme form of risk control, is used when a party decides not to incur a loss exposure or to eliminate one that already exists. For example, a family might avoid some specific liability loss exposures by deciding not to place a trampoline in its back yard or removing a trampoline that is already there. A family can decide to rent rather than buy a home, avoiding the possibility of losing the home's value through the peril of fire. A manufacturer may decide not to produce a chemical that could generate products liability claims. People who worry about poisonous snakebites or heat exhaustion can live in the Arctic or at least locate in an area with a minimum exposure to these perils. People who want to avoid the risks of airplane accidents, drownings, and sports injuries can do so largely by keeping away from airplanes, water, and sports activities, respectively.

EXAMPLE
Jack and Jean Hill have recently relocated to Naples, Florida, with their three young children. They have instructed their realtor that they do not wish to consider any home that has a swimming pool. Thus, they wish to use avoidance to treat the risk of a child's drowning in their pool.

Avoidance is not a practical solution to many risks inherent in normal activities. Some unusual risks with a high chance of loss can be avoided, but risk avoidance is a realistic alternative only for a limited number of risks. Some risks may be impossible to avoid; others may not be economically desirable to avoid because of the high costs of doing so or because avoiding one risk would create another. For example, driving rather than flying avoids the possibility that family members will be injured in a plane crash on the way to Grandma's house for the holidays, but it creates the statistically greater risk of being injured in an auto accident while making the holiday trip. For unavoidable risks, other solutions must be considered.

Loss Prevention and Reduction

loss prevention

loss reduction

Two methods of risk control, loss prevention and loss reduction, are closely related:

- *Loss prevention* refers to risk control measures intended to lower the probability of loss or the frequency with which a given type of loss occurs.
- *Loss reduction* refers to risk control measures that aim to reduce the severity of loss.

EXAMPLE
Maria's doctor has urged her to obtain a flu shot in November. He points out that the shot will lower the likelihood that she will contract the flu in the ensuing months (loss prevention) and may speed up her recovery time if she does contract the flu (loss reduction).

Some loss prevention and loss reduction measures available to families and organizations are as follows:

- building fire-resistant structures
- installing security devices in homes
- scheduling annual physical examinations and mammograms
- using auto seatbelts
- introducing wellness programs into workplaces
- using safety devices to guard against injuries from lawn mowers and other machinery

Loss prevention measures, which attempt to keep losses from occurring, are obviously used before any loss occurs. Loss reduction measures apply when a loss occurs and attempt to limit its severity. For example, immediate medical treatment can reduce the damaging effect of a heart attack or a stroke that has already occurred. However, many loss reduction measures must be put into place before losses occur. A fire extinguisher, for example, can limit the damage done by a wastebasket fire. But the fire extinguisher—a loss reduction measure—must be purchased before the fire occurs.

Noninsurance Transfers

noninsurance transfers
Some *noninsurance transfers* qualify as risk control measures. These transfers use a contract, other than an insurance contract, in which one party transfers responsibility for a specific activity and any resulting losses to another party.

Subcontracting is one example of a noninsurance transfer for risk control. A contractor may use a contract to transfer the possibility of injury to employees in a particularly dangerous part of a construction project to someone else. Subcontracting thus eliminates the original contractor's exposure to these losses.

Likewise, a homeowner might hire a pest control company rather than using a do-it-yourself approach that might subject the homeowner, family members, or neighbors to the improper application or use of poisonous chemicals.

Risk Financing Methods

risk financing
In most cases, the methods of risk control previously discussed lower the impact of losses. The one exception is risk avoidance, which eliminates the possibility of loss. With other risk control techniques, losses can still occur, and some additional choices are necessary when deciding how to pay for those losses. The alternative methods of *risk financing* may be divided into two major types:

- risk retention
- risk transfer

Risk Retention

risk retention
Risk retention is the risk financing method that is used when a person or organization keeps, or retains, the financial burden of any losses that occur rather than transferring them to

an insurer or some other party. Risk retention may be either planned or unplanned.

Planned risk retention is the result of purposeful, conscious, intentional, and active behavior. For example, a household or firm may evaluate some of its risks as having high frequency but low severity and deliberately decide to retain them. However, many pure risks are retained due to lack of planning or failure to recognize the risk rather than from a rational planning process.

Unplanned risk retention is also common. Some risks are retained because the existence or significance of the risks is not known. Lack of knowledge or inability to reach the right decision, even with adequate knowledge, may result in unplanned risk retention. Information may be available and not used, or perhaps the necessary information is unavailable. Consider the long-term care loss exposure. Retention here is often the result of (1) failing to evaluate the need for and costs of long-term care, or (2) not knowing that insurance can be obtained for such a loss exposure. Unplanned risk retention can also result from unintentional or irrational action or from passive behavior due to laziness or lack of interest in discovering possibilities of loss. Many young married people, for example, carry little or no life insurance because they view death as a problem for much later or a subject they don't want to discuss.

Some risks are intentionally retained because the risks are relatively unimportant or other alternatives are not possible. For example, retention may be the only available option for a self-employed person with a long history of heart disease who is uninsurable for life and disability insurance. Even when insurance is available, some risks are often retained because retention is more convenient, because retention provides greater control, or because the cost of insurance appears to be too high relative to the risk.

Organizations often practice risk retention because they wish to have the control or convenience of paying for their own losses. An employer may pay employees' hospital expenses directly, for example, to improve cash flow by handling expenses when they occur rather than paying a premium in advance. A manufacturer in a competitive technical field might decide to retain both property and products liability loss exposures in connection with a research laboratory's highly secret inventions. Individuals or families who have accumulated an adequate emergency fund might also choose to retain certain exposures or to self-fund smaller losses, often by purchasing insurance with a substantial deductible.

deductible A *deductible* is the initial portion of covered losses that is borne by the insured rather than by the insurance company. Deductibles are a form of partial risk retention. Having the insured receive payment only for losses over a stated amount, or only after a stated period of time has elapsed, has been accepted for many years in most types of medical expense, disability income, and property insurance. A deductible is also common in some types of liability insurance policies. Deductibles lower insurance premiums by eliminating the relatively high costs associated with processing small claims. From the insurer's perspective, deductibles also minimize attitudinal hazards by leaving an insured responsible for a portion of any loss. The policyowner who "has some skin in the game" is presumably more likely to exert an effort to minimize losses.

Some insurance policies require deductibles. Often, deductibles involve a relatively modest amount. Higher deductibles may be available at significant premium savings.

EXAMPLE
Tony Medici has a homeowners deductible of $1,000 rather than his insurer's standard amount of $250. The annual premium saving is $200. In other words, by decreasing his loss recovery by $750, he saves $200 per year. Inasmuch as the average policyowner has a homeowners loss only once every 15 to 20 years, the long-run savings could be substantial.

The appropriate deductible for a given situation varies, based on several factors. Among these factors are the nature of the perils, including the frequency and severity of loss patterns; the client's financial ability to withstand losses; the existence of reserves or funds to help finance the deductible portion of losses; the policyowner's or the insurer's desire for claims handling services; the need for loss prevention services; and the client's degree of risk tolerance. Another important consideration is the premium reduction associated with any deductible. One fundamental risk management principle is, "Don't risk a lot to save a little." Suppose $500 deductible collision coverage on an auto costs only $10 more than $1,000 deductible coverage. Even if a client is able to retain a $1,000 loss, the added retained risk of the higher deductible might not be worth the savings.

The relative costs of alternative risk treatment methods are a major consideration in most decisions to retain a risk. A comparison of the cost involved in each alternative method of financing losses is necessary. If insurance against earthquake damage is available, how much will it cost? If earthquake damage could be prevented by extra-strong building construction, how much would this cost? Would a self-insurance program with a reserve fund be feasible for a business, and what would its cost be? In each of these comparisons, the need for complete evaluation is obvious. Not only must loss frequency and severity be considered, but also all costs of the various alternatives, including indirect as well as direct costs, must be evaluated for fair comparisons. Another significant cost factor that must be evaluated is the cost of funds, which can make risk retention plans more desirable because assets are held until losses actually occur. Tax-related issues must also be considered.

Risks that a business client or a family retains must be financed in some way. The more common methods are described below.

Absorption in Current Operating Expenses. The most common method of risk financing for retained risk is to absorb losses out of regular operating expenses or family budgets. Large organizations often generate sufficient cash inflow to absorb costs, but smaller firms are less likely to be equipped to withstand ongoing losses. Businesses might consider treating glass breakage, transportation shipment damage, and auto physical damage as current operating expenses. For individuals and families, the budget usually provides even less room for absorbing unexpected losses. However, dental bills, eyeglasses, and auto towing expenses can be among the possible candidates for this type of treatment.

Funding and Reserves. For an organization, a fund of actual segregated assets or a reserve may be used to offset losses that are too large to absorb in current operating expenses but small enough that the entity can reasonably retain the risk. For a family, an emergency fund might serve the same role.

The major disadvantage of many reserve accounts is that they do not guarantee that cash will be available to meet losses. Problems with planning involving segregated funds include (1) how large the fund should be, (2) how it can be accumulated in spite of possibly disastrous losses during the accumulation period, and (3) how the fund can be maintained without raiding it for other emergencies or using it in the organization's or household's regular operations.

Many individuals and families have savings and liquid investments that provide a safety cushion, whether or not they are set aside as a segregated emergency fund. Within limits, these resources can enable a family to retain the financial consequences of a loss that is too large to handle within the monthly budget. A good example of this type of loss is short-term disability or limited periods of unemployment.

Although money is usually borrowed for other purposes, credit arrangements can also be used to finance retained losses. For example, a client who has owned a home for 10 or 20 years may have accumulated substantial equity in the house. In the event of an emergency that does not involve damage to or destruction of the house itself, this equity might be tapped by taking out a home equity loan.

self-insurance

Self-Insurance. Although the term *self-insurance* is often applied to any retention of financial risks, the proper use of the term applies to formal programs of risk retention. Self-insurance is generally appropriate only for a large business in which the business acts like an insurance company for its own risks. This involves having a large number of similar loss exposures, the ability to predict overall losses with some degree of accuracy, and the establishment of a formal fund for future losses and their possible fluctuations.

captive insurer

Captive Insurers. Another risk financing method—the use of a *captive insurer*—is closely related to self-insurance. In this risk financing method, a large organization establishes a separate subsidiary insurance company to write its own insurance. Today, many captive insurers also write insurance for unrelated outside firms as well as for their own parent companies or groups.

Risk Transfer

risk transfer

Risk transfer is the loss financing method that shifts as much as possible of the financial consequences of a risk to some other party. Individuals and organizations use risk transfer because they cannot reasonably retain the financial consequences of some risks. Often, these are risks with low loss frequency but high loss severity. The risk itself still exists, but another party will largely bear the financial consequences. Two methods of risk transfers are possible: (1) noninsurance transfers, and (2) insurance.

Noninsurance Transfers. Noninsurance transfers involve a contract through which one party transfers the legal responsibility for a specific activity and any resulting losses to another party.

When noninsurance transfer is used as a risk financing method, the financial burden of losses, rather than the ultimate legal responsibility, is transferred. For example, purchasing an extended warranty on an auto or an air conditioning system is a noninsurance transfer method that individuals and households commonly use to handle the financial consequences of pure risks. Likewise, businesses and organizations often use hold-harmless agreements to transfer the financial consequences of some of their pure risks.

hold-harmless agreement
Most noninsurance transfers to finance risk deal with liability risks. A *hold-harmless agreement* is a common type of noninsurance transfer in which the transferee agrees to hold the transferor harmless in case of legal liability to others. The transferee agrees to pay claimants or the defense costs of claims or lawsuits, or to repay these losses if they fall on the transferor. If the transferee is unable to pay the losses, the ultimate responsibility remains with the transferor.

Several types of legal contracts commonly include hold-harmless agreements. In lease contracts, a variety of legal responsibilities are transferred from one party to another. A sample hold-harmless agreement appears in the example below. This particular agreement is between a catering company and a property owner, Tucson Activities Center, Inc. The catering company wants to hold functions on this property, and the property owner wants to protect itself in the event the catering company does anything, such as injuring a guest or serving liquor to a minor, for which the property owner could be sued. A similar agreement might be signed by a couple or a family renting the facility for a wedding reception or a graduation party. For example, a lease often states that property maintenance is the responsibility of the transferee (lessee) who rents the property from the owner. Homes, apartments, autos, and many other types of property are often leased or rented subject to hold-harmless agreements.

EXAMPLE

Hold-Harmless Agreement—Sample Document

This Hold-Harmless and Indemnification Agreement ("Agreement") is entered into by and between First Class Catering, a Partnership, hereinafter "Promisor," and Tuscon Activities Center, Inc., a Corporation, hereinafter "Promisee," on this _____ day of _____, 20__, in Tuscon, Arizona.

Recitals

Promisor desires to rent Promisee's premises and building, located at 300 Party Lane, Tuscon, Arizona, for an event to be held on <date>, and at other times as mutually agreed upon between the parties. The intent of this Agreement is to indemnify Promisee from any claims arising from and related to Promisor's use and rental of these premises.

Agreement

FOR VALUABLE CONSIDERATION, the receipt of which is hereby acknowledged, Promisor and Promisee agree as follows:

Promisor will indemnify and hold harmless Promisee from any and all claims, actions, and judgments, including all costs of defense and attorney's fees incurred in defending against same, arising from and related to Promisor's use and rental of the premises located at 300 Party Lane, Tuscon, Arizona. Promisor's actions include the acts of Promisor's agents and employees.

Promisee shall be entitled, in its reasonable discretion, to settle claims prior to suit or judgment, and in such event Promisor shall indemnify and hold harmless Promisee for any such claims paid, including Promisee's reasonable attorney's fees incurred resulting from such claim.

In the event any claim or suit is brought against Promisee within the scope of this Agreement, Promisor shall pay for legal counsel chosen by Promisee to defend against same.

This Agreement shall encompass claims resulting from (i) the furnishing of alcoholic beverages, and (ii) valet parking services hired by Promisor as independent contractors.

In the event either party files suit in a court of law to interpret or to enforce the terms of this Agreement, the party prevailing in such action shall be entitled, in addition to any legal fees incurred in defending against any thirty party claim, to its reasonable legal fees and costs incurred in such action to interpret or to enforce the terms of this Agreement.

This Agreement shall be interpreted under the laws of the state of Arizona.

Tuscon Activities Center, Inc.

_____

By: Louise K. Russel, President

First Class Catering

_____

by: Manfred O. Gerzabek, General Partner

Source: www.legaldocs.com/htsgif.d/sholdhar.mv_8/26/06. Used with permission.

Insurance. Insurance is by far the most common risk financing method.

HOW INSURANCE WORKS

How can an insurance company assume a large risk for a comparatively small premium and soon thereafter make a large loss payment? For example, life insurance pays some death claims on policies issued and in force for less than a year. Fire insurance on a building may require an insurer to pay thousands of dollars in return for the payment of a few dollars in premiums. The following four concepts help explain how insurance works:

- the insurance equation
- probability and uncertainty
- the law of large numbers
- adequate statistical data

The Insurance Equation

insurance equation

The equality between the sources of income and the uses of income constitutes the *insurance equation*. An insurer receives income from three sources: (1) premium payments from policyowners, (2) investment earnings, and (3) other income. The other side of the insurance equation includes the uses of this income: (1) covered losses, (2) the cost of doing business, or expenses, and (3) covered profits (retained earnings and dividends). The tables below explain each of these cost factors.

Table 2-1 The Insurance Equation		
Sources of Income	**Equal**	**Uses of Income**
Premiums from policyowners	=	Covered losses
+		+
Investment earnings		Cost of doing business
+		+
Other income		Profits

Table 2-2 Insurance Equation Illustrated			
Life Insurance Company Annual Statement of Operations			
Premiums	$267,775,200	Covered losses	$269,314,100
Investment earnings	$303,452,600	Cost of doing business	$268,276,800
Other income	$ 10,659,000 =	Profits	$ 44,295,900
Totals	$581,886,800		$581,886,800

Losses

Insurers deal with groups. A life insurance company is not concerned with when one person will die but with how many will die each year out of a large group. Knowing this within reasonable limits, the life insurer sets its rates so that it will take in enough money to be able to pay all expected losses. With other forms of insurance, the procedure is the same, although the result might be less predictable. The fire insurer is interested not in whether specific buildings will burn but in what the ratio of losses to premiums is likely to be when a large group of buildings is insured.

The percentage of the premium used to pay losses varies with the line of insurance written. The losses per premium dollar may be 80 percent or more for group health insurance or less than 50 percent for such lines as surety bonds and equipment breakdown insurance.

Margins are included in the rates that insurers charge. These margins are required by state law to cover specific loss reserves for some lines of insurance. Insurance rates also sometimes include margins to cover possible future catastrophic losses. For example, fires have destroyed large sections in major cities; windstorms, floods, and tsunamis have damaged wide areas; and accidents and terrorist attacks have caused many people to die at one time. Insurers must take catastrophes into consideration when computing premiums.

Expenses

In addition to securing sufficient funds to meet all covered losses, insurers must collect enough money to pay business expenses, such as salaries, rents, supplies, taxes, and agents' commissions. Some insurers also provide special engineering and loss prevention services that are designed to save property or to promote healthy lifestyles. An insurer's cost of doing business is affected by the marketing system it uses and the services its agents render to policyowners.

Profits

Premiums must also be sufficient to generate profits. Profits are the amounts left after all losses and expenses have been paid out. In a stock company, insurers usually retain some profits to increase surplus, and the remainder is distributed to stockholders. Mutual insurance companies may return some of their profit to policyowners as policy dividends, with the remainder added to surplus for purposes of growth and financial stability. Insurers sometimes operate at a loss for a period of 1 or more years. But this condition obviously cannot continue indefinitely. Profits are essential if an insurance company is to survive in the long run.

Probability

Insurers try to avoid operating at a loss by applying probability concepts. Within calculable limits, the insurer can foresee the normal losses and can also estimate losses from catastrophes in order to compute the premium necessary to pay all losses, as well as to cover expenses and profits.

The ability to use probabilities gives the insurer a different perspective from the policyowner's. Without this ability, insurance would be nothing more than the accumulation of many small risks and accompanying uncertainties into one enormous risk. By using probabilities, even though the element of uncertainty is extreme for each individual insured, the insurer can estimate a somewhat predictable loss for its entire group of insured persons. Variability is not entirely eliminated, and some insurers are more successful than others in their predictions. Every insurance company endeavors to achieve reasonable predictability, but insurance companies often suffer losses and expenses beyond what they take in during any given year.

Law of Large Numbers

The law of large numbers is especially important to insurance. Also known as the law of averages, this principle states that as the number of independent events increases, the likelihood increases that the actual results will be close to the expected results.

credibility
Insurance is concerned with the number of times an event, or loss, can be expected to occur over a series of occasions. Certain events occur with surprising regularity when a large number of instances are observed. The regularity of the events increases as the observed instances become more numerous. *Credibility* is the degree of reliability placed on past experience to predict what will happen in the future.

Applying concepts such as probability and credibility to insurance in a hypothetical case, assume that we are considering the predictability of auto accidents in a given city. We have gathered data on two different classes of drivers, under age 25 and age 25 or older, in the city over the past several years. The data are shown in the table below.

Table 2-3 Data on Two Different Classes of Drivers		
	Under Age 25	**Age 25 or Over**
Average annual number of drivers	2,000	25,000
Average annual percentage involved in an auto accident	20%	12%
Range of annual percentages involved in an auto accident during the period	9%–31%	8%–16%

It is perhaps not surprising that, on average, a higher percentage of young drivers were involved in auto accidents during a year than older drivers. In addition, however, note that as a smaller group, the younger drivers showed a wider relative variation around their average from year to year than did the older, considerably larger group. If we were to use these data to predict future accident rates, we could predict only within a wide range of percentages for the younger drivers compared with the older group. As a result, there would be a rather low probability of actual experience equaling expected experience for the under-age-25 group. The relative variation in results for the 25-and-over group is smaller, so we could make predictions for the future more accurately. This is the "magic" of insurance—increasing predictability by applying the law of large numbers.

Adequate Statistical Data

mortality

morbidity
Sound application of the mathematical laws of probability and large numbers requires adequate statistical data. Predictions in the form of probabilities must be based on adequate and accurate statistical information. For each line of insurance,

insurers carefully compile statistics to accumulate experience as a basis for rate making. Important life insurance statistical data deal with *mortality,* defined as the relative incidence of death. The statistical data used in estimating the number of deaths for life insurance purposes are arranged in a mortality table that shows how many persons alive at different ages are expected to die during the coming year. Likewise, health insurers are concerned about statistics regarding *morbidity,* the relative incidence of disease. The number of individuals exposed to the risk of illness and disease at each age is shown in a morbidity table. In commercial property insurance, statistics are developed for such factors as construction, occupancy, fire protection, and location pertaining to different types of buildings. For auto insurance, data for many classifications of type and use of car, territory, age of driver, and other factors are collected. These classifications help to achieve equity in the rates charged to many policyowners with different loss probabilities.

STEPS IN RISK MANAGEMENT

The steps in risk management are:

- risk identification
- risk measurement
- choice and use of alternative methods of treatment
- risk administration

Risk Identification

risk identification　　　　The process of risk management begins with *risk identification,* the careful and systematic discovery of all risks that confront a household or an organization. Often, a risk and insurance survey form, sometimes called a loss exposure audit or fact finder, is used to organize this information. Several other effective methods of risk identification for households or small businesses are financial statement analysis, personal inspections, and contract analysis.

Table 2-4 Identification of Household/Family Loss Exposures	
Types of Loss Exposure	**Consequences**

Property
• Real property
  – Unimproved land
  – Residence premises
  – Other structures
  – Fixtures
• Personal property
  – Tangible
    ► At residence premises
    ► Elsewhere
  – Intangible
  – Property held as bailee
	Property
	• Reduction in value
	• Loss of use

Liability • Premises liability • Libel, slander, and other intentional torts • Employment of domestics • Autos • Recreational vehicles • Watercraft • Business-related liability • Personal activities (for example, hobbies, baby-sitting, serving alcohol, keeping pets)	Liability • Damages awards • Specific performance • Injunction • Fines • Costs of defense • Court costs
Illness and Injury • Related to employment • Not related to employment	Illness and Injury • Medical care expenses • Lost income • Extra expenses and loss of services • Long-term care
Death	Death • Costs associated with death (for example, funeral, taxes, estate administration fees) • Lost income for dependents • Lost employee benefits for dependents
Retirement	Retirement • Lost income
Unemployment	Unemployment • Lost income • Extra expenses (for example, relocation, job hunting)

Survey Forms

Survey forms, questionnaires, and checklists are often used to identify the loss exposures of a business or nonprofit organization. Similar forms are also available for use with individuals and families. Survey forms, questionnaires, and checklists have been prepared by insurers, financial planners, and insurance agencies. A brief exposure checklist that might be used with a family appears above.[7]

Risk and insurance survey forms involve risk detection, identification, and classification. Sometimes they also include estimates of property values, which are part of risk measurement. Survey forms may be brief or lengthy, depending on whether they are for a household or a business and on the complexity of the case under consideration.

Financial Statement Analysis

Businesses routinely prepare a balance sheet, an income statement, and other financial statements. Although most families' accounting practices are much more informal, individuals and families who are serious about their financial planning and have not already done so are often advised to prepare a balance sheet (also known as a financial position statement), an income statement, and a budget. These documents can be useful in risk identification and risk measurement.

In financial statement analysis, each account on the balance sheet, the income statement, and other financial statements is listed and analyzed to determine the potential perils that might result in losses. For example, the tangible assets listed (house, autos, jewelry, and other items) raise questions regarding the perils that could cause loss or damage to those assets, as well as liability that might result from their ownership or use. The items on the income statement and budget pinpoint the sources of income and profits subject to indirect loss when perils occur. A comprehensive analysis of financial statements thus becomes a very useful method for identifying both direct and indirect losses.

Personal Inspections

Although many methods of risk identification are valuable as checks against possible sources of loss, none of them can replace the technical knowledge that consultants or agents provide. Personal inspections of a business operation or a household remain a significant source of information about possible losses.

---

7. The checklist was created from materials in Hamilton, Karen L., and Malecki, Donald S., *Personal Insurance: Property and Liability,* 2d ed., chapter 1. Malvern, PA: American Institute for Chartered Property Casualty Underwriters, 1999.

Contract Analysis

Almost every person or organization enters into contractual agreements. Hold-harmless agreements can mean liability exposures are transferred to the client—or from the client to others. Other relevant contracts with both financial planning and insurance implications involve short-term auto rental agreements, auto lease agreements, apartment rental agreements, agreements for the purchase or sale of a house, and the master deed or declarations of a condominium complex. Legal expertise is often necessary to interpret contractual agreements.

Techniques for Risk Identification
• Survey forms • Financial statement analysis • Personal inspections • Contract analysis

Risk Measurement

The second step in risk management is risk measurement. Each risk can be measured in three basic ways: (1) loss frequency, (2) loss severity, and (3) variability. Business risk managers often estimate expected losses on the basis of past loss experience or judgment. Risk managers also try to predict variations in future losses, in both frequency and severity.

Because the law of large numbers cannot apply, past loss experience is of limited value in evaluating many of the risks facing individuals and families. Many families go 20 years or more without a homeowners insurance claim, but the risk of a serious house fire still exists. Past loss experience can be useful in predicting some expenses, such as the cost of prescription drugs for blood pressure or for a chronic illness.

Some potential losses can be so infrequent that it would be impractical to try to deal with them. Flood damage to property high on a mountain is an example of this type of loss probability. At the other extreme, some losses may be so frequent as to be regularly anticipated. If the losses are small relative to a family's or business firm's assets or income, retaining these risks by absorbing the losses in normal expenses or by reserving for the losses as they occur would be effective. For this sort of retention to work, however, not only must the frequency of loss be high and the severity low, but the variation of losses must also be regular and predictable within ranges that the household or firm can handle. We will discuss this approach further in connection with the next step in the risk management process, choice and use of methods of risk treatment.

maximum possible loss

maximum probable loss

If complete data are lacking, or if the cost of making more precise estimates is too high, other methods of measuring risks may be advisable. For example, a client might divide potential losses into various categories, such as losses that are of high, moderate, or slight importance. Estimates of *maximum possible loss* and *maximum probable loss* can also be valuable. Maximum possible loss would be the worst that could happen. Maximum probable loss would be the worst that is likely to happen.

Several dimensions of maximum probable loss are pertinent. To determine the effect of losses on a household or organization, it is worthwhile to estimate the maximum probable loss not only for a single item or life exposed to loss (such as one building or one person), but also for multiple losses that could occur together (such as a windstorm over a large area or the death or disability of both parents in an accident). In addition, the risk manager should evaluate the maximum probable loss per year in terms of its financial effect on the household's or organization's resources, budget planning, and taxes.

Choice and Use of Methods of Risk Treatment

The third step in risk management is to evaluate both the suitability and the cost of various methods of treating pure risks. Sound risk management considers all methods of dealing with risks. Even considering one peril, such as fire, usually requires a risk manager to integrate the two basic methods of risk control and risk financing.

To choose among alternatives, the risk manager must understand each alternative, the conditions under which it should be considered, its advantages, and its limitations. Can the risk be avoided, or can it be controlled by loss prevention or reduction? Can some or all of the risk be financed by risk retention or risk transfer? More important, if several methods are feasible, which one method or combination of methods will provide the most desirable result?

Factors to Consider

Elaborate mathematical models have been designed to compare the benefits and costs of the various methods, and combinations of methods, to treat various pure risks. However, these models are probably not very helpful when risk management is practiced at the level of the household or small business organization. At that level, the choice of the best technique or combination of techniques is likely to be determined by such factors as:

- the maximum probable loss associated with a particular risk in comparison to the household's or firm's financial and other capacities to bear risk
- the legal restrictions that may impose or preclude the use of one or more techniques
- the extent to which the household or firm is able to control the loss frequency or severity associated with the risk
- the loading fees (expense charges) associated with the available risk management techniques
- the value of ancillary services that may be provided as part of the risk treatment technique, especially the insurance technique
- the time value of investable funds that may be gained or lost by using certain of the available techniques
- the federal income tax treatment of losses under the various techniques
- the possible unavailability of certain techniques for dealing with some pure risks

Last, but certainly not least, the ethical implications of any risk management decision must be considered. For example, suppose the wife's employer provides a broad medical expense insurance plan for employees, with coverage available for family members at an extra cost. Meanwhile, the husband's employer provides no insurance benefits. The wife's paycheck is larger if she does not elect coverage for her husband. However, any decision to leave her husband with no medical expense coverage not only exposes the couple to financial risk but also raises ethical questions, which develop because the existence of insurance can affect one's access to health care; for instance, without insurance, the husband might need to forgo some desirable but costly treatment that would have to be paid out of pocket.

Reviewing Insurance Priorities

Reviewing insurance priorities is one of the simplest approaches to choosing a technique or combination of techniques for a household or small business. Assume that insurance will be used, if available, for each of the pure risks that has been identified and measured in the risk management process. The most suitable policy and its cost are listed for each risk as a benchmark against which to evaluate other possible techniques. Listing insurance coverages also clarifies which risks must be treated by means other than insurance—that is, the risks for which no insurance is available.

Next, insurance coverages are grouped into priority categories, such as

- essential (for example, insurance required by law or losses of possibly disastrous results for the household or business)
- desirable (for example, losses that would seriously impair but not totally wipe out the financial position of the household or business)
- available (all other types of insurance coverage)

Finally, each insurance coverage is compared with the other available techniques for treating the particular risk. For example, can some of the risks in the "essential" category be avoided? Reduced? Transferred? Can some of the risks in the "desirable" category be less expensively addressed through loss prevention and reduction? Can some of the risks in the "available" category be retained, at least partially?

Grouping by Frequency and Severity

A different approach to selecting the most appropriate technique, although it might lead to the same conclusion as the review of insurance priorities, is grouping the most logical techniques based on the probable frequency and severity of the losses associated with each pure risk.

- For risks that involve both high loss frequency and high loss severity, the most suitable technique is avoidance. Retention is not realistic, and insurance is too costly if it is even available. If avoidance is not possible, loss prevention or loss reduction measures might reduce frequency and/or severity to a more manageable level.
- For risks that involve high loss frequency and low loss severity, the most suitable technique is usually retention. Where possible, loss prevention measures might be employed to reduce loss frequency.
- For risks that involve low loss frequency and high loss severity, insurance is often the most suitable technique. Retention is not

appropriate for one individual's or business's high-severity losses, but the cost of insurance should be manageable because the insurer covers the risks of many insurance buyers and utilizes the law of large numbers.

- For risks that involve both low loss frequency and low loss severity, the most suitable technique is usually retention. Losses don't happen very often, and when they do, the consequences are not major.

The simplicity of this approach is somewhat misleading, because it implies that risks can easily be placed into one of the four categories shown in the matrix below. In reality, risks are just not that simple. The approach is especially instructive for this book on insurance planning, however, because it calls attention to the types of risks for which insurance is suited. Clearly, insurance is best suited for low-frequency, high-severity risks. Insurance is not likely to be available for high-frequency, high-severity risks, and it probably is not economically feasible for low-severity risks.

Appropriate Risk Management Techniques		
Expected Frequency	Expected Loss Severity	
	High	Low
High	Avoidance	Retention
Low	Insurance	Retention

Insurance "Building Blocks" for Individuals and Families

It can be helpful to view insurance for individuals and families as a set of three building blocks:

- social insurance
- employer-sponsored insurance
- individual insurance

Figure 2-1
Personal Insurance Building Blocks

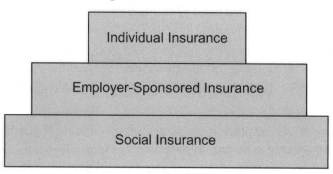

Social Insurance. Because most people are automatically covered by social insurance of some type, it provides a foundation for insurance planning upon which other forms of insurance can build. Social insurance consists of various government programs designed to help solve major social problems. Social insurance programs provide basic protection against certain types of losses. Examples include Social Security, Medicare, unemployment insurance, temporary disability insurance, and workers' compensation insurance. Social insurance programs provide compulsory employment-related coverage, partial or total employer financing, benefits prescribed by law, and benefits as a right. Emphasis is placed on social adequacy rather than individual equity.

third-party
administrator
(TPA)

Employer-Sponsored Insurance. Many individuals and families have access to a second layer of protection through an employer. Many employers provide group life, medical expense, and disability income insurance benefits to employees and their families. Many employers purchase group insurance from a commercial insurer. Other employers self-fund similar benefit programs, often with the aid of a *third-party administrator (TPA)*. A TPA is a firm that administers self-insurance programs for a fee.

Some employers automatically provide coverage for all employees and their dependents at the employer's expense. In other cases, an employee must choose to be covered and must also pay a portion of the cost; however, the employer typically pays the larger portion of the cost. Group insurance almost always costs the employee less than comparable individual coverage. Many forms of group insurance receive favorable federal income tax treatment for the employer and/or the employee.

voluntary benefits   Employers are increasingly making *voluntary benefits* available to employees. An employer makes a voluntary benefit plan available to employees, but the employer does not share in the premium cost. Voluntary benefits are referred to by various names, including *worksite products* and *mass-marketed insurance plans*. The most common products offered as voluntary benefits are various forms of life insurance, short-term and long-term disability income insurance, dental insurance, long-term care insurance, and supplemental medical policies such as cancer insurance and critical illness insurance. A few employers also offer auto and homeowners insurance as voluntary benefits.

Voluntary benefits plans have some characteristics of group insurance and some of individual insurance. As with group insurance, premiums may be payable by payroll deduction. Underwriting standards may be less stringent with insurance purchased in a voluntary benefits plan as compared with individual insurance underwriting standards, but underwriting is still done on an individual basis. As with individual insurance, each employee decides whether to purchase the optional coverage(s) his or her employer makes available. Employees should carefully examine the cost of insurance provided as a voluntary benefit. In many cases, individual coverage is available at a comparable or lower price.

cafeteria plan   A *cafeteria plan* allows employees to choose among several different types of benefits options, much as a person eating in a cafeteria decides among various available food items. In its purest form, a cafeteria plan gives employees a certain specified amount of employer-provided dollars, and the employee may select which combination of available benefits will be purchased with these funds. An employee may also be permitted to take cash in lieu of benefits. The cash option is often a sound choice for an employee whose medical expense insurance is provided through his or her spouse's employer. When an employee selects a benefit that is normally nontaxable, such as medical-expense insurance, the benefit is treated as nontaxable income to the employee. Benefits that are normally taxable—or taking cash rather than benefits—results in taxable income.

premium-conversion plan   Some cafeteria plans also permit the employee to obtain additional benefits and pay for them with salary deductions. Various cafeteria plan options enable employees to select a before-tax salary reduction to pay for their contributions to an employer-sponsored health plan or to obtain certain other types of employee benefits. This option, called a *premium-conversion plan*, may be part of a broader cafeteria plan, or the premium-conversion plan may stand alone.

flexible spending accounts (FSAs) (Sec. 125 plans) A cafeteria plan may allow *flexible spending accounts (FSAs),* also known as *Sec. 125 plans,* under which employees can fund certain types of expenses other than insurance premiums on a before-tax basis. HSAs are commonly used for medical and dental expenses not covered by an employer's plan—such as copayments and deductibles. Separate FSAs can also be established for dependent care expenses.

Forms of Employer-Sponsored Insurance
• Group insurance plans
• Voluntary benefit plans
• Cafeteria plans

Cafeteria plans are subject to complex government rules, and an in-depth discussion is beyond the scope of this book. However, they often provide a cost-effective way for individuals and families to meet some of their personal insurance needs.

Individual Insurance. Individual insurance provides the third layer of insurance protection for individuals and families, and it builds on the other two layers. Individuals and families purchase individual insurance to obtain coverage that cannot be obtained on a cost-effective basis through social insurance and employer-sponsored plans and to increase the total amount of coverage available.

Auto insurance, homeowners insurance, and umbrella liability insurance are usually purchased on an individual basis because they are not available on a group basis or because group coverage, if it is available, is not cost-effective. Individual life insurance is commonly purchased to supplement the total amount of life insurance available through an employer and to obtain permanent protection that supplements the term life insurance usually provided in employer-sponsored plans. Long-term care insurance is also commonly purchased on an individual basis.

Individual insurance generally allows the most flexibility in choosing the type and amount of insurance and selecting the insurance provider. Individual insurance can remain effective despite changes in employment or an employer's cutback or termination of group insurance plans. However, individual insurance typically has stricter underwriting requirements than group insurance plans, and individual insurance is often more expensive than comparable group insurance.

Risk Administration

The fourth step in the risk management process is risk administration. Actually, risk administration must be carried out in conjunction with each of the first three steps of risk management. New risks must be continually identified, and all risks must be frequently remeasured. Treatment alternatives, too, must be reconsidered and reviewed for their effectiveness and their actual and potential costs.

Often the process of initiating and reviewing insurance coverages for a household or small business involves shopping around for the best coverage. Agents, brokers, or financial planners are helpful in identifying and searching the available markets. Lowest costs are not the only factor to consider; the insurer's quality of service, financial strength, reputation, claims services, and loss prevention are also important, as is other business with that insurer. Shopping around may be a useful way to compare markets periodically, but it is not practical to do so every year because there is value in continued services, and there are costs involved in shopping around.

The administration of existing insurance coverages is another part of risk management. Renewal and expiration records are essential to prevent any unplanned lapse in coverage. Amounts of coverage must be kept up-to-date through frequent reevaluation of the exposures. Rate classifications and costs must be checked.

If methods of risk treatment other than insurance have been chosen, risk administration includes additional procedures and review. For example, if the client is relying on an emergency fund or on other liquid assets to cover deductibles and other retained losses, it is important to review periodically whether these assets remain both adequate and available.

EXAMPLES OF RISK MANAGEMENT DECISION MAKING

Two short case studies serve to review the steps in risk management and risk treatment techniques. The first case involves a small business firm, with emphasis on its property and liability loss exposures. The second case involves a family, with emphasis on its life and health loss exposures.

Small Business Case

This case concerns a small manufacturer of specialty plastic goods. The risk manager or consultant for the firm might apply the risk management process as described below.

Step 1—Risk Identification

Fire and products liability are relatively obvious as two major possible sources of potential loss. The risk manager or consultant also identifies and classifies other sources of loss by using a survey form covering perils or loss exposures and analyzing financial statements and contracts.

Step 2—Risk Measurement

Using past company records, the risk manager or consultant finds out that there has been extreme variation in both the frequency and severity of losses during the past 20 years. The degree of unpredictability and maximum probable loss are therefore high. Values of buildings, machinery, inventory, and other property are appraised.

Step 3—Choice and Use of Methods of Treatment

Risk control methods for this small manufacturer include

- avoiding some risks. To conserve working capital and avoid risks, the firm leases three trucks, with the rental company taking care of the fire, theft, and collision coverage. The manufacturer chooses the same risk management technique by leasing its computer.
- adopting an intensive loss prevention and loss reduction program against the perils of fire and explosion. The firm installs an automatic sprinkler system, hires night security guards, trains employees in fire prevention practices and the use of extinguishers, and conducts regular inspections.
- using noninsurance transfer of risk. The manufacturer subcontracts with another firm to produce one of the more toxic plastics necessary for the company's research department.

Risk financing methods include

- retaining some risks by

    −   setting up a reserve in the corporate accounts to cover small losses up to $5,000. Alternatively, the operating expense accounts might simply absorb these losses.

    −   selecting a deductible of $5,000 in connection with the fire insurance contract. Making the supervisors aware of the deductible may encourage loss prevention.

- transferring some risks by

    −   insuring the building and its contents for $1 million with a $5,000 deductible. Consultation with several insurers and agents will help determine the proper perils and the amount of coverage.

    −   making a noninsurance transfer of risk through a hold-harmless agreement with the firm's major sales distributor. In the agreement, the distributor agrees to pay for any products liability losses caused by negligence in the distribution process.

Step 4—Risk Administration

The manufacturer implements the risk treatment alternatives in step 3 through the following procedures: communication and discussion with other departments of the firm, rental of the trucks through the purchasing department, establishment of reserve accounts with the accounting department and the treasurer's office, explanation of deductibles to the supervisors of various departments, and coordination of the loss prevention program with the safety and security department. The manufacturer also purchases property and liability insurance through a carefully selected agent or broker who will provide appraisal services for property values at stated time intervals.

Finally, the manufacturer schedules annual reviews of all risk management methods and property values, with the option to conduct more frequent reviews if necessary. The firm also hires a consultant to evaluate the risk management decisions and arrange for reevaluation of prices for the insurance at 5-year intervals.

Family Case

Now consider how the risk management process might be applied in a family situation—in this case, to the applicable life and health pure risks. Travis and Ruth Jordan, a husband and wife, have two children: Edward and Penny.

Edward is 17 and will begin college as a full-time student in a few months. Penny is 13 and in the eighth grade. Travis is 42, and he is an executive for a chain of grocery stores. He earns about $120,000 per year. Ruth, aged 39, works part-time for an orthodontist and earns about $15,000 per year. Risk management as it relates to the family's life and health pure risks might be applied in this situation as shown below.

Step 1—Risk Identification

The Jordan family faces the following risks:

- The death or disability of Travis might cause a major loss of earnings for the support of Ruth, Edward, and Penny.
- Travis's death would result in some costs, perhaps significant, to clear his estate (funeral, probate, taxes, last illness, and so on).
- Travis's disability could cause extremely high medical bills and other costs (rehabilitation therapy, long-term care, and so on).
- Travis's unemployment could result in lost income for the support of Ruth and the children, as well as some direct costs to obtain another job.
- Several years from now, Travis's retirement from his job will cause a significant loss of income for his and Ruth's support.
- Ruth's death, disability, unemployment, or retirement would cause the same types of losses as described for Travis. The size of the income losses (and some of the estate clearance costs) would be less than for Travis, but the out-of-pocket expenses if Ruth becomes disabled could be fully as large as if Travis were disabled.
- The death of Edward or Penny would cause a loss of their future earning power, some of which might be needed eventually for the support of their parent(s). There would also be some out-of-pocket costs immediately if Edward or Penny were to die.
- The disability of Edward or Penny could lead to very high costs for medical and other types of care.

Step 2—Risk Measurement

Loss frequency rates are essentially meaningless for many of the risks facing individuals and families. Mortality and morbidity tables can be used to estimate the probability that a 42-year-old male will die or incur a disease during the next 12 months. This information is useful to insurers, who cover many 42-year-old males, but it is of limited value to Travis, who is only one 42-year-old male. Travis is concerned more with the possibility of loss than with the probability of loss. During the coming year, the possibility exists that he could die, develop a disease, become disabled, or lose his job. Sound risk management addresses all these possibilities. For example, Travis has life insurance to protect his survivors, because it is possible he could die at any time, even though the probability of death at age 42 is relatively low.

Measuring the loss severity of most risks to a family is more meaningful than measuring loss frequency. The family's loss exposures can be subjectively grouped into three broad categories based on maximum possible or maximum probable loss, as follows:

- Calamitous losses include income loss due to Travis's death, medical bills and other expenses due to his or any other family member's serious disability, income loss due to his long-term disability or unemployment, and Travis's income loss due to his retirement.
- Serious losses include income loss due to Ruth's death or long-term disability, income loss due to Travis's short-term unemployment, income loss due to Ruth's retirement, estate clearance costs due to Travis's death, and medical bills due to routine accidents or illnesses of Travis, Ruth, Edward, or Penny.
- Bearable losses include estate clearance costs due to the death of Ruth, Edward, or Penny and lost income for possible support of Travis or Ruth due to the death of Edward or Penny.

At this point, dollar values are not assigned to each of the potential losses in each category.

Step 3—Choice and Use of Methods of Treatment

The Jordan family can undertake some risk control techniques, particularly in the areas of loss prevention and loss reduction. For example, family members can schedule periodic medical checkups and take preventive measures to lower the likelihood of disability or premature death and so reduce the lost income and out-of-pocket costs associated with those two perils.

The family can also undertake some risk financing. For example, they can retain the losses listed in the "bearable" category, perhaps through the accumulation of an emergency fund and through absorption as part of normal operating expenses. The Jordans can partially retain some of the losses in the "serious" and "calamitous" categories through the use of deductibles and waiting periods in insurance policies. The household can also transfer some of these losses, perhaps through prearranged, guaranteed sources of credit in times of emergency (for example, a home equity line of credit from a bank). Of course, the best way for the Jordans to transfer the losses they cannot control or fully retain is through insurance. The family should give the highest priority to coverage of potentially calamitous losses through life insurance on Travis, major medical expense insurance on all four family members, long-term disability income coverage on Travis, and some type of retirement plan for Travis. The Jordans should also consider long-term care insurance, especially for Travis and Ruth. Life insurance and, if available, disability income coverage for Ruth are a somewhat lower priority, as is some type of retirement plan for her. The Jordans might also consider dental expense coverage for all family members.

Step 4—Risk Administration

Most of the Jordans' risk administration activities, of course, involve arranging and coordinating various forms of insurance coverage in proper amounts and with appropriate deductibles or waiting periods. They should consider three broad categories of insurance in this process: social insurance, employer-sponsored insurance, and individual insurance.

Social Insurance. The first building block for the Jordans involves social insurance programs. One of these programs is Social Security, which will provide a basic level of retirement income for Travis and Ruth. Social Security will also replace a portion of the income lost following the death of Travis or Ruth and, in certain cases, will replace some of the income lost if either of them becomes disabled.

Employer-Sponsored Insurance. The second building block for the Jordans is various insurance programs made available where Travis and Ruth work—both group insurance plans and voluntary benefit plans. Because Ruth works part-time, she may not be eligible for employee benefits. Group insurance programs—which may either be insured or self-funded by an employer—can provide specified types of coverage, such as group life insurance, group medical expense insurance, and a pension plan. In some cases, coverage is automatically given to all employees at no cost; in other cases, an employee must elect coverage and pay a portion of the cost. However, the employer often pays a significant amount of the cost, and only in rare circumstances is the cost more than that of comparable coverage in the individual marketplace.

The most common products offered as voluntary benefits are various forms of life insurance, short-term and long-term disability income insurance, dental insurance, vision insurance, and more recently, long-term care insurance. Some insurers also offer auto and homeowners insurance as voluntary benefits, although these are not a concern of the Jordan family in this case study. The Jordans should pay attention to the cost of voluntary products. In some cases, the cost of coverage may exceed the cost of comparable coverage in the individual marketplace, particularly if an employee is in good health or has a good driving record.

Individual Insurance. After the Jordans have met their economic security needs to the greatest extent possible through the first two building blocks—social insurance and employer-sponsored benefit plans—they should turn to the third building block, individual insurance. Here, the Jordans should make purchases to fill in coverage gaps left by social insurance and employer-sponsored insurance and to increase total coverage amounts to the necessary levels.

Auto insurance, homeowners insurance, umbrella liability insurance, and other forms of property-liability insurance not typically available through an employer fall in this area, together with individually purchased life insurance that provides higher limits and more permanent protection than that offered by an employer-sponsored plan. Long-term care insurance is also commonly purchased on an individual basis.

Monitoring the Risk Program. Once the Jordans have implemented each of the risk treatment methods, including the insurance method, administration of the risk management process requires ongoing monitoring of the choices and coverages by the Jordans and their financial consultant. New risks must be identified as they arise. The Jordans' insurance coverages and other risk treatment methods must also be reviewed periodically in light of their costs and their effectiveness in meeting the Jordans' needs.

CHAPTER REVIEW

Key Terms and Concepts

risk management	risk financing
enterprise risk management	risk avoidance
risk control	loss prevention

loss reduction	mortality
noninsurance transfers	morbidity
risk financing	risk identification
risk retention	maximum possible loss
deductible	maximum probable loss
self-insurance	third-party administrator (TPA)
captive insurer	voluntary benefits
risk transfer	cafeteria plan
hold-harmless agreement	premium-conversion plan
insurance equation	flexible spending accounts (FSAs)
credibility	(Sec. 125 plans)

Review Questions

Review questions are based on the learning objectives in this chapter. Thus, a [3] at the end of a question means that the question is based on learning objective 3. If there are multiple objectives, they are all listed.

1. What four steps might a client use in applying the risk management process? [4]

2. What are the objectives of risk management? [1]

3. How is the risk manager's role carried out differently in large organizations as opposed to small- and medium-sized firms? [1]

4. How do the two basic methods of treating risk—risk control and risk financing—differ from one another? [2]

5. Why is risk avoidance not a practical solution to many risks? [2]

6. Why might inadequate planning cause a client to retain pure risks? [2]

7. Why do planners often suggest that clients use higher insurance deductibles? [2]

8. Your client Sam Jones feels that if he is going to buy insurance, it should pay whenever he has a loss. As a result, his insurance program includes coverage for high-frequency, low-severity losses. For example, his health insurance program includes basic medical expense coverage that pays from the first dollar of expense when he or his family goes to the doctor or the hospital. What could you recommend to Sam that would treat his risks involving high-frequency, low-severity losses more efficiently than using first-dollar insurance? [2]

9. How do families and businesses commonly finance the risks they retain? [2]

10. Four key concepts help explain how insurance works: (a) the insurance equation, (b) probability and uncertainty, (c) the law of large numbers, and (d) adequate statistical data. Why is each concept important to the operation of the insurance mechanism? [3]

11. What are four methods of risk identification that a planner can use with households or businesses? [4]

12. What factors should a client consider in choosing the best technique(s) for dealing with a risk situation, especially for a household or a small business? [4]

13. What are two approaches a client can use in deciding which technique or combination of techniques would best handle the risks households and small businesses face? [4]

14. What are the three "building blocks" that can be used to form a client's personal insurance program? [3]

15. Norma and Sidney took an early retirement from their jobs in a northern state and purchased a condominium in the sun belt. Norma expects to remain involved in cultural and social activities while Sidney pursues his dream of writing the great American novel. They leased a convertible to enjoy the year-round sunny climate in their new area, and they also plan to travel abroad and to travel north frequently to visit their children and grandchildren. Briefly summarize the risk management process Norma, Sidney, and their financial planner might use to identify and address the risks associated with this major change in Norma's and Sidney's lives. [4]

Learning Objectives

An understanding of the material in this chapter should enable the student to

1. Distinguish among the ways private insurers may be classified and organized.

2. Compare stock and mutual insurance companies with other types of insuring organizations.

3. Explain why some mutual insurance companies are converting to stock companies.

4. Briefly describe the insurance market.

5. Describe and compare the types of marketing representatives in insurance.

6. Explain an insurance agent's legal duties to an insurer and an insurer's duties to the agent.

7. Compare the marketing systems used in insurance.

Financial planners play an important role in identifying their clients' risks and assisting their clients in risk management. A financial planner cannot function effectively without understanding one of the major tools of financial planning, insurance, and the structure of the business that produces and/or sells the insurance products that individuals, families, and businesses need.

TYPES OF PRIVATE INSURERS

The following pages summarize the characteristics of the major types of insurers that make up the United States insurance business. Throughout this book, the terms "insurer," "insurance company," and, often, "company" are used to identify the organization that issues insurance "contracts" or "policies." The choice of words often depends on the context.

As explained in this section, any private insurer—as opposed to a government insurer—can be classified according to the lines of business it writes, its state or country of domicile, and its form of organization.

Insurance companies can also be categorized in a variety of other ways not specifically discussed here. For example, a given insurer may write business within one county, within a state, within a region, or nationally. An insurer may focus on providing insurance for a particular market segment, such as farmers or teachers, or it might market its products broadly. Some insurers are very selective in their underwriting and provide low-cost insurance to applicants who qualify as preferred risks; other insurers concentrate on the high-risk or substandard-risk market. Some provide an elite set of products designed for wealthy clients, while others market heavily to wage earners. To the client, all insurance companies may seem alike. Experienced financial planners, however, discover that each insurance company has its own personality or flavor, and they often become adept at helping clients find insurers that best match their specific needs. One especially important distinguishing characteristic of any given insurer is its marketing system or systems.

Classification by Line of Business

Private insurers can be classified according to the lines of insurance they write. Any given insurer might, for example, be categorized in one of the following ways:

- a life and health insurer
- a property and liability insurer
- an all-lines insurer (writing life, health, property, and liability insurance)
- a monoline specialty insurer (specializing in one line of coverage, such as medical professional liability insurance)

Many insurers have groups of affiliated companies, often with a common field force, that write and sell all lines of insurance.

Classification by Domicile

These classifications are used to classify insurers operating in the United States:

domestic insurer

foreign insurer

alien insurer

- A *domestic insurer* is one doing business in the state where it is incorporated. For example, New York Life Insurance Company is classified as a domestic insurer when it does business in New York.

- A *foreign insurer* is one doing business in a state other than its state of incorporation. Hartford Fire Insurance Company, domiciled in Connecticut, is a foreign insurer when doing business in New York. New York Life Insurance Company is a foreign insurer when it does business in Connecticut.

- An *alien insurer* is incorporated in another country but doing business in the United States. An insurance company domiciled in Germany is an alien insurance company when it does business in New York.

Admitted versus Nonadmitted Insurers

nonadmitted insurer

An admitted insurer is one that is licensed by a state insurance department to do business in a policyowner's home state. A *nonadmitted insurer* is one that is not licensed or authorized in the policyowner's home state. However, a nonadmitted insurer might be licensed in other states, and it might even be an alien insurer (that is, it might be licensed in another country).

surplus lines insurance

Nonadmitted insurers serve a legal, valuable, and positive role in the U.S. insurance marketplace. A typical nonadmitted insurer provides *surplus lines insurance* (also referred to as *excess lines insurance*) coverages that otherwise would not be available. Consumers are permitted to buy property and liability insurance from nonadmitted insurers when they cannot purchase some needed coverage from an admitted insurer. Nonadmitted insurers generally provide insurance for policyowners that present underwriting challenges, have unique risks that are hard to evaluate, or require unusually high limits of insurance.

Because they are exempt from many regulations and laws that apply to licensed insurers, nonadmitted insurers generally have more flexibility than admitted insurers; however, the excess and surplus lines market is still subject to regulation. Many states maintain a list of nonadmitted insurers that are approved to do business in the state.

Ways to Classify Private Insurers

- By lines of insurance written—for example, life and health, property and liability, monoline, all lines
- By domicile—for example, domestic, foreign, alien
- Admitted versus nonadmitted insurers
- By legal form of organization—for example, stock, mutual, and so on
- By marketing system

Classification by Form of Organization

Private insurers can be divided into three major groups, according to their legal form of organization:

- stock
- mutual
- other

"Other" insurers include reciprocal exchanges, captive insurers, fraternal societies, banks, health associations, and Lloyd's associations.

Stock Companies

stock insurance company

A *stock insurance company* is a corporation owned by stockholders. Shares of stock companies are usually traded on an organized stock exchange. Stockholders expect to earn a profit from their investment in insurance company stock. The stockholders elect the members of the company's board of directors and vote on other major issues facing the company, such as mergers or acquisitions.

As with other types of insurers, insurance laws enacted by the various states govern the company's operations. To be licensed, stock insurers must have at least a specified amount of capital and surplus. Stock companies issue insurance contracts in exchange for a premium. The policyowner usually receives no dividends from the company's earnings. Except for participating policies (those with dividends) issued by some stock life insurers, the policyowner's first cost is usually the final cost.[8]

Stockholders are entitled to any of the residual profits declared by the board as dividends after losses and expenses have been paid and proper reserves established.

Stock insurance companies thus have the following basic legal characteristics:

- They are incorporated and owned by stockholders who supply capital funds that serve as part of the financial security for the firm's operations.
- Except for flexible-premium contracts, they usually issue contracts for a fixed cost. The contracts are usually nonparticipating.
- They can pay residual profits to the stockholders.

Mutual Companies

mutual insurance company

A *mutual insurance company* is a not-for-profit insurance company owned by its policyowners. The policyowners also participate in the operations of the company, at least through voting rights, and they share in the company's financial successes and, sometimes, its failure. A mutual insurance company is organized primarily to provide insurance for its policyowners, rather than to seek a profit. Every policyowner is an owner of the company. There are no stockholders. The mutual policyowners elect the board of directors, and the board chooses the executive officers who actually manage the company. The mutual corporation assumes the risks of its policyowners. When the premiums in a given period are more than adequate to meet losses and expenses, part or all of the excess may be returned to the policyowners as a dividend. When premiums are inadequate, dividends may be omitted and, in a few cases, assessments can be levied on policyowners.

Mutual insurers include (1) advance-premium mutuals and (2) assessment mutuals.

---

8.   In some commercial lines, such as workers' compensation insurance, the insured's first cost takes the form of a tentative deposit premium that is subject to adjustment after an audit at the end of the period of protection. Large commercial insureds might also have loss-sensitive insurance programs, in which the ultimate premium is based in part on the insured's losses during the current policy term.

advance-premium
mutuals

Advance-Premium Mutuals. Advance-premium mutuals write all but a small percentage of total mutual insurance. The operations of *advance-premium mutuals* closely resemble those of stock insurance companies. Legally, advance-premium mutuals are different because they are owned by the policyowners and have no stockholders.

Advance-premium mutuals issue nonassessable contracts in which the cost of the insurance is set when the policy begins. Legal requirements for writing nonassessable policies require these mutuals to possess specified amounts of surplus to ensure the company's financial solvency in case of temporary periods of heavier-than-normal losses or expenses.

Advance-premium mutuals may issue dividends to policyowners. At the end of the policy period, a return may be made as a dividend for any amount beyond the company's losses, expenses, and reasonable contributions to reserves and surplus. The actual amount of the return is unknown to the policyowner until after the insurance contract period ends (typically annual), and it depends on the company's experience for that policyowner classification. The actual net cost (original premium minus dividend) to the policyowner is thus uncertain until the dividend is paid.

In most states, advance-premium mutuals must comply with the same reserve, investment, policy form, and regulatory laws as stock companies. Organizational requirements are somewhat different, in that a minimum number of policyowners is required to start a company, and the board of directors must be subject to the control of policyowners rather than stockholders.

assessment
mutuals

Assessment Mutuals. Some small mutual companies are called *assessment mutuals*. Policyowners may or may not pay an advance premium, but they can be assessed for a portion of the company's losses and expenses at the end of the policy period. The policyowner's liability for the assessment may be limited or unlimited with an assessment mutual.

Choosing between the Stock and Mutual Form

From the standpoint of the insurance consumer, which type of insurer is better—a stock company or a mutual company? Neither type is inherently superior. The stock form of organization may entail lower initial premiums than the mutual form, and a stock company may be better equipped to raise the capital needed for insuring, both initially and subsequently. The mutual form, on the other hand, may charge lower premiums net of dividends because of its nonprofit status. Stock and mutual insurance companies both purchase reinsurance to ensure financial strength. The real issue for the consumer of insurance, then, is which specific insurer and which specific insurance contract to select, not which type of insurer to select.

From the standpoint of the insuring organization itself, which form is better—stock or mutual? Again, there is no definitive answer. New insurers are usually formed as stock companies because it is very difficult to form a mutual by persuading would-be policyowners to put up capital before the insurer can come into existence.

demutualization   On balance, the number of mutual insurers in the United States is decreasing due to mergers, insolvencies, and intentional shifting of mutual companies to the stock form of organization—a process called *demutualization*. Probably the most important reason for demutualization is to enable the insurer to raise capital quickly. A stock company, of course, can raise new capital by issuing stock, bonds, warrants, and other types of debt instruments, as well as by earning profits. Mutual insurers have only their profits and borrowings to provide additional capital for expansion, acquisition, or other purposes.

A second and often related reason for demutualization is to enable the insurance company to diversify its activities by merging with or acquiring other insurers or other types of financial institutions through the issuance or exchange of stock. Mutual insurers, having no stock, are less able to diversify in this way. Also, stock insurers can create upstream holding companies to facilitate diversification. Until recently, this avenue was not open to mutual insurers, and in many states it still is not available.

A third reason for demutualization is to facilitate payment of certain types of noncash compensation to the insurance company's key executives and board members. Compensation through tax-advantaged stock options and stock-ownership plans is not available in a mutual company, because it has no stock.

Reasons for Demutualizing
• Raise new capital   • Insurer diversification   • Noncash executive compensation

Nevertheless, the process of demutualization has certain significant disadvantages. The time, cost, and complexity may be enormous because of regulatory, tax, legal, and accounting requirements. Of particular importance is the regulatory requirement that the policyowners of the company seeking to demutualize be compensated adequately for loss of their ownership rights. A second disadvantage of demutualization is that, as a stock company, the insurer might become vulnerable to a hostile takeover. Third, as a stock insurer, the company would have to meet SEC and state rules relating to its equity securities. Fourth, demutualization represents a major change in corporate philosophy with the introduction of an explicit profit motive, a change that may be very difficult for senior executives and other long-standing employees of the former mutual company to accept.

mutual holding company

Several states allow mutual insurers to create a hybrid form of organization—the *mutual holding company*—to overcome some of the disadvantages of either remaining a mutual or demutualizing. The mutual holding company directly or indirectly controls a stock insurer. To be more specific, the mutual insurer creates a holding company controlled by the policyowners. The holding company then acquires at least 51 percent of the stock of a newly created stock insurance company that takes over the business of the former mutual insurer. The remaining stock can be sold to outsiders to raise additional capital for the new insurance company.

Other Types of Insuring Organizations

Most of the private insurance in the United States is written by stock companies and advance-premium mutual companies. Several other legal types of insurers also merit discussion.

fraternal insurer

Fraternal Insurers. A *fraternal insurer* is a special type of insurer providing insurance benefits, particularly life insurance, for its members. The operations of the fraternal insurer are closely related to and controlled by the bylaws of a lodge or a nonprofit social organization. Many fraternals are church oriented.[9]

reciprocal exchange

Reciprocal Exchanges. A *reciprocal exchange* is an unincorporated pool of funds owned by the policyholders and managed by an attorney-in-fact. The first reciprocal exchange was organized in 1888. At one time, in many states, reciprocals were not subject to most insurance regulation, but that distinction has now disappeared in most states. The two organizations, the pool and the manager, are now regulated as a licensed insurer.

In a reciprocal exchange's original and purest form, each policyholder was insured by all the others. In its now more popular, modified form, a reciprocal exchange may operate without individual accounts for its subscribers, and most are nonassessable. But though a reciprocal may appear to the layman to resemble a conventional mutual insurer, it is not. In a reciprocal exchange, the insured/insurer relationship is governed by a subscribers agreement or power of attorney in which policyholders assume liability as individuals and grant the attorney-in-fact the right to manage for a fee, as an insurer, the funds contributed by policyholders and others to the unincorporated association. A mutual, on the other hand, is a corporation owned by policyholders.

Reciprocal exchanges are few in number, but in certain areas and for personal lines of property and liability insurance, they have some significance. Although many are small, a few reciprocal exchanges have grown to a substantial size.

Captives. Captive insurance companies are hard to classify. Captive insurers are sometimes considered a sophisticated form of self-insurance or retention. We mention captives again here because, like a mutual insurance company, a captive insurance company is an insurance company owned by the organization or organizations it insures. In that sense, a captive insurance company resembles a mutual insurance company.

A *single-parent captive* is such an example. A single-parent captive insurance company organized for the sole purpose of insuring the "parent" company that formed it. A *group captive*, also known as an *association captive*, provides insurance to a group of corporations (often members of a trade

---

9.   The Association of America's Fraternal Benefit Societies maintains an information Web page at http://www.nfcanet.org.

association) that also own the captive. A *risk retention group* is a special type of group captive formed under the Risk Retention Act of 1986. A risk retention group provides liability insurance subject to limited state regulation.

Until recently, businesses used captive insurers primarily to finance property and liability loss exposures. However, some companies have recently been able to expand their existing captive insurance programs to finance certain employee benefits. Because the Employee Retirement Income Security Act (ERISA) prohibits transactions between an employee benefit plan and the plan's sponsor, any organization that wants to insure its employee benefits through a captive must obtain a prohibited-transaction exemption from the U.S. Department of Labor (DOL). Among other things, it is necessary to demonstrate that employees will benefit from the proposed arrangement. In recent years, the DOL has expedited the process of approving applications, and many companies now see the captive approach as a viable option for covering certain employee benefits, such as post-retirement health care. Potential benefits include lower premiums and improved cash flow, especially for benefits with claims paid over an extended time period (such as long-term disability).[10]

Banks. In recent years, the entry of banks into the business of insurance has been characterized by a considerable amount of publicity, controversy, and legal jousting. However, one particular type of bank—the mutual savings bank—has been providing life insurance for many years in a few states.

Laws in these states authorize mutual savings banks to write life insurance on residents of the state and on persons regularly employed there. The amounts that may be issued are limited. Because the coverage is written without a commissioned agent as an intermediary, premium rates for savings bank life insurance usually compare favorably with those charged by other insurers. Nevertheless, the amount of savings bank life insurance represents only a small percentage of the total amount of life insurance sold in the three states. Perhaps this is attributable to the absence of an aggressive, commission-based sales force for savings bank life insurance.

The past few years have also seen the gradual entry of banks into other aspects of the insurance business, particularly in such lines as fixed and variable annuities, homeowners insurance, auto insurance, and life

---

10. Sammer, Joanne, "The Captive Option for Employee Benefits," *Business Finance*, http://www.mag.com/magazine/ archives/article.html?articleID=14501, accessed 9/12/06.

insurance. Initially, the majority of these banks created entirely new insurance operations from scratch. Later entrants to the field, however, have tended to form alliances with existing insurers and their insurance agencies, thus becoming, rather than insurers, marketing channels for insurance "manufactured" by others.

Blue Cross and Blue Shield plans

Health Associations. *Blue Cross and Blue Shield plans* are organizations formed for the purpose of prepaying subscribers' medical care benefits. Blue Cross plans provide coverage primarily for hospital expenses, while Blue Shield plans provide coverage primarily for physicians' services. Blue Cross and Blue Shield plans and health maintenance organizations (HMOs) play a particularly important role in the field of medical expense insurance.

Blue Cross organizations have historically provided hospital care in member hospitals on a service basis, rather than on a cash reimbursement basis. Blue Shield organizations have covered the costs of member physicians and surgeons, also on a service basis. Under the service-benefit concept, benefits are expressed in terms of the services that the hospitals or physicians who participate in the plan will provide, rather than in terms of dollar maximums. For example, a Blue Cross plan might provide hospitalization in semiprivate accommodations. In contrast, an insurance company might provide reimbursement for hospital charges subject to a dollar limitation, such as $600 per day.

While Blue Cross and Blue Shield plans have traditionally operated separately in limited geographic areas, most Blue Cross and Blue Shield plans in each area have now merged into a single entity. Blue Cross and Blue Shield plans must be members of the National Blue Cross and Blue Shield Association, which sets certain standards for the local organizations. Among these standards are requirements that the local organizations have boards of directors, the majority of whom are not health care providers, and that the organizations participate in national plans that offer portability of coverage and benefit availability for insureds outside their home service areas.

Although the Blues and insurance companies were once quite different, they have evolved over the years so that they now probably have more similarities than differences. The Blues tend to exist under special enabling legislation, which gives them some advantages, such as favorable state taxation, but also limits their underwriting and rating flexibility. The majority of plans are structured as not-for-profit organizations, making them similar to mutual insurance companies. Profits are not distributed to shareholders or policyowners, but some of the Blues have accumulated a rather substantial surplus despite their nonprofit status. However, several have converted to the traditional forms of stock or mutual companies.

Lloyd's associations   ***Lloyd's Associations.*** In contrast to stock and mutual insurers, which are corporations, *Lloyd's associations* are groups of individual insurers. Insurance written by Lloyd's associations accounts for only a small percentage of the total insurance sales in the United States. However, Lloyd's organizations are significant from a historical standpoint, and in the world market, they are very important for reinsurance and for insuring unusual and difficult risks.

Lloyd's of London, one of the most famous insurance institutions, bears the name of the coffeehouse where it originated more than 300 years ago as a center of shipping news and financial information. Lloyd's itself does not directly issue insurance policies; rather, insurance is written by underwriting members who sign "each for himself and not for another." The insurer, then, is not Lloyd's but the underwriters at Lloyd's.

There are a few American Lloyd's associations, including several in Texas. These associations write primarily fire and allied lines and auto physical damage insurance. In the American Lloyd's associations, each member is ordinarily liable for only a specified maximum, and the strict regulations of Lloyd's of London that govern membership, deposits, and audits are not present. Each American Lloyd's organization depends on the financial strength of its individual members within their limited liability. The American Lloyd's and the original London organization have no connection, and the American Lloyd's associations play a relatively small role in United States insurance.

THE MARKETING PROCESS

With this background of the types of organizations that provide insurance to individuals, households, and businesses, we now turn to the process by which organizations market their insurance. Why do financial planners need to understand how the insurance business markets its contracts and services? First, financial planners are in many cases active participants in the marketing process, deriving some of their compensation from being participants. Second, working with consumers of insurance, financial planners need to understand the choices among insurers and agents that clients must make in buying insurance. Finally, financial planners need to recognize that the methods companies use to sell and service insurance contracts are significant in determining their costs and usefulness.

Marketing the Insurance Product

The following figure shows the relationship of marketing to the product design, underwriting, and loss payment functions as insurance is distributed from insurers to policyowners.

Figure 3-1
Functional Viewpoint of Insurance

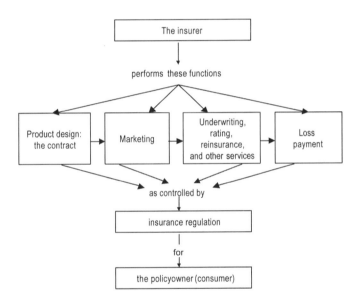

Marketing, or directing the flow of goods and services from the insurer to the consumer or user, is a particularly important business activity for insurance companies. The insurance product consists of a written legal contract plus a bundle of services. An insurer's representative may provide motivation, education, and advice both before and after an insurance policy is issued. In some ways at least, this bundle of services distinguishes insurance from tangible goods for which service often begins and ends with the sale.

The Insurance Market

A market is a meeting place where people transact business. Insurance practitioners use the term "market" in two different, almost opposite ways. On the one hand, "a market" refers to a geographic area or a group to whom a given type of insurance can be sold. For example, one might refer to the West Coast market or to the affluent market. Practitioners also use "a market" to refer to a source of insurance coverage. For example, the insurance companies that sell life insurance to people with a reduced life expectancy might be referred to as the substandard life market. As a verb, the term "market" can refer either to selling insurance to clients or to finding an insurer who will write the coverage a client needs. An insurance company will "market" insurance to the public; an insurance broker will "market" insurance to insurance companies on behalf of its clients.

To help clients facilitate effective insurance transactions, a financial planner must be familiar with the functions of the insurance market and the roles of the various participants in that market.

Types of Marketing Representatives

Many insurance buyers care more about the person with whom they deal than they do about the insurer that provides insurance coverage. A typical client is not especially concerned whether the insurer is organized as a stock insurer, a mutual insurer, or in some other form. Most are not aware what marketing system the insurer uses. Even if these distinctions seem unimportant to clients, financial planners need to distinguish among the types of insurer representatives with whom a client must deal. The applicant for insurance normally makes contact with the insurers through one or more of the following: (1) agents, (2) brokers, (3) insurance consultants and financial planners, and (4) service representatives.

Agents

agent
An insurance *agent* is often referred to as a producer because he or she produces business for the insurance company or companies that he or she represents. Legally, any agent represents a principal; an insurance agent's principal is an insurance company. Insurance companies appoint agents to solicit prospects for insurance, to negotiate with these prospects, and in some cases, to put contracts of insurance into effect. Agents are typically compensated by a commission that is a percentage of a policy premium.

The agent's powers are defined by his or her agency contract with the insurer. The agency contract spells out the agent's express authority. The agent also has implied or incidental authority to carry out those acts needed to exercise his or her express authority. An agent's acts may bind the principal even if those acts are outside the scope of the agent's express or implied authority, provided the acts are within the agent's apparent authority. Apparent authority arises when the agent, without contrary action by the principal, performs an act that appears to a reasonable person to be within the agent's express or implied authority. For example, if a life insurance agent waives a policy provision for a policyowner relating to the grace period for payment of renewal premiums, the insurance company might, if silent on the matter, be bound by the apparent authority of the agent. In an effort to prevent this from happening, insurers normally include a provision in their policies stating that only specified home office personnel have the authority to waive or modify a policy provision.

A principal may ratify an agent's actions that are outside the scope of the agent's authority and as a result be bound by those actions. For example, if an insurance contract states that renewal premiums must be sent to the insurer's home office, but the company routinely accepts premiums sent to its local agent, in the event of a dispute, the insurer would probably be found to have ratified the agent's collection of renewal premiums.

An agent owes the following legal duties to his or her principal:

- Exercise reasonable care.
- Obey the principal's instructions.
- Maintain accurate accounting records.
- Keep the principal informed.
- Comply with the agency contract.

The principal, in this case the insurance company, also owes certain duties to its agents:

- Pay for the agent's services.
- Maintain accurate accounting records.
- Reimburse the agent for expenses incurred as an agent.
- Reimburse the agent for liability incurred as an agent without the agent's fault.
- Comply with the agency contract.

Both the agent and the insurer are responsible for maintaining accounting records. The agent is responsible for properly handling any funds that belong to the insurer, such as premiums collected by the agent. The insurer, of course, is obligated to maintain accurate accounting records and to pay the agent commissions and, if applicable, other expenses provided for in the agency contract.

The liability that an agent may incur requires a comment. A customer who receives inappropriate advice, inadequate service, or incomplete coverage from an insurance agent who was allegedly negligent may bring a liability claim against that agent. These are referred to as errors and omissions claims. Insurance professionals and financial planners strive to serve their clients faithfully and avoid errors and omissions claims.

Errors and omissions can take many forms. In the principal-agent relationship, an error or omission on behalf of an agent sometimes obligates the insurer to pay a claim that should not have been covered. For example, the agent might bind coverage for which the agency contract does not provide binding authority. When the agent acted with apparent authority as an agent of the insurance company, the insurer will typically pay the claim and then seek reimbursement from the agent. Insurance agents, like other professionals, need to protect themselves against these and other claims with errors and omissions (E&O) professional liability insurance. Because E&O insurance usually includes a large deductible, even an agent who is insured faces a substantial loss in the event of an error or omission.

binder   ***Binding Authority.*** When coverage is bound, it is immediately put into effect. Written evidence that coverage is bound usually exists in the form of a written binder, but an oral binder is also valid. A *binder* is temporary evidence of insurance, and it is superseded when a written policy is issued.

Life insurance agents usually do not have binding authority, but property-liability insurance agents are normally authorized to bind insurance on behalf of the insurance companies they represent. A life insurance agent solicits life insurance applications. The agent usually collects the initial premium and gives the applicant a conditional premium receipt. The application must be approved by the insurance company before insurance becomes effective. If the applicant meets the insurer's normal underwriting standards, the insurance then becomes effective as of the date of the application or, in some cases, the date of the medical exam, whichever is later. A life insurance company issues the contract only after receiving the written, signed application and, often, a medical examination report. The agent has no authority to cover the insured immediately, and later contract modifications also require the insurance company's approval before they can become effective.

Property-liability insurance agents are usually granted binding authority, subject to any limitations set forth in the agency agreement—the contract between the agent and the insurance company. An oral or written binder is temporary evidence of insurance coverage until the insurance company issues the full insurance policy. When a client who has just purchased a car telephones an insurance agent to obtain coverage, an agent with binding authority can put coverage into effect immediately, before the client even drives the car home. A binder should identify the insurance company with which coverage is bound, any limits of insurance that apply, and the duration of the temporary coverage the binder provides.

Brokers

brokers
Brokers legally represent the policyowner rather than the insurer. Like agents, brokers can offer significant advice and counsel to their clients. The larger insurance brokerage firms are especially well equipped to handle the problems of insurance for a buyer with special requirements.

A broker is an independent contractor. The broker assists the applicant for insurance by finding coverage. A broker may be paid by the client, the insurer, or both. The duties of a broker are similar to those of an agent as described earlier, except that the broker's legal duties pertain more directly to the applicant or policyowner whom he or she represents.

Policyowners sometimes do not differentiate between an insurance broker and an agent. As explained above, an insurance agent is acting under specific and delegated authority from the insurer and is sometimes authorized to bind coverage within specific limits. A broker, on the other hand, has no such authority. Because a broker represents the applicant or policyowner, an applicant or policyowner is bound by the broker's acts. For example, any misrepresentation, mistake, breach of warranty, or fraud perpetrated by the broker on a policyowner's behalf makes the policyowner responsible as if the policyowner had committed the act. Furthermore, a statement by an applicant to a broker is not presumed to be known to an insurance company, whereas a statement by an applicant to an agent is presumed to be known by the company.

Some insurance agents are licensed as both agents and brokers. For example, a producer may act as an agent who commits the insurer for a part of a desired amount of coverage and as a broker in placing any excess coverage.

EXAMPLE
Ripley is an agent for the XYZ Insurance Company, which specializes in preferred auto insurance. Ripley also has a broker's license that includes auto insurance. Ripley may have authority to bind coverage for an applicant in XYZ, but Ripley has no authority to bind coverage that he wishes to place with another insurer for which he acts a broker.

surplus lines broker

A special type of broker, called a *surplus lines broker* (or excess lines broker), places coverage with nonadmitted insurers, who can often provide insurance when no other market is available in the state. For example, surplus lines brokers may place liability insurance for amusement parks and ski resorts, as well as many products liability coverages. A surplus lines broker often deals with the policyowner's broker rather than deal directly with the policyowner. Many states require surplus lines brokers to have a special license.

Insurance Consultants and Financial Planners

Financial planners, who help clients protect their income and assets, play a major role in the personal insurance marketing system. Financial planners are among the various other types of insurance and risk management consultants that may serve as intermediaries between insurance companies and their customers. Insurance consultants are usually compensated by the policyowner on a fee basis. Financial planners may be paid a fee by the policyowner, a commission from the insurer if they are also agents or brokers, or some combination of a fee and a commission.

Salaried Specialists

Many insurers, as well as some large insurance agencies, employ salaried service representatives to help agents sell or service the more complex lines of insurance. State insurance regulations usually do not require service representatives to be licensed.

Life insurance service representatives include advanced underwriting specialists who aid the life insurance agent in estate planning and pension or tax planning. Salaried training specialists may recruit, supervise, and assist new life insurance agents. Most companies that write group life and health coverages have salaried company representatives who assist the life insurance agent with writing group contracts. Many property and liability insurance companies use marketing representatives to initiate agency contracts, help agents with special sales problems, and keep agents informed of the insurer's new contracts and services. Engineering, appraisal, and loss prevention services are often provided by company specialists in conjunction with local agents. In addition, company claims adjusters work in cooperation with agents on many losses involving large amounts or special problems.

Marketing Systems Used in Insurance

Agency versus Direct-Response Marketing Systems

The complex and intangible nature of insurance and its significance to the policyowner make personal contact through an intermediary essential to the sale of most insurance.

direct-response marketing

Direct-response marketing provides the exception to the general rule that insurance is sold through agents. Under a direct-response marketing system, the insurer deals directly with the applicant, without agents, through employees of the insurer. In specialized lines in certain market segments of insurance, these systems assume some importance. Dread disease insurers or hospital confinement indemnity health insurers who use direct mail or television advertising are common examples. All correspondence circulates directly between the company and the prospect, and the insurance contract is written and serviced by mail or telephone without an agent.

As another example of direct-response marketing, some insurers sell such coverages as annuities and life, health, auto, homeowners, and long-term care insurance over the Internet.

Mixed marketing systems are becoming increasingly common. For example, some insurance agencies market insurance through the Internet. Some insurance companies market through agents and also market directly to consumers through the Internet or through the mail. With group life and health insurance, it is increasingly common for salaried employees to assist commissioned agents.

Life Insurance Agency Systems

general agency system

Some life insurance companies use a *general agency system*. Historically, a general insurance agent was an individual entrepreneur granted a franchise by an insurer to market the insurer's products in a specified geographic area. The general agent represented only that one insurer and was responsible for hiring, training, motivating, and supervising agents. The general agent was compensated solely by commissions on business the agency produced and was fully responsible for all expenses of operating the agency. More recently, however, insurance companies typically provide some form of financial assistance to the general agent, perhaps paying some of the costs involved in hiring and training new agents and/or providing an allowance to cover some of the operating agency's expenses.

branch office system

In contrast with the general agency system, some life insurance companies use a *branch office system*, also referred to as a managerial system. Here, the insurer establishes branch offices in the areas where it writes business, with each branch headed by a manager who is a salaried employee of the insurance company. Again, the manager is responsible for hiring, training, motivating, and supervising agents for the company, but the insurer bears all costs of operating the branch. The branch manager may also receive a bonus as part of his or her compensation, depending on the quantity and quality of business the branch writes. Payment of bonuses to branch managers, together with coverage of some general agency operating expenses, has tended to blur somewhat the historical distinctions between these two agency systems.

personal producing general agent (PPGA)

A variation of the general agency system that has become significant for many life insurance companies is the *personal producing general agent (PPGA)* system. In this system, the insurer hires an experienced agent with a proven record of sales success as its general agent in a given territory. Unlike a traditional general agent, however, the personal producing general agent's main responsibility is his or her personal production. The PPGA is expected to sell the insurer's products, rather than to build an agency force for the company. The PPGA often receives higher commissions than other agents. The PPGA may be expected to meet certain sales quotas for the company but may also be allowed to represent other insurers.

Property and Liability Insurance Agency Systems

independent agency system
The two main agency systems that dominate in the property and liability field are the independent agency system and the exclusive agency system, sometimes referred to as the captive agent system. In the *independent agency system*, the insurance agency is an independent business organization that usually represents several insurance companies or groups of companies. The head of the agency pays all his or her own operating expenses and is compensated mainly through commissions on the business the agency writes. Some independent agencies are paid fees by the insurer for settling small claims or by the policyowner for providing risk management services.

The independent agent usually has some authority to bind the insurer for a client's coverage, to collect the initial premium and in some cases the renewal premiums, to submit the application to the insurer, and to deliver the policy to the policyowner. The policyowner is, by contract, the customer of the agent. The independent agent owns the policyowner's business and has a right to place it with a different insurer when the policy comes up for renewal, if the policyowner consents. Commission rates on property and liability insurance policies tend to be the same for renewal policies as for new policies. If renewal commissions were lower, an independent agent might be inclined to place the business with a different insurer at each renewal date to earn the higher first-year commission. Another result of ownership of the customer's business is that when the independent agent elects to retire or leave the business, he or she can sell the book of business to another agent. The insurer may not interfere with the agent's ownership rights.

One of the main advantages of the independent agency system is that the agent who represents several insurers can place business with the company that offers the best coverage at the best price for each applicant. One of the disadvantages is that a conflict of interest may exist when the agent has the opportunity to place business with any of several companies that pay different commission rates.

exclusive agency system
In the *exclusive agency system*, the agent usually represents only one company or group of affiliated companies. Compensation comes mainly from commissions on the sale of new business, with lower commission rates on

renewals. One reason this is possible is that the insurance company tends to handle more of the service after the sale for exclusive agents (who are expected to devote most of their time to selling) than for independent agents (who tend to be more involved in client service). The insurer may cover some of the agent's operating expenses, particularly for new agents. The agency contract typically gives the agent either limited or no ownership, use, and control of policy and expiration data while the contract is in force. The agent has no control over what happens to the business when he or she retires or leaves the insurance field.

In the exclusive agency system, billing and collection of renewal premiums are almost always the insurer's responsibility, not the agent's. The agent may have the power, within limits, to bind the insurer on a client's coverage. The agent may also have the authority to settle small claims.

Although a clear distinction between independent agencies and exclusive agencies once existed, the lines today are blurring. Many exclusive agents have reportedly found ways to establish related independent agencies, often operated by a family member, or to participate in broker arrangements with independent agents.[11]

Main Agency Systems in Insurance

- Life insurance
  - General agent system
  - Branch office system
  - PPGA system

- Property/liability insurance
  - Independent agent system
  - Exclusive agent system

Group Insurance Systems

Marketing to consumers in the group insurance system is usually done through the employer. Payroll deductions are a convenient method of premium payment. Labor unions, credit unions, finance companies,

---

11. Barbara Bowers, "Easy Pass," *Best's Review*, March 2004, pp. 51–52.

professional associations, and other groups may also sponsor group insurance programs to lower insurance costs to the members of the group.

Group life insurance has been expanding since such plans began many years ago. Health insurance has used the group method of marketing even more extensively, especially in medical expense insurance. Annuities or insured pensions, too, have used the group system widely.

Group plans in property and liability insurance are much less common. Most of these plans have individual selection, rating, and contracts instead of group underwriting, master contracts, and certificates. However, employer participation is involved in the arrangements for the plans, premiums are collected through payroll deductions, and the objectives of the plans are similar to those of group life and health insurance. Auto and homeowners policies are the principal fields in which mass merchandising of quasi-group property and liability insurance has been tried.

CHAPTER REVIEW

Key Terms and Concepts

domestic insurer	Blue Cross and Blue Shield plans
foreign insurer	Lloyd's associations
alien insurer	agent
nonadmitted insurer	binder
surplus lines insurance	brokers
stock insurance company	surplus lines broker
mutual insurance company	direct-response marketing
advance-premium mutuals	general agency system
assessment mutuals	branch office system
demutualization	personal producing general agent
mutual holding company	(PPGA)
fraternal insurer	independent agency system
reciprocal exchange	exclusive agency system

Review Questions

Review questions are based on the learning objectives in this chapter. Thus, a [3] at the end of a question means that the question is based on learning objective 3. If there are multiple objectives, they are all listed.

1.　What are the features of stock and mutual insurance companies as to form of business, ownership, voters for the board of directors, and recipients of dividends? [2]

2. In recent years, numerous mutual insurance companies have shifted to a stock form of organization through the process of demutualization.
   a. Why do companies demutualize? []
   b. What are the potential disadvantages associated with demutualizing? [3]

3. How do reciprocal exchanges differ from mutual insurance? [1]

4. With regard to Lloyd's of London, who provides the insurance (that is, who is the insurer)? [1]

5. After you discuss an insurance policy available from a mutual insurance company, your client, Sara Lott, asks whether mutual insurance companies always provide lower-priced coverage because they do not need to earn a profit for stockholders. How would you respond? [2]

6. Why does a financial planner need to understand how the insurance business markets its contracts and services? [4]

7. What are the three powers held by an agent and the legal duties an agent and principal owe each other? [6]

8. Is binding authority generally given to each of the following by their insurers?
   a. life insurance agents [5]
   b. property-liability insurance agents [5]

9. At the advice of his financial planner, Tom Johnson meets with an agent at an all-lines agency to discuss obtaining coverage to meet his various protection needs. In each of the following cases, indicate whether or not Tom has coverage immediately and why.
   a. After gathering information about Tom's new home and its contents, the agent recommends a homeowners policy with XYZ Insurance Company. After getting satisfactory answers to questions regarding price and the claims service offered by the company, Tom tells the agent he wants the policy from XYZ. The agent tells Tom he's covered. [5]
   b. After gathering information about the needs of Tom's family in the event of his death and about Tom's existing group life coverage at work, the agent recommends a $500,000 variable universal life policy from ABC Life to meet Tom's additional needs. The agent points out the flexibility of the policy both in terms of premium payments and investment choices. Tom fills out the application and gives the agent the minimum first premium. The agent tells Tom, "You're going to like the flexibility and performance of your new policy." [5]

10. What is the difference between insurance agents and brokers in terms of
    a. whom they represent? [5]
    b. their power to bind the insurance company? [5]

11. What are the key features of the following agency systems used to market life insurance?
    a. general agent [5]
    b. branch office or managerial system [5]
    c. personal producing general agent (PPGA) [5]

12. What are the key features of the two main agency systems-the independent agency system and the exclusive agency system-used to market property-liability insurance?
    a. How many companies or groups of companies does a producer represent? [5]
    b. Who pays operating expenses? [5]
    c. What is the relative size of renewal versus initial commissions? [5]
    d. Who generally has ownership, use, and control of policy and expiration data? [5]
    e. Who generally collects premiums and settles claims? [5]

13. Your client, Bill Jones, asks your advice as a financial planner about whether it is better to purchase homeowners insurance from an independent insurance agency, which represents several insurers, or an exclusive agent, who represents only one insurance company. How would you respond? [7]

14. Mark and Liz Olson have individual life insurance policies issued by a mutual insurance company that has its corporate headquarters in their state, a homeowners policy issued by a stock insurance company based in another state, and an auto insurance policy issued by a reciprocal exchange. They also have medical expense protection through a Blue Cross/Blue Shield plan provided by their employer. Last year when their auto insurance premium increased, they decided to do some comparison shopping and were surprised to discover that some insurance agents represent may different companies while others represent only one insurance company.
    a. What different types of insurers are the Olsons dealing with? [1, 7]
    b. What different types of marketing representatives are the Olsons dealing with? [1, 5]

Learning Objectives

An understanding of the material in this chapter should enable the student to

1. Describe the nature and purpose of underwriting.

2. Explain the nature and purposes of reinsurance.

3. Explain the purpose of claims adjustment, the types of claims adjusters, and procedures for claims adjustment.

4. Describe factors involved in insurance rate making.

5. Explain the investment function and other functions of an insurance company.

Now we turn our attention to insurers' internal operations. The principal areas of internal operations for insurers are underwriting, reinsurance, claims adjusting, rate making, and investing. Financial planners need to understand the basic operation of these functions in order to help their clients make the most effective use of insurance, which is invariably a part of any sound financial plan.

UNDERWRITING

Insurers are not usually required to sell insurance to every person who applies for it.[12] This fact puzzles many people. Something seems wrong with a business that can refuse to sell its product or service to the people who need and want it most. In the case of insurance, these are the people most likely to have losses. Insurers are more interested in finding and accepting the clients who are least likely to have losses.

---

12. Exceptions apply in some cases. For example, insurers are required in some states to provide an insurance policy to all applicants for auto insurance. However, behind the scenes, the insurer can transfer an undesirable risk to a residual market facility.

Insurance is legally viewed as a "business affected with the public interest."[13] Insurers serve the public interest not only by providing a wide variety of coverages to most applicants, but also by remaining, or at least attempting to remain, financially solvent so that they can deliver on the promises made in the insurance contracts they sell. Financial planners need to recognize and appreciate the delicate balancing act insurers face in meeting these sometimes conflicting objectives.

Purpose

underwriting   *Underwriting* is the selection and pricing of insurance applications that are offered to an insurer. The insurer attempts to accept only applicants who, on average, will have actual loss experience comparable to the expected loss experience for which the company has set its premium rates. Selection implies that there are some acceptances and some rejections, or that not all applicants will be accepted for insurance. Most other businesses welcome virtually all paying customers and do not attempt to screen them. However, banks and other institutions that lend money practice a selection process that resembles insurance underwriting. The selection process lenders use is, in fact, referred to as credit underwriting or loan underwriting.

Most insurance prices are based on an average rate for an entire class or group, such as 30-year-old female nonsmokers or owners of 2008 Buick Lucernes in Philadelphia with no youthful drivers. Some applicants within each class will be better than average and some worse than average. Which type of policyowners will an insurer that does no selection tend to have? Those persons who are better than average are most likely not to want or need the insurance at the price quoted for the class, and conversely, those persons who know they are worse than average will be most likely to desire the insurance contract at that price. The result is obvious: The bad applicants at the average rate would be getting a bargain.

This is known as adverse selection and is found throughout insurance. *Adverse selection* refers to the natural tendency for those who know they are highly vulnerable to loss from a specific risk to be most likely to acquire and retain insurance that covers that risk or to select insurance options that best fit their situations. Insurers, on the other hand, are most eager to sell insurance to the people least likely to suffer a covered loss. Insurers attempt

---

13. See *German Alliance Insurance Co. v. Lewis*, 233 U.S. 389 (1914).

to avoid adverse selection in order to prevent the financial disaster that results when an insurer ends up with a customer base of worse-than-average applicants, who will have worse-than-average losses, but collects premiums based on applicants whose loss experience would be average. Underwriters attempt to avoid adverse selection by selecting a large, safely diversified, profitable group of applicants.

The major need for insurance underwriting stems from this tendency toward adverse selection, which, without underwriting, would ruin insurers. An insurer can be profitable only by exercising careful selection that reasonably offsets the natural economic forces which lead to adverse selection in insurance applications. The insurer needs adequate and accurate information about its applicants to determine fair classifications and to charge sufficient prices

Underwriting is the process by which the insurer evaluates the applicants it has been asked to accept. A compromise is often necessary between two objectives: (1) to obtain a large number of individual insureds within each classification so that reasonable predictability of losses is possible, and (2) to obtain a homogeneity of insureds within each classification so that reasonable equity between the better and the more loss-prone individual insureds is achieved. The care with which an insurer combines these objectives is vital to its underwriting success and thus to its entire operations.

Underwriters are the backbone of the insurance business. They must decline many applications, but they are also often able to help consumers become insurable and thereby have their applications accepted. Proper rate classes and prices, coupled with good risk control practices, help make insurance available to most people who need it.

Selection of Applicants

The selection of applicants and the pricing of insurance contracts are closely related. If an adequate price for a class of insureds has been established, the insurer must underwrite to secure at least an average group of insureds within that class. Otherwise, the insurer's losses will exceed the premium income available to pay claims for this group of insureds' losses. If the pricing for an insurance contract is inadequate, even reasonably careful selection can produce an unprofitable group of applicants. When rates are inadequate, insurers respond with strict underwriting, accepting only the very best applicants in each rate class.

The Agent and Insurer As Underwriters

field underwriting   For most insurers and most lines of insurance, the choice of applicants begins with the underwriting done by the agent, sometimes referred to as *field underwriting*. Each time an agent prepares a prospect list or, for example, telephones Mr. Brown instead of Mr. Green to sell insurance, the agent is performing the first step in field underwriting. Well-qualified agents usually try to choose clients that meet the insurer's underwriting rules. Even though the agent does some underwriting for the insurer, most of the underwriting is an insurance company function, performed by salaried employees in the home office or branch office.

Underwriting does not involve rejecting all difficult or doubtful applications. Both the agent and the insurer frequently explain how a borderline applicant can become acceptable through loss prevention or other methods. Good judgment and good information are needed in this process. For example, an auto insurance underwriter whose company rules do not permit him or her to write a teenaged driver with a high-performance sports car might suggest that the parents purchase a more conservative vehicle that would meet underwriting standards at a standard rate. Or the underwriter might suggest that an applicant for disability income insurance, whose type of work occasionally involves minor injuries, would be acceptable for coverage with a waiting period longer than the one indicated on the original application.

Generally, the insurer determines the underwriting rules to be carried out by its agents and its company personnel in the underwriting department. Agents receive instructions on what types of applicants are unacceptable, as well as encouragement through directives and sales contests that specify what types of contracts and what kinds of business the company particularly desires. Other types of applicants may be specified as insurable only after the insurer has detailed information.

Types of Underwriting
• Field underwriting
• Initial home office or branch office underwriting
• Renewal underwriting

Underwriting by the insurer and the agent takes place not only at the time of the original application but also at each renewal of the insurance contract.

During renewal underwriting, loss experience and other new information are considered in most insurance lines.

Sources of Underwriting Information

The sources of underwriting information on which insurers rely, depending on the line of insurance, include (1) the applicant, (2) the agent, (3) the insurer's own inspection or claims department, (4) insurer bureaus and associations, and (5) outside agencies.

The applicant for an insurance contract often makes both written and oral statements. Signed written statements are standard in life and health insurance, and the application becomes a part of the contract. Auto and business insurance applicants also frequently complete written application forms that give the insurer basic underwriting details. Agents in many kinds of insurance give their companies reports, opinions, and recommendations that are valuable aids in selecting or rejecting applications. Many insurers maintain separate inspection departments to give the underwriters physical inspection and engineering reports on applicants' properties. The insurer's claims department, too, can be a source of important underwriting data for renewal decisions.

Insurers also combine efforts to maintain bureau or association lists of insurance applicants. For example, the MIB Group, Inc. (MIB) offers a centralized source of information about medical and other impairments of individual applicants for life insurance. Other service organizations provide regular inspection and rating services in regard to property insurance.

Insurance companies often use outside agencies to supplement the information gathered from the applicants, agents, and other insurer representatives. For example, physicians supply life insurance companies with medical reports after physical examination of the applicants. Standard financial rating services, such as Dun & Bradstreet (D&B), are used for many insurance applications from businesses. Life insurers have used credit investigations by outside firms for many years. Auto insurers have used external agencies to check motor vehicle reports and court records of new applicants, especially for younger drivers. Agencies that develop a credit score or an insurance score, such as Fair Isaac and ChoicePoint, have become increasingly important sources of information in several other personal lines of property and liability insurance as well.

Inspection agencies are valuable for gathering factual data and for identifying a prospect's poor habits or moral problems through such sources as employers, neighbors, or associates. The evaluation of moral and attitudinal hazards is crucial, yet difficult, for many kinds of insurance. The aim of these investigations is not only to gather negative information but also to obtain positive character reports that will permit insurance to be written. The independent investigative companies must comply with federal legislation that deals with credit reporting and privacy. Insurers must also meet these requirements, as well as laws on the state level, such as the NAIC (National Association of Insurance Commissioners) Health Information Privacy Protection Model Act, adopted by many states.

Automation in Underwriting

The increasing complexity of computer systems has enabled insurers to automate many underwriting activities, especially for high-volume lines of business such as auto and homeowners insurance, that involve many routine transactions. The insurer's experience and underwriting expertise is translated into complex computer algorithms that automate the decision-making process. This reduces the need for human intervention, and consequently reduces the insurer's underwriting expenses while it expedites the handling of insurance applications. Based on information in the application and other underwriting sources, automated systems can determine the eligibility, acceptability, and rate classification of a routine insurance policy almost instantaneously and offer an immediate quote. Borderline cases or others that are not routine in some manner may still be referred to a human underwriter for evaluation. The extent to which automated underwriting processes are used and the nature of those processes vary substantially among insurers.

REINSURANCE

reinsurance   Financial planners must recognize how underwriters' ability to accept applications is both broadened and limited by reinsurance available to the insurer. *Reinsurance* is an arrangement in which an insurance company transfers to another insurance company some or all of the risks it has taken on by writing primary insurance. With reinsurance, the primary insurer or ceding company that issues the policy transfers all or part of the risk to another insurer, the reinsurer.

Purposes

How can an insurer accept large loss exposures that sometimes exceed many millions of dollars in a single building, a ship, or an airplane? How can liability contracts for business firms have policy limits of $100 million or more? How can a person obtain in excess of $10 million of life insurance? When hurricanes affect many policyowners at one time, how can insurers survive the concentration of loss that occurs? Gigantic losses do not occur frequently, but when they do occur, they illustrate the real reason for insurance—protection against losses that perhaps only the private insurance system can provide.

Catastrophes illustrate the most important purpose of reinsurance: the spread or diversification of losses. One insurer can write large amounts of insurance on a single life or property or in a concentrated area, then use reinsurance to shift part of the loss exposure to perhaps several other insurance companies. Large losses are thus shared, and excessive losses in one occurrence are less likely to cause financial instability for individual insurers. Without reinsurance, each insurer would be limited to its own financial ability to pay losses. Reinsurance enhances financial strength by spreading losses throughout the insurance business.

Reinsurance also has other purposes. Mandatory reserve requirements drain surplus and restrict growth, a particularly severe problem for newer or smaller companies. These companies can achieve more rapid growth by transferring part of the responsibility for maintaining reserves from the insurer to a reinsurer, permitting the insurer to increase its writing of new business. Reinsurers also offer many technical advisory services to new insurers or those expanding to new types of insurance or territories.

Significance to Financial Planners

Insurance companies usually obtain reinsurance from two basic types of organizations: (1) professional reinsurers, which sell only reinsurance, and (2) other insurance companies that write some reinsurance in addition to issuing policies directly to consumers. The financial planner should recognize that the policyowner is not a party to a reinsurance agreement. Reinsurance is usually transparent to policyowners. Neither the policyowner nor the financial planner is usually aware of the primary insurer's specific reinsurance arrangements. Reinsurance operates in the background as a separate contract between the primary insurer and the reinsurer. The policyowner or other claimant looks to the primary insurer that wrote the policy for claims payment. This primary insurer is responsible for paying the entire claim and is then reimbursed by the reinsurer, if reinsurance applies.

Reinsurance agreements are often highly complex, and the typical financial planner does not need to understand the many types of such agreements. However, the planner should at least be aware of the difference between treaty, or automatic, reinsurance agreements and facultative agreements.

treaty (automatic) reinsurance

Treaty (automatic) reinsurance exists when the primary insurer agrees in advance to transfer, or cede, some types of loss exposures and the reinsurer agrees to accept them. The reinsurer agrees to insure an amount or a proportionate part of a designated class of past or future business written by the primary insurer. The reinsurer participates in the risk as soon as the primary insurer accepts the loss exposure. Automatic protection is thus ensured for the primary insurer because the reinsurer has agreed beforehand to accept all loss exposures within the terms of the treaty. Usually, the policyowner will not even be aware of the existence of treaty (automatic) reinsurance.

facultative reinsurance

Facultative reinsurance, on the other hand, is optional for both the insurer and the reinsurer. Each facultative reinsurance contract is written on its own merits and is a matter of individual bargaining between the primary insurer and the reinsurer. The primary insurer may or may not offer part of a loss exposure to the reinsurer. The reinsurer is under no obligation to accept the loss exposure if it is offered. Each party thus retains the "faculty" or privilege of accepting or rejecting the reinsurance agreement. For large or unusual cases, the availability of facultative reinsurance may be the deciding factor in the underwriting process as to whether an application for insurance is acceptable to the primary insurer. Delays in obtaining coverage for a client often result from the primary insurer's need to obtain a facultative reinsurance commitment.

CLAIMS SETTLEMENT

Settling claims, often referred to as claims adjusting, is certainly the most obvious function of insurance. Without covered claims that lead to loss payments, there would be no insurance business. The claims process applies with all lines of insurance, and it includes paying covered claims and denying claims that are not covered. Specific claims-handling details naturally vary substantially depending on the line of insurance, the nature and size of the claim, and the insurer involved in any specific case.

Thousands of claim checks are delivered to insureds, third-party claimants, or beneficiaries every day. Most claims are routine, but some are unique and spectacular. Losses from hurricanes or epidemics can affect thousands of people. Tornadoes, earthquakes, floods, explosions, nuclear accidents, terrorism, and other natural and man-made catastrophes can cause huge numbers of deaths and injuries and massive damage, producing covered claims that cost insurers billions of dollars.

When policyowners receive claims payments, they quite clearly recognize the value of their insurance. Up to that time, some might only have had a feeling that they were complying with some vague duty. When they actually receive insurance proceeds that make it possible for them to rebuild their homes, to replace lost income, or to pay nursing home expenses, they come to appreciate insurance. Those who were inadequately insured often realize belatedly that they should have purchased more coverage, and they may blame—or even sue—their agents or financial planners.

Apart from routine medical expense claims, most individuals and families experience relatively few claims. Experienced financial planners, because they deal with many clients, usually have more opportunities to recognize the value of adequate insurance in the financial planning process. Unfortunately, claims experience can also demonstrate the problems that result from inadequate insurance.

Financial planners usually discover that claims provide an extremely rewarding opportunity to see insurance in action. Tremendous personal satisfaction results when a family receives steady income during a long period when the primary breadwinner cannot work, because the family took the planner's advice and purchased disability income protection. It is highly gratifying to see a dream home rebuilt, with homeowners insurance proceeds, on the ashes of a fire that otherwise would have caused a loss of lifetime savings. Experienced financial planners point with quiet pride to families whose sons and daughters have been able to attend college without financial hardship, despite the unexpected early death of family breadwinners. Because experienced financial planners and insurance agents have seen firsthand the value of insurance, it is easy to understand their missionary zeal in urging clients to have adequate coverage.

Purpose

The claims settlement process is set in motion when a notice of loss is filed with an insurer. The purpose of the claims settlement process is to confirm whether the insurer has an obligation to pay for a given loss and to reach an agreement on the amount of any covered loss or damage that is payable under the insurance contract.

Insureds and beneficiaries have a legally enforceable contractual right to seek payment for any covered claim. Arriving at a fair and equitable measure of the loss should be the objective of both insurers and claimants. There are sometimes areas of disagreement, but if both parties resolve to reach an equitable adjustment, disagreements can usually be reconciled.

Claims adjusters have been advised to follow the "4F rules": Be fair, frank, friendly, and firm. New claims adjusters are taught that their responsibility is to settle claims equitably and not, as policyowners sometimes believe, to pay the smallest dollar amount to which claimants will agree. Adjusters are also advised to give reasonable assistance to claimants during the traumatic days immediately following a serious loss—for example, helping the family relocate to temporary housing following a fire, providing names of reputable repair shops after an auto accident, or helping injured or disabled claimants find properly qualified medical or rehabilitation facilities. Adjusters are further instructed, when claimants do not know what is due them under their contracts, to fully explain what items or expenses to include in their claims. In the interest of equity, adjusters are also trained to recognize unethical practices and to resist padded claims or fraudulent demands. Fairness to uninformed claimants and resistance to wrongful claims benefit both insurers and their policyowners, who in the long run must pay premiums based on loss experience.

An insurer's reputation rests not only on how satisfied the claimants are but also on how many other persons they tell about their experience. Satisfied claimants often take their payments as a matter of course, but dissatisfied policyowners tell everyone why they believe they were unfairly treated, and they often file complaints with state insurance commissioners. Insurer's complaint data is publicly available on the National Association of Insurance Commissioners (NAIC) Web site at naic.org.

Insurance Adjusters: Types and Organization

The parties most directly involved in the claims settlement process fall into four general categories:

- agents
- company employees
- independent adjusters
- consumer advocates

Agents' Role

Many property-liability insurers permit their agents to settle claims that involve small losses. This practice is common for fire, windstorm, and medical payments under homeowners and auto insurance contracts. The agent usually is close to the client, is familiar with the policyowner's insurance contracts, and has the earliest facts concerning the claim. The agent also has a prime interest in seeing that the consumer receives prompt and fair treatment in the claims adjustment process. Most claims involve larger losses or more complex adjusting methods, and in these cases the insurer handles the settlement process.

With life insurance, the agent is often involved in loss payment as an intermediary but not as an adjuster. The claims procedure for smaller contracts is simple. Notice to the company and a death certificate are often all that is required before the policy's death benefit can be paid. The life insurance agent usually forwards the death notice and certificate to the insurer. In some cases, especially those involving smaller amounts, the insurer may issue a check for the agent to deliver to the beneficiary, or the company may simply mail the check. When larger amounts are involved, instead of issuing a check, the company will usually open a money market account, funded with policy proceeds, and provide the beneficiary with a checkbook on that account. Unlike property insurers, life insurers do not usually have the problem of determining the extent of loss payment because there is no such thing as a partial loss, and the contract itself states the amount to be paid upon loss. For larger life insurance policies, the agent may need to explain various settlement options that provide alternatives to a lump-sum cash payment.

Insurance agents usually are not involved in medical expense, disability, or long-term care insurance claims, but in unusual cases the agent who sold the policy might become involved in resolving matters with personnel from the insurer's claims department.

Company Employees

Many insurance claims are settled by insurance company employees, who may be referred to by various titles, such as *staff adjuster, claims examiner,* or *claims analyst.*

With property and liability insurance, staff adjusters usually devote their entire time to handling loss settlements. Sometimes they investigate claims by inspecting the scene of an accident or property damage, interviewing claimants and witnesses, and consulting hospital and police records. Some auto insurers in larger cities have drive-in claims locations where immediate estimates and payments for covered damage to autos are made by staff adjusters known as *physical damage appraisers.* Small, uncomplicated claims may be handled by telephone and mail.

Claims examiners or claims analysts handle life, medical, disability, and long-term-care insurance claims. When handling life insurance claims, for example, they typically review the cause of death, since many policies pay additional benefits for accidental death but not for a death by natural causes. Medical expense claims are reviewed to determine whether or to what extent they qualify for benefits, and payment is made accordingly.

Staff adjusters, claims adjusters, and claims analysts often consult with other professionals, such as accountants, architects, construction workers, engineers, lawyers, and physicians, to get expert advice as they investigate and evaluate various claims.

Independent Adjusters

independent adjusters   Insurance companies often outsource certain aspects of the claims settlement process. Property-liability insurers, for example, often use *independent adjusters* to settle claims. Independent adjusters are experts who have made loss adjusting a business. Some specialize in particular fields. Others have a general knowledge and understanding of adjustment procedures and handle losses whenever it is impossible or inconvenient for the insurance company's staff or other types of adjusters to do so. Independent adjusters include both individuals and adjusting firms that are in the business of providing claims adjusting services for a fee. National adjusting firms include rather sizable organizations.

Independent adjusters work for the insurers who purchase their services. A typical use is in auto insurance when the insurer has only a small volume of business in an area. Independent adjusters are also used frequently to supplement staff adjusters when catastrophic events, such as a major hurricane, give rise to a large number of separate claims. Independent adjusters can also be used by insurers to settle claims in highly technical areas in which the staff adjusters lack the necessary skills or expertise. Independent adjusters often develop continuing working relationships with particular insurers, in addition to accepting infrequent adjusting assignments from other insurers.

Although routine life, medical expense, disability, and long-term care claims are typically handled by insurance company employees, insurers may also outsource some or all of their claims-handling process to persons or organizations that specialize in this activity, especially when more complex claims, large disability claims, or long-term care claims are involved.

Consumer Advocates

public adjuster   In contrast to staff adjusters and independent adjusters, who represent insurers, a *public adjuster* represents members of the public in settling property insurance claims against an insurer. Even though most insurers do their utmost to settle claims fairly, people sometimes assume that adjusters who represent the insurer are biased in favor of the insurer and will make borderline decisions to the insurer's advantage. Claimants who wish to have somebody represent their interests sometimes turn the claim over to a public adjuster, who charges a fee for his or her services.[14]

Attorneys sometimes perform a similar function with property insurance and often represent claimants with liability insurance claims.

Claims assistance professionals often assist individuals and families in keeping track of their claims and ensuring that they are properly handled and accurately represent the treatments provided. A service of this type can be especially useful to senior citizens who find it difficult to stay on top of complex medical bills and insurance coverages while also battling health problems.[15]

---

14. For further information on public adjusters, see the National Association of Public Insurance Adjusters Web site at www.napia.com.

15. For further information on claims assistance professionals, see the Alliance of Claims Assistance Professionals Web site at www.claims.org.

Claims Procedures

The process by which claims are settled varies by line of insurance. Each policy spells out the steps that the policyowner or other claimant must follow, as well as his or her responsibilities following a loss. In general, there are four main steps in the claims adjustment process:

- the policyowner furnishes a notice of loss to the insurer
- the insurer investigates the claim
- the policyowner files a proof of loss with the insurer
- the insurer pays or denies the claim, sometimes after negotiating the amount to be paid

Notification to the insurer must be provided as spelled out in the policy. Often, the time frame is specified as "immediately," "promptly," or "as soon as practicable." A few types of policies may be more specific, such as "within 30 days after the occurrence of a loss."

Claims investigation determines whether a loss occurred and, if so, whether the policy covers it. In life insurance, this process is usually quite simple, but complicating factors can arise in some cases. For example, what if the insured has mysteriously disappeared, so that at best it can only be presumed that he or she is dead? What if there is evidence that the insured died by his or her own hand, in which case the policy's suicide clause might come into play? What if there was a material misrepresentation in the application for the coverage, in which case the incontestable clause may be applicable?

In other lines of insurance, the investigation phase can be more complex. Some of the questions that may have to be resolved include the following:

- Did a loss actually take place?
- Did the loss occur while the policy was in force?
- Did the loss occur at a location covered by the policy?
- Was the loss caused by a covered peril or activity?
- Do any policy exclusions apply to the loss?
- Do any exceptions to policy exclusions apply to the loss?
- Has the policyowner fulfilled all necessary conditions?
- Is there any evidence of fraud?
- Is the claimant entitled to recover under the policy?
- Does the policy cover the particular type of loss consequence?

The third step in the process of adjusting a claim is filing a proof of loss. In life insurance, the proof of loss may be a death certificate. In many cases, medical expense claims are submitted directly by the health care provider, who also furnishes the necessary proof of loss, often as part of the preapproval process that must be followed before treatment is provided. In other lines, a written and sworn statement may be required that details all the specifics of the loss.

Finally, the amount to be paid must be determined in one of three ways: (1) denial of the claim, (2) payment of the claim in full, or (3) payment of a different amount than the claimant initially seeks. Life insurance claims are usually simple because there are no partial losses. Complicating factors, however, can affect the amount to be paid, including an accidental death benefit provision, a misstatement-of-age clause, or a settlement option the policyowner or the beneficiary selects.

In some cases, the amount to be paid, if any, can involve complex issues. Numerous policy provisions may be applicable. These include provisions that

- deal with other insurance covering the same loss
- provide for a deductible
- specify that recovery will be affected by the amount of insurance carried relative to the value of the covered property
- give the insurer the choice of two or three methods of calculating the amount of the loss
- impose a specific limit on the insurer's liability for certain types of losses

RATE MAKING

rate making   *Rate making* refers to the process of establishing the price to be charged for insurance. Insurance rates are based on the costs of providing the product, plus a margin for profit. The rate-making task is complicated because the insurer does not know the amount or timing of the largest cost element—the claims to be paid—in advance. Claims can only be estimated. Predicting future loss costs—and in long-term contracts (such as life insurance), their timing—and adding necessary margins for expenses and profit to those predictions are all involved in the rate-making process. Rate making is carried out by actuaries, who are specialists in the mathematics of insurance.

Components of the Insurance Premium

rate   The insurance *rate* is the price charged for each unit of coverage, called an exposure unit, the policy provides. Units of coverage differ by line of insurance. For example, in life insurance, the rate is determined using a unit of coverage which is $1,000 of face amount. For long-term disability income insurance, it is usually $100 of monthly income. For medical expense insurance, it is an individual or family. For most property insurance, it is $100 of value. For auto liability insurance, it is one covered vehicle.

premium   The insurance *premium* is the price charged for the amount of coverage the policy provides. The premiums are the rates multiplied by the number of units of coverage. For example, in life insurance, the rate for a particular category of insureds might be $30 per $1,000 of face amount per year. The annual premium for a $50,000 policy, then, is $30 × 50 units, or $1,500. In fire insurance, the annual rate might be $.25 per $100 of coverage. Therefore, the annual premium for coverage of a $200,000 building is $.25 × 2,000 units of coverage, or $500.

pure (net) rate

gross rate   How is an insurance rate derived? Usually, the rate is developed by the pure premium method, which first requires an estimate of the future loss costs per unit of coverage during the policy period. The portion of the rate that is designed to cover future loss costs is called the *pure rate* or *net rate*. Then a factor, called a *loading*, is added to cover the insurer's expected operating expenses and to provide a margin for profit and contingencies. The sum of the pure (net) rate and the loading is called the *gross rate*.

Determining the gross rate leads first to an examination of a logical question: How is the pure (net) rate derived? Most lines of insurance use a statistical analysis of past loss data for each class of insureds and a projection of that loss experience into the future time period during which the rate to be charged for each class will be in effect.

The rate-making task is complicated in some lines of insurance by a scarcity of data on past loss experience. This scarcity of data can exist either for all insureds (as in a newer line of coverage, such as long-term care insurance) or for particular classifications of insureds (such as very elderly auto drivers). In most lines of insurance, such as homeowners coverage or disability income insurance, loss data must also be sufficient to allow accurate predictions of both loss frequency and loss severity. An explanation of how actuaries deal with these and other rate-making complexities is well beyond the scope of this introductory text.

Property Insurance As an Example

advisory organization

Property insurance offers insight into the many rate-making factors. Here, insurance advisory organizations play a key role. An insurance *advisory organization* is an organization that assists insurers by collecting and furnishing loss statistics or by submitting rating recommendations. These advisory organizations, such as Insurance Services Office (ISO), are permitted under state statutes in order to allow cooperation for property and liability insurance, subject to state regulation of their activities. Reasonable competition is achieved by permitting individual insurers to file separate rates or to add separate loadings to published loss costs or net rates.

A property insurance contract usually covers more than just the fire peril. The advisory organization develops separate prices for such allied perils as windstorm, hail, smoke, explosion, riot, and others; loss of income, rents, and extra expenses; water damage and sprinkler leakage; and earthquake.

The price of property insurance also varies with the location or territory of the property, the construction of the building, the use or occupancy of the property, the loss prevention or reduction facilities, and the proximity or exposure to other properties from which a peril might spread. The advisory organizations carefully define standards for the classes, so there is a higher rate for a frame building than for a brick or a fire-resistant building.

Two types of property insurance rates are set: (1) class rates for groups of similar properties and (2) specific rates for individual properties with unique characteristics. Having some rates for groups of applicants with similar characteristics and separate individual rates for applicants that differ widely in their specific characteristics is common to many types of insurance.

Class Rates

class rates

Class rates are group rates with an average price per unit of insurance that applies to each category or classification of similar insureds. A common example is class rating of separate dwellings or residential homes. Class-rated dwellings are subdivided into groups according to their construction, and a rate is assigned to such classes as frame or brick and to combustible or noncombustible roofs. The rate also varies as to the fire protection classification of the city or town and the number of families that occupy the property. In addition, many jurisdictions apply class rates to commercial buildings when the elements of construction and occupancy are similar enough to permit a ready grouping into rate classes. ISO filings expand class rating to most smaller buildings in general classes, such as mercantile, churches, schools, warehouses, and offices, and to habitational classes, such as apartments, motels, and boardinghouses. Class rates must be used for properties to which the rates apply.

Class rates provide not only economy and simplicity but also reasonable equity, provided that the individual properties within a given class do not vary too much with regard to potential loss-causing characteristics. Thus, for example, all one-family brick dwellings in a midwestern town of 200,000 in population and with fire hydrants within 1,000 feet might have a 1-year fire insurance rate of $.30 per $100 of insurance.

Specific or Schedule Rates

specific rate   When class rates do not apply, the rate is said to be specific. A *specific rate* is created for one particular insured based on that insured's own risk characteristics. Specific or schedule rates are set for larger mercantile and manufacturing properties, educational institutions, public buildings, and many types of business establishments. Specific rates are determined by applying a schedule that measures the relative fire hazard for the particular loss exposure. Most larger buildings use specific rates developed after a physical inspection of the individual property.

The process of developing a specific rate considers differences in hazards for different properties. This process takes into consideration the various items that contribute to the insured perils, including the construction of the building, its occupancy or use, its protection, and its exposure to nearby buildings. Credits and charges that represent departures from standard conditions for each of these items are incorporated into the rate.

Life Insurance As Another Example

Life insurers collect voluminous amounts of data on mortality rates. The most important basis for classifying these data are the age and gender of insureds and whether they are smokers or nonsmokers.

net single
premium

net level annual
premium

A large percentage of life insurance is sold on a
level-premium basis. Death rates, on the other hand,
rise with increasing age. Most claims on these policies
occur years after the policies are issued. To deal with the
imbalance of level premiums in traditional life insurance
products and rising claim costs, life insurers first compute a *net single
premium* per $1,000 of face amount for the policy. This net single premium
is an amount that the insurer would need today from all insureds in a
classification, together with future investment earnings, to pay all claims
within that class of insureds as those claims arise. The net single premium
per $1,000 of face amount is then spread or leveled over the policy's
premium-paying period on an actuarial basis to produce a *net level annual
premium* per $1,000 for each insured. The net level annual premium is a
charge that is based on spreading the net level premium over the policy's
premium-paying period. Finally, a level annual loading amount is added
to cover such insurer expenses as commissions, premium taxes, general
administrative expenses, and an allowance for contingencies and profit.

The establishment of rates for nontraditional life insurance products, such
as universal life insurance and variable life insurance, is considerably more
complex. A detailed description is well beyond the scope of this book.

Loss Ratio Method for Adjusting Rates

We previously described the pure premium method, which entails
development of a pure or net rate plus a loading. For many property and
liability insurance lines in which rate changes upward or downward are
common, the loss ratio method of rate making is used to adjust rates.
Emphasis in the loss ratio method is not on calculating a new rate directly but
on determining the necessary change to an existing rate.

loss ratio

Loss ratios can be calculated in various ways, but the
most common way is to divide losses incurred plus loss
adjustment expenses incurred by earned premiums. The needed change
from an existing insurance rate is found by comparing the actual loss ratio
experienced with the expected (or desired) loss ratio. The difference is then
divided by the expected or desired loss ratio.

EXAMPLE

The present rate in a particular auto liability insurance classification is $700 per year. The insurer's expected loss ratio in that classification is 75 percent. During the latest experience period, that classification generated $4.5 million of incurred losses, $400,000 of expenses allocated to settle specific claims, and $7 million of earned premiums. The actual loss ratio was, therefore, 70 percent:

$$\left(\frac{\text{Incurred losses} + \text{Loss adjustment expenses}}{\text{Earned premiums}}\right) \times 100 =$$

$$\left(\frac{\$4,500,000 + \$400,000}{\$7,000,000}\right) \times 100 = 70\%$$

The needed rate change, then, is a reduction of 6.7 percent, determined as follows:

$$\left(\frac{\text{Actual loss ratio} - \text{Expected loss ratio}}{\text{Expected loss ratio}}\right) \times 100 =$$

$$\left(\frac{70 - 75}{75}\right) \times 100 = \left(\frac{-5}{75}\right) \times 100 = -6.7\%$$

Therefore, the indicated new rate will be $653, determined as follows:

$$\$700 \times (1 - .067) = \$700 \times .933 = \$653$$

Note, however, that because of expected inflation in the future and other variables, the rate might not be lowered by the full 6.7 percent.

Rate Classifications

The previous discussion implied the use of different rate classifications. Not all applicants for any type of insurance will be charged the same rate. Insurers must establish overall rates so that they have sufficient funds to pay losses and expenses. At the same time, they must provide reasonable equity among policyowners and charge rates that reflect quantifiable characteristics which affect losses. For example, because smokers have shorter life expectancies than nonsmokers, most life insurers have both smoker and nonsmoker rates. Life insurance rates also vary by age and gender. At the opposite extreme is auto insurance, where rate classifications may reflect many factors, including age, gender, marital status, geographic location, miles driven, vehicle use, and driving record. In a given state, an insurance company may have more than a thousand classifications when all combinations of these factors are considered.

The degree to which rate classifications are refined depends on available and reliable statistics, the administrative costs of establishing classifications, and government regulations. For example, some states require the use of unisex rates for certain types of insurance even though loss statistics can justify gender-specific rates. The number of exposure units to be insured is also highly relevant in determining how many rating classifications to use. It would be possible to develop a classification plan so detailed that each insured was in his or her own rating category. This would obviously defeat the purpose of having a large number of similar exposure units in each class so that an average rate for that class can be developed. Auto insurance classification plans can be highly refined because each rating territory contains many insured drivers.

INVESTING

Insurers accumulate huge amounts of capital, most of it collected as policyowner premiums. Except for amounts needed for the insurer's operating expenses, those funds will be used primarily to pay claims. Funds not immediately needed are invested, both as a means of lowering the cost of insurance and as a source of profit for the insurer.

State laws closely regulate the ways an insurer can invest the funds it holds. Emphasis is on safety, both of principal and of income.[16] An additional objective is an adequate yield, or rate of return. Life insurers guarantee a minimum rate of return to policyowners in many of their products, so they must earn at least that much. Perhaps more important, a life insurance company's rate of investment earnings must be high enough to enable its insurance contracts to be competitively priced. In most states, property and liability insurers are not required by law to build investment income into their rate making, but investment income still is essential. In many years and for

---

16. These regulations apply to the insurer's general investment account that supports obligations for guaranteed, fixed-dollar benefits, life traditional life insurance and annuities. Life insurers also have substantial amounts of funds in separate accounts, in cases where policyowners choose more aggressive investment goals. Examples of separate accounts are those that underlie a life insurer's variable life insurance business, variable annuities, and much of its pension business.

lines of insurance in which loss experience is unfavorable, investment income is the insurer's only source of profit.

Life Insurer Investments

Because life insurance claims are usually paid many years after the policy is put into force, life insurers tend to invest heavily in long-term securities, which produce better yields, all other things being equal. Liquidity of the investments—the ability to convert them into cash quickly without loss of value—is not a major consideration.

Table 4-1 shows the latest data available as this text was being prepared (2009 data). United States life insurers had over $5 trillion of invested funds, when combining the general and separate account assets. About 52 percent of it was invested in government and corporate bonds. A much smaller percentage—2.3 percent—was invested in corporate stocks. Other investment assets took the form of cash equivalents, real estate mortgage loans, policy loans, and miscellaneous assets.

Table 4-1 Insurance Company Investments			
	Life Insurers General Account	Life Insurers Separate Account	Property/Casualty Insurers
Total amount of invested assets	$3.3 Trillion	$1.6 Trillion	$1.3 Trillion
Distribution of invested assets			
Cash and cash equivalents	1.2%	1%	6.96%
Bonds			68.82
Government	8.8	2.3	
Corporate	45.0	5.2	
Stocks	2.3	80	18.4
Mortgages	9.8	.6	0.36
Policy Loans	3.7	0	0
Other	3.9	2.0	4.57

Totals do not add up to 100 percent due to rounding.

Sources: *Life Insurers Fact Book 2010*, American Council of Life Insurers, Washington, DC, pp. 7–11, and *The Fact Book 2011*, Insurance Information Institute, New York, pp. 27, 28, 44, 45.

Property and Liability Insurer Investments

United States property and liability insurers' invested assets show a somewhat different pattern. The aggregate amount invested, $1.3 trillion, is smaller than for life insurers because property and liability contracts are of short duration and do not build up a savings element. Moreover, in many property and liability policies, large reserves are not needed because claims are settled soon after they arise.[17] As with life insurers, the invested assets of property and liability insurers heavily emphasize bonds and common stocks, vehicles that are attractive because of their usually generous yields.

OTHER FUNCTIONS OF INSURERS

Other departments of insurers perform numerous other important functions that support the primary operating functions of marketing, underwriting, reinsuring, adjusting claims, and investing.

The legal department, for example, often works closely with the property and liability insurers' underwriting and claims departments. The legal department is generally also responsible for meeting general incorporation, licensing, and taxation requirements of the many states in which insurers do business. Often, the legal department helps design insurance contracts, drafts agency agreements, and provides general legal counsel for the insurer. In life insurance, the department offers substantial aid to the sales and underwriting departments by reviewing cases that involve complex tax problems.

The actuarial department is closely related to insurers' rating and underwriting departments. Life insurance companies need a separate actuarial staff to diagnose mortality trends, determine costs for various contracts, and provide research for many phases of their activities. Although separate research departments are not common for most insurers, companies are increasingly realizing the need for economic and social research. Many insurers also maintain public relations departments. Education and training is another important area for insurance companies.

Other functional areas within an insurance company are also critical to the organization's success. The accounting department prepares the

---

17. An important exception to this general rule exists in some liability lines, such as products liability insurance, where claims may not even arise until long after the period of coverage has expired and ensuing claim payments may be spread over many years.

insurer's financial statements, both for regulators and for the general public. Accountants also prepare various internal financial reports for managers and in preparation of the company's state and federal tax returns. The information technology department is responsible for automating many of the formerly manual tasks in policy issuance, premium billing, and claims payment, to mention just a few. Loss control departments in property and liability insurance companies provide advice and inspection services in many areas of loss prevention and minimization. Finally, many general administrative functions are performed within an insurance company, such as personnel management and purchasing.

CHAPTER REVIEW

Key Terms and Concepts

underwriting	premium
field underwriting	pure (net) rate
reinsurance	gross rate
treaty (automatic) reinsurance	advisory organization
facultative reinsurance	class rates
independent adjusters	specific rate
public adjuster	net single premium
rate making	net level annual premium
rate	loss ratio

Review Questions

Review questions are based on the learning objectives in this chapter. Thus, a [3] at the end of a question means that the question is based on learning objective 3. If there are multiple objectives, they are all listed.

1. As a financial planner, you are working with a client, Bill Jackson, on meeting his various protection needs. Answer the following questions asked by Bill:
   a. Bill asks, "Why can't insurance companies insure every applicant since they seem to charge pretty high premiums?" [1]
   b. After you answer that question, Bill asks, "Even if you qualify for insurance, sometimes companies charge a much higher rate than they charge other similar insureds. Why?" [1]

2. Your client, Nancy Hall, asks how an underwriter obtains the information necessary to evaluate her insurance application. What sources of underwriting information do insurers typically use? [1]

3. Although reinsurance is transparent to the client, it is often helpful to explain the extra security it provides. What are the key purposes of reinsurance? [2]

4. What is the difference between facultative and treaty reinsurance? [2]

5. Contrary to the opinion of some clients, it is *not* the purpose of the claims department to minimize claims payments. What is the purpose of the claims (loss) settlement process? [3]

6. How does the role of the agent in property insurance compare with that of the life insurance agent regarding the claims settlement process? [3]

7. What are the four main steps in the claims settlement process, and how does their implementation differ in life insurance versus other lines of insurance? [3]

8. During a discussion of insurance needs with a financial planning client, Sally Johnson, she asks the following questions:
   a. What is the difference between an insurance rate and an insurance premium? [4]
   b. How is an insurance rate derived? [4]

9. Financial planning client Penny Wise observes that the insurance company that provides her coverage holds huge amounts of capital.
   a. From what sources do insurers receive the huge amounts of capital they hold as assets? [5]
   b. How do insurers use the funds they hold? [5]

Learning Objectives

An understanding of the material in this chapter should enable the student to

1. Explain the general purpose of insurance regulation.
2. Describe the methods of insurance regulation.
3. Describe the kinds of insurance regulation by the states, and explain the issue of state versus federal regulation.
4. Discuss the criteria for selecting an insurer and agent or broker.

Financial planners clearly need to understand insurance regulation in order to understand the regulatory environment in which they work. Insurance is a highly regulated business, and insurance regulation is subject to frequent change. Financial advisors also must understand why and how the business of insurance is regulated, and the factors a client should consider in evaluating and selecting an insurance company, agent or broker.

The value of insurance contracts depends on the insurer's ability to fulfill these policies' promises to the public, sometimes many years after the policies are issued. Ability to carry out contract provisions depends on many factors, including the efficient operation of the insurer, satisfactory underwriting, proper premium rates, and wise investment of adequate reserves.

The general purpose of insurance regulation is to protect the public against insurer insolvency or unfair treatment by insurers. From the state's viewpoint, regulation is also important because state taxes on insurance premiums are a substantial source of revenue.

The insurance business is generally considered to be "affected with a public interest." This characteristic explains why many types of government supervision of insurance are deemed necessary. Uncontrolled competition in insurance could impose a hardship on insurance buyers and insurance claimants or beneficiaries who do not understand insurance contracts.

SOURCES OF INSURANCE REGULATION

State governments undoubtedly play the most important role in regulating insurance. Before we consider this and other phases of government insurance regulation, however, we will summarize insurance self-regulation.

Self-Regulation of Insurance

The concept of self-regulation in general is clearly described in the following excerpt from remarks made in 1998 by Robert Pitofsky, chairman of the Federal Trade Commission:[18]

> An industry group may engage in self-regulation to enhance its reputation for fair and honest service by establishing ethical standards and disciplining those who do not abide by the standards. Professional associations, for example, often exclude unqualified applicants to assure the public that practitioners possess a minimum level of competence and to protect the associations' reputations as well. Self-regulation often may deter conduct that would be universally considered undesirable, but that the civil or criminal law does not prohibit. For example, cheating in sporting contests may not violate the law because the improper conduct is not considered sufficiently serious or because no injured party is likely to appear to bring suit. As a result, industry self-regulation may provide the only meaningful deterrent to would-be cross checkers and bean ball artists.
>
> From a public policy perspective, self-regulation can offer several advantages over government regulation or legislation. It often is more prompt, flexible, and effective than government regulation. Self-regulation can bring the accumulated judgment and experience of an industry to bear on issues that are sometimes difficult for the government to define with bright line rules. Finally, government resources are limited and unlikely to grow in the future. Thus, many government agencies, like the FTC, have sought to leverage their limited resources by promoting and encouraging self-regulation.

---

18. *Self-Regulation and Antitrust*, prepared remarks of Robert Pitofsky, Chairman of the Federal Trade Commission, DC Bar Association Symposium, February 18, 1998, Washington, DC (www.ftc.gov/speeches/pitofsky/self4.htm, accessed 9/26/06).

Cooperation by insurers to regulate themselves is permitted by law and is practiced extensively. Many insurers and trade association groups exercise considerable control or provide advice with regard to each of the major functions of insurance. For example, Insurance Services Office (ISO) compiles loss data and drafts and files forms for many property and liability types of insurance on behalf of individual insurers for approval by the state insurance departments, saving duplication of effort and reducing costs. In claims administration, independent adjusting firms handle some losses involving several insurers, so that several insurers involved in the same losses do not need to provide separate loss investigation and payment services. Many insurers cooperate with one another to coordinate loss prevention. Examples include the Insurance Institute for Highway Safety and the National Fire Protection Association. The MIB Group, Inc. gathers information needed in life insurance and disability income insurance underwriting. Rules that apply to members of numerous organizations of insurance agents, brokers, and companies regulate marketing activities. Insurers' joint efforts with LIMRA International and the Society of Insurance Research (SIR) enhance research. The American Council of Life Insurers (ACLI), the Insurance Information Institute, and the Risk and Insurance Management Society (RIMS) promote better public relations and legislation. To improve insurance education and set standards for professional courses and designations, the following organizations are important: the American Academy of Actuaries, The American College (and the related LUTC), the American Institute for CPCU (and the related Insurance Institute of America), and the Life Office Management Association (LOMA). Professors of insurance and other industry personnel exchange much valuable information through conferences and publications of the American Risk and Insurance Association (ARIA). Many insurers and these types of organizations supply representatives directly to industry committees that work in conjunction with government regulatory bodies to draft legislation, coordinate programs, and improve both self-regulation and public regulation of insurance. For example, the National Association of Insurance and Financial Advisors (NAIFA) has encouraged much legislation for implementation in state legislative bodies.

Self-regulation works extremely well in some aspects of insurance, while in others it is disappointingly ineffective. Difficult areas for self-regulation include competitive practices that involve such factors as production costs, commissions, advertising, selling practices, and rates.

Ethical Standards

In the area of individual life insurance, annuities, and long-term care insurance sales, the Insurance Marketing Standards Association (IMSA) has been active for over a decade in setting ethical standards. IMSA is a voluntary not-for-profit organization, and its mission is to strengthen trust and confidence in the life insurance industry. IMSA member companies are required to demonstrate commitment to high ethical marketplace standards. IMSA-qualified companies commit to maintaining high ethical standards and to being fair, honest, and open in the way they advertise, sell, and service their products.

No direct counterpart to IMSA exists in the property-liability area. However, organizations such as the CPCU Society have been especially visible in promoting ethical behavior among Society members and within the insurance industry as a whole. Many other insurance industry associations, as well as individual companies, have also developed codes of ethics to which their members must adhere.

As a review of this section on self-regulation and as an introduction to the next section on government regulation, see the following figure, which summarizes the methods of insurance regulation.

Figure 5-1
Sources of Insurance Regulation

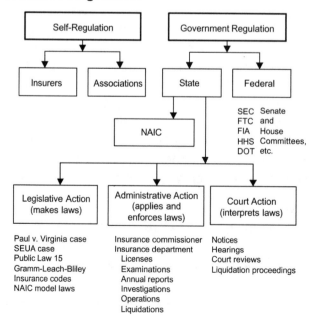

Government Regulation of Insurance

Three basic methods of government insurance regulation are available: (1) legislative action, (2) administrative action, and (3) court action. These correspond to the three main branches of the government. Legislation is the foundation of insurance regulation because it creates the insurance laws. The insurance laws of each state are often combined in what is known as an insurance code.[19] The application and enforcement of insurance laws are left in the hands of the insurance commissioner, the administrative official in each state. Court action provides detailed interpretations of troublesome parts of the law.

Legislative Action

State regulation of the insurance business was well established by the late 1800s and continues today as the predominant form of regulation. The practice is based on a series of court decisions, and it has been continued despite some contention that insurance might better be regulated by the federal government. In the classic 1868 case *Paul v. Virginia,* the Supreme Court decided that insurance "is not a transaction of commerce" and thus can be neither interstate commerce nor subject to federal regulation.[20] Until 1944, a period of about 75 years, the Supreme Court upheld the *Paul v. Virginia* decision.

In 1941, the Department of Justice heard complaints that certain insurance company practices violated the Sherman Antitrust Act. In 1944, the U.S. Supreme Court handed down a momentous four-to-three decision before one of its largest audiences in history. This case, *U.S. v. South-Eastern Underwriters Association (SEUA) et al.,*[21] now known to the legal profession and to the insurance business as the *SEUA* case, held that insurance is commerce. Thus, because of its interstate nature, it would be subject to federal regulation.

---

19. The insurance code for an individual state can exceed several hundred pages.

20. Today it is difficult to rationalize such a decision, but in 1868 the now famous decision stated, "Issuing a policy of insurance is not a transaction of commerce. They are not commodities to be shipped or forwarded from one state to another and then put up for sale. . . . Such contracts are not interstate transactions, though the parties may be domiciled in different states. They are, then, local transactions and are governed by local law." From *Paul v. Virginia,* 231 U.S. 495.

21. 64 United States 1162.

However, because of delegation of authority by Congress, the regulation of the business of insurance remains primarily a state function. The specific delegation to the states of the power to regulate insurance occurred with the passage of Public Law 15, also known as the McCarran-Ferguson Act or simply the McCarran Act, in 1945.[22] Congress made the Sherman Act, the Clayton Act, and the Federal Trade Commission Act applicable to the business of insurance after January 1, 1948, "to the extent that such business is not regulated by state law." In other words, the jurisdiction for regulating interstate insurance was left with the individual states as it had been for many years, but the important proviso was added permitting the federal government to take over insurance regulation if state regulation should become inadequate.

The enactment of the Financial Services Modernization Act, also referred to as the Gramm-Leach-Bliley Act, again addressed the regulation issue as a result of a growing number of affiliations between banks and insurance. Traditionally, the federal government and, in some cases, the states regulated banking activities, while only the states regulated insurance. The act indicated that each segment of the financial services business is to be regulated separately and that states continue to have primary regulatory authority for all insurance activities.

National Conference of Insurance Legislators (NCOIL)

Many state legislators whose primary focus is insurance legislation and regulation belong to an organization known as the *National Conference of Insurance Legislators*. The purpose of the National Conference of Insurance Legislators (NCOIL) is to help legislators make informed decisions on insurance issues that affect their constituents and to declare opposition to federal encroachment of state authority to oversee the business of insurance, as authorized under the McCarran-Ferguson Act of 1945. Toward that end, NCOIL works to:

- educate state legislators on current and perennial insurance issues
- help state legislators from different states interface effectively with each other
- improve the quality of insurance regulation
- assert the prerogative of legislators in making state policy regarding insurance

---

22. C 20, 79th Cong., 1st sess.

- speak out on Congressional initiatives that attempt to encroach upon state primacy in overseeing insurance

Many legislators active in NCOIL chair or are members of the committees responsible for insurance in their respective state houses across the country.

Today, most insurance regulation remains with the states. However, federal legislators, consumer advocates, and various insurance industry associations frequently question whether all or some of these regulatory activities should instead take place at the federal level, reducing the challenges and inefficiencies both U.S. and alien insurers currently face in meeting the requirements of more than 50 jurisdictions. Issues recently discussed at the federal level include such diverse topics as the role of banks in insurance, terrorism coverage, and underwriters' use of credit scoring.

Although most insurance regulation takes place at the state level, the role of federal insurance regulation has been gradually expanding.

Landmark Events in the History of Insurance Regulation

- U.S. Supreme Court decision in the case of *Paul v. Virginia*, 1868
- U.S. Supreme Court decision in the case of *U.S. v. South-Eastern Underwriters Association*, 1944
- Public Law 15 (McCarran-Ferguson Act), 1945
- Financial Services Modernization Act's reaffirmation of states' primary role in insurance regulation, 1999

Administrative Action

The insurance commissioner[23] of each state has broad powers. The commissioner's authority extends to licensing insurers and agents; requiring annual reports from the insurers; approving forms and rates in some, but not all, lines of insurance; and investigating complaints of many kinds. According to data released by the National Association of Insurance Commissioners (NAIC), the top five reasons consumers filed formal complaints against their insurance companies in one recent year were delays, denials of claims,

---

23. Most of the states use this title of "commissioner of insurance," eight use "director of insurance," and three use "superintendent of insurance."

unsatisfactory settlement offers, policy cancellations, and premium/insurance rating issues.[24]

In most states, the insurance commissioner is appointed by the governor and is a member of the governor's cabinet. The rationale behind this method of choosing the head insurance regulatory official is that the governor is ultimately responsible for the business success of his or her term of office and therefore should be able to appoint a person to carry out this responsibility. In about 10 states, insurance commissioners are elected by voters in a general election. Recent history has not demonstrated whether voters or governors have done a better job of selecting commissioners of high caliber and integrity. Both methods of selecting and retaining insurance commissioners clearly involve a political process.

The insurance department within which insurance commissioners carry out their duties may vary from a few persons in some states to several hundred employees in a state such as New York. Many departments have existed for a century or more. Some states have relied on New York as their guide for insurance legislation and administrative action. Some New York laws apply to all insurers licensed there, wherever they do business, a provision called extraterritoriality. This provision has played an important role in creating a degree of uniformity in practice among many states.

The insurance commissioner's major powers involve licensing, examination, and investigation. In addition to following the required incorporation procedure for domestic organizations, each insurer that wishes to do business in the state must be licensed for the lines of business it plans to write. The commissioner has broad interpretive powers to decide whether an insurer is qualified, financially and otherwise, to operate in the state. Licenses are usually renewable on an annual basis. The insurance commissioner has considerable power to refuse to issue a renewal license, as well as the power of suspension or revocation. Tests are also administered for licensing insurance agents or brokers.

On-site examination of insurers once they have been licensed is also an important responsibility of the commissioner. Insurers' continued solvency is the major objective of detailed examinations that are conducted according to

---

24. NAIC Cites Top Insurance Complaints for 2007," NAIC News Release, posted January 31, 2008; http://www.namic.org/topnews/080131st1.asp?utm_source=weekly& utm_medium=email, accessed 2/7/08.

law, at intervals usually from 3 to 5 years. Checking assets, liabilities, and reserves is part of this procedure, as is reviewing the insurer's underwriting, investment, and claims practices. A regional zone system is used in cooperation with the National Association of Insurance Commissioners (NAIC) to avoid unnecessary redundant examination of multistate insurers by many states. In this way, the examination of insurers licensed in many states is standardized and simplified, and all states in which the insurer does business accept the results of the regular zone examination. In the intervening years between complete examinations of insurers, every state requires the filing of an Annual Statement with the insurance commissioner. This filing reports current financial conditions and changes that have occurred during the year. A standard NAIC form is used that, for most details, provides uniformity of the information the statement requests. These Annual Statements are available to the public in the state insurance department offices.

National Association of Insurance Commissioners (NAIC)

model law

model regulation

We previously mentioned NCOIL, an association of state legislators. Insurance regulators also have an association. The *National Association of Insurance Commissioners (NAIC)* is a voluntary nonprofit association of state insurance administrators. The NAIC itself has no regulatory authority. It is important, however, not only for the zone examination procedures but also for its influence through the commissioners on uniformity of insurance laws in the various states. The NAIC assists state insurance departments by developing model laws and regulations. A *model law* is a draft bill—the suggested wording of a new law—for consideration by state legislators. Any state may choose to adopt the model bill or adopt it with modifications. A *model regulation* is a draft regulation that may be implemented by a state insurance department if the model law is passed. The insurance laws and regulations of many states incorporate at least the primary concepts of NAIC model laws, resulting in some degree of uniformity among the states.

The NAIC has been criticized for its inability to bring about greater uniformity in state insurance legislation. A program under which the NAIC accredits state insurance regulatory bodies, based largely on the extent to which the state has adopted certain of the NAIC's model laws and regulations, has been developed to counter some of this criticism. The NAIC has recommended many model laws and regulations for such areas as holding companies, variable contracts, guaranty funds, life insurance replacement, and unfair advertising. In addition, the NAIC has been instrumental in developing risk-based capital requirements. These requirements call for differing minimum amounts of capital that insurers must maintain, based on the riskiness of their insurance and investment operations. Other NAIC model laws or regulations deal with unfair claims practices, privacy protection, unfair sex discrimination, and long-term care policies, among numerous other topics. Major research projects have covered such topics as auto insurance, premium taxation, competitive rating, credit life and health insurance, and mass marketing. Statistical reporting systems both for testing company solidity and for measuring profitability have been operational for several years.

The insurance commissioners' investigative powers help determine whether insurers and their representatives meet statutory requirements. Open access to insurers' records and books and hearings on such matters as rate violations and unfair trade practices are examples of this authority. As a result of such procedures, which are often informal, the commissioner may issue administrative rulings or advisory opinions with regard to the business conduct of insurers or their agents. In extreme cases, the commissioner can declare an insurer insolvent and order its liquidation. All these investigative powers have as their major goal the protection of insurance policyowners and claimants.

Financial planners must realize that insurance regulation does not serve as a guarantee against any and all possible insolvencies and abuses, but the commissioner's insurance regulatory powers do serve as an important means of reducing such problems.

Judicial Action

The broad authority of insurance commissioners is subject to review and interpretation by the courts. To determine whether the commissioner's duties conform with state statutes, the courts may review the notice and hearing procedures that commissioners use to arrive at official rulings. Examples are actions to compel the commissioner to issue a license to an insurer or to prevent its cancellation, and court review of decisions to permit or refuse rate increases. The courts may be used in private actions or by the attorney general of the state against an insurance commissioner, and the commissioner may also, for example, petition the courts to enforce compliance with laws or rulings. Courts also resolve disputes between insurers and policyowners or insurance claimants.

WHAT IS REGULATED BY THE STATES

The insurance codes, as well as the general business laws, vary among the 50 states. This section summarizes the regulation typically found in the more important insurance jurisdictions, such as New York state.

Insurance regulation by each state is largely aimed at the insurers that conduct an insurance business within the state's jurisdiction. Some regulation is also provided for agents, brokers, and other persons who are part of the marketing of insurance contracts and provide certain other services to insurance policyowners. The regulation of insurers falls into the following categories:

- formation and licensing of insurers
- supervision of insurer operations
- rehabilitation and liquidation of insurers

Truly, the birth, life, and death of an insurance company are in the hands of the state regulators.

Formation and Licensing of Insurers

Insurance companies are required to meet specific standards that are often higher than those set for general business organizations. Standards that ensure the solvency, competence, and integrity of the insuring organization are necessary. The first step is incorporation,[25] an introductory process in which the state recognizes and approves the existence of a new legal identity.

The next step, licensing, is a check on the insurer's financial condition to determine that it has the required initial capital and surplus for the kinds of insurance permitted in the license. Domestic, foreign, and alien insurers that wish to become "admitted" insurers in the state must meet the statutory requirements for licensing. The laws usually specify standards for foreign and alien insurers at least as high as those for domestic insurers. Standards vary by legal type of insurer, with requirements for mutual insurers somewhat different from those for stock insurers. These standards also vary widely in the different states.

---

25. Reciprocal exchanges, Lloyd's associations, fraternals, and some health insurance associations do not legally become incorporated by this process. They do, however, file similar statements of their present status and proposed activities as stated in their charters and bylaws.

The licensing procedure is not dependent on financial requirements alone. Many states give the insurance commissioner leeway to apply considerable judgment in acting, or refusing to act, on a license application. The objective of licensing is to provide a preliminary method to lessen the chance of insurer insolvency, particularly during the difficult formative years. A license may be denied for many other reasons, including the bad faith or reputation of the proposed incorporators or management of an insurer. General managerial ability is undoubtedly as important as capital and surplus requirements for an insurer to achieve sustained financial stability. For that reason, the insurer's license is no more a guarantee against failure than an auto driver's license is a guarantee against an accident.

Insurer Operations

Insurance regulation continues after the formation and licensing of an insurer. Continual regulation is needed because most insurer obligations extend years into the future, and the state should provide supervision so that the contractual promises are fulfilled. The ways in which insurer operations are supervised are strikingly different among the states and among the various kinds of insurance. Most states provide some regulation contracts and forms, rates, reserves, asset and surplus values, investments, agents' licensing and trade practices, claims practices, and taxation.

Contracts and Forms

Because insurance policies are complex legal documents that consumers often do not fully understand, they could be used to mislead or unfairly treat policyowners. Consequently, in many lines of insurance, policy forms must be approved by, or at least filed with, the insurance commissioner. The task of gaining approval is simplified if an insurer uses a standard policy form developed by an insurance advisory organization, such as ISO or the American Association of Insurance Services (AAIS). Independent insurers may have individualized contracts that vary significantly.

Life and health insurance contracts are not standard contracts in the sense that similar forms or benefits are required. Most states do, however, impose some uniformity by requiring standard provisions in life and health contracts pertaining to such items as loan and surrender values and the grace period.

Many insurance forms are subjected to little or no regulatory review. For example, the contracts that cover property in transit are not at all uniform, and policyowners should review their benefits, conditions, and exclusions carefully.

Rates

The regulation of insurance pricing varies by line of business. In some lines of insurance, such as aviation insurance, practically no state regulation exists. In life insurance, regulation involves maintaining minimum reserves, rather than setting prices. Many kinds of insurance are subject to some direct rate regulation.

Insurance rating laws usually require that rates be

- *adequate.* Rates are considered adequate rates when, along with investment income, they are expected to produce sufficient revenue to pay all losses and expenses of doing business, along with a reasonable profit.
- *not excessive.* Rates are considered nonexcessive rates if they do not generate an unreasonably high profit for the insurer. This, however, does not guarantee that rates will be affordable to consumers.
- *not unfairly discriminatory.* Rates are considered not unfairly discriminatory rates if they reflect the expected loss costs and expenses of the homogeneous group of insureds to whom they apply.

Discrimination and Insurance. It is important to distinguish between discrimination and unfair discrimination.

For example, in the United States, age discrimination is considered inappropriate for many business purposes. However, age discrimination is commonly practiced in insurance rates, especially with regard to life insurance. Age discrimination in life insurance rates is not *unfair* discrimination, because it reflects the differing mortality rates of people of different ages and enables insurers to charge equitable premiums.

Any rebate of the insurance premium to an insured, other than dividends to a class of policyowners, is considered discriminatory in most states. A rebate is usually contrary to the law, whether it is made in the form of a direct payment or a credit against the premium or by means of any deception. The statutes do not, however, prohibit the payment by one broker or agent of a part of his or her commission or other compensation to other licensed agents or brokers.

Proposed rates for property and liability insurance are often based on loss data accumulated by advisory organizations, formerly called rating bureaus. Subscribing insurers add loss data to margins for covering expenses, contingency reserves, and desired profits. Some large insurers do not subscribe to these organizations' services and instead base rates on their own independent loss and expense data. Individual insurer rate making has increased in recent decades and has become an important factor in auto insurance and homeowners contracts.

Many of the states passed rating laws some 50 years ago, following a model bill the NAIC developed. In these states, the laws provide specifically that there is no intent to prohibit or discourage reasonable price competition, and they do not prohibit or discourage price uniformity. The laws permit, but do not require, concerted rate making. The state insurance department passes on the reasonableness of the rules and regulations of rating advisory organizations that furnish insurers with loss statistics and other material for rate making. An advisory organization may not exclude or withhold its facilities from any insurers, each of which has the statutory right to become a subscriber by paying reasonable fees.

Types of Rating Laws. Several different types of rating laws are used in different states and lines of insurance. The most common types are (1) prior approval laws, (2) file-and-use laws, (3) open competition laws, (4) use-and-file laws, and (5) flex-rating laws.

prior approval law   A *prior approval law* requires that the proposed rates be filed with the insurance commissioner. The rates may not be used by the insurer unless and until the commissioner approves them. With increased competition, potentially lower rates, and deregulation of insurance, prior approval laws have come under heavy fire. Although some states have adopted other types, regulation through prior approval laws remains predominant.

file-and-use law   Several states employ a *file-and-use law,* which permits the immediate use of filed rates without the insurance commissioner's affirmative approval. The commissioner, however, may disapprove the rates within a certain time period, such as 30 or 60 days. Some states use this method for one type of insurance while retaining the prior approval rule for other kinds of insurance.

use-and-file law   Numerous states have a *use-and-file law*. Rates must be filed with the insurance commissioner within a specified time after they are first used. The rates may be disapproved if not in compliance with the law.

flex-rating law   A few states have enacted *flex-rating laws* for some lines of insurance. Under these laws, no regulatory approval is needed if a proposed new rate represents a change of less than 5 or 10 percent or some other stated percentage of the existing rate. Other rate changes require prior approval.

open competition   From time to time for some lines, some states have also adopted *open competition,* which was pioneered in California. Open competition, which relies on competition to set rates, actually represents the absence of government regulation. A broader movement toward open rate competition for commercial insurance exists.

Instead of directly regulating insurance prices, some state laws supervise the cost of life insurance by limiting the portion of the premium that can be used for expenses other than claims. The New York law applicable to life insurance is most influential in this regard because, under the extraterritoriality provision, all insurers that do business in that state must conform to its regulations for all insurance contracts, regardless of where they are written.

Types of State Laws Affecting Insurance Rates

- Prior approval laws
- File-and-use laws
- Use-and-file laws
- Flex-rating laws
- Open competition
- Expense limitation laws

Reserves

The states require insurers to maintain, as a liability on their balance sheets, a minimum reserve considered adequate to meet policy obligations as they mature.

legal reserve   ***Life Insurance.*** In life insurance, the *legal reserve* is an amount that, augmented by premium payments under outstanding contracts and interest earnings, is sufficient to enable the life insurer to meet its expected policy obligations. These include death benefits and nonforfeiture benefits, such as policy loans and surrender values. Insurers need to charge premiums sufficient to pay expenses and meet the legal reserve requirement. Requiring these minimum reserves therefore indirectly regulates life insurance rates, or at least reduces the likelihood of inadequate rates.

unearned premium reserve

Property and Liability Insurance. In property and liability insurance, the *unearned premium reserve* must always be adequate to pay a return premium to all policyowners if their policies are canceled prior to expiration. The unearned premium reflects the proportion of the written premium that the insurer has not earned by providing protection for the full policy period. The purpose of this reserve is to meet all liabilities under the contract and to pay expenses in the future. At the same time, it accounts for income the insurer has received but not yet fully earned.

EXAMPLE
Assume that an insurer issues a 1-year homeowners policy on October 31 of a particular year. On December 31 of that year, the insurer has an unearned premium equal to five-sixths of the annual premium for the policy. This and the unearned premiums for other unexpired policies make up the unearned premium reserve shown as a liability on the insurer's balance sheet.

loss reserve

A second type of reserve required of property and liability insurers is the *loss reserve*. The loss reserve reflects the insurer's liability for losses that have already occurred but have not yet been paid or otherwise settled. Because many claims do not result in immediate payment of all incurred losses, the insurer must set up a reserve to ensure their payment. For example, a workers' compensation claim may be made against the insurer today. However, payments to the claimant are made gradually over a long future period of disability. In auto liability cases, several years may elapse after a loss before a court decides who is liable and for how much. In these cases, an estimate of the reserve that will be needed to pay the insurer's obligation is made and carried on its books as a loss reserve. In this way, losses and loss expenses for claims that are incurred but not yet paid are provided for by the insurer under the loss-reserve laws of the states.

Simply put, even if the money has already been collected, property-liability insurers may not count premiums as earned until the period for which they purchase coverage is completed. Collected premiums are an asset, but any premiums that have not been earned are an offsetting liability—the unearned premium reserve. Insurers are also required to count as a liability—the loss reserve—the full estimated value of all losses as soon as they happen, even if the actual claims payment occurs much later.

Assets and Surplus Values

The value of assets that appear on insurers' balance sheets must be correct and conservative in order for liabilities, other reserves, and residual surplus items to be meaningful. Securities insurers hold are valued according to practices adopted by a committee of the NAIC. Stocks are usually given year-end market values, while most bonds are carried at amortized values. The valuations are only advisory to the states, but the result is a good example of voluntary and state regulation working together. For some insurers, such as mutual insurers, both surplus accumulation and distribution are subject to regulation aimed at providing equitable treatment for all policyowners.

nonadmitted asset Insurance companies are required to file detailed financial information with insurance regulators in a form known as an Annual Statement. Insurance companies are required to characterize some assets on their Annual Statements as nonadmitted assets. *Nonadmitted assets* are thought to be of marginal quality or of little liquidity for policyowners if their insurers should get into financial difficulty. Examples of nonadmitted assets are most office furniture and supplies, as well as premiums that are 90 days or more past due.

Investments

To protect insurer solvency, most states have laws that govern the types of securities that may be purchased for investment. The strictest regulations apply to life insurers because they retain many billions of dollars of assets for many years for their policyowners.

Life insurers' investment portfolios are subject to rigorous supervision. Each Annual Statement lists every investment with detailed information about its date of acquisition, costs, values, and earnings. Bonds and common stocks are the prime investments in life insurers' portfolios, constituting a large majority of total assets. Most states grant limited permission for certain investments. Stocks may be limited, for example, to a stated percentage of assets or to 100 percent of surplus. Real estate holdings, especially commercial properties and housing projects, are also limited to a maximum in various states. The legality of all the insurer's holdings is checked carefully in periodic audits of the insurer's portfolio.

Property and liability insurers' investment portfolios are also supervised, although the laws are more lenient and vary greatly among the states. The laws of each state specify the investment restrictions. The general practice aims at requiring the safest types of investments for all assets held as reserves, both for unearned premiums and losses, and for other liabilities. Cash, high-grade bonds, and perhaps preferred stocks of proven quality may be permitted for such assets. The remainder of assets (representing capital and surplus) may be invested in a wider range of securities, including common stocks that meet certain standards. Limitations on real estate holdings, the size of single investments in relation to total assets or surplus, and investments in foreign companies, as well as many other restrictions, are also common.

Producer Licensing

Laws in all states require insurance agents and brokers to be licensed. The insurance departments usually administer these laws. The objective is insurer representation that is competent and trustworthy. All states require a comprehensive written examination before agent licensing. The examinations are often divided into separate tests for different lines of insurance. Some adjusters and consultants also must be licensed in a few states. All states now require continuing education as a condition for license renewal.

Financial planners per se are not regulated by federal or state governments. However, the activities and conduct of financial planners are subject to government regulation, because most of the individual components of the financial planning process are regulated. Thus, federal or state securities regulators oversee financial planners in their capacity as investment advisors; federal or state securities agencies also regulate those financial planners who sell securities. Additionally, many engaged in financial planning are subject to state regulation of insurance brokers and agents, accountants, or attorneys.

Financial planning often includes an analysis of a client's insurance needs. Financial planners, therefore, may find themselves subject to government regulation of insurance, which primarily means state regulation. In some states, financial planners are even subject to regulation if they recommend a generic insurance product or a specific amount of insurance without referring the client to an insurance agent or acting as insurance agents themselves. Some states, however, make insurance licensing easier for accredited financial planners by exempting individuals holding the CFP or other designations from insurance testing requirements.

Unfair Trade Practices

unfair trade practices

The McCarran-Ferguson Act left insurance regulation to the states with the stipulation that the federal government could take over if state regulation should become inadequate. To help maintain adequate state regulation, the NAIC developed the model Unfair Trade Practices Act, and almost all U.S. jurisdictions have adopted *unfair trade practices* acts. The acts prohibit unfair trade practices in insurance, including the following:

rebating

twisting

misappropriation

commingling of funds

- *rebating:* Rebating is the return of any part of the premium, except in the form of dividends, to the policyowner by the insurer or agent as a price-cutting sales inducement

- *twisting:* Twisting is a special form of misrepresentation in which an agent may induce the policyowner to cancel the contract of another insurer in order to take out a new contract based on an unfair or incomplete comparison of the contracts.

- *misappropriation:* Misappropriation is an agent's unlawful keeping of funds belonging to others

- *commingling of funds,* which occurs when an agent mixes the insured's or the insurer's funds with the agent's personal funds; commingling of funds is prevented in some states by requiring a separate bank account for the agent's premium funds held in trust for the insurer

- *misleading advertising:* Misleading advertising is restrained by many regulations that require full and fair information in advertisements by insurance companies and agents

Avoiding Insurance Fraud

FIGHT FAKE INSURANCE

Stop. Call. Confirm.

Fake Insurance Consumer Awareness Tips

Take the following steps to avoid becoming a victim of a fake insurance scam:

- When you are offered a policy, call the Department of Insurance [in your state] and check to see if your agent is licensed, and if the insurance company is legitimate.

- Never pay cash!

- Don't be pressured into signing anything you do not understand.

- Look for "red flags," such as high-pressure marketing tactics or an extreme sense of urgency. Be skeptical of sales pitches contending that you "must act now," or those that say, "this is a one-time offer."

- Be wary of policies pushed by high-pressure newspaper ads, fax flyer solicitations, hotel sales meetings, and via internet marketing.

- Ask questions! If the sales agent or representative is evasive, that's a warning signal. Make sure you get all of the important information about the policy.

- Be aware of premiums that are at least 25 percent below the average price for comparable insurance products.

- After you purchase your policy, call the Insurance Company to verify the company and your insurance policy number. Call the Insurance Company if you have not received your policy within 30 days.

- "Fake health insurance" is difficult to manage and more often than not, the advertising clearly states that "this is not insurance." Consumers and small business owners must read the fine print to avoid scams.

- With rising health care costs a big concern, fraudulent health insurance plans thrive by victimizing small businesses and consumers.

- Illegal discount health cards and plans are also widely offered to the public through newspaper ads, flyer solicitations, hotel sales meetings, and via the internet.

- The premise is that the buyer usually pays a one-time or monthly fee and, in return, will receive a discount off the medical practitioner's normal fee by simply presenting the card. Generally, a list of practitioners is part of the process.

The bottom line: If it seems too good to be true, it probably is!

The insurance commissioner has broad powers to prevent unfair practices. The commissioner exercises this authority by investigating complaints, as well as by initiating investigations of any questionable acts of insurance companies or their representatives. Any individual or organization found to have violated an unfair trade practices act is subject to penalties that include fines and suspension or revocation of a license.

unauthorized entity　　Licensed insurance agents are responsible for determining that the carriers for which they are selling are approved by the department of insurance in that state. Any agent who sells coverage from an unauthorized entity faces the risk of regulatory penalties, liability for unpaid claims, and imprisonment on a felony charge. An *unauthorized entity* is an insurance company (or other organization either real or fictitious) that has not gained approval to place insurance business from a department of insurance in the jurisdiction where it or a producer wants to sell insurance.

To help consumers avoid buying insurance from unauthorized entities, the California state insurance department has provided the tips in the list above titled "Avoiding Insurance Fraud."[26]

Unfair Claims Practices

An insurer's practices in adjusting claims represent a major source of possible mistreatment of insureds and other claimants. Most states have laws patterned after the NAIC's model laws and regulations pertaining to unfair claim settlement practices. Some of the practices that are regarded as unfair are the following:

- failing to investigate claims promptly
- failing to communicate with or acknowledge communications from clients on a timely basis
- failing to provide a reasonable explanation as to why a claim was denied
- failing to maintain procedures for handling complaints about claims
- misrepresenting pertinent policy provisions that affect claims
- failing to try to settle a claim once the insurer's liability becomes clear

---

26. From the California Department of Insurance web site (www.insurance.ca.gov/0400-news/ 0100-press-releases/0080-2005/release085-05.cfm, accessed 9/27/06).

- attempting to settle a claim for far less than a reasonable person would expect based on the insurer's advertising material

Other Areas of Consumer Protection

In some lines of insurance, insurers are required to use policies that meet specified readability standards. These standards relate not just to the size of the print font used but also to expressing policy provisions in terms that a typical high school graduate should understand. Some states require that insurance consumers be given shopper's guide booklets for certain lines of insurance. These booklets help consumers make comparisons of the costs and benefits of different policies. Various state insurance departments also publish an abundance of consumer information on their Web pages.

Taxation

premium tax   Like other businesses, insurance companies are subject to federal income taxation. Insurers are also required to pay a *premium tax* to the state, usually at a rate of about 2 percent of the gross premiums policyowners pay. This premium tax resembles a sales tax on insurance premiums. Although insurers pay the tax, its cost, of course, is built into the price of insurance and thus is paid by the policyowners.

Premium taxes primarily generate revenue for the state rather than pay for the cost of insurance regulation. The state premium tax usually goes into the state's general revenue fund, with insurance department expenses being based on separate appropriations from that fund. Only a small percentage of the total tax revenue and fees is used to operate the state insurance department.

Rehabilitation and Liquidation of Insurers

The insurance commissioner of a state not only officiates at the birth and oversees the ongoing operation of an insurer but also presides over its demise if necessary. An insurer may be liquidated for numerous reasons, including financial insolvency.

rehabilitation   The insurance commissioner acts under the insurance laws as the official in charge of supervising *rehabilitation.* Rehabilitation is the process of restoring an insurer to financial stability through reorganization. Or the commissioner might choose *liquidation,* the process of dissolving a financially troubled insurer. The purpose of both actions is to conserve as much of the insurer's assets as possible for fair distribution to claimants, policyowners, and investors. Sometimes an insurer's license is suspended temporarily for not meeting financial solvency standards or for other noncompliance with department rulings on rates, advertising, and so on. This suspension may be a prelude to liquidation proceedings or may be a temporary action to force changes in the insurer's operations.

guaranty fund   A *guaranty fund* is a state fund designed to at least partially protect consumers against insurer insolvency. In recent years, all 50 states have adopted insurance guaranty fund plans. Model legislation promulgated by the NAIC encouraged states to adopt these laws. A "guaranty" is an agreement by which one party assumes another's debts. Guaranty funds should not be confused with guarantees, which assure the performance of a product or a service. Guaranty plans, administered on a state-by-state basis, usually assess solvent insurers in order to pay an insolvent company's unpaid claims and to return unearned premiums to its policyowners. Insurers each pay a proportional share of the losses, based on their premium volume in the state.

To date, the guaranty funds have done a reasonably good job of protecting the consumer, and some states have adopted several improvements. These improvements concern (1) giving the guaranty funds immediate access to the insolvent insurer's assets, rather than waiting until liquidation proceedings are complete; (2) giving the guaranty funds priority over general creditors to obtain the insolvent insurer's assets; and (3) permitting a tax offset against premium taxes to solvent insurers for money paid into the guaranty funds. Even with these improvements, however, some problems remain, including lengthy delays before consumers receive their money and dollar limits on some types of claims.

Guaranty funds do not guarantee that an insurer will be able to pay its claims. A system to pay for insolvencies does not completely protect insurance buyers against insurer insolvencies. Detecting troubled insurers in advance of insolvency proceedings is an important goal. The NAIC has developed an "early warning system" based on a series of financial ratio tests. These tests have dealt mainly with the adequacy of the insurer's reserves, changes in its surplus, its rate of growth, and the adequacy of its prices. Other tools for the early detection of insurer financial difficulty include the risk-based capital standards and the on-site examination system developed by the NAIC.

CURRENT FEDERAL REGULATION OF INSURANCE

Most government legislation, administrative action, and court decisions that pertain to insurance have been at the state level. The McCarran-Ferguson Act reaffirmed the states' predominant role in insurance regulation. This role still continues because the law conditionally exempts insurance from such major federal statutes as the Sherman Antitrust Act (except for boycotts, coercion, or intimidation), Clayton Act, Robinson-Patman Act, and other laws. Federal laws apply only to the extent that state legislation is inadequate.

The federal government has increased its regulation of insurance in some specific and limited, but nonetheless important, areas of insurance. For example, federal agencies have regulated some aspects of interstate advertising and mergers through the Federal Trade Commission (FTC), variable life insurance and annuities through the Securities and Exchange Commission (SEC), occupational safety under various rules of the Occupational Safety and Health Administration (OSHA), and pensions and other employee benefits under the Employee Retirement Income Security Act (ERISA) administered mainly by the U.S. Department of Labor.

The Financial Services Modernization Act (Gramm-Leach-Bliley Act) addresses the role of banks in insurance—is a relatively recent example of federal legislation that directly affects insurance and other financial services organizations. This act makes it clear that banking regulators regulate banking activities, but states continue to have primary regulatory authority for banks' insurance activities.

In October 2005, the Financial Crimes Enforcement Network (FinCEN), an agency of the United States Department of the Treasury, announced rules requiring certain U.S. insurance companies to establish anti-money-laundering programs and file suspicious-activity reports. The rules apply to insurance companies that issue or underwrite certain products that present a high degree of risk for money laundering or the financing of terrorism or other illicit activity, including the following products:

- permanent life insurance policies, other than group life insurance policies
- annuity contracts, other than group annuity contracts

- any other insurance products with cash value or investment features[27]

Money laundering involves disguising financial assets so they can be used without detection of the illegal activity that produced them. Through money laundering, the criminal transforms the monetary proceeds derived from criminal activity into funds with an apparently legal source.[28] The concern is that money laundering can be used to finance terrorism or other illicit activity. The requirement to identify and report suspicious transactions applies only to insurance companies, not their agents or brokers. However, agents and brokers must be integrated into an insurance company's anti-money-laundering program and monitored for compliance.

In compliance with these rules, insurance companies are required to train their agents to be alert for the following "red flags" to possible money-laundering activity:

- The purchase of an insurance product that appears to be inconsistent with a customer's needs.
- Any unusual method of payment, particularly by cash or cash equivalents (when such method is, in fact, unusual).
- The purchase of an insurance product with monetary instruments in structured amounts.
- The early termination of an insurance product, especially at a cost to the customer, or where cash was tendered and/or the refund check is directed to an apparently unrelated third party.
- The transfer of the benefit of an insurance product to an apparently unrelated third party.
- Little or no concern by a customer for the investment performance of an insurance product, but much concern about the early termination features of the product.
- The reluctance by a customer to provide identifying information when purchasing an insurance product, or the provision of minimal or seemingly fictitious information.

---

27. "Insurance Companies Required to Establish Anti-Money Laundering Programs and File Suspicious Activity Reports," U.S. Department of the Treasury, Financial Crimes Enforcement Network, FinCen News, October 31, 2005, p. 1 (http://www.fincen.gov/ newsrelease10312005.pdf, accessed 9/27/06).

28. From the Frequently Asked Questions page of the FinCEN web site (www.fincen.gov/af_faqs.html, accessed 9/27/06).

- The borrowing of the maximum amount available soon after purchasing the product.[29]

Over the years, the states have taken some steps toward "modernizing" insurance regulation, such as implementing measures for national uniformity of producer licensing. A number of bills have been introduced proposing a variety of changes to the current system, but none have become law. The Dodd-Frank Wall Street Reform and Consumer Protection Act (2010) established a Federal Insurance Office within the Department of Treasury and gives it tasks such as studying and reporting on how to modernize and improve the system of insurance regulation in the United States. The Act mandates that the Director consider the ability of any federal regulation or federal regulator to provide consumer protection for policyholders. The Act also gives the Office the authority to coordinate federal efforts, and develop federal policy on international insurance matters and assist the Secretary of Treasury in negotiating covered agreements pertaining to insurance or reinsurance between the United States and one or more foreign governments, authorities or regulatory entities.

FEDERAL VERSUS STATE REGULATION

Proposals to modify the insurance regulatory system are often discussed but rarely implemented. One proposal recently introduced in Congress would create an optional federal charter that would give individual insurance companies the choice to adopt a federal charter or remain with the current state regulatory system. Why should regulation of insurance be performed mainly by the states? Advocates of state regulation have pointed out the following reasons:

- the local nature of many insurance transactions, for which any difficulties can best be resolved on a state basis
- the reasonable success of state regulation for many years, during which insurance has become an important and sound business
- the value of regulation on a state-by-state basis, which permits gradual changes and innovations in regulation without applying them to the entire country all at once
- the NAIC's help in recommending model legislation to the states to achieve some uniformity in insurance regulation

---

29. *Federal Register* , "Rules and Regulations," Vol. 70, No. 212 (Thursday, November 3, 2005), p. 66759 (www.fincen.gov/amlforinsurancecompany.pdf, accessed 9/27/06).

While supporters recognize that state regulation is not perfect, they claim that federal regulation would be much worse. It would, they argue, be cumbersome, expensive, less effective, and fragmented among dozens of agencies.

Conversely, the proponents of federal regulation of insurance have criticized state regulation on many points:

- inconsistencies and lack of uniformity in regulation of insurers
- inadequate funding for the important tasks of the insurance commissioners, and the short-term and political aspects of their terms of office
- the need for greater standardization in insurance contracts to cover many interstate exposures
- the desire for increased competition to ensure availability and lower, fairer insurance prices

The threat of federal regulation wherever the states fail to perform adequately is a constant incentive to improve state insurance regulation.

EVALUATING INSURERS

In order to properly advise clients, a planner should be aware of the various criteria that can be used in evaluating both insurance companies and insurance producers.

Criteria for Selecting an Insurer

A financial planner may assist the client in the selection of insurers. Probably the single most important criterion is the insurer's financial strength. Because an insurer's basic function is to pay claims, care must be taken to select insurers that are most likely to be able to do so. In light of the number of insolvencies and near insolvencies among insurers in recent decades, and the limitations of state insurance guaranty funds noted earlier, an insurer's claims-paying ability cannot simply be taken for granted.

The size of an insurer is not always the most relevant factor, as financial strength and size are not necessarily equivalents. Many primary insurers—especially the smaller ones—are financially strong because of reinsurance. State insurance departments can provide some current information about insurers, including records about consumer complaints against specific insurers, risk-based capital compliance, and early warning financial ratios (described earlier). Many states make this information available through the Internet. A link to state insurance department web sites appears at the NAIC web site, naic.org.

Several rating organizations publish the financial history, ratings, and analyses of individual insurers. These organizations include A.M. Best Company, Demotech, Fitch Ratings (formed by a merger of Duff & Phelps and Fitch IBCA), Moody's, Standard & Poor's, and Weiss Ratings. However, a few words of caution are in order:

- Criteria and methodology differ among rating organizations, so an insurer may receive different ratings from different organizations.
- A rating of "A" may sound like an excellent grade, but "A" is not necessarily the highest possible rating. Best's has two ratings higher than "A," and Standard and Poor's has five ratings higher than "A."
- Some rating organizations seem to be more generous in their ratings than others.
- Not all insurers are rated by all of the rating organizations.

In light of all of these differences, it is probably wise advice to choose insurers that have very high ratings from at least two or three of the rating organizations. It is important also to remember, however, that financial ratings are based on past performance. A good rating does not ensure that an insurer will remain solvent for years to come, and a poor rating does not always mean that the insurer is about to become insolvent.

Insurer selection should consider willingness and ability to pay claims. Companies' attitudes toward claims may differ, and the applicant should be concerned with the company's viewpoint on technicalities, as well as the claims department's reputation for satisfactory dealings with insureds. Consumer complaint files that state insurance departments maintain can be helpful.

Service is another criterion that should be used in evaluating insurers. The insurer must be able to provide proper protection for the applicant. Does the insurer specialize in a few lines of insurance, or does it sell all coverages that the purchaser may need and want? Is the insurer experienced in offering all the contracts it will write? Will the insurer individualize contracts to meet the insurance buyer's particular needs? Does it have capacity and adequate reinsurance for the amount of insurance the buyer may require? Is it licensed in all states where the buyer needs coverage? In addition to indemnification for losses, can the insurer provide any engineering and loss prevention services that the purchaser may need? And again, what is the insurer's general attitude and reputation with regard to prompt and fair settlement of all reasonable claims?

The applicant should be interested in knowing whether the insurer is liberal with respect to underwriting. A company that is selective in underwriting may prove unsatisfactory when a consumer has a difficult situation, such as poor health or extremely hazardous business activities. Conversely, a consumer with very favorable risk characteristics may benefit by dealing with a highly selective insurer.

An important criterion in the evaluation of an insurer, of course, is the cost of its products. Cost should usually be considered and compared only after the above criteria are analyzed. Exorbitant rates are obviously undesirable. Lower rates are beneficial to the purchaser; however, rates that are too low could reflect an unduly strict attitude toward claims payment, inadequate financial reserves, restrictive policy provisions, highly selective underwriting, or minimal services.

Criteria for Selecting an Insurance Company

- Financial strength
- Attitude concerning claims payment
- Lines of coverage offered
- Service before and after a claim
- Underwriting standards
- Cost of the coverage

Initial costs are only part of the necessary analysis; final costs over a longer period of protection must be considered, including possible rate changes, dividends, assessments, or premium adjustments under some types of rating plans. In life insurance, net cost comparisons over a period such as 20 years, considering dividends, cash values, and interest factors, may be appropriate. Also, all insurance costs should be analyzed along with other risk management costs, such as those of loss prevention.

Criteria for Choosing an Agent or Broker

One of the most important decisions in the insurance-buying process involves selection of a competent and reliable insurance agent or broker. If an exclusive agent who represents one insurer only is chosen, this selection also determines the insurer with which business is conducted. If an independent agent is chosen, the insurance buyer often leaves the selection of the insurer up to the agent, or at least relies heavily on the agent's recommendations.

Part of the insurance premium represents commission or salary to the agent or broker. If no service or inadequate service is rendered for this part of the premium, the policyowner is paying for something he or she did not receive. If the agent or broker is only an order taker, the policyowner is getting less than full value.

Some applicants place insurance with numerous agents. Frequently, this is done to create goodwill or to distribute business among a number of friends. Sound practice suggests selecting one agent or broker, or as few as possible, to handle an entire insurance portfolio. Both the insurance buyer and the agent should prefer this practice. Most agents would rather have fewer accounts for which they are fully responsible than to participate in many accounts to which they contribute little service. Sometimes an account may be split so that one agent handles the property and liability lines and another agent the life, health, and annuity business. Regardless of the number of agents, the more information that an agent has about the client's total insurance account, the better he or she may be able to analyze the risks and recommend coordinated protection for the client's needs.

The insurance consumer or financial planner who allows friendship to govern the selection of an agent may receive inadequate protection or pay an exorbitant amount for excessive or duplicate coverages. Placing insurance only on the basis of personal friendship is as foolish as selecting a doctor, a lawyer, or an architect on that basis. Because of the complex nature of various risks, insurance coverages, and rates, the insurance agent or broker should be selected with the same care and discrimination used to choose other professional advisors.

Some buyers solicit competitive bids every year for their property and liability insurance or their group employee benefits. Lower costs for insurance may come at the price of less satisfactory service from the agent, who may not regard the policyowner as a permanent client. Policyowners have found the competitive approach detrimental because in a period of losses, a business firm may have no assurance of continued coverage and competing insurers will be reluctant to participate. Thus, insurance buyers who shop too aggressively may seriously limit their market. This is less likely to occur if an insurer may expect to recoup over a period of years losses incurred in an unfavorable year. From the buyer's standpoint, as well as the agent's, a long-term relationship on a professional basis seems to work best in the long run.

Choosing an agent or a broker is an essential step toward a sound insurance and risk management program. Criteria used to evaluate insurance agents and brokers include knowledge and ability, willingness, integrity and character, and representation.

Knowledge and Ability

The agent must have the background and experience necessary to identify, analyze, and treat risks properly. One method to evaluate the agent's knowledge and ability is to ask such questions as, "Are you a CFP, ChFC, CLU, or CPCU? If not, are you working toward these or other educational objectives on a regular basis?" "Are you a full-time agent?" Agents who are fully committed to the insurance business are more likely to do a really successful job for their clients by developing their professional skills and keeping abreast of rapidly changing knowledge requirements.

The insurance consumer needs a technically competent agent who performs the wide variety of services essential to proper insurance protection. These services may include understanding needs, analyzing significant possibilities of loss, finding markets, comparing alternative coverages and contracts, arranging for credit or installment payments, checking on the accuracy of classifications and rates charged, providing loss prevention or engineering services, making evaluation appraisals, seeing that claims payments are made promptly, reviewing changing needs frequently, and many other important duties.

Willingness

Is the agent willing to take the time to apply his or her knowledge conscientiously and fully evaluate all the client's needs and alternatives? If not, the client won't receive the benefit of that knowledge. The agent must take the time to see that services, including those of agency staff and insurance companies, are performed as effectively as possible.

The agent should recommend additional legal, accounting, or consulting services as needed. Loss prevention suggestions and help with filing claims are also important to the insurance buyer. The best qualified agent who is too busy to provide service is of no value to the client. The time and desire to perform necessary services must be present when the client needs them.

Integrity and Character

Willing and able agents and brokers should be able to command the policyowner's confidence and trust. Because insurance is purchased to reduce uncertainty, agents or brokers must be able to give their clients both psychological and actual security. Consumers need someone with whom they can identify closely in discussing their financial needs and goals. The values of agent and client, if similar, can help them establish a good rapport. The agent's age in relation to the policyowner's can be a factor in this regard, but differences in age are probably less important than differences in philosophy and lifestyle. Confidential information from the purchaser is often required to provide good insurance counseling services. Thus, the agent or broker must respect the buyer's trust with complete honesty as would a doctor, a lawyer, or an accountant.

Representation

Good agents generally do not represent weak insurers. They must represent or have contacts with one or many insurers that can provide the required protection and services for the policyowner. Ideally, all necessary coverages, including even special or unusual ones, should be available through the agent(s) at a reasonable cost. The insurer or insurers represented should be capable of writing many different kinds of insurance with a progressive attitude toward newer coverages and forms designed to meet individual buyers' particular needs.

Insurance agencies and brokerage firms vary from the individual agent to organizations that have large staffs and offer a wide range of specializations. Some agencies consist of one person, others have a half-dozen agents and office personnel, while still others have 100 or more employees and operate much like a small insurance company. These organizations differ in the services they are able to offer, their methods of doing business, and the types of insurance they handle. Frequently, the members of an agency who handle life insurance limit their activities to this field. Also, in a large agency certain persons become recognized experts in such lines as pensions, liability, workers' compensation, or surety coverages. When selecting the agent or broker, the insurance consumer should consider whether the particular agent and agency office have the needed experience and service facilities.

CHAPTER REVIEW

Key Terms and Concepts

National Conference of Insurance Legislators (NCOIL)

National Association of Insurance Commissioners (NAIC)

model law

model regulation

prior approval law

file-and-use law

use-and-file law

flex-rating law

open competition

legal reserve

unearned premium reserve

loss reserve

nonadmitted asset

unfair trade practices

rebating

twisting

misappropriation

commingling of funds

unauthorized entity

premium tax

rehabilitation

guaranty fund

Review Questions

Review questions are based on the learning objectives in this chapter. Thus, a [3] at the end of a question means that the question is based on learning objective 3. If there are multiple objectives, they are all listed.

1. Your financial planning client asks why insurance seems to be so highly regulated. How would you explain the general purpose of insurance regulation to this client? [1]

2. Insurers participate in many activities that are forms of self-regulation. What are two ways that insurers engage in self-regulation? [2]

3. What are the three basic methods of government insurance regulation? [2]

4. What are the three key categories of state regulation of insurance? [3]

5. How do each of the following aspects of insurer operations tend to be regulated? Point out any differences between regulation applying to life insurers and that applying to property-liability insurers.
   a. contracts and forms [3]
   b. rates [3]
   c. reserves [3]
   d. assets and surplus values [3]
   e. investments [3]
   f. agents' licensing [3]
   g. trade practices [3]
   h. claims practices [3]

6. Maria Rodriguez, your client, is reluctant to buy whole life insurance, because she has heard of some insurers becoming insolvent. She is concerned that her insurance company might not be able to perform its obligations by the time she dies and her heirs need the insurance proceeds. How does insurance regulation seek to protect insurance buyers like Maria when an insurance company becomes insolvent? [3]

7. What are the arguments for and against regulation of insurance by the states? [3]

8. What criteria can a financial planner use to help clients select insurers for their insurance programs? [4]

9. What criteria can a financial planner use to help clients choose reliable and competent agents or brokers for their insurance programs? [4]

Learning Objectives

An understanding of the material in this chapter should enable the student to

1. Describe the unique aspects of an insurance contract that differentiate it from other goods and services.

2. Explain the general legal requirements of an insurance contract.

3. Describe the special legal characteristics of an insurance contract.

4. Explain how to analyze the various provisions in an insurance contract.

Financial planners must understand some fundamental attributes of insurance to make effective use of insurance as a financial planning tool. Some of these attributes are, in a sense, so obvious that they almost go without saying. But it is necessary to state them in order to understand the nature and importance of insurance.

Private insurance is usually provided through a written contract, known as an insurance policy. (Sometimes, insurance begins with a binding oral agreement between the insurer, or its agent, and the insurance applicant; the oral binder is later replaced by a written contract.) The most tangible product resulting from the insurance transaction is the insurance policy—a legally enforceable written contract. The effectiveness of insurance depends to a high degree on contract law, which governs the making and enforcement of contracts. Most financial planners are not attorneys, and they should not therefore deal in depth with legal issues. However, financial planners need to understand basic principles of contracts.

INSURANCE: AN INTANGIBLE CONTRACT

The insurance policy consists of tangible pieces of paper. However, insurance is more than mere pieces of paper; those pieces of paper contain the insurer's promise to pay money. Unlike tangible assets that have intrinsic value, an insurance contract is an intangible asset that represents value. Other intangible assets include stock certificates and savings bonds.

Unlike most physical goods, which are purchased for immediate use, consumers usually view insurance as a product that provides future benefits when loss payments are made. A hurricane, an auto accident, a premature death, or a retirement are all *future* possibilities for the insurance purchaser. A policyowner who focuses on the future benefits, however, is likely to overlook the significant immediate benefit of insurance: freedom from worry about financial losses.

Many people who buy insurance are convinced they will never have a loss. They buy insurance "just in case," but at the same time they think, "It will never happen to me." It's true that most families carry insurance for many years without having serious illness and/or without experiencing serious damage to their homes. Only the unfortunate minority who suffer losses come to realize the substantial benefits of insurance. Insurance is activated by contingencies that might or might not occur, contingencies that normally do not happen very often.

Insurance transfers the financial risk of losses to the insurer, an organization that is in the business of bearing risks. Insurance is affordable because it involves an exchange of unequal values. The insurance buyer pays a relatively small premium, or a series of premiums, in exchange for the insurer's promise to pay for a potentially large loss.

GENERAL LEGAL REQUIREMENTS

The rights and obligations of the parties to an insurance agreement are determined largely by the general laws that govern contracts. The agreement by which insurance is effected is a contract in which the insurer, in consideration of the policyowner's payment of a specified sum, agrees to make good the losses suffered through the occurrence of a designated unfavorable contingency.

A contract has been defined as "an agreement enforceable by law." A more complete definition would include the following essentials required by law:

- offer and acceptance
- legal purpose
- competent parties

- consideration

Absence of any of the essential elements prevents enforcement of any contract. To be valid and enforceable, insurance contracts must meet these four general legal requirements.

Offer and Acceptance

The first requirement of a legally enforceable contract involves offer and acceptance. A contract requires both an offer by one party to the contract and acceptance of that offer by another party. In insurance, the offer is usually made in a request for coverage by the prospect, or applicant. The simplest method, used for many types of property and liability insurance, is an oral request to an agent either in person or by telephone. In life insurance and in many forms of health insurance, the offer must be made in a written application.

Before a contract is effective, acceptance of the offer is necessary. As noted earlier, with property and liability insurance, the agent often has authority to bind coverage, or accept the offer, even before receiving any payment from the applicant. The protection may commence immediately, if desired, based entirely on the oral request of the applicant and the oral acceptance by the agent.

In life insurance, the method and timing of legal acceptance are different. The applicant usually submits the written application and the first premium payment as the offer to the insurer through the agent, who issues a conditional receipt. Acceptance is held by most courts to occur if the applicant meets the normal underwriting standards of the insurer, including a medical examination if required. Then coverage becomes effective as of the time of the application and premium payment. If the applicant does not meet the underwriting standards of the insurer, the insurer may make a counteroffer with a different contract, which the prospect may accept or reject upon delivery by the agent. If the premium is not paid with the application, the offer to insure is made by the insurer after reviewing the application. The insurance is accepted and becomes effective when the contract is delivered to the applicant while the applicant is in good health and the premium is paid.

EXAMPLE 1
Shelley completed an application for $25,000 of nonmedical (no examination required) life insurance on her own life and gave it to the insurer's agent with a check for the first premium. Shelley died in an auto accident 2 days later. Three weeks later, the insurer reviewed the application and found that Shelley, at the time of the application, met the insurer's normal underwriting standards. The insurer is obligated to pay $25,000 to Shelley's beneficiary.

EXAMPLE 2
Same facts as above, except that Shelley did not pay the premium. In this case, the insurer is not obligated to pay anything.

Legal Purpose

To be legally binding, any contract must meet the second requirement—a legal purpose or object. The courts will not enforce an insurance contact if it has an illegal purpose or is contrary to public policy. For example, a thief might purchase a property insurance policy listing stolen property. The courts will not require the insurer to pay a claim brought by the thief if that property is then lost or destroyed. Likewise, the courts will not enforce a life insurance contract if it is proven that the applicant who purchased the insurance did so intending to murder the insured and collect the insurance proceeds.

Punitive damages claims provide a good example of the public policy issue. Courts award punitive damages, in some cases, to punish the defendant in a liability claim who has committed some particularly egregious act. Some states do not permit insurance to pay punitive damages claims on behalf of an insured on the basis that the insured is not really punished unless the insured pays punitive damages with his or her own funds. Some liability insurance policies exclude coverage for punitive damages, but even a policy without an exclusion cannot be enforced in states where insurers are not permitted to pay punitive damages claims on behalf of their policyowners.

Competent Parties

Valid contracts require that the party making the offer and the one accepting the offer be legally competent to make the agreement. In insurance, the most common problem arises in connection with applicants who are under the age of legal majority, which differs by state. Minority age applicants may have the option of repudiating contracts up to the time they reach legal adulthood, unless the contracts are for necessities, such as food, shelter, or clothing.

Some insurance contracts are thus voidable by applicants who are minors, and these applicants will receive a full return of the premiums paid if they later decide to make them void. Some states have made exceptions for life, health, and auto insurance contracts by establishing special age limits of 14 or 16; beyond this age, minors are considered to have the legal capacity to insure themselves, and a contract is binding on them.

A similar problem may occur when insurance is purchased by legally insane or intoxicated persons. They cannot make legal contracts, because they fail to understand the agreement.

Insurers, too, must be competent to enter into a legal contract by meeting state charter and license requirements. In cases where legal capacity is lacking, many courts have nevertheless held the contracts binding on the insurer, or on its corporate officers personally, rather than penalizing a good-faith purchaser of the coverage.

Consideration

The final requirement for a valid contract is some "consideration" exchanged by both parties to the agreement—a right or something of value given up or an obligation assumed. In insurance, the applicant typically makes a premium payment, or the contract may become effective on the basis of the applicant's promise to pay and to meet other conditions of the contract. The insurer's consideration is its promise to pay for specified losses or to provide other services to the policyowner.

SPECIAL LEGAL CHARACTERISTICS

This section concerns special legal characteristics of the insurance contract. These are not necessarily unique to insurance contracts, but they help describe the fundamental ideas on which insurance contracts are based. A good understanding of these characteristics should help the financial planner, insurance advisor, and consumer to read insurance contracts and comprehend the underlying legal concepts that are essential to most insurance contracts. The following figure summarizes the characteristics.

Figure 6-1
Special Legal Characteristics of Insurance Contracts

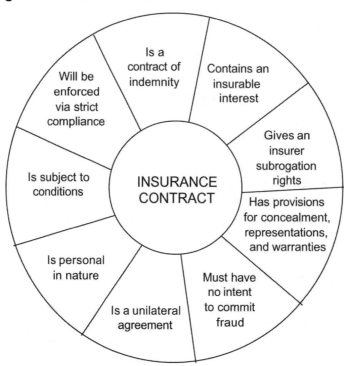

Unilateral Nature

unilateral contract   A *unilateral contract* is one in which only one party to the contract makes a binding promise that, if broken, gives rise to an action against that party for breach of contract. An insurance contract is a unilateral contract because only one party, the insurer, makes a legally enforceable promise. If the insurer fails to fulfill the promises it makes, such as to pay the specified benefits at the death of the insured, it may be held legally liable for breach of contract. After the premium is paid and the insurance is in force, the policyowner has no further promises to keep, although, of course, failure by the policyowner to live up to policy conditions may release the insurer from the contract.

Unlike an insurance contract, most contracts are bilateral. If Able agrees to sell a car to Baker for $7,000 and Baker agrees to buy it for that amount, they have formed a bilateral contract. If Able later decides not to sell the car, Baker can sue him to enforce the contract or, if the contract is breached, to pay damages. Likewise, if Baker changes his mind and decides not to buy the car, Able can insist that Baker honor his contract.

Personal Nature

An insurance contract is personal and covers the person rather than the property concerned. We may speak of insuring property, but this is not technically accurate. An insurer cannot guarantee that possessions will not be lost, or even guarantee replacement with items of like quality and kind. The insurer can, however, indemnify the person who has incurred the loss. We, therefore, speak of the personal nature of insurance. Consider an individual who pays for a property insurance contract and later sells the property without canceling the insurance. In the event of subsequent loss to the property, the insurer will make no payment, because the insured has suffered no loss. Insurance payment is contingent on loss to an insured party, not merely on loss of the property described in the policy.

One result of the personal nature of insurance is that many insurance contracts are not freely assignable, or transferable, by the policyowner to other parties. Most insurance contracts, with the exception of life insurance, represent a personal agreement between the insurer and the policyowner. To permit a property or liability insurance contract to be assignable without the insurer's approval would be unfair to the insurer. Only by knowing and investigating each policyowner can the insurance company accurately calculate the potential losses it is insuring.

A life insurance policy can be assigned to another party, such as a charity. Assigning ownership of a life insurance policy does not generally change the insured's life expectancy.

Conditional Nature

conditional contract   A *conditional contract* is an agreement in which one party has an obligation to perform only if the other party meets certain conditions specified in the agreement. Insurance is a conditional contract, because the insurer is obligated to pay claims, defend the insured against liability claims, or perform other services only if the insured (or the life insurance policyowner) has complied with policy conditions. Insurance policy conditions place some limitations on the insurer's obligations to perform by paying claims. Any failure by the insured to comply with policy conditions may relieve the insurer of its obligation.

An insurance contract condition is usually regarded as either precedent (before) or subsequent (after) the time at which a promise becomes binding on the promisor. An illustration of a common condition precedent, which must take place before a promise becomes binding, is the requirement in many insurance contracts that an insurer must have proper notice and proof of loss before the claim is payable. Note that the policyowner who has a loss has no contractual obligation to file an insurance claim, but the insurer is not obligated to pay unless the policyowner makes a claim in the proper manner. An example of a condition subsequent is an insured's obligation to cooperate with the insurer in defending a liability claim. If the insured does not cooperate, that failure subsequently relieves the insurer of its earlier obligation to pay.

Contract of Adhesion

contract of adhesion

A *contract of adhesion* is prepared in all its details by one party, in contrast to a bargaining contract, in which the terms are negotiated between the parties to the contract. An insurance contract is usually characterized as a contract of adhesion because the insurer ordinarily prepares all its details. The policyowner has no part in drafting its clauses or determining its wording. When applying for insurance, the applicant either accepts the policy as prepared by the insurer (adheres to it) or does not purchase the insurance.

The insurer does not always create the wording for the contract. Sometimes legislation requires that specific wording be used. State regulators often approve policy wording.

Sometimes the policyowner is a large corporation that asks for and obtains special contract provisions. In these cases, the intent of the entire contract, and of both the insurer and the policyowner, will probably be considered in court interpretations of any contract ambiguities.

The insurer that drafts an insurance contract has an opportunity to represent its intentions clearly. If the terms of an insurance policy are ambiguous, obscure, or susceptible to more than one reasonable interpretation, the construction most favorable to the policyowner generally prevails. It is nearly impossible for insurers to draft contracts that clearly describe every possible situation that might develop. Therefore, in cases of ambiguity in insurance contracts, this principle often helps policyowners.

Where there is no ambiguity, an insurance contract is to be enforced in accordance with its terms. If the contract is clear and understandable, few interpretations are necessary. Readers must consider the generally understood meaning of the terms used and examine the entire context to determine the nature and extent of coverage.

The law holds persons to be bound by the terms of a written contract that they sign or accept, regardless of whether they have acquainted themselves with all of its terms and conditions.[30]

Most people do not read their policies. Insurance contracts are complicated and difficult to understand. Policyowners assume that a policy meets their needs and let it go at that. However, when a loss occurs, claiming ignorance of the policy's terms because of failure to read the agreement is no defense. The policyowner's failure to read the contract does not change or extend the rights of the policyowner as stated in the written policy. A financial planner's advice to insurance buyers should be: "To avoid problems (and uncertainties), know what is in your insurance policy by reading it, having it explained, or both."

Oral Evidence

parol evidence
rule

The *parol evidence rule* is a legal principle that specifies that oral contemporaneous evidence may not be used to contradict or vary the terms of a valid written contract. Thus, with the parol evidence rule, for example, a policyowner may not usually contradict the written contract by saying that the agent promised that the policy covered a specific type of loss.[31]

Although the written contract is not ordinarily subject to modification by oral evidence, the language of the policy is nevertheless not binding in clear cases of mutual mistake of fact. In some cases, the injured party has a right in equity to ask that the contract be reformed to the true agreement. An example might be a contract that misspells the name of the insured.

---

30. This is the general rule-see *Grace v. Adams,* 100 Mass. 505. However, some cases seem to say that the policyowner does not have to read his or her policy. Special situations sometimes occur, such as those in which the policyowner has reasonably relied upon advice of a professional agent, but it is unwise for policyowners to assume that courts will be lenient in excusing policyowners from a contract's written terms.

31. *Northern Assurance Co. v. Grand View Building Assn.,* 182 U.S. 380 (1902).

Contract of Indemnity

contract of indemnity

A *contract of indemnity* is one in which the insurer agrees, if a covered loss occurs, to pay an amount directly related to the amount of the loss. Most property, liability, and health insurance contracts are contracts of indemnity. A policyowner is entitled to payment only to the extent of financial loss or legal liability. The policyowner might not be made completely whole because of policy limits and other policy provisions and limitations, such as deductibles. Indemnity refers to financial compensation. According to the *principle of indemnity*, the purpose of insurance is to indemnify (financially compensate) people entitled to insurance benefits in an attempt to make them financially whole; however, people should not profit from an insured loss.

EXAMPLE
Assume an insured has an individual major medical policy with a $1 million lifetime limit. Also assume that the policy limits hospital room and board benefits to the cost of semiprivate accommodations. Furthermore, assume that the insured is hospitalized and incurs $25,000 in hospital bills, $1,200 of which is for the extra cost of a private room occupied at the insured's request. The policy will reimburse the insured for $23,800 of the hospital expenses, minus policy deductibles and percentage participation. Therefore, the insured has been reimbursed to the extent of his or her financial loss, subject to policy limits and provisions.

---

valued contract

A *valued contract* specifies the amount the insurer will pay in the event of a specified loss—usually a total loss. This amount does not depend on the actual value of the loss. Although most insurance contracts are contracts of indemnity, some are valued contracts. Life insurance is the most common example. The insurer must pay the stated death benefit if the insured dies. The insurer cannot, for example, deny full payment under a $1 million life insurance policy by arguing that the insured's life was worth only $650,000.

Insurable Interest

insurable interest

Most insurance contracts contain an element of *insurable interest*. An insurable interest is a right or relationship with regard to the subject matter of the insurance contract such that the policyowner would suffer financial loss from its damage, loss, or destruction.

The purposes of requiring an insurable interest in insurance contracts are to prevent gambling and to decrease moral hazard. Without an insurable interest, an insurance contract might be a wager or gambling contract. The contract also could provide an undesirable incentive to cause losses or injuries purposely. When an insurable interest exists, no profit results from an insurance claim settlement, because policyowners merely receive repayment for the loss they have suffered.

A property owner has an insurable interest in that property, because the owner could suffer a financial loss if the property is destroyed by fire, windstorm, or some other peril. Mortgagees, bailees, and creditors may have insurable interests, and often several persons have an insurable interest in the same property. A homeowner may insure his or her interest in property, for example, while at the same time the policy insures the mortgagee's interest up to the value of the mortgage loan.

The continuance of life and good health serves as the basis for many other examples of insurable interest. Death, injury, or sickness may result in financial losses to the persons insured or to their families, creditors, business partners, or employers. The right of persons to insure their own lives, as well as the right of close family members to insure blood relatives, is based on a presumed insurable interest. Other insurable interests for life or health insurance are based on potential losses, either increased expenses or reduced income potential, resulting from the relationship to the insured. For example, a creditor may insure the life of a debtor, normally up to the amount of the loan, or a business person may insure a partner's life for the potential loss that his or her death would cause for the partnership.

When must an insurable interest exist? The situation is different with life insurance than with property insurance. Life insurance requires an insurable interest only when the insurance contract is purchased. The insurer is obligated to pay a life insurance claim even if the current policyowner does not have an insurable interest in the insured's life at the time of the insured's death. This long-standing life insurance principle has raised recent questions and ethical concerns in light of the growing market for life insurance settlement agreements, in which a life insurance policy is sold for a portion of its face value to a third party who has no insurable interest in the life of the insured but acquires the policy as an investment that is expected to return a profit when the insured dies.

With property insurance, an insurable interest must exist at the time of the loss. It is not enough for an insurance policy to be in force that lists the property that was damaged. The policy must also provide coverage for a party who has an insurable interest in that property. Without an insurable interest, that party would have no loss. In practice, people do not usually buy property insurance unless they have an insurable interest, and insurers do not usually sell property insurance to people with no insurable interest in the property.

Insurable interest never becomes an issue in liability insurance. Unless a claim is made, there is no need to raise the issue. If a claim is made, the claim itself proves that the insured could have a liability claim that would result in financial loss.

Subrogation Rights

subrogation   The common-law doctrine of *subrogation* provides that an insurer who has paid a claim under a contract of indemnity takes over any rights of recovery that the insured might have against another party responsible for the loss. In common law, a person who causes a loss to another is responsible for that loss.

EXAMPLE
Jonathan's negligent burning of trash sets fire to his neighbor Laura's house. Therefore, Jonathan will be held responsible for paying for the damage to Laura's house. Laura will probably submit a claim to the insurance company that provided her homeowners policy. The insurer will pay Laura's claim, subject to any deductible, and then take over Laura's rights to recover from Jonathan. (Jonathan might be protected by liability insurance that ultimately pays the claim on Jonathan's behalf, but that is not the issue here.)

The right of the insurer against other negligent persons usually does not rest on any contractual relationship. As a general rule, an insurer has the right of subrogation even when there is no subrogation clause in the indemnity contract. For the most part, an insurance policy's subrogation clause merely makes the policyowner aware of this common-law doctrine. In some cases, however, the clause might also modify the insurer's subrogation rights.

The right of subrogation by the insurer is limited in amount to the loss payment made to the insured. The insurer may not make a profit by subrogating against the person who caused the loss and recovering a larger amount than the insurer has paid. In fact, subrogation rights are often of little value to the insurance company. There may be no doubt that someone else was responsible for the loss, but to recoup its loss payments (1) the insurer must prove the liability of the wrongdoer and (2) the negligent party must have the financial ability to pay for the loss he or she caused. In many cases, the expense or difficulty of legal proof may prevent the insurer from exercising its subrogation rights. If it might cost $1,000 to collect a $600 claim, the subrogation right may be worthless.

The importance of subrogation differs greatly for various types of insurance. In life insurance, which is a valued contract rather than a contract of indemnity, subrogation is not used at all. Subrogation is commonly used in property and liability insurance and, to a lesser extent, in health insurance.

A common illustration of subrogation is found in auto insurance. If the insurer first pays under collision coverage for damage to the insured's car caused by the negligent driver of another car, then the insurer takes over the rights of the policyowner by subrogation and files a claim against the other driver involved in the accident to receive reimbursement. If the insured does not receive full payment from the insurer because of a deductible in the policy, the insured retains the right to file a claim against the other driver for that deductible. Often the insurer files a joint suit for the loss on its own behalf and on behalf of the insured, but the insurer is not obligated to do so.

Three final points should be made about subrogation. First, insurers often agree in their contracts that they will not pursue a subrogation claim against anyone who is an insured under the policy.

EXAMPLE
Suppose Theresa lends her car to Jared, who causes an accident while driving it. Assuming Theresa has collision coverage on her auto policy, the insurer will pay Theresa, the car owner with the insurable interest in the car. The insurer will not subrogate against Jared, because he is also an insured.

Second, some insurance contracts permit an insured to waive rights of recovery before any loss occurs.

EXAMPLE

An insured signed a lease agreement that the landlord is not responsible for any damage to the tenant's property. If the landlord's negligence causes a fire that damages the tenant's property, the tenant then has no right to recover from the landlord. The tenant's fire insurance will pay for the tenant's loss. Because the tenant has no rights of recovery to transfer to the insurer, the tenant's insurer cannot take over those (nonexistent) rights and recover from the landlord.

Third, the policy or court interpretations of subrogation may specify the insured's right to retain any subrogation proceeds if the insured has not been fully indemnified for a loss because of deductibles, copayments, exclusions, or inadequate limits. In some cases, the insurer and the insured will share the proceeds on a pro rata basis. In other cases, the insured must be fully indemnified before the insurer is entitled to any recovery.

Effect of Concealment, Misrepresentations, and Fraud

concealment   Concealment and misrepresentation are easily confused. *Concealment* is failure to affirmatively disclose relevant information. Concealment occurs, for example, if an applicant for property insurance knows that the building is in imminent danger of collapsing but does not disclose this fact to the insurer. This building's condition is obviously a material fact that would affect the insurer's underwriting decision.

misrepresentation   *Misrepresentation*, on the other hand, occurs when an insurance applicant makes a false statement of a material fact. The applicant who owns the about-to-collapse building would be guilty of misrepresentation if he or she stated that the building was in sound structural condition. To clarify the distinction between concealment and representation, concealment is concealing material information and misrepresentation is knowingly providing false information. An applicant conceals by maintaining silence when there is an obligation to speak; he or she misrepresents by making an untrue statement.

voidable contract   Either concealment or misrepresentation may make an insurance contract a voidable contract. A *voidable contract* may be affirmed or rejected at the option of one of the parties, although it is binding on the other. If an insurance applicant has concealed or misrepresented material information, the insurer may have a right not to honor the contract. But the insurer may also choose to honor the contract. A policyowner rarely has the right to treat an insurance policy as voidable. Such a situation could arise if the insurer or its agent has grossly misrepresented the contract benefits, or the contract was offered by an unauthorized insurer.

Elements of Fraud
Courts consider six elements when evaluating allegations of fraud. The first five elements must be present to rescind a contract on the basis of fraud. The sixth element must also be necessary for a plaintiff to obtain damages. The six elements of fraud are as follows: • *False representation*—A party must misrepresent a past or existing fact. • *Knowingly made*—A party must know a fact to be false or must have made the representation in reckless indifference toward the truth or falsity of the statement made. • *Intent to influence or deceive*—One party must have intended to influence or deceive another party. • *Material fact*—The misrepresented fact must have influenced or induced the other party to enter the contract or affected the terms under which the other party would have been willing to contract. • *Reasonable reliance*—The innocent party must show justification in relying on the statement. • *Detriment*—In a suit for damages, the plaintiff must show injury or loss.
Source: Wiening, Eric A., *Foundations of Risk Management and Insurance,* Malvern, PA: American Institute for CPCU, 2002, p. 9.10.

void contract

A *void contract* has no legal effect, and neither party may enforce it. A void contract is void from the beginning; it never existed. For example, an illegal gambling contract cannot be enforced through the courts; strong-arm enforcement systems are sometimes used, but that is not the point here. Concealment and misrepresentation make insurance contracts voidable, not void.

fraud

Concealment and misrepresentation often involve *fraud*, as the above text box explains. If an applicant commits fraud in procuring an insurance policy, the policy may be voidable by the insurer. A policyowner's fraud in connection with a loss or at any other time may also make an insurance contract voidable by the insurer.

Warranties and Representations

warranty

When an application for insurance is made a part of the policy, the answers to specific questions on the application may be considered *warranties*. If false, they make the policy voidable by the insurer regardless of their materiality. Some warranties may also be specifically added in the policy, such as the promise of the policyowner in a burglary policy that an alarm system will be maintained or a security guard will be required.

representation

The difference between a warranty and a representation is that a warranty is a part of the contract itself and must therefore be strictly complied with, whereas a *representation* is usually an incidental statement preceding the contract, although it may be an inducement to it. The difference, in effect, is that to make the contract voidable, a warranty need only be false, whereas a representation must be both false and material.

To constitute a warranty, a statement must not only be intended, but must also be definitely indicated as a warranty, either by its incorporation into the policy or by specific reference. Where there is any doubt as to whether a warranty was intended, the statement is to be regarded as a representation and must be shown to be material in order to defeat the policy.

Many states have modified by legislative act the strict application of the doctrine of warranties for most kinds of insurance except ocean marine insurance. When the doctrine has been thus modified, the insurance is sometimes voidable only if a loss occurs during a breach of warranty or is caused thereby, or if the breach materially increases the risk. In effect, this causes most statements in insurance contracts today to be considered representations. In some lines of insurance, the application itself specifies that statements contained in it are representations, not warranties. This is the case in life insurance. Warranties incorporated into insurance policies should be complied with to the letter, for some courts still tend to enforce the original strict rule of declaring the policy voidable when a warranty is breached, regardless of how trivial or immaterial the loss.

ANALYZING AN INSURANCE CONTRACT

The typical insurance contract appears to be a long, complex, formidable legal document. However, an insurance policy is much less formidable to a financial planner who has learned a system or framework for analyzing insurance contracts. The following discussion includes some examples that involve insurance policy extracts taken out of context.

The provisions of the typical insurance contract can be grouped into the following categories, depending on the purposes they serve: declarations, definitions, insuring agreements, exclusions, conditions, and miscellaneous provisions. The contract also may be modified by adding endorsements or riders.

Declarations

declarations

Every insurance contract has a set of declarations, although they are not always labeled. *Declarations* are factual statements that identify the specific person, property, or activity being insured and the parties to the insurance transaction; they also provide descriptive information about the insurance being provided. They are usually grouped together in the initial section of the policy and are computer-printed for the individual contract, rather than preprinted for all contracts of the same type.

The declarations section of a life insurance policy typically shows the names of the insurer and the agent, the name and age of the insured, the name of the policyowner if different from the insured, the type of policy, the amount of insurance, the policy number, the effective date, the premium, and a listing of attachments to the policy showing such items as supplementary benefits and the beneficiary designation. In property and liability insurance contracts, the declarations section of the policy shows similar types of information as well as the address of the property or activity covered, a listing of endorsements attached to the policy, the names of additional persons or organizations whose interests are insured (such as a mortgagee), the period of coverage, and any applicable deductibles.

Definitions

definitions

Because an insurance policy is a contract of adhesion, the insurer must define carefully what it covers or does not cover. Ambiguities in the contract are likely to be construed against the insurer. The *definitions* in the policy explain the key policy terms and are a major help in precisely defining the insured's intentions.

Often words or phrases that are included among the definitions appear in boldface type or quotation marks elsewhere in the policy. The definitions are usually grouped together in an early section of the policy or appear near the end of the policy, serving as a kind of glossary. Examples of a few terms that may appear in the definitions section of insurance contracts are as follows:

- in *life insurance*—"you," "we," "designated office (of the insurer)," "beneficiary," and "new policy"
- in *disability income insurance*—"monthly earnings," "qualifying period," and "total disability"
- in *auto insurance*—"bodily injury," "family member," "occupying (an auto)," "your covered auto," and "trailer"
- in *homeowners insurance*—"business," "insured," "insured location," "occurrence," and "residence employee"

One of the more important definitions in many policies stipulates who is an insured. In homeowners policies, an "insured" includes the person named in the declarations, his or her spouse and relatives if residents of the household, and persons under age 21 residing in the household and in the care of the named insured, spouse, or resident relatives. Full-time students are also included as insureds, provided they were residents of the household before moving out to attend school, are relatives under the age of 24, or are under the age of 21 and in the care of the named insured or another relative.

In the liability section of the personal auto policy, the definition of "insured" includes the named insured and his or her spouse if a resident of the household and for up to 90 days after ceasing to be a member of the household. The definition also includes family members (as defined in the policy) who are residents of the household, anyone using a covered auto, and any person or organization that might be held vicariously liable for use of the auto. Thus, Tom's personal auto policy protects even Tom's employer, as an insured, against liability claims involving Tom's car. If Tom strikes a pedestrian while using his car on business, and the pedestrian sues Tom's employer, Tom's employer is covered as an insured.

Words and phrases not specifically defined in the contract are interpreted according to the following general principles:

- Everyday language is given its ordinary or normal meaning.
- Technical terms are assigned their technical definitions.
- Terms that have an established legal meaning are given that meaning.

- Where appropriate, meanings of words take into account local, cultural, and trade usage considerations.

Insuring Agreements

insuring agreement

The *insuring agreement* is the core of any insurance policy. This insuring agreement (or agreements, as many contracts contain several insuring agreements) spells out the basic promise of the insurance company. Examples of these promises are to pay the face amount of the policy in the event of the insured's death, to defend the insured in any suit alleging liability associated with an auto accident, to pay the actual cash value of personal property damaged by a covered peril, and to pay up to $250 per day for loss of earnings because of the insured's attendance at a court hearing at the insurer's request.

The main insuring agreements in insurance policies are usually either the *open-perils* type or the *named-perils* type. An open-perils agreement, also known as an all-risks agreement, covers all losses except those that the policy specifically excludes. All policies have at least a few exclusions, and some have many. For example, a whole life insurance policy is an open-perils policy because it covers death from any cause except a few specified ones, such as death by suicide during the policy's first 1 or 2 years and, in some policies, death by war or specifically excluded activities, such as skydiving or crop dusting.

The named-perils or specified-perils policy approach to the insuring agreement is used in the personal property coverage of most homeowners policies. This agreement covers only losses that arise from one of the listed perils. If the peril is not listed, the loss is not covered. For example, one homeowners policy form states that it covers direct physical loss caused by fire; lightning; windstorm; hail; explosion; riot; civil commotion; aircraft; vehicles; smoke; vandalism; malicious mischief; theft; falling objects; weight of ice, snow, or sleet; accidental discharge or overflow of water or steam from certain household systems; and a few other perils. Flood is not contained in the list, so loss to personal property due to flood is not covered.

Exclusions

exclusions

Every insurance policy has *exclusions* identifying types of claims that the insurer does not cover. The exclusions usually apply either to certain perils, types of losses, types of property, or types of activities. For example, in major medical expense insurance, loss due to the peril of occupational injury or illness is usually excluded because the loss is covered under workers' compensation insurance. In long-term care insurance, costs of care for which the insured is reimbursed under a government program are excluded. In homeowners insurance, the property of unrelated boarders is excluded. And in auto insurance, losses arising from use of the vehicle in a prearranged or organized racing contest in a facility designed for racing are excluded.

The following are the principal reasons for the presence of exclusions in insurance policies:

- Some perils are uninsurable by private insurers. Examples of such perils are wear-and-tear losses to auto and losses due to war.
- Some conditions pose a major increase in risk not contemplated in the basic premium for the coverage. Examples of these conditions are, in auto insurance, the use of an auto to carry persons for a fee other than in a simple carpooling arrangement and, in medical expense insurance, the cost of long-term custodial care.
- Some losses are best covered by other types of policies. For example, collision damage to an auto is not covered by a homeowners policy, and losses due to occupational injury may be excluded by a disability income insurance policy.
- Coverage of some losses would pose too great a potential moral hazard. For example, loss of more than a specified dollar amount of cash is excluded by homeowners policies.
- Some coverages are not needed by most policyowners, so they should not have to pay for them. For example, most individual medical expense insurance policies exclude or limit maternity coverage.

A practical reason for exclusions is to hold down the cost of coverage for policyowners.

Conditions

The insuring agreement is not an absolute promise by the company with "no strings attached." Instead, the promise is a qualified one, enforceable only if the policyowner fulfills the conditions spelled out in the policy. Those conditions may be grouped together in a section of the policy labeled "Conditions," or they may be scattered throughout the policy and its endorsements or riders.

The policyowner must fulfill most of the conditions in an insurance policy before the insurer may be held liable for a loss. An example of one of these conditions, called a condition precedent, is timely payment of premiums.

Many conditions relate to claims. Most policies, with the exception of life insurance, contain provisions pertaining to the time period within which the insurer must be notified of a loss and the time period within which the insured must file a formal proof of loss. The information that must be included with the formal proof of loss may also be specified.

The insured must fulfill other conditions, called conditions subsequent, after the insurer has become liable in order to avoid releasing the insurer from liability. All policies specify that the insured must cooperate with the insurer. As an example of a condition subsequent, disability income insurance policies include the condition that the insurer can require the insured to submit to examinations by an insurer-selected physician at reasonable intervals during the continuation of a claim. Property and liability insurance policies include the condition that the insured must do nothing to jeopardize the insurer's right to recover from responsible third parties and the condition that the insured must cooperate with the insurer in legal proceedings against the insurer by a third-party claimant.

Miscellaneous Provisions

Some provisions in insurance contracts do not fall into any of the preceding categories. These provisions may deal with policy continuation, valuation of losses, or other administrative aspects of the policy.

Policy Continuation Provisions

Some of the more important miscellaneous provisions in an insurance policy relate to the policyowner's right to continue the coverage in force. Although policies can be issued for a specific term and terminate at the end of that term, many policies allow the policyowner to renew the policy and/or allow the insurer to refuse renewal. These policy renewal provisions fall into four categories: noncancelable, guaranteed renewable, nonrenewable for stated reasons only, and optionally renewable. In addition, some policies are cancelable.

noncancelable   ***Noncancelable.*** Some types of insurance policies are *noncancelable*, giving the policyowner the right to renew the coverage at each policy anniversary date, although possibly only until some stated age, such as age 65. A noncancelable policy may not be terminated by the insurer during the period of coverage, and future rates for the coverage are guaranteed in the contract itself. Examples of noncancelable policies are whole life insurance policies and some disability income insurance contracts.

guaranteed
renewable

Guaranteed Renewable. A guaranteed renewable policy provides a bit less certainty for the policyowner regarding the right to continue coverage. Guaranteed renewable policies are most often found in the health insurance area. Like a noncancelable policy, a *guaranteed renewable* policy gives the policyowner the right to renew the coverage at each policy anniversary date, but usually only until a stated age, such as age 65. The coverage may not be canceled by the insurer during the period of coverage. However, in a guaranteed renewable policy, the insurer does not guarantee future rates for the coverage. Instead, the insurer retains the right to raise the rates for broad classes of insureds, but not just for individual insureds with poor claims experience.

EXAMPLE

Several years ago, Eric Burton bought long-term care insurance for himself and his wife, Claire. They didn't want all their life savings to be depleted by the cost of nursing home or custodial care if they later needed it. They also wanted to leave their assets to their children and not burden them with providing health care for their parents.

The Burtons were extremely satisfied with their guaranteed renewable policies until a couple months ago when their premiums soared from $3,250 per year to almost $5,000. They were shocked, especially because they had believed that the premiums would never increase.

Although the guaranteed renewable provision in their contracts stated that their premiums would never rise based on Eric's and Claire's age or claims history, the insurer had reserved the right to increase premiums based on broad classes of insureds. Experience with long-term care insurance revealed that the insurer had initially underestimated its cost of providing the coverage, so a rate increase became necessary. Unlike in a noncancelable contract, future premium rates are not guaranteed.

Nonrenewable for Stated Reasons Only. Some policies that are otherwise guaranteed renewable allow the insurer to refuse to renew the policy for reasons specifically listed in the policy. These policies are referred to as nonrenewable for stated reasons only. These might include the attainment of a certain age. However, if this is the only condition, the policy still often qualifies as guaranteed renewable. Other possible conditions for nonrenewal include termination of the policyowner's employment in some disability income insurance policies and the nonrenewal of all policies bearing the same form number as the policyowner's.

optionally renewable

Optionally Renewable. Provisions in most property and liability insurance policies give the insurer the unilateral right to refuse to renew a policy at the end of any period for which premiums have been paid. These policies are referred to as optionally renewable. Even if the insurer agrees to renew the policy, it has the right to alter the policy's provisions. Some states have enacted legislation that allows an insurer to nonrenew only on annual anniversary dates. Regulations may also require the insurer to give specified periods of advance notice to policyowners whose coverage will not be renewed.

Cancelable. A few property and liability policies are cancelable during the period for which premiums have been paid. However, midterm cancellation by the insurer is not allowed for auto and homeowners policies in many states. When a policy can be canceled, the policy and/or state law determines the period of advance notice that must be given to the policyowner. If the policy is cancelled by the insurer, a pro rata share of the premium must be returned.

Table 6-1 Renewal Provisions in Insurance Policies	
Cancelable	The insurer may terminate the policy at any time for any reason by notifying the policyowner (advance notice is usually required) and refunding any unearned premium. Some states prohibit midterm cancellation for some policy types.
Optionally renewable	The insurer has a right to refuse to renew the policy on its anniversary or premium-due date. Advance notice must be given to the policyowner.
Nonrenewable for stated reasons only	The insurer may refuse to renew the policy, but only for one of the specific reasons stated in the policy.
Noncancelable	As long as premiums are paid, the insurer must renew the policy at a guaranteed premium rate specified in the policy, at least until the insured reaches a specified age.

Loss-Sharing Provisions

Another type of miscellaneous provision in several types of insurance policies requires insureds to share in the amount of the loss. For example, dollar *deductibles* are common in homeowners insurance, auto physical damage insurance, and medical expense insurance. Most common is an initial deductible, under which the insurer will pay claims to the extent that they exceed a specified amount. The amount, such as $500, may apply to each claim, as is common in property insurance policies, or to a period of time, such as a calendar year, as in medical expense policies. A similar provision is a time deductible in the form of a *waiting or elimination period*, during which no benefits are payable. Time deductibles are common in equipment breakdown insurance, disability income insurance, and long-term care insurance.

Other loss-sharing provisions are the *coinsurance clause* and copayment requirement in major medical and other types of medical expense coverage. Under these types of provisions, the insured is required to assume a portion of certain covered expenses. For example, the insurer may pay 80 percent of certain medical expenses under a coinsurance clause, while the insured assumes 20 percent. Or the insured may pay a $10 or $20 copayment for each doctor's visit.

Several types of insurance contain a miscellaneous provision that explains how the insurer will respond if other insurance covers the same loss. This might be referred to as an *other insurance clause*. For example, the property insurance portion of homeowners policies provides that the insurer will pay only that proportion of the loss that the limit of liability applicable in the homeowners policy bears to the total amount of insurance in all policies covering the loss. The liability section specifies that the homeowners coverage is excess over other valid and collectible insurance, except insurance written specifically to provide excess coverage over that of the homeowners policy. An umbrella policy is the most common example of a liability insurance policy specifically written to provide excess liability coverage. Group health insurance often contains a *coordination-of-benefits provision* to prevent duplication of benefits when an insured is covered by more than one group health insurance plan. For example, if a wife has coverage as an employee under her own plan and is a dependent under her husband's plan, her coverage as an employee is primary and her coverage as a dependent is excess.

Endorsements or Riders

endorsement

rider

An *endorsement*, or in life insurance a *rider*, is a provision added to the policy, sometimes for an extra premium charge or a premium reduction, by which the scope of its coverage is clarified, enlarged, or restricted. An endorsement may alter the declarations, such as identifying a mortgage holder in a homeowners policy. Endorsements also may add new definitions to the policy, or modify exclusions in the policy, such as removing earthquake from the list of excluded perils in a homeowners policy. Endorsements may even modify a policy condition, such as amending a 30-day notice of nonrenewal to conform with the statute of a particular state that requires a 60-day notice, or a miscellaneous provision, such as limiting the insurer's right to cancel the policy to only specified reasons. Similarly, a rider may modify the insuring agreement—for example, adding to a life insurance policy a waiver-of-premium benefit that eliminates the need for a disabled policyowner to pay premiums.

As a general legal principle, whenever the wording in an endorsement or rider conflicts with the terms of the policy to which it is attached, the endorsement or rider takes precedence. This principle is based on the assumption that an alteration of the basic agreement between the policyowner and insurer more accurately reflects the true intent of the parties than does the basic agreement itself.

Contents of an Insurance Contract

- Declarations—statements of fact that identify the parties to the insurance transaction, the amount of insurance, the property or activity being covered, the effective date of the coverage, etc.
- Definitions—precise meanings of terms used in the contract, like "family member," "disability," "covered auto," etc.
- Insuring agreements—the promises made by the insurer, such as to pay, to defend, to reimburse, etc.
- Exclusions—the perils, properties, types of losses, circumstances, etc. that the insurance does not cover
- Conditions—the duties that (usually) the insured must fulfill before the other party is held to the terms of the contract
- Miscellaneous provisions—other clauses that do not fall into the above categories, such as those concerning policy continuation, loss valuation, optional modes of settlement, etc.
- Endorsements or riders—provisions added to the policy to modify or clarify the coverage, sometimes for an extra premium or a reduced premium

---

CHAPTER REVIEW

Key Terms and Concepts

unilateral contract	fraud
conditional contract	warranty
contract of adhesion	representation
parol evidence rule	declarations
contract of indemnity	definitions
valued contract	insuring agreement
insurable interest	exclusions
subrogation	noncancelable
concealment	guaranteed renewable
misrepresentation	optionally renewable
voidable contract	endorsement
void contract	rider

Review Questions

Review questions are based on the learning objectives in this chapter. Thus, a [3] at the end of a question means that the question is based on learning objective 3. If there are multiple objectives, they are all listed.

1. Your client, Maria, complains that buying insurance is just like buying a new car in that you shop around, trying to get the best deal, but you don't get to enjoy the new car until you actually close the deal and drive it home. What unique aspects of an insurance contract differentiate it from other goods and services? [1]

2. Define the following legal requirements of an enforceable contract:
    a. offer and acceptance [2]
    b. legal purpose [2]
    c. competent parties [2]
    d. consideration [2]

3. Define the following legal characteristics of an insurance contract:
    a. unilateral nature [3]
    b. personal nature [3]
    c. conditional nature [3]

4. Your client, Sue Litigator, would like to know her legal rights concerning the following situations:
    a. Sue claims that one of the provisions in the insurance contract is unclear. [3]
    b. Sue wants to ignore a portion of the contract she did not read. [3]
    c. Sue claims that the insurance agent told her something that contradicts the language of the contract. [3]

5. Teddy, your client's son, says he has heard that if he has an accident with his old car, the insurance company will buy him a new car. How does Teddy's insurance work as a contract of indemnity? [3]

6. After her accident-prone cousin's second car accident within 2 months, your client, Julie, asks you if she could buy insurance on the cousin's new car. Julie thinks this might be a good investment, because the cousin is such a bad driver that she will probably have another accident, and the insurance company will then have to pay Julie if Julie has insured the car. You tell Julie that she cannot insure somebody else's car. What are three reasons for requiring an insurable interest in insurance contracts? [3]

7. Does your client have an insurable interest in the following situations?
    a. Your client lent a large amount of money to a friend who is starting a business. [3]
    b. Your client owns and drives a fancy red sports car. [3]
    c. Your client owned a precious stone that was destroyed soon after he gave it to his girlfriend. [3]

8. Cheryl Eng, a client of yours, was responsible for an auto accident that damaged the other driver's car. Cheryl was pleased to hear that the other driver had insurance that paid for the damage to his car. Cheryl has just learned that the other driver's auto insurance company has asked Cheryl's insurer for reimbursement. "Can they do that?" she asks you. How does the doctrine of subrogation applies to insurance contracts? [3]

9. What is the difference between concealment and misrepresentation by an applicant for insurance? [3]

10. What is the purpose of each of these components of a typical insurance contract?
    a. declarations [4]
    b. definitions [4]
    c. insuring agreements [4]
    d. exclusions [4]
    e. conditions [4]

11. What is the major distinction between a noncancelable policy and a guaranteed renewable policy? [4]

12. The wording in an endorsement to your client's insurance policy conflicts with the terms of the policy itself. What is the significance of this conflict for your client? [4]

Learning Objectives

An understanding of the material in this chapter should enable the student to

1. Describe the extent of coverage under the Social Security and Medicare programs, and explain how the programs are financed.

2. Explain the requirements for eligibility under Social Security, and identify the types and amounts of benefits available.

3. Explain the requirements for eligibility under Medicare, and describe the benefits available under Parts A and B.

4. Describe the Medicare Advantage program.

5. Describe the prescription drug coverage available under Medicare.

6. Explain how to deal with Social Security and Medicare.

7. Discuss the adequacy of Social Security and Medicare financing, and identify the ways in which long-term financial stability might be maintained.

8. Describe the federal income tax treatment of Social Security and Medicare contributions and benefits.

9. Describe the nature of unemployment insurance, temporary disability income insurance, and workers' compensation insurance.

Financial planners and insurance agents should understand social insurance because it lays a foundation of basic coverages on which private employer-provided and individual insurance plans are built. Nearly one-quarter of employee benefit dollars spent by employers are for mandated social insurance programs. And the most significant insurance expense for most individuals is their contribution to Social Security and Medicare. For many Americans, this contribution exceeds the cost of all other types of insurance paid for by the individual.

Social insurance programs in the United States fall into several categories:

- Social Security
- Medicare
- unemployment insurance
- temporary disability insurance
- workers' compensation insurance

Two other programs are established by the Railroad Retirement Act and the Railroad Unemployment Insurance Act. These acts provide benefits to railroad workers that are similar to the benefits provided to other persons by Social Security and state unemployment insurance programs. Social Security and Medicare, which are totally federal programs, are the focus of this discussion. The other three social insurance programs that vary from state to state are touched upon in a more general manner.

SOCIAL SECURITY AND MEDICARE

In a broad sense, the term *social security* can be used to refer to any of several programs resulting from the Social Security Act of 1935 and its frequent amendments over the years. The act established four programs aimed at providing economic security for the American society: (1) old-age insurance, (2) unemployment insurance, (3) federal grants for assistance to certain needy groups (the aged, the blind, and children), and (4) federal grants for maternal and child welfare, public health work, and vocational rehabilitation.

OASDHI   Benefits have been added to the Social Security insurance program over the years. These additional benefits include survivors insurance (1939), disability insurance (1956), hospital insurance (1965), and supplementary medical insurance (1965). Taken together, these programs constitute the old-age, survivors, disability, and health insurance *(OASDHI)* program of the federal government. This program is often separated into two broad parts. The first part is the old-age, survivors, and disability insurance (OASDI) program. Over the years OASDI has become commonly referred to as Social Security. The remainder of the OASDHI program is called Medicare.

The following discussion of Social Security and Medicare begins with a description of the extent of coverage under the programs and the way the programs are financed. It then focuses on the eligibility requirements and benefits under the various parts of the programs. Because of the many differences between Social Security and Medicare, the discussion largely treats each program separately. This is followed by a discussion of the adequacy of the funding of these programs. Finally, there is a description of the tax implications of Social Security and Medicare benefits and contributions.

More detailed information about Social Security and Medicare can be found on the web at socialsecurity.gov and medicare.gov. Dollar amounts indicated as of 2011 are subject to annual indexing, and are posted on these respective web sites in October or November for the next year.

Extent of Coverage

Over 95 percent of the workers in the United States are in covered employment under the Social Security program and over 98 percent under the Medicare program. These workers have wages (if they are employees) or self-employment income (if they are self-employed) on which Social Security and Medicare taxes must be paid. The following are the major categories of workers who are not covered under the programs or who are covered only if they have met specific conditions:

- civilian employees of the federal government who were employed by the government prior to 1984 and who are covered under the Civil Service Retirement System or certain other federal retirement programs. This exclusion applies only to Social Security benefits. *All* federal employees have been covered for purposes of Medicare since 1983.

- railroad workers. Under the Railroad Retirement Act, employees of railroads have their own benefit system that is similar to Social Security. However, they are covered under Medicare.

- some state and local government employees. Historically, employees covered under state and local government retirement plans have been covered under Social Security only if a state entered into a voluntary agreement with the Social Security Administration. Under such an agreement, the state may either require that employees of local governments be covered or allow the local governments to decide whether to include their employees. In addition, the state may elect to include all or only certain groups of employees. It is estimated that more than 80 percent of state and local government employees have Social Security and Medicare coverage as a result of such agreements. In addition, coverage under Medicare is compulsory for state and local employees hired after March 1986, and coverage under Social

Security is compulsory for employees hired after July 1, 1991, if they do not participate in a public retirement system.

- American citizens working abroad for foreign affiliates of U.S. employers, unless the employer owns at least a 10 percent interest in the foreign affiliate and has made arrangements with the Secretary of the Treasury for the payment of Social Security and Medicare taxes. However, Americans working abroad are covered under Social Security and Medicare if they work directly for U.S. employers rather than for their foreign subsidiaries.

- ministers who elect out of coverage because of conscience or religious principles

- workers in certain jobs such as student nurses, newspaper carriers under age 18, and students working for the school at which they are regularly enrolled or doing domestic work for a local college club, fraternity, or sorority

- certain family employment. This includes a parent's employment of a child under age 18. This exclusion, however, does not apply if the employment is for a corporation owned by a family member.

- certain workers who must satisfy special earnings requirements. For example, self-employed persons are not covered unless they have net annual earnings of $400 or more.

Tax Rates and Wage Bases

Part B of Medicare is financed by a combination of monthly premiums paid by persons eligible for benefits and contributions from the federal government. Part A of Medicare and all the benefits of the Social Security program are financed through a system of payroll and self-employment taxes paid by all persons covered under the programs. In addition, employers of covered persons are also taxed. These taxes are often referred to as FICA taxes because they are imposed under the Federal Insurance Contributions Act.

In 2011, an employee and his or her employer pay a tax of 7.65 percent each on the first $106,800 of the employee's wages. Of this tax rate, 6.2 percent is for Social Security, and 1.45 percent is for the hospital insurance portion of Medicare. The Medicare tax rate of 1.45 percent is also levied on all wages in excess of $106,800. The tax rates are currently scheduled to remain the same after 2011, but the $106,800 Social Security wage base is adjusted annually for changes in the national level of wages. Therefore, if wage levels increase by 4 percent in a particular year, the wage base for the following year will also increase by 4 percent. The tax rate for the self-employed is 15.3 percent on the first $106,800 of self-employment income and 2.9 percent on the balance of any self-employment income. This is equal to the combined employee and employer rates.

Over the years, both the tax rates and wage bases have risen dramatically to finance increased benefit levels under Social Security and Medicare as well as new benefits that have been added to the program. In 1950, a tax rate of 1.5 percent was levied on the first $3,000 of wages. These figures increased to 4.8 percent and $7,800 in 1970, and 7.65 percent and $51,300 in 1990. Starting in 1991, a two-tier program was introduced with a tax of 7.65 percent (6.2 percent for Social Security and 1.45 percent for Medicare) on the first $53,400 of wages and the Medicare tax of 1.45 percent on the next $71,500. By 1994, all wages were subject to the Medicare tax.

Paying for Social Security and Medicare

- Social Security—Employees pay 6.2 percent of the first $106,800 (2011) of earnings. Employers pay the same. Self-employed persons pay 12.4 percent of first $106,800 (2011) of self-employment income.

- Medicare Part A—Employees pay 1.45 percent of all earnings. Employers pay the same. Self-employed persons pay 2.9 percent of all self-employment income.

- Medicare Part B—Covered persons pay at least a $96.40 (2011) monthly premium. General revenues of the federal government cover the remainder (about 75 percent) of the program's cost.

The adequacy of the current funding structure to pay for Social Security and Medicare benefits continues to be a source of public concern and political debate. This issue is addressed in more detail after the programs are described.

SOCIAL SECURITY: ELIGIBILITY

credit   To be eligible for benefits under Social Security, an individual must have credit for a minimum amount of work under the program. For 2011, a worker receives one *credit* (also referred to as a quarter of coverage) for each $1,120 in annual earnings on which Social Security taxes were paid. However, no more than four credits may be earned in any one calendar year. Consequently, a worker who pays Social Security taxes on as little as $4,480 ($1,120 × 4) at any time during the year will receive the maximum four credits. As in the case of the wage base, the amount of earnings necessary for a credit under Social Security is adjusted annually for changes in the national level of wages.

Credits are the basis for establishing an insured status under Social Security. The three types of insured status are fully insured, currently insured, and disability insured.

Fully Insured

fully insured   A person is *fully insured* under Social Security if either of two tests is met. The first test requires 40 credits of coverage. Once a person acquires this credit, he or she is fully insured for life even if covered employment under Social Security ceases.

Under the second test, a person who has a minimum of six credits is fully insured if he or she has at least as many credits as there are years elapsing after 1950 (or after the year in which he or she reaches age 21, if later) and before the year in which he or she dies, becomes disabled, or reaches age 62, whichever occurs first. Therefore, a worker who reached age 21 in 1997 and died in 2009 would need 11 credits for his or her family to be eligible for survivors benefits.

[handwritten notes in margin: 1st Are they fully Insured? If fully then for sure disability!]

Currently Insured

currently insured   If a worker is not fully insured, certain survivors benefits are still available if a *currently insured* status exists. To be currently insured, it is only necessary that a worker have earned at least six credits during the 13 calendar quarters ending with the quarter in which his or her death occurs.

Disability Insured

disability insured   To receive disability benefits under Social Security, it is necessary to be *disability insured*. At a minimum, a disability-insured status requires that a worker (1) be fully insured and (2) have a minimum amount of work under Social Security within a recent time period. In connection with the latter requirement, workers aged 31 or older must have earned at least 20 credits during the 40 calendar quarters ending with the quarter in which disability occurs; workers aged 24 through 30 must have earned credits equal to at least one-half the number of calendar quarters from the time they turned 21 and the quarter in which disability begins; and workers under age 24 must have earned six credits during the 12 calendar quarters ending with the quarter in which disability begins.

A special rule for blind persons states that they are exempt from the recent-work rules and are considered disability insured as long as they are fully insured.

SOCIAL SECURITY: TYPES OF BENEFITS

The Social Security program provides three principal types of benefits: retirement (old-age) benefits, survivors benefits, and disability benefits.

Retirement Benefits

A worker who is fully insured under Social Security is eligible to receive monthly retirement benefits as early as age 62. However, the election to receive benefits prior to the full Social Security retirement age results in a permanently reduced benefit.

full retirement age   *Full retirement age* (sometimes referred to as *normal retirement age*), or the age at which nonreduced retirement benefits are paid, is 65 for workers born in 1937 or before. As shown in the table below, a gradually increasing full retirement age applies to workers born in 1938 and later.

In addition to the retired worker, the following dependents of persons receiving retirement benefits are also eligible for monthly benefits:

- a spouse aged 62 or older. Benefits are permanently reduced, however, if this benefit is elected prior to the spouse's reaching full retirement age. This benefit is also available to a divorced spouse under certain circumstances if the marriage lasted at least 10 years.
- a spouse of any age if the spouse is caring for at least one child of the retired worker as long as the child is (1) under age 16 or (2) disabled and entitled to a child's benefit as described below. This benefit is commonly referred to as a *mother's* or *father's benefit.*
- dependent, unmarried children under age 18. This child's benefit will continue until age 19 as long as a child is a full-time student in elementary or secondary school. In addition, disabled children of any age are eligible for benefits as long as they were disabled before age 22.

It is important to note that retirement benefits, as well as all other benefits under Social Security and Medicare, are not automatically paid upon eligibility but must be applied for.

Table 7-1 Retirement Age for Nonreduced Benefits	
Year of Birth	**Full Retirement Age**
1937 and before	65 years
1938	65 years, 2 months
1939	65 years, 4 months
1940	65 years, 6 months
1941	65 years, 8 months
1942	65 years, 10 months
1943–54	66 years
1955	66 years, 2 months
1956	66 years, 4 months
1957	66 years, 6 months
1958	66 years, 8 months
1959	66 years, 10 months
1960 and later	67 years

In addition to the retired worker, the following dependents of persons receiving retirement benefits are also eligible for monthly benefits:

- a spouse aged 62 or older. Benefits are permanently reduced, however, if this benefit is elected prior to the spouse's reaching full retirement age. This benefit is also available to a divorced spouse under certain circumstances if the marriage lasted at least 10 years.
- a spouse of any age if the spouse is caring for at least one child of the retired worker as long as the child is (1) under age 16 or (2) disabled and entitled to a child's benefit as described below. This benefit is commonly referred to as a *mother's* or *father's benefit*.
- dependent, unmarried children under age 18. This child's benefit will continue until age 19 as long as a child is a full-time student in elementary or secondary school. In addition, disabled children of any age are eligible for benefits as long as they were disabled before age 22.

It is important to note that retirement benefits, as well as all other benefits under Social Security and Medicare, are not automatically paid upon eligibility but must be applied for.

Survivors Benefits

All categories of survivors benefits are payable if a worker is fully insured at the time of death. However, three types of benefits are also payable if a worker is only currently insured. The first is a lump-sum death benefit of $255, payable in the following order of priority:

- to a surviving spouse who was living with the deceased worker at the time of death
- to a surviving spouse (other than a divorced spouse) who was not living with the deceased worker at the time of death if the surviving spouse is eligible for or entitled to benefits based on the deceased wage earner's record for the month of death
- to children who are eligible for or entitled to benefits based on the deceased wage earner's record for the month of death

If none of these categories of survivors exists, the benefit is not paid.

Two categories of persons are eligible for income benefits as survivors if the deceased worker was either fully or currently insured at the time of death:

- dependent, unmarried children under the same conditions as previously described for retirement benefits
- a spouse (including a divorced spouse) caring for a child or children under the same conditions as described for retirement benefits

The following categories of persons are also eligible for benefits, but only if the deceased worker was fully insured:

- a widow or widower aged 60 or older. However, benefits are reduced if taken prior to the widow's or widower's full retirement age. This benefit is also payable to a divorced spouse if the marriage lasted at least 10 years. In addition, the widow's or widower's benefit is payable to a disabled spouse at age 50 as long as the disability commenced no more than 7 years after (1) the worker's death or (2) the end of the year in which entitlement to a mother's or father's benefit ceased
- a parent aged 62 or over who was a dependent of the deceased worker at the time of death

Social Security Blackout Period
No benefits are payable for the surviving spouse of a deceased covered worker from the time the youngest child reaches age 16 (or is no longer disabled in certain cases) until the surviving spouse is 60.

Disability Benefits

A disabled worker under full retirement age is eligible to receive disability income benefits under Social Security as long as he or she is disability insured and meets the disability definition under the law. The definition of disability is very rigid and requires a mental or physical impairment that prevents the worker from engaging in any substantial gainful employment. The disability must also have lasted (or be expected to last) at least 12 months or be expected to result in death. A more liberal definition of disability applies to blind workers who are aged 55 or older. They are considered disabled if they are unable to perform work that requires skills or abilities comparable to those required by the work they regularly performed before reaching age 55 or becoming blind, if later.

Disability benefits are subject to a waiting period and are payable beginning with the sixth full calendar month of disability. In addition to the benefit paid to a disabled worker, the other categories of benefits available are the same as those described under retirement benefits.

Certain family members not otherwise eligible for Social Security benefits may be eligible if they are disabled. Disabled children are subject to the same definition of disability as workers. However, disabled widows or widowers must be unable to engage in any gainful (rather than substantial gainful) employment.

Eligibility for Dual Benefits

In many cases, a person is eligible for more than one type of Social Security benefit. Probably the most common situation occurs when a person is eligible for both a spouse's benefit and a worker's retirement or disability benefit based on his or her own Social Security record. In this and any other case when a person is eligible for dual benefits, only an amount equal to the higher benefit is paid.

Termination of Disability Benefits

Monthly benefits to any Social Security recipient cease upon his or her death. When a retired or disabled worker dies, the family members' benefits that are based on the worker's retirement or disability benefits also cease, but the family members are then eligible for survivors benefits.

A worker technically has a termination of benefits at full retirement age, but these benefits are then replaced by comparable retirement benefits. Any benefits payable because of disability cease at an earlier date if medical or other evidence shows that the definition of disability is no longer satisfied. However, the disability benefits continue during a readjustment period that consists of the month of recovery and 2 additional months. As an encouragement for them to return to work, disabled beneficiaries for whom there is no evidence that their disability has otherwise terminated are allowed a 9-month trial work period during which benefits are not affected regardless of how much the beneficiary earns. At the end of that period, a beneficiary's earnings are evaluated to determine if the earnings are substantial ($1,080 per month in 2011). If earnings then exceed this amount for 3 months, benefits are suspended but can be reinstated during the next 36 months without starting a new application process should the earnings fall below this level.

As long as children are not disabled, benefits usually terminate at age 18 but may continue until age 19 if the child is a full-time student in elementary or secondary school.

A surviving spouse's benefit terminates upon remarriage unless remarriage takes place at age 60 or later.

SOCIAL SECURITY: BENEFIT AMOUNTS

Calculating Benefits

primary insurance amount (PIA) Except for the $255 lump-sum death benefit, the amount of all Social Security benefits is based on a worker's primary insurance amount. The *primary insurance amount (PIA)* is the monthly amount a worker receives if he or she retires at full retirement age or becomes disabled, and it is the amount on which benefits for family members are based. The actual PIA calculation is complex and performed by the Social Security Administration when a beneficiary is eligible for benefits. It involves indexing past wages on which taxes were paid to current wage levels, eliminating some years with the lowest or no earnings, and averaging the indexed wages for the remaining years. The result is then put into a formula that is weighted in favor of lower-income workers.

The average PIA for a worker who retires in 2011 at the full retirement age is about $1,177. A worker who has continually earned the maximum income subject to Social Security taxes can expect to have a PIA for retirement purposes of about $2,366 if he or she retires in 2011. The maximum retirement benefit depends on the age a worker chooses to retire. For example, for a worker retiring at age 66 in 2011, the amount is $2,366. This figure is based on earnings at the maximum taxable amount for every year after age 21. The following table shows the Social Security Administration's estimated average monthly benefit that various categories of beneficiaries receive in 2011.

Table 7-2 Estimated Average Monthly Social Security Benefits, 2011	
Category of Beneficiary	**Amount**
All retired workers	$1,177
Aged couple, both receiving benefits	1,907
Widowed mother and two children	2,409
Aged widow(er) alone	1,133
Disabled worker, spouse, and one or more children	1,813
All disabled workers	1,067
Source: Understanding the Benefits, 2011 at socialsecurity.gov	

If a worker is retired or disabled, these benefits are paid to family members, as shown below.

Table 7-3 Benefits for Family Members of a Disabled or Retired Worker	
Family Member	**Percentage of Worker's PIA**
Spouse at full retirement age	
Spouse caring for disabled child or child under 16	50%
	50%
Child under 18 or disabled	50% each

If the worker dies, survivors benefits are as shown below.

Table 7-4 Benefits for Survivors of a Deceased Worker	
Family Member	**Percentage of Worker's PIA**
Spouse at full retirement age	100%
Spouse caring for disabled child or child under 16	75%
Child under 18 or disabled	75% each
Dependent parent	82.5 for one, 75% each for two

However, the full benefits described above may not be payable because of a limitation imposed on the total benefits that may be paid to a family. This family maximum is again determined by a formula and is usually reached if three or more family members (including a retired or disabled worker) are eligible for benefits.

If the total amount of benefits payable to family members exceeds the family maximum, the worker's benefit (in the case of retirement and disability) is not affected, but the benefits of other family members are reduced proportionately.

EXAMPLE

Sam Chen died, leaving a spouse aged 42 and three children. All four family members are eligible for 75 percent of Sam's PIA of $1,200. Ignoring the family maximum, the benefits total $3,600 ($900 for each family member). However, the family maximum using the prescribed formula for 2011 is $2,105. Therefore, each family member has his or her benefit reduced to $526 (rounded to the next lower dollar). When the first child loses benefits at age 18, the other family members' benefits increase to $701 (ignoring any automatic benefit increases, including the family maximum).

When a second family member loses eligibility, the remaining two family members each receive the full benefit of $900 because the total benefits the family receives are now less than the $2,105 calculated by the formula

Other Factors Affecting Benefits

Benefits Taken Early

If a worker elects to receive retirement benefits prior to full retirement age, benefits are permanently reduced by 5/9 of 1 percent for each of the first 36 months that the early retirement precedes full retirement age and 5/12 of 1 percent for each month in excess of 36. For example, for a worker who retires 3 years before full retirement age, the monthly benefit is only 80 percent of that worker's PIA. A spouse who elects retirement benefits prior to full retirement age has benefits reduced by 25/36 of 1 percent per month for each of the first 36 months and 5/12 of 1 percent for each month in excess of 36. A widow or widower has benefits reduced proportionately from 100 percent at full retirement age to 71.5 percent at age 60. If the widow or widower elects benefits prior to age 60 because of disability, there is no further reduction.

Many Americans retire before the age at which they are eligible for nonreduced Social Security benefits. In some cases, an individual may need the Social Security benefits to meet regular living expenses. In other cases, however, an individual may have income or investments to bridge the gap until full retirement age. Then the decision becomes: Do I elect early benefits at a reduced amount for a longer period of time or larger benefits that will start later? There is no precise answer. As a general rule, if a person expects to live to 78 years or older, the better decision is to wait until full retirement age. However, the "break-even age" will vary by such factors as when early benefits start, gender, the category of Social Security benefits, and the interest rate at which funds can be invested.

Delayed Retirement

Workers who delay applying for benefits until after full retirement age are eligible for an increased monthly benefit. Benefits are increased for each month of late retirement until age 70. For persons born in 1943, for example, the increase is 2/3 of 1 percent per month, which equals 8 percent for delaying application for benefits for one full year. To encourage later retirement, the monthly percentage gradually increases. *Table 7-5* shows the percentage for each month of deferral as well as the maximum percentage increase that is available if the worker postpones retirement until age 70.

These increases apply to a worker's PIA as determined at the time he or she applies for retirement benefits. If a person continues to work during the period of delayed retirement and covered wages are sufficiently high, it is possible for a worker's PIA to exceed the dollar amount applicable at normal retirement age. Therefore, the increased monthly retirement benefit from working past full retirement age may be greater than the percentages in the table.

Table 7-5 Increase for Delayed Retirement		
Year of Birth	**Monthly Percentage Increase**	**Maximum Percentage Increase**
1939	7/12	32 1/3
1940	7/12	31 1/2
1941	15/24	32 1/2
1942	15/24	31 1/4
1943-54	2/3	32
1955	2/3	30 2/3
1956	2/3	29 1/3
1957	2/3	28
1958	2/3	26 2/3
1959	2/3	25 1/3
1960 and later	2/3	24

Earnings Test

earnings test   The *earnings test* is a process for determining whether income benefits of Social Security beneficiaries under full retirement age should be reduced because earned income exceeds a specified amount. For the earnings test, earned income includes wages and net self-employment income. It does not include interest and dividends.

Through the 1999 tax year, benefits were reduced for Social Security beneficiaries under age 70 if they had wages (but not interest and dividends) that exceeded a specified level. For tax years beginning after 1999, Congress repealed this earnings test in and after the month in which a beneficiary attains the full retirement age. However, the earnings test still applies to beneficiaries under full retirement age. They are allowed annual earnings of up to $14,160 in 2011, and this figure is subject to annual indexing for later years. If a beneficiary earns more than this amount, his or her Social Security benefit is reduced by $1 for each $2 of excess earnings. There is one exception to the test: The reduction is $1 for every $3 of earnings in excess of $37,680 (in 2011) in the calendar year a worker attains the full retirement age for earnings in months prior to such age attainment. Once the beneficiary reaches full retirement age, he or she can earn any amount without a Social Security reduction.

Any reduction is based on estimated earnings for the year. A final adjustment is made the following year, based on income tax information. If the prior year's payments were too high, future monthly benefits cease entirely until the deficit is made up. If the prior year's payments were too low, the beneficiary receives a check for any balance due.

Social Security Earnings Test

- Beneficiaries who have reached full retirement age—no loss of benefits regardless of annual wages
- Beneficiaries who are under full retirement age—$1 of benefits lost for every $2 of annual wages in excess of $14,160 (2011). A more liberal test applies in the calendar year a worker attains the full retirement age.

The reduction in a retired worker's benefits that results from excess earnings is charged against the entire benefits that are paid to a family and based on the worker's Social Security record. If large enough, this reduction may totally eliminate all benefits otherwise payable to the worker and family members. In contrast, excess earnings of family members are charged against their individual benefits only. For example, a widowed mother who holds a job outside the home may lose her mother's benefit, but any benefits her children receive are unaffected.

Cost-of-Living Adjustments

Social Security benefits increase automatically each January as long as there has been an increase in the Consumer Price Index (CPI) for the 1-year period ending in the third quarter of the prior year. This inflation protection is the same as the increase in the CPI since the last cost-of-living adjustment, rounded to the nearest 0.1 percent. Benefits do not automatically decrease if the CPI declines.

Offset for Other Benefits

Disabled workers under full retirement age who also receive workers' compensation benefits or disability benefits from certain other federal, state, or local disability programs will have their Social Security benefits reduced to the extent that the total benefits received (including family benefits) exceed 80 percent of their average current earnings at the time of disability. In addition, the monthly benefit of a spouse or surviving spouse is reduced by two-thirds of any federal, state, or local government pension that is based on earnings not covered under Social Security on the last day of employment.

SOCIAL SECURITY: REQUESTING BENEFIT INFORMATION

Social Security Statement

The Social Security Administration annually sends a *Social Security Statement* to all persons aged 25 or older who have covered employment under Social Security and are not currently receiving monthly benefits. The Social Security Statement enables an employee to verify his or her contributions to the Social Security and Medicare programs. It also contains an estimate of benefit amounts that are available upon retirement, disability, or death for that person.

The statement helps employees to understand their total benefit package as well as facilitate the correction of any errors in earnings records while information is readily available. As a general rule, requests for corrections must be made within 3 years, 3 months, and 15 days following the year in which wages were paid or self-employment income was earned. However, clerical or fraudulent errors can be corrected after that time.

DEALING WITH SOCIAL SECURITY

With private insurance, the provisions pertaining to the coverage are spelled out in the policy itself or in a plan document if a person still has employer-provided coverage. This is not the case with Social Security. Its provisions are contained in the relevant laws, rules, and regulations that pertain to the program. Seniors, their families, and professionals dealing with older or disabled clients need to be aware of the mechanics of dealing with both Social Security and Medicare.

Social Security's official web site, socialsecurity.gov, contains numerous publications about benefits, how to apply for benefits, and what to do when a beneficiary dies. There are also calculators to estimate benefits.

Filing for Benefits

Social Security benefits do not begin until an application for benefits is made. Applications can be made by phone, online, or in person. To ensure timely commencement of retirement benefits, an individual should apply at least 3 months before he or she wants benefits to begin. Application for disability and survivor benefits should be made as soon as possible after the onset of disability or the death of a covered worker. However, retirement and survivor benefits can be paid retroactively for up to 6 months after a claim is filed, and certain disability claims can be paid retroactively for up to 12 months.

An individual will have to file certain specified information and records to prove eligibility for benefits. These records must generally be original or certified copies, and they are returned after the Social Security Administration makes photocopies. For example, the list of required information to file for retirement benefits includes the following:

- Social Security number
- birth certificate
- W-2 forms or self-employment tax return for the prior year
- military discharge papers if applicant had military service
- spouse's birth certificate and Social Security number if he or she is applying for benefits
- children's birth certificates and Social Security numbers, if applying for children's benefits
- proof of U.S. citizenship or lawful alien status if applicant was not born in the United States.
- name of bank and account number so benefits can be directly deposited

Proof of death is required for receipt of survivors benefits, and verification of disability is needed to begin disability benefits.

Benefit Appeals

If Social Security denies a claim for benefits, it sends the applicant a letter explaining its decision. If the applicant wishes to appeal the decision, he or she can do so in writing within 60 days after receiving the letter.

The first level of appeal is called a *reconsideration* and is a complete review of the claim by someone who did not take part in the first decision. Old as well as newly submitted evidence is reviewed.

If an applicant disagrees with the reconsideration decision, the applicant may request a hearing. The hearing is conducted by an administrative law judge. Hearings are generally held within 75 miles of the applicant's home. In most cases, applicants will attend such hearings, either in person or by video conference. They may bring representatives and witnesses, and the government may also have expert witnesses. The administrative law judge may question the applicant and witnesses, and the applicant and his or her representative may also question the government witnesses.

If an applicant disagrees with the hearing decision, he or she may ask for a review by Social Security's Appeal Council. It may refuse to hear the case, return it to an administrative law judge, or make a decision itself. If the applicant disagrees with the Appeal Council's decision or the Appeal Council refuses to hear the case, the applicant may file a lawsuit in federal district court.

MEDICARE: TYPES OF BENEFITS

The current Medicare program consists of four parts:

- Part A—Hospital Insurance
- Part B—Medical Expense Insurance
- Part C—Medicare Advantage
- Part D—Prescription Drug Coverage

original Medicare   Parts A and B are often referred to as the original Medicare program. Part C is a series of options that beneficiaries can elect in lieu of the original program. Most of the available options are forms of managed care. However, most beneficiaries remain in the original program. In 2006, Part D became effective for all Medicare beneficiaries.

MEDICARE: ELIGIBILITY

Part A, the hospital portion of Medicare, is available at no monthly cost to any person aged 65 or older as long as the person is entitled to monthly retirement benefits under Social Security or the railroad retirement program. Civilian employees of the federal government aged 65 or older are also eligible. It is not necessary for these workers actually to be receiving retirement benefits, but they must be fully insured for purposes of retirement benefits. The following persons are also eligible for Part A of Medicare at no monthly cost:

- persons aged 65 or older who are spouses (including certain divorced spouses) of fully insured workers aged 62 or older
- survivors aged 65 or older who are eligible for Social Security survivors benefits

- disabled persons at any age who have been eligible to receive Social Security benefits for 2 years because of their disability. This includes workers under age 65, disabled widows and widowers aged 50 or over, and children 18 or older who were disabled prior to age 22.
- workers who are either fully or currently insured and their spouses and dependent children with end-stage renal (kidney) disease who require renal dialysis or kidney transplants. Coverage begins either the first day of the third month after dialysis begins or earlier for admission to a hospital for kidney-transplant surgery.

Most persons aged 65 or over who do not meet the previously discussed eligibility requirements may voluntarily enroll in Medicare. However, they must pay a monthly Part A premium and also enroll in Part B. The monthly Part A premium in 2011 is $450. The premium is adjusted annually, and the $450 amount reflects the full average cost of providing benefits to a Part A beneficiary.

Any person eligible for Part A of Medicare is also eligible for Part B. A monthly premium must be paid for Part B. The minimum premium ($96.40 in 2011 if enrolled in 2009, $110.50 if enrolled in 2010, and $115.40 for all others) is adjusted annually and represents only about 25 percent of the cost of the benefits provided. The general revenues of the federal government finance the remaining cost of the program. As a result of the Medicare Prescription Drug, Improvement, and Modernization Act, the Part B premium will continue to equal 25 percent of Part B benefit costs, but only for beneficiaries with modified adjusted gross income of $85,000 or less for a single person and $170,000 for a couple (in 2011 and subject to indexing). Higher-income persons pay a larger premium that increases with income. Persons with income above $214,000 ($428,000 for a couple) have a Part B premium equal to 80 percent of the cost of the benefits provided. These income figures are also indexed annually.

Persons who receive Social Security or railroad retirement benefits are automatically enrolled in Medicare if they are eligible. If they do not want Part B, they must reject it in writing. Other persons eligible for Medicare must apply for benefits. As a general rule, anyone who rejects Part B or who does not enroll when initially eligible may later apply for benefits during a general enrollment period that occurs between January 1 and March 31 of each year. The monthly premium is increased by 10 percent for each 12-month period during which the person was eligible but failed to enroll.

Table 7-6 Medicare Part B Premiums (2011)		
Modified Adjusted Gross Income (Individual Tax Return)	Modified Adjusted Gross Income (Joint Tax Return)	Premium
$85,000 or less	$170,000 or less	$115.40
$85,001 to $107,000	$170,001 to $214,000	161.50
$107,001 to $160,000	$214,001 to $320,000	230.70
160,001 to $214,000	$320,001 to $428,000	299.90
over $214,000	over $428,000	369.10

Medicare secondary rules make employer-provided medical expense coverage primary to Medicare for certain classes of individuals who are over 65, who are disabled, or who are suffering end-stage renal disease. These persons (and any other Medicare-eligible persons still covered as active employees under their employer's plans) may not wish to elect Medicare because it largely constitutes duplicate coverage. When their employer-provided coverage ends, these persons have a 7-month special enrollment period to elect Part B coverage, and the late enrollment penalty is waived.

Medicare is also secondary to benefits received by persons (1) entitled to veterans' or black lung benefits, (2) covered by workers' compensation laws, or (3) whose medical expenses are paid under no-fault insurance or liability insurance.

MEDICARE PART A: HOSPITAL BENEFITS

Medicare Part A   *Medicare Part A* provides benefits for expenses incurred in hospitals, skilled-nursing facilities, and hospices. Some home health care benefits are also covered. In order for benefits to be paid, the facility or agency providing benefits must participate in the Medicare program. Virtually all hospitals are participants, as are most other facilities or agencies that meet the requirements of Medicare.

Medicare Part A, along with Part B, provides a high level of benefits for medical expenses. As described in the next few pages, however, deductibles and copayments may be higher than in prior group or individual coverage. In addition, certain benefits that were previously provided may be excluded or limited. For this reason, persons without supplemental retiree coverage from prior employment may wish to consider purchasing a Medicare Advantage plan or Medicare supplement (medigap) policy in the individual marketplace.

Hospital Benefits

Part A pays for inpatient hospital services for up to 90 days in each benefit period. A benefit period begins the first time a Medicare recipient is hospitalized and ends only after the recipient has been out of a hospital or skilled-nursing facility for 60 consecutive days. A subsequent hospitalization then begins a new benefit period.

In each benefit period, Medicare pays covered hospital expenses in full for 60 days, subject to an initial deductible ($1,132 in 2011). This deductible is adjusted annually to reflect increasing hospital costs. Benefits for an additional 30 days of hospitalization are also provided in each benefit period, but the patient must pay a daily copayment ($283 in 2011) equal to 25 percent of the initial deductible amount. All recipients also have a lifetime reserve of 60 additional days that they may use if they exhaust the regular 90 days of benefits. However, once a reserve day is used, it cannot be restored for use in future benefit periods. When using reserve days, patients must pay a daily copayment ($566 in 2011) equal to 50 percent of the initial deductible amount.

There is no limit on the number of benefit periods a person may have during his or her lifetime. However, there is a lifetime limit of 190 days of benefits for treatment in psychiatric hospitals.

Covered inpatient expenses include the following:

- room and board in semiprivate accommodations. Private rooms are covered only if required for medical reasons.
- nursing services (except private-duty nurses)
- use of regular hospital equipment, such as oxygen tents or wheelchairs
- drugs and biologicals ordinarily furnished by the hospital
- diagnostic or therapeutic items or services
- operating room costs
- blood transfusions after the first three pints of blood (or three units of blood cells). Patients must pay for the first three pints of blood unless they get donors to replace the blood.

There is no coverage under Part A for the services of physicians or surgeons.

Skilled-Nursing Facility Benefits

In many cases, a patient may no longer require continuous hospital care but may not be well enough to go home. Consequently, Part A provides benefits for care in a skilled-nursing facility if a physician certifies that the patient needs skilled-nursing care or rehabilitative services for a condition that was treated in a hospital within the last 30 days. In addition, the prior hospitalization must have lasted at least 3 days. Benefits are paid in full for 20 days in each benefit period and for an additional 80 days with a daily copayment ($141.50 in 2011) equal to 12.5 percent of the initial hospital deductible. Covered expenses are the same as those described for hospital benefits.

A skilled-nursing facility may be a separate facility for providing such care or a separate section of a hospital or nursing home. The facility must have at least one full-time registered nurse, and it must provide nursing services at all times. Every patient must be under the supervision of a physician, and a physician must always be available for emergency care.

One very important point should be made about skilled-nursing facility benefits. Custodial care is not provided under any part of the Medicare program unless skilled-nursing or rehabilitative services are also needed and covered. Older individuals often need custodial care to help them with such personal needs as walking, bathing, dressing, or taking medication. This care may be short-term in nature, but often it is long-term and a major health care expense.

Home Health Care Benefits

If a patient can be treated at home for a medical condition, Medicare pays the full cost for an unlimited number of home visits provided by a home health agency. To receive these home health care benefits, a person must be confined at home and treated under a home health plan set up by a physician. The care needed must include skilled-nursing services, physical therapy, or speech therapy. In addition to these services, Medicare pays for the cost of part-time home health aides, medical social services, occupational therapy, and medical supplies and equipment provided by the home health agency. There is no charge for these benefits other than a required 20 percent copayment for the cost of such durable medical equipment as oxygen tanks and hospital beds. Medicare does not cover home services that are furnished primarily to assist people in activities of daily living (ADLs), such as housecleaning, preparing meals, shopping, dressing, or bathing.

If a person has only Part A of Medicare, Part A covers all home health care benefits. If a person has both Parts A and B, Part A covers the first 100 visits that commence within 14 days of a hospital stay of at least 3 days. Part B covers all other home health visits.

Hospice Benefits

Hospice benefits are available under Part A of Medicare for beneficiaries who are certified as being terminally ill with a life expectancy of 6 months or less. Although a hospice is thought of as a facility for treating the terminally ill, Medicare benefits provided by a Medicare-approved hospice are available primarily to patients in their own homes. However, a hospice can provide inpatient care if the patient needs it. In addition to including the types of benefits described for home health care, hospice care benefits include drugs, bereavement counseling, and inpatient respite care when family members need a break from caring for the ill person.

To qualify for hospice benefits, a Medicare recipient must elect such coverage in lieu of other Medicare benefits, except for the services of the attending physician or services and benefits that do not pertain to the terminal condition. There are modest copayments for some services. A beneficiary may cancel the hospice coverage at any time (for example, to pursue chemotherapy treatments) and return to regular Medicare coverage. The beneficiary can elect hospice benefits again but must be recertified as terminally ill.

Part A Exclusions

There are some circumstances under which Part A of Medicare does not pay benefits. In addition, there are times when Medicare acts as the secondary payer of benefits. Part A exclusions include the following:

- services outside the United States and its territories or possessions. However, there are a few exceptions to this rule for qualified Mexican and Canadian hospitals. Medicare pays benefits if an emergency occurs in the United States and the closest hospital is in one of these countries. However, persons living closer to a hospital in one of these countries than to a hospital in the United States may use the foreign hospital even if an emergency does not exist. Finally, there is coverage for Canadian hospitals if a person needs hospitalization while traveling the most direct route between Alaska and another state in the United States. This latter provision does not apply to persons vacationing in Canada.
- elective luxury services, such as private rooms or televisions

- hospitalization for services that are not necessary for the treatment of an illness or injury, such as custodial care or elective cosmetic surgery

Under certain circumstances, Medicare is the secondary payer of benefits. Medicare pays only if complete coverage is not available from these sources, and then only to the extent that benefits are less than would otherwise be payable under Medicare.

MEDICARE PART B: MEDICAL EXPENSE BENEFITS

Benefits

Medicare Part B   *Medicare Part B* provides benefits for most medical expenses not covered under Part A. These Medicare Part B benefits include

- physicians' and surgeons' fees. Under certain circumstances, Medicare also provides benefits for the services of chiropractors, podiatrists, and optometrists.
- diagnostic tests
- X rays
- physical therapy
- cardiac and pulmonary rehabilitation
- blood transfusions
- drugs and biologicals that cannot be self-administered
- radiation therapy
- medical supplies, such as surgical dressings, splints, and casts
- rental of medical equipment, such as oxygen tents, hospital beds, and wheelchairs
- prosthetic devices, such as artificial heart valves or lenses after a cataract operation
- ambulance service if a patient's condition does not permit the use of other transportation methods
- mammograms and Pap smears
- diabetes glucose monitoring and education
- diabetic screening for persons at risk of diabetes
- screening blood test for early detection of heart disease
- colorectal cancer screening

- bone mass measurement
- prostate cancer screening
- pneumococcal vaccination and flu shots
- dilated eye examinations for beneficiaries at high risk for glaucoma
- home health care services as described for Part A when a person does not have Part A coverage or when Part A benefits are not applicable

Part B Exclusions

Although the preceding list may appear to be comprehensive, there are numerous medical products and services Part B does not cover, some of which represent significant expenses for the elderly. These exclusions include

- most drugs and biologicals that can be self-administered except drugs that are used for osteoporosis, oral cancer treatment, and immunosuppressive therapy under specified circumstances. However, benefits are now available under Part D, which is discussed later.
- most routine physical, eye, and hearing examinations except those previously mentioned. However, all Medicare beneficiaries are eligible for a one-time physical examination within one year of enrolling in Part B.
- routine foot care
- immunizations except pneumococcal vaccinations or immunization required because of an injury or immediate risk of infection
- cosmetic surgery unless it is needed because of an accidental injury or to improve the function of a malformed body part
- dental care unless it involves jaw or facial bone surgery or setting fractures
- custodial care
- eyeglasses, hearing aids, or orthopedic shoes

In addition, benefits are not provided to persons eligible for workers' compensation or to those treated in government hospitals. Benefits are provided only for services received in the United States, except for physicians' services and ambulance services rendered for a hospitalization that is covered in Mexico or Canada under Part A. Part B is also a secondary payer of benefits under the same circumstances described for Part A.

Amount of Benefits

The benefits available under Part B are subject to a number of different payment rules. A few charges are paid in full without any cost sharing. These include (1) home health services, (2) pneumococcal vaccinations and flu shots, (3) certain outpatient surgical procedures that are performed in lieu of hospitalization, (4) outpatient diagnostic preadmission tests performed within 7 days prior to hospitalization, (5) mammograms, (6) Pap smears, and (7) the onetime physical examination.

For other charges, there is a $162 calendar-year deductible in 2011. When the deductible is satisfied, Part B pays 80 percent of approved charges for most covered medical expenses other than professional charges for mental health care and outpatient services of hospitals and mental health centers. Until 2009, Medicare paid only 50 percent of approved charges for the mental health services of physicians and other mental health professionals. This will gradually increase to 100 percent by 2014.

There is a separate payment system under which Medicare determines a set payment for each type of service for outpatient services of hospitals and mental health centers. This amount varies across the country to reflect such factors as the level of hospital wages. For some services, Medicare patients are required to pay an amount equal to 20 percent of the set payment amount, and Part B pays 80 percent. For other services, there is a fixed copayment that may be more or less than 20 percent of the set payment amount. In no case can the amount a Medicare patient pays for a single service exceed a dollar figure equal to the Part A hospital deductible ($1,132 in 2011).

The approved charge for doctors' services covered by Medicare is based on a fee schedule issued by the Centers for Medicare & Medicaid Services, the federal agency that administers Medicare. A patient will be reimbursed for only 80 percent of the approved charges above the deductible—regardless of the doctor's actual charge. Most doctors and other suppliers of medical services accept an assignment of Medicare benefits and therefore are prohibited from charging a patient more than the fee schedule. They can, however, bill the patient for any portion of the approved charges that Medicare does not pay because of the annual deductible and/or the 20 percent percentage participation for which the beneficiary is responsible. They can also bill for any services that Medicare does not cover.

If a doctor does not accept assignment, the patient will receive a reimbursement directly from Medicare. However, this reimbursement is only 95 percent of what Medicare would have paid to a participating doctor. Doctors who do not accept assignment of Medicare benefits cannot charge a Medicare patient more than 115 percent of this amount. The effect is that a doctor who does not accept an assignment of Medicare benefits can charge a fee that is only 9.25 percent greater than if an assignment had been accepted (115 percent × 95 percent = 109.25 percent). As a result, some doctors either do not see Medicare participants or limit the number of such patients they treat.

The previous limitation on charges does not apply to providers of medical services other than doctors. Although a provider that does not accept assignment can charge any fee, Medicare pays only what it would have paid if the provider accepted assignment. For example, if the approved charge for medical equipment is $100 and the actual charge is $190, Medicare reimburses $80 (.80 × $100), and the Medicare recipient must pay the balance.

MEDICARE PART C: MEDICARE ADVANTAGE

In 1985, Congress amended the Medicare program to allow a beneficiary to elect coverage under a health maintenance organization (HMO) as an alternative to original Medicare. In 1999, Medicare Part C (originally called Medicare+Choice) went into effect. It expanded the choices available to most Medicare beneficiaries by allowing them to elect health care benefits through one of several alternatives to original Medicare, as long as the providers of these alternatives enter into contracts with the Centers for Medicare & Medicaid Services. However, beneficiaries were (and still are) required to pay the Part B premium. It is important to emphasize that these are private insurance plans. Although some plans market directly to Medicare beneficiaries, others use agents or brokers to sell their products.

Medicare Advantage   The initial reaction to Medicare+Choice was less than overwhelming. Few new providers of alternative coverage entered the marketplace, and enrollment had decreased after several years of growth. The situation, however, changed in 2005 as a result of provisions in the Medicare Prescription Drug, Improvement, and Modernization Act. The act changed the name of Medicare+Choice to *Medicare Advantage*. The act also made numerous administrative changes to the program aimed at increasing participation. The method for calculating payment to participating plans changed, and many plans received larger payments. This prompted some plans to increase benefits and/or lower premiums. And participation began to increase. Today, about one out of every seven Medicare beneficiaries is enrolled in a Medicare Advantage plan. About 85 percent of these enrollees are in HMO plans; the remainder are scattered among the other types of plans. The participation rate varies significantly among states, with some states having almost no participants and other states having participation rates over 20 percent. To some extent these statistics have been influenced by the fact that most Medicare Advantage plans are HMOs, and some parts of the country are either served by a single Medicare Advantage plan or have no such plans. In other parts of the country, there is a very competitive market.

Beneficiaries are generally able to enroll in a Medicare Advantage plan or switch plans (including reenrollment in Parts A and B) from November 15 to December 31. The new plan is effective the following January 1. Between January 1 and February 1, if you're in a Medicare Advantage Plan, you can leave your plan and switch to Original Medicare.

Types of Plans

There are currently five types of Medicare Advantage plans. It is important to emphasize that, if one of these options is selected, a beneficiary is still technically covered by Medicare. However, benefits are paid by the Medicare Advantage plan, not original Medicare. Any medical expenses not covered by the Medicare Advantage plan are the responsibility of the plan member.

- *HMOs.* As with health maintenance organizations for persons who are not eligible for Medicare, beneficiaries typically must select a primary care physician from the plan's network. This physician must usually make referrals for specialty care. Some Medicare Advantage HMOs have a point-of-service option, under which a beneficiary can elect to go outside the plan's network, but the beneficiary will pay a portion of the cost of these services.

- *preferred-provider organizations (PPOs).* Beneficiaries can elect out-of-network care if they are willing to pay the additional cost for such care, which can be substantial.

- *private fee-for-service (PFFS) plans.* Beneficiaries can go to any provider who agrees to accept the payment rates determined by the plan, but they may be required to pay a portion of these rates in the form of cost sharing. If a provider does not accept the PFFS plan rates, the beneficiary is responsible for the entire balance above what the plan pays. PFFS plans, which are similar to traditional major medical plans, were not widely purchased until recently. They are becoming increasingly popular with consumers, and more insurers are marketing such products. However, federal legislation will decrease payments to these plans, starting in 2009, and this may affect their growth.

- *Medicare medical savings account (MMSA) plans.* These are similar to health savings accounts (HSAs). A beneficiary has a high-deductible policy, with the size of the deductible varying from plan to plan. Medicare then puts an annual amount into a medical savings account that can be used for unreimbursed medical costs. MMSA plans are not yet widely purchased and are offered by only a small number of insurers in limited parts of the country.

- *special needs plans (SNPs).* SNPs are designed primarily to meet the needs of beneficiaries who are eligible for both Medicare and Medicaid (or who have certain chronic conditions) and who live in institutions such as nursing homes, or continue to live at home but need the level of care provided by such institutions. These plans help manage and coordinate the many services and providers needed by such beneficiaries. These plans are available only in limited geographic regions.

These plans must provide all benefits available under Parts A and B of Medicare. They typically include broader benefits as part of the basic coverage at no additional cost or for an additional premium. These include coverage for the deductibles, copayments, and percentage participation of original Medicare. They may also include some benefits for vision, hearing, or dental care as well as some wellness benefits. As a result, beneficiaries have little or no reason to have a Medicare supplement policy. In fact, they are ineligible to purchase one. However, they still have a need for Medicare prescription drug coverage.

Is a Medicare Advantage Plan an Appropriate Option?

The original Medicare program provides less than complete protection for medical expenses. As a result, many retirees have some type of medical expense coverage to provide additional benefits. Some retirees have this coverage under employer-provided postretirement medical expense plans; other retirees purchase a Medicare supplement (medigap) policy.

The selection of a Medicare Advantage plan is also a viable option that may provide broad coverage at a relatively modest cost. However, Medicare Advantage plans are not available in all parts of the country, and the number of plans in a given area may be very limited. In addition, most of the plans that currently exist are structured as HMOs. For a retiree who was covered by an HMO plan while working, the nature of the coverage will be familiar, and the HMO plan may even be with the same insurer that provided coverage previously. For other retirees, the inherent nature of such plans may be less than desirable. For example, HMOs control the selection of physicians that a member can use. The selection of a Medicare Advantage plan may require a retiree to stop seeing a long-time trusted physician and select a physician who participates in the HMO network. On the other hand, the retiree's physician may already be in the HMO network and no change will be necessary. HMOs also have limited coverage when a member receives medical care outside the plan's relatively small geographic service area. Retirees who plan to spend winter or summer months at another location may have limited coverage except in emergency situations unless they return home for treatment.

The decisions regarding HMO coverage are essentially the same for retirees as they are for actively working persons.

MEDICARE PART D: PRESCRIPTION DRUG COVERAGE

Medicare Part D   Along with numerous other changes to Medicare and the establishment of health savings accounts, the Medicare Prescription Drug, Improvement, and Modernization Act added a prescription drug program to Medicare—*Medicare Part D*. The act also gives employers a financial incentive to provide or continue to provide drug coverage to retirees as an alternative to enrollment in Part D.

Eligibility

Part D consists of voluntary prescription drug plans available to all Medicare beneficiaries enrolled in either Part A and/or Part B or enrolled in any of the various Medicare Advantage plans. Each enrollee must pay a monthly premium. No one can be denied coverage because of income level or for health reasons. Hereafter, Part D benefits are referred to as Medicare prescription drug plans.

Types of Plans

Medicare prescription drug plans are private plans offered by insurance companies, managed care plans, Blue Cross and Blue Shield plans, and other organizations. These sponsors typically contract with pharmacy benefit managers to design plan formularies. The plans must meet certain standards and be approved by the Secretary of Health and Human Services.

There are two basic types of Medicare prescription drug plans. One type of plan is for persons enrolled in most Medicare Advantage plans. As long as the Medicare Advantage plan has such a prescription drug program, members can obtain their prescription drug coverage only through that program. The other type of plan, referred to as a *stand-alone plan*, is available to persons enrolled in original Medicare or in Medicare Advantage plans without prescription drug programs. The main differences between these two types of plans are in the process of enrollment and premium payment.

Standard Benefit Structure

The act provides for a standard prescription drug plan but also allows for alternative plans to be approved if certain requirements are met and the plans are at least as generous as the standard plan. Most plans that are now available provide broader coverage than the standard plan, as explained later.

The standard prescription drug program has an initial annual deductible of $310 in 2011. This amount and other dollar figures mentioned below will increase in later years if the expenditures for prescription drugs by Medicare beneficiaries increase.

coverage gap (doughnut hole)
This is the standard Part D drug prescription plan for 2011 required by Medicare.[32]

- If a beneficiary joins a Medicare prescription drug plan, he or she must pay the deductible—the first $310 of drug costs.
- During the initial coverage phase, the beneficiary pays a copayment or coinsurance, and Part D drug plan pays its share for each covered drug until your combined amount (including your deductible) reaches $2,840.
- Once the beneficiary and the Part D drug plan have spent $2,840 for covered drugs, the beneficiary will be in the donut hole. Previously, the beneficiary had to pay the full cost of prescription drugs while in the donut hole. However, in 2011, the beneficiary gets a 50% discount on covered brand-name prescription medications. The

---

32. "Understanding the Medicare Part D Donut Hole", About.com Health Insurance, updated Nov. 23, 2010, from Michael Bihari, MD, Accessed 3/1/2011, www.healthinsurance.about.com/medicare.

donut hole continues until total out-of-pocket cost reaches $4,550 (referred to as TROOP or true out-of-pocket costs). This annual out-of-pocket spending amount includes the yearly deductible, copayment, and coinsurance amounts.

- When the beneficiary spends more than $4,550 out-of-pocket, the coverage gap ends and the drug plan pays most of the costs of your covered drugs for the remainder of the year. The beneficiary will then be responsible for a small copayment ($2.50 for generic and $6.30 for brand name drug). This is known as catastrophic coverage.

It is important to point out that all of the above limits apply to drug costs covered by the plan. If a beneficiary purchases a drug that is not covered by the plan, the beneficiary must pay the full cost for the drug and cannot apply this amount toward the initial deductible or use it to satisfy the previously mentioned limits. In addition, certain other drug costs do not count toward the limits. These include the cost for drugs purchased outside the United States, the cost of drugs specifically excluded by Medicare, and any payments made by most other private or government drug programs. However, drug costs paid by family members and certain state assistance programs count toward these limits.

EXAMPLE 1

Charley Smith takes three medications to treat his high blood pressure and high cholesterol. These medications will cost him about $1,200 in 2011. Charley is switching to a Medicare prescription drug plan that has a low premium and offers the standard Medicare drug benefit, including a deductible and no drug coverage in the donut hole.

This is what his prescription medications will cost in the plan he has selected:

- Charley will pay a deductible of $310

- He will then pay 25% (coinsurance) of the remaining $890 cost of his medications ($1,200 – $310 = $890). His additional out-of-pocket cost during this initial coverage period will be $223 ($890 X 25% = $223)

- Since Charley did not reach the $2,840 initial coverage limit, he will not enter the donut hole.

Charley's total estimated annual out-of-pocket prescription drug cost with his Medicare Part D plan will be $310 + $223 = $533 (plus his monthly premiums for the Medicare Part D plan).[33]

---

33. "Understanding the Medicare Part D Donut Hole", About.com Health Insurance, updated Nov. 23, 2010, from Michael Bihari, MD, Accessed 3/1/2011, www.healthinsurance.about.com/medicare.

EXAMPLE 2

Mary Jones takes three medications to treat her type 2 diabetes, high blood pressure, and high cholesterol—all of them brand name drugs. These medications will cost her about $3,800 in 2011. Mary is planning to join a Medicare prescription drug plan that offers the standard Medicare drug benefit, including a deductible and no coverage for generic medications in the donut hole.

This is what her prescription medications will cost in the plan she has selected:

- Mary will pay a deductible of $310

- She will then pay 25% of the cost of her medications for the next $2,530, until she reaches the coverage gap. Her additional out-of-pocket cost during this initial coverage period will be $633 ($2,530 X 25% = $633)

- Since Mary did reach $2,840 in drug spending ($310 + $2,530 = $2,840), she will enter the donut hole. Prior to 2011, Mary would have been responsible for 100% of the remaining cost of $970. However, since all of Mary's medications are brand names, she will only have to pay about 50% of the drug costs while in the donut hole.

Mary's total estimated annual out-of-pocket prescription drug cost with her Medicare Part D plan will be $310 + $633 + $485 = $1,428 (plus her monthly premiums for the Medicare Part D plan).[34]

Covered Drugs

formulary
Each Medicare prescription drug plan has a *formulary,* which is a list of approved drugs that the plan will cover. A formulary does not need to cover every prescription drug. By law, it must include at least two drugs in every therapeutic class. Most plans cover more than the minimum required number of drugs. Medicare drug plans, however, are required to cover a majority of drugs in certain classes. These classes include antidepressant, antipsychotic, anticonvulsant, antiretroviral, anticancer, and immunosuppressant drugs.

Some drugs are excluded from Medicare coverage by law. These include nonprescription drugs, prescription vitamins and minerals, certain barbiturates and benzodiazepines, and drugs for anorexia, weight loss or weight gain, fertility, cosmetic purposes, hair growth, and relief of such symptoms of cold as cough and stuffy nose. Plans may provide enhanced

---

34. "Understanding the Medicare Part D Donut Hole", About.com Health Insurance, updated Nov. 23, 2010, from Michael Bihari, MD, Accessed 3/1/2011, www.healthinsurance.about.com/medicare.

benefits and cover some of these excluded drugs. However, charges for the excluded drugs will not count towards meeting out-of-pocket limits.

A prescription drug plan is allowed to make formulary changes during the year as long as the changes are approved by the Centers for Medicare & Medicaid Services. Such changes must be posted on the plan's web site at least 60 days prior to the change. However, persons already taking a drug removed from the formulary continue to have coverage for refills until the end of the calendar year. If a prescription drug is not on a plan's formulary, a beneficiary has the right to request that the plan cover a medically necessary drug.

Plan Variations

Very few Medicare prescription drug plans are exactly like the standard benefit plan. There are several major ways in which most plans might provide more comprehensive benefits, but there are significant variations in how they do this.

Formulary Drugs

Most, if not all, plans have more drugs on their formularies than required by law. In some cases, the additional drugs are mostly generics; in other cases, there are both generic and brand name drugs.

Reduced Deductibles

Although many drug plans have an annual calendar-year deductible of $310, the majority of drug plans have no initial deductible. There are also a small number of plans that have a deductible under $310, often $100.

Tiered Copayments

In lieu of paying 75 percent of the cost of each drug after meeting the deductible, most plans have a tiered copayment structure. This is acceptable as long as the average amount paid by the plan for the initial level of benefits is at least 75 percent.

The following examples show some of these variations.

EXAMPLE 1
The plan has a three-tiered copayment structure. Tier I consists of generic drugs and has no copay. Tier II is preferred brand name drugs and has a $15 per-prescription copay. The copay is $50 for other brand name drugs, which make up tier III.

EXAMPLE 2
The plan has a four-tiered copayment structure. It is similar to the plan in example 1, except there is a fourth tier for certain unique and expensive specialty drugs. The copays for the first three tiers are $7, $30, and $60, respectively. The beneficiary must pay 25 percent of the cost of drugs in tier IV.

Where Prescriptions Can Be Filled

Prescription drug plans use a network of providers to dispense drugs. Some plans operate on a national basis; others operate within defined regions. In some case, the network may include many local pharmacies; in other cases, it may consist of a single large retail claim.

Beneficiaries are allowed to use out-of-network pharmacies only if they cannot reasonably be expected to use a network pharmacy and they do not regularly get their drugs from the out-of-network pharmacy.

All plans must include walk-in pharmacies. They can, and most plans do, also fill prescriptions through mail-order pharmacies that can be accessed by mail, telephone, fax, or Internet. Unlike other types of prescription plans, Medicare plans do not allow prescriptions to be filled for longer periods of time if a mail-order pharmacy is used. For example, if a 90-day supply can be obtained by mail order, a 90-day supply must be available at local pharmacies. However, some plans have a financial incentive, such as lower copayments, to use mail order.

Cost

The federal government pays a significant subsidy out of general tax revenue to each Medicare prescription drug plan. On the average, this subsidy is about 75 percent of the cost for a plan with the standard benefit structure. There are, however, significant variations in the premiums that a beneficiary must pay. Nationally, the premiums average about $38 per month in 2009 for the broad spectrum of stand-alone plans, but some stand-alone plans cost less (particularly if they have the standard benefit structure) and other plans cost significantly more. Premiums for drug coverage under Medicare Advantage drug plans are generally somewhat lower.

These variations are a function of several factors, including the drugs covered, deductibles, copays, the pharmacies used, and the ability of the plan to negotiate with manufacturers of drugs. Some lower-cost plans are also attempting to buy market share.

Subsidies in the form of waiver of premiums and copayments are available to beneficiaries who have low incomes and limited assets.

Enrollment

The initial enrollment period for a person who becomes eligible for Medicare prescription drug coverage is the 7-month period that includes the month of eligibility and 3 months before and after that date. This is the same as the enrollment period for Part B. If an individual enrolls during the first 3 months of this period, coverage begins on the first day of the month of Medicare eligibility. If the individual enrolls later, coverage begins the first day of the month after the plan receives the application.

creditable prescription drug coverage

If an individual fails to enroll in a Medicare prescription drug plan at the time of initial eligibility, there is a penalty unless the person had prior *creditable prescription drug coverage.* (The penalty is waived, however, for persons eligible for subsidized coverage.) For coverage to be creditable prescription drug coverage, it must be at least as good as Medicare's. These other plans, such as an employer or union plan, must certify the actuarial equivalency of their plan benefits with Medicare. It is not necessary that these plans meet the Medicare prescription drug plan rules; they only must be at least as good. For example, an employer plan might have higher copays than permitted for Medicare plans when prescription costs exceed a specified amount, but this might be offset by no coverage gap. By law, health plans that provide prescription drug coverage must notify persons aged 65 or older whether their prescription drug coverage is creditable or not.

If an individual fails to enroll in a prescription drug plan and has not had creditable coverage, there is a penalty added to the premium. The penalty equals 1 percent of the average national Medicare prescription drug plan premium for each month of late enrollment. The percentage does not change after an individual enrolls, but the size of the penalty changes each year as the average premium changes.

An individual may change prescription drug plans, without evidence of insurability, during an annual election period that runs from November 15 until December 31 of each year. The new plan is effective on the following January I.

There are also special enrollment periods when certain events take place. These include

- moving out of the plan's service area
- losing creditable prescription drug coverage by retirement or any other reason that is not the beneficiary's fault
- returning to original Medicare from a Medicare Advantage plan
- entering or leaving a long-term care facility
- losing coverage because a Medicare prescription drug plan stops offering coverage, fails to provide timely benefits, or misled the beneficiary about benefits

Making Choices

It is obvious from the prior discussion that the Medicare prescription drug plan is very complex. Seniors need to make decisions on whether to obtain coverage, and if so, which plan to purchase. Some seniors will need help in making their decisions. Information is available on Medicare's web site (medicare.gov) and those of consumer groups, such as AARP (aarp.org), as well as from financial services professionals.

Many factors that should enter into these decisions have previously been addressed. In this final section on Medicare prescription drug plans, these factors are summarized.

Necessity of Coverage

Seniors fall into three categories as to the necessity for coverage: those with creditable coverage, those with less-than-creditable coverage, and those with no drug coverage.

Those with Creditable Coverage. Some seniors are eligible for prescription drug coverage from an employer or union health plan. If this coverage is creditable, there is probably little reason to join a Medicare prescription drug plan. There may be some circumstances when a senior may find that the Medicare plan has features that make it more attractive than the current coverage. However, seniors must be cautious in deciding to drop existing coverage, because the individual may not be able to rejoin the plan at a later date. The individual may also be unable to drop the drug coverage without also dropping the entire medical expense coverage under the employer or union plan.

EXAMPLE
Wilma is retired. She has prescription drug coverage from her previous employer. That employer notifies her that her current coverage on average is at least as good as Medicare prescription drug coverage. She reviews the information provided by her previous employer and decides to keep the coverage. Because her current coverage is at least as good as Medicare prescription drug coverage, if she later decides to get Medicare prescription drug coverage, she won't have to pay a penalty. If her employer later stops offering prescription drug coverage, she can join a Medicare drug plan within 63 days after her current coverage ends and avoid paying the penalty.

One concern of Congress is that employers or unions that provide prescription drug coverage to retirees will drop this coverage, and possibly other retiree medical expense coverage, because Medicare prescription drug coverage is available. To prevent this, Medicare provides a subsidy to employers or unions that continue drug coverage as long as it is at least actuarially equivalent to the coverage under a standard prescription drug program. The annual subsidy equals 28 percent of the cost of providing a retiree with coverage equal to the standard plan.

Those with Less-Than-Creditable Coverage. Some seniors have employer or union drug coverage that is not creditable. In this case the individual has several choices:

- Keep the current plan and join a Medicare drug plan to obtain more complete protection. If an employee is subject to the Medicare secondary rules, the employer's plan pays its drug benefit first and Medicare is secondary.
- Drop the current plan and purchase a stand-alone plan along with original Medicare or join a Medicare Advantage plan that has prescription drug coverage. The same caveats previously mentioned for dropping coverage apply in this situation as well.
- Do nothing. Unfortunately, the penalty premium will be charged if a Medicare prescription drug plan is later needed and purchased.

Those with No Coverage. Some seniors without prescription drug coverage prior to enrollment in Medicare will easily realize the importance of prescription drug coverage—particularly if they are already incurring significant drug expenses. Other seniors may question the need for coverage if they currently incur few or no prescription drug expenses. They need to be aware that the use of medications increases with age and the failure to purchase coverage when initially eligible will result in increased premiums if purchased in the future. Some who advise seniors suggest that they be encouraged to buy the least expensive plan available; they can always change to a different plan if their circumstances change.

Cost

The premiums and cost sharing for Medicare prescription drug plans vary considerably. In comparing costs, however, keep in mind that a lower-cost plan may not be the best choice if it does not cover all the drugs an enrollee is taking, has higher copayments, or requires prescriptions to be filled at inconvenient locations.

Covered Drugs

Not all formularies are alike. Before purchasing a Medicare prescription drug plan, an individual needs to evaluate whether the drugs he or she is taking are included on the drug plan's formulary. Plans have web sites where this can be determined. If the drugs are not available, perhaps a different plan is better. Alternatively, the individual might consult his or her physician to see if a formulary drug is an acceptable substitute.

EXAMPLE
Ian takes a relatively expensive drug for his arthritis. He is considering purchasing a Medicare prescription drug plan that does not include this drug on its formulary. Ian's physician says he should not take the drugs that are on the plan's formulary because of possible side effects. The physician says he can request an exception but feels Ian should try to find a plan that includes the current drug on its formulary. Ian finds another plan, but it is slightly more expensive.

Convenience. Convenience is important to many seniors. For example, they need to be able to obtain prescription drugs easily and in the way they prefer.

EXAMPLE
Claire, a widow, has been in frail health for the last few years. When she became eligible for Medicare, her sister who lives in another state suggested a prescription drug plan that she liked very much and felt provided excellent benefits at a reasonable cost. Unfortunately, the plan uses the pharmacies of a large discount chain, and the store nearest to Claire is 18 miles away. She is also reluctant to use mail order. Claire checks with her local pharmacy that is only a block's walk away and finds that it participates in two plans that cover the drugs she takes. She has a modest fixed income and selects the lower-cost plan that uses the local pharmacy.

DEALING WITH MEDICARE

State Health Insurance Assistance Plan (SHIP)

Each state also has a *State Health Insurance Assistance Plan (SHIP)*. These are state programs that get money from the federal government to give free health insurance counseling and assistance to people with Medicare. State Health Insurance Assistance Plan counselors can answer questions about Medicare on such topics as Medicare benefits, dealing with denials and appeals, Medicare rights and protections, sending complaints about care or treatment, and selecting the appropriate Medicare and prescription drug plan. A SHIP also should be able to offer guidance about enrolling in Medicaid, selecting a Medicare supplement policy, and buying long-term care insurance. Phone numbers for each state's SHIP can be found on the Medicare web site.

Enrollment

Enrollment in Medicare Advantage plans and Medicare prescription drug plans is with the private insurers that offer these coverages, and enrollment requires action on the insured's part. The process of enrolling in original Medicare is relatively simple and may be automatic.

Individuals who are already receiving retirement benefits from Social Security or the Railroad Retirement Board prior to age 65 are automatically enrolled in both Parts A and B. The Part B premium is then deducted from their retirement benefit. In some cases, individuals may not want Part B. This usually occurs when they are still working and covered under an employer-provided medical expense plan that is primary to Medicare. These individuals must notify Medicare and reject the coverage. Automatic coverage begins the first day of the month an individual turns age 65.

If an individual is nearing age 65 and applies for retirement benefits to begin at that time, Part A is automatic and he or she can elect whether or not to have Part B. Anyone else must contact the Social Security Administration to enroll.

EXAMPLE 1
Flora retired in 2010 at age 65. She is not eligible for full Social Security retirement benefits until she is age 66 and decided not to take a reduced benefit by starting benefits earlier. However, she needs to apply for Medicare so that its benefits begin at age 65.

EXAMPLE 2
Bob is still working at age 65 and plans on continuing to work for several more years. His employer-provided medical expense coverage costs him $170 per month and has high deductibles and copayments. Bob is convinced that he will have better coverage at a lower cost under Medicare. Even though he does not plan to apply for Social Security retirement benefits, Bob can drop his employer-provided coverage and elect Medicare. However, he must apply. Bob also needs to be aware that he will need a Medicare supplement policy to fill in the gaps of Medicare. The cost of this policy may cause him to change his mind.

If an individual needs to take action to enroll in Part B, there is a 7-month initial enrollment period that begins 3 months before the month a person turns 65. As long as an individual signs up during the first 3 months of this period, coverage begins at the beginning of the month the person turns 65. Application during the last 4 months of the period will delay the effective date of Part B coverage beyond age 65.

If an individual does not elect Part B coverage during the initial enrollment period and is not covered under an employer-provided plan, there is a general enrollment period during the first 3 months of each calendar year. Coverage begins on July 1, and the Part B premium is increased by 10 percent for each full 12-month period of late enrollment.

EXAMPLE
Gus retired at age 64 and had significant financial resources. Therefore, he decided not to apply for Social Security until age 70, when he would receive much higher benefits because of the delayed retirement credit. Unfortunately, he procrastinated about applying for Medicare when his retiree coverage terminated at age 65 because he was in excellent health and rarely saw a doctor. At age 66, Gus was hospitalized and found himself without medical expense protection. When he did apply, he found out that coverage was not retroactive and that his future Part B premium would be 10 percent higher than normal.

Individuals who do not elect Part B because they are still working and covered under an employer-provided medical expense plan can enroll in Part B with no increase in cost as long as they apply within 8 months of losing the employer-provided coverage. However, they should apply as soon as possible to avoid a gap in their medical expense protection.

ADEQUACY OF FINANCING

partial advance funding

Social Security and Medicare are based on a system of funding that the Social Security Administration refers to as *partial advance funding*. Under partial advance funding, taxes are more than sufficient to pay current benefits and thus provide some accumulation of assets for the payment of future benefits. Partial advance funding falls somewhere between pay-as-you-go financing, which was once the way Social Security and Medicare were financed, and full advance funding, as used by private insurance and retirement plans. Under pay-as-you-go financing, taxes are set at a level to produce just enough income to pay current benefits; under full advance funding, taxes are set at a level to fund all promised benefits from current service for those making current contributions.

All payroll taxes and other sources of funds for Social Security and Parts A and B of Medicare are deposited into four trust funds: an old-age and survivors fund, a disability fund, and two Medicare funds. Benefits and administrative expenses are paid out of the appropriate trust fund from contributions to that fund and any interest earnings on accumulated assets. The trust funds have limited reserves to serve as emergency funds in periods when benefits exceed contributions, such as in times of high unemployment. However, current reserves are relatively small and could pay benefits for only a limited time if contributions to a fund ceased. In addition, the reserves consist primarily of IOUs from the Treasury because the contributions have been "borrowed" to finance the government's deficit.

In the early 1980s, considerable concern arose over the potential inability of payroll taxes to pay promised benefits in the future. Through a series of changes, the most significant being the 1983 amendments to the Social Security Act, these problems appeared to have been solved for the Social Security program—at least in the short run. The changes approached the problem from two directions. On one hand, payroll tax rates were increased; on the other hand, some benefits were eliminated and future increases in other benefits were scaled back. However, the solutions of 1983 have not worked. Without further adjustments, the trust funds will have inadequate resources to pay claims in the foreseeable future. Although the old-age and survivors fund will continue to increase—it will be quite large by the time the current baby boomers retire—and benefits will then exceed income, the fund balance will begin to decrease as the percentage of retirees grows rapidly. Current projections indicate that the assets of the combined old-age and survivors trust fund and the disability trust fund will run out about 2040.

Because of an increasing number of persons aged 65 or older and medical costs that continue to grow at an alarming rate, there is also concern about the Medicare portion of the program. Estimates are that its trust funds will be depleted by about 2020.

The depletion of the trust funds does not mean that Social Security and Medicare will be unable to pay any benefits. However, currently projected revenue to the two programs will be sufficient to pay only about 80 percent of what has been promised. It is obvious that changes must be made—either now or later—in the Social Security and Medicare programs. Probably the most important step in finding a solution is to convince the public that changes in this very popular entitlement program are necessary. Changes, of course, have significant political implications. Although most members of Congress realize the need for reform, neither political party has been willing to compromise and take the necessary initiative for fear of losing public support.

In the broadest sense, the solution lies in doing one or both of the following: increasing revenue into the trust funds or decreasing benefit costs. Changes that would increase revenue include the following:

- increasing the Social Security and/or Medicare tax rate
- increasing the Medicare Part B premium beyond its projected levels
- increasing the wage base on which Social Security taxes are paid
- using more general tax revenue to fund the programs
- subjecting a greater portion of income benefits to taxation and depositing the increased tax revenue into the trust funds
- investing all or a portion of trust fund assets in higher-yielding investments than Treasury securities

Suggested changes that have been made for decreasing benefit costs include the following:

- increasing full retirement age beyond the planned increase to age 67

- raising the early retirement age beyond 62
- lowering the benefit formula so that future retirees will receive somewhat reduced benefits
- reducing cost-of-living increases
- imposing a means test for benefits
- shifting more of the inflation risk to workers through the use of separate accounts for all or part of each worker's contributions. This would give the worker some control over his or her account.
- increasing the Medicare eligibility age beyond 65
- raising Medicare deductibles and copayments
- lowering or slowing the growth of payments to Medicare providers
- encouraging or requiring Medicare beneficiaries to enroll in managed care plans

Any single change to the Social Security and Medicare programs will probably offend one important group of voters or another. As a result, the ultimate solution will probably involve a combination of several of the suggestions for change so that everyone will bear a little of the pain.

TAX TREATMENT OF SOCIAL SECURITY AND MEDICARE

Deductibility of Premiums

Employer contributions to the Social Security and Medicare program are tax deductible for federal income tax purposes. Any employee contributions are paid with after-tax dollars. Self-employed persons are able to deduct one-half of their Social Security and Medicare taxes as business expenses. In addition, Medicare premiums are treated the same as other medical expense premiums for individual insurance and may be deductible.

Tax Treatment of Benefits

Benefits received in the form of monthly income under Social Security are partially subject to income taxation for some Social Security recipients. To determine the amount of Social Security benefits subject to taxation, it is necessary to calculate modified adjusted gross income, which is the sum of following:

- the taxpayer's adjusted gross income (disregarding any foreign income and savings bond exclusions)

- the taxpayer's tax-exempt interest received or accrued during the year
- one-half of the Social Security benefits for the year

If the modified adjusted gross income is $25,000 or less for a single taxpayer ($32,000 or less for married taxpayers filing jointly), Social Security benefits are not taxable. If the modified adjusted gross income is between $25,001 and $34,000 ($32,001 to $44,000 for married taxpayers filing jointly), up to 50 percent of the Social Security benefit is includible in taxable income. If the modified adjusted gross income exceeds $34,000 ($44,000 for married taxpayers filing jointly), up to 85 percent of the Social Security benefit is includible in taxable income. The exact amount of the taxable Social Security benefit is determined by complex formulas that are beyond the scope of this discussion.

Medicare benefits and any lump-sum Social Security benefits are received tax free.

OTHER SOCIAL INSURANCE PROGRAMS

Unemployment insurance is a joint federal and state program, and workers' compensation insurance and temporary disability laws are solely under state control. Because the programs of each state are unique, readers should familiarize themselves with the programs in their own states and not assume that these programs will always conform to the generalizations that follow. Detailed information on a specific state's program can be obtained from the state agency that administers the program.

Unemployment Insurance

unemployment insurance
Prior to the passage of the Social Security Act in 1935, relatively few employees had any type of protection for income lost during periods of unemployment. The act stipulated that a payroll tax was to be levied on covered employers for the purpose of financing *unemployment insurance* programs that were to be established by the states under guidelines issued by the federal government. Essentially, the federal law levied a federal tax on certain employers in all states. If a state established an acceptable program of unemployment insurance, the taxes used to finance its program could be offset against up to 90 percent of the federal tax. If a state failed to establish a program, the federal tax would still be levied, but no monies collected from the

employers in that state would be returned for purposes of providing benefits to the unemployed there. Needless to say, all states quickly established unemployment insurance programs. These programs (along with a federal program for railroad workers) now cover over 95 percent of all working persons, but major gaps in coverage exist for domestic workers, agricultural workers, and the self-employed.

There are several objectives to the current unemployment insurance program. The primary objective is to provide periodic cash income to workers during periods of involuntary unemployment. Benefits are generally paid as a matter of right, with no demonstration of need required. Although federal legislation has extended benefits during times of high unemployment, the unemployment insurance program is basically designed for workers whose periods of unemployment are short-term; the long-term and hard-core unemployed must rely on other measures, such as public assistance and job-retraining programs, when unemployment insurance benefits are exhausted.

A second major objective of unemployment insurance is to help the unemployed find jobs. Workers must register at local unemployment offices, and they receive unemployment benefits through these offices. Another important objective is to encourage employers to stabilize employment. As described below, this is accomplished through the use of experience rating to determine an employer's tax rate. Finally, unemployment insurance contributes to a stable labor supply by providing benefits so that skilled and experienced workers are not forced to seek other jobs during short-term layoffs, thereby remaining available to return to work when called back.

Financing Benefits

Unemployment insurance programs are financed primarily by unemployment taxes levied by both the federal and state governments. The federal tax is equal to 6.2 percent of the first $7,000 of wages for each worker, but this tax is reduced by up to 5.4 percentage points for taxes paid to state programs. The practical effect of this offset is that the federal tax is actually equal to 0.8 percent of covered payroll. A few states levy an unemployment payroll tax equal to only the maximum offset (5.4 percent on the first $7,000 of wages), but most states have a higher tax rate and/or levy their tax on a higher amount of earnings.

No state levies the same tax on all employers. Rather, states use a method of experience rating whereby all employers, except those that have been in business for a short time or those with a small number of employees, pay a tax rate that reflects their actual experience, within limits. Thus, an employer who has laid off a large percentage of employees will have a higher tax rate than an employer whose employment record has been stable.

An employer that has good experience often has to pay a state tax of less than 1 percent of payroll and possibly even as little as 0.1 percent. On the other hand, some employers pay a state tax as high as 9 or 10 percent. Regardless of the amount of actual state tax paid, the employer still pays the 0.8 percent federal tax.

The major argument for experience rating is that it provides a financial incentive for employers to stabilize employment. Those who oppose its use, however, contend that many employers have little control over economic trends that affect employment. In addition, they argue that tax rates tend to escalate in bad economic times and thus may actually be an obstacle to economic recovery.

Individual states collect the entire unemployment insurance tax and deposit it in the Federal Unemployment Insurance Trust Fund, which is administered by the Secretary of the Treasury. Each state has a separate account that is credited with its taxes and its share of investment earnings on assets in the fund. Unemployment benefits in the state are paid from this account. The federal share of the taxes the fund receives is deposited into separate accounts and used for administering the federal portion of the program and for giving grants to the states to administer their individual programs. In addition, the federal funds are available for loans to states whose accounts have been depleted during times of high unemployment.

Eligibility for Benefits

The right to benefits depends on the worker's attachment to the labor force within a prior base period. In most states, this base period is the 52 weeks or 4 quarters prior to the time of unemployment. During this base period, the worker must have earned a minimum amount of wages or worked a minimum period of time, or both.

The right to benefits is also contingent on an unemployed worker's being both physically and mentally capable of working. The worker must also be available for work. Benefits may be denied if he or she refuses suitable work or places substantial restrictions on the type of work he or she will accept. In addition to registering with a local unemployment office, most states require a worker to make a reasonable effort to seek work.

Most unemployment programs have a 1-week waiting period before benefits commence. Benefits are not paid retroactively for that time of unemployment.

All states have provisions in their laws under which a worker may be disqualified from receiving benefits. This disqualification may take the form of (1) a total cancellation of benefit rights, (2) the postponement of benefits, or (3) a reduction in benefits. Common reasons for disqualification include voluntarily leaving a job without good cause, discharge for misconduct, refusal to accept suitable work, involvement in a labor dispute, and receipt of disqualifying income, such as dismissal wages, workers' compensation benefits, benefits from an employer's pension plan, or primary insurance benefits under Social Security.

Benefits

The majority of states pay "regular" unemployment insurance benefits for a maximum of 26 weeks; the remaining states pay benefits for slightly longer periods. In most states, the amount of the weekly benefit is equal to a specified fraction of a worker's average wages during the highest calendar quarter of the base period. The typical fraction is 1/26, which yields a benefit equal to 50 percent of average weekly earnings for that quarter. Other states determine benefits as a percentage of average weekly wages or annual wages during the base period. Some states also modify their benefit formulas to provide relatively higher benefits (as a percentage of past earnings) to lower-paid workers. Benefits in all states are subject to minimum and maximum amounts. Minimum weekly benefits typically fall within the range of $20 to $100, maximum benefits in the range of 275 to $500, and average benefits in the range of $250 to $350. In addition, a few states currently provide additional benefits if there are dependents who receive regular support from the worker.

States also provide reduced benefits for partial unemployment. Such a situation occurs if a worker is employed less than full-time and has a weekly income less than his or her weekly benefit amount for total unemployment.

There is also a permanent federal-state program of "extended" unemployment benefits for workers who exhaust regular benefits during periods of high unemployment. When a state's unemployment rate exceeds a specified level, it automatically triggers the availability of these benefits. The federal government and the states involved finance the benefits equally, and they can be paid for up to 13 weeks, as long as the total of regular and extended benefits does not exceed 39 weeks.

In periods of severe economic conditions on a national basis, the federal government often enacts legislation to provide additional benefits that are financed with federal revenue. The most recent program, enacted in 2008 and extended in 2010, provides up to 13 weeks of benefits to persons who had exhausted regular benefits.

Temporary Disability Laws

temporary disability law

At their inception, state unemployment insurance programs were usually designed to cover only unemployed persons who were both willing and able to work. Programs denied benefits to anyone who was unable to work for any reason, including disability. Some states amended their unemployment insurance laws to provide coverage to the unemployed who subsequently became disabled. Five states—California, Hawaii, New Jersey, New York, and Rhode Island—and Puerto Rico each went one step further by enacting *temporary disability laws* under which employees can collect disability income benefits, regardless of whether their disability begins while they are employed or unemployed. Although variations exist among the states, these temporary disability laws (often referred to as nonoccupational disability laws because benefits are not provided for disabilities covered under workers' compensation laws) are generally patterned after the state unemployment insurance law and provide similar benefits.

Eligibility

Every jurisdiction requires that an employee must have worked for a specified time and/or have received a minimum amount of wages within some specific period prior to disability to qualify for disability income benefits. The usual waiting period for benefits is 7 days. In some jurisdictions, the waiting period is waived if the employee is hospitalized.

Benefits

Benefits are a percentage, ranging from 50 percent to 66 2/3 percent, of the employee's average weekly wage for some period prior to disability, subject to maximum and minimum amounts. Benefits are generally paid up to 26 weeks if the employee remains disabled that long.

Workers' Compensation Laws

Prior to the passage of workers' compensation insurance laws, it was difficult for employees to receive compensation for their work-related injuries or diseases. Group benefits were meager and the Social Security program had not yet been enacted. The only recourse for employees was to sue their employer for damages. In addition to the time and expense of such actions (as well as the possibility of the employee's being fired), the probability of a worker's winning such a suit was small because of the three common-law defenses then available to employers. Under the contributory negligence doctrine, a worker could not collect if his or her negligence had contributed in any way to the injury sustained. Under the fellow-servant doctrine, the worker could not collect if his or her injury had resulted from the negligence of a fellow worker. And finally, under the assumption-of-risk doctrine, a worker could not collect if he or she had knowingly assumed the risks inherent in the job.

workers' compensation laws To help solve the problem of uncompensated injuries, *workers' compensation laws*—a form of both social insurance and liability insurance—were enacted to require employers to provide benefits to employees for losses resulting from work-related accidents or diseases. These laws are based on the principle of liability without fault. Essentially, an employer is absolutely liable for providing the benefits prescribed by the workers' compensation laws, regardless of whether the employer would be considered legally liable in the absence of these laws. Benefits, with the possible exception of medical expense benefits, are subject to statutory maximums.

All states have workers' compensation laws. In addition, the federal government has enacted several similar laws. The Federal Employees Compensation Act provides benefits for the employees of the federal government and the District of Columbia. Other federal acts require benefits for various groups of persons who might be exempt from state workers' compensation laws.

Type of Law

Most workers' compensation laws are compulsory for all employers covered under the law. A few states have elective laws, but the majority of employers do elect coverage. If they do not, their employees are not entitled to workers' compensation benefits and must sue for damages resulting from occupational accidents or diseases. However, the employer loses the right to the three common-law defenses previously described.

Financing Benefits

Most states allow employers to comply with the workers' compensation law by purchasing coverage from insurance companies. Several of these states also have competitive state funds from which employees may obtain coverage, but these funds usually provide benefits for fewer employers than insurance companies do. Five states have monopolistic state funds that are the only source for obtaining coverage under the law.

Almost all states, including some with monopolistic state funds, allow employers to self-insure their workers' compensation exposure. These employers must generally post a bond or other security and receive the approval of the agency that administers the law. Although the number of firms using self-insurance for workers' compensation is small, these are large firms that account for approximately one-half of the employees covered under such laws.

Ways to Comply with Workers' Compensation Laws

Depending on the state, the ways to comply with workers' compensation laws include the following:

- Purchase insurance from a private insurance company
- Purchase insurance from a competitive state fund
- Purchase insurance from a monopolistic state fund
- Qualify as a self-insurer

In virtually all cases, the employer bears the full cost of providing workers' compensation benefits. Insurance premiums are set at a level that covers both the costs of expected claims and the insurer's sales and administrative expenses and other services. Obviously, if an employer self-insures benefits, the ultimate cost will include the claims paid plus any administrative expenses.

Employers who purchase coverage pay a premium that is calculated as a rate per $100 of payroll, based on the occupations of their workers. For example, rates for office workers may be as low as $.10, and rates for workers in a few hazardous occupations may exceed $50. Most states also require that employers with total workers' compensation premiums above a specified amount be subject to experience rating. That is, the employer's premium in part is a function of benefits paid for past injuries to the employer's workers. To the extent that savings in workers' compensation premiums offset or eliminate safety costs, experience-rating laws encourage employers to take an active role in correcting conditions that may cause injuries.

Covered Occupations

Although it is estimated that about 90 percent of the workers in the United States are protected by workers' compensation laws, the percentage varies among states from less than 70 percent to more than 95 percent. Many laws exclude certain agricultural, domestic, and casual employees. Some laws also exclude employers with a small number of employees. Furthermore, coverage for employees of state and local governments is not universal.

Eligibility

In order for an employee to receive benefits under a workers' compensation law, he or she must work in an occupation covered by that law and be disabled or killed by a covered injury or illness. The typical workers' compensation law provides coverage for accidental occupational injuries (including death) arising out of and in the course of employment. In all states, this includes injuries arising out of accidents, which are generally defined as sudden and unexpected events that are definite in time and place. Every state has some coverage for illnesses resulting from occupational diseases. Although the trend is toward full coverage for occupational diseases, some states cover only those diseases that are specifically listed in the law.

Benefits

Workers' compensation laws typically provide four types of benefits: medical care, disability income, death benefits, and rehabilitation benefits.

   Medical Care. Benefits for medical expenses are usually provided without any limitations on time or amount. They are not subject to a waiting period.

   Disability Income. Disability income benefits are payable for both total and partial disabilities. It does not matter whether a disability is temporary or permanent.

Most workers' compensation laws have a waiting period for disability income benefits that varies from 2 to 7 days. Benefits in many states are paid retroactively to the date of the injury if an employee is disabled for a specified period of time or is confined to a hospital.

Disability income benefits under workers' compensation laws are a function of an employee's average weekly wage over some time period, commonly the 13 weeks immediately preceding the disability. For total disabilities, benefits are a percentage (usually 66 2/3 percent) of the employee's average weekly wage, subject to maximum and minimum amounts that vary substantially by state. Benefits for temporary total disabilities continue until an employee returns to work; benefits for permanent total disabilities usually continue for life but have a limited duration (such as 10 years) in a few states.

Benefits for partial disabilities are calculated as a percentage of the difference between the employee's wages before and after the disability. In most states, the duration of these benefits is subject to a statutory maximum. Several states also provide lump-sum payments to employees whose permanent partial disabilities involve the loss (or loss of use) of an eye, an arm, or other body part. These benefits, determined by a schedule in the law, may be in lieu of or in addition to periodic disability income benefits.

Death Benefits. Most workers' compensation laws provide two types of death benefits: burial allowances and cash income payments to survivors.

Burial allowances are a flat amount in each state and vary from $300 to $5,000; benefits of $1,000 and $1,500 are common.

Cash income payments to survivors, like disability income benefits, are a function of the worker's average wage prior to the fatal injury. Benefits are usually paid only to a surviving spouse and children under 18. Some states require employees to pay benefits until the spouse dies or remarries and all children reach 18. Other states require benefits for a maximum time, such as 10 years, or until a maximum dollar amount has been paid, such as $50,000.

Rehabilitation Benefits. All states have provisions in their workers' compensation laws for rehabilitative services for disabled workers. These rehabilitation benefits are included for medical rehabilitation as well as for vocational rehabilitation, including training, counseling, and job placement.

Federal Taxation of Other Social Insurance Benefits

Unemployment insurance benefits are included in a recipient's gross income. Workers' compensation benefits are received free of income taxation.

Benefits received under temporary disability laws must be included in gross income. However, disabled persons with gross incomes below a specified level may be eligible for a federal tax credit. In jurisdictions where unemployed persons can also receive disability income benefits, any benefits paid to them are considered unemployment insurance benefits and taxed accordingly.

CHAPTER REVIEW

Key Terms and Concepts

OASDHI	Medicare Advantage
credit	Medicare Part D
fully insured	coverage gap (doughnut hole)
currently insured	formulary
disability insured	creditable prescription drug coverage
full retirement age	State Health Insurance Assistance
primary insurance amount (PIA)	Plan (SHIP)
earnings test	partial advance funding
Social Security Statement	unemployment insurance
original Medicare	temporary disability law
Medicare Part A	workers' compensation laws
Medicare Part B	

Review Questions

Review questions are based on the learning objectives in this chapter. Thus, a [3] at the end of a question means that the question is based on learning objective 3. If there are multiple objectives, they are all listed.

1. How are the Social Security and Medicare programs financed? [1]

2. As of this year, Evelyn, aged 37, had 28 credits under Social Security. She earned 24 of these credits prior to the birth of her first child 11 years ago. She has earned 4 credits since she reentered the labor force 1 year ago.
    a. Is Evelyn fully insured? Explain. [2]
    b. Is Evelyn currently insured? Explain. [2]
    c. Is Evelyn disability insured? Explain. [2]

3. What are the retirement benefits available under Social Security? [2]

4. What categories of persons are eligible for Social Security survivors benefits? [2]

5. a. What is the definition of disability under Social Security? [2]
    b. What categories of persons may be eligible for disability benefits? [2]

6. a. What is the relationship between a worker's PIA and the benefits available for dependents and survivors? [2]
    b. What happens if the total benefits for a family exceed the maximum family benefit? [2]

7. How is a worker's retirement benefits under Social Security affected if that person elects early or delayed retirement? [2]

8. Describe the earnings test applicable to the Social Security program. [2]

9. Describe the automatic cost-of-living-adjustment provision under Social Security as it relates to benefit amounts. [2]

10. Describe the filing process for Social Security benefits. [6]

11. What is the process for appealing the denial of Social Security claims for benefits? [6]

12. With respect to Part A of Medicare:
    a. What types of benefits are available? [3]
    b. To what extent are deductibles and copayments required? [3]
    c. What are the major exclusions? [3]

13. With respect to Part B of Medicare:
    a. What types of benefits are available? [3]
    b. To what extent are copayments required? [3]
    c. What are the major exclusions? [3]

14. How does Medicare Advantage increase the options available to Medicare beneficiaries for obtaining medical expense coverage? [4]

15. Describe the prescription drug coverage available under Part D of Medicare with respect to each of the following:
    a. eligibility [5]
    b. types of plans [5]
    c. standard benefit structure [5]
    d. covered drugs [5]

16. What are the variations among Medicare prescription drug plans? [5]

17. a. What is the nature of the Social Security and Medicare trust funds? [7]
    b. What are the possible actions that can better ensure the adequacy of these trust funds? [7]

18. To what extent are Social Security benefits taxed to recipients? [8]

19. a. What are the objectives of unemployment insurance? [9]
    b. How is the program financed? [9]
    c. How is benefit eligibility determined? [9]

20. What is the nature of temporary disability laws? [9]

21. a. What is the purpose of workers' compensation insurance? [9]
     b. What types and amounts of benefits are available? [9]

22. To what extent, if any, are benefits from unemployment insurance, temporary disability insurance programs, and workers' compensation insurance included in a recipient's gross income for federal income tax purposes? [9]

A human life has value for religious, relational, and social reasons that defy measurement. From a religious standpoint, for example, human life is regarded as immortal and endowed with a value beyond the comprehension of mortal man. In a person's relationship with other human beings, a set of emotional and sentimental attachments is created that cannot be measured in monetary terms or supplanted by material things. A human may be capable of artistic achievements that contribute in a unique way to the culture of a society.

human life value Life insurance, however, is primarily concerned with the economic value of human life, which can be measured to some degree in financial terms. A person's *human life value* is derived from earning capacity and the financial dependence of other lives on that earning capacity. More precisely, a person's human life value can be measured in terms of the present value of that portion of estimated future earnings, which, if he or she lives long enough to achieve all of the earnings, will be used to support dependents. Financial planners must understand the concept of human life value in order to evaluate their clients' life insurance needs.

EXAMPLE 1

Vance is a 30-year-old male whose estimated average earnings will be $50,000 per year until he retires at age 65. If we assume that one-half his income will be used to support dependents, his economic value to dependents is $25,000 per year for 35 years or $875,000 ($25,000 × 35 = $875,000). However, at age 30 his human life value is not this $875,000 total, but the present value of a stream of income in the amount of $25,000 for 35 years. Using a rate of 6 percent compound interest, the present value of this cash flow is calculated at $362,456.

Stated differently, if Vance's dependents had $362,456 today and invested it at 6 percent compound interest, they could withdraw $25,000 per year for the next 35 years before running out of money. Based on these assumptions, Vance's current human life value is $362,456.

Although this simple example illustrates the human life value concept that equates the value of a person's life with the income stream that person generates, the human life value concept has many obvious flaws that limit its usefulness as a financial planning tool. Perhaps most obvious is the assumption that income will be level over a number of years. This basic concept can be refined.

Life insurance is a valued contract, not a contract of indemnity. When an insured person dies, the beneficiaries of his or her life insurance receive the face amount of the policy or some other benefit that depends on provisions within the insurance contract. The amount paid by the insurer does not depend on any external measure of the insured's worth but rather on the life insurance benefit that was purchased. Financial planners need to help their clients understand what type and amount of life insurance will provide a benefit that compensates survivors for the economic loss associated with the death of an insured.

Because the human life value may arise out of a family or a business relationship, it is important to understand the purposes of life insurance for families and businesses, the basic methods of providing life insurance protection, and the types of individual life insurance policies. Three traditional types of life insurance are term insurance, whole life insurance, and endowment policies. Some of the newer variations of life insurance policies include current assumption whole life insurance, variable life insurance, universal life insurance, variable universal life insurance, indexed universal life insurance, joint-life insurance, and group insurance, a marketing variation.

PURPOSES OF LIFE INSURANCE

When measured in terms of his or her lifetime earning capacity, an individual's life may be worth millions of dollars. However, earning power alone does not create a need for life insurance. The financial value of any human life lies in the purposes for which the individual's earnings might be used.

A person's life clearly has an economic value if some other person or organization expects to benefit financially from the person's existence. Most income producers either have dependents or expect to acquire some during their lifetimes. People without legal dependents often intend to voluntarily provide financial support to relatives, friends, and charitable or religious organizations. Whether provided during one's lifetime or through an inheritance, this support may come from income earned during the person's lifetime or through life insurance proceeds payable upon the person's death.

Life insurance also serves a wide variety of purposes in the business world. The primary purposes of life insurance in business are key person indemnification, business continuation, and protection for employees and executives.

METHODS TO PROVIDE LIFE INSURANCE PROTECTION

There are two basic approaches to life insurance:

- term insurance, which is temporary
- cash value insurance, which provides permanent protection and involves a reserve or savings component

Premiums are usually guaranteed for the duration of the policy, but some policy types offer flexible premiums.

Term Insurance Approach

yearly renewable term insurance

Yearly renewable term insurance is the simplest form of life insurance. Yearly renewable term insurance provides protection for a period of 1 year and permits the policyowner to renew the policy for successive 1-year periods without furnishing a medical examination or other evidence of insurability. Term life insurance can also be written for longer periods, such as 5 or 10 years. A 10-year renewable term life insurance policy has a level premium for 10 years and may then be renewed for another 10 years at a higher premium. However, the right to renew is usually limited to a stated number of years or up to a specified age. If the insured dies while the term policy is in force, the face amount is paid to the designated beneficiary. If the insured does not die during the period of protection, no benefits are payable at the expiration of the policy or on the insured's subsequent death.

To clarify the term insurance approach, the following discussion deals only with the net premium and ignores the insurer's operating expenses. The net premium for term insurance is determined by the death rate for the attained age of the individual involved. Subject to minor exceptions, death rates increase with age, so the term insurance policy's net premium needed to pay death claims increases at the start of each new term. Moreover, because death rates rise at an increasing rate as ages increase, the net premium also rises at an increasing rate, much like a flight of stairs with successively higher risers.

If the surviving members of the insured group continue to renew their term insurance, the steadily rising premiums necessary to cover death claims become increasingly unaffordable. As premiums increase, healthy individuals will tend to give up their protection, while those in poor health may sacrifice to renew their policies, regardless of cost. This is a type of adverse selection. The withdrawal of the healthy members accelerates the increase in the death rate among the continuing members, and it can produce death claims in excess of premiums unless the insurance company's net premium rates provide ample margins. An insurer cannot adjust its term insurance rates if they prove to be inadequate, because the rates at which the policy can be renewed are usually guaranteed for the entire period of renewability. For these reasons, companies that offer term insurance on an individual basis limit the time during which the insurance can be renewed, such as up to age 65.

At older ages, the premium rates for term insurance are extremely high. However, many individuals need coverage that extends throughout their lifetime. This need led to the development of cash value or permanent life insurance.

Cash Value Approach

cash value life insurance

With *cash value life insurance*, premiums are sufficient not only to pay the insurer's mortality costs (death claims) and expenses but also to build a cash value (or savings fund) within the policy. That fund's growth depends in part on the premiums paid, and it is designed to equal the face amount of the policy at some point, such as age 100 or 120.

Life insurance calculations are based on mortality tables. Until recently, these mortality tables assumed that few people would live past the age of 100. If the insured is still alive at age 100, the policy's maturity date, the face amount is paid to the policyowner. Many insurance policies based on this assumption remain in force. However, currently issued policies are based on the 2001 Commissioners Standard Ordinary (CSO) mortality table, which is a mandatory minimum standard insurers must use for all policies issued on or after January 1, 2009. Reflecting improvements in longevity, this table runs to age 120. Newly issued cash value life insurance policies have a maturity date of 121; in the event an insured survives to age 121, the face amount is paid.

In many cash value policies, the annual premium does not increase from year to year but remains level throughout the premium-paying period. This does not mean that the policyowner must pay premiums as long as insurance protection is in force, but only that all required premiums will be the same amount.

Net premiums tend to rise as a result of increasing death rates. If premiums are leveled out, those paid in the early years of the contract must be more than sufficient to meet current death claims, while those paid in the later years generally will be less than adequate to meet incurred claims. The net premiums beyond those needed for death claims in the early years of the contract create an accumulation that is held in trust[35] by the insurance company for the benefit of, and to the credit of, the policyowners. This accumulation is usually called a legal reserve. The legal reserve is an amount that, augmented by premium payments under outstanding contracts and interest earnings, is sufficient to enable the life insurer to meet its expected future obligations. These obligations include death benefits and nonforfeiture benefits such as policy loans and surrender values. Because the 2001 CSO mortality table assumes premiums may be paid over a longer period of time, use of the later table reduces statutory legal reserve requirements by approximately 20 percent.

---

35. This is not a trust fund in the legal sense, which would require the insurance company to establish separate investment accounts for each policyowner and render periodic accountings.

The manner in which the reserve fund is accumulated and invested is strictly regulated by law. Technically, the reserve is a liability account on the insurer's balance sheet. The reserve is not allocated to individual policies, but it may be viewed as an aggregate of individual savings accounts established for the benefit of the policyowners.[36]

Figure 8-1 compares the net level premium for a type of cash value policy known as whole life with the net premium that would be required for a yearly renewable term policy. The age of issue in both cases is 25. Assume that an annual net level premium of $6.09 per $1,000 of insurance is paid for the whole life policy as long as the insured lives. This premium is the actuarial equivalent of a series of increasing net premiums on the yearly renewable term basis, ranging from $1.16 per $1,000 of insurance at age 25 to $956.94 at age 99.

Figure 8-1

**Annual Net Premium Comparison per $1,000 of Coverage—
Whole Life and Yearly Renewable Term (YRT)**

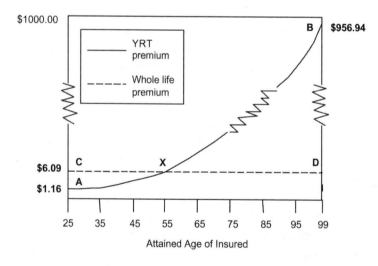

The mortality table used in this example assumes that everyone who survives to age 99 will die during the following year, producing a net premium at age 99 on the yearly renewable term basis equal to the face of the policy, minus

---

36. In practice, each policy is credited with a cash value or surrender value, which is not the same as the reserve but also has its basis in the redundant premiums of the early years.

the interest earned on the premium during the year. New policies use a mortality table that extends through age 120.

In *Figure 8-1*, line CD, the net level premium for the whole life policy, bisects the curve AB, the rising net premiums for the term policy, between the ages of 53 and 54. The disparity between the areas bounded by AXC and BXD shows that excess net premiums (AXC) in the early years of a whole life contract (or, for that matter, any type of insurance contract except term) will offset the deficiency in the net premiums of the later years when the term insurance net premium is in the hundreds of dollars. In addition, with the aid of compound interest, the excess premium will accumulate a reserve equal to the face of the policy by the time the insured reaches age 100 or 121. In contrast, a yearly renewable term contract will have no reserve at the expiration of the contract. So long as premiums are paid, a permanent or cash value life insurance contract must provide for a death claim that is certain to occur, the only uncertainty being the time of its occurrence.

net amount at risk   Under a cash value contract, the accumulated reserve becomes part of the face amount payable at the insured's death. From the standpoint of the insurance company, the effective amount of insurance is the difference between the face amount of the policy and the reserve. This amount is called the net amount at risk. As the reserve increases, the *net amount at risk* decreases if the face amount remains constant.

A cash value life insurance policy does not provide pure insurance but a combination of protection and cash values, the sum of which is always equal to the face amount of the policy. This is illustrated in the figure below for a level-premium whole life policy of $1,000 issued at age 25. Because of the accumulated reserve, a $1,000 permanent life insurance policy does not provide $1,000 of pure insurance, and the company is not "at risk" for the face amount of the policy. The amount of actual insurance is always the face amount, minus the policyowner's total excess net premium payments, plus interest. From the insurance company's perspective, the accumulation is the reserve, and from the policyowner's perspective, it is the cash value, which is slightly less than the reserve in the early years. Because the policyowner can withdraw the excess net premium payments in the form of the cash value at virtually any time, these excess net premium payments can be regarded as a savings or accumulation account.

The area below the curve represents the reserve under the contract or, as mentioned above, the policyowner's equity in the contract. The area above the curve represents the company's net amount at risk and the policyowner's amount of protection. As the reserve increases, the amount of pure protection decreases. At any given age, the two combined will equal the face amount of the policy. By the insured's age 95, the protection element of the contract has become relatively minor, and by age 100—frequently, the end of the contract—it has completely disappeared. At age 100, the policyowner will receive $1,000, composed entirely of the policy's cash value element. The illustrations here are based on an in-force policy with a maturity date of 100. The same principles apply to a policy with a maturity date of 121 except that the accumulated reserve builds more slowly.

Figure 8-2

Proportion of Protection and Savings Elements per $1,000 of Coverage in Ordinary Whole Life Contract, Issued at Age 25

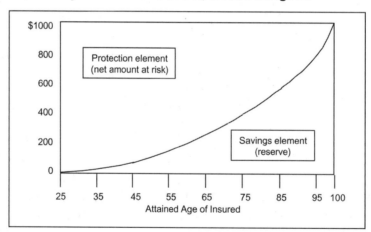

This combination of protection and accumulated cash values is characteristic of all permanent life insurance. Fundamentally, one contract differs from another only by the proportions in which they combine the two elements.

Yearly renewable term insurance is all protection with no cash value, while single-premium life insurance is at the other end of the spectrum, with the highest cash values and the lowest net amount at risk. Accumulated cash values should be thought of as a degree of prefunding. Single-premium policies are fully prefunded, and lower-premium policies that develop cash values are only partially prefunded. The shorter the premium-paying period, the higher the relative proportion of cash value to death benefit.

Nearly all operations of a life insurance company feel the effect of cash value or permanent life insurance plans. The reserve accounts for a major portion of the aggregate assets of life insurance companies. The need to invest funds presents the life insurance institution with a challenge but also enables it to materially contribute to economic expansion. The cash value makes a life insurance contract one of the most flexible and valuable contracts in existence, and one of the most acceptable forms of collateral for credit purposes. A cash value or permanent life insurance plan provides the only practical arrangement to provide insurance protection for an individual's entire life span, without the possibility that the cost will become prohibitive.

Effect of the Cash Value

- Serves as a major source of an insurer's investable funds
- Adds to the flexibility of the life insurance policy
- Is useful as collateral for credit purposes
- Makes permanent death protection possible

Guaranteed Premiums

modified whole life insurance

With most types of life insurance policies, the periodic premiums to be paid throughout the premium-paying period of coverage are known in advance and guaranteed by the insurance company. However, these premiums are not necessarily level over time. For example, in a yearly renewable term policy, the annual premium increases are usually guaranteed by the insurer at the issue of the contract. A similar guarantee is provided with respect to the renewal premiums for 5-year, 10-year, and other renewable term policies. Even in cash value policies, the annual premiums can be both nonlevel and guaranteed. An example would be *modified whole life insurance*. Modified whole life insurance guarantees a level premium for the first few policy years, with a higher guaranteed level premium thereafter.

Flexible Premiums

In several types of life insurance policies the premium is flexible, at the option of either the policyowner or the insurance company.

- With universal life insurance, the policyowner can elect to pay, within limits, more or less than the target premium established at the issue of the contract.
- With current assumption whole life insurance, the insurer periodically redetermines the premium, based on experience and assumptions for mortality, expenses, and interest.

Flexible premiums naturally affect the cash value of permanent insurance.

TRADITIONAL TYPES OF LIFE INSURANCE

There are three traditional types of life insurance:

- term insurance
- whole life insurance
- endowments

Term Insurance

Term life insurance provides life insurance protection for a limited period only. The face amount of the policy is payable if the insured dies during the specified period, and the insurer pays nothing if the insured survives.

Like most property and liability insurance contracts, term insurance provides temporary insurance. A person who buys a 1-year property insurance policy pays for 1 year of insurance coverage. The insurer pays for any covered claims that occur during that year. At the conclusion of that 1-year period, the insurer has no further obligation unless the policy is renewed for another year. Likewise, if a person insures his or her life under a 5-year term contract, no obligation is incurred by the insurance company unless the death of the insured occurs within the term. The company considers all premiums paid for the term protection to be fully earned by the end of the term, whether or not a loss has occurred, and the policy has no further value.

return of premium term insurance   A variation on traditional term insurance, known as *return of premium term insurance*, returns all premiums if the insured is still alive at the end of the policy term. A portion of the premium may also be returned if the policy is surrendered during the policy term after some minimum time period has elapsed. To many people return of premium term insurance feels like free insurance but this view, of course, ignores the time value of money.

The premium for term insurance is initially relatively low, even though it includes a relatively high expense loading and an allowance for adverse selection. Premiums can be low because most term contracts do not cover the period of old age when death is most probable and the pure cost of insurance is high. Depending in part on the age of the insured and the length of the term, return of premium insurance can cost 25 to 50 percent more than traditional term insurance.

Renewability

Many term insurance contracts contain an option to renew for a limited number of additional periods, usually of the same length. The simplest policy of this type is the yearly renewable term policy, which is a 1-year term contract renewable for successive periods of 1 year each. Longer term contracts, such as 10-year term, may also be renewable.

renewability *Renewability* refers to the right to renew the contract without a medical examination or other evidence of insurability. The renewability feature protects the insurability of the insured. When a term policy contains no renewal privilege, or when it can be renewed only upon evidence of insurability satisfactory to the company, the insured may find that he or she cannot continue coverage as long as needed. Because of poor health, a hazardous occupation, or some other reason, the insured might be unable to secure a renewal of the contract or to obtain any other form of life insurance.

reentry term insurance A variation is known as *reentry term insurance*. Reentry term insurance permits the insurer to use one schedule of renewal premiums if the insured can prove his or her continuing insurability and a higher schedule of renewal premiums if the insured's health has declined.

Under a term insurance policy, the premium increases based on the insured's attained age at the time of each renewal. Within each contract period, however, the premium is level. The schedule of renewal rates is included in the original contract, and the company cannot change these rates while the contract remains in force. As a safeguard against adverse selection, companies historically did not permit renewals beyond a specified age, such as 65. Renewals that continue the coverage to later ages are now commonly available.

Convertibility

convertibility

Convertibility is the policyowner's right to replace term coverage with permanent individual coverage, within a specified time frame, without having to show evidence of insurability. Convertible term insurance enables a policyowner to obtain temporary insurance with the option to purchase permanent insurance. This feature serves the needs of those who want permanent insurance but are temporarily unable to afford the higher premiums that whole life and other types of cash value life insurance require. Convertibility is also useful when the policyowner desires to postpone the final decision as to the type of permanent insurance until a later date when, for some reason, it may be possible to make a more informed choice.

The conversion from term to permanent insurance may be effective as of the date of the conversion or as of the original date of the term policy. If the term policy is converted as of the current date, conversion is usually referred to as the *attained age method* because the current age determines the premium rate. A conversion using the original date of the term policy is referred to as the *original age method* or a *retroactive conversion*. When the conversion is effective as of the original date, the premium rate for the permanent contract is the lower rate that would have been paid had the new contract been taken out originally, and the policy form is that which would have been issued originally. The advantage of the lower premium is obvious, and in many cases, the contract issued at the original date contains actuarial assumptions or other features that are more favorable than those incorporated in current policies.

Attained Age versus Retroactive Method

- **Attained age method of conversion**: New premium is based on insured's age at time of conversion; policy form is one that the insurer issues at that time.

- **Retroactive (original age) method of conversion**: New premium is based on the insured's age when the term insurance was first taken out; policyowner must make a lump-sum payment equal to the difference in the reserves or premiums plus interest on the old and new policies; policy form is one that the insurer issued when the term insurance was first taken out.

Offsetting the advantages of the original age method, however, is the financial adjustment—a payment by the policyowner to the company—which may be quite substantial if the term policy has been in force for several years.

The financial adjustment can be computed on a variety of bases, but many companies specify that the payment will be the larger of (1) the difference in the reserves under the policies being exchanged or (2) the difference in the premiums paid on the term policy and those that would have been paid on the permanent plan, with interest on the difference at a stipulated rate. The purpose of the financial adjustment, regardless of how it is computed, is to place the insurance company in the same financial position that it would have been in had the permanent contract been issued originally.

Nonlevel Term Insurance

decreasing term insurance

Normally, the amount of term insurance is level or uniform throughout the term of the policy. The amount of insurance, however, may increase or decrease throughout the period of protection. This is referred to as nonlevel term life insurance. Some term insurance provides systematic decreases in the amount of insurance from year to year. This type of term is appropriately called *decreasing term insurance*. Decreasing term insurance is often used to provide the funds necessary to pay off a mortgage loan if the insured dies, and it is mainly sold through mortgage lenders.

EXAMPLE

Jonathan, aged 34, and his wife Laura, aged 30, buy a house with the aid of a 20-year $200,000 mortgage. Jonathan is the primary breadwinner, and they qualified for the mortgage based on his salary. They plan to begin a family, and it would be unmanageable for Laura to be burdened with the mortgage payments if Jonathan were to die. To address this specific need, Jonathan purchases a 20-year decreasing term insurance policy through the mortgage company.

It might have been more cost-effective for Jonathan to purchase level death benefit term life insurance to meet this temporary need. The decreasing term insurance issued through lenders tends to be relatively expensive, because the rates anticipate a substantial amount of adverse selection.

---

increasing term insurance

Increasing term insurance is occasionally provided in a rider to another policy. Increasing term insurance is intended to increase insurance protection in order to keep pace with inflation or to meet additional future responsibilities which the insured expects to have.

Term insurance is suitable in two situations:

- *The need for protection is purely temporary.* Term insurance is the complete answer to a temporary need, but it should be *renewable* in case the temporary need lasts longer than originally expected.

- *The need for protection is permanent, but the policyowner temporarily cannot afford the premium for permanent insurance.* In this case, the policy should be *convertible*. By enabling the policyowner to convert the term policy to a permanent policy, the conversion privilege spans the gap between the need for permanent insurance and the financial ability to meet the need.

Renewability and convertibility serve quite different functions, and it might be appropriate for a term policy to include both features.

Term Insurance

- Protection during the term of the policy (for example, 1 year, 5 years)
- Premium that covers current mortality and expenses (no cash value)
- Renewability

  - "Renewable term," which may be renewed for subsequent terms, without evidence of insurability, at a higher premium

    - Premium based on attained age
    - Becomes expensive at higher ages
    - Common to have age limit, such as 65, on renewals

  - Level premium for each term

- Convertibility (option to convert to permanent insurance)

  - Attained age—premium based on age at conversion
  - Retroactive (original age)—lump-sum catch-up premium

- Nonlevel term

  - Decreasing term (for example, to pay off mortgage)
  - Increasing term (for example, to keep pace with inflation)

Whole Life Insurance

whole life
insurance

In contrast with traditional term insurance, which pays benefits only if the insured dies during a specified period of years, *whole life insurance* provides for the payment of the policy's face amount at the death of the insured, regardless of when death occurs. This characteristic—protection for the whole of life—gives the insurance its name. Whole life insurance offers permanent protection, and it accumulates a cash value. Some whole life policies also pay a dividend; these are known as participating policies. Whole life insurance may be subdivided into two categories that depend on the length of time during which premiums are paid:

- *Ordinary life* premiums are paid throughout the insured's lifetime.
- *Limited-payment life* premiums are paid only during a specified period.

Characteristics of Whole Life Insurance

Whole life insurance has two key characteristics:

- It offers permanent protection.
- It accumulates a cash value.

A whole life policy can be either participating or nonparticipating.

Permanent Protection. A whole life contract provides permanent protection that never expires in a policy that never has to be renewed or converted. As long as the policyowner continues to pay premiums when they are due, protection lasts for as long as the insured lives, regardless of his or her health; eventually, the policy's face amount will be paid as a death benefit. Most people need some life insurance until their death, if only to pay for last-illness and funeral expenses.

Cash Value or Accumulation Element. As level-premium permanent insurance, whole life insurance accumulates a reserve that gradually reaches a substantial level and eventually equals the face amount of the policy. The contract emphasizes protection, but it also accumulates a cash value that can be used to accomplish a variety of purposes.

Cash values are not generally available during the first year or two of the insurance contract because of the insurer's cost of putting the business on the books. Common exceptions are single-premium policies and some durations of limited-payment whole life policies where initial premiums exceed all first-year expenses incurred to create the policy and maintain policy reserves. The cash values that accumulate under a whole life policy can provide the basis for a policy loan, or they can be used to support one of the nonforfeiture options.

participating
policy

nonparticipating
policy

Participating versus Nonparticipating. A *participating policy* is a life insurance policy that may pay dividends. A *nonparticipating* policy does not pay dividends. Dividends, which are not guaranteed, enable the policyowners to participate in the insurance company's favorable experience.

Historically, stock life insurance companies did not pay dividends to policyholders but shared gains only with their shareholders. Participating policies had their origin with mutual life insurance companies, which were owned by their policyholders.

Whole life policies issued as participating policies anticipate charging a small extra margin in the fixed premium with the intention of returning part of the premium later in the form of policyowner dividends. This approach allows the insurance company to maintain a stronger contingency margin and still adjust the ultimate cost to policyowners downward after periods of coverage have been evaluated. Policyowner dividends are based on favorable experience, such as higher-than-expected investment returns or lower-than-expected mortality and/or expenses for operations.

Although participating policies were originally offered by mutual life insurers, the consumer appeal of policyowner dividends prompted stock life insurance companies to offer participating policies. Many stock life insurance companies now offer a choice of both participating and nonparticipating policies. Most of the policies mutual companies sell are participating policies. Policyowner dividends are generally declared annually, based on the insurance company's experience. Investment results usually account for the largest portion of dividends. The policyowner chooses among several dividend options for the use of his or her dividends.

The amount of dividends cannot be guaranteed, and it is illegal for an agent to present projections of future dividends as if they were guaranteed or certain. If insurance company experience turns unfavorable, policyowner dividends may decline or cease.

Types of Whole Life Insurance

There are two types of whole life insurance: ordinary life insurance and limited-payment life insurance.

ordinary life
insurance

Ordinary Life Insurance. *Ordinary life insurance* (also called *continuous-premium whole life*) is a type of whole life insurance with premiums that are assumed to be paid until the insured's death. We define ordinary life insurance this way because, in an increasing number of cases, policyowners purchase life insurance without intending to pay premiums for the duration of the insured's life. In many cases, they purchase the insurance intending to use dividends to pay up the insurance before the insured reaches his or her normal life expectancy. In other cases, they plan to eventually surrender the insurance for an annuity or for a reduced amount of paid-up insurance. Ordinary life should not be envisioned as insurance on which the policyowner must pay premiums for a lifetime, or even into the insured's extreme old age. Rather, it should be viewed as a contract that provides permanent protection along with some flexibility to meet changing needs and circumstances for both long-lived persons and those with average-duration life spans. Ordinary life is the most basic lifelong coverage any life insurance company offers.

Basing the premium rate for an ordinary life contract on the assumption that premiums will be payable throughout the insured's life produces the lowest premium rate for any type of whole life policy. Naturally, the longer the period over which the premium payment is spread, the lower each periodic premium will be. However, lower premiums also result in lower cash values than other types of whole life policies. Nevertheless, many financial advisors believe that an ordinary life contract offers the optimal combination of protection and savings.

If the objective is to secure the maximum amount of permanent insurance protection per dollar of premium outlay, then an ordinary life contract is the best choice. Its moderate cost can bring the policy within reach of most purchasers except those in the older age brackets. However, limited-payment insurance contracts provide benefits that justify the higher premium rates.

limited-payment
life insurance

Limited-Payment Life Insurance. *Limited-payment life insurance* is a type of whole life insurance for which premiums must only be paid for a specified number of years, as specified in the contract. The extreme end of the limited-payment life insurance policies spectrum is the single-premium whole life policy.

single-premium
whole life policy

As the name suggests, a *single-premium whole life policy* is fully paid up upon the payment of a single, substantial premium. However, few people can afford the premium required by a single-premium whole life policy, and even fewer are willing to pay that much in advance.

The limitation in limited-payment policies can be expressed in terms of the number of annual premiums or the age beyond which premiums will not be required. Policies with premiums limited by number usually stipulate 1, 5, 7, 10, 15, 20, 25, or 30 annual payments. These policies are usually referred to as, for example, *20-pay life.* The greater the number of premiums payable, naturally, the more closely the contract approaches the ordinary life design. For those who prefer to limit their premium payments to a period measured by a terminal age, companies make policies available that are paid up at a specified age—typically, 60, 65, or 70. These policies are often referred to, for example, as *life paid up at 65*, or more simply, *life at 65.* The objective of these age-related premium horizons is to confine premium payments to the insured's working years.

Because the value of a limited-payment whole life contract at the date of issue is precisely the same as that of a contract purchased on an ordinary life basis, and it is presumed that there will be fewer premium payments under the limited-payment policy, it follows that each premium must be larger than the comparable premium under an ordinary life contract. Moreover, the fewer the premiums specified or the shorter the premium-paying period, the higher each premium will be. The higher premiums, however, are offset by greater cash values. Thus, a limited-payment policy will provide a larger fund for use in an emergency and will accumulate a larger fund for retirement purposes than will an ordinary life contract issued at the same age. On the other hand, if the insured dies during the first several years after a limited-payment policy is issued, the policyowner will have paid more in premiums than under an ordinary life contract that provides the same death benefit. However, the total premiums required to cover a comparatively long-lived insured will be considerably less under a limited-payment plan than on an ordinary life basis.

The limited-payment policy contains the same types of surrender options, dividend options, settlement options, and other features as ordinary life policies.

vanishing premium It is important to differentiate between a limited-payment policy, which guarantees paid-up status at the end of the premium-paying period, and a *vanishing premium* approach, which uses policyowner dividends to pay all the remaining premiums as soon as the dividends are adequate to do so. Vanishing premium approaches were popular during the early 1980s when the high interest rates insurers could earn made possible a rapid buildup in cash values. However, dividends are not guaranteed. By the early 1990s, customers who had purchased policies expecting the premiums to vanish found that they had to make continuing premium payments to keep these policies in force. It is important to remember that dividends are not guaranteed and may decline in the future, and if dividends are inadequate to pay the premiums under the vanishing premium approach, the policyowner will have to resume actual premium payments out of pocket or let the policy lapse. There is no guarantee that so-called vanishing premiums will actually vanish or, if they do vanish, that they will never reappear.

Whole Life Insurance

- Permanent protection—never expires if premium is paid
- Level premium—does not increase with age
- Premium in early years that exceeds current mortality and expenses
- Accumulation of cash value
- Participating versus nonparticipating

    – Participating—extra premium returned as dividend
    – Nonparticipating—no dividends

- Ordinary life insurance (continuous-premium whole life)—premiums paid until insured's death

    – Lowest premium for permanent insurance
    – Lower cash values than other types

- Limited-payment life insurance

    – Premiums paid for a specified number of years or to a specified age
    – Goal—premiums confined to working years

Endowment Policies

endowment life insurance

Endowment life insurance policies are a variation of cash value life insurance. They not only provide level death benefits and cash values that increase with duration so that a policy's cash value equals its death benefit at maturity, but they also allow the purchaser to specify the policy's maturity date. Among the wide variety of endowments available are 10-, 15-, 20-, 25-, 30-, 35-, and 40-year endowments (or longer), or the maturity date can be a specific age of the insured, such as 55, 65, 70, or older. Whole life insurance is identical in design to an endowment at age 100 or 121, when the cash value equals the death benefit.

Endowment life insurance contracts were designed with a target accumulation amount that would equal the death benefit at the end of the specified accumulation period. An endowment policy with a face amount equal to the desired accumulation amount ensures that the policy's face amount will be available whether or not the insured survives to the target date. In the past, endowment policies were popular for policyowners who were beyond the chronological midpoint of their careers and sought accumulation for retirement or other objectives.

Although endowment contracts were readily available, sales were declining in the United States even before a 1984 federal income tax law change eliminated the tax-advantaged buildup of most endowment policies' cash values. Congress was concerned that life insurance policies (especially endowments) with high cash values relative to their death benefit amounts were being used as tax-advantaged accumulation vehicles by the wealthy.

Since 1984, sales of new endowment contracts have been very limited. Although contracts are still available from a few insurers, most new sales are for policies used in tax-qualified retirement plans where other factors control the tax treatment.

Outside the United States, especially in countries with high savings rates, endowment policies are still quite successful and widely purchased to accumulate funds for a variety of purposes, including to fund retirement or children's higher education.

VARIATIONS OF TRADITIONAL POLICIES

Numerous variations of traditional life insurance policies have developed, including

- current assumption whole life insurance
- variable life insurance
- universal life insurance
- variable universal life insurance
- indexed universal life insurance
- joint-life insurance

Current Assumption Whole Life Insurance

current assumption whole life insurance

A *current assumption whole life insurance* (CAWL) policy is a whole life policy with a premium charge that varies with changes in the insurer's actual or anticipated mortality, expense, and investment earnings experience. The insurer makes actuarial *assumptions* regarding the policy's mortality, investment returns, and expenses. If the insurer's assumptions are accurate, the policy performs as expected. If the insurer's results exceed the assumptions, the premiums drop, or the cash value or the death benefit increases. The opposite occurs if the insurer's results are worse than it assumed. Whatever the premium charge is at a given time, that premium is a fixed obligation for the policyowner. If the premium is not paid, the policy will lapse after the grace period. CAWL policies are usually issued on a nonparticipating basis.

As each premium is paid, it is added to the policyowner's accumulation account. An expense charge and a mortality charge to cover the policy's share of current death claims are deducted. Also, an interest credit is added to the account. These charges and the credit are based on current mortality, expense, and interest assumptions, subject to a guaranteed maximum charge for mortality and expenses and a guaranteed minimum interest rate credit. The cash surrender value of the policy at any point is equal to the value of the accumulation account minus a surrender charge that gradually reduces to zero after a specified time, such as after the first 15 or 20 years of the policy's life. A *surrender charge* is a fee imposed on the owners of certain types of life insurance policies and annuities at the time they surrender their contracts.

CAWL policies have been marketed in low-premium and high-premium designs. Both reflect the general features described above.

Low-Premium Design

With the low-premium design, sometimes called interest-sensitive whole life insurance or indeterminate-premium whole life insurance, the policyowner initially pays a low-level premium in comparison to that paid for a traditional nonparticipating whole life policy. This premium is guaranteed for the first few (generally 3 or 5) policy years. At the end of the guarantee period, the insurer redetermines the premium required to keep the CAWL policy in force under then-current assumptions, given the amount already available in the accumulation account. Redetermination of the required premium will again occur on specified policy anniversary dates or at specified intervals, such as every 5 years.

If, on a particular redetermination date, the premium charge increases because the insurer's experience has been worse than the assumptions anticipated, the policyowner has the option of paying the new, higher premium and keeping the policy's death benefit unchanged. Alternatively, he or she may continue to pay the old, lower premium and accept a reduction in the death benefit.

If the premium charge is reduced because assumptions were too conservative, the policyowner may pay the new, lower premium with no change to the death benefit. Alternatively, he or she may elect to continue to pay the old, higher premium with the same death benefit as formerly but with a more rapid buildup of the accumulation account. The policyowner may even have the option, if he or she can provide satisfactory evidence of insurability, to continue to pay the old, higher premium and increase the policy's death benefit. Therefore, with a low-premium CAWL policy, changes in current mortality, expense, and, especially, interest assumptions can affect the policy's premium, cash value, and death benefit.

Distinctive Features of Current Assumption Whole Life Insurance

- Usually nonparticipating, but favorable experience may reduce or eliminate premium charges
- Guaranteed maximum premium based on maximum mortality and expense charges and minimum interest rate credit
- Premiums that must be paid when due, or policy lapses
- Low-premium design—premiums redetermined periodically as current conditions warrant
- High-premium design—policy may reach paid-up status for a time, perhaps even permanently

---

High-Premium Design

With the high-premium design of CAWL insurance, the policyowner pays a relatively high level premium compared to that of traditional whole life insurance. The high premium charge causes a much more rapid buildup of the accumulation account than would occur in the low-premium design. If the insurer's mortality, expense, and investment results are favorable enough, the accumulation account will grow to an amount that eventually equals or exceeds the net single premium needed to pay up the policy under then-current assumptions. At that time, the policyowner can elect to stop paying premiums. However, unlike a traditional paid-up whole life policy, which guarantees that premiums will never have to be paid again, the CAWL does not guarantee that premiums will not have to be resumed if experience and assumptions worsen sufficiently. Indeed, the CAWL policy does not guarantee that premiums will ever completely vanish.

Variable Life Insurance

variable life
insurance

With a *variable life insurance* (VLI) policy, the policyowner directs how the cash value will be invested, the policyowner bears the investment risk, and the death benefit is linked to the policy's investment performance. Variable life insurance was the first type of life insurance designed to shift the uncertainty of investment gains or losses to policyowners. This product had a long and expensive gestation period. It not only had to run the gauntlet of state insurance department approvals but also needed, and finally acquired after many years of negotiations, approval by the Securities and Exchange Commission (SEC).

The premium in a variable life policy is fixed and guaranteed not to increase. A variable life insurance policy provides no guarantee of either interest rate or minimum cash value. Theoretically, the cash value can go down to zero, and if it does, the policy will terminate. As the SEC pointed out, in order for policyowners to gain the additional benefit of better-than-expected investment returns, they also must assume all the risk of investment losses. Consequently, the SEC requires that variable life policies be registered and that all sales be subject to the requirements imposed on other registered securities. In other words, policy sales may be made only after the prospective purchaser has been given the policy prospectus. The SEC also requires that the insurance company be registered as an investment company and that all sales agents be registered with the SEC for the specific purpose of variable life insurance policy sales. Agents who sell variable life insurance policies must be licensed both as life insurance agents and as securities agents.

Investment Choices

A variable life insurance policy gives the policyowner several investment options into which the cash value can be directed. The policyowner is free to put all of the funds into one of these choices or to distribute the funds among the options in whatever proportions he or she desires. Some insurance companies have more than a dozen funds from which to choose. There are usually a variety of stock funds, including growth stock funds, income stock funds, balanced stock funds, and international stock funds. Bond fund offerings include different durations and different types of issuers (large corporations, small corporations, state governments, and the federal government).

In addition, many insurance companies offer a managed fund as one of the portfolio choices. The policyowner can put all of the policy funds into a managed portfolio fund and have a professional money manager working for the insurance company make the investment allocation decision. This option appeals to policyowners who do not want to spend a lot of time learning about the market and making investment decisions.

Some insurance companies have allied with large mutual fund groups that make their entire range of mutual funds available. These agreements enable smaller life insurance companies to gain access to the administrative services already in place in these large mutual fund family groups.

With variable life insurance, the policyowner benefits directly from better-than-expected results and bears the risk of poor investment performance. The results of the investment performance are credited directly to the policy's cash values.

   Ability to Tolerate Investment Fluctuations. Individuals who are already experienced in equity investments are generally comfortable with a variable life insurance policy. However, the policy is subject to daily portfolio fluctuations that can provoke great anxiety in individuals who are not accustomed to or risk tolerant enough to be comfortable with market value fluctuations.

A variable life policy is a market-driven product, and its popularity, to some extent, is influenced by general investment market conditions. This type of policy becomes more acceptable to consumers after a long period of market increases and falls out of favor when the market experiences a general price decline.

Insurance Charges

Variable life insurance contracts are not exclusively investments. They are, in fact, life insurance contracts, and they include mortality charges for the death benefits. Consequently, the return on the invested funds within a variable life insurance contract will never equal the return on a separate investment fund that invests in assets of a similar type and quality but does not provide a death benefit.

Variable life insurance is not a short-term investment vehicle. The combination of sales load, mortality charges, and surrender charges significantly limits any potential gains in the policy's early years.

Distinctive Features of Variable Life Insurance
• The policyowner selects the types of investments into which the savings element will be directed.
• Premiums are fixed.
• Policies can be sold only with a prospectus.
• The death benefit depends on the investment performance of the policyowner-selected separate account(s).
• Policy loans are allowed, but to a smaller percentage of the cash value than in traditional contracts.
• Contracts contain the usual range of nonforfeiture options.

Policy Cash Values

Premiums paid under variable life insurance contracts are often subject to an administrative charge. The balance of the premium payment goes into the cash value account, from which mortality charges are deducted. The actual value of the cash component is determined by the net asset value of the separate account funds that make up the policy portfolio. The cash value of a variable life policy fluctuates daily. Each day's net asset value is based on the closing price for the investments in the portfolio on that trading day.

As with traditional life insurance contracts, the policyowner has access to the cash value via policy loans. Variable life insurance policies usually limit maximum policy loans to a slightly smaller percentage of the total cash value than is traditionally available in whole life policies. Policy loans may be repaid at any time in part or in full, but there is no requirement that policy loans be repaid at any time during the existence of the life insurance contract. Interest accrues on any unpaid loan balance. As with other types of whole life insurance, policy loans under a variable life insurance policy reduce the death benefit payable. The policy loan is always fully secured by the remaining cash value in the policy. Whenever the outstanding loans plus accrued interest equal the remaining cash value, the net cash value becomes zero and the policy terminates. Variable life insurance contracts provide the same range of nonforfeiture options as do traditional whole life policies.

Prospectus

Variable life insurance policies must be sold with an accompanying prospectus. The prospectus the SEC mandates is similar in many respects to the prospectus required for new stock issues. This prospectus contains a full and accurate disclosure of all the contract provisions, including expenses, surrender charges, and investment options. Although the prospectus is a long and detailed document that most purchasers are reluctant to read, it is an important source of information not available elsewhere.

Expense Information. The prospectus has very detailed information about all the expense charges the insurance company levies against variable life insurance contracts. These charges include commissions paid to soliciting agents, state premium taxes, administrative charges, collection charges, and any fees for specific future transactions.

In addition, the prospectus sets forth the manner in which charges are made against the asset account to cover the cost of insurance under the contract. This is usually referred to in the prospectus as the cost-of-insurance charge. The prospectus specifies exactly what rate will be used to determine cost-of-insurance charges and explicitly specifies if there is any maximum rate above the intended rate. The prospectus also explains the manner in which charges are levied against the separate account itself—essentially the fees associated with managing the various investment accounts from which the policyowner may choose. Part of that charge is always some specified percentage (usually less than 1 percent) of the assets in the separate accounts themselves. There also may be specific charges to establish and maintain the trusts necessary for managing those assets.

Surrender Charges. The prospectus clearly spells out the charge applicable to policy surrenders. In most cases, this information is set forth in a schedule, listing each policy year with its applicable percentage surrender charge. Surrender charges are applicable only if the policy is surrendered for its cash value, allowed to lapse, or (under some contracts) adjusted to provide a lower death benefit. Surrender charges are commonly levied during the first 10 to 15 years of the contract.

Investment Portfolio Information. The prospectus sets forth the objectives of each of the available investment funds and a record of their historical performance. There is detailed information on the current holdings of each of the available portfolios, usually supplemented by information about trades of equities or debt instruments over the previous 12 months. It gives further information about earnings during that same period of time and usually for longer intervals of prior performance if those portfolio funds have been in existence for 5 or 10 years. The prospectus fully discloses any investment restrictions applicable to these portfolios as indicated in the trust instruments themselves.

The prospectus also includes projections of future performance under the contract if portfolio funds generate an assumed level of investment earnings over the projected interval. Under SEC regulations, the permissible rates of return that can be projected are the gross annual rates after tax charges but before any other deductions at 0, 4, 6, 8, 10, or 12 percent. The insurer decides which of those permissible rates to project.

Universal Life Insurance

universal life insurance

Universal life insurance policies are characterized by the following features:

- flexible premiums
- shift of some investment risk to the policyowner even though the policyowner does not direct the investment portfolio
- ability to withdraw part of the cash value without having the withdrawal treated as a policy loan
- choice of level or increasing death benefit designs

The universal life policyowner receives detailed periodic reports from the insurer that generally include current information concerning each of the following:

- the death benefit
- the cash value
- the cash surrender value, if different from the cash value
- the amount of interest earned on the cash value
- mortality charges deducted
- expense charges deducted
- premiums paid during the reporting period

- outstanding policy loans
- any cash value withdrawals

The open disclosure associated with universal life policies eliminates some of the doubts about fair treatment sometimes directed at whole life insurance policies.

Flexible Premiums

Universal life insurance has the unusual feature of completely flexible premiums after the first year—the only time a minimum level of premium payments for a universal life policy is rigidly required. As usual, the first year's premium can be arranged on a monthly, quarterly, semiannual, or annual basis. The insurance company requires only that the premium equal or exceed a minimum specified level of first-year premium payments. After the first policy year, the policyowner can determine how much premium to pay and even whether or not to pay premiums—with one constraint.

The one constraint regarding premium payments is that the aggregate premiums paid, regardless of their timing, must be adequate to cover the costs of maintaining the policy. Consider the analogy of an auto's gas tank, where premium payments are like filling the tank. Premium payments (tank refills) can be made frequently to keep the tank nearly full at all times. With that approach, the auto is never likely to run out of gas. The same auto, however, can operate on a just-in-time philosophy, where premium payments (additional fuel) of minimal amounts are made only as frequently as necessary to keep the policy (the car) from running out of gas.

Under a universal life insurance policy, if the policy's cash value is allowed to drop too low (the cash value is inadequate to cover the next 60 days of expense and mortality charges and any surrender charge), the policy will lapse. If an additional premium payment is made soon enough, the policy may be restarted without a formal reinstatement process. However, if an injection of additional funds comes after the end of the grace period, the insurance company may force the policyowner to request a formal reinstatement before accepting any further premium payments.

Prefunding

The higher the amount or proportion of prefunding through premium payments, the more investment earnings will be credited to the policy where they can be utilized to cover mortality and administrative costs. All premium suggestions are based on some assumed level of investment earnings, and the policyowner must accept the possibility that actual investment earnings might be less than necessary to support the suggested premium. Even though investment earnings cannot go below the guaranteed rate, a long-term shortfall may eventually necessitate either an increase in premiums or a reduction in coverage.

Under traditional contracts with cash values, policyowner dividends provide the only mechanism for returning policy overfunding in the early years. With universal life policies, however, the accumulations from prefunding are credited to the policy's cash value. The earnings rates applied to those accumulations are also clearly visible in the policy's periodic reports, and they fluctuate with current economic conditions.

Withdrawal Feature

Universal life policies permit the policyowner to make partial withdrawals from the policy's cash value without incurring any indebtedness. In other words, money can be taken out of the policy's cash value just like a withdrawal from a savings account. There is no obligation to repay those funds, nor is interest incurred on the amount withdrawn. Withdrawals do affect the policy's future earnings because the fund still intact to earn interest for future crediting periods is reduced by the amount of the withdrawal. The extent to which the withdrawal reduces the death benefit depends on the type of death benefit.

Target Premium Amount

Nearly every universal life policy is issued with a target premium amount. The target amount is the suggested premium to be paid on a level basis throughout the contract's duration or for a shorter period of time if a limited-payment approach is intended to fund the policy. The target premium amount is merely a suggestion, and there is no guarantee it will be adequate to maintain the contract.

In some insurance companies, the target premium is actually sufficient to keep the policy in force (under relatively conservative investment return assumptions) through age 95 or 100 and to pay the cash value equivalent to the death benefit amount if the insured survives either to age 95 or 100. On the other hand, some companies with a more aggressive marketing stance have chosen lower target premiums, which may not be adequate to carry the policy in force to advanced ages even under more generous (if questionable) assumptions of higher investment returns over future policy years. If, in fact, the investment return credited to the policy's cash value falls short of the amount assumed to derive the target premium, the policy may essentially run out of gas before age 95 or 100. In these cases, the policyowner will be faced with two options: (1) to increase the premium level or (2) to reduce the death benefit amount. Neither one of these options is necessarily desirable, but they are the only acceptable ways under the contract's provisions to correct for unfulfilled optimistic assumptions about investment returns in the contract's early years.

Some insurance companies have introduced a *secondary guarantee* associated with their target premium. These companies have pledged contractually to keep the policy in force for, say, 15 to 20 years and to pay the full death benefit as long as the premium has been paid in an amount equal to or greater than the target premium amount at each suggested premium-payment interval. These guarantees ensure that the premium suggested as a target will be adequate to provide the coverage for at least as long as the guarantee period.

The flexible features of universal life premiums allow policyowners to make additional premium payments above any target premium amount at any time and without prior negotiation or agreement with the insurance company. The only limitation on paying excess premiums is associated with the income tax definition of life insurance. However, the insurance company reserves the right to refuse additional premium payments under a universal life policy if the policy's cash value is large enough to encroach on the legal upper limit (Sec. 7702) allowed for cash values relative to the level of death benefit granted in the policy.

The premium flexibility also allows the policyowner to skip premium payments, again without any prior negotiation or notification, or to pay premium amounts lower than the target premium suggested at the time of purchase. The lower limitations on premium payments have two constraints. The first is that nearly every company specifies a minimum acceptable amount for any single payment. The second is that there must be enough cash value in the contract to meet the mortality and administrative charges for the next 60 days. In other words, if the tank is running on empty, more premium is required.

Distinctive Features of Universal Life Insurance
• Premium flexibility
• Market rates of interest credited
• Unbundling of cost elements
• Partial withdrawals allowed
• Differential interest crediting rates if policy loans are outstanding
• "Back-end" expense loads in case of surrender
• Choice of death benefit designs (level or increasing)

Death Benefit Type

Universal life insurance gives policyowners a choice between level death benefits and increasing death benefits.

The *level death benefit design* (also referred to as option A or option 1) is much like the traditional whole life design. When the death benefit stays constant and the cash value increases over the duration of the contract, the net amount at risk—the protection element—decreases. The one new aspect of a level death benefit design under universal life policies is not really a function of universal life itself but a function of the tax law definition of life insurance (Sec. 7702) requiring that a specified proportion of the death benefit be derived from the net amount at risk. Whenever the cash value in the contract gets high enough that this proportion is no longer satisfied, the universal life policy starts increasing the death benefit, even though the contract is called a level death benefit contract. This phenomenon, illustrated below, does not occur until ages beyond normal retirement, and it is not a significant aspect of this design.

Figure 8-3
Universal Life Insurance—Level Death Benefit Design

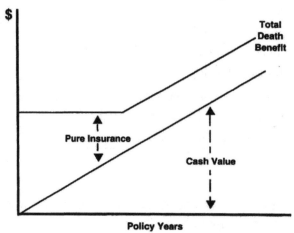

Policy Years

The *increasing death benefit design*, also known as option B or option 2, was introduced with universal life policies. Under this approach, illustrated below, there is always a constant net amount at risk that is superimposed over the policy's cash value. As the cash value increases, so does the total death benefit payable under the contract. A reduction in the cash value will reduce the death benefit. This design pays the policy's stated face amount plus its cash value at the insured's death. Policies with an increasing death benefit design overcome the criticism of whole life policies that the death benefit consists partially of the contract's cash value. By selecting the increasing death benefit option under a universal life policy, the policyowner is ensuring that the death benefit will be composed of the cash value and an at-risk portion equal to the original face value of the contract.

Figure 8-4
Universal Life Insurance—Increasing Death Benefit Design

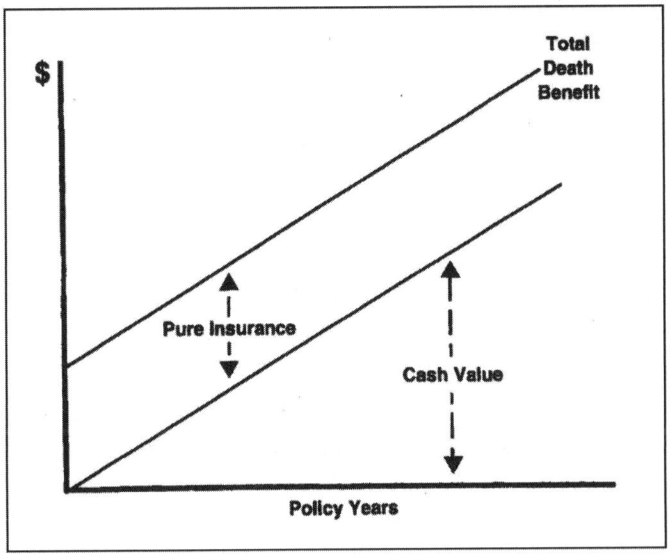

Effect of Policy Loans

Another aspect of policy design in universal life policies is the differential crediting rate on the cash value, depending on whether there are policy loans outstanding. Most insurance companies credit current interest rates on the cash value as long as there are no policy loans outstanding. Once the policyowner borrows funds from the cash value, the insurance company usually credits a lower interest rate or earnings rate to the portion of the cash value associated with the policy loan.

Internal Funds Flow

Universal life insurance policy designs constantly evolve in response to the economy, competitive pressures, and market demand.

Most of the first generation of universal life policies were heavily front-end loaded products. They consumed a significant proportion of each premium dollar as administrative expenses, and the remaining portion was then credited to the policy's cash value account. In most insurance companies, the mortality rate then charged against the cash value for the amount at risk was often about 50 percent of the guaranteed maximum mortality rate set forth in the policy contract for the insured's attained age. The difference between the mortality rate actually charged and the maximum permitted mortality rate published in the policy represents the safety margin the life insurance company holds in reserve. If future mortality costs for the block of policies turn out to be more than initially assumed, the insurance company can increase the mortality charge, as long as it does not exceed the guaranteed maximum rates specified in the contract.

From each premium dollar paid for universal life insurance, deductions are made for expenses and mortality. In addition, the universal life cash value account is increased at the current crediting rate to reflect investment earnings on that cash value. These dollars help to reduce the policyowner's current and future out-of-pocket premium expenses. The actual rate credited is discretionary on the part of the insurance company, and it tends to fluctuate, reflecting current market conditions.

Cash Value Account for a Universal Life Policy	
	Ending account balance, previous period
plus	Flexible premium paid
minus	Current expense charge (guaranteed maximum)
minus	Current mortality charge (guaranteed maximum)
plus	Interest credit at current rate (guaranteed minimum)
minus	Partial withdrawal (if any)
equals	Ending account balance, current period

Interest crediting rates have been the focal point of most of the competition among companies that sell universal life policies. There has been very little emphasis on the mortality rates charged or the expense charges levied against incoming premiums. In reality, all three factors constitute the total cost of insurance. Interest rates can be (and have been) intentionally elevated to a level above what the investment portfolio actually supports, but they are still viable for the company because of compensating higher levels of mortality charges and expense deductions. When consumers choose to focus on only one of the three elements, it is not surprising that marketing efforts zero in on that element. Assessment of overall policy efficiency requires that all factors be considered in concert.

Most universal life insurance policies are now based on a back-end loading design. In other words, they lower or eliminate up-front charges levied against incoming premium amounts and, instead, impose new or increased surrender charges applicable to the cash value of a policy surrendered during the contract's first 7 to 15 years. The dollar amount of any surrender charges usually increases during the first policy years and then decreases on a straight-line basis over the remaining years until the year in which the insurance company expects to have amortized all first-year expenses. At that point, the surrender charge is reduced to zero and is not applicable at later policy durations.

Competitive pressures have caused many insurance companies to minimize front-end loading in order to demonstrate that nearly all premium dollars go directly into the cash value account. The actual expenses are still being exacted internally, but it is not easy for the consumer to discern the manner in which they are handled. For example, expenses can be embedded in the spread between actual mortality costs and current mortality charges or in the spread between investment earnings and the interest rate credited to the cash value account.

Variable Universal Life Insurance

variable universal life insurance

Variable universal life insurance (VUL) incorporates the premium flexibility features of universal life insurance with the policyowner-directed investment aspects of variable life insurance.

Variable universal life insurance incorporates the death benefit designs applicable to universal life policies—either a level death benefit or an increasing death benefit design where the policy provides a constant fixed amount of protection in addition to the cash accumulation account. Under the first option, the death benefit usually does not change, regardless of how positive or negative the investment performance under the contract is. If the policyowner wants to vary the death benefit with the performance of the investments under the contract, he or she must choose the increasing death benefit design. Any increase or decrease is then a direct result of the accumulation balance.

Distinctive Features of Variable Universal Life Insurance

- Premium flexibility of universal life
- Death benefit design flexibility of universal life
- Investment flexibility of variable life

Variable universal life policies offer the policyowner a choice among a specified group of separate investment accounts that the insurance company itself usually creates and maintains. Some insurance companies have made arrangements with other investment companies to utilize separate account portfolios that those investment management firms create and maintain.

Like variable life insurance, variable universal life insurance policies are classified as securities and subject to regulation by the SEC. The SEC requires registration of the agents who market the product, the separate accounts that support the contracts, and the contracts themselves. In addition, policies must conform with the SEC requirements that the investment funds be in separate accounts that are segregated from the insurance company's general investment portfolio and are therefore not subject to creditors' claims on the insurer's general portfolio should the company face financial difficulty. As with all insurance, variable universal life contracts are also subject to regulation by state insurance commissioners.

Because variable universal life is a registered investment product, policies must be accompanied by a prospectus, which is governed by the same rules that are applicable to prospectuses for variable life insurance policies. The prospectus provides the necessary information for a meaningful evaluation and comparison of policies.

Variable universal life insurance is similar to universal life insurance, but with the added feature that the policyowner chooses the investments, as under fixed-premium variable life insurance contracts. Variable universal life offers the policyowner both flexibility and the potential for investment gain or loss. There are no interest rate or cash value guarantees and very limited guarantees on the applicable maximum mortality rates. Policyowners have wide-open premium flexibility under a variable universal contract and can fund it at whatever level they desire, as long as it is at least high enough to create coverage similar to yearly renewable term insurance and not in excess of the amount that would drive the cash accumulation account above the maximum threshold set forth in the Internal Revenue Code. Policyowners do not need to negotiate with or inform the insurer in advance of any premium modification or cessation.

Variable universal life contracts permit partial withdrawals that work like those under universal life policies. Early partial withdrawals may be subject to surrender charges, which apply to surrenders during the policy's early years, when the insurance company is still recovering excess first-year acquisition costs. The surrender charges vanish at a specified policy duration.

Policyowners can aggressively prefund variable universal life insurance so that later the policy can completely support itself from its cash value. If large premiums are contributed to the contract, this self-support can be accomplished in a relatively short period. As with universal life insurance, variable universal life policies have no guarantee that once the cash value is large enough to carry the policy, it will always be able to do so. The policyowner assumes the uncertainty of investment return and, to a limited extent, some of the uncertainty of mortality rate charges. Consequently, the policyowner may either pay more premiums or reduce the death benefit at some future time if, in fact, the cash value subsequently dips below the level needed to totally prefund the remaining contract years.

Choosing the increasing death benefit option under a variable universal life contract affords policyowners an automatic hedge against inflation. This inflation protection is general in nature and subject to a timing mismatch in that investment experience may not keep pace with short-term bursts of inflation. Over the long haul, however, the investment-induced increases in coverage should equal, if not exceed, general increases in price levels.

As with variable life, the policyowner is able to switch investment funds from one of the available choices to any other single fund or combination whenever desired. Some insurance companies limit the number of fund changes permitted before charging the policyowner for additional changes. Policyowners can switch investment funds without incurring any internal or external taxation of inherent gains in the funds. The internal buildup of the cash value is tax deferred at least as long as the policy stays in force and will be tax exempt if the policy matures as a death claim.

Indexed Universal Life Insurance

indexed universal life insurance (IUL)

An *indexed universal life insurance* policy receives interest crediting based on the performance of some external index, such as the Standard & Poor's 500. A policyowner's risk in an indexed universal life policy falls somewhere between the fixed and the variable universal life products previously discussed. Although it is a relatively new product innovation, the number of insurers providing indexed universal life insurance is growing rapidly. In a low-interest environment, an indexed universal life product can produce higher yields than a fixed universal life product with earnings based on the insurer's investment in bonds and mortgages, but it does not compete with the yields available with variable universal life.

Indexed universal life insurance is currently classified as a fixed investment product that can be sold by licensed life insurance agents without a securities license. The Dodd-Frank Wall Street Reform and Consumer Protection Act of 2010 withdrew the SEC Rule 151A (making indexed annuities registered securities products), to ensure that indexed annuities and life insurance would continue to be regulated as fixed insurance products.

IUL has been gaining market share over the last several years, as more companies offer this product. According to LIMRA[37], IUL sales jumped 47% in 2010, representing almost 20% of the 2010 annualized premium sales.

Joint-Life Insurance

joint-life policy The typical life insurance contract is written on the life of one person and is technically known as *single-life insurance*. A contract written on more than one life is known as a *joint-life policy*.

A joint-life policy written on the lives of two or more persons and payable upon the death of the first person to die is called a *first-to-die policy*. A first-to-die policy is not very common, but these policies have sometimes been used for funding business buy-sell agreements.

survivorship (second-to-die) policy If the face amount is payable upon the death of the last of two or more lives, the policy is called either a *survivorship policy* or a *second-to-die policy*. A survivorship policy (second-to-die policy) has become quite popular as a means of funding federal estate taxes of wealthy couples whose wills make maximum use of estate tax deferral at the first death.

Joint-life policies are usually some form of cash value insurance. A term insurance rider may be used to increase the overall amount of protection in the cash value policy.

GROUP LIFE INSURANCE

The discussion up to this point focuses on individual life insurance. However, for many people, group insurance is their principal, or perhaps only, source of life insurance protection. One indication of the important role of group life insurance is that, of the total life insurance in force in the United

---

37. U.S. Individual Life Sales Survey, Insurance Networking News, March 1, 2011, Ruthie Ackerman, www.insurancenetworking.com/news/life insurance sales distribution.

States, almost 39 percent is group coverage. Thirty-seven percent of U.S. Households rely only on group insurance to provide financial protection for the family if a wage-earner dies.[38] Group insurance also represents the fastest-growing portion of life insurance sales.

By far the most common type of coverage issued under group life plans is term insurance, accounting for about 95 percent of the total. The remainder consists mainly of universal life insurance or variable universal life insurance.

State law establishes the groups that are eligible for group life insurance. In general, the minimum size required is ten lives. Five types of groups are usually eligible: individual employer groups, negotiated trusteeships (also known as Taft-Hartley trusts), trade associations, creditor-debtor groups, and labor union groups. The most common insured group is the employees of a common employer.

In a typical group term life insurance plan covering employees, a benefit schedule defines the classes of employees that are eligible for coverage and specifies the amount of life insurance that will be provided to the members of each class. The employee also is given a conversion privilege.

Eligibility

To be eligible, an employee must be in a covered classification of workers, work on a full-time basis, and be actively at work. He or she may be required to fulfill a probationary period and, in some cases, to show insurability and meet premium contribution requirements.

The employer defines the classes of workers eligible for the group life insurance. Eligibility is usually restricted to full-time workers, such as those who work at least 30 hours per week. Many group life insurance master contracts also contain an actively-at-work requirement, meaning that the employee is not eligible for coverage if absent from work due to sickness, injury, or other reasons on the otherwise effective date of coverage. Coverage commences when the employee returns to work.

probationary period
The master contract may also specify a *probationary period* of employment with the employer, such as 6 months, that an employee must satisfy before he or she is eligible for coverage.

---

38. LIMRA, Household Trends in U.S. Life Insurance Ownership, 2010, LLGlobal Inc., p. 19.

Most group life coverage is provided without individual evidence of insurability. However, evidence is required in some cases, such as when an employee decides after the eligibility period has expired that he or she wants the coverage.

If the group plan is contributory, meaning that covered employees pay a portion of the premium, the coverage will not take effect until the employee properly authorizes payroll deduction. Usually, a 31-day eligibility period is provided, during which the employee may make the decision on this matter without having to show evidence of insurability.

Benefit Amounts

The amount of group life insurance on each covered worker is normally set according to a schedule, rather than chosen by the employee. The most common schedules are based on earnings. In an earnings schedule, the amount of insurance is equal to some multiple of earnings, such as two times the employee's annual earnings, rounded up to the next $1,000 and subject to a maximum benefit, such as $200,000. Benefits may also be a flat amount (such as $50,000) for all employees, or they may be based on position. In a position schedule, different benefit amounts are provided based on each employee's position within the firm. For example, the president and vice presidents might have $200,000 of coverage, managers $100,000, salespersons $50,000, and other employees $30,000.

Convertibility

Any employee whose group life insurance ceases has the right according to the master contract to convert to an individual insurance policy. For example, an individual who terminates his or her employment or ceases to be a member of an eligible classification of employees has the right to convert. Conversion does not require proof of insurability and must occur within the first 31 days of eligibility to convert. The individual policy usually can be any type the insurer offers, except term insurance. Some insurers also make term coverage available. A few states require that employees be allowed to purchase term coverage for a limited time, after which an employee must convert to a cash value coverage. The face amount may not exceed the amount of group life insurance being terminated, and the premium for the individual policy is based on the employee's attained age at the time of conversion.

Supplemental Benefits

A group life insurance plan may provide certain supplemental benefits. For example, the plan may make additional amounts of insurance available to some or all classes of employees. Proof of insurability is usually required to obtain the additional amount except when the amount of coverage is small, and the employer does not usually pay any part of the premium for it. Employees who need additional protection can pay premiums for supplemental coverage by payroll deduction. However, the premium is not necessarily any less expensive than coverage that an employee might be able to purchase in the individual marketplace.

Dependent life insurance may also be available as a supplemental benefit. Coverage is generally optional, with the employee paying the entire cost. The amount of insurance is usually modest, such as $5,000 on the employee's spouse and $1,000 on each dependent child over 14 days of age and under age 21. The employee typically is not allowed to select which of his or her eligible dependents will be covered but must decide on an all-or-none basis.

COMPARISON OF LIFE INSURANCE TYPES

Though variations exist within each type of individual life insurance plan, some generalizations can be made. The following table is arranged in a sequence that roughly reflects the increasing complexity of various types of life insurance, ranging from term insurance to variable universal life insurance.

Table 8-1 Types of Life Insurance				
Type	**Protection Period**	**Premium**	**Death Benefit**	**Cash Value**
Term	Temporary, often renewable	Increases with each renewal as scheduled and guaranteed	Level, increasing, or decreasing	None
Return of premium term	Temporary	Increases with each renewal as scheduled and guaranteed	Level	None, but premium is returned at expiration and may be returned upon surrender
Reentry term	Temporary	Fixed for 1 or more years, then increases based on one of two schedules, depending on insured's health	Usually level	None

Type	Protection Period	Premium	Death Benefit	Cash Value
Whole life Single-premium whole life Modified whole life Ordinary whole life Limited-pay whole life	Permanent	Fixed and level One up-front premium payment Level for first few years, then higher guaranteed premium Premiums payable for life Premiums payable for specified period	Fixed and level	Guaranteed and scheduled
Endowment life insurance	Specified maturity date	Payable until maturity date	Fixed and level	Guaranteed and scheduled; equals death benefit at maturity
Current assumption whole life Low-premium design High-premium design	Permanent	Can vary, depending on insurer's mortality, expense, interest experience; guaranteed maximum Premiums redetermined periodically Relatively high premium, which may cease	Fixed and level Insured may decrease death benefit to avoid premium increase Fixed and level	Guaranteed and scheduled plus accumulation fund High premiums speed cash buildup, possibly to a point where no premium is required
Variable life	Permanent	Fixed and level	Depends on cash value; guaranteed minimum but may lapse if cash value drops too low	Not guaranteed; depends on investment performance; policyowner chooses investment account(s)
Universal life	Permanent	Flexible after first year	Level or increasing	Guaranteed minimum interest rate plus excess interest; insurer chooses investments; partial withdrawals permitted

Type	Protection Period	Premium	Death Benefit	Cash Value
Indexed universal life	Permanent	Flexible after first year	Level or increasing	Depends on an external index, such as S&P 500
Variable universal life	Permanent	Flexible after first year	Depends on cash value	Depends on investment performance; policyowner chooses investment account(s); no guarantees; partial withdrawals permitted

CHAPTER REVIEW

Key Terms and Concepts

human life value
yearly renewable term insurance
cash value life insurance
net amount at risk
modified whole life insurance
return of premium term insurance
renewability
reentry term insurance
convertibility
decreasing term insurance
increasing term insurance
whole life insurance
participating policy
nonparticipating policy

ordinary life insurance
limited-payment life insurance
single-premium whole life policy
vanishing premium
endowment life insurance
current assumption whole life
    insurance
variable life insurance
universal life insurance
variable universal life insurance
indexed universal life insurance (IUL)
joint-life policy
survivorship (second-to-die) policy
probationary period

Review Questions

Review questions are based on the learning objectives in this chapter. Thus, an [3] at the end of a question means that the question is based on learning objective 3. If there are multiple objectives, they are all listed.

1. Your client, Marty Gibson, is an auto mechanic in his 30s with two children in elementary school. His wife, Cindy, works part-time as a cosmetologist. The Gibsons struggle to meet daily expenses and to pay off the substantial medical bills resulting from Cindy's serious case of Lyme disease. Why, Marty asks, should he incur an additional expense by buying life insurance? Explain to Marty the purposes of life insurance, and identify the type of life insurance that would provide the most protection at the lowest cost. [1]

2. What are the differences between yearly renewable term insurance and level-premium cash value insurance? (Ignore the loading to cover expenses, profit, and contingencies.) [2]

3. Your financial planning client requires some life insurance to meet various needs. You begin to discuss some products available to meet those needs. How would you answer the following questions?
   a. What is the difference between term and whole life insurance regarding
      (1) the permanence of death protection provided? [3]
      (2) the benefit promises if the client lives until the end of the policy? [3]
      (3) the use of premiums to save money as well as provide death protection? [3]
   b. If your client buys a 10-year term policy, can the client extend it at the end of 10 years to satisfy new needs? [3]
   c. If the client buys a 10-year term policy and then needs a more permanent form of insurance, can the client switch the policy to whole life insurance? [3]
   d. Is there a policy that would pay the balance of the client's mortgage when the client dies to relieve the family of that burden? [3]
   e. What is the difference between ordinary life and limited-payment whole life in terms of the
      (1) permanence of protection? [3]
      (2) amount of premium outlay per year? [3]
      (3) relative size of their cash values? [3]

4. Your financial planning client says she's heard that some life insurance policies pay dividends and others don't. Why is this the case? [4]

5. Your financial planning client tells you that his grandmother bought a $50,000 20-year endowment policy 30 years ago that paid her even though she didn't die. The client asks you:
   a. How does that type of policy work? [3]
   b. Would it make sense for him to buy one today? [3]

6. How does each of the following relate to variable life insurance?
    a. guarantees with respect to interest rate or minimum cash value [4]
    b. SEC requirements [4]
    c. investment choices [4]
    d. insurance charges [4]
    e. linkage of death benefits with investment performance [4]
    f. policy cash values [4]
    g. contents of the prospectus [4]

7. How does each of the following relate to universal life insurance?
    a. flexible premiums [4]
    b. prefunding [4]
    c. withdrawal [4]
    d. target premium amount [4]
    e. death benefit type
      (1) level death benefit design [4]
      (2) increasing death benefit design [4]
    f. effect of policy loans [4]
    g. internal funds flow [4]

8. How can a universal life policy with a level death benefit design take on an array of different forms (depending on how much premium is paid to the insurance company), ranging from being comparable to yearly renewable term insurance to being comparable to limited-payment whole life insurance? [4]

9. Why does a universal life policy with
    a. the level death benefit design not always provide a level death benefit? [4]
    b. the increasing death benefit design not always provide an increasing death benefit? [4]

10. How is variable universal life insurance similar to each of the following?
    a. variable life insurance [4]
    b. universal life insurance [4]
    c. indexed universal life insurance [4]

11. Martha and Steve Miller have a handicapped daughter who is dependent on them for daily care. If either Martha or Steve dies, they would need to hire somebody to help with their daughter's care. This creates a specific need for funding. If both of them die, the daughter would be institutionalized and would need a much larger amount of funding to pay for her care. How might a survivorship or second-to-die life insurance policy meet the Millers' needs? [4]

12.   Your client, Jane, took your advice and purchased individual life insurance
      when she was a self-employed management consultant. She has just taken
      a full-time position with a large corporation that provides a benefits package,
      including group life insurance. Jane asks you to explain how group life
      insurance works so she can decide whether to make any changes in her
      individual life insurance program. What should you tell her about the following
      features of a typical group life insurance plan covering employees?
      a. employee eligibility requirements [5]
      b. evidence of insurability requirements [5]
      c. benefit amounts [5]
      d. convertibility [5]
      e. supplemental benefits [5]

Learning Objectives

An understanding of the material in this chapter should enable the student to

1. Describe the policy declarations page.

2. Explain the effect of standard policy provisions laws, and describe the provisions that are required in life insurance policies.

3. Indicate the provisions that are prohibited in life insurance policies.

4. Identify the optional provisions found in many life insurance policies.

5. Describe three types of riders that policyowners often add to their life insurance policies.

6. Describe the effect of state requirements for policy filing and approval.

Financial planners must understand the provisions and riders in life insurance contracts in order to help their clients make use of available contract privileges.

There are two parties to the life insurance contract: the insurance company and the policyowner. The applicant is normally, but not necessarily, the owner and the person whose life is the subject matter of the insurance contract. The person whose life is insured is not a party to the contract unless he or she is also the policyowner. Additionally, the beneficiary is not a party to the contract unless he or she is also the policyowner. Often there are additional interested parties involved in a life insurance policy and one of these parties can also serve two roles.

beneficiary

- The *insured* is the person whose life is insured. Life insurance benefits are paid if that person dies.

- The *policyowner* is the party that owns the insurance contract and that generally has the right to change, renew, or cancel a policy. In individual insurance, this also includes the right to name the beneficiary. Often, the policyowner of an individual policy is also the insured. However, a parent may be the policyowner of a life insurance policy that covers a child, and one spouse may own a policy that insures the other spouse. In group insurance, the policyowner is an entity, such as an employer, and each insured typically can name his or her own beneficiary.

- The *beneficiary* or *beneficiaries* are the person or persons who are entitled to receive death benefits. In individual life insurance, the policyowner may also be the beneficiary. Of course, the insured who dies cannot also be the beneficiary. However, the insured's estate may be the beneficiary.

Most insurance contracts, including life insurance contracts, are contracts of adhesion, which means that the policyowner and the insurer do not negotiate the contract's terms.

By completing an application, the applicant is making an offer, thereby taking the first step to create an enforceable contract. The applicant specifies what type and amount of insurance he or she would like to purchase. Based on this information, the insurer will decide whether it wishes to accept the offer and issue an insurance contract.

The applicant cannot negotiate the wording of the insurance policy. Because the prospective policyowner can only accept or reject the contract the insurer issues, the contract of adhesion rule provides that all ambiguities in the contract of insurance will be resolved in favor of the policyowner and against the insurer. This rule of law is not entirely fair to insurance companies, because there are substantial limitations on the insurer's freedom to draft the insurance contract as it wishes. Insurers are required by law to include many types of provisions and in some cases are required to use or not use certain words.

Many states require that the contracts avoid complex sentences and arcane legal terminology in order to make the contracts easier for the consumer to read and understand. Although laudable, this requirement for simplicity can conflict with an insurer's need to be certain that a contract will be interpreted exactly as the drafter intended. Over many years, courts have given certain legal terms specific meanings on which lawyers have come to rely in drafting contracts. This legalese may be difficult for the uninitiated to understand, but it offers a degree of consistency that lawyers prefer. The United States trend to simplify insurance contracts by using less technical language involves a trade-off that will continue to evolve as the courts interpret the simplified language of modern contracts.

State law controls a variety of required, prohibited, and optional life insurance policy provisions. Before an insurer can sell a policy in a particular jurisdiction, it must file the policy provisions with that state's insurance department for approval.

POLICY DECLARATIONS PAGE

Although the placement of the provisions may vary from company to company, the declarations pages of most life insurance contracts are quite similar and have the following information:

- the name of the insurance company
- details specific to the policy. These include the name of the insured and the name of the policyowner, the identity of the beneficiary or beneficiaries, the face amount of the policy, the policy number, and the policy date or issue date (some declarations pages include both dates).
- a general description of the type of insurance the policy contract provides. For example, the declarations page of a traditional participating whole life policy might read as follows:

  Whole Life—Level Face Amount Plan. Insurance payable upon death. Premiums payable for life. Policy participates in dividends. Dividends, dividend credits, and policy loans may be used to help pay premiums.

- a statement about the policy's free-look provision. This is a provision that gives the policyowner a period of time, usually 10 days, to return the policy after acceptance. The following is an example of such a provision:

  You may return this contract no later than 10 days after you receive it. All you have to do is take it or mail it to one of our offices or to the agent who sold it to you. The contract will be canceled from the start, and a full premium refund will be made promptly.

- the insurer's promise to pay. This is the core of the insurance contract. A typical statement reads as follows:

> We will pay the beneficiary the sum insured under this contract promptly if we receive due proof that the insured died while this policy was in force. We make this promise subject to all of the provisions of this contract.

The remainder of the required and optional provisions are not usually included on the declarations page.

REQUIRED PROVISIONS

standard policy provisions laws

The *standard policy provisions laws* of the various states require that life and health insurance policies include certain provisions but allow the insurance companies to select the actual wording as long as it is at least as favorable to the policyowner as the statutory language. However, companies must submit the wording to the state insurance department and have it approved. Some of the standard policy provisions laws do not apply to certain types of insurance contracts, such as term, single-premium, and nonparticipating policies. Insurers are not required to include standard policy provisions in policies to which they would not apply. For example, because term policies do not build a cash value, these policies are not required to include nonforfeiture provisions that would preclude loss of the cash value when a policy terminates.

Grace Period

grace period

The *grace period* provision grants the policyowner an additional period of time to pay any premium after it has become due. Although the provision is now required by law, acceptance of a slightly overdue premium was a common practice among insurers before laws compelled insurers to include the provision in the contract. Because of the provision, a policy that would have lapsed for nonpayment of premiums continues in force during the grace period. The premium remains due, however, and if the insured dies during the grace period, the insurer may deduct the overdue premium from the death benefit.

Although insurers could charge interest on the unpaid premium for the late period, they do not typically do so. If the insured survives the grace period but the premium remains unpaid, the policy lapses. However, cash value life insurance policies are required to include a nonforfeiture provision that may enable the policyowner to continue coverage.

As with all renewal premiums, the policyowner has no obligation to pay the premium for the insurance coverage provided under the grace period clause. Thus, it might be said that the policyowner has received "free" insurance during that time, but only when the insured does not die within the grace period.

The standard length of the grace period is 30 or 31 days in fixed-premium policies. In flexible-premium policies, such as universal life insurance, a grace period of 60 or 61 days is common. If the last day of the grace period falls on a nonbusiness day, the period is usually extended to the next business day.

Late Remittance Offers

late remittance offer It is important to distinguish between the grace period rules and a *late remittance offer* that the insurer makes after the grace period expires. They are not the same, and there is usually no provision in the contract concerning a late remittance offer. Such an offer is made solely at the insurer's option. It is not a right of the policyowner or an obligation of the insurer included in the insurance contract under the requirements of the law.

Some insurers will make a late remittance offer to a policyowner whose coverage has lapsed after the grace period has expired. This is not an extension of the grace period, and coverage is not continued as a result of the offer. A late remittance offer is intended to encourage the policyowner to reinstate the policy; it does not extend coverage. The inducement from the insurer is that coverage may be reinstated without providing evidence of insurability. The policyowner accepts a late remittance offer by paying the premiums due and meeting any other conditions the insurer imposes. The most common condition is that the insured must be alive when the late premium payment is made.

EXAMPLE
Hope misplaced her life insurance bill, and as a result she failed to pay her term life insurance premium when it was due. Because Hope's life insurance policy has a 30-day grace period, as required by law, she can continue her life insurance coverage without interruption as long as she pays the premium before the 30-day period has run out. If she dies during that period and has not paid the premium before she dies, the insurance company will deduct the overdue premium from the death benefit.

Suppose Hope is also strapped for cash and does not pay her term life insurance premium within the grace period. Hope's coverage would normally lapse at this point, and the insurer would have no further obligation to Hope. However, in an effort to retain Hope as a customer, the insurer may voluntarily make a late remittance offer to accept her payment belatedly without requiring evidence of insurability. Of course, Hope must be alive when the premium is paid.

Policy Loans

policy loans

The law requires that a life insurance contract permit policy loans if the policy generates a cash value. *Policy loans* give the policyowner access to the cash value that accumulates inside the policy without having to terminate the policy. The policyowner merely requests a loan, and the life insurer lends the funds confidentially. The loan provisions in the policy specify what portion of the cash value is available for loans and how interest will be determined. In most policies, over 90 percent of the cash value is available for loans—some policies may restrict the amount of loanable funds to 90 percent of the cash value—and the policyowner may borrow any portion of the available cash value. Policyowners indicate in their request the amount desired. A policyowner can take more than one policy loan as long as the aggregate amount of all outstanding loans plus accrued interest does not exceed the policy's cash value available for loan.

Policy loans accrue interest on the borrowed funds. When purchasing a policy, the policyowner usually selects one of two different approaches to setting the policy loan interest. The policy will contain either (1) a fixed rate as specified in the policy or (2) a variable interest tied by formula to some specified index. One variable approach is to use Moody's composite yield on seasoned corporate bonds or some other index that is regularly published in the financial press, such as *The Wall Street Journal* or *The Journal of Commerce*. Another index may be the interest rate being credited to the cash value plus a specified spread.

Policy Loan Provision

- No credit questions asked
- Policyowner may borrow up to 90 percent to 100 percent of cash value
- Technically, insurer can delay lending for up to 6 months
- Fixed or variable interest rates charged
- Unpaid interest added to the loan balance
- No repayment schedule or requirement
- Indebtedness repaid when policy is surrendered or matures as a claim
- May include automatic premium loan feature

The policyowner has the option of paying loan interest in cash or adding the unpaid interest charge to the balance of the outstanding loan. The policyowner can choose to pay any part of the loan and interest he or she desires; there is no repayment schedule or repayment requirement. If the policyowner makes any repayments, they are totally at his or her discretion as to both timing and amount. If the policyowner does not pay the policy loan and accrued interest in cash, the life insurer recovers the outstanding balance of the loan and accrued interest either from (1) the death benefits if the insured dies or (2) the cash surrender value if the policy terminates. In fact, the policy automatically terminates if the policy loan balance plus unpaid interest ever exceeds the policy's cash value.

automatic premium loan option

Some whole life policies give policyowners an *automatic premium loan option*. When the policyowner selects the automatic premium loan option, any delinquent premium is automatically paid by a new policy loan. This keeps the policy in force as long as there is adequate cash value to cover each delinquent premium. The policy, however, will terminate if the cash value is exhausted.

A policy loan has negative consequences on benefits and can reduce the amount credited to the cash value and/or the level of policyowner dividends. The death benefit payable to the beneficiary is reduced by the full amount of policy loans outstanding and accrued interest under most types of policies. Policy loans also reduce nonforfeiture benefits.

direct recognition

Policy loans result in the life insurer's release of funds that would otherwise have been invested. If investment return on the insurer's portfolio exceeds the rate paid on the policy loan, the insurer experiences a reduction in earnings. Therefore, the insurance company usually takes steps to offset such loan-induced losses to preserve an approximate equity between policyowners who leave their cash values invested and those who preclude the insurer from reaping the higher yield. In traditional participating whole life policies, policyowner dividends were not affected by policy loans, but most participating whole life policies sold today use *direct recognition* to reduce dividends on policies with outstanding loans. With direct recognition, dividends are reduced to reflect the amount of the cash value encumbered by the policyholder's loan. The more the policyowner borrows, the less the policy earns. This not only adjusts for the differential in earnings but also discourages policy loans. Policy loans can be more expensive than they appear.

State statutes allow life insurers to delay lending funds for up to 6 months after they are requested. Although insurers almost never exercise this right, it serves as a form of emergency protection in case policyowners' demands for loans accelerate to the point that the insurer must liquidate other assets at significant losses to satisfy the loan demands.

EXAMPLE

Helen and Gary desperately need a new car. They do not qualify for an auto loan because they already have substantial medical bills due to their children's illnesses, as well as credit card debt. Helen remembers the cash value in her whole life insurance policy and wonders whether that might provide a way to finance the car.

The law requires that Helen's policy include a loan provision that Helen can access with no credit-check requirements. The insurer will charge interest on the loan, but Helen will not be required to make payments on a fixed schedule. Although these features seem attractive, Helen must also realize that the loan reduces not only the current and future cash value of the policy but also the benefits payable upon her death. If she does not repay the loan and the amount she has borrowed plus unpaid interest exceeds the policy's cash value, her life insurance policy will terminate. In short, Helen should probably think twice about taking steps that could impair the important protection her life insurance policy provides. Insurance on Helen's life might be especially important if her children have medical problems and the family is financially strapped.

Incontestable Clause

incontestable clause
     The life insurance policy provision called the *incontestable clause* prohibits the insurer from disputing or *contesting* the validity of the policy after it has been in force for a

certain time period. State laws differ as to the form of the clause prescribed, but no state permits a clause that would make the policy contestable for more than 2 years.

The following is a sample incontestable clause:

> Except for nonpayment of premium, we will not contest this contract after it has been in force during the lifetime of the insured for 2 years from the date of issue.

After a policy has been in effect for the period of time the incontestable clause prescribes (normally 2 years), the insurance company cannot have the policy declared invalid. The courts have generally recognized three exceptions to this rule, deeming that the incontestable clause does not apply because the contract was void from its inception. These three exceptions are as follows:

- The applicant had no insurable interest at the inception of the policy.
- The policy was purchased with the intent to murder the insured.
- There was a fraudulent impersonation of the insured by another person (for example, for purposes of taking the medical exam).

The incontestable clause exists due to a belief that a life insurance policy's beneficiaries should not suffer for mistakes made in the application. The beneficiary is protected by the incontestable clause even if the error in the application is based on a fraudulent or material misrepresentation by the applicant or by a failure to meet a condition precedent to the existence of the contract.

After the insured's death, it would be extremely difficult, if not impossible, for the beneficiary to disprove the allegations of the insurance company that there were irregularities in procuring the policy. If there were no time limit on the insurance company's right to question the accuracy of the information in the application, there would be no certainty during the life of the policy that the benefits promised would be payable at maturity. Honest policyowners need assurance that at the insured's death, the beneficiary will receive a check. The incontestable clause gives policyowners that assurance. The clause is based on the theory that, after the insurance company has had a reasonable opportunity to investigate the circumstances surrounding issuance of a life insurance policy, it should thereafter relinquish the right to question the validity of the contract.

The typical incontestable clause makes the policy incontestable after it has been in force during the lifetime of the insured for a specified period.

This means that if the insured dies during that period, the policy never becomes incontestable. As a result, if the insured dies a few days before the contestable period expires, the policy remains contestable by the insurer even if it is not notified of the death claim until after that period expires.

EXAMPLE

Donald took out a life insurance policy on February 16, 2005, naming his wife as the beneficiary. The policy contained the typical 2-year incontestable clause. Donald dies on February 9, 2007. Knowing that Donald had lied about his health on the insurance application, Donald's wife waits until February 17, 2007, before filing the claim. Will she collect the proceeds? Probably not. Because the life insurance policy was not in force for 2 years *during Donald's lifetime,* it never became incontestable.

Other points are worth noting. First, refusal to pay a claim because of nonpayment of the premium is not governed by the incontestable clause. Second, some insurers specify in their incontestable clause that it does not apply to disability benefits or accidental death benefits that may be provided as part of the life insurance policy. Third, the policy provision relating to misstatement of the insured's age or gender takes precedence over the incontestable clause.

Divisible Surplus

divisible surplus

An insurer's *divisible surplus* is that portion of an insurer's surplus declared as a dividend to be distributed to the owners of participating policies. The divisible surplus provision appears only in participating policies, because it would not be relevant in a nonparticipating policy. The provision requires the insurer to determine and apportion any divisible surplus among the insurer's participating policies at frequent intervals.

A typical divisible surplus provision reads as follows:

While this policy is in force, except as extended term insurance, it is entitled to the share, if any, of the divisible surplus that we shall annually determine and apportion to it. This share is payable as a dividend on the policy anniversary.

In addition, some contracts provide that payment of a dividend is conditional on payment of all premiums then due. The provision in most contracts notes that a dividend is not likely to be paid before the second anniversary of the policy.

Dividend Options

dividend options

The application for a participating life insurance policy asks the policyowner to select from among several of the following *dividend options*, thus indicating how any available dividends are to be used:

fifth dividend
option

- *cash option.* The policyowner receives dividends in cash.

- *reduction of premiums.* The policyowner simply subtracts the amount of the dividend from the premium currently due and remits the difference to the insurer.

- *accumulation at interest.* The dividends are maintained in the equivalent of an interest-bearing savings account for the policyowner. A minimum rate of interest is guaranteed, but a higher rate of interest may be credited if conditions warrant. The accumulated dividends may be withdrawn at any time. If not withdrawn, they are added to the death proceeds or to the nonforfeiture value if the policy is surrendered.

- *purchase of paid-up additions.* Each dividend is used to purchase, on an attained age basis, a small amount of additional, fully paid-up whole life insurance. The purchase is made at rates that do not contain a loading for expenses, and no evidence of insurability is required.

- *purchase of term insurance.* Some insurers that offer what is sometimes called a *fifth dividend option* use a portion of the dividend to buy 1-year term insurance equal to the policy's then cash value, with the remainder used to buy paid-up additions or to accumulate at interest. Other insurers use the entire fifth dividend option to buy 1-year term insurance. In either case, the term insurance is purchased on the basis of the insured's attained age.

Other dividend options that may be available enable the policyowner to shorten the premium-paying period or to cause the policy to mature as an endowment. In the former case, the policy becomes paid up when its reserve, together with the reserve value of the dividends, equals the net single premium for a paid-up policy that the company could issue to the insured on the basis of his or her attained age. In the latter case, the insurer pays the face amount of the policy when the reserve, together with the reserve value of the dividends, equals the policy's face amount.

Entire Contract

One might ordinarily expect that any written contract includes all the provisions that bind the parties to the contract. Sometimes, however, a contract refers to the terms of another document without actually including that document in the contract. This practice is known as incorporation by reference. An insurance contract, for example, might refer to provisions in the insurer's procedural rules or manuals without including these external documents in the contract itself. Any changes to the insurer's rules or manuals might then result in a change to the contract. Entire contract statutes prohibit this practice and ensure that the policyowner receives all documents that constitute the contract, and they also protect the policyowner against changes in the contract after the contract has been issued.

entire contract provision
States deal with this matter in different ways. Some require that the policy include an *entire contract provision,* which states that the policy (including any attached riders) and the application constitute the entire contract.

A sample provision is as follows:

> This policy and any attached copy of an application form the entire contract. We assume that all statements in an application are made to the best of the knowledge and belief of the person who makes them; in the absence of fraud, they are deemed to be representations and not warranties. We rely on those statements when we issue the contract. We will not use any statement, unless made in an application, to try to void the contract, to contest a change, or to deny a claim.

Other states simply provide that the policy, riders, and application are the entire contract, regardless of what the policy might say. Either approach makes it clear that an agent's oral statements are not a part of the policy. This supports the parol evidence rule.

Reinstatement

reinstatement provisions

Reinstatement provisions allow a policyowner to reacquire coverage under a policy that has lapsed. This right is valuable to both the policyowner and the insurer. The various state laws and the insurance contracts impose certain requirements that the policyowner must meet to reinstate the policy.

A typical reinstatement clause is as follows:

> This policy may be reinstated within 3 years after the due date of the first unpaid premium, unless the policy has been surrendered for its cash value. The conditions for reinstatement are that (1) the insured must provide evidence of insurability satisfactory to us, (2) the policyowner must pay all overdue premiums plus interest at 6 percent per year, and (3) the policyowner must repay or reinstate any policy loan outstanding when the policy lapsed, plus interest.

Generally, insurers do not permit reinstatement of a policy that has been surrendered for its cash value, and this prohibition is often included in the contractual definition of the requirements for reinstatement.

EXAMPLE

When Rick completed a life insurance application, he mentioned his high blood pressure, controlled with medication, but disclosed no other health problems. Soon after the policy was issued, a colonoscopy, given as part of a routine physical, led Rick to discover that he had colon cancer, which had apparently been developing over the past few years. Rick was surprised at this discovery.

misrepresentation

A *representation* is a statement in an insurance application that is substantially true to the best of the applicant's knowledge and belief. A false representation of a material fact is a *misrepresentation*. It now seems clear that Rick already had colon cancer when he completed the insurance application. He did not know it, however, and he represented his condition to the best of his knowledge. This was not a case of misrepresentation. Rick did not warrant that he had no health problems. The *entire contract provision* makes it clear that the insurer cannot use Rick's statement to void Rick's policy unless the insurer can prove that Rick was aware of his condition and intentionally misrepresented it.

Rick also had another life insurance policy that lapsed 2 years earlier when he failed to pay a renewal premium. Given his serious health problem, Rick decides to reinstate the policy since he is still within the 3-year reinstatement period. The *reinstatement provision* in Rick's policy requires that he provide satisfactory evidence of insurability. Because he may no longer be able to do so, Rick might not be able to reinstate this policy.

Misstatement of Age or Gender

misstatement of age or gender clause

The insured's age and gender are fundamentally important factors in the evaluation of the risk the life insurance company assumes. Rather than voiding the contract based on any misrepresentation of any insured's age or gender, the practice is to adjust the policy's premium or benefits to reflect the truth. The incontestable clause does not preclude adjustments in the policy's premiums based on a misstatement of age or gender; the incontestable clause only precludes disputes over the policy's validity. Also, because a *misstatement of age or gender clause* (often called a misstatement of age or sex clause) appears in the contract, an adjustment based on that clause would be an attempt to enforce the terms of the contract, not to invalidate it.

The question of how to settle a misstatement of age discovered during the insured's lifetime depends on (1) policy language, (2) insurance company practices, and (3) whether the age was overstated or understated. If an individual life insurance policy does not stipulate in detail how the lifetime adjustment is to be made, then the insurer's established procedure will dictate. Most cases involve understatement of age, and insurers are inclined to require the payment of additional funds to make up for the past underpayments. A few insurers would instead adjust the death penalty downward. In the rarer cases where the age was overstated, there is still a preference to adjust the premium by providing a refund, but some insurers may instead increase the death benefit. With group insurance, the insurer pays the benefit and adjusts the premium with the employer.

A sample provision in an individual life insurance policy might read as follows:

> If the age or gender of the insured has been misstated, we will adjust all benefits payable under this policy to that which the premium paid would have purchased at the correct age or gender.

EXAMPLE
Jim took out an individual life insurance policy for an annual premium of $1,300. He stated that his age was 41, when in fact he was 46. When he died, the company discovered the misstatement of age. The insurer will pay an amount less than the face of the policy to Jim's beneficiary-specifically, the amount of insurance that an annual premium of $1,300 would have bought for a 46-year-old male.

However, if the insured is still alive when the age or gender misrepresentation is discovered, the parties typically will agree to adjust the premium to the correct amount, rather than to adjust the benefits. An adjustment of premium is also the method used in group life insurance, whether the insured is living or not. A majority of states require a provision that adjusts for misstatements of age, but fewer than half require a provision that applies to misstatement of gender.

Nonforfeiture Provisions

A nonforfeiture provision in a cash value life insurance policy provides alternative ways in which the policy's cash value can be taken out or utilized if the contract is terminated during the insured's lifetime.

When insurers developed the concept of insurance policies with level premiums over the insured's lifetime, the goal was to make life insurance more affordable to older policyowners. In the early years of the policy, the level premium was higher than necessary to cover the mortality costs. The excess portion of the premium in the policy's early years, and the interest it earned, built up a cash reserve that was used to help pay the mortality costs at older ages, which then exceeded the attained age level premium. A question soon arose over who was entitled to those reserves when a policy lapsed in the early years. Initially, the policyowner forfeited these reserves, but this was clearly inequitable, and the practice was soon modified. Today, that question has been answered by nonforfeiture laws.

The states require that insurers assure policyowners who voluntarily terminate their contracts a fair return of the value, if any, built up inside their policies. These laws are known as *nonforfeiture laws*. As late as the middle of the 19th century, insurance policies in the United States made no provision for refunds of excess premiums paid on cash value policies upon the policyowner's termination of the policy before maturity. However, in 1861, Massachusetts recognized that the policyowner had a right to at least a portion of those funds, and the first nonforfeiture law was enacted in that state. By 1948, that idea had evolved into the Standard Nonforfeiture Law, and subsequent versions of the law have become effective in all jurisdictions. Policies issued since that date have provided at least the minimum surrender values prescribed by the version of the law in effect when the policy was issued.

The NAIC Standard Nonforfeiture Law for Life Insurance, which has been widely adopted by the states, does not require specific surrender values. The only requirement is that surrender values are at least as large as those that would be produced by the method the law prescribes. In addition, each policy must contain a statement of the method used to determine the surrender values and benefits provided under the policy at durations not specifically shown.

nonforfeiture options
After a traditional cash value policy has been in effect for a minimum number of years—usually 3—the insurer must use part of the reserved excess premium to create a guaranteed minimum cash value. Nonforfeiture laws require that a life insurance policy must make certain options available regarding how a policyowner can use the policy's cash value. The insurer must make that value available to the policyowner in cash as a surrender value and must give the policyowner a choice of two other *nonforfeiture options:* (1) paid-up insurance at a reduced death benefit amount or (2) extended term insurance for the net face amount of the policy. These options are illustrated below. If the policyowner has not elected a nonforfeiture option, the policy must provide that one of these two options will be effective automatically if the policy lapses. Under most plans and issue ages, nonforfeiture values are made available by the end of the second policy year.

Figure 9-1
Face Value with Various Nonforfeiture Options

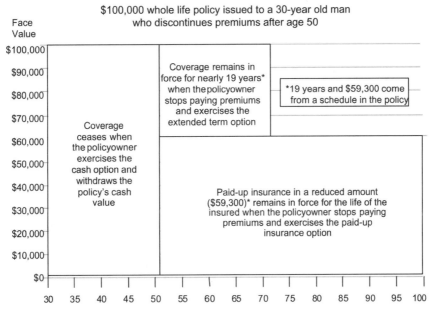

$100,000 whole life policy issued to a 30-year old man
who discontinues premiums after age 50

Face Value

Coverage remains in force for nearly 19 years* when the policyowner stops paying premiums and exercises the extended term option

*19 years and $59,300 come from a schedule in the policy

Coverage ceases when the policyowner exercises the cash option and withdraws the policy's cash value

Paid-up insurance in a reduced amount ($59,300)* remains in force for the life of the insured when the policyowner stops paying premiums and exercises the paid-up insurance option

Cash Surrender Option

Under the cash surrender option the policyowner may surrender the policy at any time for its cash value, minus any policy indebtedness, plus accumulated dividends. In that event, the protection terminates and the company has no further obligation under the policy. As with policy loans, a 6-month delay clause applies to cash surrenders, although it is extremely rare for an insurer to exercise this right to delay payment.

Reduced Paid-up Insurance Option

The reduced paid-up insurance option permits the policyowner to take a reduced amount of paid-up whole life insurance, payable upon the same conditions as the original policy. The amount of the paid-up insurance is the amount that can be purchased at the insured's attained age with the net cash value (cash value, minus any policy indebtedness, plus any dividend accumulations) applied as a net single premium. Note that the paid-up insurance is purchased at net rates, meaning they contain no expense loading, which may constitute a sizable savings to the policyowner.

Extended Term Insurance Option

The extended term option provides term insurance in an amount equal to the original face amount of the policy, increased by any dividend additions or deposits, and decreased by any policy indebtedness. The length of the term is that which can be purchased at the insured's attained age with the net cash value applied as a single premium. If the policyowner fails to elect an option within a specified period after default of premiums, this option usually goes into effect automatically.

Annuity Alternative

Surrender values may also be used to purchase an annuity for retirement income. If the life insurance policy does not specifically give the policyowner the right to take the cash value in the form of a life income, purchased at net rates, the insurer will usually grant the privilege on request. Some policyowners purchase ordinary life insurance to protect their families during the child-raising period with the objective of eventually using the cash values for their own retirements. The cash value, supplemented by Social Security benefits, private retirement plan benefits, and income from other savings, could provide a policyowner with an adequate retirement income.

Nonforfeiture Options

- Surrender the policy for cash.
- Buy a reduced amount of paid-up permanent insurance.
- Buy the same amount of extended term insurance.
- If the insurer allows, purchase an annuity.

The nonforfeiture options in universal and variable life insurance policies have special characteristics that differentiate them from traditional whole life policies. First, variable life policies provide no guarantees as to the minimum nonforfeiture values available under any of the three options. Second, universal and variable life policies in force under the reduced paid-up option or the extended term option may require further adjustments of the coverage if investment earnings or interest crediting rates fall significantly.

EXAMPLE

Following the death of her invalid husband, Rob, who was the beneficiary on her life insurance policy, Becky no longer wishes to pay premiums on the whole life insurance policy she has carried for the past 20 years. She contacts her financial advisor, who reminds her that her policy has accumulated a substantial cash value and that she will not need to forfeit this value because she has several options. Becky must select one of them:

- She can surrender the policy and take the money in cash.

- Rather than taking cash, Becky can probably arrange to surrender the policy and take the money as an annuity (periodic payments for the remainder of her life).

- She can stop paying premiums but keep permanent insurance in force with a reduced face limit.

- She can stop paying premiums and keep the full face limit of the insurance in force as term insurance that will expire at the end of a specified term.

If Becky chooses to keep life insurance in force, she will need to change the beneficiary to, perhaps, her children, her grandchildren, and/or a charity.

Settlement Options

settlement options

Settlement options provide alternative ways of taking the death proceeds of a life insurance policy. The policyowner can select the settlement option, and the beneficiary may or may not be permitted to change it following the insured's death. Sometimes it is desirable to give the beneficiary some flexibility, but in other cases the policyowner may wish to keep the beneficiary from using proceeds unwisely. If the policyowner has not selected a settlement option, then the selection is made by the beneficiary upon the insured's death. The standard policy provisions of the various states require that a life insurance policy include certain settlement option tables for the policy's death proceeds if the *settlement options* include installment payments or annuities. These tables must show the minimum amounts of the applicable installment or annuity payments.

The types of settlement options, other than the lump-sum or cash option, most commonly found in life insurance policies are the interest option, the fixed-period option, the fixed-amount option, and one or more life income options.

Interest Option

Under the interest option, the insurer temporarily retains the death proceeds and pays only the interest to the beneficiary periodically, such as monthly or annually. The policy guarantees a minimum rate of interest, although insurers frequently pay a higher rate if investment earnings warrant it. The company pays the death proceeds at a specified later date at the request of the beneficiary, or on the occurrence of a specified event, such as the beneficiary's death.

Fixed-Period Option

Under the fixed-period option, the insurer makes installment payments consisting of both the death proceeds and interest to the beneficiary over a specified period of time, such as 10 years following the insured's death. Again, there is a guaranteed minimum interest rate. If the insurer pays a higher rate than the guaranteed rate, the amount of the installment payment increases accordingly.

Fixed-Amount Option

The insurance company makes level periodic installments of a specified amount to the beneficiary under the fixed-amount option. The payments consist of a portion of the death proceeds and interest earnings, and they continue for as long as the funds that the insurer holds last. Unlike the fixed-period option, excess interest earnings under the fixed-amount option do not increase the size of the periodic payments. Rather, they extend the length of time during which the payments will continue.

Life Income Options

Under a life income option, the policy's death proceeds are used as a single premium to purchase an annuity for the beneficiary. Various forms of annuities may be available, but the most common ones are a straight life income, a life income with a period certain, a life income with some type of refund feature, and a joint-and-survivor life income.

EXAMPLE

As the beneficiary on his late wife Edna's $250,000 life insurance policy, Bob is entitled to receive benefits. He consults his financial advisor to decide how best to handle these policy proceeds; the advisor informs Bob that he can take the money in cash but that the policy also provides these other options:

- *interest option.* Bob can let the insurer keep the $250,000 for now, in effect lending it to the insurer, and have the insurer pay him interest at a rate no lower than the rate specified in the policy. Bob can receive the death proceeds later or arrange for them to be payable at his death.

- *fixed-period option.* Rather than taking the money as a lump sum, Bob can take it in payments over a fixed period of, say, 10 years, with the insurer paying at least a guaranteed minimum rate of interest.

- *fixed-amount option.* Instead of taking the money over a fixed period of time, Bob can choose to receive periodic payments in a fixed amount for as long as the money lasts, with the insurer paying at least a minimum guaranteed rate of interest. (The money will last longer if interest rates are higher.)

- *life income option.* Bob can use the $250,000 death proceeds to provide him with an income for as long as he lives.

Bob's choice among these options will depend on a variety of factors, such as his age, his health, other income sources, and his interest in leaving an estate for his heirs or other beneficiaries.

PROHIBITED PROVISIONS

Although state laws are not uniform, most states prohibit insurers from including certain provisions in their policies. For various reasons, courts or state legislatures have determined that these prohibited contract provisions violate public policy. There are five generally prohibited provisions:

- The insurance producer, who is the agent of the insurance company, may not be made the agent of the policyowner for purposes of filling out the application for insurance. If the producer were acting as an agent of the applicant, then any concealment or misrepresentation in the application would be binding on the policyowner even if the producer was aware of the true facts

- Nonpayment of a loan cannot cause a forfeiture. The state laws generally provide that as long as the cash value of the insurance policy exceeds the total indebtedness on the policy, the policyowner's failure to repay the loan or to pay interest on the loan may not cause a forfeiture of the policy.

- An insurer cannot promise something on the declarations of the policy and take it away in the "fine print." This is spelled out in laws called less value statutes because the insurer is prohibited from providing a settlement option that is of less value than the death benefit of the policy.

- The insurance laws of several states prohibit use of a policy provision that gives the policyowner too short a time in which to bring suit against the insurer. Statutes of limitations place an upper limit on the time during which legal action can be brought for alleged wrongs of various types, but sometimes parties to a contract can agree on a shorter period. Some states allow insurers to include a shorter time period in their policies; the permissible periods vary from 1 to 6 years. Other states do not allow insurers to reduce the time specified in the statute of limitations. These laws protect the interests of the insurers and the public. Insurers are protected because the laws allow them to impose shorter limitation periods than otherwise permitted in the state. This benefits insurers because it requires plaintiffs to sue while information relevant to the insurance policy is still easy to obtain. The public is protected because the statutes do not allow insurers to shorten the limitation period so much that the public does not have sufficient time to determine whether a lawsuit is worthwhile.

- Although not directly related to a policy provision, state laws typically include a limitation concerning the effective date of the policy as specified on its declarations page. The limitation involves the practice of *backdating*, which means to issue the policy as if it had been purchased when the insured was younger. The consumer advantage is that the policyowner pays lower periodic premiums for the policy because the premium is based on the younger age. The consumer disadvantage is that the policyowner must pay the premium for the backdated period, during which no coverage existed. Statutes generally limit backdating to no more than 6 months.

OPTIONAL PROVISIONS

Numerous other provisions are neither required nor prohibited. Some of these relate to the beneficiary designation.

Beneficiary Provisions

Several provisions in a life insurance policy relate to designating the beneficiary who receives policy proceeds upon the death of the insured. The first reference to the beneficiary appears on the policy's declarations page. There, the policyowner names the primary, and perhaps a contingent, beneficiary.

primary beneficiary

The *primary beneficiary* is the person or organization that is to receive the proceeds if he, she, or it survives the insured. The policyowner may name more than one person or organization, with a percentage of the proceeds allocated to each. The policyowner may even name the insured's estate as the primary beneficiary, although naming the estate is usually unwise because it subjects the proceeds to transfer taxes and costs that can be avoided. Naming the estate as primary beneficiary may be acceptable, however, if the proceeds are small and/or designed to pay only last-illness costs, funeral expenses, estate debts, and taxes. Among the parties often named as primary beneficiaries are the policyowner (if different from the insured), the heirs of the insured, other donee beneficiaries (such as charitable organizations), and creditors of the insured.

contingent beneficiary

A *contingent beneficiary* is a person or organization that is to receive the proceeds only if the primary beneficiary predeceases the insured or loses entitlement to any of the proceeds for some other reason (for example, if a charity named as primary beneficiary goes out of existence or if the primary beneficiary murders the insured). If the primary beneficiary is eligible to receive the policy proceeds, that extinguishes the rights of the contingent beneficiary.

contingent payee

When life insurance proceeds are payable under a settlement option (other than the lump-sum cash option), a contingent payee, as contrasted with a contingent beneficiary, may have a claim on the proceeds. For example, assume that the primary beneficiary begins receiving the policy's death proceeds under the life income with a 10-year period certain. If he or she dies after, say, 7 years, the remaining 3 years of income would go to the named *contingent payee*, who may or may not be the same person or organization as the contingent beneficiary.

Whether primary or contingent, beneficiaries may be named specifically (for example, "my wife, Anne J. Kirby") or as a class (for example, "the children born to my wife, Anne J. Kirby, and me"). In either case, the policyowner should make every effort to be clear in spelling out who is to receive the proceeds. For example, simply designating "my husband" is unclear, as the policyowner may have more than one husband during her lifetime. Or simply designating "my grandchildren" is unclear because the policyowner's children may have adopted children, children from different marriages, or children from outside the state of marriage. Class designations present many possible problems in identifying who is a member of the class; therefore, insurers often limit the use of such designations.

EXAMPLE

Dolores named her husband to receive the death proceeds of her life insurance policy. She also specified that if her husband predeceased her, the proceeds would be paid to her brother. The settlement option Dolores selected was the 10-year fixed period option. Dolores dies in 2005, her husband in 2004, and her brother in 2008.

Who gets what:

- The husband is the *primary beneficiary* but he gets nothing because Dolores outlived him.

- The brother is the *contingent beneficiary* but became the primary beneficiary when the husband died. The brother gets 3 years of death benefit payments.

- The brother's heirs or his estate are the *contingent payees* and get 7 years of death benefit payments.

The declarations page of the life insurance policy, in addition to identifying the beneficiaries, may also state whether they are named revocably or irrevocably. If the policyowner names a revocable beneficiary , the policyowner can change the designation at any time prior to the insured's death without the beneficiary's consent. If the policyowner names the beneficiary irrevocably, however, the policyowner must obtain the beneficiary's consent before making a beneficiary change. Usually, an irrevocable beneficiary designation also requires that the beneficiary consent to the policyowner's exercise of other ownership rights in the policy, such as surrendering it for cash or borrowing against the cash value.

Provisions in the body of the life insurance policy concerning the beneficiaries are not standardized. Policies often contain provisions that specify the conditions under which a policyowner can change the beneficiary designation. Also, the policy may describe the right of the beneficiary to name or change the contingent payee, who will receive the remaining proceeds if the beneficiary dies before all the death proceeds have been distributed. The policy can also specify that, if the beneficiary predeceases the insured and if no contingent beneficiary has been named or is alive when the insured dies, the proceeds will be paid to the policyowner or to his or her estate.

Other Optional Provisions

Life insurance policies usually contain optional provisions concerning suicide, ownership, assignment, and changes of plan. Increasingly, they also include a provision concerning accelerated benefits. Common optional provisions are as follows:

suicide provision

ownership provision

assignment provision

plan change provision

accelerated benefits provision

- *suicide provision.* An insurer can elect to cover suicide from the day it issues the policy. However, this is unusual, and most insurance contracts do not provide coverage for a death by suicide within the first 1 or 2 years after the policy issue date. If the policy does not contain a suicide exclusion provision, then the policy covers a death by suicide, and the death benefit is payable to the beneficiary regardless of when the suicide occurs.

The following is a typical insurance contract suicide provision:

Suicide of the insured, while sane or insane, within 2 years of the issue date, is not covered by this policy. In that event, we will pay only the premiums paid to us, minus any unpaid policy loans.

- *ownership provision.* Ordinarily, the insured is the applicant and owner of the policy. The ownership provision in the life insurance contract describes the rights of the owner. The typical ownership provision stipulates that the owner of the policy is the insured unless the application states otherwise. The provision usually states that the policyowner may change the beneficiary, assign the policy to another party, and exercise other ownership rights. If the provision describes these powers, it will also define how such powers are to be exercised in order to be recognized by the insurance company.

- *assignment provision.* In contract law, assignment is the act of transferring a property right. As with most contracts and most interests in property, the policyowner has, as a matter of law, the right to assign some or all of his or her rights to another person or an entity. The right to assign an ownership interest in a life insurance policy exists even without an assignment provision in the contract and even if the assignee has no insurable interest. However, most contracts include an assignment clause that clearly specifies the conditions under which the policyowner may make an assignment. The purpose of these conditions in a life insurance contract is to make the insurer aware of the assignment to eliminate future disputes. A sample assignment clause might provide the following:

  > You may assign this policy if we agree. We will not be bound by an assignment unless it has been received by us in writing at our home office. Your rights and the rights of any other person referred to in this policy will be subject to the assignment. We assume no responsibility for the validity of an assignment. An absolute assignment will be the same as a change of ownership to the assignee.

- *plan change provision.* This provision acknowledges that the parties may agree to change the terms of the contract. A sample plan change provision might read as follows:

  > Subject to our rules at the time of a change, you may change this policy to another plan of insurance, you may add riders to this policy, or you may make other changes if we agree.

- *accelerated benefits provision.* Some insurers have added a provision that permits the policyowner to withdraw a portion of death benefits under certain circumstances. These accelerated benefits or living benefits provisions state that if the insured becomes terminally ill, then the policyowner may withdraw a portion of the policy's death benefit. According to the NAIC Accelerated Benefits Model Regulation, the condition that permits the payment of the accelerated benefits must be a medical condition that drastically limits the insured's life span expectation (for example, to 2 years or less). The regulation also lists several examples of a qualifying medical condition: acute coronary artery disease, a permanent neurological deficit resulting from a cerebral vascular accident, end-stage renal failure, AIDS, or other such medical condition as the commissioner may approve. To qualify as accelerated benefits, the lifetime payments must reduce the death benefit otherwise payable under the contract. About half of the states have adopted regulations or statutes similar to the NAIC model.

RIDERS

Common riders that policyowners can add to their life insurance policies include those concerning accidental death benefits, the guaranteed purchase option (also known as the guaranteed insurability option), and waiver of premium in the event of the insured's disability. With the possible exception of an accidental death benefit rider, these riders are typically available only at the time a new policy is purchased.

Accidental Death Benefits

add accidental death benefits

Insurers *add accidental death benefits* to some contracts in the form of a rider, or amendment, to the policy. The rider is also known as the *double indemnity provision* because it usually doubles the standard death benefit if the insured dies accidentally.

In the absence of a specific definition of accidental death, accident means an unintentional event that is sudden and unexpected. An accidental death is one that is caused by an accident. This statement seems quite clear, but it is not always easy to apply. An insured may have been mortally injured in an accident, then died from a disease. The accidental death benefit is payable only if the accident was the cause of death. If the insured is in an auto accident but dies from a heart attack, the accidental death benefit is payable only if the accident is proven to have triggered the heart attack.

The standard practice of including a time limit in the accidental death benefit provision somewhat mitigates the problems caused by cases in which there may be more than one cause of death. In the most common type of provision, the death must occur within 90 days of the accident said to have caused the injury.

These basic definitions preclude coverage for any death that is the natural and probable result of a voluntary act. An unchallenged principle of law is that people are presumed to expect and intend the probable or foreseeable consequences of their actions. This concept is sometimes described by the term *assumption* of risk. If an individual plays Russian roulette, jumps off buildings, or runs with the bulls in Pamplona, Spain, his or her death as a result of those activities cannot be described as accidental.

A sample accidental death benefit provision is as follows:

> We will pay this benefit to the beneficiary when we have proof that the Insured's death was the result, directly and apart from any other cause, of accidental bodily injury, and that death occurred within 1 year after that injury and while this rider was in effect.

Some life insurance agents routinely include an accidental death benefit rider in virtually every life insurance contract they sell. The cost of the rider is small because a small percentage of all deaths occur as a result of accident. On the other hand, there is little reason for an individual to carry more insurance for an accidental death than for any other type of death, except perhaps as an appeal to the policyowner's gambling instinct.

Guaranteed Purchase Option

guaranteed purchase (insurability) option
Another popular policy provision is the *guaranteed purchase option,* also called the *guaranteed insurability option.* This provision helps policyowners protect themselves against the possibility that the insured might become uninsurable. Under the typical guaranteed purchase option, the policyowner may purchase the right to acquire additional insurance in specified amounts at specified times or ages. Typically, this provision allows additional purchases every 3 years, upon marriage, and after the birth of a child, provided the events occur before the insured reaches a specified maximum age, often age 45. This right to purchase additional insurance can be valuable because the insured need not provide evidence of insurability to exercise the option. Another benefit of the guaranteed purchase option is that the new coverage is usually not subject to a new suicide provision or a new incontestable clause.

There is a ceiling on the maximum amount of insurance available under the guaranteed purchase option and a maximum age at which the option may be exercised. Once the insured passes an age or event that triggers the right to purchase additional insurance and does not exercise the option, that option lapses, but future options are not affected.

Guaranteed Purchase Option
• Allows purchase of specified additional amounts of insurance at specified times and ages
• No need to show evidence of insurability
• No new suicide exclusion or incontestable period
• Options not cumulative

Waiver of Premium

waiver-of-premium rider

A *waiver-of-premium rider* in the event of the insured's disability is another commonly available rider. According to a typical waiver-of-premium rider, if the insured becomes totally disabled as defined in the rider or policy, the insurance company will waive payment of premiums on the policy during the continuance of the insured's disability.

The disability waiver of premium has some limitations. For example, the insurer will not grant the waiver if the insured's disability begins after a specified age. In addition, the provision usually will not waive premiums if the disability is self-inflicted or the result of an act of war.

In any contract, it is important to pay close attention to the wording of the waiver-of-premium rider. For example, these riders usually require that the disability last for at least 6 months before premiums will be waived. Some riders specify that only premiums due thereafter will be waived, while others provide that the insurer will refund premiums that were paid during the 6 months, as well as waive premiums due thereafter.

Care should be taken to examine the definition of total disability used in the rider. A common definition of total disability is the inability to perform the essential duties of the insured's own job or of any job for which he or she is suited by reason of training or experience. However, some riders contain definitions that are less liberal to the insured.

POLICY FILING AND APPROVAL

A policy may not be issued or delivered in a state until the policy language has been approved by the state insurance department. In some states, the insurer can assume that the policy has been approved if it has not been advised otherwise within a fixed period of time, such as 30 days, after submission to the state insurance department. In other states, the insurer may not issue the policy until it has received notice of approval from the department.

If an insurer issues a policy that the insurance department has not approved, the policyowner can seek a refund of premiums (because the contract is voidable) or seek enforcement of the policy. If there is a suit, the courts will enforce the unapproved contract against the insurer on behalf of the beneficiary. If the unapproved policy does not include a provision that would have been required for approval, the courts will treat the policy as if it did contain such a provision. Furthermore, if a required provision is more favorable to the policyowner than one actually included in the contract, the courts will treat the contract as if it included the more favorable provision. The insurer that violates the laws requiring filing of the policy and approval of its provisions by the state is also subject to fines or other penalties, such as revocation of the insurer's right to do business in that state.

CHAPTER REVIEW

Key Terms and Concepts

beneficiary
standard policy provisions laws
grace period
late remittance offer
policy loans
automatic premium loan option
direct recognition
incontestable clause
divisible surplus
dividend options
fifth dividend option
entire contract provision
reinstatement provisions
misrepresentation
misstatement of age or gender clause

nonforfeiture options
settlement options
primary beneficiary
contingent beneficiary
contingent payee
suicide provision
ownership provision
assignment provision
plan change provision
accelerated benefits provision
add accidental death benefits
guaranteed purchase (insurability)
   option
waiver-of-premium rider

Review Questions

Review questions are based on the learning objectives in this chapter. Thus, a [3] at the end of a question means that the question is based on learning objective 3. If there are multiple objectives, they are all listed.

1.   What information appears on the declarations page of most life insurance policies? [1]

2.   Do state standard policy provision laws require all life insurance policies to have identical wording? [2]

3.   Frank purchased a participating whole life policy many years ago, and over time, several questions have arisen regarding his coverage. Which policy provision should be reviewed to clarify each of the following questions, and what would that provision typically suggest?
     a. Frank just discovered that his premium was due 2 weeks ago. Is the coverage still in force? [2]
     b. Frank is facing a liquidity crunch. He needs some cash but does not want to exercise a nonforfeiture option. Can his life insurance policy help? [2]
     c. When Frank purchased the policy, he lied about his health history. Will this prevent his beneficiary from collecting the face amount of the coverage? [2]
     d. Frank has been using his dividends to help pay premiums. Are other options available to him? [2]

4.   When Sara purchased her $500,000 life insurance policy five years ago, she indicated in the application that she was 45 years old. She has been paying an annual premium of $480. When she died this year, the insurance company learned that she was actually 50 years old when she completed the application and should have been paying a premium of $720. What amount, if any, is due to the beneficiary on Sara's policy. [2]

5.   Describe the two options, in addition to cash surrender values, that life insurance companies are required to provide under the Standard Nonforfeiture Law. [2]

6.   Describe the settlement options that life insurance policies most commonly provide. [2]

7.   What types of provisions do not appear in life insurance policies because they are legally prohibited in most states? [3]

8.   What is the difference between
     a. a primary beneficiary and a contingent beneficiary? [4]
     b. a continent beneficiary and a contingent payee? [4]
     c. the rights of the policyowner when the beneficiary is named revocably versus irrevocably? [4]

9.   Bill purchased a $500,000 whole life policy 10 years ago. When his marriage and business recently failed, he became distraught and committed suicide. Would Bill's beneficiary receive the $500,000 policy death benefit? [4]

10. Harold has the AIDS virus. His prognosis is not good, and he has exhausted all of his financial resources on treatment. His life insurance contract includes an accelerated benefits (living benefits) provision. How can this provision benefit Harold? [4]

11. When Rita purchased a whole life policy, she added a double indemnity rider and was surprised to learn that adding the rider did not double her premium. Rita believes that she "slipped one past" the insurance company. Is Rita overlooking something? [5]

12. How does a guaranteed purchase option protect an insured policyowner who may need additional life insurance protection in the future? [5]

13. Susan, a 61-year-old widow, has decided to stop paying the premiums on the $250,000 whole life policy that named her late husband as primary beneficiary and her three grandchildren as contingent beneficiaries. It's not that she needs the money she would receive by cashing in the policy, because Susan was the beneficiary of a substantial life insurance policy on her late husband, but rather that she no longer sees a need for life insurance. Susan had thought of taking the life insurance policy's cash surrender value and using it to set up a trust to fund her grandchildren's college expenses, but she has just learned that the policy also provides other nonforfeiture options. What factors should Susan consider in evaluating her other options? [2]

14. Antea Insurance Company developed a new life insurance policy with some innovative features, then conducted a national advertising program on morning television. Robin and Diane saw the TV commercials, contacted Antea, and purchased these life insurance policies. Neither they nor the insurance company representative handling their application realized that these new policies had not yet been approved by insurance regulators in the state where Robin and Diane lived. What rights do Robin and Diane have? [6]

Learning Objectives

An understanding of the material in this chapter should enable the student to

1. Explain the key approaches to determining the amount and type of life insurance appropriate for a client.

2. Explain the key methods for measuring the cost of life insurance.

3. Describe the issues involved in illustrations and in the replacement of a life insurance policy.

4. Explain the reason for and methods used to treat substandard risks.

5. Explain the regulation, ethics, taxation, and planning considerations of policy viatication and life settlements.

6. List and explain business uses of life insurance.

7. Describe the taxation of life insurance benefits and premiums.

8. Describe the uses of life insurance in estate planning.

Clients who are considering the purchase of life insurance must make a variety of decisions with which the financial planner should be able to provide assistance. Proper guidance for financial planners regarding making life insurance recommendations, considering the implications of those recommendations, assumes that clients are serious about their financial futures and that the financial services professional has established enough trust for the information-gathering and analysis process to proceed. Problem solving in this arena requires complete and accurate information about the client's finances. In addition, the planner must understand the client's goals or objectives and priorities. The planner must gather this information before making any recommendations.

Key considerations include determining the appropriate amount and type of life insurance to provide future income for persons who depend on the insured for support, weighing estate and gift taxation strategies, and understanding tax rules to appreciate the role life insurance can play in estate planning.

LIFE INSURANCE PLANNING

Life insurance planning includes determining both how much and what type of insurance is needed. The first of these tasks is usually based on an analysis of the client's needs. The second task begins with a decision between temporary and permanent coverage and proceeds to the selection of a particular type of policy.

Appropriate Amount of Life Insurance

Many different approaches are used to determine the amount of life insurance appropriate for any given client. Some of these approaches include the following:

- *human life value approach*—an approach that measures a person's human life value in terms of the present value of that portion of estimated future earnings which, if he or she lives long enough to achieve all the earnings, will be used to support dependents.
- *multiple of income approach*—a simplistic approach that determines life insurance needs based on the client's current annual income
- *financial needs analysis approach*—an approach that determines how much life insurance is needed to provide a principal sum that will be liquidated to meet survivors' lump-sum and ongoing income needs
- *capital needs analysis approach*—an approach that determines how much life insurance is needed to provide a principal sum adequate to fund survivors' needs while preserving the principal

Multiple of Income Approach

How much life insurance should a client purchase? Some financial journalists recommend that people have life insurance and liquid assets in amounts ranging from five to seven times their annual income. This simplistic approach is easy to explain, and it requires few computations. However, this approach ignores specific information about assets the client has already accumulated and any external sources of funds, such as trusts and inheritances. This approach can err in either direction—that is, it can either overinsure or underinsure the client.

More sophisticated approaches to determine needs are described below. These approaches translate the client's needs into estimated costs, then evaluate assets and existing coverage to determine how much of the funding is already in place. Any deficit between the intended goals and objectives and current financial sources is usually a candidate for additional coverage.

Financial Needs Analysis Approach

financial needs analysis
The financial needs analysis approach is commonly used to determine how much life insurance a person should carry. The financial needs analysis approach identifies survivors' immediate cash needs and ongoing income needs and assumes life insurance policy proceeds will be liquidated to meet them. The financial needs approach begins with estimates of the family's financial needs if the client were to die today. The two main categories of financial needs are lump-sum needs at death and ongoing income needs.

Lump-Sum Needs at Death. This lump-sum need category deals with needs at the client's death that require immediate cash. These needs include

- final illness costs that insurance does not cover
- repayment of outstanding debt, perhaps including a home mortgage loan that becomes due and payable upon death
- estate taxes, if applicable
- probate and attorney's expenses
- funeral, burial, or cremation expenses, as applicable
- operational expenses to cover survivors' ongoing, short-term household expenses, such as mortgage or rental payments, utility bills, property insurance premiums, property taxes, food, clothing, transportation costs, and the costs of childcare or education
- an emergency fund

Although it does not address specific identifiable expenses, an emergency fund provides an important safety net or shock absorber that will help survivors cope with unexpected costs that could otherwise devastate a family in a strained financial situation. An emergency fund enables the family to meet emergencies without sacrificing funds it needs for ongoing expenses. Determining emergency fund needs should take into consideration any liquid or near-liquid assets that survivors could use to cover emergencies. Money market accounts and listed securities that can readily be liquidated can reduce the extent to which life insurance proceeds are needed to address emergencies.

Children's educational needs might be considered either a lump-sum need or an ongoing income need, depending on the specific situation. Both the amount of the need and the timing of the need depend on the number of children and their ages, the costs associated with the educational institutions they will attend, the number of years for which educational support is to be provided, and the portion of educational expenses the parents intend to fund. Some families' educational goals include a public school education, while others intend to pay for private preparatory schools and an Ivy League college education that includes a graduate degree.

Ongoing Income Needs. In addition to a lump-sum cash need to manage specific, immediate expenses, most clients' surviving dependent family members have ongoing financial needs that require a flow of income that continues until the dependents can support themselves. Some families can reasonably expect all members to become self-sufficient soon after the head of the household dies. In other families, such an expectation is so unrealistic that a client who does not provide for the survivors' support is guilty of neglect. Some surviving spouses never become self-sufficient, and there often is no intent that the surviving spouse support himself or herself.

Many families wish to prefund survivors' income needs at least until the youngest child becomes self-sufficient, typically when the child completes his or her formal education. Some families have special-needs children who never will become self-sufficient; these children can have ongoing income needs that extend for many years beyond the death of both parents.

Survivors' ongoing income needs are commonly analyzed in four categories:

- readjustment income for the period immediately after death
- adjusted income starting after the initial transition period, continuing until the youngest child becomes self-sufficient
- income for the surviving spouse, if any, after the children have become self-sufficient and before the spouse is again eligible for Social Security benefits
- surviving spouse's income after renewed eligibility for Social Security benefits and initial eligibility for private pension benefits

Because the purpose of life insurance is to fund the previously unfunded portion of these objectives, all existing resources that can provide part or all of these needs should be considered. For simplicity and efficiency, most planners suggest using a percentage of the insured's current income as the target income level, rather than calculating a composite of each separate anticipated need. That the survivors will need about 70 percent of the predeath income to carry on after the insured's death is often assumed, but a higher or lower percentage may be more accurate depending on a particular family's circumstances.

Social Security benefits are the most commonly available source of income for survivors. Other potential sources of income include employer-provided plan benefits—such as deferred compensation, group life insurance, and any qualified plan participation funds that are not forfeited or terminated upon the employee's death—and perhaps the surviving spouse's earnings.

At this point in the process, a financial planner has helped the client determine the income necessary to provide a readjustment income and meet each of the other income objectives. The planner has also identified existing benefits or sources of income and estimated their anticipated levels. The gap between needs and income for each period is a deficit that must be addressed. The next step in the planning process is to determine the present value of all future additional income needs. The total income need is simply the sum of the present values of income deficiencies for each separate period. This entire process is illustrated in the following example.

Case Example of Financial Needs Analysis

A simplified case situation will illustrate the use of the financial needs analysis method to determine the amount of life insurance needed.

Ted and Maggie Stringer are a young married couple with a 4-year-old daughter, Laura. Ted, aged 31, is a bank employee earning $48,000 per year. Maggie, aged 27, is an administrative assistant earning $28,000 per year.

Following a series of conversations with Ted and Maggie, their financial planner has summarized their objectives or needs in today's dollars, if Ted were to die today, as follows:

- Lump-sum needs at Ted's death

– Funeral expenses	$5,000
– Estate clearance (attorney's fees, debts, taxes, etc.)	5,000
– Mortgage retirement	140,000
– Emergency fund	15,000
– Education fund for Laura	100,000
Total	$265,000

- Income needs after Ted's death

– Readjustment period income for 1 year	$ 65,000
– Dependency period income per year for 17 years	$ 50,000
– Life income per year for Maggie after Laura finishes college	$ 40,000

The financial planner next gathers information about the sources of funds Ted and Maggie already have for meeting the above needs. Their principal resources are as follows:

• Group term life insurance on Ted provided by the bank (face amount)	$96,000
• Individual universal life insurance on Ted (face amount)	$50,000
• Investments (mutual funds and 401(k) plan, market value)	$20,000
• Checking account (average balance)	$ 2,045
• Social Security lump-sum death benefit	$ 255
• Social Security survivorship benefits (Laura until she finishes high school at age 18)	$ 6,000/yr.
• Maggie's income	$28,000/yr.
• Maggie's combined Social Security retirement benefits and miscellaneous income at age 65 for life	$15,000/yr.

Notice that no specific amount of Social Security survivorship benefits is identified for Maggie. Instead, Maggie's earned income is assumed to cause her to forfeit these benefits as long as she is working. A further assumption for purposes of simplicity is that Maggie's income is shown as an annual average, rather than an estimated amount year by year. Also, notice that a combined income of $15,000 per year is assumed for Maggie beginning at her projected retirement age of 65 from her pension, Social Security benefits, and miscellaneous sources. Maggie will not be eligible for full Social Security retirement benefits until age 67.

As noted earlier, the family needs a total of $265,000 as a lump sum at Ted's death. The present sources of funds with which to meet this need total only $166,000, consisting of group insurance of $96,000, individual insurance of $50,000, and investments of $20,000. The checking account and Social Security lump-sum death benefit are ignored. Thus, a first need is for an additional $99,000 to meet the lump-sum needs (the difference between $265,000 and $166,000).

A time line, as shown in the figure below, is useful for planning the income needs of the family. The uppermost set of lines shows the desired income level of $65,000 for the readjustment period of 1 year, followed by $50,000 per year for the dependency period of 17 years until Laura is 22, followed by $40,000 per year as the life income Maggie needs, beginning when she is 45 and continuing for the rest of her life. Below the lines are the various sources of income available to provide the desired income, consisting of a Social Security benefit for Laura until age 18, an unspecified mix of Maggie's Social Security benefits and earned income until age 65, and Maggie's pension, Social Security benefits, and miscellaneous income beginning at age 65 and continuing for life.

Figure 10-1
The Stringers' Income Needs and Available Resources

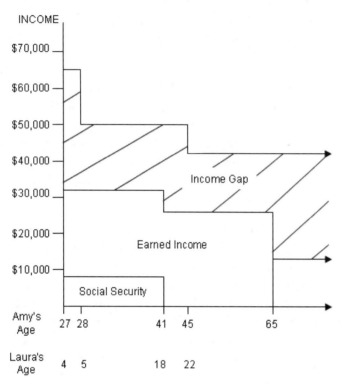

The period of time in this graph, spanning 40 years or more, can be broken into five component segments. For each segment, the figure shows the income gap, or the difference between the desired or needed income during each period and the available income at that time. This gap amounts to

$65,000 minus $34,000, or $31,000, for 1 year; followed by
$50,000 minus $34,000, or $16,000, for 13 years; followed by
$50,000 minus $28,000, or $22,000, for 4 years; followed by
$40,000 minus $28,000, or $12,000, for 20 years; followed by
$40,000 minus $15,000, or $25,000, for the rest of Maggie's life

The amount of life insurance proceeds needed today to fill the income gap is the present value of each of the separate gaps. If discounted at an assumed after-tax rate of return of 6 percent per year, the total present value can be found with a calculator's net present value (NPV) function, or by using an Excel® spreadsheet as shown in the following table. As indicated, assuming Maggie lives to age 85, the net present value is approximately $294,000.

Table 10-1 Maggie's Needs Analysis Calculation upon Ted's Death				
1				
2	A	B	C	D	E
3	**Maggie's Age**	**Year**	**Need**	**Income**	**Gap**
4	27	1	$65,000	$34,000	$31,000
5	28	2	$50,000	$34,000	$16,000
6	29	3	$50,000	$34,000	$16,000
7	30	4	$50,000	$34.00	$16,000
8	31	5	$50,000	$34,000	$16,000
9	32	6	$50,000	$34,000	$16,000
10	33	7	$50,000	$34,000	$16,000
11	34	8	$50,000	$34,000	$16,000
12	35	9	$50,000	$34,000	$16,000
13	36	10	$50,000	$34,000	$16,000
14	37	11	$50,000	$34,000	$16,000
15	38	12	$50,000	$34,000	$16,000
16	39	13	$50,000	$34,000	$16,000
17	40	14	$50,000	$34,000	$16,000
18	41	15	$50,000	$28,000	$22,000
19	42	16	$50,000	$28,000	$22,000
20	43	17	$50,000	$28,000	$22,000
21	44	18	$50,000	$28,000	$22,000
22	45	19	$40,000	$28,000	$12,000
23	46	20	$40,000	$28,000	$12,000
24	47	21	$40,000	$28,000	$12,000
25	48	22	$40,000	$28,000	$12,000
26	49	23	$40,000	$28,000	$12,000
27	50	24	$40,000	$28,000	$12,000
28	51	25	$40,000	$28,000	$12,000
29	52	26	$40,000	$28,000	$12,000
30	52	27	$40,000	$28,000	$12,000
31	54	28	$40,000	$28,000	$12,000
32	55	29	$40,000	$28,000	$12,000
33	56	30	$40,000	$28,000	$12,000
34	57	31	$40,000	$28,000	$12,000
35	58	32	$40,000	$28,000	$12,000
36	59	33	$40,000	$28,000	$12,000
37	60	34	$40,000	$28,000	$12,000
38	61	35	$40,000	$28,000	$12,000
39	62	36	$40,000	$28,000	$12,000
40	63	37	$40,000	$28,000	$12,000
41	64	38	$40,000	$28,000	$12,000
42	65	39	$40,000	$15,000	$25,000
43	66	40	$40,000	$15,000	$25,000
44	67	41	$40,000	$15,000	$25,000
45	68	42	$40,000	$15,000	$25,000

	A	B	C	D	E
	Table (Continued)				
	Maggie's Age	**Year**	**Need**	**Income**	**Gap**
46	69	43	$40,000	$15,000	$25,000
47	70	44	$40,000	$15,000	$25,000
48	71	45	$40,000	$15,000	$25,000
49	72	46	$40,000	$15,000	$25,000
50	73	47	$40,000	$15,000	$25,000
51	74	48	$40,000	$15,000	$25,000
52	75	49	$40,000	$15,000	$25,000
53	76	50	$40,000	$15,000	$25,000
54	77	51	$40,000	$15,000	$25,000
55	78	52	$40,000	$15,000	$25,000
56	79	53	$40,000	$15,000	$25,000
57	80	54	$40,000	$15,000	$25,000
58	81	55	$40,000	$15,000	$25,000
59	82	56	$40,000	$15,000	$25,000
60	83	57	$40,000	$15,000	$25,000
61	84	58	$40,000	$15,000	$25,000
62	85	59	$40,000	$15,000	$25,000
63	86	60	$40,000	$15,000	$25,000
64	87	61	$40,000	$15,000	$25,000
65	88	62	$40,000	$15,000	$25,000
66	89	63	$40,000	$15,000	$25,000
67	90	64	$40,000	$15,000	$25,000
68	91	65	$40,000	$15,000	$25,000
69	92	66	$40,000	$15,000	$25,000
70	93	67	$40,000	$15,000	$25,000
71	94	68	$40,000	$15,000	$25,000
72	95	69	$40,000	$15,000	$25,000
73	96	70	$40,000	$15,000	$25,000
74	97	71	$40,000	$15,000	$25,000
75	98	72	$40,000	$15,000	$25,000
76	99	73	$40,000	$15,000	$25,000
77	100	74	$40,000	$15,000	$25,000

Basis of NPV calculation:

PV to age 85: $293,552.86 = E4 + NPV (0.06, (E5:E62))

PV to age 100: $301,823.13 = E4 + NPV (0.06, (E5:E77))

On this basis, the total additional life insurance that should be written on Ted's life is $99,000 for the lump-sum needs plus $294,000 for the survivors' income needs, or approximately $393,000. (A similar approach can be used to determine the amount of life insurance Maggie should have.) There are two difficulties with this amount of insurance:

- Maggie could outlive this income because an assumption was made that she would live for no more than 20 years, or to age 85, after she retired. As shown in the last line of the table, the insurance needs would increase by approximately $8,000 if a life expectancy of age 100 were used. Note how little additional insurance is required to guarantee income for a longer time if that time is far in the future.

- No inflationary increase in the annual income is provided to the survivors.

As to the first point, additional life insurance on Ted at a later date, if he does not die soon, or electing a life income settlement option for a portion of the life insurance death proceeds could provide a partial solution. Alternatively, at some point, Maggie could use the then-unliquidated capital sum from the life insurance proceeds to purchase an annuity. Annuities can provide an income for Maggie's lifetime. Then, too, if all else fails, perhaps Laura will be able and willing to help support her mother in Maggie's later years.

As for the latter point regarding inflation, several approaches can alleviate the problem. For example, Social Security benefits for survivors and retirees are automatically adjusted annually for inflation. Also, a rate of interest lower than 6 percent could be used to calculate the present value of the income. The lower discount rate would create a larger amount of additional life insurance needed but would allow for modest periodic increases in the income it provides. Alternatively, Ted's life insurance could be increased later by including a guaranteed insurability option in the policy and/or by using policy dividends to buy additional insurance. Another possible approach is for Ted to buy a variable, variable universal, or indexed universal type of life insurance policy. The premium cost, however, may be prohibitive at this point in light of the Stringers' present income and the large amount of life insurance needed.

The financial needs analysis approach requires estimating the beneficiary's likely age at death and planning for the capital sum to be fully liquidated at that date or later. The problem is that the person might live longer than the plan has projected. Any liquidation planning predicated on the beneficiary's death at an early age runs a high probability of using all the proceeds while the beneficiary still needs them.

Capital Needs Analysis Approach

capital needs analysis

The *capital needs analysis* approach resembles the financial needs analysis approach, just described. However, the capital needs analysis approach relies on meeting income needs with the earnings on a principal sum, without liquidating that sum. Capital is therefore retained rather than being consumed.

The capital needs analysis approach is most appropriate for a client who wishes not only to meet the financial needs of surviving family members but also to leave an estate that will pass to other heirs or be used for charitable purposes. It should be pointed out that preserving capital requires a substantially larger capital sum than consuming it during the survivor's remaining lifetime. When used to assess a client's life insurance needs, the capital needs approach is therefore likely to require a much higher insurance recommendation than the financial needs analysis approach, as shown in the following example.

EXAMPLE

Based on a 5 percent interest assumption, a $1 million capital sum will provide a monthly income of approximately $10,500 for 120 months under the financial needs approach. At the end of that period, the capital sum will have been liquidated.

Under the capital needs analysis approach, a $1 million capital sum will provide a monthly income of about $4,200, but the income will continue indefinitely. To provide a monthly income of $10,500 would require a capital sum of about $2.5 million.

If capital is to be retained, determination of the amount of life insurance to own based on needs proceeds as in the capital liquidation approach. Then a personal balance sheet of the client is prepared. All the liabilities, immediate cash needs, and all assets that do not produce income, such as the residence, are subtracted from the total assets. The remainder is the client's present income-producing capital. The last step is to compute the amount of additional capital needed to achieve the desired income objective net of all other income sources.

The amount of additional capital needed to meet the desired objective is found by dividing the amount of additional income needed by the applicable interest rate that represents the after-tax rate of investment return anticipated on the capital sum. For example, if $100,000 per year of additional income is desired, and the capital sum generating those income payments can realistically be expected to generate a 5 percent return after taxes, a $2 million fund is sufficient ($100,000 ÷ .05 = $2,000,000).

Obviously, the lower the after-tax investment return rate, the higher the capital fund needed to produce the same amount of income. Similarly, higher marginal tax rates will lower the after-tax return rate and increase the size of the fund needed to generate the income.

The choice between capital liquidation and capital retention is not necessarily an all-or-nothing decision. A planner may use a combination of the two approaches, liquidating some of the client's capital and retaining some of it, as a compromise approach to filling the gap between the income needs of the survivors and the other available sources of income.

Life Insurance and Retirement Needs

The income needs described to this point do not include the client's own retirement. The client who survives long enough to retire does not need to fund most of the needs previously described, but he or she then has a need for retirement income. Financial planners need to consider this contingency in determining not only the amount but also the type of insurance a family head should carry. Term insurance can provide the necessary capital sum upon the death of the insured, but permanent insurance can not only meet the family's capital needs upon the client's death but also build a cash value that helps address the postretirement needs of the insured and his or her spouse.

Appropriate Type of Life Insurance

After the needed amount of life insurance has been determined, there is a question about the most appropriate types of life insurance for the client. Too often, this question resolves itself into the highly debatable and often emotional matter of term life insurance versus permanent life insurance. In fact, each of these types has a legitimate role in life insurance planning for a client.

The characteristics of term insurance include

- the temporary nature of the coverage; even the right to renew or to convert expires at some point
- the low initial premium cost per $1,000 of coverage because of the absence of a savings element
- the rising premium, at an increasing rate, at the expiration of each period of coverage
- the inclusion in the rate of a margin to offset the adverse selection among term insurance purchasers
- the availability of a death benefit that can be level over time, decreasing, or, in some cases, increasing

Needs that term insurance can and should meet are encountered daily. One of the most obvious is to hedge a loan. A term policy in the amount of the loan payable to the lender protects the lender against possible loss, and it relieves the insured's estate of the burden of repaying the loan if the insured dies. An entrepreneur who has invested heavily in a speculative business venture should protect his or her family and estate by obtaining term insurance in the amount of the investment. A parent with young children is likely to need more insurance while the children are dependent than he or she will need when they are grown and self-sufficient. Additional insurance during the child-raising period can be provided through term insurance, frequently through decreasing term insurance superimposed on a permanent policy.

On the other hand, some needs for life insurance are permanent, or at least extend over a very long period. For example, a client's need for funds with which to provide a life income for his or her spouse may not arise in the next few years, or even by age 65. A wealthy client's need for a substantial sum with which to meet estate clearance costs at his or her death or that of his or her spouse is likely to extend for several decades. Permanent life insurance is an efficient, cost-effective way to partially fill these needs.

Nonetheless, some financial planners find virtually no legitimate role for permanent insurance in life insurance planning for their clients. They argue that clients are best served by providing for their death protection needs initially through low-premium term coverage and by meeting their other needs through investing the premium dollars saved in a separate fund. Buying term and investing the difference, or separating the savings and protection elements of the life insurance contract, is based on the assumption that an individual can invest his or her surplus funds more wisely and with a greater return than the life insurance company can. This argument should be analyzed in terms of the objectives of any investment program: safety of principal, yield, and liquidity.

Regarding safety of principal, the life insurance industry has compiled a solvency record over the years that is unmatched by any other type of business organization. Losses to policyowners have been relatively rare despite periods of war, depression, and inflation. Even the few insurance companies seized by regulators in recent years have been able to honor most of their policyowners' contracts.

Life insurance companies unquestionably obtain the highest possible yield commensurate with the standard of safety they have set for themselves and the regulatory constraints within which they operate. Precise measurement of their yield is complicated by several aspects of life insurance accounting. Comparisons of the returns earned by life insurers depend on which invested assets are being considered, and whether they are total invested assets or various separate blocks of assets supporting variable insurance and annuity products.

At certain times, many individuals may be able to secure a higher yield than that provided by a life insurance company by investing in common stocks or other equity investments, and some exceptional investors will be able to do it under virtually any circumstances. The typical life insurance policyowner is unlikely, over a long period, to earn a consistently higher yield than a life insurance company without taking on a greater degree of speculative investment risk. Annual increases in cash values are not subject to federal income taxes as they accrue, while the earnings from a separate investment program are often taxed as ordinary income.

With respect to the third objective of an investment program, the liquidity of a life insurance contract is unsurpassed. Although surrender charges may apply during a policy's early years, the policyowner's cash value can be taken out at any time through surrender for cash, policy loans, or in many newer life insurance products, partial withdrawals.

More important perhaps than any of the preceding factors is the question of whether savings under a separate investment program will actually take place. Fixed-premium life insurance that develops cash values is a form of "forced" saving. Periodic premiums provide a simple and systematic mechanism for saving, and when the savings feature is combined with the protection feature, there is also far more incentive for the policyowner to save consistently than otherwise might be present. An individual who voluntarily buys a bond per month, who purchases a flexible-premium form of life insurance, or who sets aside a certain amount per month in another type of savings program might skip a month or two if some other use of money is more appealing. If, however, failure to set aside the predetermined contribution to a savings program would result in loss of highly prized insurance protection that might be irreplaceable, he or she will be far more likely to make the savings effort.

Buy Term and Invest the Difference? Factors to Consider
• Safety of principal and income • Rate of return • Liquidity • Assurance that saving will be done

The foregoing is not meant to disparage other forms of investment. All have their place in an individual's financial program. Permanent life insurance, however, can be the foundation for funding lifelong financial needs, particularly if there is a long-term need for life insurance.

If permanent life insurance is to play a role in financial planning for a client, each of the types of such insurance should be considered. Among the distinguishing characteristics that may make one type of permanent life insurance preferable over another for a particular client are the following:

- *length of the planned premium-paying period.* The shorter this period, the higher the periodic premium. The client should consider limited-payment whole life to confine premium payments to his or her years of earned income. Alternatively, the client could purchase ordinary life but use dividends or a nonforfeiture option to avoid the need for lifelong premium payments.

- *emphasis on saving versus protection.* Limited-payment life builds up the savings component more rapidly than ordinary life. If heavy emphasis is to be placed on the savings element, the client should consider a very short premium-paying period, perhaps single-premium whole life or an endowment, although some of the advantage of the tax-deferred buildup of the savings element can be lost.

- *time when death benefits are needed.* If the principal need for funds is at the death of the main income earner, a single-life policy is appropriate. However, if the principal need for funds is to provide estate liquidity when the surviving spouse dies, the client should consider a joint-life or survivorship (second-to-die) policy.

- *desire for inflation protection.* Variable life, universal life, indexed universal life, or variable universal life insurance can provide increasing amounts of death benefit protection. In other types of insurance, the use of dividends to buy additional insurance or the use of a guaranteed insurability option is also helpful.

- *importance of yield versus safety in the savings component.* If the client's risk tolerance permits, variable, universal, indexed universal, or variable universal life may be appropriate as a way to achieve a higher yield.

- *unbundling of cost components.* If the client wants to know where his or her premium dollars go, he or she should consider variable, universal, indexed universal, or variable universal life insurance.

- *premium-payment flexibility.* Universal, indexed universal, or variable universal life can be appropriate if premium flexibility is important to the client.

MEASURING THE COST OF LIFE INSURANCE

Of course, one important factor in a rational life insurance purchasing decision is the cost of life insurance. If all other factors are equal, low-cost insurance obviously is preferable. If the other factors are unequal, the prospective purchaser needs to weigh price differentials against the differences in other factors that are important to him or her. Therefore, meaningful cost information is an essential element in intelligent decision-making.

At one time, it was common for insurers and their agents to show the net cost of a policy as equal to the sum of the premiums to be paid during the first, for example, 20 years of the policy, minus the sum of the dividends anticipated during that period, and minus the cash value available at the end of that period. The rather ludicrous result of this traditional net cost method was often a net cost of less than zero. Purchasers were asked to believe not only that their insurance for the 20 years would be free but also that the insurer would pay them for the privilege of giving them the coverage!

EXAMPLE

Under the traditional 20-year net cost method, if the annual premium for a $100,000 policy is $1,600, the 20th-year cash value is $28,000, and the projected dividends total $7,200, the annual net cost per $1,000 of coverage would be shown as

Premiums ($1,600 × 20)	$32,000
Minus dividends	7,200
Minus cash value	28,000
Net cost	–$ 3,200
Net cost per $1,000 (–$3,200 ÷ 100)	–$ 32.00

The weakness of the traditional net cost method was the disregard for the time value of money. Specifically, the method ignored that premiums must be paid out by purchasers every year, whereas most of the dividends and cash values are not available until much later. Also, dividend growth patterns, and perhaps those of cash values, can differ significantly for different insurance companies.

The National Association of Insurance Commissioners (NAIC) has developed a model regulation to improve the quality of the cost information prospective life insurance buyers receive. The NAIC model regulation for cost information requires insurers to give the prospective purchaser a buyer's guide that contains a clear explanation of products and how to shop for them, and a policy summary that contains essential information pertaining to the particular policy under consideration. The policy summary is required to disclose two interest-adjusted cost indexes that reflect the time value of money by recognizing that money is paid and received at different times and that costs can be better compared by using a specified interest assumption. These two indexes, referred to as a surrender cost index and a net payment cost index, do not reflect actual net costs to the individual policyowner, but the prospective cost estimates can be valuable in giving the applicant a *relative* sense of which similar policies are high or low in cost. Note, however, the actual cost of a life insurance policy to an individual depends on his or her own circumstances and the actual cash flows experienced under the policy. This actual cost cannot be ascertained until the contract expires by death, maturity, or surrender.

Surrender Cost Index

surrender cost index   The *surrender cost index* indicates the cost of surrendering the policy for the cash value at some future point in time, such as 20 years. The index shows the average amount of each annual premium that is not returned if the policy is surrendered for its cash value. This index is useful when the client's main concern is the level of cash values.

To compute the surrender cost index, the usual steps are:

1. Assume that each annual premium, paid at the beginning of the year, is placed in an account to accumulate at 5 percent interest until the end of a 20-year period.

2. Assume that each annual dividend, paid at the end of the year, is placed in an account to accumulate at 5 percent interest until the end of the 20-year period.

3. Subtract the 20th-year cash value and the result of step 2 from the result of step 1.

4. Divide the result of step 3 by 34.719. This interest factor converts it into an equivalent level annual amount that, if paid at the beginning of each year over a 20-year period, would accrue to the value in step 3. With this computation, the cost is discounted over 20 years at 5 percent to a beginning-of-year annuity.

5. Divide the result of step 4 by the number of thousands of dollars in the policy's death benefit. The result is the estimated level annual cost per $1,000 of coverage.

Net Payment Cost Index

net payment cost index

The other interest-adjusted cost index is the *net payment cost index*. This index evaluates the cost of insurance protection based on the assumption that the insured dies at the end of the policy's 20th year. It is useful for a client who is more concerned with the death benefit rather than the cash value. The procedure for calculating the net payment cost index is identical to that for the surrender cost index, except that in step 3 there is no subtraction of the 20th-year cash value.

EXAMPLE

This example illustrates both surrender cost and net payment cost indexes. Assume that a policy has a $100,000 death benefit. Assume also that the level annual premiums, if accumulated at 5 percent compound interest from the time of payment until the end of the 20th policy year, would amount to $75,931. Further assume that the 20th-year cash value is $35,900. Last, assume that the anticipated dividends, if accumulated at 5 percent compound interest from the time of receipt until the end of the 20th policy year, would amount to $14,119. The 20-year *surrender cost index* would be

Accumulated premiums	$75,931.00
Minus accumulated dividends	14,119.00
Minus cash value	35,900.00
Cost	$25,912.00
Discounted over 20 years at 5 percent, to a beginning-of-year annuity =	$746.33
Divided by 100 units of coverage =	$7.46

The *net payment cost index* would not entail subtraction of the cash value. It would therefore be

Accumulated premiums	$75,931.00
Minus accumulated dividends	14,119.00
Cost	$61,812.00
Discounted over 20 years at 5 percent, to a beginning-of-year annuity =	$1,780.34
Divided by 100 units of coverage =	$17.80

By themselves, these index numbers are not especially useful. However, the index numbers of two or more similar policies can be used as one basis of comparison.

LIFE INSURANCE ILLUSTRATIONS

illustration   Insurance sales representatives often use tabular or graphic illustrations to depict the performance of a life insurance policy over a period of years. An *illustration* is a presentation or depiction that includes nonguaranteed elements of a life insurance policy over a period of years. Illustrations are useful for showing how a policy works and how sensitive the policy is to changes in such factors as interest, mortality, and expenses. However, illustrations are of limited value for comparing different policies.

Unethical sales representatives have misused life insurance illustrations that present unfettered pie-in-the-sky optimism, painting unrealistic pictures of future performance that vastly exceed the guarantees in the policy. To protect consumers, the NAIC promulgated a model regulation pertaining to life insurance illustrations for policies with a face amount of $10,000 or more.

Each illustration used in the sale of a life insurance policy covered by the new regulation must be clearly labeled "life insurance illustration" and must include the following:

1. name of the insurance company
2. name and business address of the insurer's agent
3. name, age, and gender of the proposed insured
4. the underwriting or rating classification upon which the illustration is based
5. the generic name of the policy (for example, whole life, universal life, and so on)
6. the initial death benefit amount

7. the dividend option election or application of nonguaranteed elements if applicable

The NAIC model regulation prohibits insurers and their agents from the following:

1. representing the policy as anything other than a life insurance policy
2. using or describing nonguaranteed elements in a manner that is misleading or has the capacity or tendency to mislead
3. stating or implying that the payment or amount of nonguaranteed elements is guaranteed
4. using an illustration that does not comply with the illustration regulation
5. using an illustration that is more favorable to the policyowner than the illustration based on the illustrated scale of the insurer
6. providing an applicant with an incomplete illustration
7. representing in any way that premium payments will not be required for each year of the policy in order to maintain the illustrated death benefits, unless that is the fact
8. using the term "vanish," "vanishing premium," or a similar term that implies the policy becomes paid up, to describe a plan for using nonguaranteed elements to pay a portion of future premiums
9. using an illustration that is not "self-supporting

The NAIC model illustration regulation specifies that all illustrations must be dated as of the date prepared. All pages must be marked to indicate both the individual page number and the total number of pages in the illustration (for example, "page 3 of 7"). The illustration must clearly indicate which elements are guaranteed and which are nonguaranteed. Any amount available upon surrender shall be the amount after deduction of surrender charges. Items presented in illustrations can be in the form of charts, graphs, or tabular values.

Each illustration must be accompanied by a narrative summary that describes the policy, premiums, and features, and defines column headings used in the illustration. The summary should also state that actual results might be more or less favorable than those shown in the illustration.

The regulation further states that illustrations for universal life policies must comply with the regulation requirements and additionally that the insurance company must issue annual reports to policyowners after the policy is issued.

These annual reports must specify the beginning and ending dates for the reporting period.

The content of the annual reports is specified in the NAIC model regulation:

- all transactions affecting the policy during the reporting period (debits and credits) and a description of each (for example, premiums paid, interest credited, loan interest debited, mortality charges, expenses debited, rider transactions, and so on)
- cash values at the beginning and end of the period
- death benefit at the end of the reporting period (for each life covered)
- the cash surrender value at the end of the period after deduction of surrender charge (if any)
- the amount of outstanding policy loans, if any, at the end of the report period
- a special Notice to Policyowners if the policy will not maintain insurance in force until the end of the next reporting period unless further premium payments are made

The regulation also stipulates that policyowners have the right to request an in-force illustration annually without charge. The insurer must provide information regarding where and how to direct such requests and must supply a current illustration within 30 days of the request. Such illustrations are to be based on the insurer's present illustrated scale. The model regulation also sets forth limits on the methodology for calculating illustrations.

LIFE INSURANCE POLICY REPLACEMENT

replacement   In life insurance, *replacement* refers to the process of replacing an existing life insurance policy with a new policy, a move that might or might not be advantageous to the policyowner. Agents and insurers must follow certain prescribed procedures for a policy replacement to avoid harm to policyowners.

An existing insurance policy may be replaced by another policy from the same insurer or by a policy issued by a different insurer. Twisting, an illegal practice, takes place when a policyowner is induced to discontinue and replace a policy through agent or insurer distortion or misrepresentation of the facts. However, replacement can occur in the absence of any distortion or misrepresentation.

Traditionally, most replacements were considered detrimental to the policyowner for at least three reasons:

- The policyowner had already incurred the high first-year expenses associated with a new policy.
- Premiums under the new policy might be higher due to the insured's increased age.
- The suicide and incontestable provisions under the existing policy might expire sooner, if they have not already done so, than those in the replacement policy.

More recently, however, life insurance rates dropped so dramatically that many policyowners can save money by replacing current policies, despite the insured's increased age. In some cases, for example, term insurance rates dropped as much as 50 percent within one decade. These decreases resulted from Americans' increased longevity and insurers' increased price competition.

1035 exchange   Policy replacement also has tax implications, which may be mitigated when the replacement qualifies as a *1035 exchange*. Sec. 1035 of the Internal Revenue Code permits a policyowner who exchanges one insurance contract for another in a "like-kind exchange" to receive certain tax advantages.

Although the terms "replacement" and "1035 exchange" are sometimes used interchangeably, not all replacements qualify as 1035 exchanges. For example, the old and the new contract must cover the same insured and have the same policyowner. A life insurance contract may be exchanged for a life insurance contract or an annuity, and an annuity may be exchanged for an annuity, but an annuity may not be exchanged for life insurance. Certain procedures must also be followed in effecting a 1035 exchange.

If an agent accurately discloses the facts and the replacement works to the policyowner's benefit, replacement does not present an ethical problem. Agents may have another motive for suggesting a life insurance policy be replaced. Because of high first-year commissions on new policies, agents have financial incentives not only to take business away from another insurer but also to replace a policy in their own company to generate another first-year commission. Furthermore, insurers who seek new business may not be averse to taking it away from a competitor, even when doing so may not benefit the policyowner. Consequently, proposed replacements need to be carefully evaluated.

To protect policyowners' interests, the NAIC developed the Unfair Trade Practices Act, which contains prohibitions against misrepresentation, including misrepresentations to induce the lapse, forfeiture, exchange, conversion, or surrender of any life insurance policy. The NAIC has also adopted what is now called the Life Insurance and Annuities Replacement Model Regulation, which focuses on giving the buyer full disclosure of information in a fair and accurate manner and providing ample time to review the information before making a final decision.

When an agent submits an application for life insurance or an annuity to the insurer, he or she must include a statement about whether the policy is a replacement. If a replacement is involved, the agent must give the applicant a prescribed notice that alerts the applicant to the need to compare the existing and the proposed benefits carefully and to seek information from the agent or insurer from whom he or she purchased the original policy. The replacing insurer must advise the other insurer of the proposed replacement and provide information on the new policy. The replacing insurer must also give the applicant at least a 20-day free look at the new policy, during which time he or she has an unconditional right to a full refund of all premiums paid if he or she decides not to retain the policy. The existing insurer or agent has 20 days to furnish the policyowner with information on the existing policy, including the premium, cash values, death benefits, and dividends. Both insurers and agents are responsible for the accuracy of the information submitted to the person whose policy is being considered for replacement.

Some Issues in Policy Replacement
• Pay high first-year expenses again?
• Higher premium?
• New suicide clause?
• New incontestable clause?
• More or less favorable policy terms?

SUBSTANDARD COVERAGE

In life insurance, an individual who belongs to a class with a higher-than-standard mortality rate is referred to as a substandard risk. Insurance on these individuals is referred to as substandard coverage. In this context, substandard refers to the applicant's underwriting characteristics, not the quality of the insurance policy. The individual may still be considered insurable by an insurer's underwriter, but only on a substandard basis. This situation occurs in about 6 percent to 7 percent of all new policies issued, and it introduces some additional complexities into the life insurance purchasing decision.

A group or classification that an insurer rates as substandard, such as male applicants who have elevated blood pressure readings, is expected to produce a higher mortality rate than a group of normal lives. The group concept must be emphasized because, as with insuring standard applicants, there is no certainty about any individual's longevity expectations. All assumptions therefore are based on the anticipated average experience of a large number of individuals.

The law of large numbers should be reiterated in any consideration of substandard insurance, involving as it does extra cost or restricted benefits for the policyowner or beneficiary. Some believe that if an individual is placed in a substandard classification and subsequently lives to a ripe old age, the company erred in its treatment of the case. However, if 1,000 persons, each of whom is suffering from a particular physical impairment, are granted insurance, the death rate among them will be greater than the death rate among a group of people the same age who are free of any discernible impairments. To allow for the higher death rates or extra mortality that will certainly occur within the substandard group, the company must collect an extra premium from or impose special terms on all who are subject to the extra mortality. The insurer does not expect that every member of the group will survive for a shorter period than the normal life expectancy, just that a larger proportion of the people in a substandard group will fail to reach normal life expectancy.

Incidence of Extra Mortality

If a group of substandard applicants is to be fairly treated, the degree of extra mortality the group represents and the approximate period in life when the extra mortality is likely to occur must both be known within reasonable limits. The timing of claims makes a great deal of difference financially to the insurer, whether the extra claims are expected to occur primarily in early life, middle age, old age, or at a level rate throughout the individuals' lifetimes. If the extra mortality occurs during the early years of the policies, when the net amount at risk is relatively large, the burden on the insurance company will be greater than if it occurs later, when the net amount at risk is relatively small. Therefore, between two substandard groups representing the same aggregate amount of extra mortality, the group whose extra mortality is concentrated later in life should pay a smaller extra premium than the group whose extra mortality occurs earlier.

The majority of companies assume that each substandard applicant falls into one of three broad groups:

- additional hazard increases with age (example: high blood pressure)
- additional hazard remains approximately constant (examples: occupational hazard, some physical impairments)
- additional hazard decreases with age (examples: past illnesses, surgical operations)

Treatment of Substandard Applicants

Several methods have been devised to provide insurance protection to people with impaired health. In general, companies make an effort to adapt the method to the type of hazard the substandard applicant represents.

Increase in Age

rate-up age method   The rate-up age method of dealing with substandard applicants is often used when the extra mortality is decidedly increasing and will continue to increase indefinitely. Under the *rate-up age method*, the applicant is assumed to be a number of years older than his or her real age, and the policy is written accordingly. For example, if a male applicant, aged 25, is placed in a classification that is expected to produce an extra mortality equivalent to the rate for a male aged 33, the applicant would be rated up 8 years and thereafter treated in all respects as if he were 33 years of age. His policy would contain the same surrender and loan values and would be entitled to the same dividends, if any, as any other similar contract issued at age 33.

The chief appeal of this method for the insurance company is its simplicity. Policies can be dealt with for all purposes as standard policies issued at the assumed age. No separate set of records is required; no special calculations of premium rates, cash and other surrender values, reserves, and dividends are involved. For the applicant, the method is attractive because the higher premium is accompanied by correspondingly higher surrender values and dividends, if the policy is participating.

Extra Percentage Tables

extra percentage tables

Extra percentage tables provide the most common method of dealing with substandard applicants who present an increasing hazard. These extra percentage tables classify applicants into groups based on the expected percentage of standard mortality and charge premiums that reflect the appropriate increase in mortality. The number of substandard classifications can vary from three to twelve, depending to some extent on the degree of extra mortality the company is willing to underwrite. For example, a company might establish three acceptable substandard classifications with expected average mortalities of 150, 175, and 200 percent of standard, respectively. In effect, a special mortality table that reflects the appropriate degree of extra mortality is prepared for each substandard classification, and a complete set of gross premium rates is computed for each classification. Depending on company practice and state law, surrender values may be based on the special mortality table or may be the same as surrender values under policies issued to standard applicants.

Flat Extra Premium

flat extra premium

A third method of underwriting substandard applicants is to assess a *flat extra premium*. Under this method, the standard premium for the policy in question is increased by a specified number of dollars per $1,000 of insurance. Assessed as a measure of the extra mortality involved, the flat extra premium does not vary with the age of the applicant. The extra premium may be paid throughout the premium-paying period of the policy, or it may be terminated after a period of years when the extra hazard has presumably disappeared.

The flat extra premium method is generally used when the hazard is thought to be constant, for example, deafness or partial blindness, or decreasing, as with a family history of tuberculosis or the aftermath of a serious illness or surgical operation, in which case the flat extra premium is usually temporary. The flat extra premium is widely used to cover the extra mortality associated with certain occupations and avocations.

The flat extra premium is not reflected in policy values and dividends. It is assumed that the entire amount of the extra premium is needed each year to pay additional claims and expenses. The dividends and guaranteed values are identical to those of a comparable policy without the flat extra premium.

Liens

lien

When the extra mortality to be expected from an impairment is of a distinctly decreasing and temporary nature, such as that associated with convalescence from a serious illness, an insurer may create a *lien* against the policy for a number of years, with the amount and term of the lien depending on the extent of the impairment. If this method is utilized, the policy is issued at standard rates and is standard in all respects except that, should death occur before the end of the period specified, the amount of the lien is deducted from the proceeds otherwise payable. Consequently, the death benefit is reduced during the first few years of coverage.

The lien method has a psychological appeal in that few persons who are refused insurance at standard rates believe themselves to be substandard applicants, and most tend to resent the company's action in classifying them that way. If the only penalty involved is a temporary reduction in the amount of protection, most applicants are willing to go along with the company's decision, confident that they will survive the period of the lien and thus prove the company wrong.

A practical and serious disadvantage of the method is that the reduction in coverage occurs in the early years of the policy, when the need for protection is presumably the greatest. The beneficiary usually has no knowledge of the lien, and the company's failure to pay the face amount of the policy can be the source of great disappointment and resentment, to the detriment of the company's reputation in the community. There is also a possibility that the lien is in conflict with laws in certain states that prohibit any provision that permits the company to settle a death claim with a payment smaller than the policy's face amount.

Other Methods

When the degree of extra mortality is small or when its nature is not well known, the insurer may make no extra charge but, if the policy is participating, place all members of the group in a special class for dividend purposes, adjusting the dividends in accordance with the class's actual experience. Alternatively, the insurer may simply limit the plan of insurance to one with a high savings component.

Ways to Deal with Substandard Applicants

- Hazard increases with age
  - Age rate-up
  - Extra percentage table
- Hazard remains constant
  - Flat extra premium
- Hazard decreases with time or is temporary
  - Flat extra premium
  - Lien
  - Special dividend class
  - Limit policy type to one with high savings component

Removal of Substandard Rating

Frequently, a person who is classified as substandard and insured on that basis by one company subsequently applies for insurance with another company, or even the same company, and is found to be standard in all respects. Under these circumstances, the person's natural reaction is to request the removal of the substandard rating. The insurer must then determine whether to remove the rating.

Theoretically, the rating should not be removed unless the impairment on which it was originally based was known to be temporary or was due to occupation or residence. At the time the policy was originally issued, the insured was placed in a special classification whose members were presumably impaired to approximately the same degree. The company knew that some of the members of the group would die within a short period, while others would survive far beyond their normal expectancy. If the company reduces the premiums for those whose health has improved, the insurer should also be permitted to increase the premiums of those whose health has deteriorated. Because the premiums of those in the latter category cannot be adjusted upward, the premiums of those in the former category should not logically be reduced.

As a practical matter, however, the company is virtually forced to remove the substandard rating of a person who can demonstrate current insurability at standard rates. If the insurer does not do so, the policyowner will almost surely surrender the substandard insurance and replace it with insurance at standard rates with another company. Thus, the common practice is to remove the extra premium upon proof that the insured is no longer substandard.

Value of Substandard Insurance

Substandard insurance is of great social importance because it makes insurance protection available to millions of American families that would otherwise be without it. It is perhaps fair to conclude that life insurance is now available to all except those subject to such excessive rates of mortality as to entail premiums beyond their ability or willingness to pay.

VIATICAL AGREEMENTS

Financial planners realize that part of insurance planning pertains to alternative uses of the life insurance policy. At certain times, the benefits payable at the insured's death may become less important than the cash that may be available from the policy during the insured's last months. The policyowner may need access to funds during the insured's final months for funding experimental treatments or other treatments insurance does not cover, for keeping the insured comfortable at home rather than in an institution, or simply for financing enjoyable final experiences.

Numerous alternatives may be available if the policyowner needs funds prior to the insured's death. First, the policyowner can access the cash value in the form of a loan. Alternatively, the policyowner may use the cash value as collateral for a loan from a bank or from a family member, possibly from the beneficiary against the future death benefit. In both of these cases, the policy will remain in force and premiums, which may be prohibitive for the policyowner, will continue to be due. Another alternative to accessing additional funds is to utilize the policy's accelerated benefits provision. The policyowner may need to check with the insurance company to see whether this alternative is available, as some insurers will pay an accelerated death benefit even when the provision is not included in the policy.

viatical settlement   Finally, the policyowner may enter into a *viatical settlement*. A viatical settlement involves the sale of a terminally ill insured's life insurance policy in exchange for a percentage of the face amount. The agreement is a contract for the policyowner, or viator, to sell the life insurance policy to a third party, the viatical settlement provider, who purchases the policy as an investment. The settlement provider becomes the new policyowner, is responsible for future premium payments, and is entitled to receive the death benefit at the insured's death.

In a viatical settlement purchase agreement, in exchange for the rights to the insurance policy, the viator receives a lump-sum cash settlement from the settlement provider. This lump sum is a percentage of the death benefit, based on various factors, such as the insured's life expectancy, the premiums that will be required to keep the policy in force, the insurer's financial strength, and the settlement provider's required rate of return. Settlements generally are paid in the range of 40 to 80 percent of the death benefit.

The policyowner may engage a viatical settlement broker to comparison shop for the best offer and negotiate the agreement between the viator and the viatical settlement provider. The broker will usually charge a fee of 5 to 7 percent of the policy's face amount. Alternatively, policyowners can comparison shop on their own to find the best offer. Most life insurance policies can be viaticated, including (under some circumstances) term insurance and group policies. Any policy must have been in force for at least 2 years so that the contestability period is past.

Regulation and Ethics

Viaticals for Viators

Viatical settlements became available in the mid-1980s in response to a new demand created by the AIDS epidemic. AIDS patients, as well as patients with other terminal illnesses such as cancer, use viatical settlements to help with expenses during the insured's final months. Regulation of these transactions did not follow until years after their introduction and, as discussed in this section, remains inadequate to protect the public.

Viatical settlements are not considered securities and are not subject to SEC regulation. Regulation of viaticals is left to the states. The NAIC developed the 1993 Viatical Settlement Model Regulation Act, which provides guidelines to help state insurance commissioners protect viators. The act mandated full disclosure to consumers and established fair payment guidelines based on the estimated life expectancy of the insured. The act requires that the viatical settlement provider grant a 15-day cooling off period during which the viator can rescind the viatical agreement. Nearly half of the states have adopted the act. Additionally, some, but not all, states require licensing of viatical settlement brokers and viatical settlement providers.

Due to the lack of disclosure requirements, the provider's financial strength may not be known. Because there is little financial protection to the viator, consumer groups recommend that the viator insist that an independent escrow agent hold the funds to ensure that they will be available to pay the viator.

Viaticals for Investors

After the settlement is complete, viatical settlement providers may retain the insurance as an asset in their investment portfolios. Alternatively, the settlement provider may offer the insurance contract to a third-party investor, who will pay the settlement provider cash in exchange for the ownership rights to the policy. Depending on the conditions of sale, the investor or, more commonly, the settlement provider may pay any remaining premiums.

Investment in insurance policies as the result of viatication is not well regulated, and fraudulent practices have tainted the industry. Viatical salespeople have promised investors high returns with no risk, and they have often misrepresented the life expectancy of the insured. Furthermore, such dishonest practices as the sale of nonexistent policies to investors have made front page news in the past few years. Additionally, the fraudulent practice of clean sheeting, or inducing terminally ill individuals to apply for life insurance and then selling those policies to investors, has been identified.

The current inadequacy of regulation has created a climate with potential for abuse of both the viator and the investor. The viator is not assured of a fair and adequate payment at a time of physical, emotional, and financial vulnerability. The ethics of investing in a viatication contract may be difficult for some investors because the earlier the insured dies, the higher the return to the investor.

When a life insurance policy is viaticated, the new policyowner has no insurable interest in the life of the insured. Current insurance laws require that insurable interest exists only at the time of application, not throughout the life of the policy. However, the ownership of the policy by a complete stranger could create an incentive for the investor to encourage the death of the insured. Although there has been no evidence in the United States of homicide of an insured by an investor, some experts caution that the contract could encourage murder for profit.

Tax Treatment

The Health Insurance Portability and Accountability Act of 1996 (HIPAA) defined situations under which viatical and accelerated death benefits are tax exempt on the federal level. The insured must be terminally ill, having been certified by a physician as having a life expectancy of 24 months or less, or chronically ill, defined as permanently and severely disabled. Also, if the viator's state requires licensing, the viatical settlement provider must be licensed with the state. If the state does not require licensing, the settlement provider must meet selected requirements of the NAIC Model Act. Most, but not all, states also exempt these settlements from taxation if they meet these conditions.

Planning Considerations

A major weakness in using a viatical settlement is that at the death of the insured, the policy will not provide death benefits to the surviving family but rather to the investor. Thus, income and burial protection will not be provided to the survivors. However, needs may have changed since the policy was purchased, and the death benefit may no longer be necessary for the surviving family.

Other weaknesses of the viatical approach are less obvious. First, the proceeds may make the viator ineligible for assistance for which he or she otherwise would be eligible. This assistance may include Medicaid, Supplemental Social Security Income, Aid for Families with Dependent Children, food stamps, and state prescription programs. The proceeds may also be subject to creditors' claims.

Another weakness of viatical settlements is that personal and medical information may be passed along to the investor. This information may include the insured's identifying information, life expectancy, and other medical information. With no privacy regulation, the policyowner has no control over who may have access to this information. A contractual agreement regarding privacy should be a consideration to a potential viator who is comparison shopping for a settlement provider.

Viatication can provide much needed financial relief to a dying client. The financial planner should help the client explore all other options available and consider both the benefits and the shortcomings of viatication. The client should compare provider offers as to the amount of cash offered as well as other factors, such as reputation, financial strength, state licensure, and privacy provisions. A thorough review of the client's tax situation should also be undertaken to ensure that the settlement will be tax exempt. The financial planner should help the client reach the solution that will best serve the client's needs and provide for the client's wishes as to the financial security of the surviving family.

LIFE SETTLEMENTS

life settlement

A *life settlement* involves transferring the ownership of a life insurance policy to a third-party investor, much like a viatical settlement, but in cases where the insured is not chronically or terminally ill. Life settlements provide a relatively new way for seniors to convert their life insurance policies to cash. Policyholders typically receive more than the policy's cash surrender value but less than they would get in a viatical settlement available to a terminally ill insured.

Life settlements can be appropriate for a relatively small number of seniors with an urgent need for cash who have absolutely no further need for life insurance and no wish to leave an inheritance to heirs, loved ones, or charities. However, studies have shown that most seniors who used a life settlement received a relatively small portion of the intrinsic value of the policy—20 cents on the dollar in one recent study.[39] Advisors generally advise seniors to sell other assets or borrow against the life insurance policy rather than decide to sell it. Another alternative would be asking beneficiaries to pay the premium and keep the policy in force.

Life settlements raise a number of ethical issues. One is the substantial profit available to investors who purchase life insurance policies for a small fraction of their intrinsic value, often taking advantage of senior citizens. As with viaticals, a life settlement also involves a third party whose profit depends upon the death of the insured—and the sooner the better. A client may not find it comforting to know that some unrelated party literally has a contract on his or her life!

stranger-originated
life insurance
(STOLI)

A controversial segment of the life settlement market involves *stranger-originated life insurance (STOLI)*. In a STOLI arrangement, speculators initiate coverage on older

---

39. Deloitte Consulting LLP and the University of Connecticut, The Life Settlements Market: An Actuarial Perspective on Consumer Economic Value, p. 1. Copyright (c) 2005 Deloitte Development LLC (www.lifesettlementseducation.com/pdf/Life_Settlements_Mrkt_3.pdf, accessed 11/13/06).

persons and fund the premium payments with intentions of profiting upon the death of the insured. In one such scheme, ownership of the policy is transferred to investors after the policy's two-year incontestability period has passed.

Because they have no relationship to the insured, in stranger-originated life insurance these speculators violate the intent behind insurable interest laws, which is to ensure that the person taking out a life insurance policy has an interest in the insured's continuing good health. Several states have enacted statutes specifically banning stranger-originated life insurance, and it may well violate insurable interest statutes in other states.

BUSINESS USES OF LIFE INSURANCE

The discussion of life insurance in this chapter has explicitly or implicitly assumed its use for family purposes. Life insurance also serves a number of functions in the business world, and for these purposes, additional factors bear on the purchase decision. In this text, only a few of the many ways in which life insurance can be used in a small business situation are described—namely, indemnifying a small business for death of a key employee; funding a business *buy-sell agreement*; serving as a group employee benefit plan; and furnishing an executive compensation benefit under a split-dollar plan. Other uses and the sometimes intricate tax aspects of business life insurance are described in more advanced texts.

Key Person Indemnification

The success of a closely held business often depends on the personal services of a key employee. The loss of a key employee's services due to death or disability will probably result in a loss of income, at least temporarily, to the closely held business. In addition, the business could incur increased expenses if a replacement employee has to be recruited at a higher salary and requires extensive training.

What makes someone a key employee? He or she might have a specialized skill critical to the success of the particular closely held business. Potential replacements may possess this same skill, but replacement employees might have to be recruited at higher salary levels. Or perhaps the employee has a significant customer or client base and is responsible for attracting significant amounts of business. As another example, the employee might be a source of capital if his or her loss would damage the closely held business's credit rating.

Valuing the Key Employee

Determining the key employee's value to the closely held business is very speculative. The actual valuation method depends on the characteristic of the employee that creates the key employee status. Determining the value of the key employee who attracts substantial business might be relatively easy. The net income resulting from the business he or she produces in excess of the amount of net income that could be expected from a similarly situated but less effective employee could be capitalized in some manner. In other cases, the firm may have to consider various subjective factors to arrive at a proxy for the key employee's value. For example, the firm should consider replacement salaries and the training required for a replacement employee to become effective.

Key Employee Life Insurance

key employee life insurance   *Key employee life insurance* protects a business against the possibility of an income loss and/or increase in expenses resulting from a key employee's death. Term insurance can be purchased if the primary concern is the key employee's dollar value to the business. Decreasing term might be appropriate because the key employee loss exposure decreases as the insured approaches retirement. Key employee life insurance, however, is usually coupled with some other purpose, such as providing a retirement benefit for the key employee. Permanent life insurance is typically purchased to meet this objective. The business receives the life insurance death benefit as compensation for the income loss and/or increase in expenses resulting from the key employee's death. If the insured survives to retirement, the corporation can use the cash surrender value to fund a retirement benefit. Another approach is for the business to transfer the policy to the employee at retirement.

EXAMPLE

Chuck Keller is a key employee of Pontco. What makes him a key employee? Because of Chuck's ebullient personality and his vast technical knowledge, he sells more industrial cranes than Pontco's five other salesmen combined. If Chuck were to die or become disabled before his normal retirement age, Pontco's sales revenues would suddenly plummet, at least in the short run. Pontco can purchase key employee life insurance to protect against this possibility. The death benefit Pontco receives in the event of Chuck's demise will stabilize Pontco by helping to offset this drop in revenue. Two approaches are possible:

- Yearly renewable term insurance, with a term long enough to last until Chuck's normal retirement age, can be used to protect Pontco.

- A permanent life insurance policy could both protect Pontco and reward Chuck by funding some additional retirement benefits if he survives to retirement.

The business should be the owner and beneficiary of key employee life insurance. The premiums for key employee life insurance are nondeductible, and death benefits are not taxable as long as the employer complies with the best practices provisions of the Pension Reform Act of 2006. Detailed rules require employers to notify the employee in writing of the employer's intentions to insure the employee's life for a stated maximum face amount and that the employer will be the beneficiary of any death benefits. The employee must consent to the insurance in writing and confirm that he or she is aware that coverage may continue after the employment terminates. If these notice and consent provisions are met and at the time of death the insured is either a highly compensated employee as defined in the rules or was employed by the employer within the last 12 months, policy proceeds will be excludable from taxable income. Death benefit proceeds paid to the insured's heirs (or trust for the benefit of the heirs) or used in a stock redemption of an insured's interest in the company will also be free of income taxation.

Funding Buy-Sell Agreements

The death or disability of an owner of a closely held business typically disrupts the business and often leads to its failure. Life insurance can be used to provide the funds necessary to finance a buy-sell agreement that preserves the value of the business. When a business owner dies, the executor of his or her estate must collect, preserve, and distribute the decedent's assets. Of course, these assets include both the business and personal assets owned by the decedent at the time of his or her death. The closely held business presents many difficulties for the executor unless the decedent has appropriately planned for business continuation.

buy-sell agreement   A properly designed buy-sell agreement ensures that the estate can sell its interest in the closely held business for a reasonable price. A *buy-sell agreement* is a contract that binds the owner of a business interest to sell at his or her death, and a designated buyer to buy at that time, the business interest for a specified or determinable price. The purchasers of the business interest, perhaps the surviving co-owners of the business, will obtain the business interest and avoid the difficulties associated with passing it through probate. Without an appropriate continuation plan, the executor may be compelled to sell the business interest to pay the estate's settlement costs and federal estate taxes and/or state inheritance taxes. The settlement costs must be paid in cash promptly after the business owner's death. Under these circumstances, the executor has a tenuous bargaining position, and a forced sale of the business interest may yield far less than its full fair market value. The surviving co-owners also face a great deal of uncertainty. The survivors may be pressured to provide distributions of business income to the decedent's heirs. They may also face the prospect that the executor or the heirs will choose to sell the business interest to outsiders.

Benefits of a Buy-Sell Agreement

Proper estate planning with a buy-sell agreement offers several advantages, which include:

- a guarantee that there will be a market for the closely held business interest
- liquidity for the payment of death taxes and other estate settlement costs
- establishment of the estate tax value of the decedent's business interest, making the estate planning process more reliable for the owner
- continuation of the business in the hands of the surviving owners and/or employees
- improved credit risk because the probability of continuation of the business is enhanced

Basic Structure of a Buy-Sell Agreement

A properly designed buy-sell agreement has several provisions that are generally included. Among these are the following:

- *purpose of the agreement.* A buy-sell agreement should contain a statement indicating its purpose. One advantage of including a statement of purpose is to document the intent of the agreement should a dispute arise later.

- *commitment of the parties.* The agreement should clearly state the obligation of all parties. For example, it should be clear that the estate of the deceased business owner will sell the business interest to the parties who become purchasers under the terms of the agreement.

- *lifetime transfer restrictions.* Most buy-sell agreements contain a first-offer provision that prevents the parties to the agreement from disposing of the business interest to outsiders while all the parties are living.

- *purchase price.* The buy-sell agreement should specify a purchase price or, as an alternative, a method for determining the purchase price at which the business interest will be bought and sold.

- *funding provisions.* The terms of the agreement should specify how the purchase price will be funded. For example, if the agreement is funded with life insurance, the agreement should indicate how such life insurance will be structured and paid for. A first-to-die joint life policy is often used for this purpose.

Continuation Agreements for Partnerships and Corporations

entity agreement   In the case of a partnership or closely held corporation, the agreement may be structured under either an entity agreement or a cross-purchase approach. Under an *entity agreement*, the firm itself enters into an agreement with each owner specifying that, on the death of an owner, the firm will buy the business interest of the deceased and the deceased's estate will sell it. Technically, the firm liquidates the interest of the deceased partner or redeems the stock of the deceased stockholder. The firm carries life insurance on each owner, with the firm as beneficiary, to provide the money to fund the entity agreement.

cross-purchase agreement   Under a *cross-purchase agreement*, each partner or stockholder is both a seller and a purchaser. The cross-purchase buy-sell agreement provides that, on the death of one owner, his or her estate will sell the deceased's interest, and the other owners will buy it. To fund this type of agreement, each owner should carry and be the beneficiary of insurance on the lives of the other owners. For example, if there are three equal partners, the two surviving partners will each purchase one-half, or another agreed-upon share, of a deceased partner's interest.

Continuation Agreements for Sole Proprietorship

The sole proprietorship is by far the most common form of business organization. By definition, there is only one owner of the firm, so on his or her death, there are no surviving co-owners to serve as purchasers of the deceased's business interest. Nevertheless, the advantages of having a binding buy-sell agreement are as important for a sole proprietorship as they are for a closely held corporation or a partnership.

The new issue in a proprietorship is the challenge of finding an appropriate purchaser. Often, the sole proprietor has no family successors who are capable and/or willing to step in at the sole proprietor's death. However, there may be a key employee or group of employees who would like to be purchasers of the business. Such individuals, if available, are logical choices for two reasons. First, the key employee or employees of the sole proprietorship are familiar with the business. This is particularly important if the business requires unique skills to perform its function. Second, the key employees may be willing to enter into a buy-sell agreement to protect their own future employment. Without a buy-sell agreement, the sole proprietorship is often liquidated or sold to outsiders at the death of the proprietor. This could leave the key employees unemployed and without a future in the proprietorship. If there are no key employees or natural successors to the sole proprietor, the sole proprietor could seek a buyer from competitors who might want to take over the proprietor's business at some point in the future.

The life insurance arrangements for a sole proprietorship buy-sell agreement are relatively simple. The purchasing party is obligated to provide sale proceeds to the deceased proprietor's estate. Accordingly, the owner and beneficiary of the life insurance should be the purchasing party. The purchaser should obtain sufficient coverage on the life of the sole proprietor to make the required payments to the estate.

Life Insurance as an Employee Benefit

Sec. 79 plan   Group term life insurance is a benefit plan provided by an employer to a group of participating employees. Almost all plans are designed to receive favorable federal income tax treatment. Such plans are also known as *Sec. 79 plans*, referring to the section of the Internal Revenue Code that applies to them. These Sec. 79 plans allow the employer a tax deduction for premium payments on behalf of a participant unless the premium amounts exceed the tax code's reasonable compensation test, which is unlikely.

If the coverage provided by the plan is nondiscriminatory, the first $50,000 of coverage is provided tax free to all plan participants. The taxable amounts of coverage—that is, amounts above $50,000—are taxed according to a premium rate schedule, referred to as Table I, provided by IRS regulations. These rates are as shown in the following table. If a plan is contributory, an employee's taxable income is reduced by any employee contributions for the entire amount of coverage.

Table 10-2 Uniform Premium Table I	
Age	**Cost per Month per $1,000 of Coverage**
24 and under	$ .05
25–29	.06
30–34	.08
35–39	.09
40–44	.10
45–49	.15
50–54	.23
55–59	.43
60–64	.66
65–69	1.27
70 and over	2.06

EXAMPLE

Jill, aged 55, has a salary of $60,000 and receives $120,000 in group term life insurance as an employer-paid fringe benefit. The first $50,000 of this insurance is tax free. The remaining $70,000 is treated as taxable income. The amount her employer actually pays the insurance company is irrelevant. For tax purposes, the amount of taxable income Jill receives is determined based on the Sec. 79 cost per month, which, as shown in the table above, is $.43 per thousand per month for a person aged 55. As far as the Internal Revenue Service is concerned, Jill receives a taxable income of 70 × $.43 × 12, or $361.20, in addition to her taxable salary. Her employer reports this additional income to the IRS on her W-2 form.

If Jill paid $20 per month for her coverage, her annual taxable income for this benefit would be reduced by $240 to $121.20.

If the plan discriminates in favor of key employees with respect to coverage or benefits, the actual premiums paid on behalf of these key employees for their entire amount of coverage are taxable as ordinary income to them, but other employees still receive the previously mentioned favorable tax treatment. A key employee generally includes the shareholder-employees and officers of a closely held corporation. The actual nondiscrimination rules are complex and beyond the scope of this book. However, a plan is generally nondiscriminatory if (1) it covers at least 70 percent of a firm's employees, (2) key employees make up fewer than 15 percent of plan participants, and (3) benefits are either a flat amount or a uniform percentage of salary.

Split-Dollar Life Insurance Plans

split-dollar life
insurance

Split-dollar life insurance is a form of permanent life insurance frequently used prior to 2003 as an executive compensation benefit. In a traditional split-dollar plan, a corporation and an employee split a life insurance policy covering the life of the employee. The corporation contributes an amount equal to the annual increase in the cash surrender value, while the executive pays the remainder of the annual premium. In the past, the executive was taxed only for the PS 58 cost of 1-year term insurance funded by the employer. PS 58 rates are 1-year term insurance rates the federal government uses to measure the taxable economic benefit employees receive from the pure insurance protection split-dollar plans and qualified retirement plans provide.

Under split-dollar, the death benefit is split between the participating executive and the corporation as follows:

- The corporation receives a return of its contributions, which equals the cash surrender value.
- The beneficiary named by the insured receives a death benefit equal to the net amount at risk.

The Sarbanes-Oxley Act, enacted in 2002 to bar insider loan transactions, struck a major blow to split-dollar life insurance. Sarbanes-Oxley prohibits a publicly traded company from using corporate funds to make personal loans to its directors or officers. A second blow took place when the IRS and the Treasury Department issued final regulations in December 2003. The new regulations clearly make split-dollar plans less attractive.

Under current regulations, split-dollar arrangements are treated in one of two ways for tax purposes. If the employee owns the policy and the employer pays part of the premium, the employer's contribution is treated as a loan, and the employee is taxed on the difference between the market interest rate and any interest being charged by the employer. If the employer owns the policy and pays the premium, the employee is taxed based on the economic benefit he or she receives; the value of the current life insurance protection and the employee's interest in the policy's cash value increase are treated as taxable income to the employee.

TAX TREATMENT OF LIFE INSURANCE

Quite often, especially for affluent clients, financial planners recognize that a life insurance purchase can legitimately serve to reduce the client's federal tax burden. In the following discussion we will summarize some of the common tax aspects of individual life insurance.

Income Taxation of Death Proceeds

In general, and subject to some exceptions, proceeds paid under a life insurance contract by reason of the insured's death are excludible from gross income for federal income tax purposes. The basic requirement for the income tax exclusion for life insurance proceeds is that they be paid because of the death of the insured. Current law also extends the exclusion to certain viatical settlements and accelerated death benefits made on behalf of an insured who is terminally ill and expected to die within 24 months.

Transfer-for-Value Rule

transfer-for-value rule
The most important exception to the general rule of exclusion of life insurance death proceeds from federal income taxation is the *transfer-for-value rule*. This rule provides that if a policy is transferred from one owner to another for valuable consideration, the income tax exclusion is lost. When the insured dies in these cases, the policy beneficiary will recover income tax free only the amount the transferee-owner paid for the policy, plus any premiums subsequently paid. The transfer-for-value rule is not limited to an outright sale of a policy. This rule can also apply when a noncash consideration for a policy transfer can be inferred.

Thus, the transfer-for-value rule is an exception to the general rule of exclusion for policy proceeds. There are also exceptions to the exception (a common phenomenon in tax law). Policy transfers that are not jeopardized by the transfer-for-value rule are as follows:

- transfers in which the transferee-owner is the insured
- transfers to a partner of the insured
- transfers to a partnership in which the insured is a partner
- transfers to a corporation of which the insured is a shareholder or officer
- transfers in which the transferee's tax basis of the policy is determined by reference to its basis to the transferor, as discussed later

Income Tax Definition of Life Insurance

The full exclusion for life insurance death proceeds depends in part on whether the policy itself meets the definition of life insurance under the Internal Revenue Code. A policy qualifies as life insurance for income tax purposes if it satisfies either of two tests. The determination whether a policy qualifies is not performed by the consumer or agent, but rather by the insurance company that makes this information available.

cash value accumulation test
The first test, the *cash value accumulation test*, generally applies to more traditional cash value policies, such as whole life policies. Under this cash value accumulation test, the cash value generally may not exceed the net single premium that would be needed to fund the policy's death benefit. The insurance company

calculates the net single premium using an assumed interest rate and certain mortality charges.

guideline premium and corridor test

The second, two-pronged test is the *guideline premium and corridor test*. Policies that are designed to pass the guideline premium and corridor test must meet both of the requirements. The guideline premium requirement limits the total premium that may be paid into the policy at any given time. This limit varies with each life insurance company based on its own expenses and its own mortality experience. The limit also varies with the insurer's own interest assumptions, subject to specified IRS limits. The policy meets the corridor or death benefit requirement, the second prong of the test, if the contract's death benefit exceeds a specified multiple of its cash value at all times. This multiple varies according to the insured's attained age. Generally, universal life and other similar types of policies are tested under this second, two-pronged test.

Settlement Options

Death proceeds distributed as a series of payments under a settlement option generally include an element of interest earned after the death of the insured, which is taxable. However, the portion of a settlement option payment that represents principal (the policy's face amount) still qualifies for the income tax exclusion.

The portion that represents the death benefit is calculated by prorating the face amount over the option's payment period. This is the excludible portion. Any excess amount of each payment represents interest. If the interest-only option is used, all interest paid or accrued is taxable. If the fixed-amount option is used, the payment period is calculated by determining the number of fixed payments needed to exhaust the policy's face amount at its guaranteed interest rate. If a life-income option is used, the present value of any refund or period-certain feature is subtracted from the excludible amount to be prorated.

Income Taxation of Living Proceeds

inside buildup

The *inside buildup* is, the increase in the cash value of a permanent life insurance policy. The inside buildup is not subject to taxation as long as it is left inside the policy. However, amounts taken out of the policy during the insured's life may be subject to taxation, as discussed in this section.

Amounts paid under a life insurance contract while the insured is still living can take several forms. The most common of these are policy loans, policy dividends, proceeds from a cash surrender, and withdrawals from the policy's cash value.

To determine the income tax effect of most of these transactions, the policyowner's tax basis in the policy must be known. A policyowner's basis is initially determined by adding the total premiums paid into the policy and subtracting the dividends, if any, that the insurer has paid. If nontaxable withdrawals have previously been made from the policy, such amounts also reduce the policyowner's basis.

Policy Loans

Generally policy loans have no effect on basis unless the policy is a modified endowment contract (MEC), as defined later. However, if a policy is surrendered, the principal amount of any outstanding loan is includible in the surrender value of the policy for tax purposes.

Policy Dividends

Policy dividends are treated as a nontaxable return of premium, and they therefore reduce the policyowner's basis. If total dividends exceed total premiums, dividends are taxable to that extent. If dividends are used to reduce premiums or otherwise paid back into the policy (for example, to buy paid-up additions), the basis reduction caused by payment of the dividend is offset by a corresponding basis increase, because the dividend is then treated as an additional premium payment.

Cash Surrender

If a policy is surrendered for cash, the taxable amount is the total surrender value minus the policyowner's current basis in the policy. Dividends left with the insurer to accumulate at interest are not included in the surrender value for tax purposes because they have already reduced the policyowner's basis in the contract.

EXAMPLE	

Aaron Sloan, aged 40, owns a level-premium whole life policy. He has paid $25,000 in premiums and has received $4,000 in dividends from the policy. The face amount of the policy is $100,000. Its total cash value is $29,000. The policy is also subject to an outstanding loan of $15,000. Aaron decides to surrender his policy for cash. The tax effects of Aaron's surrender of his policy are as follows:

Surrender Value	
Policy loan	$15,000
Plus net cash value ($29,000 total value minus $15,000 policy loan)	14,000
Total surrender value	$29,000
Basis	
Premium paid	$25,000
Minus dividends	4,000
Total basis	$21,000
Taxable Gain	
Surrender value	$29,000
Minus basis	21,000
Taxable gain	$ 8,000

Cash Withdrawal

If a policyowner withdraws funds from a policy's cash value, the general rule is that the withdrawal is first treated as a nontaxable return of basis. The excess, if any, of the amount of the withdrawal over the policyowner's current basis is taxable in the year of withdrawal. However, there are important exceptions to this general rule. These exceptions include certain withdrawals from universal life policies and withdrawals from policies classified as modified endowment contracts (MECs).

Universal Life Policies. If a cash withdrawal results in a reduction in the policy's death benefit during the first 15 years of the policy, the withdrawal may first be taxed as income to the extent of income earned within the contract. This income-first, or LIFO (last-in, first-out), method of taxation is the reverse of the general FIFO (first-in, first-out) taxation that life insurance typically enjoys.

**modified
endowment
contract (MEC)**

Modified Endowment Contracts (MECs). A policy is treated as a *modified endowment contract* if it fails a test called the 7-pay test. This test is applied at the inception of the policy and again if the policy experiences a material change. A material change generally includes most increases and certain decreases in future benefits. A common example of a material change is an increase in death benefits under the policy, resulting from a flexible premium payment.

The 7-pay test is designed to impose modified endowment contract (MEC) status on policies that take in too much premium during the first 7 policy years, or in the 7 years after a material change. For each policy, a net level premium is calculated. If the total premium actually paid into the policy at any time during the 7-year testing period is more than the sum of the net level premiums that would be needed to result in a paid-up policy after 7 years, the policy is a MEC. Simply stated, the 7-pay test is designed to discourage a premium schedule that would result in a paid-up policy before the end of a 7-year period.

Any life insurance policy that falls under the definition of a MEC is also subject to an income-first or LIFO tax treatment with respect to loans and most distributions from the policy. A 10 percent penalty tax also generally applies to the taxable portion of any loan or withdrawal from a MEC unless the taxpayer has reached age 59½. With respect to loans (not withdrawals) from a MEC, the policyowner does receive an increase in basis in the policy equal to the amount of the loan that is taxable. However, as shown in the example, the nontaxable portion of a loan from a MEC will not affect the policyowner's basis. A nontaxable portion of a withdrawal, on the other hand, will reduce the basis.

EXAMPLE
Assume that Aaron Sloan's policy in the previous example is a MEC and that he takes the $15,000 loan from the policy this year. Prior to the loan, Aaron has a total of $8,000 in untaxed gain in the policy. However, the withdrawal of any untaxed gain from the policy triggers a taxable event. Therefore, the loan will first be treated as a taxable event to the extent of $8,000. The remaining $7,000 of the loan is not taxable to Aaron. The $8,000 taxable portion of the loan will also be subject to the 10 percent penalty tax because Aaron is under age 59½. Aaron's basis in the policy will be increased by $8,000 (the taxable portion of the loan). Therefore, Aaron's basis is now $29,000 ($21,000 + $8,000).

1035 Exchanges

A taxable event usually occurs when an existing insurance policy with a cash value is surrendered. However, Sec. 1035 of the Internal Revenue Code provides that replacing one life insurance policy with another is a nontaxable event when certain requirements are met. A policyowner may therefore exchange a life insurance policy for a new policy, insuring the same person, without paying tax on the investment gains earned in the original contract. Only certain exchanges qualify and a qualifying exchange is referred to as a 1035 exchange. Also, the policyowner may not simply receive a check from one insurer and use the proceeds purchase a new contract from another. An actual exchange must take place between the two insurance companies. The old policy is assigned to the new insurer who then surrenders the policy to the old insurer and applies the proceeds of the surrender to the new contract.

Deductibility of Premium Payments

As a general rule, premium payments for individual life insurance policies are not deductible for federal income tax purposes. This rule applies, regardless of who owns the policy and whether it is used for personal or business purposes. In certain situations, however, life insurance premiums can be deductible because they also fit the definition of some other type of deductible expense, not because they are premium payments. For example, a premium payment for a policy on behalf of a charitable organization is deductible by the payor if the charity owns the policy outright. The premium is deductible because it is treated as a charitable contribution, not because it is a life insurance premium. Similarly, in cases where a corporation pays the premium on a policy that covers an employee and the death benefit is payable to the employee's beneficiary, the employer can deduct the premium as compensation paid to the employee. Another situation in which premium payments can fit the definition of a particular deductible expense is when premium payments constitute alimony, made on behalf of an ex-spouse.

Transfer Taxation of Life Insurance

Gift taxes and estate taxes are part of the federal transfer tax system. This section briefly reviews these two transfer taxes, with emphasis on their life insurance implications.

Federal Gift Tax

gift tax

gift

The federal *gift tax* is a tax imposed on transfers of property by gift during the donor's lifetime. The gift taxes are levied on the donor, not the gift's recipient. This tax applies only if both of the following two elements of a *gift* are present:

- a completed transfer and acceptance of property, including money
- a transfer for less than full and adequate consideration

The taxation of a transfer does not require an element of donative intent, only that the transfer be made for less than full consideration.

The lifetime amount that a person can gift on a tax-exempt basis is $5 million. This amount remains constant through 2011, then increases with inflation thereafter.

annual exclusion

Annual Exclusion. Much of the planning and complexity associated with gift tax planning involves the *annual exclusion*. In 2011, qualifying gifts of $13,000 or less can be made annually by a donor to any number of donees without gift tax. The exempt amount can be increased to $26,000 if the donor is married and the donor's spouse elects to split gifts on a timely filed gift tax return. With gift splitting, each spouse gives half the gift. The annual exclusion amount is indexed to inflation, and it increases in $1,000 increments. The annual exclusion is in addition to the lifetime tax-exempt amount of $5 million described in the previous paragraph.

Nontaxable Gifts. Although most gifts are taxable, the following are not taxable gifts:

- gifts that do not exceed the annual exclusion
- gifts to the donor's spouse
- gifts to charities
- tuition paid directly to an educational institution for someone
- medical expenses paid directly to a medical institution for someone
- gifts to a political organization for its use

Federal Estate Tax

estate tax

The federal *estate tax* is a tax imposed on the transfer of property at death. The most difficult task in calculating the estate tax is often the determination of the assets included in the decedent's estate tax base. Some of the included assets are obvious, such as individually owned property, but the estate tax rules often cause the inclusion of property in surprising circumstances. For example, property previously transferred by a decedent can be brought back to the estate tax base by provisions in the statute.

gross estate

Gross Estate. The starting point in the federal estate tax calculation is determining the property included in the decedent's gross estate. The *gross estate* includes the property in the probate estate, which is all property that passes under the deceased's will or, in the absence of a valid will, under the state intestacy law, but it also includes property transferable by the decedent at death by other means. The decedent's gross estate includes, among other things, the following:

- property individually owned by the decedent at the time of death
- (some portion of) property held jointly by the decedent at the time of death
- insurance on the decedent's life if either (1) the decedent held an incident of ownership or transferred it by gift within 3 years of death or (2) the proceeds are deemed payable to the estate
- property transferred by the decedent during his or her lifetime if the decedent retained (1) a life interest in the property, (2) a reversionary interest valued at greater than 5 percent of the property at the time of death, or (3) a right to revoke or amend the transfer at the time of death

Items Deductible from the Gross Estate. Certain items are deductible from the gross estate for estate tax calculation purposes: legitimate debts of the decedent, reasonable funeral and other death costs of the decedent, and the reasonable cost of estate settlement, such as the executor's commission and attorney fees. Moreover, the federal estate tax charitable deduction provides that transfers at death to qualifying charities are fully deductible from the estate tax base.

As with the gift tax, qualifying transfers to a surviving spouse are deductible under the marital deduction rules. Because the marital deduction is unlimited, the usual dispositive scheme (100 percent to the surviving spouse) for married individuals results in no federal taxes for a married couple until the death of the second spouse. As a client's wealth increases, sophisticated planning is needed to make optimal use of the marital deduction.

The Taxable Estate. The 2001 Economic Growth and Tax Relief Reconciliation Act significantly revised federal estate taxation. The act increased the exclusion amount, which can pass by death on a tax-exempt basis, to the levels indicated in the following table. The act also reduced the marginal tax rates, which were applied on the amount in excess of the exclusion amount. Furthermore, the exclusion amount increased and the marginal tax rate decreased for larger estates periodically through 2009. In 2010 the estate tax was eliminated.

Table 10-3 Exclusion Amounts for Estate Taxation	
Year of Death	**Exclusion Amount**
2003	$1,000,000
2004–2005	1,500,000
2006–2008	2,000,000
2009	3,500,000
2010	Unlimited
2011–2012	5,000,000

In December of 2010, Congress passed and the President signed the Tax Relief, Unemployment Insurance Reauthorization and Job Creation Act of 2010 (2010 Tax Relief Act). It provides a top federal estate tax rate of 35 percent with a $5 million exclusion amount for 2011 and 2012, at which point it sunsets (expires). The applicable exclusion amount is adjusted for inflation beginning in 2012. The 2010 Tax Relief Act also provides for "portability" of the estate tax applicable exclusion amount, allowing a surviving spouse to elect to take advantage of the unused portion of the estate tax exclusion amount of his or her predeceased spouse.

Federal Gift Taxation of Life Insurance

Gifts of life insurance are treated in the same manner as gifts of any other assets as far as the annual exclusion ($13,000 for 2011) is concerned.

Sometimes there is an inadvertent gift of life insurance policy proceeds. This can happen when a policy one individual owns on another's life matures by reason of the insured's death and a person other than the policyowner has been named as beneficiary. For example, if a wife purchases a policy on her husband's life and names her children as beneficiaries, the proceeds that otherwise would have been payable to her are payable instead to her children at her husband's death. The transaction is treated as if the policyowner—the wife—had received the proceeds and made a gift in that amount to her children. Moreover, gift splitting will not be allowed because there is no longer a spouse with whom to split the gift.

Federal Estate Taxation of Life Insurance

Estate taxes are payable on property included in a decedent's gross estate if the decedent's estate exceeds the available deductions and credits. Frequently, life insurance is the single largest asset or group of assets in the gross estate. Including life insurance can often mean the difference between a federal estate tax liability and no tax liability. For this reason, it is important to look at the factors that determine when life insurance is included in the decedent-insured's gross estate for federal estate tax purposes:

- Life insurance proceeds payable to the executor, that is, to or for the benefit of the insured's estate, are includible in the estate, regardless of who owned the contract or who paid the premium.
- Life insurance proceeds are included in the estate of an insured if he or she possessed an incident of ownership in the policy at the time of his or her death.
- Life insurance proceeds are included in the gross estate of an insured who transferred incidents of ownership in the policy by gift within 3 years of his or her death.

Life Insurance Payable to the Executor. In general, life insurance should not be made payable to a decedent's estate. There are many reasons in addition to avoiding federal estate taxation why estate planners seldom recommend such a beneficiary designation. These reasons include the following:

- Insurance payable to a decedent's estate subjects the proceeds to the claims of the estate's creditors.
- Insurance payable to a decedent's estate subjects the proceeds to costs of probate administration, such as executor's fees, but provides no corresponding advantages.

incident of
ownership

Possession of Incidents of Ownership. When insurance proceeds are paid to a named beneficiary other than the insured's estate, incidents of ownership in the policy at the time of death are the key criteria for determining inclusion. If the insured held an incident of ownership at the time of his or her death, the policy is included in his or her gross estate. An *incident of ownership* is broadly defined as an element of ownership or degree of control over a policy. Incidents of ownership include, but are not limited to, the power to

- change the beneficiary
- assign the policy
- borrow on the policy
- surrender the policy
- exercise any of the other essential contract rights or privileges

Merely being the beneficiary of a policy's death benefit is not an incident of ownership.

Like any other property, a life insurance policy is an asset that a policyowner can freely assign in a gift or sale. Thus, the policyowner may transfer limited interests to others while retaining some of the privileges and rights in the policy. However, to remove the proceeds from the scope of the federal estate tax, the insured must divest himself or herself of all significant rights and privileges under the contract.

Transfers of Policies within 3 Years of Death. Life insurance policies are often transferred to others so that policy proceeds will not be in the insured's gross estate when he or she dies. Inclusion will still result, however, if the insured dies within 3 years of a gratuitous transfer. Under this 3-year rule, life insurance transferred to a third party for less than full consideration within 3 years of the insured's death is automatically includible in the insured's gross estate. Transfers made more than 3 years before the insured's death are not normally includible in the insured's estate if the insured has retained no incidents of ownership. In addition, a sale to a third party for the full fair market value of the policy will not be included even if the sale occurs within 3 years of the insured's death.

Life Insurance and the Federal Estate Tax Marital Deduction. Life insurance proceeds payable at the insured's death to his or her surviving spouse can qualify for the federal estate tax marital deduction. Because the marital deduction is unlimited, the full value of life insurance proceeds payable in a qualifying manner to the surviving spouse is deductible from the insured's gross estate.

USES OF LIFE INSURANCE IN ESTATE PLANNING

The goal of life insurance in an estate plan depends on many factors specific to the client. The goals for life insurance in general, however, can be divided into two categories:

- estate enhancement
- estate liquidity/wealth replacement

The goals of a specific client for his or her life insurance planning depend on age, family circumstances, and financial status.

Estate Enhancement Purposes

In many cases, a client's estate at death will not be sufficient to provide for the basic needs of his or her heirs. This is particularly true for (1) young clients, (2) clients with family members dependent on their income, and/or (3) clients with small- to moderate-sized estates. They may still have their peak earning years in front of them. The basic support needs of their family, such as educational, medical, and retirement savings programs, depend on this income. It is essential for these clients to investigate their life insurance coverage needs and secure sufficient insurance to enhance their estates to a size that is, at the very least, adequate to handle their dependent family members' basic needs. Life insurance is the perfect estate enhancement device to replace the financial loss created by premature death.

Estate Liquidity/Wealth Replacement Purposes

For older clients or clients with large estates, estate liquidity/wealth replacement is often the primary goal of life insurance coverage. Their children's support and educational expense needs are usually things of the past. Older clients are nearing the end of their income-producing years and should, presumably, have less future income to replace. Their needs for estate enhancement from life insurance should have diminished in importance relative to their estate liquidity/wealth replacement needs.

A prospective insured may need coverage for estate liquidity/wealth replacement for the following purposes:

- *probate expenses.* Estate settlement costs usually increase with the size of the estate. The cost for such professionals as executors, attorneys, accountants, and appraisers to settle an estate is often based on a percentage of the total size of the probate estate. Generally, the larger the estate, the greater the complexity and need for costly professional help. One advantage of life insurance is that it avoids probate if paid to a named beneficiary.
- *death taxes.* As discussed above, federal estate taxes, as well as other taxes, also increase with the size of the estate. Federal estate taxes, and state death taxes in many states, are based on a

progressive rate schedule. Thus, wealthy individuals often desire life insurance to replace the wealth lost to taxes.

- ***liquidity needs.*** Wealthy clients often face an additional problem. Frequently, their accumulated wealth contains assets that are not liquid. For example, wealthy individuals often own closely held businesses that may be unmarketable to outsiders. Death taxes and other estate settlement costs are based on the full value of such assets the estate owns and must be paid in cash. The liquidity problems an estate faces often result in the forced sale of estate assets on undesirable terms.

Estate Planning Techniques with Life Insurance

There are many practical uses for life insurance in the estate planning context. Three are described briefly here:

- gifts of policies to family members
- providing estate liquidity
- the second-to-die policy

Gifts of Policies to Family Members

Although the 3-year rule causes estate tax inclusion if the insured transfers incidents of ownership within 3 years of his or her death, transferring or assigning a life insurance policy to family members might still be an appropriate planning step. The insured simply has to live more than 3 years following the transfer to avoid inclusion of the proceeds in his or her estate. Even if the insured dies within 3 years, he or she will be no worse off from an estate tax standpoint, because the policy would have been included in any event had the transfer or assignment not occurred.

There are many reasons why estate planners recommend a life insurance policy gifting program. Some of the reasons are as follows:

- The donee feels no richer after the gift of the life insurance policy and will seldom dispose of it foolishly.
- The donor-insured's financial position is not markedly affected by making a gift of life insurance.
- The gift tax cost to transfer a policy is usually nominal compared to the potential estate tax savings if a person is in a situation where the gift tax applies. Through efficient use of the donor-insured's annual exclusion, the gift of the policy and subsequent premiums can actually avoid gift taxes entirely.

- The gift of a life insurance policy is particularly advantageous for older donors whose estate planning concerns have risen in priority in relation to their other financial planning goals. Usually, older insureds can select appropriate beneficiaries with more certainty, and they are less concerned about a policy's cash surrender value. If a life insurance policy is gifted more than 3 years before the donor's death, the transfer tax savings is substantial.

Providing Estate Liquidity

Unless the executor of an estate wishes to go through a series of complex and burdensome requests for an extension, the estate tax due must be paid within 9 months of the date of death. If the gross estate is composed of liquid assets, the executor or administrator faces no problem in meeting the 9-month deadline successfully. For example, if the estate is composed of sufficient cash, marketable securities, or life insurance proceeds, there will be ample liquidity to ensure that the tax can be paid within the required time. Conversely, if the federal estate tax liability exceeds the amount of liquid assets available, there will be an estate liquidity deficit. To meet the 9-month deadline, a forced liquidation of assets, possibly at a loss, will be necessary.

Life insurance is the most effective way to supply needed dollars to meet federal estate tax obligations for several reasons. First, the dollars, in the form of death proceeds, are free of federal income taxation. Second, if someone or some entity other than the insured owns the life insurance, the policy's face amount will not be included as part of the decedent's gross estate. Finally, a sizable death benefit may be purchased for pennies on the dollar in the form of premium payments.

Second-to-Die Policy

The federal estate tax marital deduction is now unlimited in nature and scope. Consequently, there is a propensity by estate owners to leave their entire estates to their surviving spouses, which ensures no estate tax liability at the first death. There is, unfortunately, a serious flaw in this approach.

The concept of the federal estate tax marital deduction is based on deferral, rather than complete avoidance, of estate tax liability. Although the deduction is unlimited, to use the deduction to its fullest extent creates a stacking of estate taxes at the second death. The estate tax liability from the first to die is added to that of the second to die. The result is a higher estate tax liability overall.

**Survivorship Life Insurance
(Second-to-Die Coverage)**

- Pays the death benefit only at the death of the surviving spouse
- The federal estate tax system allows an unlimited marital deduction
- Problem: the estate tax bill at the death of the surviving spouse
- Solution: death benefit payable at the second death on a far less costly basis than two separate policies

---

The unlimited marital deduction has created a need for greater planning for the death of the second spouse. That is why the second-to-die policy was instituted. At the death of the first spouse, no death benefit is paid; at the death of the second spouse, the policy proceeds are paid to the named beneficiary.

Second-to-die coverage is often a perfect fit in a married couple's estate plan. The most common use of second-to-die coverage is in an estate plan in which taking the unlimited marital deduction after the death of the first spouse will result in more substantial taxes at the death of the second spouse. With second-to-die coverage, policy benefits will be paid when the insured married couple incurs these more substantial taxes—at the second death of the two spouses.

CHECKLIST FOR EVALUATING AND COMPARING LIFE INSURANCE POLICIES

- What are the provisions concerning premium payments?

  ___ Are they level or rising at each renewal date?

  ___ Are they flexible at the policyowner's option at each renewal date?

  ___ Are they payable for life or for a specified number of years?

- What is the initial policy premium?

  ___ What is the 20-year surrender cost index?

  ___ What is the 20-year net payment cost index?

- Is the duration of death benefit protection for a limited number of years? If yes,

___ Is the policy renewable for additional periods? If yes, until when?

___ Is the policy convertible to permanent coverage? If yes, until when?

- What is the initial amount of death benefit protection?
- How does the amount of death protection change thereafter?
- Does the policy contain a cash value? If yes,

  ___ Is there a minimum guaranteed amount?

  ___ Is there a minimum guaranteed interest rate?

  ___ In what year is it first available?

  ___ Will it grow with inflation?

  ___ What nonforfeiture options are available?

  ___ Are withdrawals permitted?

  ___ Are policy loans allowed?

  ___ What is the interest rate for policy loans?

  ___ Is an automatic premium loan option available?

  ___ Is the inside buildup tax deferred?

  ___ Are policyowner-directed types of investments available?

- Is the policy participating? If yes,

  ___ When are dividends likely to be available for the first time?

  ___ Are dividends usable to buy additional term or permanent insurance?

  ___ Are dividends affected by policy loans?

  ___ What is the interest rate if dividends are left to accumulate?

  ___ What is the insurer's track record of meeting dividend projections?

- What is the length of time available to reinstate?
- What settlement options does the policy contain?
- How soon can the policy be made to mature as an endowment?
- What is length of the contestable period?
- What is length of the suicide exclusion?
- Are accelerated benefits available?
- Is an accidental death benefit rider available?
- Is a guaranteed purchase (insurability) rider available?

  ___ What is the amount that may be bought?

___ What is the frequency of purchase dates?

• Is a waiver-of-premium rider available?

___ What is the definition of disability?

___ What is the length of the waiting period?

___ Are premiums waived retroactively to the start of disability?

___ Is there an age before which disability must occur?

CHAPTER REVIEW

Key Terms and Concepts

financial needs analysis
capital needs analysis
surrender cost index
net payment cost index
illustration
replacement
1035 exchange
rate-up age method
extra percentage tables
flat extra premium
lien
viatical settlement
life settlement
stranger-originated life insurance (STOLI)
key employee life insurance

buy-sell agreement
entity agreement
cross-purchase agreement
Sec. 79 plan
split-dollar life insurance
transfer-for-value rule
cash value accumulation test
guideline premium and corridor test
inside buildup
modified endowment contract (MEC)
gift tax
gift
annual exclusion
estate tax
gross estate
incident of ownership

Review Questions

Review questions are based on the learning objectives in this chapter. Thus, a [3] at the end of a question means that the question is based on learning objective 3. If there are multiple objectives, they are all listed.

1. Life insurance plays a key role in most clients' financial plans. What two basic tasks are involved in life insurance planning? [1]

2. Before gathering the information required for determining the amount of additional life insurance your client needs, explain to your client the key steps involved and types of information required in the financial needs analysis approach. [1]

3. Sophie Jones, a single mother and corporate manager on the "fast track," needs help to determine the amount of additional life insurance she needs to provide support for her children if she should die before they finish college. After gathering information regarding the family's needs in the event of Sophie's death, you find that support for the children, including college educations, would require $300,000 to meet lump-sum needs. Also, taking into account reasonable assumptions regarding inflation, after-tax investment returns, and Social Security benefits for the children, you calculate that a present value of $200,000 would be required to meet the children's income support needs if Sophie were to die today. Fact-finding indicates that Sophie already has $200,000 of group term life insurance and $50,000 in savings. How much additional life insurance would Sophie need if the principal will be liquidated to help meet the family's needs? [1]

4. What are the steps in the capital needs analysis approach for determining the amount of additional life insurance your client needs, and how does that approach differ from the financial needs analysis approach? [1]

5. Many clients have heard the "buy term and invest the difference" argument against the use of permanent life insurance. This argument is based on the assumption that an individual can invest his or her surplus funds more wisely and with greater returns than a life insurance company can. Analyze this argument in terms of the following objectives of an investment program: safety of principal, yield, and liquidity. [1]

6. What distinguishing characteristics may make one type of permanent life insurance preferable over another type for a particular client? [1]

7. A financial planning client of yours received a buyer's guide and policy summary from an agent trying to sell him some additional life insurance. Your client asked the agent several questions, but the agent said, "Don't worry about that detail. We're just required by law to give it to you. Our policy is a good buy." Answer the following questions your client asked:

    a. "The summary says the policy has a surrender cost index of $7.35 per $1,000 of coverage. What does that number indicate, and generally how was it calculated?" [2]

    b. "How does the net payment cost index shown in the summary differ from the surrender cost index?" [2]

    c. "Why is there so much concern with taking interest into account in these calculations? Why can't you just calculate the cost of a life insurance policy by adding the premiums for 20 years and subtracting the sum of the illustrated dividends for 20 years and the 20th-year cash value?" [2]

8. What are the major elements of the NAIC model regulation that applies to life insurance policy illustrations? [3]

9. You suggested to a financial planning client that she might want to consider replacing a life insurance policy she already owns with a new one. She quickly replied, "An agent told me at a cocktail party last week that you should never replace a life insurance policy. In fact, it's against the law." Advise her by answering the following questions:

    a. Why might replacement of an existing policy be advantageous to a client? [3]

    b. If replacement itself is not illegal, what type of replacement is illegal? [3]

    c. What requirements are typically imposed on the replacing agent, the replacing insurer, and the existing insurer or agent by state law? [3]

10. A client of yours applies for life insurance, and he is placed in a substandard classification. He says, "So my job is hazardous. I'm in great health as the underwriting showed. Besides, no one has ever died on a job site where I've worked except from bad health. What's the deal?" Explain to your client the rationale for substandard insurance. [4]

11. What methods life do insurers use to handle substandard risks? Be sure to indicate the type(s) of substandard risk for which each method is most commonly used. [4]

12. What are the benefits and pitfalls of a policyowner's viaticating an insurance policy? [5]

13. Compare accelerated benefits, viatical agreements, and life settlements as alternatives for converting a life insurance policy to cash. [5]

14. Suzie Pomeranz, a financial planning client, owns her own rapidly growing business with two minority stockholders. As CEO, she asks for advice in dealing with the following:

a. The firm has a number of salespersons, but one, Betty, is the superstar in terms of generating and closing deals. Suzie is concerned with the loss of income, the extra expenses, and the potential effect on the corporate credit rating if Betty were to die. What can you suggest as a solution, and how might it be funded? [6]

b. The two minority stockholders who own a total of 40 percent of the voting stock are also corporate vice presidents. They have expressed concern to Suzie about their futures because, if she were to die, her majority shares would currently pass to her playboy son Lance, who has already indicated he would change operations significantly to focus on current return to the owners rather than on long-term growth. What could you suggest as a means to financially protect the interests of both Suzie's estate and the two minority stockholders in the event of Suzie's death? How might your recommended solution be funded? [6]

c. Suzie feels that because the business is growing rapidly due to the very productive contributions of her employees, as an employee benefit, they should all be provided with life insurance protection equal to two times their salary. What would you suggest as a cost-effective way to accomplish this objective? [6]

15. What provisions are generally included in a properly designed buy-sell agreement? [6]

16. What are the general rules and key exceptions with regard to the federal income tax treatment of the following aspects of life insurance?
a. death proceeds distributed in a lump sum [7]
b. death proceeds distributed under a settlement option [7]
c. policy dividends [7]
d. inside buildup of a policy's cash value [7]
e. withdrawal of funds from a policy's cash value [7]
f. policy loans [7]
g. loans and most other distributions from a policy that falls under the definition of a MEC [7]
h. premium payments [7]

17. Describe the following aspects of the federal gift tax system:
a. the essential elements of a taxable gift [7]
b. the annual exclusion [7]
c. deductions from the gift tax base [7]

18. What key factors are taken into account in calculating the federal estate tax? Explain each. [7]

19. In each of the following situations, are the proceeds of the life insurance policy included in your client John's estate for federal estate tax purposes upon his death, and if so, why?
    a. John's wife purchased a policy on John's life. She was the policyowner and paid all the premiums. She named John's estate as primary beneficiary so there would be sufficient liquidity to pay estate taxes and she would not be required to sell the family home upon his death. [8]
    b. John purchased a policy on his own life and named his children as beneficiaries. Although he was initially the policyowner, he transferred all the rights in the policy to his wife 5 years ago except the right to change the beneficiary. [8]
    c. John purchased a policy on his own life and named his children as beneficiaries. Although he was initially the policyowner, he gave all the rights in the policy to his wife 2 years before his death. [8]

20. Discuss some key uses of life insurance in estate planning. [8]

Learning Objectives

An understanding of the material in this chapter should enable the student to

1. Explain the nature of annuities, and compare and contrast them with life insurance.

2. Contrast the various types of annuities, and explain their key features.

3. Describe actuarial considerations, fees, and charges for annuities.

4. Describe the taxation of annuities during the accumulation and liquidation periods.

5. Explain uses of annuities, including charitable gift annuities, structured settlements, and impaired risk annuities.

6. Explain the major ethical issues involved in annuity sales.

Besides selling life insurance, many life insurers also sell annuity contracts, in which they promise to pay an income to the annuitant for a fixed period of time or for life. Based on mortality tables similar to those used in life insurance, which pays benefits when the insured dies, annuities were originally developed to provide a fixed stream of income that persists until the death of the annuitant. Because the internal buildup of earnings within an annuity is not taxed until funds are withdrawn, tax deferral is an important feature, perhaps the most important feature in many annuity sales. Clients and financial planners sometimes regard annuities as a tax-advantaged alternative to other investments, although the fees associated with annuities often offset the advantages.

This discussion does not focus on the use of annuities as investments, but on the structure of various annuity products that clients may use to accumulate and disperse assets. The tax treatment of annuities is briefly discussed.

TERMS ASSOCIATED WITH ANNUITIES

annuity

annuitant

An *annuity* is a periodic payment that will begin at a specified or contingent date and continue throughout a fixed period or for the duration of a designated life or lives. The person on whose life the duration of the payments is based is called the *annuitant.* The annuitant is usually but not always the person who receives the periodic payments. Payments under the annuity contract may be on an annual, semiannual, quarterly, or monthly basis, depending on the conditions of the agreement. Usually, payments are made monthly.

Annuity Definitions

- annuitant—the person on whose life the duration of payments may be based; usually also the person receiving the payments
- annuity certain—payments made for a definite period of time; no relationship to how long the annuitant lives
- life (whole life) annuity—payments made until the annuitant dies; the word "life" in the title indicates that payments are based on life contingencies
- temporary life annuity—payments made until the annuitant dies or for a specified period of time, whichever time period is shorter

---

annuity certain

life (whole life) annuity

temporary life annuity

If annuity payments are to be made for a definite period of time without being linked to the duration of a specified human life, the agreement is known as an *annuity certain* or fixed-period annuity. If the payments are to be made for the duration of a designated life, the agreement is called a *life annuity* or, more accurately, a single-life annuity. This life annuity is also referred to as a *whole life annuity* to distinguish it from a *temporary life annuity*, under which payments are made during a specified period of time, but only for as long as a designated person is alive. In other words, a temporary life annuity terminates with the death of the designated individual or at the expiration of the specified period of time, whichever occurs earlier. The temporary life annuity concept is used in determining premiums for life insurance policies and is not used as a product sold to the public. The whole life annuity is for the entire duration of the designated life. The word *life* in the title of an annuity indicates that the payments are based on life contingencies; that is, they continue only as long as a designated person is alive. Life annuities are created by life insurance companies.

NATURE OF ANNUITIES

Comparison with Life Insurance

The primary function of life insurance is to *create* an estate or principal sum; the primary function of an annuity is to *liquidate* a principal sum, regardless of how it was created. Despite this basic dissimilarity in function, both life insurance and annuities are based on the same fundamental pooling, mortality, and investment principles.

Both life insurance and annuities can protect against loss of income. Life insurance furnishes protection against loss of income arising out of premature death; an annuity provides protection against loss of income arising out of excessive longevity. While life insurance can provide a financial hedge against dying too soon, an annuity can provide a hedge against living too long. From a financial standpoint, both contingencies are undesirable.

Life Insurance Compared with Annuities	
Life Insurance	**Annuities**
• Protects against loss of income resulting from premature death	• Protect against loss of income arising out of excessive longevity
• Pooling arrangement in which those who live beyond their life expectancy compensate dependents of those who die prematurely	• Pooling arrangement in which those who die prematurely contribute to the income of those who live beyond their life expectancy
• Premiums based on a mortality table	• Premiums based on a different mortality table
• Premiums discounted to reflect interest earned by the insurer	• Premiums (deposits) discounted to reflect interest earned by the insurer

A second common feature that life insurance and annuities share is the pooling technique. Insurance is a pooling arrangement where all members contribute so that the dependents of those who die prematurely are partially compensated for loss of income. An annuity is a pooling arrangement where those who die prematurely contribute so that those who live beyond their life expectancy will not outlive their income.

A third common feature that life insurance and annuities share is that contributions are based on probabilities of death and survival derived from a mortality table. For reasons that will be apparent later, the same mortality table is not used for both sets of calculations. Finally, for both life insurance and annuities, premiums are discounted for the compound interest that the insurance company will earn on them.

Annuity Principle

Like life insurance, the annuity principle is founded on the unpredictability of any given human life. A person may have accumulated a principal sum to be liquidated for income over the person's remaining years. However, the individual must accurately predict the number of years remaining. With average health and vitality for his or her age, the individual could expect to live exactly the calculated life expectancy, based on a mortality table. But because survival beyond this predicted life expectancy is possible, to be conservative, the accumulated principal would have to be adequate to fund a longer period than the annuitant is likely to live. Even then, there is some danger of finding the assets and income totally consumed prior to death.

On the other hand, the annuitant might die after only a few years, leaving funds to the estate that could have been used to provide more comforts during the decedent's lifetime. If the annuitant is willing to pool savings with those of other people in the same situation, the administering agency, relying on the laws of probability and large numbers, can provide all the participants with an income of a specified amount as long as they live—regardless of longevity. In this way none of the participants could outlive their income. This arrangement relies on participants' willingness to have all or a portion of their unliquidated principal at the time of death used to supplement the principal of those who live beyond their life expectancy. Therefore, each payment to the annuitant is composed partly of the annuitant's principal, the unliquidated principal of other annuitants who die early, and investment income on these funds.

Classifications of Annuities

As the following figure shows, annuities can be classified in many different ways, depending on the point of emphasis.

The distribution of benefits may extend only for the life of the annuitant or may include some minimum guaranteed total payout. The annuity may cover only one life, or it may depend on the longevity of two (or more) persons. The benefit payments may begin immediately or at some future date. The annuity may be purchased through a single premium or through installment premiums. Last, the amount of each annuity payment may be fixed or variable. The discussion that follows provides details on the types and characteristics of annuities.

Figure 11-1
Classification of Types of Individual Annuities

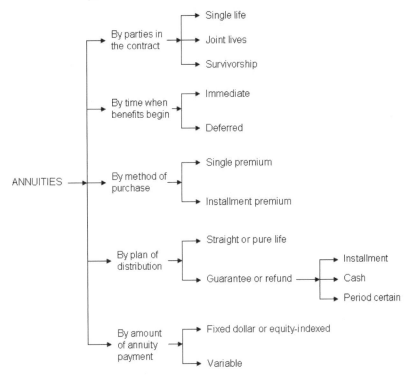

Number of Lives Covered

joint (joint-life)
annuity

joint-and-last-survivor
annuity

An annuity may cover a single life or more than one life. A single-life annuity is most common. A contract that covers two or more lives may be a joint annuity or a joint-and-last-survivor annuity. The seldom-issued *joint* or *joint-life annuity* provides that the income ceases at the first death among the lives covered. A *joint-and-last-survivor annuity*, on the other hand, provides that the income ceases only at the last death among the lives covered. In other words, payments under a joint-and-last-survivor annuity continue for as long as either of two or more specified persons lives. This annuity contract is very useful, and widely marketed, especially for husband and wife couples. Annuity contracts that involve more than two lives are uncommon.

Time When Benefit Payments Commence

immediate
annuity

Annuities can also be classified as immediate or deferred. An *immediate annuity* makes the first benefit payment one payment interval after the date of purchase. If the contract provides for monthly payments, the first benefit payment is due 1 month after the date of purchase; if annual payments are called for, the first payment is due 1 year after the date of purchase. An immediate annuity is always purchased with a single premium; the annuitant exchanges a principal sum for a lifetime income or some other payment promise.

deferred annuity

Under a *deferred annuity*, a period longer than one payment interval must elapse after purchase before the first benefit payment is due. Normally at least several years elapse between the date of purchase and the time when payments commence. A deferred annuity is suitable for many people, including those of ordinary means who want to accumulate a sum for their old age.

longevity
insurance

Longevity insurance refers to a class of pure deferred annuities that provide a future income stream during the distribution period, which typically begins at a relatively advanced age such as 85. Although longevity insurance tends to offer bigger payouts than other alternatives, survivors receive no benefit if the annuitant dies before the distribution period begins.

Method of Premium Payment

Deferred annuities can be purchased with either single premiums or periodic premiums. Originally, an annuity was developed as a contract purchased with a lump sum, perhaps accumulated from a successful business venture or an inheritance. The lump sum was paid in exchange for an immediate periodic income of a stipulated amount. Immediate annuities are still purchased with a lump sum, but most annuities today are purchased on an installment basis. Periodic payments may be scheduled level deposits or may be flexible deposits with the amount and timing at the purchaser's discretion. A deferred annuity provides an attractive and convenient method of accumulating over time the necessary funds for an adequate old-age income.

Nature of the Insurer's Obligation

accumulation period

liquidation period

pure (straight life) annuity

When discussing deferred annuities, it is important to distinguish between the *accumulation period*, during which premiums (deposits) are paid *to* the insurer, and the liquidation period, during which benefits are paid *by* the insurer. During the *liquidation period*, a *pure annuity*, also known as a *straight life annuity*, provides periodic—usually monthly—income payments that continue as long as the annuitant lives and terminate at that person's death. Most deferred annuities sold to individuals provide that all premiums paid will be refunded, with or without interest, if the insured dies during the accumulation period. In any case, a pure annuity or straight life annuity is considered to be fully liquidated upon the death of the annuitant, regardless of how soon after the beginning of the liquidation period death may occur. There is no guarantee that the insurer will pay any particular number of monthly payments during the liquidation period. This nonrefund feature applies to the liquidation period of not only deferred annuities but also immediate annuities.

refund annuity

A pure annuity will make no additional payments after the death of an annuitant, even if the annuitant dies very early in the liquidation period. In contrast, a *refund annuity* includes a promise to return all, or at least part, of the purchase price of the annuity in some manner. As might be expected, refund annuities are far more popular than pure annuities. A refund annuity contract take several forms, as discussed in the following sections.

EXAMPLE

Betsy, aged 60, is retiring and wants to take the $100,000 in vested funds from her employer's retirement plan in a lump sum. She plans to use this money to purchase an annuity to fund her retirement.

She learns that the insurer offers a life annuity that will pay her $558 per month until she dies, whether she lives for 1 month or 50 years. Betsy is not thrilled with the idea that her $100,000 retirement fund could pay as little as $558 in benefits (or even nothing at all if she dies within the first month).

She also learns that the insurer offers a refund annuity that will pay her a little less money, $551 per month for life, *and* guarantee payments for at least 10 years, even if she does not live that long. Betsy chooses the 10-year certain annuity.

Fixed or Variable Benefit Amounts

fixed annuity

variable annuity

Annuities may provide a fixed number of dollars for each benefit payment (fixed annuity) or a varying payment (variable annuity) based on the investment performance of the assets underlying the annuity. The conventional *fixed annuity* provides periodic payments of a fixed dollar amount over a specified period or throughout the lifetime of one or more persons. Significant inflation during some recent periods, however, focused attention on the need to protect the purchasing power of benefits. In response to this need, *variable annuity* contracts were developed to provide benefits that vary with changes in investment performance.

Liquidation Period

The liquidation period is the period during which the capital sum is paid out. The capital sum here is either (1) the single premium that funds an immediate annuity or (2) the periodic premiums paid during the accumulation period, plus interest accrued on those payments, that fund a deferred annuity. Because of the nature of an annuity, the total amount paid out—or liquidated—in any specific case may actually be less or more than the principal sum, plus accumulated earnings. If the annuitant lives longer than expected, the amount ultimately paid may exceed the principal sum plus earnings, and vice versa. Although this discussion refers specifically to annuities, the same principles apply to the liquidation of a principal sum under the life-income settlement option of a life insurance policy. These principles also apply when an annuity is used in lieu of a lump-sum payment to settle a liability claim, referred to as a structured settlement.

Pure Annuities

A pure annuity provides periodic benefit payments for the lifetime of the annuitant. The premium paid for the annuity is fully earned by the insurance company when the benefit payments begin; no refund is possible. Periodic benefit payments can be made monthly, quarterly, semiannually, or annually. The more frequent the periodic payments, the more costly the annuity for the owner. The insurer must charge more due to the greater expense of writing frequent checks, the loss of interest earnings by the insurance company, and the greater probability that the annuitant will live to receive at least some of the payments. For example, if the annuitant dies 6 months and 1 day after purchasing the annuity, he or she would have received six monthly payments if the benefit payment is monthly but no benefit payments if the benefit is payable annually.

A pure annuity provides the maximum income per dollar of outlay, and for that reason, it is perhaps most suitable for people with only a limited amount of capital. According to typical actuarial assumptions, $1,000 of capital will provide monthly income between $7 and $10 for males aged 65 and between $6 and $9 for females aged 65 under a straight life annuity. If payments are guaranteed for 10 years, whether the annuitant lives or dies, the monthly income will be reduced approximately $.50 for each $1,000 increment. On an investment of $100,000, the difference in monthly income will be $50, which might be the difference between dependency and self-sufficiency for an elderly person. For a person aged 70, the difference in monthly income from $100,000 will be $100, and at 75, the difference will be $175—too large to ignore.

At younger ages, because of the high probability of survival, the difference in income between an annuity without a refund feature and one with a refund feature is extremely small. A person aged 35 can obtain an annuity with a 5-year guarantee for the same cost as a pure annuity and an annuity with a 10-year guarantee at the sacrifice of only a few cents of monthly income per $1,000 of outlay. Even someone aged 55 can obtain a 10-year guarantee at a reduction in monthly income of less than $.50. In general, the chances for males under 60 and females under 65 to survive the typical periods of guaranteed payments are so high that little in monthly income is gained by giving up the refund feature. Even so, if a particular younger-aged annuitant does die early during the liquidation period and he or she has not opted for a refund feature, the financial loss to the heirs can be substantial.

Refund Annuities

Most people have strong objections to placing a substantial sum of money into a contract that promises little or no benefit to their heirs if the annuitant dies at an early age. Therefore, to make annuities marketable, insurance companies add a refund feature. The refund feature in a refund annuity can take two general forms: a promise to provide at least a certain number of annuity payments whether the annuitant lives or dies, or a promise to refund all or a portion of the purchase price in the event of the annuitant's early death.

The table below summarizes these refund features.

Table 11-1 Refund Features During Liquidation		
	Annuitant Dies:	**Then:**
Pure annuity	During liquidation	No further payments
Life annuity certain	During period certain	Payments to contingent payee for remainder of period certain
	After period certain	No further payments
Installment refund	When total payments < purchase price	Payments to contingent payee until purchase price is recovered
	When total payments ≥ purchase price	No further payments
Cash refund annuity	When total payments < purchase price	Lump sum paid to contingent payee equal to purchase price minus total payments
	When total payments ≥ purchase price	No further payments
50 percent refund annuity	When total payments < 50% × purchase price	Payments on lump sum paid to contingent payee equal to (50% × purchase price) minus total payments
	When total payments ≥ 50% × purchase price	No further payments

life annuity certain

Life Annuity Certain. One type of contract goes under various names, including *life annuity certain*, life annuity certain and continuous, life annuity with installments certain, life annuity with a period certain guarantee, and life annuity with minimum guaranteed return. This annuity pays a *guaranteed minimum number of monthly payments*, regardless whether the annuitant lives or dies, and payments continue for the whole of the annuitant's life if he or she lives beyond the guaranteed period. Contracts can be written with payments guaranteed for 5, 10, 15, 20, or even 25 years, although not all insurers offer such a wide range of choices.

As the following figure illustrates, the life annuity certain can be viewed as a combination of two components: an annuity certain and a pure deferred life annuity. The annuity certain covers the period of guaranteed payments and provides the payments regardless of whether the annuitant is living. The pure deferred life annuity becomes effective if the annuitant is still alive at the end of the period of guaranteed payments, and it provides continuing lifetime benefits. If the annuitant does not survive the period of guaranteed payments, no payments are made under the deferred life annuity, and no refund is forthcoming.

Figure 11-2
Two Components of a Life Annuity Certain

Annuity Liquidation Period (Years)	
Annuity Certain	**Pure Deferred Life Annuity**
Payments will be made whether annuitant is dead or alive.	If annuitant is still alive, payments will be made until annuitant dies.
1 2 3 4 5	6 7 8 9 10, etc.
As the annuity certain period is reduced, the refund annuity provides a higher benefit for a given purchase price (or lower price for a given benefit).	As the annuity certain period is increased, the refund annuity provides a lower benefit for a given purchase price (or higher price for a given benefit).
The cost for this period varies directly with the length of the term for which payments are guaranteed.	The cost for this period decreases as the age at which the commencement of the deferred life annuity increases.

All other things being equal, an annuity with a period certain is always more expensive per dollar of income than a straight life annuity because it is not based solely on life contingencies. Some of the payments are a certainty; the only cost-reducing factor is the compound interest earned on the unliquidated portion of the purchase price. Therefore, the longer the term of the period certain (the period of guaranteed payments), the more costly this type of refund annuity is or the lower the yield on the purchase price. Because the annuity certain is not based solely on life contingencies, the cost of an annuity certain does not depend on the age of the annuitant; it varies directly with the length of the term. At any particular age, however, the longer the period of guaranteed payments, the less expensive the deferred life annuity will be because the higher the age at which the deferred life annuity commences, the smaller the probability that the annuitant will survive to that age. This means that the larger the number of guaranteed payments, the smaller the portion of the purchase price going into the deferred life annuity.

installment refund
annuity

Installment Refund Annuity. Under an *installment refund annuity,* if the annuitant dies before receiving monthly payments equal to the purchase price of the annuity, the payments will continue to a designated beneficiary or beneficiaries until the full cost is recovered. Of course, payments to the annuitant continue as long as he or she lives, even if the purchase price has long since been recovered in full.

EXAMPLE
Assume that Stan, aged 65, purchases an immediate annuity for $100,000. This annuity will provide a monthly life income of about $750 on an installment refund basis. If Stan dies after receiving 100 payments ($75,000), the payments will continue to a designated beneficiary until an additional $25,000 is paid out, for a total of $100,000. If Stan dies after 13 years, there will be no further payments because the entire purchase price already will have been recovered.

Cash Refund Annuity. A *cash refund annuity* promises, at the death of the annuitant, to pay to the annuitant's estate or to a designated beneficiary a lump sum amounting to the difference, if any, between the purchase price of the annuity and the sum of the monthly payments. The only difference between installment refund annuities and cash refund annuities is this:

- In an *installment refund* annuity, monthly payments (installments) continue until the purchase price has been recovered in full.
- In a *cash refund* annuity, the unrecovered portion of the purchase price is refunded in a lump sum at the time of the annuitant's death.

A cash refund annuity is naturally somewhat more expensive than the installment refund because the insurance company loses the interest it would have earned while liquidating the remaining portion of the purchase price on an installment basis. Under a cash refund annuity, the insurer uses the interest earnings on the unliquidated portion of the premiums of all annuitants receiving benefits to fund benefit payments in excess of any particular annuitant's purchase price.

50 Percent Refund Annuity. A *50 percent refund annuity* contract guarantees a minimum return of one-half of the purchase price, a compromise between a straight life annuity and a 100 percent refund annuity. Under the 50 percent refund annuity contract, if the annuitant dies before receiving benefits equal to half of the cost of the annuity, monthly installments continue until the combined payments to both the annuitant and a designated beneficiary equal half of the cost of the annuity. If available, and if the beneficiary so elects, he or she can receive the present value of the remaining payments in a lump sum. Because the guarantee under this contract is smaller than that under a 100 percent refund annuity, the income per dollar of purchase price is larger.

Another form of annuity sometimes provides that, regardless of the number of payments received prior to the annuitant's death, 50 percent of the cost of the contract will be returned in the form of a death benefit. This contract is not a refund annuity in the strict sense. Instead, the company uses one-half of the premium to provide a straight life annuity and holds the other half on deposit. It uses earnings from the half it holds on deposit to supplement the annuity benefits the other half of the premium provides. At the annuitant's death, the insurer returns the premium deposit to the annuitant's estate or to a designated beneficiary in the form of a death benefit.

Comparisons. Monthly income amounts one insurer provides under various forms of annuities per $1,000 of premium accumulations are shown in the following table. This table illustrates the small cost of a refund feature at age 60 or 65 and the high cost at more advanced ages. Note that at the highest age shown, the refund form is less expensive—or, conversely, purchases a higher monthly benefit—than a life annuity with a 10-year guarantee. Remember, however, that the benefits under each of the forms are the actuarial equivalent of those under all the other forms, and the annuitant must choose the form that is most appropriate to his or her financial and family circumstances.

Insurance companies can design annuity contracts with any period certain or with a refund guarantee for any specified percentage from 0 to 100 percent of the purchase price. In practice, however, each insurer is likely to offer only a few options, primarily due to the costs of getting regulatory approval for each type of contract.

The figures shown in the table remain fixed over the liquidation period. However, an annuitant may want benefit payments to increase with rises in the cost of living. One alternative is to purchase a variable annuity. There is no guarantee, however, as to the level of future payments. Another alternative is to select a fixed income payment that is adjusted for inflation. Only a few insurers offer such payment options, and they are not widely selected by annuitants when they are available. For example, one insurer allows the annuitant to select an inflation factor of 1, 2, 3, 4, or 5 percent. For an annuitant aged 65, the initial payment is reduced by 25 percent if he or she selects a 3 percent inflation factor and 43 percent for a 5 percent inflation factor. Each year, however, the payment amount increases by the selected inflation factor, regardless of the actual inflation rate. This insurer also allows the annuitant to select an income that will be adjusted by changes in the consumer price index, subject to a maximum 10 percent annual increase.

Table 11-2 Monthly Annuity Benefits Available per $1,000 of Purchase Price (Immediate Annuities)					
Type	**Male Age**				
	60	65	70	75	80
Life	$5.85	$6.54	$7.47	$8.89	$10.90
10-year certain + life	5.73	6.32	6.98	7.79	8.65
Refund	5.62	6.18	6.49	7.74	8.90
Type	**Female Age**				
	60	65	70	75	80
Life	$5.81	$6.16	$6.91	$8.07	$9.71
10-year certain + life	5.51	6.03	6.62	7.40	8.33
Refund	5.45	5.93	6.49	7.28	8.36

Accumulation Period

The preceding discussion of annuities related entirely to their liquidation phase, with no discussion concerning how the funds for payout had been accumulated. With deferred annuities, during an *accumulation period,* funds are invested at the insurance company to grow to the amount necessary to fund benefits promised at a specified future date.

Annuity contracts that allow flexible premium payments during the accumulation phase cannot specify in advance the level of benefit payments that will be paid during the liquidation phase. Instead, these annuities specify the amount of benefit for each $1,000 of fund balance when the annuity switches over to the liquidation phase.

Almost without exception, deferred annuities sold to individuals promise to return all premiums, with or without interest, if the annuitant dies during the accumulation period. The usual contract provides for a return of either gross premiums without interest or the cash value, whichever is larger. This contract is a type of refund annuity with respect to the period of accumulation.

Structuring the Annuity Contract

The premiums for an annuity contract bought with periodic premiums can be quoted in units of $100 of annual premium or in terms of the annual premium needed to provide a monthly life income of $10 at a designated age.

In every deferred annuity except a variable annuity, a minimum rate of interest on the cash value is guaranteed throughout the accumulation period. Some annuities also provide a short-term (such as 2, 3, or 5 year) interest rate guarantee that is competitive with current investment yields and higher than the guaranteed long-term rate.

After the short-term guaranteed rate expires, some contracts contain a bail-out provision that allows the contract to be terminated without a surrender charge if the interest rate falls below a stipulated rate, often 2 percentage points below the short-term guaranteed rate. The bail-out provision may seem much more attractive than it really is for two reasons: (1) Competitors are unlikely to be able to pay higher rates if and when the release is triggered, and (2) interest on a cash-out will be subject to income taxes and possibly a 10 percent penalty tax. In the event of the annuitant's death before age 65 or other scheduled start of the liquidation period, the company will return the accumulated gross premiums without interest or the cash value, whichever is larger. The cash value is equal to the gross premiums plus interest at a guaranteed rate, after deducting an expense charge. After about 10 years, the cash value exceeds the accumulated value of premiums paid without interest, and it becomes the effective death benefit. Note that, although this is an annuity contract, there is an insurance element during the accumulation period in that the death benefit can exceed the cash value.

Evaluating a Short-Term Guaranteed Interest Rate

- At what rate will funds accumulate?
- For how long does the rate apply?
- After the rate expires, is a subsequent rate guaranteed?
- What will the effect of withdrawals be on the rate?
- After the rate expires, can the contract be terminated without a surrender charge?

The annuitant can withdraw the full cash value at any time before the liquidation period, whereupon the contract terminates and the company has no further obligation. Under some contracts, the annuitant can borrow against the cash value, and the loan will not bring about a termination of the contract.

cash option
Liquidation Options. At the maturity date, the annuitant can elect to have the accumulation applied under any of the annuity forms the company offers. Depending on the option the owner elects at maturity, the actual monthly income might be more or less than the amount originally anticipated, based on the owner's payout option selection at the time of issue. Moreover, the annuitant usually has a *cash option* of taking a lump sum in lieu of an annuity. The cash option exposes the company to serious adverse selection. Persons in poor health tend to withdraw their accumulations in cash, while those in excellent health usually choose an annuity. To offset this selection, if the annuitant selects the cash option, some companies provide a retroactive reduction in the investment earnings rate applied to accumulations under a deferred annuity. The resulting penalty can be a substantial dollar amount.

Under most contracts, the annuitant can choose to have the benefit payments commence at an earlier or a later date than the one originally specified in the contract, with a subsequent adjustment in the amount of monthly benefits. Beginning the income at an earlier age than the age specified in the contract amounts to converting the cash value to an immediate annuity. There is usually no age limit below which the benefit payments must not begin, although the option is subject to the general requirement that the periodic income payments equal or exceed a stipulated minimum amount.

There is usually an upper age limit, sometimes as high as age 80 or as low as age 70, beyond which commencement of the income benefits cannot be postponed. The option to postpone the commencement of benefit payments can be particularly attractive if the annuitant is still in good health at the original maturity date and plans to work for a few more years.

JOINT ANNUITIES

Joint annuities involve more than one annuitant. The two basic types of joint annuities accomplish the following:

- A joint-life annuity provides income benefits only until the death of the first of two or more annuitants.
- A joint-and-last-survivor annuity continues benefit payments until the last of the named annuitants dies.

Joint-Life Annuity

A joint-life annuity provides an income as long as the two or more persons named in the contract live. Because the income ceases at the first death among the covered lives, the coverage is relatively inexpensive. This contract is always sold as a single-premium immediate annuity.

This contract has a very limited market. It might be appropriate for two persons—elderly sisters, for example, who have an income from a stable source large enough to support one but not both of the sisters. If they can purchase a joint-life annuity in an amount adequate to support one sister without disturbing the other income, the combined income will be adequate for their needs while both sisters are alive. Upon the death of one of the sisters, the income from the original source will meet the survivor's needs.

Joint-and-Last-Survivor Annuity

A joint-and-last-survivor annuity is a far more marketable contract than a joint-life annuity because the income under this form of annuity continues as long as any of two or more persons live. This arrangement is often ideal for a husband and wife.

For most combinations of ages, the joint-and-last-survivor annuity is the most expensive of all annuity forms. According to one insurer, an accumulation of $18,469 is required to provide an income of $100 per month on a joint-and-last-survivor basis to a man and a woman both aged 65. If the man is 65 and the woman 60, a sum of $19,068 is needed to provide $100 per month on a joint-and-last-survivor basis. Compare those figures to the approximate amount of $15,290 that is required, according to the $6.54 rate shown in the previous table, to provide a life income of $100 per month with no refund feature only to a man aged 65.

A joint-and-last-survivor annuity can be purchased as a single-premium immediate annuity at a cost somewhat higher than the accumulation figures quoted above, as an optional form under an annual-premium deferred annuity, or in conjunction with the settlement of life insurance or endowment proceeds.

Although a typical joint-and-last-survivor contract does not contain a refund feature, most insurance companies offer a contract that guarantees 120 monthly installments, and a few offer 240 guaranteed installments. Under these contracts, if the last survivor dies before the minimum number of payments has been made, the remaining installments continue to a designated beneficiary. As with single-life annuities, the designated beneficiary may be permitted to take the present value of the remaining installments as a lump sum. When both husband and wife are 65, a life income of $100 per month with 120 guaranteed installments requires an accumulation of $18,589—only $120 more than a similar annuity without a refund feature.

The conventional joint-and-last-survivor annuity continues the same income to the survivor as was paid while both annuitants were alive. A common modification, which reduces the cost, decreases the income to the survivor to two-thirds of the original amount. This contract, the *joint-and-two-thirds annuity*, is based on the assumption that the survivor does not require as much income as the two annuitants. This contract written in an original amount of $100 per month on the lives of a husband and wife, both aged 65, requires an accumulation of slightly more than $15,960.

In a *joint-and-one-half annuity*, the income to the survivor is reduced to one-half of the original amount. This form has not had the popular appeal of the joint-and-two-thirds annuity. Many insurers have introduced other options besides the two-thirds and one-half options for continuation at the death of the first annuitant.

The joint-and-last-survivor form is widely used by private pension plans to pay retirement benefits to married plan participants. When the employee elects the joint-and-two-thirds annuity, many plans reduce the income only if the employee dies first. If the employee's spouse dies first, the employee continues to receive the full income. Federal law requires written consent of the nonemployee spouse in order to eliminate the survivorship benefit.

VARIABLE ANNUITIES

To offer benefits with stable purchasing power, an annuity contract should provide more dollars if prices rise and fewer dollars if prices decline. Theoretically, benefits could be adjusted as an appropriate price index, such as the consumer price index, changes. From the standpoint of insurance companies, however, there is no mechanism by which the value of the assets backing the annuity can be adjusted automatically to reflect changes in consumer price levels. As a practical solution, variable annuity contracts have been developed that provide benefits adjusted to changes in the market value of the assets—typically common stocks—in which the annuity reserves are invested. The tie to common stock is based on the theory that over a long period of time, the market value of a representative group of common stocks tends to conform rather faithfully to changes in the consumer price level. Moreover, inasmuch as the insurance company's liabilities to its annuitants are expressed in terms of the market value of the assets offsetting the liabilities, funds for the payment of annuity benefits are available in the appropriate proportions at all times.

Variable annuity proponents believe that annuitants need protection against inflation and that a common stock investment program administered by a life insurance company is the best approach yet developed. Critics of the variable annuity approach question whether continuing inflation is inevitable, and even if it is, whether common stock investments provide an effective hedge against rising prices in the short run. These critics also cite the absence of any guaranteed minimum interest rate credit as an important disadvantage of the variable annuity.

Accumulation Units

accumulation
units

At present, variable annuities are most often issued on a deferred basis. During the accumulation period, premium payments are applied to the purchase of *accumulation units*. The accumulation unit is assigned an arbitrary value, such as $10, at the inception of the plan, and the initial premiums purchase accumulation units at that price. Thereafter, the units are revalued each month to reflect changes in the market value of the common stock that makes up the company's variable annuity portfolio. On any valuation date, the value of each accumulation unit is determined by dividing the market value of the common stock underlying the accumulation units by the aggregate number of units. Dividends are usually allocated periodically to the participants and applied to the purchase of additional accumulation units, although they may simply be reinvested without allocation and permitted to increase the value of each existing accumulation unit. Capital appreciation or depreciation is always reflected in the value of the accumulation units, rather than in the number of units. (In other words, both realized and unrealized gains and losses are reflected for individual participants through an increase or decrease in the value of their accumulation units.) A portion of each premium payment is deducted for expenses, and the remainder is invested in accumulation units at their current market value.

Table 11-3 Variable Annuity Accumulation Units—Deferred Annuity Purchased at Age 35 at $200 per Month

Year	Age	Unit Value*	New Units	Total Units	Total Value
1	35	$1.00	2,400.00	2,400.00	$2,400.00
2	36	1.08	2,232.56	4,632.56	4,980.00
3	37	1.16	2,076.80	6,709.36	7,753.50
4	38	1.24	1,931.91	8,641.26	10,735.01
5	39	1.34	1,797.12	10,438.38	13,940.14
6	40	1.07	2,242.99	12,681.37	13,569.07
7	41	1.15	2,086.50	14,767.88	16,986.75
8	42	1.24	1,940.93	16,708.81	20,660.76
9	43	1.88	1,276.60	17,985.41	33,812.56
10	44	2.12	1,132.08	19,117.48	40,529.06
11	45	2.28	1,053.09	20,170.57	45,968.74
12	46	2.45	979.62	21,150.20	51,816.39
13	47	2.63	911.28	22,061.47	58,102.62
14	48	2.83	847.7	22,909.17	64,860.32
15	49	3.04	788.56	23,697.73	72,124.84
16	50	3.27	733.54	24,431.27	79,934.21
17	51	3.52	682.36	25,113.63	88,329.27
18	52	3.78	634.76	25,748.39	97,353.97
19	53	3.5	685.71	26,434.10	92,519.37
20	54	3.25	738.46	27,172.57	88,310.84
21	55	3	800	27,972.56	83,917.70
22	56	3.6	666.67	28,639.23	103,101.24
23	57	4.01	598.5	29,237.74	117,243.32
24	58	4.97	482.9	29,720.63	147,711.55
25	59	5.76	416.67	30,137.70	173,590.85
26	60	6.25	384	30,521.30	190,758.13
27	61	7.16	335.2	30,856.50	220,932.51
28	62	7.9	303.8	31,160.29	246,166.32
29	63	8.09	296.66	31,456.96	254,486.78
30	64	8.14	294.84	31,751.80	258,459.62

*Rounded to two decimal places

A hypothetical accumulation is shown in the previous table. In this example, the initial purchase is made at age 35 with a premium high enough to cover a $200 purchase of units each month after paying insurer expenses. The assumptions behind the table numbers are that the accumulation units change value once each year and that a full $200 is available each month to acquire more units. The units in this example grow at approximately 7.5 percent in most years but fluctuate more or less than that in some years as stock prices are prone to do over short intervals. In this case, there is an accumulation of $258,459.62 at the end of the 30th year (end of age 64 or beginning of age 65) consisting of 31,751.80 accumulation units.

Annuity Units

annuity units   At the beginning of the liquidation period, a variable annuity's accumulation units are exchanged for *annuity units*. The number of annuity units the annuitant acquires depends on the company's assumptions as to mortality, dividend rates, and expenses, and on the market value of the assets underlying the annuity units. The number of annuity units is determined by dividing the dollar value of the accumulation units ($258,459.62 in the example above) by an actuarial factor (assumed to be $35 in this case) designed to provide a benefit of $1 per year for the annuitant's remaining lifetime. While the owner's number of accumulation units increases with each premium payment and each allocation of dividends during the accumulation period, the number of annuity units remains constant throughout the liquidation period (7,384.6 annuity units in this case). However, the units are revalued each year, to reflect the current market price of the common stock and the mortality, investment, and expense experience for the preceding year.[40] The dollar income payable to the annuitant each month is determined by multiplying the number of units the annuitant owns by the current value of one unit. During the liquidation period, the higher the market price of the stock and the greater the dividends, the greater the dollar income of the annuitant.

Some of the more recent variable annuity contracts differ from the above by using only one unit throughout the contract period, by discounting for

---

40. More precisely, the value of an annuity unit at the end of each fiscal year is obtained by dividing the current market value of the funds supporting the annuity units by the total number of annuity units expected to be paid over the future lifetimes of all participants then receiving annuity payments, in accordance with the assumptions as to mortality, investment earnings, and expense rates for the future.

mortality before as well as after retirement, and by limiting variations in the unit value to investment experience only.

Accumulation Units versus Annuity Units in a Variable Annuity
• Accumulation units: The number of units bought and the value of each unit vary depending on when the purchases are made.
• Annuity units: The number of annuity units distributed periodically is constant, but the value varies depending on when the distributions are made.

Surrender Provisions

When a variable annuity is sold as an individual contract, surrender privileges are made available but on a much more restricted basis than in connection with ordinary annuities. When a variable annuity is used as part of a pension plan, surrender values are not generally made available. Under all plans, the current value of the accumulation units is payable to a designated beneficiary, if any, or to the estate, usually as a continuing income. However, a lump-sum settlement is possible at the death of the participant during the accumulation period.

Regulation

In a landmark decision,[41] the United States Supreme Court held that an individual variable annuity contract is a security within the meaning of the Securities Act of 1933 and that any organization that offers such a contract is an investment company subject to the Investment Company Act of 1940. Any company that offers individual variable annuity contracts is subject to dual supervision by the Securities and Exchange Commission (SEC) and the various state insurance departments. Persons selling variable annuities must pass the Series 6 licensing exam of the Financial Industry Regulatory Authority (FINRA).

INDEXED ANNUITIES

indexed annuities

Indexed annuities (also referred to as equity-indexed annuities) are a variation of fixed-interest, traditional deferred-annuity products. These annuities were introduced in the mid-1990s. Fixed-interest annuities were very attractive during the high-interest-rate era

---

41. *Securities and Exchange Commission v. Valic* , 359 U.S. 65 (1959).

of the 1980s and early 1990s. Their appeal waned, however, as interest rates dropped and stock market yields significantly surpassed the yields in traditional fixed-interest annuities.

An indexed annuity offers guaranteed minimum interest rates and, at the same time, pays a higher return if a specified stock index increases enough to provide a higher yield. They are designed to appeal to persons who want to participate in high equity investment yields without bearing the full downside investment risk they assume through the purchase of a variable annuity.

The indexed annuity provides only a portion of the capital gain of the stocks that make up the applicable index, commonly Standard & Poor's composite index of 500 stocks (S&P 500). Variable annuities are still the only annuity products that provide most of the full yield of the equity investments to the owner/annuitant.

Participation Rate Formula

Prospective purchasers of indexed annuities should understand that their potential return based on increases in the value of the index is determined by the formula approach set forth in the contract. Generally, this formula includes a participation rate as well as the increase in the index from the beginning of the term to the verified anniversary-date value of the index. The participation rate is a percentage of the defined increase that will be used to calculate the crediting amount. The insurer sets this participation rate, which is subject to change. Some companies do not even specify the current participation rate in their promotional materials. Often, the participation rate is guaranteed for a specified term, such as the first 5 or 7 years. The insurance company reserves the right to change the participation rate at the expiration of each term, but the company usually guarantees the then-current rate for the subsequent term.

Most contracts anticipate a series of terms of uniform length, much like renewals of 5-year term life insurance. However, some contracts reserve the insurer's right to modify the term period available for continuation at the expiration of any existing term. In most designs, a higher increase from the index calculation is available only at the end of the applicable term unless the owner dies or the contract is converted to benefit-payout status (annuitized) before the end of the term. The higher value based on the index will not apply if the contract is terminated before the end of the term.

The participation rate restricts the amount of the index gain, if any, that can be applied to produce more than the guaranteed yield. The participation rate and the guaranteed interest rate are linked. Higher participation rates may be available from some insurers if the purchaser accepts a lower guaranteed interest rate. One company guarantees that the participation rate will never be lower than 25 percent. Illustrations are often based on 80 percent or 90 percent participation rates. The participation rate cannot be changed more than once per year under most contracts.

Another aspect of the indexed benefit is that some contracts include a cap on the crediting rate that is applied to the accumulated value of the contract. This cap prevents full formula participation in times of very rapid index increases.

As downside protection, most contracts specify a floor of 0 percent as the minimum extra interest crediting rate applicable to the accumulated value. This prevents the application of a negative percentage in the formula to reflect plunges in the index value. The intent is that the fixed-interest-rate guarantee is the worst possible outcome, and if the equity index does better, the accumulation can be even better than the guaranteed accumulation.

No Securities and Exchange Commission Regulation

The Securities and Exchange Commission approved a new rule in December, 2008, which clarified the status of indexed annuities under federal securities laws. SEC Rule 151A established that investors in indexed annuities are exposed to investment risk and are thus entitled to regulatory protection the same as other investors in all types of securities. A Congressional amendment was added to the Dodd-Frank Wall Street Reform and Consumer Protection Act of 2010 to withdraw SEC Rule 151A and ensure that indexed annuities would continue to be regulated as fixed insurance products permanently.

Guarantees

The minimum guarantees under indexed annuities are lower than those for traditional fixed-interest annuities. In fact, the rates actually guaranteed apply to less than the full amount paid as a premium. The guaranteed rate is usually applied to 90 percent of the amount paid to purchase the annuity. The percentage (10 percent in this example) not included in the guarantees can be used to cover insurer expenses. With this approach, usually 3 or 4 years elapse before the guaranteed amount equals or exceeds the original purchase amount. The contract indicates the specified interest rate applied each year to the contract value. This rate remains fixed unless both the contract owner and the insurance company later agree to a negotiated change. Many of the existing indexed annuities have guaranteed rates in the range of 2 percent to 3.5 percent.

Value of Contract at End of Term

At the end of each term or participation period, the value of the annuity is the greatest of the following three amounts:

- the contract value based on the minimum interest rate guarantees
- the accumulated value derived by applying the participation rate to the increase in the index on the applicable anniversary. This amount is subject to any cap on the maximum crediting rate and to any floor on the minimum crediting rate.
- the premiums paid through the end of the term, minus any withdrawals

In many contracts, the same procedures are used to calculate the death benefit payable if the owner dies during the deferral phase of the contract.

Terminating an indexed annuity before the end of a specified term usually results in loss of the index-crediting option. The termination is usually the greater of the following two amounts:

- the guaranteed-interest contract value
- the aggregate purchase amount minus adjustments for any partial withdrawals previously taken

Indexes

Although the most commonly used index is the S&P 500, some insurers use another index specified in the contract. These are generally established indexes that regularly appear in financial publications, such as the *Wall Street Journal*. However, some insurers use international indexes or a composite of two or more established indexes. The definition of the index is under the insurance company's control. Theoretically, the company could change the definition of the index after the contract is created, leaving open the possibility of intentional manipulation of the index in the future.

Asset Match

All financial products involve risks to the issuer, and the indexed annuity is no exception. The issuer needs to invest in assets that will provide an adequate return to honor the contractual promises.

Because the index participation promises some results that are above those of bond returns when the stock index outperforms the bond market, how can a company invest assets to produce the higher return? The closest match is achieved by investing the funds in the same stocks that make up the index. However, some insurers have chosen to invest in derivatives and other financial assets that they believe will track well with the index, even though these choices are not a composite of the items that make up the index. Over the long run, there could be a significant difference between investment results and contractual obligations. If the investment results exceed the contractual obligations, there will be no problem honoring the annuity contract terms. Conversely, underperformance of asset returns relative to obligations could threaten the insurer's financial viability. Purchasers should feel more comfortable with issuing companies whose investments closely resemble the index to which the benefits are related.

ACTUARIAL CONSIDERATIONS FOR ANNUITIES

The insurance company's cost of providing annuity benefits is based on the probability of survival, rather than the probability of death. In itself, this fact would seem to have no greater significance than that the insurance company actuaries, in computing premiums for annuities, have to refer to the actuarial probabilities of survival rather than probabilities of death. As a matter of fact, however, writing annuities poses a unique set of actuarial problems.

First, insurance companies have found that the mortality, or probability of death, among annuity purchasers tends to be lower, age for age, than that of persons who purchase life insurance, due mainly to adverse selection against the company. Individuals who know that they have serious health impairments rarely, if ever, purchase annuities. In fact, many persons contemplating the purchase of immediate annuities subject themselves to a thorough medical examination to make sure that they have no serious impairments before committing their capital to annuities. On the other hand, people who know or suspect that they have an impairment usually seek life insurance. Whatever its origin, the mortality difference between life insurance insureds and annuitants is so substantial that special annuity mortality tables must be used to calculate annuity premiums.

Second, the trend toward lower mortality, resulting in longer life spans, has been a favorable development for insurers with respect to life insurance but an unfavorable development with respect to annuities. Many annuity contracts, including the accumulation period, run for 60 to 75 years, and rates that were adequate at the time of issue can, with the continued increase in longevity, prove inadequate over the years. All mortality tables, of course, contain a safety margin—which, for life insurance mortality tables, means higher death rates than those likely to be experienced, and for annuity mortality tables, lower rates of mortality than anticipated. Although long-run decline in mortality rates increases the safety margin in life insurance mortality tables, this decline shrinks the margin in annuity mortality tables, sometimes to the point of extinction. Therefore, an annuity mortality table that accurately reflects the mortality among annuitants at the time it was compiled gradually becomes obsolete and eventually overstates the expected mortality.

Finally, a high percentage of annuitants are women, who as a group enjoy greater longevity than men. This gender difference in longevity forced companies to use a rate differential between male and female annuitants long before a rate differential based on gender was applied to the sale of life insurance policies. However, court decisions have required insurers to base some group annuity contracts on unisex mortality rates.

Annuitants Never Die—Well, Hardly Ever

- Purchasers of annuities have generally lower mortality rates than others (adverse selection).
- Mortality rates for most people, including annuitants, have been declining.
- A high percentage of annuitants are women, who have greater average longevity than men.

Revised Mortality Tables

Life insurance companies cope with these mortality differences in various ways. First, the insurers can compute annuity premiums on the basis of mortality tables that reflect annuitants' lower mortality.

For many years, companies used age setbacks for rates. The setbacks were used to recognize mortality differences between annuity and life insurance purchases. For example, the rate for an age-65 applicant may have been based on a 2-year age setback, thereby increasing the premium for a given amount of income to that based on the mortality of an age-63 individual. Ages for females were usually set back 4 or 5 years in addition to the setback for males, in recognition of the gender differential in mortality.

The 2000 Annuity Mortality Table enables insurers, by means of projection factors, to make long-range adjustments for future reductions in mortality rates. Modern annuity tables all contain a set of projection factors that can be used to adjust the mortality assumptions for all ages from year to year or, instead, to project the basic rates of mortality to some future date. The projections make allowances for anticipated future improvements in mortality.

Interest Assumptions

Historically, insurance companies attempted to hedge future improvement in annuitant mortality by using an unrealistically low interest assumption in the premium formula. The rates were substantially lower than those used to calculate life insurance premiums. This technique can be quite effective because an interest margin of 25 basis points can absorb a general reduction in mortality of 6 or 7 percent. Intensified competition among insurance companies and between insurance companies and investment media, however, has now caused companies to adopt interest assumptions much closer to the level of their actual investment earnings.

Use of Participating Basis

A third approach to adjusting annuity prices for anticipated future increases in life expectancy is to compute the premiums and/or benefits on a participating basis, which permits conservative assumptions with respect to all factors in the premium calculations. Annual-premium annuities issued by mutual companies are almost invariably participating during the liquidation period. Some stock companies also issue annuities that are participating during the accumulation period. Single-premium immediate annuities, whether written by mutual or stock companies, are usually not participating.

FEES AND CHARGES

Our discussion to this point has concentrated on the distributions made by various types of annuities and the premium payments and investment earnings that accumulate to fund an annuity. However, the discussion has largely ignored the various fees and expenses that contribute to the cost of an annuity. Most insurance companies and insurance agents are in business to make a profit. The profit in annuities results from the extent to which premiums, investment earnings, and fees exceed the pure cost of providing annuity benefits.

In their annuity designs, insurers expect to derive some profit from the spread between investment earnings and the amounts reflected in annuity benefits. To reflect the costs involved in providing the annuity and as an additional source of revenue, an insurer may also charge various fees. The types of fees and charges that may be associated with an annuity are briefly described below:

- *Mortality and expense charge.* This charge covers the guarantees provided by the contract—guarantees that a certain amount will be paid for the life of the annuitant, any death benefits payable to the beneficiary, and any expense limitation guarantees.
- *Investment management fee.* This fee is assessed to cover investment management services.
- *Administrative charge or maintenance fee.* A charge may be assessed to cover the cost of record-keeping and mailing periodic reports to the annuity owner.
- *Front-end load.* An amount may be charged when the annuity is purchased to compensate the insurer for sales commissions and other expenses involved in marketing and setting up the account.
- *Surrender charge* or *back-end load.* An annuity owner who withdraws money during the early years of an annuity's accumulation period may face a substantial penalty. This charge is designed to offset the insurer's costs of paying sales commissions and setting up the policy, and it also serves to discourage annuitants from cashing in their accounts. Annuities do not usually impose both a front-end load and a back-end load.

The fees and charges associated with an annuity are not trivial. The annual fees and charges associated with a typical variable annuity can easily exceed 2 percent of the assets. A client evaluating an annuity strictly for its short-term investment value will find that annuity fees and charges substantially reduce the return as compared with many other investments. However, annuities also provide guarantees—such as a lifetime income—as well as tax-deferral features that are not available through other investments but are often desirable for clients concerned about their long-term income needs.

FEDERAL INCOME TAX TREATMENT

Annuities enjoy a significant federal income tax advantage of accumulating on a tax-deferred basis, with the investment income that is credited to the contract not taxable until the annuitant or beneficiary receives it.

Amounts Received during Accumulation Period

Amounts received as loans and withdrawals during an annuity's accumulation period are taxable to the extent of income earned on the contract. This represents a kind of LIFO (last-in, first-out) tax treatment.[42] Also, a 10 percent penalty tax generally applies to the taxable portion of these amounts unless they are made after the taxpayer reaches age 59½ or by reason of the taxpayer's death or disability.

Amounts Received during Liquidation Period

exclusion ratio   The portion of benefit payments taxable during the liquidation period depends on the applicable exclusion ratio. This ratio is calculated by dividing the amount invested in the annuity by the total amount expected to be received. The exclusion ratio is then multiplied by the amount of each payment to the annuitant to determine the excluded amount, which is presumed to be a return of the investment in the contract. The balance of each payment is taxable.

The amount invested in the contract is generally the premiums paid, minus any previous nontaxable distributions and minus the actuarial value of any period certain or other guarantee feature. The amount the annuitant can expect to receive depends on the type of payout option he or she selected. If the annuity provides payments for a fixed period of time, the total payments to be received constitute the expected amount to be received. If the annuity provides a life income, the expected amount to be received is based on life expectancy tables from the U.S. Treasury Department.[43]

After the annuitant has received excludible amounts equal to the investment in the contract, he or she has fully recovered the basis in the annuity. Thereafter, under current tax law, any remaining benefit payments are fully taxable to the annuitant. If he or she dies before the basis is fully recovered,

---

42.   Different treatment is applicable for amounts invested in an annuity before August 14, 1982.

43.   Special rules apply to the calculation of the exclusion ratio for equity-based annuity contracts.

a deduction is applicable for the unrecovered amount in the taxpayer's final return.

USES OF AN ANNUITY

The market for annuities comprises two broad categories of individuals:

- those who have already accumulated an estate, either through inheritance or by their own personal efforts
- those who are seeking to accumulate an estate

Wealthy individuals purchase annuities as a hedge against adverse financial developments. Business reverses, unwise investments, and reckless spending can destroy large estates. Insurance company records abound with cases of individuals who at one time were wealthy but whose fortunes melted away, leaving payments from annuities they purchased in their more affluent days as their sole source of income. There are also numerous cases of individuals who are dependent on relatives for whom they had purchased annuities during a more solvent period. Wealthy people, then, purchase annuities in a search for security, with yield a secondary consideration.

Yield is a primary consideration for those individuals, often middle-aged or elderly, who have accumulated a modest estate and envision this estate as the source of financial security during the remaining years of their lives. The life annuity, or the joint-and-last-survivor form for couples, promises a continuation of the benefit payments and some deferral of income taxes as long as the annuitant or annuitants live. Although some people are reluctant to invest their capital in an annuity because they want to leave an estate to their children or other close relatives, others feel that a greater responsibility is to provide for their own old-age maintenance, relieving the children of that burden.

A retired couple might not need to invest their entire capital accumulation in an annuity to provide for their old-age support. In fact, such a move would generally be ill-advised. Instead, the couple might purchase an appropriate annuity with the remainder of the estate to be distributed to their children, or to a charitable cause, either during the couple's lifetime or after their deaths. Annuities can also be used to provide a living bequest to a charitable, educational, or religious organization.

The annuity is also an attractive savings medium for the person who has not yet accumulated an estate but wants to achieve financial independence in old age. He or she can make premium payments on a flexible schedule, and the accumulation grows on a tax-deferred basis.

Finally, annuities may be structured to provide benefits to finance long-term care. Some annuities contain a long-term care rider. With such a rider, the periodic payment increases when the annuitant is determined to need long-term care. For the most part, this involves satisfying the same criteria that trigger benefits under a long-term care insurance policy.

ETHICAL ISSUES

Many news reports have recently described incidents of questionable or unethical behavior in annuity sales, and a number of insurers and agents have been sanctioned for unethical sales practices. Although most concern over ethical issues centers on unsuitable variable annuity sales to seniors, they are not the only affected group. Some insurance agents have been enticed by high sales commissions to recommend annuities—especially variable annuities—in cases where they were clearly inappropriate. Aggressive sales presentations tout the fact that annuities produce higher income than other investments and provide payments the annuitant cannot outlive. Many people discover belatedly that much of their initial investment is eroded through fees and that they can no longer tap their assets for illness or other needs without paying a stiff surrender charge.

In response to concerns such as these, the NAIC drafted a model regulation designed to protect senior consumers. Subsequently, the NAIC amended the model regulation by removing specific reference to senior consumers, thereby making it applicable to all annuity sales. The model regulation requires that the insurance producer or insurer should have reasonable grounds for believing that the proposed annuity is suitable for the consumer based on facts the consumer provides concerning his or her needs, financial situation, investments, and other insurance products. Before executing an annuity sale, the producer or insurer should also make reasonable efforts to obtain information concerning the consumer's financial status, tax status, and investment objectives as well as other reasonable information. FINRA has also proposed consumer protection rules specifically focused on the sale of variable annuities. State insurance departments are enacting additional oversight rules to help ensure suitable sales to protect consumers. In order to achieve this, states will incorporate specific annuity courses into their required training regimen, and will also require the insurance companies to verify that the producers selling their products are knowledgeable on each specific product.

None of these rules prescribe the specific situations in which fixed or variable annuities are suitable or unsuitable. Indeed, many considerations are involved, and annuities serve a valuable need for many clients. However, financial planners should be sure to take a client's entire financial picture, health, and other relevant factors into account when making annuity recommendations.

CHARITABLE GIFT ANNUITIES

The goals of many financial planning clients include contributing to a religious organization, an educational organization, or another charity while also providing an adequate life income for themselves or others and, of course, minimizing taxes. Charitable gift annuities can simultaneously address all three goals.

A client who enters into a gift annuity agreement donates cash or other assets to a sponsoring charity. In exchange for the gift, the charity enters into a contract to provide the donor or other beneficiaries with fixed payments for the life of the annuitant(s).

Because a client's donation is an irrevocable gift, the client is entitled to an immediate income tax deduction based in part on the value of the donated asset. The client's tax deduction is not the value of the donated asset, but rather the difference between the date-of-gift value of the asset and the present value of the annuity contract as determined by IRS tables that take into account both the age of the donor and the applicable federal interest rate. Clients who own property that has appreciated in value receive an added tax benefit if they donate the property itself rather than selling it and donating the cash proceeds. Subject to limitations beyond the scope of this discussion, the client, in effect, is allowed to spread payment of capital gains taxes on the appreciation in asset value over an extended period of time. A further benefit results from the fact that assets used to fund the gift annuity are generally removed from the client's taxable estate.

Besides receiving immediate tax benefits, the client receives a periodic annuity payment. The payment may be annual, monthly, or at some other interval. Only part of these payments is taxable income, because a portion of the payments is deemed to be a tax-free return of the donor's gift during the donor's expected lifetime under federal tax regulations. In the case of gifts of appreciated capital assets, the taxable component of each annuity payment consists of ordinary income and a statutorily defined share of the unrealized capital gains inherent in the gift asset, taxed at applicable capital gains tax rates.

Virtually any kind of annuity arrangement—immediate, deferred, single-life, joint-life, and so forth—may be used. Gift annuity rates are a bit lower than the rates available from an insurance company. The charity benefits from this differential. From the client's standpoint, part of this financial disadvantage is offset by the tax advantages of a charitable gift annuity. Remember also that clients purchase a charitable gift annuity in large part because they want the charity to receive a benefit.

Benefits to the charity include any difference between its earnings and its costs of providing periodic payments. The charity also benefits from the residual value of the donated property, if any, after the death of the annuitant(s). Sometimes, of course, a client will substantially outlive his or her normal life expectancy. In such cases, the charity may not realize net gift proceeds from that particular annuity transaction.

Benefits to the client include the following:

- The client receives an immediate income tax deduction when making the initial donation.
- The client or the client's designee receives an income stream for the duration of his or her life with a rate of return higher than the rate available through interest or dividends alone.
- Only a portion of the income stream is taxable, and, in some cases, that portion may be taxed at preferential long-term capital gains rates.
- The client's charity receives a benefit.
- No commission is involved in the sales transaction.

Although they provide many benefits, charitable gift annuities are not without their disadvantages, nor do they completely solve the problem of providing an adequate cash stream for retired clients. Gift annuities provide a fixed income stream that is not adjusted for inflation. Clients should also invest in securities or maintain an additional source of funds that enables them to cope with increasing future expenses.

Even more significant, in many cases, is the fact that charitable annuities may provide fewer financial safeguards than the annuities from insurance companies. It is very important to evaluate the charity's long-term solvency. If a charity goes bankrupt or faces financial difficulty, the annuitant is merely a general creditor, and the client may have neither income nor recourse.

Clients who would like to donate property outright but cannot do so because they also need to provide for their own needs during retirement often use charitable gift annuities. Property can be willed to a charity, but this produces no immediate income tax benefit. Some clients also find that a charitable gift annuity is a useful means of disposing of appreciated property or other assets that a surviving spouse would be unwilling or unable to manage.

EXAMPLE

Polly, aged 75, decides to donate $100,000 to her university under a gift annuity agreement. The payment rate at her age is 7.1 percent, so she will receive a payment of $7,100 each year for the remainder of her life. More than two-thirds of each annual payment will be free of federal income tax. Polly will also receive a substantial income tax deduction in the year of her gift.

If Polly wished, she could also name her brother or another loved one to continue to receive annual payments, for his or her life, after Polly dies. The payment rates and tax benefits in this case would be reduced because payments are likely to be made for a longer period. There may also be transfer tax obligations flowing from the creation of an income gift in favor of nonspousal income beneficiaries.

STRUCTURED SETTLEMENTS

structured settlements

The courts have been involved in thousands of cases involving bodily injury or wrongful death in which the negligent party was required to pay at least $1 million in damages. It is usually acceptable to the court for large awards of this type to be paid as *structured settlements*, which are periodic payments instead of, or in addition to, a single lump-sum payment. Insurance companies issue immediate annuity contracts that guarantee the payments over the required lifetime or over the mandated support period. These contracts are specifically tailored to the needs of the claimants, who are the injured or wronged parties.

Although making periodic payments over time for claimants' damages can be traced to the 1950s, independent full-time structured settlement specialists were not common until the 1970s. Since then, the number of cases using structured settlement contracts to satisfy plaintiffs' claims has grown substantially. The most frequent cases in which a structured settlement can be appropriate involve general liability, medical malpractice, defective products, auto accidents, or workers' compensation injuries.

Liability claims adjusters and/or defense attorneys work together with a structured settlement specialist to arrange appropriate settlements. Suitable structured settlements provide an adequate amount of immediate cash for liquidity needs, as well as reimbursement for past expenses, legal fees, and other cash needs. If the recipient is unable to work, an income stream can be designed to fund his or her normal living expenses, custodial and medical services, rehabilitation costs, and where appropriate, tuition for educational programs.

Annuities Utilized in Structured Settlements

The customary structured settlement uses an annuity to provide periodic payments that meet the recipient's financial needs as much as possible. The claimant receives periodic payments of income that are tax free during his or her life, and thereafter, the claimant's beneficiaries receive payments for the balance of any guarantee period. Two of the requirements for the claimant's income-tax-free treatment are the absence of any evidence of ownership by the annuitant of the annuity that funds the structured settlement and the absence of constructive receipt or economic benefit in the annuity itself. Therefore, the defendant, who is the legal owner of the annuity, and the insurer predetermine all timing decisions, as well as the exact amount of money.

step-rate annuity   If the claimant has no reduction in life expectancy from the injuries that caused the claim, standard rates are applied for life annuities. Likewise, standard rates are used for fixed-period annuities because there is no life contingency. An example of a fixed-period annuity is payment of $1,000 per month for 5 years and $2,000 per month during years 6 through 10. This is also referred to as a *step-rate annuity*. The step-rate annuity takes the payment to the annuitant up a set level (or levels) over the years. Annuity benefit payments can generally be increased on a compound annual rate, ranging from 3 percent to 6 percent. In addition to life income guarantees, period-certain and joint-life guarantees can be used, depending on the circumstances. The insurer may issue a rated-age or substandard life annuity if the claimant's life expectancy has been reduced.

In a catastrophic injury case, the structured settlement broker submits the medical data to different insurance companies for evaluation. Each company makes its own judgment as to the claimant's life expectancy and bases its annuity quotes on that opinion. Life expectancy estimates vary among companies, just as substandard life insurance varies among insurers. The lower the life expectancy, the lower the annuity cost. Then the broker presents the bids to the defendant and his or her legal counsel to make an informed selection.

Generally, only defendants in bodily injury and wrongful death cases or their insurers can purchase this kind of annuity, and the number of insurance companies that issue such contracts is rather small.

Advantages of Structured Settlements

The following figure describes the structured settlement approach from the perspective of a liability claims adjuster. The advantages for each of the other involved parties are described below.

Structured Settlements—A Liability Claims Adjuster's Perspective

A structured settlement is a method of resolving a claim that gives the claimant some payment immediately but defers much of the payment into the future. The future payment is usually disbursed over a period time rather than in one lump sum. A liability insurer normally arranges a structured settlement by purchasing an annuity from a life insurance company and naming the claimant as "beneficiary" so that the claimant will receive periodic payments for a set number of years. The advantage to the claimant is that the interest earned on these annuities is tax-free, whereas if the claimant invests the lump-sum payment, interest on those investments is taxable. The advantage to the insurer is that the additional tax-free income may make the settlement more attractive to the claimant. This tax-free feature may be enough to help parties overcome an impasses, because the claimant receives more money in total than with a lump-sum payment.

Structured settlements are useful for addressing the following claimant needs:

- ongoing regular medical treatments
- adequate income to replace wages that can no longer be earned
- ongoing household help
- occupational therapy and rehabilitation
- educational needs for children
- lump-sum needs on an occasional basis for medical equipment replacement
- payment of legal fees on a lump-sum or an extended basis
- trusts, endowments, or annuities to take care of dependents or contingencies that may arise

Factors to consider in determining the amount and terms of a structured settlement are

- the life expectancy of the claimant
- the likely cost of future medical expenses, including rehabilitation, physical therapy, future surgeries, nursing home costs, home services, prosthetic devices, wheelchairs, and other equipment
- cost of reasonable monthly living expenses, including mortgages, taxes, maintenance, food, clothing, and similar items
- cost of dependents' needs
- legal fees
- lump sums for special contingencies

Source: Jones, James R. *Liability Claim Practices*, Malvern, PA: Insurance Institute of America, 2001. Phone: 800-644-2101. Web site: aicpcu.org.

For the Injured Party

Financial Security. The major advantage of a structured settlement for the injured party is financial security. A lifetime income is especially practical and desirable when a minor or someone acknowledged to be incompetent is involved or whenever there is reason to be concerned about protecting the injured party's, or the surviving family's, future finances.

Benefits That Match Needs. An injured party needs regular income to meet living expenses and medical care costs. On occasion, when future medical costs are estimated to be substantial but the timing of these costs is unknown, a medical trust, similar to an emergency fund, can be created with the defendant as grantor under the trust agreement.

Management of Benefits. Claimants and their families or guardians are usually not trained to manage large sums of money. The use of periodic payments in a structured settlement significantly reduces the risk of dissipation of funds through mismanagement, imprudent investment, unwise expenditures, misuse, or even neglect.

Guaranteed Payment. Because the income payments are guaranteed for life or for a fixed period, the settlement can never be prematurely exhausted.

Income-Tax-Free Payments. Whether payments are in a lump sum or periodic, they represent bodily injury damages, which are excluded from income tax.[44]

For the Plaintiff's Attorney

Attorneys are assured that their client's settlement is guaranteed and will not be subject to the potential dissipation of a lump-sum settlement. Some attorneys even believe that recommending a structured settlement insulates them from exposure to legal malpractice because they are not taking a sizable portion of the total value of the entire benefit payable as a lump sum right in the beginning.

---

44. IRC Sec. 104(a)(2). Also see Rev. Ruls. 79-220, 79-313, and 77-230.

For the Judge

Under the structured settlement, guaranteed periodic payments for life ensure the plaintiff's ongoing financial security for a lifetime. The judge or jury simply identifies the amount of monthly need rather than the actuarially equivalent lump-sum present value of payments over an uncertain number of years.

For the Public

The public benefits from the structured settlement because the injured party does not become a ward of the state and is assured a guaranteed income and proper care. In addition, a structured settlement avoids the delay of prolonged litigation, reducing court costs and placing fewer burdens on the already overloaded judicial system.

Disadvantages of Structured Settlements

If the life insurance company becomes insolvent, the annuitant may have a delay of benefit payments. Also, the annuitant will absorb all of the losses in excess of any state guaranty fund limitations. Furthermore, the benefit payments may be reduced with the new insurer. Therefore, structured settlement specialists should select only the most secure and well-managed insurance companies.

The periodic payment schedule cannot be changed, so problems can occur if more immediate cash is needed than the stream of payments provides. This may be due to an unprecedented financial reversal, a medical necessity, an educational need, or greater-than-expected inflation. The original design of the structured settlement should therefore anticipate increasing payments annually (or at least periodically), build in periodic deferred lump sums, or include a medical trust for future medical and custodial needs.

Structured settlements do not necessarily accomplish their intended purpose. As with life insurance, various organizations have emerged that are willing to pay a discounted lump sum in exchange for the stream of future income expected from structured settlements, lottery winnings, or other annuities. By engaging in such a transaction, a claimant who has received a structured settlement can circumvent the provider's intention to provide an income stream rather than a lump sum that can be used unwisely and leave the injured annuitant without a life income.

IMPAIRED RISK ANNUITIES

Annuities are generally purchased by people who anticipate a long life span. However, some structured settlements that use annuities involve victims whose life expectancy has been reduced as a result of their injuries. Annuities can also be used to provide for specific long-term care needs, often when an individual is unable to qualify for long-term care insurance. Individuals who need long-term care have life expectancies, on the average, that are of shorter duration.

impaired risk annuity   An *impaired risk annuity* takes into account the annuitant's reduced life expectancy. The applicant's health is considered in the impaired risk annuity underwriting process, and the annuity payments are increased (or the premium lowered) in relation to the shorter life expectancy.

CHECKLIST FOR EVALUATING AND COMPARING ANNUITIES

Accumulation Period

- Is the annuity funded with a single premium? If yes, how much?
- Is the annuity funded with periodic premiums? If yes,

  ___ Are premiums fixed or flexible?
  ___ What is the periodic premium?
  ___ What is the premium frequency?
  ___ For how many years are premiums payable?

- Is a minimum interest rate guaranteed for the length of the accumulation period?
- Is a short-term interest rate guaranteed? If yes,

  ___ What is the rate?
  ___ How long is it guaranteed?
  ___ What happens after it expires?
  ___ Is a bail-out option provided?

- What is the benefit amount for death or surrender of the contract?

  ___ If there is a return of premiums, is it with interest?
  ___ When will the cash value exceed premiums paid?

___ Are there surrender charges? If yes, describe.

Liquidation Period

- When does the liquidation period begin?

  ___ Is there an option to accelerate the starting date? If yes, by how much?

  ___ Is there an option to delay the starting date? If yes, how long?

  ___ Is a cash option available at the start of the liquidation period?

- How much is the periodic benefit payment?
- Is the periodic benefit amount guaranteed or variable?
- Is the benefit payment based on the insurer's investment results?
- Is the benefit payment based on a stock market index? If yes,

  ___ What is the participation rate?

  ___ What is the index?

  ___ Is there a cap on participation?

  ___ Is there a guaranteed minimum?

- How frequently is the periodic benefit paid?
- Do the benefit amounts continue for only a specified number of years? If yes, how many?
- Do the benefit payments continue for only one lifetime? If yes,

  ___ Is there any period certain? If yes, how long?

  ___ Are there any installment or cash refund features? If yes, how much?

- Do the benefit payments continue for two lifetimes? If yes,

  ___ Are the benefit payments reduced after the first death? If yes, by how much?

  ___ Is there any guaranteed minimum amount of the total benefit payments? If yes, what is the amount?

CHAPTER REVIEW

Key Terms and Concepts

annuity	life (whole life) annuity
annuitant	temporary life annuity
annuity certain	joint (joint-life) annuity

joint-and-last-survivor annuity
immediate annuity
deferred annuity
longevity insurance
accumulation period
liquidation period
pure (straight life) annuity
refund annuity
fixed annuity
variable annuity

life annuity certain
installment refund annuity
cash option
accumulation units
annuity units
indexed annuities
exclusion ratio
structured settlements
step-rate annuity
impaired risk annuity

Review Questions

Review questions are based on the learning objectives in this chapter. Thus, a [3] at the end of a question means that the question is based on learning objective 3. If there are multiple objectives, they are all listed.

1. A client seems surprised when you mention that annuities have a lot in common with life insurance, because she thought annuities were more like mutual funds. Explain how annuities and life insurance are
    a. dissimilar in function [1]
    b. based on the same principles [1]

2. Ben Thayer is retiring and plans to live off a combination of Social Security and investments made during his working years, but he worries that he might outlive his investments. How can an annuity guarantee a lifetime income to an individual? [1]

3. How are annuities classified by each of the following?
    a. plan of distribution [2]
    b. parties in the contract [2]
    c. time when benefits begin [2]
    d. method of purchase [2]
    e. amount of annuity payment [2]

4. Penny Youngman's employer provides no 401(k) plan or other retirement program, but Penny is investing roughly one-third of her current income in savings bonds and other investments. When she retires, she plans to use most of her life savings to buy an annuity that will pay her living expenses. A friend has suggested that Penny consider a deferred annuity, rather than purchasing an immediate annuity when she retires. Explain how immediate and deferred annuities differ with regard to
    a. the method of premium payment possible [2]
    b. the existence of accumulation and/or liquidation periods [2]

5. Your client, Jim Smith, wishes to supplement, over time, the funds he is accumulating in his corporate pension so that he will be able to more adequately meet the anticipated needs for him and his wife after he retires in 20 years. Jim has indicated in his discussions with you that he is willing to take sufficient investment risk in an attempt to protect his retirement savings and benefits from inflation. What features would you have Jim consider in purchasing an annuity to accomplish his goal? [2]

6. Ann Peterson purchased an immediate annuity for $300,000 at retirement, received two monthly payments, and died. What would happen after Ann died if her annuity was
    a. a pure annuity? [2]
    b. a life annuity with 20 years certain? [2]
    c. an installment refund annuity? [2]

7. Alan Sands, a financial planner and close personal friend, advised Kenny Drane and his wife Shirley, both aged 70, to pool their life savings and invest them in a joint-and-two-thirds annuity.
    a. How does this type of annuity operate? [2]
    b. Why might this type of annuity be appropriate for the Dranes? [2]
    c. What ethical issues are involved in this recommendation? [6]

8. Describe the operation of a variable annuity issued on a deferred basis in terms of the role of accumulation units and annuity units. [2]

9. What are the key features of indexed annuities? [2]

10. What three approaches do life insurance companies use to adjust annuity prices for anticipated future increases in life expectancy? [3]

11. Lynn Straw's financial goals, as a recent retiree with substantial assets and no dependents, include providing a retirement income and making a major donation to her favorite educational institution. Explain how a charitable gift annuity might simultaneously accomplish both of Lynn's goals while also providing tax advantages. [5]

12. How is an annuity used in a typical structured settlement? [5]

13. What are the advantages and disadvantages of structured settlements? [5]

14. What type of annuity would be most advantageous for a client whose life expectancy has been reduced by various health problems? [5]

Learning Objectives

An understanding of the material in this chapter should enable the student to

1. Describe the development of medical expense coverage.

2. Describe traditional major medical expense coverage, and explain how this approach has incorporated managed care provisions.

3. Identify the reasons for the use of managed care, and describe the various types of managed care plans.

4. Describe the nature and purpose of consumer-directed medical expense plans.

5. Explain why benefit carve-outs are used with medical expense plans, and describe the carve-outs used for prescription drugs, vision benefits, and behavioral health.

6. Describe the provisions found in medical expense plans that pertain to eligibility, coordination of benefits, Medicare, and claims.

7. Describe the nature of limited-benefit medical expense plans.

8. Describe the nature of dental insurance plans.

9. Explain the rationale for supplemental medical expense plans for executives, and describe the nature of such plans.

10. Explain the tax implications of employer-provided medical expense premiums and benefits for employers and employees.

health insurance

medical expense insurance

Although the term *health insurance* is often used in a narrow sense to mean protection against financial loss resulting from medical bills, the term actually has a much broader meaning. In this book, health insurance refers to protection against the financial consequences of poor health. These financial consequences can result from incurring medical bills as the result of an accident or illness (including dental expenses) for which *medical expense insurance* provides protection. Poor health can also result in lost income and additional expenses. Protection against lost income is provided by disability income insurance, and long-term care insurance covers another significant expense that can be a result of poor health. Health insurance is also provided by the Social Security and Medicare programs.

Medical expense insurance is arguably the most important type of insurance protection to most Americans and the type of protection that causes the most anxiety if it is lost or unaffordable. It is also a type of insurance for which a significant dollar outlay is made. However, approximately 90 percent of the persons who have medical expense insurance obtain it as an employee benefit, and their employers pay a major portion of the cost of coverage for most working persons. Employer-provided coverage is the focus of this chapter. It is important for the financial planner to understand a client's coverage to determine whether it is adequate. If it is not, sometimes the client can obtain supplemental coverage. It is equally important to know when supplemental coverage, such as a dread disease policy, may be inappropriate because it only duplicates employer-provided coverage or provide poor or inadequate protection for the client's actual needs.

It is also important for financial planners to know what alternatives are available when a client's employment or insurance coverage terminates. Various forms of individual coverage can be used for clients who are self-employed or work for employers that do not have a group insurance plan.

Medical expense insurance is the most significant type of employee benefit in terms of both the number of persons covered and the dollar outlay. Almost all employers with 200 or more employees offer some type of medical expense plan. However, in 2010 69 percent of firms offered health benefits, which is a statistically significant increase from the 60 percent reported in 2009. The smallest firms are least likely to offer health benefits, particularly employers with fewer than 10 employees.[45] In almost all cases, coverage identical to that offered for employees is also available for eligible dependents. Even with employee contributions, the cost of providing medical coverage for employees is several times greater for most employers than the combined cost of providing life insurance and disability income insurance.

In contrast to other types of employer-provided coverage, such as group life insurance and group disability income insurance, group medical expense

---

45. The Henry J. Kaiser Family Foundation and Health Research & Educational Trust, *Employer Health Benefits Survey, 2010*, p. 36.

coverage is not as standardized. Coverage may be provided through Blue Cross and Blue Shield plans, health maintenance organizations (HMOs), and preferred-provider organizations (PPOs), as well as insurance companies. In addition, a large and increasing percentage of the benefits is provided under plans that are partially or totally self-funded (self-insured) by the employer. A medical expense plan may be limited to specific types of medical expenses, or it may be broad enough to cover almost all medical expenses. Even when broad coverage is available, it may provide benefits either under a single contract or under a combination of contracts. Furthermore, in contrast to other types of group insurance, benefits may be in the form of services rather than cash payments.

Finally, the skyrocketing cost of providing medical expense benefits over a long period of time has led to changes in coverage and plan design aimed at controlling these costs. Many of these changes have resulted in more similarities among providers of medical expense coverage than existed in the past.

Over the last two decades, two major issues—affordability and accessibility of medical care—have led to profound changes in the health care industry. Not only has there been a continued shift to managed care plans but the entire character of the health care industry has also changed. Where once there was a distinction among the providers of care (such as doctors and hospitals) and the organizations that financed the care (such as insurers, the Blues, and HMOs), this distinction is now blurred. For example, physicians and hospitals have established HMOs and PPOs, and physicians may be employees of managed care plans. There are those who feel that in the not-too-distant future most Americans will receive their medical expense coverage from one of a small number of large organizations that both provide medical care and finance the cost of that care.

The issues surrounding medical care have also become a concern of government. Many states have enacted programs to make coverage available to the uninsured, including those who work for employers with a small number of employees. At the federal level, lively debate over health care continues to occur.

The Patient Protection and Affordable Care Act (PPACA) and the Health Care and Education Reconciliation Act of 2010 (HCERA) are the health care reform bills passed into law by the Obama administration. The law includes numerous health-related provisions to take effect over a 4-year period, including expanding Medicaid eligibility, subsidizing insurance premiums, providing incentives for businesses to provide health care benefits, and prohibiting denial of coverage or paying claims based on pre-existing conditions. Additionally, annual limits on coverage will be phased out over the next few years, starting in 2010. Effective September 23, 2010, a ban on lifetime limitations on all insurance plans that begin or are renewed after that date took effect. There are many other provisions that are expected to affect all Americans in some way.

It is expected that changes will be made to these laws over time due to political debate as well as practical issues relating to implementing their provisions. Provisions relevant to this discussion include prohibitions on pre-existing conditions and the banning of lifetime maximums on the dollar value of coverage. People who have been without insurance because of pre-exisiting conditions will be eligible for subsidized coverage through a new, high risk insurance program.

In 2010 the law provided a $250 rebate to Medicare beneficiaries who reach the Part D prescription coverage gap, and a gradual elimination of the Part D coverage gap by 2020. The act will establish in 2011 a national, voluntary insurance program for purchasing community living assistance services and support (CLASS program). It will be important for all pre-retirees and retirees to monitor the changes that may impact their health care.

HISTORY OF MEDICAL EXPENSE INSURANCE

Development of Medical Expense Coverage

Until the 1930s, medical expenses were borne primarily by ill or injured persons and their families. Blue Cross and Blue Shield plans, as well as HMOs, were developed during the Great Depression, and the Blues were the predominant providers of medical expense coverage through the 1940s. HMOs remained only a small player in the marketplace for medical expense coverage until the last three decades.

Insurance companies were only modestly successful in competing with the Blues until a new product was introduced in 1949—major medical insurance. By the mid-1950s, insurance companies surpassed the Blues in premium volume and number of persons covered.

The number of persons with medical expense insurance plans grew rapidly during the 1950s and 1960s. For the first time, the federal government became a major player in providing medical expense coverage by creating national health insurance programs for the elderly and the poor. The first program—Medicare—provides benefits for persons aged 65 and older. The second program—Medicaid—provides medical benefits for certain classes of low-income individuals and families.

By 1970, expenditures for health care equaled 7.3 percent of GDP (gross domestic product), and the country saw the first large-scale debate over national health insurance. The result was legislation to encourage HMOs. The Employee Retirement Income Security Act (ERISA) also freed self-funded plans from state regulation and hastened the growth of this financing technique. Growth in national health expenditures (NHE) in the United States over the coming decade is expected to be slightly higher as a result of the implementation of the Patient Protection and Affordable Care Act (PPACA). Many of the major ACA provisions go into effect in 2014, resulting in substantive differences in projected growth of NHE compared to estimates made prereform. An expansion of Medicaid coverage (to all persons under age 65 in households with incomes less than 138 percent of the federal poverty level), combined with the advent of state-level health insurance exchanges, is expected to result in NHE growth of 9.2 percent in 2014. Over the latter stages of the projection period (2015 through 2019), the impact of PPACA on health coverage is anticipated to continue as more people acquire, or shift, into new or different coverage. By 2019, 92.7 percent of the U.S. population is expected to have health insurance—an increase of 10 percentage points—driven, in part, by growth in Medicaid, which when combined with the Children's Health Insurance Program (CHIP), is projected to cover 82 million persons. Also by 2019, 30.6 million people are expected to be enrolled in health insurance exchange plans.

Attempts to rein in the cost of medical care since the 1970s seemed to have little effect, and health care expenditures now account for over 16 percent of GDP and are projected to rise to nearly 20 percent by 2019.[46] Still, over 45 million Americans, including many employed persons and their families, remain uninsured.

The many efforts by employers to contain these rising health care costs include the following:

- increased use of employer self-funding

---

46. Centers for Medicare & Medicaid Services, Office of the Actuary, *National Health Expenditure Projections, 2008–2019*, 2010–, p. 1.

- cost-shifting to employees. Employers raise deductibles and require employees to pay a larger portion of their medical expense coverage.

- requiring or encouraging managed care plans. Many employers have dropped traditional medical expense plans, and offer managed care alternatives only. Another prevalent approach is for employers to offer employees a financial incentive to join managed care plans.

- increased use of managed care plans that are alternatives to HMOs, such as PPOs and point-of-service (POS) plans

- introduction of consumer-directed medical expense plans

- discontinuance of medical expense coverage by some small employers or shifting to limited-benefit plans

- increased emphasis on wellness and healthy lifestyles

Data collected by the Kaiser Family Foundation[47] show that enrollment in medical expense plans that can be characterized as traditional indemnity plans has dropped from over 70 percent to 12 percent since the early 1990s. During the same period, the number of enrollees in plans that use PPOs has increased significantly to 58 percent. HMOs and point-of-service plans have grown more slowly and now account for about 19 percent and 8 percent, respectively, of the number of enrollees. Consumer-directed health plans now account for about 13 percent of the market, up from 8 percent in 2009.

One important change is hidden in these statistics—the increasing trend toward self-funding of medical expenses by employers. It is estimated that over 50 percent of all workers are covered under plans that are totally or substantially self-funded. Note that the way benefits are provided under a self-funded plan can vary—the employer may design the plan to provide benefits on an indemnity basis or as an HMO or a PPO.

A Look at the Future

As in past decades, the health care system will continue to evolve. A few observations can be made about the current environment:

- Premiums for employer-provided medical expense plans are increasing at the highest percentage since the early 1990s and are predicted to continue in the foreseeable future. As a result, employers will continue to look for ways to control their costs,

---

47. The Henry J. Kaiser Family Foundation and Health Research & Educational Trust, *Employer Health Benefits Survey, 2010, p. 66.*

including cost-shifting to employees. Higher premiums have resulted in a slight decrease in the number of employees that have employer-provided coverage available to them. The effects of the Healthcare Reform of 2010 will evolve as the key provisions in the law are implemented over the next several years. Opinions vary as to whether these initiatives will increase or lower health care costs.

- Surveys indicate that a large majority of Americans, including those with HMO coverage and other forms of managed care, are satisfied with their own health care plan. The relatively low degree of dissatisfaction, however, is higher among plans with the greatest degree of managed care.

- Surveys also indicate that despite satisfaction with their own coverage, Americans are becoming less satisfied with and less confident about the health care system.

- There is a growing backlash against managed care, particularly HMOs. Many persons appear to have based their opinions on media reports and stories from friends, not on their own experiences. This backlash has attracted the attention and legislation from Congress and the states. However, managed care plans are becoming increasingly flexible and consumer friendly.

- Federal legislation continues to change the character of medical expense insurance plans. For example, the Medicare Prescription Drug, Improvement, and Modernization Act was passed in 2003. In addition to making significant changes in Medicare, the act also encouraged the growth of consumer-directed medical expense plans with the creation of health savings accounts.

- The political changes in Washington as a result of the 2010 elections and the passage of the Healthcare Reform Bill will lead to increased debate over health care reform and the implementation of The Patient Protection and Affordable Care Act and the Health Care and Education Reconciliation Act of 2010. Issues such as the constitutionality of some provisions, the funding of reform provisions and the specific definitions of certain elements of health care reform will need to be resolved as the provisions come up for implementation.

TRADITIONAL PLANS

Prior to the mid-1970s, most employees were covered by what are commonly referred to as traditional, or indemnity, plans. However, these plans have evolved. Although they are still far from what might be called managed care plans, these plans increasingly contain provisions designed to control costs and influence the behavior of persons who need medical care.

Historically, medical expense coverage consisted of separate basic benefits for hospital expenses, surgical expenses, and physicians' visits. Coverage was limited, and many types of medical expenses were not covered. However, the available coverage was "first dollar," in that covered expenses were paid in full without deductibles and coinsurance. Over time, employers began to offer more extensive benefits to employees. Although this broader coverage was usually provided through a single major medical contract, some employees were still covered under medical expense plans that consisted of selected basic coverages typically provided by Blue Cross and/or Blue Shield. In most cases, these basic coverages were supplemented by a major medical contract so that the effect was essentially the same as if a single major medical contract was used.

Three comments need to be made about the importance of traditional plans. First, interest in various types of plans varies by the state in which a reader resides. Only about 1 percent of employees and their families are still covered under traditional plans. However, this percentage varies significantly by state. For example, HMO enrollments are small (10 percent or less) in about 20 percent of the states—mostly states with small and heavily rural populations. In these states, most employees and their families are covered by traditional plans or PPOs. In another 20 percent of the states—typically populous and urban states—35 to 50 percent of employees and their families are covered by HMOs, and almost all of the remaining employees and families are covered by other forms of managed care.

Second, the discussion of traditional medical expense plans largely follows their historical development. Much of the terminology and coverage of legislation introduced here also applies to the managed care approaches to medical care.

Third, traditional major medical plans are the basis on which most PPOs and high-deductible medical expense plans are based. PPOs can be viewed as traditional plans that have adopted a wide range of managed care characteristics. High-deductible health plans also usually incorporate certain managed care features as well as features unique to consumer-directed health care.

Major Medical Coverage

major medical insurance

Major medical insurance protects against catastrophic medical expenses, with few exclusions or limitations. The distinguishing features of major medical insurance plans include a broad range of covered expenses, deductibles, and coinsurance.

Basic Characteristics of Major Medical Expense Insurance
• Wide range of covered expenses • Use of deductibles • Use of coinsurance

Covered Expenses

Major medical plans give broad coverage for expenses incurred for necessary medical services and supplies that a physician has ordered or prescribed. These services and supplies, which are specified in the contract, generally include the following:

- hospital room and board. Traditionally, coverage has not been provided either for confinements in extended care facilities or for home health care. However, major medical plans now often include such coverage. Some plans also provide benefits for room and board in alternative facilities, such as birthing centers.
- other hospital charges
- charges of outpatient surgical centers
- anesthetics and their administration
- services of doctors of medicine (M.D.) or osteopathy (D.O.). Coverage for the services of other medical practitioners (such as chiropractors or podiatrists) may also be included.
- professional services of registered nurses. The services of other nurses (such as nurse midwives) may also be covered.
- prescription drugs
- physical and speech therapy
- diagnostic X-ray and laboratory services
- radiation therapy
- blood and blood plasma
- artificial limbs and organs
- pacemakers

- casts, splints, trusses, braces, and crutches
- rental of wheelchairs and hospital beds
- ambulance services

Even though coverage is broad, major medical contracts contain certain exclusions and limitations.

Exclusions. The list varies, but exclusions in most major medical contracts preclude coverage for charges arising from the following:

- occupational injuries or diseases to the extent that benefits are provided by workers' compensation laws or similar legislation
- care provided by family members or when no charge would be made for the care received in the absence of the insurance contract
- cosmetic surgery, except as required by the Women's Health and Cancer Rights Act (discussed later), unless such surgery is to correct a condition resulting from either an accidental injury or a birth defect (if the parent has dependent coverage when the child is born). Depending on the contract, complications that arise from pregnancy may or may not be covered.
- most physical examinations, unless such examinations are necessary for the treatment of an injury or illness. However, plans are increasingly providing preventive medicine that might involve specific types of physical examinations. PPACA will also require an increasing amount of preventative care excluded in the past.
- convalescent, custodial, or rest care
- dental care except for (1) treatment required because of injury to natural teeth and (2) hospital and surgical charges associated with hospital confinement for dental surgery
- eye refraction, or the purchase or fitting of eyeglasses or hearing aids
- expenses either paid or eligible for payment under Medicare or other federal, state, or local medical expense programs
- experimental services

preexisting-conditions provision   Most major medical plans also contain an exclusion for preexisting conditions. However, such a *preexisting-conditions provision* applies only for a limited time, after which the condition is no longer considered preexisting and is covered in full, subject to any other contract limitations or exclusions.

A *preexisting condition* is typically defined as any illness or injury for which a covered person received medical care during the 3-month period prior to the person's effective date of coverage. Usually, the condition is no longer considered preexisting after the earlier of (1) a period of 3 consecutive months during which no medical care is received for the condition or (2) 12 months of coverage under the contract by the individual.

It is also not unusual, particularly with large employers, for the preexisting-conditions provision to be waived for persons who are eligible for coverage on the date a master contract becomes effective. However, future employees will be subject to the provision, but its effect may be shortened or eliminated by the portability provision of the Health Insurance Portability and Accountability Act (HIPAA). HIPAA also limits the use of preexisting-conditions provisions with respect to newborn or adopted children. Preexisting-conditions provisions also cannot apply to pregnancy.

The Patient Protection and Affordable Care Act (PPACA) introduces several modifications to the pre-existing conditions clause in health insurance. Effective September 23, 2010, insurers are prohibited from excluding pre-existing medical conditions (except for grandfathered individual health insurance plans) for children under the age of 19. By January 1, 2014, insurers will be prohibited from discriminating against or charging higher rates for any individuals based on pre-existing medical conditions.

The exclusion for cosmetic surgery is subject to the Women's Health and Cancer Rights Act, which amended ERISA and applies to all types of group health plans as well as individual medical expense insurance. Under the provisions of the federal act, any benefit plan or policy that provides medical and surgical benefits for mastectomy must also provide coverage for the following: (1) reconstruction of the breast on which the mastectomy has been performed, (2) surgery and reconstruction of the other breast to produce a symmetrical appearance, (3) prostheses, and (4) physical complications of the mastectomy.

The federal Pregnancy Discrimination Act requires that benefit plans of employers with 15 or more employees treat pregnancy, childbirth, and related conditions the same as any other medical condition. In the absence of a state law to the contrary, pregnancy may be and is sometimes excluded under group insurance contracts written for employers with fewer than 15 employees.

Limitations. Traditional, as well as managed care plans, have placed some limitations on the amounts that may be paid under the plan. These include "internal limits", or limitations on certain types of medical expenses, annual maximum limits and lifetime maximum medical expenses.

Major medical plans contain "internal limits" for certain types of medical expenses. Although the expenses are covered, the amounts paid under the contract are limited. For example, benefits are rarely paid for charges that exceed what are reasonable-and-customary charges, room-and-board benefits are generally limited to the charge for semiprivate accommodations unless other accommodations are medically necessary, and benefits for infertility treatments might be subject to 50 percent coinsurance or a maximum dollar limitation.

Beginning on September 23, 2010, lifetime limits for all plans that begin or are renewed after that date are prohibited for employer-sponsored and individual medical expense policies under the 2010 Healthcare Reform package (PPACA). Exclusion of all benefits for a condition is not considered to be a lifetime or annual dollar limit. Insurance companies can not longer cut off policyowners when their medical expenses reach a lifetime limit. Annual limits on coverage will be phased out over the next several years: in 2010, insurers must provide medical expense coverage for at least up to $750,000. That coverage limit increases to $1.45 million for September 23, 2011, and $2 million after September 23, 2012. Limits will be completely banned starting January 1, 2014.

The ban on annual and lifetime limits apply to both individual and employer-sponsored plans, but only for what are called "essential health benefits". Essential health benefits include minimum benefits in general categories, to be determined by the Department of Health and Human Services. These exceptions do not apply to "grandfathered" plans, which are insurance policies in existence before March 23, 2010, when the reform bill was signed into law. Essential health benefits include:

- emergency services
- ambulatory patient services
- hospitalization
- maternity and newborn care
- mental health and substance abuse services
- prescription drugs
- rehabilitative services

- laboratory services
- preventive and wellness services and chronic disease management
- pediatric services, including oral and vision care

Treatment of Mental Illness, Alcoholism, and Drug Addiction. It was historically common for employer-sponsored major medical plans to provide limited benefits for treatment for mental and nervous disorders, alcoholism, and drug addiction. Unless state laws required that these conditions be treated like any other medical condition, inpatient coverage was often limited to a specific number of days each year (commonly 30 or 60). Outpatient benefits, which were even more limited, were often subject to 50 percent coinsurance and to a specific dollar limit per visit.

It was also historically common for major medical plans to impose an annual maximum (such as $1,000) and/or an overall maximum lifetime limit (such as $25,000) on benefits for mental and nervous disorders, alcoholism, and drug addiction. However, the provisions of the Mental Health Parity Act of 1996, which apply only to employers with more than 50 employees, prohibit a group health plan, insurance company, or HMO from setting annual or lifetime *dollar* limits on mental health benefits that are less than the limits that apply to other medical and surgical benefits. Besides imposing no dollar limitations on benefits for alcoholism or drug addiction, the act is noteworthy for other things it does not do. It does not require employers to make any benefits available for mental illness, and it does not impose any other restrictions on mental health benefits. Employers can still impose limitations, such as an annual maximum on number of visits or days of coverage, and different cost-sharing provisions for mental health benefits than those that apply to other medical and surgical benefits. This will change under PPACA, and annual limits will phase out over the next several years.

The situation changed as a result of amendments to the Mental Health Parity Act passed in 2008 that must be incorporated into certain medical benefit plans, effective for plan years beginning after October 3, 2009. The new rules apply only to plans of employers with more than 50 employees and still do not require employers to offer benefits for mental health or substance abuse. However, if plans do offer such benefits, there must be financial equity between these benefits and benefits for medical and surgical procedures. This equity applies to all financial requirements, including deductibles, copayments, percentage participation, and out-of-pocket expenses. The act also requires equity with respect to all treatment limitations, including frequency of treatment, number of visits, and days of coverage.

Also note that states may require more comprehensive coverage than the federal act and/or mandate that benefits provided under insurance contracts be made available for employers with a smaller number of employees.

Deductibles

deductible   A *deductible* is the initial amount of covered medical expenses an individual must incur before he or she receives benefits under a major medical plan. For example, if a plan has an annual deductible of $200, the covered person is responsible for the first $200 of medical expenses incurred each year. The major medical plan then pays covered expenses in excess of $200, subject to any limitations or coinsurance.

The simplest and most common form of deductible is the initial deductible. Essentially, a covered person must satisfy this deductible before the plan will pay any insurance benefits. However, the deductible can vary with respect to (1) the amount of the deductible, (2) the frequency with which it must be satisfied, and (3) the expenses to which it applies.

Deductible Amounts. Deductible amounts for any covered person under benefit plans of large employers tend to be relatively small. Most deductibles are fixed-dollar amounts that apply separately to each person and usually fall within the range of $200 to $500. Higher deductibles (such as $1,000) are often found in plans of small firms. In addition, large deductibles are frequently used for coverage written in conjunction with consumer-directed medical expense plans. PPACA will limit annual deductibles for single individuals to $2,000 and $4,000 for any other plan beginning January 1, 2014.

In most major medical expense plans, the deductible must be satisfied only once during any given time period (usually a calendar year), regardless of the number of causes from which medical expenses arise.

Deductibles apply to each covered individual, including an employee's dependents. To minimize the family's burden of satisfying several deductibles, however, most major medical expense plans contain a family deductible. Once the family deductible is satisfied, future covered medical expenses of all family members are paid just as if every member of the family had satisfied his or her individual deductible.

The most common type of family deductible waives any future deductible requirements for other family members once a certain number of family members (generally two or three) have satisfied their individual deductibles.

EXAMPLE
A family deductible might specify that the first $100 per year for each covered family member is the deductible. However, if three of five covered members of the family have each satisfied the deductible in a given year, the family needs to meet no further deductibles for that year. Thus, after Mom, Dad, and child #1 each incur $100 or more of covered expenses during the year, no further deductible applies to the expenses of child #2 and child #3 incurred after the family deductible is satisfied.

common accident provision

Most major medical expense contracts also contain a *common accident provision*. If two or more members of the same family are injured in the same accident, the common accident provision specifies that covered medical expenses for all family members are at most subject to a single deductible, usually equal to the individual deductible amount.

Deductible Frequency. A deductible usually applies to medical expenses incurred within a specified 12-month period, typically a calendar year. Under such a calendar-year deductible, expenses incurred from January 1 on apply toward the deductible. Once the deductible has been satisfied, the balance of any covered expenses incurred during the year is then paid by the major medical plan, subject to limitations and coinsurance.

Many plans with a calendar-year deductible also have a carryover provision that allows any expenses (1) applied to the deductible and (2) incurred during the last 3 months of the year to also be applied to the deductible for the following year.

Expenses to Which the Deductible Applies. Most major medical plans have a single deductible that applies to total medical expenses. However, some plans have two (or more) deductibles that apply separately to different categories of medical expenses. In some major medical plans, the deductible does not apply to certain expenses, in effect giving the covered person first-dollar coverage for these charges.

Effective 9/23/2010, insurers are prohibited from charging copayments or deductibles for Level A and Level B preventative care and medical screenings on all new insurance plans. These preventative services include annual check-ups, healthy child visits, bone density tests, breast cancer screenings for women and immunizations.

Coinsurance

coinsurance (medical expense insurance)

Major medical expense plans contain a coinsurance provision whereby the plan pays only a specified percentage (in most cases, 80 percent) of the covered expenses that exceed the deductible. For purposes of medical expense insurance, the term *coinsurance* refers to the percentage of covered expenses a medical expense plan pays. Thus, a plan with 80 percent coinsurance, sometimes referred to as an 80/20 plan, pays 80 percent of covered expenses while a person who receives benefits under the plan must pay the remaining 20 percent. In most plans, a percentage participation, such as 20 percent, is specified. The term *percentage participation* refers to the percentage of covered medical expenses that a medical expense plan does not pay and that a person receiving benefits must pay. Percentage participation is sometimes referred to as a *copayment,* but copayment usually implies a fixed-dollar amount that an insured must pay for a covered service. Some insurers refer to the percentage participation, rather than their portion of the benefit payment, as coinsurance.

EXAMPLE

If a comprehensive major medical expense plan has a $200 calendar-year deductible and an 80 percent coinsurance provision that applies to all expenses, an individual who incurs $1,200 of covered medical expenses during the year (assuming no limitations) will receive an $800 reimbursement, calculated as follows:

Covered expenses	$1,200
Minus deductible	200
	$1,000
Multiplied by coinsurance percentage	.80
	$ 800

Just as deductibles vary, so do coinsurance provisions. Sometimes different coinsurance percentages apply to different categories of medical expenses. For example, outpatient psychiatric charges may be subject to 50 percent coinsurance, while other covered medical expenses are subject to 80 percent coinsurance. In addition, certain medical expenses may be subject to 100 percent coinsurance (and usually no deductible), which in effect means that the expenses are paid in full, subject to any limitations. An example is preventative care under PPACA. Such full coverage is most likely to exist (1) for those expenses over which an individual has little control (such as hospitalization), (2) when there is a desire to provide first-dollar coverage for certain expenses, or (3) when there is a desire to encourage the use of the most cost-effective alternative treatment (such as outpatient surgery, preadmission testing, or birthing centers).

stop-loss limit   In the case of catastrophic medical expenses, the coinsurance provision could result in an individual's having to assume a large dollar amount of his or her own medical expenses. Consequently, many major medical expense plans place a limit, often called a *stop-loss* (or coinsurance) *limit* or cap, on the amount of out-of-pocket expenses that a covered person must bear during any time period. For example, a plan with an 80 percent coinsurance provision might have an annual stop-loss limit of $2,000. As long as aggregate claims for the year subject to coinsurance are $10,000 or less, the insured will be required to assume 20 percent of his or her own medical expenses. At $10,000 of claims, the insured will have reached the stop-loss limit of $2,000, and additional claims during the year will be paid in full.

Most plans apply the stop-loss limit only to amounts paid by the insured because of the coinsurance provision. However, some plans also include any deductibles that have been paid in determining when a stop-loss limit has been reached.

Stop-loss limits commonly range from $1,000 to $5,000. Like deductibles, the stop-loss limit is often waived for other family members after two or three family members satisfy their individual limits.

Maximum Benefits

Many major medical contracts contain a lifetime maximum benefit that applies to all medical expenses paid (after the application of deductibles and coinsurance) during the entire period an individual is covered under the contract. Benefit maximums are rarely less than $1 million and are usually $2 million or more. In some instances, the benefit amount is unlimited. This is an area of PPACA of 2010 that will have a significant effect on health care costs. Lifetime benefit limits are banned for all new plans that take effect on or after September 23, 2010. Annual limits will be phased out over the next few years and will be completely banned by January 1, 2014.

In addition to the overall lifetime maximum, major medical contracts sometimes have *internal maximums*. For example, a plan may have a $2 million overall lifetime maximum but a $20,000 lifetime maximum for benefits relating to alcoholism and drug addiction as long as the employer is not subject to state and federal laws that prevent such internal maximums. The Health care reform legislation (PPACA) has essentially ended these maximum benefit limitations.

Managed Care Provisions in Traditional Plans

Historically, medical decisions were between the covered persons and their health care providers, and medical expense plans did little to manage or control patients' treatment. Over time, however, medical expense plans have gradually increased their control. For years, many plans have required preadmission certification of the need for hospital treatment and supported the cost of second opinions for surgical treatment. It is also common to cover treatment provided in facilities other than hospitals. Other managed care provisions and practices that traditional plans may contain include the following:

- preapproval of visits to specialists
- increased benefits for preventive care
- carve-outs of benefits that can be provided cost effectively under arrangements that employ various degrees of managed care. Examples include prescription drugs, treatment of mental illness, and substance abuse treatment. These types of carve-outs are discussed later as part of managed care plans.

Some traditional major medical plans actually make wide use of managed care techniques; the primary factor that prevents them from being called managed care plans is that there are few restrictions on access to providers.

Preadmission Certification

preadmission certification   As a method of controlling costs, medical expense plans have adopted utilization review programs. One aspect of these programs is *preadmission certification*. Such a program requires that a covered person, or his or her physician, obtain prior authorization from the plan for any non-emergency hospitalization.

Authorization usually must also be obtained within 24 to 48 hours of admissions for emergencies.

Most plans reduce benefits if the preadmission certification procedure is not followed. If a patient enters the hospital after a preadmission certification has been denied, many plans do not pay for any hospital expenses, whereas other plans provide a reduced level of benefits.

Under PPACA, a group health plan may not require preauthorization or referral for a woman covered under the plan who seeks obstetrical or gynecological care. Additionally, a group health plan may not require preauthorization for emergency services, whether in or out of network.

Second Surgical Opinions

second surgical opinions
Most major medical expense policies provide benefits for *second surgical opinions* in an attempt to control medical costs by eliminating unnecessary surgery. A voluntary approach for obtaining second surgical opinions is often used. If a physician or surgeon recommends surgery, a covered person may seek a second opinion and the medical expense plan bears the cost. Some plans also pay for a third opinion if the first two opinions disagree. When there are divergent opinions, the final choice is up to the patient, and the plan's regular benefits are usually paid for any resulting surgery.

Some medical expense plans require mandatory second opinions, which may apply to any elective and non-emergency surgery but frequently apply only to a specified list of procedures. In most cases, a surgeon selected by the insurance company or other provider of benefits must give the second opinion. If conflicting opinions arise, a third opinion may be obtained. The costs of the second and third opinions are paid in full. In contrast to voluntary provisions, mandatory provisions generally specify that benefits are paid at a reduced level if surgery is performed either without a second opinion or contrary to the final opinion.

Alternative Facilities for Treatment

Many traditional medical expense plans provide coverage for treatment in facilities that are alternatives to hospitals. Initially, this coverage was provided primarily to the extent that it reduced hospital benefits that were otherwise covered. Although this is still the primary effect of this coverage, it is often an integral part of medical expense plans, and benefits are provided even if they might not have been covered under a plan limited solely to treatment received in hospitals.

extended care facilities

Extended Care Facility Benefits. Many hospital patients recover to a point where they no longer need the full level of care a hospital provides but still require a medically supervised period of convalescence. *Extended care facilities* (often called convalescent nursing homes or skilled-nursing facilities) have been established in many areas to provide this type of care. Treatment in these facilities, which are sometimes adjacent to hospitals, can reduce daily room-and-board charges—often substantially. As a result, an increasing number of contracts include benefits for situations when extended care facilities are used in lieu of hospitalization to contain medical care costs.

Extended care facility coverage provides benefits to inpatients in an extended care facility, which is typically defined as an institution that furnishes room and board and 24-hour-a-day skilled-nursing care under the supervision of a physician or a registered professional nurse. It does not include facilities that are designed as a place for rest or domiciliary care for the aged. Facilities for the treatment of drug abuse and alcoholism are often excluded from the definition.

The maximum length of time for which extended care benefits will be paid is usually limited to a specific number of days; 60 days is fairly common.

home health care

Home Health Care Benefits. *Home health care* coverage is similar to extended care facility benefits but designed for when the necessary part-time nursing care ordered by a physician following hospitalization can be provided in the patient's home. Coverage is for (1) nursing care (usually limited to a maximum of 2 hours per day) under the supervision of a registered nurse; (2) physical, occupational, and speech therapy; and (3) medical supplies and equipment, such as wheelchairs and hospital beds.

In most cases, the home health care benefits payable are equal to a percentage, frequently 80 percent, of reasonable-and-customary charges. Benefit payments are limited to either a maximum number of visits (such as 60 per calendar year) or to a period of time (such as 90 days after benefits commence).

hospice care   ***Hospice Benefits.*** Hospices for the treatment of terminally ill persons are a recent development in the area of medical care. *Hospice care* does not attempt to cure medical conditions but is devoted to easing the physical and psychological pain associated with dying. In addition to providing services for the patient, hospice care may offer counseling to family members. Although a hospice may be a separate facility, this type of care is frequently provided on an outpatient basis in the dying person's home.

birthing centers   ***Birthing Centers.*** Another recent development in medical care is *birthing centers,* which are designed to provide a homelike facility for the delivery of babies. Nurse-midwives perform deliveries in a facility separate from a hospital, and mothers and babies are released from birthing centers shortly after birth.

Preapproval of Visits to Specialists

Many persons elect to bypass their primary care physicians, such as family physicians and pediatricians, and use specialists as their main access to medical care. This practice results in additional costs but, in the opinion of much of the medical community, does not improve medical outcomes. To counter this practice, some medical expense plans require that a visit to a specialist be preceded by a visit to a primary care physician. It is not necessary for the primary care physician to actually certify that a trip to a specialist is needed, only that he or she has been told that the patient plans to make such a visit. The rationale for this procedure is that the primary care physician may convince the patient that the primary care physician is able to treat the condition and that a specialist is unnecessary, at least at that time. If a specialist is needed, the primary care physician is also in a better position to recommend the right type of specialist and to coordinate health care for persons seeing multiple specialists.

The patient's failure to use the primary care physician as a quasi-gatekeeper will result in a reduction in benefits. Usually, benefits will still be paid but at a lower level.

Benefits for Preventive Care

Most traditional medical expense plans provide at least a few benefits for preventive care. PPACA requires that group health plans and insurers in the group and individual markets provide certain preventive services without imposing any cost-sharing. As a result, no deductibles, copays, coinsurance, or other cost-sharing may be imposed on these services.

MANAGED CARE PLANS

Managed care plans take a much more direct approach to controlling patient care costs. Over the last few years, the number of persons having medical expense coverage from managed care plans has grown rapidly. Almost 60 percent of managed care participants are enrolled in PPOs, and the remaining participants are split between traditional HMOs and point-of-service plans.

managed care   Although managed care plans have evolved over the last few years, it is generally felt that a true *managed care* plan should have five basic characteristics:

- *controlled access to providers.* It is difficult to control costs if participants have unrestricted access to physicians and hospitals. Managed care plans attempt to encourage or force participants to use participating-provider networks. By limiting the number of providers, managed care plans are better able to control costs by negotiating provider fees. Because a major portion of medical expenses results from referrals to specialists, managed care plans tend to use primary care physicians as gatekeepers to determine the necessity and appropriateness of specialty care.

- *comprehensive case management.* Successful plans perform utilization review and other forms of case management at all levels. This involves reviewing a case to determine the type of treatment necessary, monitoring ongoing care, and assessing the appropriateness and success of treatment after it has been given.

- *preventive care.* Managed care plans encourage preventive care and the attainment of healthier lifestyles.

- *risk sharing.* Managed care plans are most successful if providers share in the financial consequences of medical decisions. Newer managed care plans have contractual guarantees to encourage cost-effective care. For example, a physician who minimizes diagnostic tests may receive a bonus. Ideally, such an arrangement will eliminate unnecessary tests, not discourage tests that should be performed.

- *high-quality care.* A managed care plan will not be well received and selected by participants if there is a perception of inferior or inconvenient medical care. In the past, too little attention was paid to this aspect of cost containment. Newer managed care plans not only select providers more carefully but also monitor the quality of care on a continuing basis.

This section on managed care first looks at the issue of quality of care and discusses some recent developments. It then describes the types of managed care plans.

Basic Characteristics of Managed Care Plans

- Controlled access to specialists and hospitals
- Emphasis on case management, including utilization review
- Encouragement of preventive care and healthy lifestyles
- Sharing by medical care providers in the financial consequences of medical decisions
- Careful selection and monitoring of medical providers

Quality of Care

A difficult question to answer is whether persons covered by managed care plans receive the same quality of care as persons covered under traditional medical expense plans. If the sole objective of a managed care plan is to offer coverage at the lowest possible cost, there may be a decline in the quality of care. However, some type of quality assurance program is one aspect of any managed care plan.

The results of numerous surveys and studies on the quality of medical care plans have been mixed. Some studies show that persons in managed care plans are less likely than persons in traditional medical expense plans to receive treatment for a serious medical condition from specialists, and they are also likely to have fewer diagnostic tests. There are those who argue that family physicians can treat a wide variety of illnesses and avoid unnecessary diagnostic tests and referrals to specialists. An opposing argument contends that the decline in the use of diagnostic tests indicates a corresponding decline in the level of medical care. Other studies show that persons in managed care plans are much more likely than the rest of the population to receive preventive care and early diagnosis and treatment of potentially serious conditions, such as high blood pressure and diabetes. In addition, managed care plans are viewed as having been successful in coordinating care when it is necessary for a person to see several different types of specialists. There is no doubt that there are some small provider networks with a limited choice of specialists, but most networks are relatively large or allow persons to select treatment outside the network. There are also many managed care plans that do refer patients to highly regarded physicians and hospitals or include these providers in their network.

Recent Developments

The majority of employers and employees are reasonably satisfied with managed care plans but have increasing concerns. However, physicians and other providers are much less satisfied, primarily because of decreased control over medical decisions for their patients and a loss of income. Some of the public's concerns, such as lack of complete mental health parity and inadequate coverage for certain preventive medical screenings, apply to the entire health care system, not just to managed care. Additionally, although some dissatisfactions are aimed at all types of managed care plans, many are targeted solely at practices of HMOs. As a result, states continue to enact legislation to address many of the concerns, and managed care organizations voluntarily modify their practices in light of legislative activity and competitive forces.

State Reform

State legislatures in recent years have passed several types of laws aimed at managed care reform. These changes often bring managed care plans closer to traditional indemnity plans in both coverage and cost. Some of these laws, passed by anywhere from a dozen to almost all states, include

- rules that prohibit managed care organizations from including anti-gag clauses in their contracts. Such clauses prevent doctors from having discussions with patients about treatment options that may not be covered under their health plans or from referring patients who are very ill for specialized care by providers outside the plan.
- grievance, review, and appeal procedures
- mandatory point-of-service options that require managed care organizations to permit enrollees to seek treatment from nonnetwork providers by paying a portion, but not all, of the expenses incurred with these providers. In effect, such legislation transforms a traditional HMO into a point-of-service plan.
- emergency room coverage that requires a plan to pay emergency room charges whenever a prudent layperson considers a situation to be an emergency

- mental health parity laws that require either complete parity for benefits arising from physical illnesses and mental illnesses or complete parity for physical illnesses and certain severe mental illnesses, such as schizophrenia, depression, and bipolar disorder
- minimum stays for certain procedures, such as maternity or breast cancer surgery
- plastic surgery mandates that require all health insurance contracts or health plans to provide coverage for certain types of reconstructive surgery. This legislation may apply to the repair of birth defects only, or it may apply to a broader list of situations in which reconstruction might be needed as a result of mastectomies, trauma, infections, tumors, or disease.
- legislation that allows women covered under managed care plans to have direct access to obstetricians/gynecologists without obtaining approval or a referral from their health plan. A few states require direct access to other types of providers, such as dermatologists.

Voluntary Reform by Managed Care Organizations

Many managed care organizations have voluntarily initiated reforms. Some reforms are a result of the natural evolution of a new form of financing and providing health care; other changes have occurred because of competition among managed care organizations for market share. Most reforms are reactions to legislation that is proposed or passed by the states. After a few states enact a certain type of managed care legislation, managed care organizations nationwide often revise their plans to address the concerns that resulted in the legislation. The threat of legislation, at either the state or federal level, is also a major impetus for voluntary changes by managed care plans. Such voluntary reform may forestall more restrictive government regulation.

Federal Reform

The Patient Protection and Affordable Care Act (PPACA) and the Health Care and Education Reconciliation Act (HCERA) were two massive statutes enacted in 2010 that address health care reform. These laws made changes to the Internal Revenue Code, ERISA, The Social Security Act, and the Fair Labor Standards Act, while leaving COBRA unchanged. These laws set new minimum standards for health coverage and impose an array of new requirements on individuals, employers and health plans. Among other things, health care reform will require individuals to have health insurance, encourage employers to provide group health benefits, and provide health care exchange markets to help facilitate these changes.

Many of the health care reform provisions will not take place until 2014. Many provisions have already taken effect, while others will be phased in over the next several years. At the core of health care reform is the requirement that, beginning in 2014, individuals maintain health insurance through individual insurance, group insurance, a grandfathered plan, or a federal program such as Medicare of Medicaid. This is the most controversial and politically charged aspect of health care reform. A tax penalty will be imposed on any applicable individual for any month after 2013 that he or she fails to maintain minimum essential coverage.

To make it easier for individuals to purchase coverage, states are provided with funds to operate health benefit "exchanges" by 2014. The exchanges will offer insurance plans to individuals, families and employers. Individuals will be able to buy four levels of coverage: bronze (60% coverage), silver (70% coverage), gold (80% coverage) and platinum (90% coverage). Low income earners will receive a tax credit. Although employers are not required to provide health insurance, certain employers with 50 or more full-time employees may be required to pay a penalty if they do not provide coverage, or provide coverage that does not meet certain requirements.

Health Maintenance Organizations

health maintenance organizations (HMOs)

Health maintenance organizations (HMOs) are generally regarded as organized systems of health care that provide a comprehensive array of medical services on a prepaid basis to voluntarily enrolled persons or members who live within a specified geographic region. Like insurance companies and the Blues, health maintenance organizations finance health care. Unlike insurance companies and the Blues, however, they also deliver medical services. HMOs can be either profit or not-for-profit organizations. They may be sponsored or owned by insurance companies, the Blues, consumer groups, physicians, hospitals, labor unions, or private investors.

Even though the term health maintenance organization is a relatively modern term, the concept of the HMO is not. For many years, prepaid group practice plans have operated successfully in many parts of the country. However, growth was relatively slow until the passage of the Health Maintenance Organization Act of 1973. This act resulted from a belief by the federal government's that HMOs were a viable alternative method of financing and delivering health care and thus should be encouraged with grants for feasibility studies and development and loans (or loan guarantees) to assist them in covering initial operating deficits. Many HMOs were formed as the result of these grants and loans.

Characteristics of HMOs

HMOs have several characteristics that distinguish them from traditional medical expense contracts that are offered by insurance companies and the Blues.

Comprehensive Care. HMOs offer their members a comprehensive package of health care services, generally including benefits for outpatient services as well as for hospitalization. Members may get these services at no cost except the periodically required premium. However, in most cases, a copayment, such as $10 or $20 per physician's visit, may be imposed for certain services. HMOs emphasize preventive care and provide such services as routine physicals and immunizations. Under PPACA, some preventative care services are required beginning in 2010 without cost sharing that are rated A or B by the Preventative Services Task Force of the Department of Health and Human Services. By 2018, all existing plans must cover approved preventative care and checkups without copayments.

Delivery of Medical Services. HMOs provide for the delivery of medical services performed by salaried physicians and other personnel the HMO employs, or by providers on a fee-for-service basis. Members are required to obtain their medical care services from providers who are affiliated with the HMO. Because HMOs may operate in a geographic region no larger than a single metropolitan area, this requirement may result in limited coverage for members if treatment is received elsewhere. Most HMOs do have out-of-area coverage but only in the case of medical emergencies.

HMOs emphasize treatment by primary care physicians to the greatest extent possible. These practitioners fulfill a gatekeeper function and historically have controlled access to specialists. The traditional HMO covers benefits provided by a specialist only if the primary care physician recommends the specialist, who may be a fellow employee in a group-practice plan or a physician who has a contract with the HMO. The member has little or no say regarding the specialist selected, one of the more controversial aspects of HMOs and one that has discouraged larger enrollment. In response to consumer concerns, many HMOs now make the process of seeing a specialist easier. Referrals can often be made by nurses in physicians' offices or by HMO staff members whom members can contact by telephone. Some HMOs, referred to as direct-access or self-referral HMOs, allow members to see network specialists without going through a gatekeeper. However, the specialist may have to contact the HMO for authorization before proceeding with tests or treatment. A variation of an HMO, called a point-of-service (POS) plan, allows even more choice.

Cost Control. HMOs emphasize control of medical expenses. By providing and encouraging preventive care, HMOs attempt to detect and treat medical conditions at an early stage, thereby avoiding expensive medical treatment in the future.

The use of salaried employees by many HMOs may also result in lower costs because the physician or other care provider has no financial incentive to prescribe additional, and possibly unnecessary, treatment. In fact, the physicians and other medical professionals in some HMOs may receive bonuses if the HMO operates efficiently and generates a surplus.

Types of HMOs

There are several types of HMOs: closed-panel HMOs, individual practice associations, and mixed-model HMOs.

Closed-Panel HMOs. The earliest HMOs can be described as closed-panel plans under which members must use physicians employed by the plan or by an organization with which it contracts. Because most closed-panel plans have several general practitioners, members can usually select their physician from among those accepting new patients and make medical appointments just as if the physician was in private practice. However, there may be little choice among specialists because a plan may contract with a limited number of physicians in a given specialty.

capitation   These HMOs may operate in a variety of ways with respect to providing physicians' services. They may own their own facilities and hire their own physicians, who are paid a salary and possibly an incentive bonus. They are more likely, however, to enter into contracts with one or more groups of physicians to provide services. In many cases, these groups are paid on a *capitation* basis, which means that they receive a predetermined fee per year for each member and must provide any and all covered services for this fee. Closed-panel plans may own their own hospitals, laboratories, or pharmacies or contract with other entities to provide their services.

Individual Practice Associations. Many HMOs have been formed as individual practice associations (IPAs). This type of plan has more flexibility with respect to members' ability to choose physicians and physicians' ability to participate in the plan.

In IPAs, participating physicians practice individually or in small groups at their own offices. In most cases, these physicians accept both nonmanaged care patients (on a traditional fee-for-service basis) and HMO members. IPAs are often referred to as open-panel HMOs, because members choose from a list of participating physicians. The number of physicians participating in this type of HMO is frequently larger than the number participating in group practice plans and may include several physicians within a given specialty. Because most of the newer HMOs are IPAs, the percentage of HMO members served by these plans continues to grow.

Several methods may be used to compensate physicians who participate in an IPA. The most common is a fee schedule based on the services provided to members. To encourage physicians to be cost effective, it is common for plans to have a provision for reducing payments to physicians if the experience of the plan is worse than expected. On the other hand, the physicians may receive a bonus if the experience of the plan is better than expected. Particularly with respect to general practitioners, some IPA plans pay each physician a flat annual capitation for each member who has elected to use him or her. For this annual payment, the physician must see these members as often as necessary during the year.

It is unusual for IPAs to own their own hospitals or other medical facilities. Usually, they enter into contracts with local hospitals or other organizations to provide the necessary services for their members.

Mixed-Model HMOs. Some HMOs operate as mixed-model plans. This means that the organization of the plan is a combination of the approaches previously described. Such a combination generally occurs as a plan continues to grow. For example, a plan might have been established as a closed-panel HMO but at a later time decided to expand its capacity or geographic region by adding physicians under an IPA arrangement. Some mixed-model plans have also resulted from the merger of two plans that each used a different organizational form.

Types of HMOs
• Closed-panel HMOs
• Individual practice associations
• Mixed-model HMOs

Preferred-Provider Organizations

A concept that continues to receive considerable attention from employers and insurance companies is the preferred-provider organization (PPO). Since the early 1980s, PPOs have grown steadily in number and in membership. Today, preferred-provider organizations provide coverage for medical expenses to more Americans than do HMOs, primarily because of the flexibility covered persons have in choosing their own medical providers.

PPOs are regulated by the states but somewhat less strictly than HMOs. Most PPO contracts also meet the regulatory definition of insurance and are subject to the same regulation by state insurance departments as traditional insurance contracts with respect to contract provisions and benefit mandates.

What Is a PPO?

preferred-provider organization (PPO) The term *preferred-provider organization (PPO)* tends to be used in two ways. One way is to apply it to health care providers that contract with employers, insurance companies, union trust funds, third-party administrators, or others to provide medical care services at a reduced fee. Using this definition, a PPO may be organized by the providers themselves or by other organizations, such as insurance companies, the Blues, HMOs, employers, third-party administrators, private investors, and groups of physicians and/or hospitals. Like HMOs, they may take the form of group practices or separate individual practices. They may provide a broad array of medical services, including physicians' services, hospital care, laboratory costs, and home health care, or they may be limited only to hospitalization or physicians' services. Some of these types of organizations are very specialized and provide specific services, such as dental care, mental health benefits, substance abuse services, maternity care, or prescription drugs. In this book, these providers are referred to not as *PPOs* but as *preferred providers* or *network providers*.

The second use of the term *PPO,* and the one generally assumed when the term is used, is to apply it to benefit plans that contract with preferred providers to obtain lower-cost care for plan members. Most such PPOs are offered by insurance companies or the Blues. Some are also offered by HMOs to diversify their portfolios.

PPOs typically differ from HMOs in several respects. First, the preferred providers are generally paid on a fee-for-service basis as their services are used. However, fees are usually subject to a schedule that is the same for all similar providers within the PPO contracts, and providers may have an incentive to control utilization through bonus arrangements. Second, employees and their dependents are not required to use the practitioners or facilities that contract with the PPO; rather, they can make a choice each time they need medical care, and benefits are also paid for care from nonnetwork providers. Employees are offered incentives to use network providers; they include lower or reduced deductibles and copayments as well as increased benefits, such as preventive health care. Third, most PPOs do not use primary care physicians as gatekeepers; employees do not need referrals to see specialists.

Characteristics of a Typical PPO

- A network of medical care providers contracts to offer medical services to plan participants at reduced rates.
- Medical care providers are usually paid on a fee-for-service basis.
- Members have a choice of using network or nonnetwork providers.
- Members who opt to use a network provider pay lower deductibles or copayments or receive broader types of covered care.

Variations. Over time, PPOs have continued to evolve. Some PPOs compensate providers on a capitation basis, while others perform a gatekeeper function. If a member's primary care physician does not recommend a specialist, benefits may be reduced. With these changes, it is sometimes difficult to determine the exact form of a managed care organization. However, those that operate as traditional HMOs generally provide medical expense coverage at a slightly lower cost than those that operate as traditional PPOs, but there are wide variations among HMOs as well as among PPOs. Therefore, a careful analysis of quality of care, cost, and financial stability is necessary before selecting a particular HMO or PPO.

Benefit Structure

The basic benefit structure of a PPO is similar to that of the traditional major medical contract. The most significant difference is that PPOs include a higher level of benefits for care received from network providers than for care received from nonnetwork providers. Many PPOs have extensive networks of preferred providers, particularly in the geographic areas in which they operate; so there is little reason to seek care outside the network. However, other PPOs have more limited networks, so their members' need for treatment from nonnetwork providers is greater.

The level of benefits under PPOs may vary because of differences in deductibles, coinsurance, copayments, maximum lifetime benefits, and precertification rules. There may also be a few additional benefits that are available only if care is received from a network provider. Finally, procedures for filing claims also differ. The major purpose of these differences is to encourage an employee or dependent to receive care from preferred providers who have agreed to charge the plan a discounted fee.

Deductibles. A PPO may have annual deductibles that apply separately to network and nonnetwork charges—for example, $250 and $1,000, respectively for an individual. In some cases, there is only a single deductible that applies in the aggregate to both network and nonnetwork charges. However, some PPOs have no deductible for network charges or waive this deductible for certain medical services, such as emergency or preventive care.

Copayments and Coinsurance. The use of a copayment structure and coinsurance after an insured satisfies the deductible differs according to whether care is received from a network or nonnetwork provider. The level of copayments and coinsurance vary among plans.

Under the most common approach, copayments apply to network charges and coinsurance applies to nonnetwork charges. For example, a plan may have a copayment of $20 for doctor's visits and $100 for an emergency room visit. It is also common for such plans to have a copayment for hospitalizations—for example, a $50 or $100 flat fee per day. If an insured uses a nonnetwork provider, the same plan may pay 80 percent of allowable charges. Allowable charges are sometimes pegged to what the plan pays network providers, rather than actual charges. As a result, the insured will be responsible for 20 percent of allowable charges as well as any provider charges in excess of allowable charges. Instead of copayments, some PPOs use coinsurance for both network and nonnetwork charges. However, the coinsurance percentage is lower for the latter. For example, 90 percent coinsurance may apply to network charges and 70 percent to nonnetwork charges. Different stop-loss limits, such as $1,000 and $3,000, typically apply to network and nonnetwork charges.

Precertification Rules. PPOs often have precertification requirements for many types of hospitalizations, outpatient procedures, and medical supplies. For network benefits, the person responsible for obtaining the needed precertification is the network provider, and the covered person is not penalized if the network provider fails to obtain the proper precertification. However, this responsibility shifts to the employee or family member for nonnetwork services. If precertification is not obtained when required, there usually is a reduction in benefits for whoever should have obtained the certification.

Additional Network Benefits. For the most part, PPOs pay benefits for the same medical procedures, whether they are performed by a network or nonnetwork provider. A few procedures, however, may be covered only if they are received from network providers. For example, routine physical exams may be covered only in the network. In addition, there might be coverage for more outpatient psychiatric visits if a network provider is used.

Claims. No forms are required for claims as long as the insured receives network services. The covered person merely pays any required copayment, and the provider of medical services does the paperwork needed to receive the additional amounts payable by the plan.

Point-of-Service Plans

point-of-service (POS) plan

Another type of managed care arrangement is the *point-of-service (POS) plan*. A *POS plan* is a hybrid arrangement that combines aspects of a traditional HMO and a PPO. With a point-of-service plan, participants in the plan elect, at the time medical treatment is needed, whether to receive treatment within the plan's tightly managed network, usually an HMO, or outside the network. Expenses received outside the network are reimbursed in the same manner as described earlier for nonnetwork services under PPO plans.

There are two basic types of POS plans: the open-ended HMO and the gatekeeper PPO. An open-ended HMO is by far the most common form and is the HMO industry's response to the demand for more consumer flexibility in the choice of providers, even though it increases costs somewhat. It essentially consists of traditional HMO coverage with an endorsement for nonnetwork coverage. It can take the basic form of any of the HMOs previously described. However, at any time, a member can elect to go outside the HMO network of medical care providers.

It can be argued that any PPO is actually a POS plan. However, the normal usage of the term POS implies a higher degree of managed care than is found in most PPOs. A gatekeeper PPO requires the PPO participant to elect a primary care physician in the manner of an HMO participant. This physician acts as a gatekeeper to control utilization and refer members to specialists within the PPO network. At any time care is needed, however, a covered person can elect to go outside the network.

Under some POS plans, a covered person can go outside the plan's network without informing the plan. In other POS plans, the person must notify the gatekeeper that he or she is seeking such treatment.

COMPARISON OF TYPICAL MEDICAL EXPENSE PLANS

Thus far, we have discussed the various types of medical expense plans and how they differ. Although variations within each type of plan exist, some generalizations, which are summarized in the following table, can be made. The degree of managed care increases as one moves from left to right in the table. However, the cost of the plans, on the average, decreases as the degree of managed care increases. In addition, a higher degree of managed care is generally associated with lower annual premium increases by a plan.

Table 12-1 Comparison of Health Insurance Plans				
	Traditional Major Medical Contracts	**PPOs**	**POS Plans**	**HMOs**
Provider choice	Unlimited	Unlimited, but benefits are greater if network provider is used	Unlimited, but benefits are greater if network provider is used	Network of providers must be used; care from nonnetwork providers covered only in emergencies
Use of gatekeeper	None	None	Used for access to network specialists	Used for access to specialists
Out-of-pocket costs	Deductibles and percentage participation	Deductibles, copayments, and percentage participation, which may be lower if network providers are used	Copayments for network services; deductibles and percentage participation for nonnetwork services	Copayments for some services
Utilization review	Traditionally little, but a few techniques are likely to be used now	More than traditional plans, but less than HMOs; network provider may be subject to some controls	Like HMOs for network services; like PPOs for nonnetwork services	Highest degree of review, including financial incentives and disincentives for providers
Preventive care	The least generous coverage	Usually more coverage than traditional major medical plan but less coverage than HMOs and POS plans	Covered	Covered
Responsibility for claims filings	Covered person	Plan providers for network services; covered person for nonnetwork services	Plan providers for network services; covered person for nonnetwork services	Plan providers

CONSUMER-DIRECTED MEDICAL EXPENSE PLANS

consumer-directed medical expense plan
In recent years there has been considerable interest in the concept of the *consumer-directed medical expense plan*. Such plans, also referred to by such names as consumer-driven health care and consumer-choice plans, give the employee increased choices and responsibilities for their medical care. Some consumer-directed models also have a greater accountability for health plans and providers.

There are two general approaches to consumer-directed medical expense plans—defined-contribution medical expense plans and the use of savings accounts.

Defined-Contribution Medical Expense Plans

defined-contribution medical expense plan
Even though some consumer-directed approaches for medical expense plans are relatively new, they have existed in the form of the *defined-contribution medical expense plan* for some time. For example, many employers make two or more medical expense plans available to their employees, such as an HMO, a PPO, and an indemnity plan. Under such a defined-contribution medical expense plan, the employer contribution to the cost of coverage for each available option may be a defined dollar amount that is pegged to a fixed percentage of the cost of the least expensive option, usually an HMO. Therefore, employees who elect a more expensive PPO or indemnity plan must make a greater out-of-pocket contribution for coverage than if they had selected the HMO.

EXAMPLE

The Weir Corporation makes three medical expense plans available to its employees—an HMO, a POS plan, and a PPO. For a single employee, the corporation pays an amount equal to 90 percent of the cost of the least expensive plan, which is the HMO. For the three plans, the employee contribution is as follows:

	Total Monthly Premium	Employer Premium	Employee Contribution
HMO	$300	$270	$30
POS plan	363	270	93
PPO	461	270	191

A similar approach is used to determine the cost of dependent coverage, for which the corporation contributes an amount equal to 50 percent of the cost of HMO coverage.

Use of Savings Accounts

high-deductible health plan

Newer types of defined-contribution medical expense plans have features other than just fixed employer contributions. At a minimum, these approaches force employees to make financial decisions that involve their health care. Typically, an employer might provide employees with a medical expense plan that has a very high deductible, perhaps as much as $5,000 per year. This type of plan is often referred to as a *high-deductible health plan*. The employer often also contributes a lower or equal amount, such as $2,500 per year, to some type of savings account from which the employee can make tax-free withdrawals to pay medical expenses that are not covered because of the deductible under the high-deductible health plan. The employee can carry forward any unused amount in the account and add it to the next year's employer contribution. Such a plan gives the employee an immediate incentive to purchase medical care wisely because, if medical expenses exceed the amount in the account, the employee will have to pay the full cost of medical expenses out of his or her own pocket until the deductible is satisfied. The plan often incorporates a preferred-provider network of health care professionals. As long as an employee receives medical treatment within the network, any charges that the employee must pay because of the deductible are limited to the amount negotiated with the preferred provider. Employers might use this approach for all employees, but most employers make it available as an option to a more traditional medical expense plan.

The rationale for using a high-deductible medical expense plan along with a savings account is that significant cost savings can occur for two primary reasons.

1. First, the expensive cost of administering and paying small claims is largely eliminated, since a major medical policy with a $2,500

deductible can often be purchased for about one-half the cost of a policy with a $250 deductible.

2. Second, employees now have a direct financial incentive to avoid unnecessary care and to seek out the most cost-effective form of treatment.

A small number of employers have used this approach for some time with positive results. Costs have been lowered or have risen less rapidly than would otherwise be expected. Employees' reactions have generally been favorable. But, as with almost any approach to cost containment, this type of medical expense plan has its critics. It is argued that employees will minimize treatment for minor medical expenses and preventive care that would have been covered under a plan without a high deductible. Critics contend that this avoidance of medical care may lead to major expenses that could have been averted or minimized with earlier treatment. However, some types of consumer-directed medical expense plans waive the deductible for preventive care. Another criticism is that a high-deductible plan tends to favor healthy individuals and those in high income tax brackets. A final criticism is that this type of medical expense plan does not focus on the problem of the uninsured. In rebuttal to this criticism, proponents argue that any technique that lowers costs for employers will ultimately benefit everyone and encourage small employers to provide coverage that would have previously been unaffordable.

health reimbursement arrangement

There are two major types of savings accounts. One of these—called a *health reimbursement arrangement* (HRA)—is an unfunded arrangement. There are no restrictions on the type of underlying policy used with a health reimbursement arrangement, and the employer makes an annual credit to an employee's account. The employee can use these credits to pay his or her medical expenses as well as those of a spouse and dependents to the extent these expenses are not reimbursed by any other insurance plan. If an employee does not use the amount credited to an account during the year, the balance rolls over to the following year. At termination of employment, the account usually terminates and any remaining balance belong to the employer.

The other major type of savings accounts is the health savings account (HSA). Persons other than employees can also establish these accounts.

BENEFIT CARVE-OUTS

The use of benefit carve-outs by medical expense plans has grown in recent years, often as a method of cost containment via managed care techniques. In addition, many medical expense plans have come to realize that they cannot always provide as high a quality of care as a well-managed specialty provider. Carve-outs for prescription drugs, vision care, dental care, and behavioral health have been common for a number of years. Increasingly, carve-outs are being used to better manage a wide variety of medical conditions, such as pregnancy, asthma, and diabetes.

**carve-out
(medical expense
insurance)**
A benefit *carve-out* can best be defined as coverage under a medical expense plan for a health care service that has been singled out for management by a party other than the employer or the employer's primary health plan provider. Some types of carve-outs predate managed care as it is now known. For example, many employees have long been covered under separate prescription drug plans. The early emphasis under these carve-out plans was on discounts with preferred providers of prescription drugs. Today, prescription drug plans and other types of carve-outs use a wider variety of managed care techniques.

An employer can purchase a medical expense plan to provide benefits to its employees for most types of medical care and then enter into a separate contract with another provider for the carved-out benefit. However, in many cases, it is the health care provider that enters into the carve-out arrangement with a "subcontractor" that manages the benefits. From the standpoint of employers and employees, the benefit is part of the employer's plan.

Vendors who provide carve-outs often act as managed care plans for a single medical expense benefit and take on characteristics of HMOs or PPOs. They also have learned over time that their type of specialty care should sometimes be accompanied by a unique benefit structure. This is one reason why certain benefits, such as prescription drugs, are often subject to different deductibles, copayments, or benefit limitations than those used for most types of medical expenses.

There are numerous types of benefit carve-outs. The three discussed here are prescription drugs, vision benefits, and behavioral health.

Prescription Drugs

Although separate prescription drug plans have existed for many years, the initial focus was on obtaining lower costs through discounts with participating pharmacies and mail-order suppliers of drugs. The situation changed significantly in the early 1980s when pharmacy benefit managers (PBMs) appeared in the marketplace. Today, most persons with prescription drug coverage obtain their drugs through PBMs. PBMs may be affiliated with pharmaceutical companies or health benefit providers, such as insurance companies. They may also be independently owned.

PBMs administer prescription drug plans on behalf of health care providers. PBMs' online capabilities enable them to offer considerable flexibility in designing a prescription drug program for a specific employer or benefit plan provider. PBMs have been leaders in the integration of formularies into prescription drug plans. A formulary is a list, developed by a committee of pharmacists and physicians, of preferred medications for a specific medical condition.

The typical prescription drug plan covers the cost of drugs (except those dispensed in a hospital or in an extended care facility) that are required by law to be dispensed by prescription. Drugs for which prescriptions are not required by law are usually not covered even if a physician orders them on a prescription form. One frequent exception to this general rule is injectable insulin, which is generally covered despite the fact that in many states it is a nonprescription drug. No coverage is provided for charges to administer drugs or the cost of therapeutic devices or appliances, such as bandages or hypodermic needles. It is also common to limit an order for drugs to a specified amount each time a prescription is filled.

Contraceptive drugs are usually covered but may be excluded. Some prescription drug plans take a middle approach by covering these drugs only when they are prescribed for treating some medical condition rather than for preventing conception. Recent court decisions and the position of the Equal Employment Opportunity Commission indicate that an employer will have a more difficult time defending a legal challenge by female employees over the failure to provide complete coverage for prescription contraceptives. Drugs for treatment of infertility or erectile dysfunction, such as Viagra, may or may not be covered. These drugs, too, have been subjects of recent lawsuits.

Drug plans are increasingly requiring precertification for the use of certain expensive drugs.

Most prescription drug plans have a copayment that a covered person pays for any prescriptions filled; in a few cases, it may be a flat amount that usually varies from $10 to $30 per prescription. Other plans have one copayment amount for generic drugs and a higher one for brand-name drugs. A three-tier structure, such as a $10 copayment for brand-name generic drugs, $20 for brand-name formulary drugs, and $35 for nonformulary drugs, is now the most common approach. Nonformulary drugs are brand name drugs that are not commonly prescribed for a specific condition where a suitable generic is available. A few plans have a four-tier structure under which a higher copayment or a significant percentage participation applies to a list of lifestyle and/or expensive drugs. For these drugs, the copayment may be $50 or $100. Some plans provide financial incentives for prescriptions filled by mail-order pharmacies or on the Internet.

Two basic methods are used to provide prescription drug coverage: a reimbursement approach and a service approach. Under plans using a reimbursement approach, a covered individual personally pays the cost of prescription drugs and files a claim for reimbursement.

The majority of prescription drug plans use a service approach. Under this approach, participating pharmacies provide drugs to covered persons upon receipt of prescriptions, proper identification (usually a card issued by the plan), and any required copayments. The pharmacy then bills the provider of coverage (usually electronically) for the remaining cost of any prescription filled. Prescriptions filled at nonparticipating pharmacies are often covered but on a reimbursement basis.

Vision Benefits

Over half of the persons covered under employer-provided medical expense plans have some type of vision coverage, and the majority of this coverage is provided under a carve-out arrangement. Normally, a benefit schedule is used that specifies the types and amounts of certain benefits and the frequency with which they will be provided. An example of one such schedule is shown below. Under some plans, most benefits are provided on a service basis rather than being subject to a maximum benefit. These plans usually cover only the cost of basic frames, which the covered persons can upgrade at an additional expense.

Table 12-2 Example of Benefit Schedule	
Type of Benefit	**Maximum Amount**
Any 12-month period	
Eye examination	$ 75
Lenses, pair	
single vision	45
bifocal	75
trifocal	125
lenticular	200
contact (when medically necessary)	300
contact (when not medically necessary)	125
Any 24-month period	
Frames	60

There are usually exclusions for any extra charge for plastic lenses or the cost of safety lenses or prescription sunglasses. Benefits are generally provided for eye examinations by either an optometrist or an ophthalmologist, and larger benefits are sometimes provided if the latter is used. Vision care plans do not pay benefits for necessary eye surgery or treatment of eye diseases because these services are covered under a medical expense plan's regular coverage. However, many vision plans make benefits available for elective procedures to improve vision, such as LASIK surgery. This benefit is usually in the form of a discounted fee from a provider who has a relationship with the plan.

Behavioral Health

Behavioral health benefits have always presented a challenge for medical expense plans. There is less uniformity in treatment standards for mental health, alcoholism, and drug addiction than for most other medical conditions. This, and the difficulty of monitoring treatment, has often led to unnecessary, expensive, and dangerous treatment by less-than-scrupulous providers of behavioral health care. Historically, benefit plans addressed these problems by having very limited benefit levels. But even these benefit levels had a tendency to encourage more expensive inpatient care over outpatient treatment, which in most cases appears to be as clinically effective. Moreover, there was little follow-up care after treatment. With rapidly increasing costs for behavioral health, employers and providers of benefit plans are increasingly carving out this benefit by contracting with vendors that use managed care techniques. Even with the use of carve-outs, plans continue to limit behavioral health benefits to a level significantly below that for other medical conditions. PPACA prohibits individual and group plans from placing lifetime limits on the dollar value of coverage and prior to 2014, plans may only pose annual limits on coverage as determined by of Secretary of HHS.

Characteristics of a successful behavioral health program, whether or not it is a carve-out arrangement, include the following:

- the use of case management to design and coordinate treatment plans and to monitor the need for follow-up care
- a mechanism for referring a patient to the program. In many cases, this is through a primary care physician gatekeeper.
- the development of a provider network that specializes in behavioral health. In addition to physicians, the network will include psychologists and therapists. It will also include alternatives to hospital treatment, such as residential centers, halfway houses, and structured outpatient programs. Benefits may or may not be provided if patients seek nonnetwork treatment. If it is covered, there is usually a lower benefit level than for network treatment.
- 24-hour patient access to care. Persons who have behavioral health problems often need immediate crisis intervention. Of course, the availability of such care needs to be well communicated to patients.

PLAN PROVISIONS

Medical expense plans have numerous provisions that concern financial planners. This section discusses provisions that pertain to eligibility, coordination of benefits, the relationship with Medicare, and claims.

Eligibility

The eligibility requirements for medical expense coverage are essentially the same as those for other types of group insurance—an employee must usually be in a covered classification, must satisfy any probationary period, and must be employed full-time. If an employer changes insurance companies, however, eligible employees who were covered under the old plan are automatically covered under the new plan and are exempt from any probationary periods.

Under PPACA, the plan sponsor of a group insurance plan cannot base eligibility rules for health care coverage on salaries or wages that create health care plans that discriminate in favor of higher wage employees.

Dependent Eligibility

Typically, the same medical expense benefits that are provided for an eligible employee are also available for that employee's dependents. If the employee does not elect dependent coverage under a contributory plan within 31 days after dependents are eligible, future coverage is available only during an open enrollment period or when satisfactory evidence of insurability is provided. Newly acquired dependents (by birth, marriage, or adoption) are eligible for coverage as of the date they gain dependent status. As a general rule, the employee must take a positive action to enroll such new dependents in order for their coverage to become effective. However, a newborn child is automatically covered for the first 31 days following birth.

The term *dependents* most commonly refers to an employee's spouse who is not legally separated from the employee and any unmarried dependent children (including stepchildren, adopted children, and children born out of wedlock) under the age of 26, under PPACA (Patient Protection and Affordable Care Act). Under PPACA, dependents include children who no longer live with their parents, are no longer a dependent on the parent's tax return, are no longer a student or are married.

In addition, coverage may also continue (and is required to continue in some states) for children who are incapable of earning their own living because of a physical or mental infirmity. Such children are considered dependents as long as this condition exists, but periodic proof of the condition may be required.

If an employee has dependent coverage, all of the employee's newly acquired dependents (by birth, marriage, or adoption) are automatically covered.

A few plans define "dependent" more widely to include grandchildren, parents, and siblings who live with the employee.

Portability

The Health Insurance Portability and Accountability Act (HIPAA) also affects eligibility for medical expense coverage. HIPAA's provisions, which apply to both insured and self-funded plans, do not allow an employee to take specific insurance from one job to another. Rather, they put limitations on preexisting-conditions exclusions and allow an employee to use evidence of prior insurance coverage to reduce or eliminate the length of any preexisting-conditions exclusion when the employee moves to another employer-provided medical expense plan. The act's provisions on portability generally override state laws unless state laws provide more liberal portability.

Restrictions under a preexisting-conditions provision are limited to a maximum of 12 months (18 months for late enrollees). In addition, the period for preexisting conditions must be reduced by the length of coverage under a prior medical expense plan as long as there has not been a break in coverage of 63 days or more. The prior coverage can have been under an individual policy, an employer-provided group plan (either insured or self-funded), an HMO, Medicare, or Medicaid. Under PPACA, insurers are prohibited from discriminating against or charging higher rates for any individuals based on pre-existing medical conditions as of January 1, 2014.

The act requires an employer to give persons who lose group coverage a certificate that specifies the period of coverage under the plan they are leaving, including any period of COBRA coverage.

Benefits for Domestic Partners

In the mid-1980s, a few employers' plans began to define the term *dependent* broadly enough to include unmarried domestic partners. For example, one plan covers unmarried couples as long as they live together, show financial interdependence and joint responsibility for each other's common welfare, and consider themselves life partners. This type of requirement is fairly typical, as is the additional requirement that the employee's relationship must have lasted some specified minimum period of time, such as 6 or 12 months. The employee must usually give the employer an affidavit that these requirements have been satisfied.

About half of employers now provide medical expense benefits to domestic partners, and they may be required to do so as a result of state and local legislation. Since there are no current federal guidelines that state what a domestic partnership is, that answer is up to each individual state or local jurisdiction. No laws prohibit a private-sector employer from offering partner health benefits, but federal and state laws do affect certain other benefits and the taxation of health and retirement benefits. It is becoming common practice for states to recognize a domestic partnership (A smaller percentage of employers offer other types of group benefits.) Most plans provide benefits to domestic partners engaged in either heterosexual or homosexual relationships. Some plans provide benefits only to persons of the opposite sex of the employee, while other plans limit benefits only to persons of the same sex. The rationale for the latter is that persons of opposite sexes can obtain benefits by marrying, whereas this option is not generally available to persons of the same sex.

Coordination of Benefits

In recent years, the percentage of individuals who have duplicate group medical expense coverage has increased substantially and is estimated to be about 10 percent. Probably the most common situation is one in which a husband and wife both work and have coverage under their respective employers' noncontributory plans. If the employer of either spouse also provides dependent coverage on a noncontributory basis, the other spouse (and other dependents if both employers provide such coverage) is covered under both plans. If dependent coverage is contributory, it is necessary for a couple with children to elect such coverage under one of their plans. Because a spouse is considered a dependent, he or she also has duplicate coverage when the election is made. Duplicate coverage may also arise when an employee has two jobs, or children are covered under both a parent's and a stepparent's plans.

coordination-of-benefits (COB) provision   In the absence of any provisions to the contrary, each group medical expense plan is obligated to provide benefits in cases of duplicate coverage as if no other coverage exists. To prevent individuals from receiving benefits that exceed their actual expenses, most group medical expense plans contain a *coordination-of-benefits (COB) provision,* which establishes priorities for the payment of benefits by each plan covering an individual.

The typical coordination-of-benefits provision is based on the NAIC Group Coordination of Benefits Model Regulation. This regulation is periodically revised, and almost all states have adopted all or portions of one of the versions. As with all NAIC model legislation and regulations, some states have adopted the COB provisions with variations.

Although some flexibility is allowed, virtually all COB provisions apply when other coverage exists through another employer's group insurance plans or group benefit arrangements. They may also apply to no-fault automobile insurance benefits and to student coverage that educational institutions either sponsor or provide. However, these provisions virtually never apply (and cannot in most states) to any other coverages provided under contracts purchased on an individual basis outside of the employment relationship.

As a general rule, coverage under multiple policies will allow a person to receive benefits equal to 100 percent of his or her medical expenses. The coverage determined to be primary will pay as if no other coverage exists. If some expenses are not reimbursed (because, for example, of deductibles, copayments, or policy limitations), the secondary coverage will pick up the balance as long as it is less than what that coverage would have paid if it were the only coverage in existence.

Determination of Primary Coverage

The usual COB provision stipulates that any plan without the COB provision is primary and that any other plan with it is secondary. If more than one plan has a COB provision, the following priorities are established:

- Coverage as an employee is usually primary to coverage as a dependent. The exception occurs if a retired person is covered (1) by Medicare, (2) under a retiree plan of a former employer, and (3) as a dependent of a spouse who is an active employee. In this case, coverage as a dependent is primary, Medicare is secondary, and the retiree plan pays last.
- Coverage as an active employee (or as that person's dependent) is primary to coverage as a retired or laid-off employee (or as that person's dependent).
- Coverage as an active employee (or that person's dependent) is primary to a plan that provides COBRA continuation benefits.
- If the specific rules of a court decree state that one parent must assume responsibility for his or her child's health care expenses, and the plan of that parent has actual knowledge of the terms of the court decree, then that plan is primary.
- If the parents of dependent children are married or are not separated (regardless of whether they have ever been married) or if a court awards joint custody without specifying that one parent has the responsibility to provide health care coverage, the plan of the parent whose birthday falls earlier in the calendar year is primary and the plan of the parent with the later birthday is secondary.
- If the parents of dependent children are not married, are separated (regardless of whether they have ever been married), or are divorced and if there is no court decree allocating responsibility for the child's health care expenses, the following priorities apply:

- – The plan of the parent with custody is primary.
- – The plan of the stepparent who is the spouse of the parent with custody is secondary.
- – The plan of the parent without custody is tertiary.
- – The plan of the stepparent who is the spouse of the parent without custody pays last.

- If none of the previous rules establishes a priority, the plan covering the person for the longest period of time is primary. However, if this rule also fails to determine the primary plan, then benefit payments are shared equally among the plans.

Relationship with Medicare

Because most employees and their dependents are eligible for Medicare upon reaching age 65 (and possibly under other circumstances), a provision that eliminates any possible duplication of coverage is necessary. The simplest solution is to exclude any person eligible for Medicare from eligibility under the group contract. In most cases, however, this approach conflicts with the Age Discrimination in Employment Act, which prohibits discrimination in benefit plans for active employees.

Medicare Secondary Rules

Under the Medicare secondary rules, employers with 20 or more employees must make coverage available under their medical expense plans to active employees aged 65 or older and to active employees' spouses who are eligible for Medicare. Unless an employee elects otherwise (by not enrolling in the employer's plan), the employer's plan is primary and Medicare is secondary. Except in plans that require large employee contributions, it is doubtful that employees will elect Medicare because employers are prohibited from offering active employees or their spouses a Medicare carve-out, a Medicare supplement, or some other incentive not to enroll in the employer's plan.

Medicare is the secondary payer of benefits in two other situations. The first situation involves persons who are eligible for Medicare benefits to treat end-stage renal disease with dialysis or kidney transplants. Medicare provides these benefits to any insured workers (either active or retired and regardless of age) and to their spouses and dependent children, but the employer's plan is primary during the first 30 months of treatment only; after that time, Medicare is primary and the employer's plan is secondary.

Medicare is also the secondary payer of benefits to disabled employees (or disabled dependents of employees) under age 65 who are eligible for Medicare and covered under the medical expense plan of large employers (defined as plans with 100 or more employees). The rule applies only if an employer continues medical expense coverage for disabled persons; there is no requirement for such a continuation.

Medicare Carve-Outs and Supplements

An employer's plan may cover certain persons aged 65 or older who are not affected by the provisions of the Age Discrimination in Employment Act—specifically, retirees and active employees of firms with fewer than 20 employees. Although there is nothing to prevent an employer from terminating coverage for these persons, some employers provide them with either a Medicare carve-out or a Medicare supplement.

Medicare carve-out

Medicare supplement

With a *Medicare carve-out,* plan benefits are reduced to the extent that benefits are payable under Medicare for the same services. As an alternative, some employers use a *Medicare supplement* that provides benefits for certain specific expenses not covered under Medicare. These include (1) the portion of expenses Medicare does not pay because of deductibles, coinsurance, or copayments and (2) certain expenses that Medicare excludes. Such a supplement may or may not provide benefits similar to those available under a carve-out plan.

Claims

Medical expense contracts that provide benefits on a service basis (such as HMOs and the Blues) or that use preferred providers generally do not require covered persons to file forms for claims. Rather, the providers of services perform any necessary paperwork and are then reimbursed directly.

Medical expense contracts that provide benefits on an *indemnity basis* indemnity basis typically require that the insurance company (or other provider) be given a written proof of loss (a completed claim form) concerning the occurrence, character, and extent of each claim. This form usually contains portions that must be completed and signed by the employee, a representative of the employer, and the provider of medical services.

The period during which an employee must file a claim depends on the provider of coverage and any applicable state requirements. An employee generally has at least 90 days (or as soon as is reasonably possible) after medical expenses are incurred to file. Some insurance companies require that they be notified within a shorter time (such as 20 days) about any illness or injury on which a claim may be based, even though they give a longer time period for the actual filing of the form itself.

Individuals have the right under medical expense plans to assign their benefits to the providers of medical services. Such an assignment, which authorizes the insurance company to make the benefit payment directly to the provider, may generally be made by completing the appropriate portion of the claim form. In addition, the insurance company has the right to examine any person for whom a claim is filed at its own expense and with the physician of its own choice.

LIMITED-BENEFIT PLANS

limited-benefit plan   Medical expense plans provide broad and comprehensive benefits to pay the medical bills of covered persons. Even with deductibles, copayments, and percentage participation, such plans typically pay from 80 percent to almost all of medical expenses incurred. Plans that provided more limited benefits were once more common but had largely disappeared over the years. More recently, such plans have begun to reappear. These *limited-benefit plans*, often referred to as mini-med plans, are not yet common but do play a role in providing medical expense coverage to some Americans at a cost significantly less than more comprehensive coverage.

The usual purchasers of limited-benefit plans are small employers that cannot afford to provide more comprehensive coverage to their employees. Often, low-income or part-time employees do not have the resources to purchase broader coverage in the individual marketplace. The limited benefits of such plans are controversial, and a few states restrict their use. However, these plans do provide some benefits to persons who would otherwise lack coverage.

Although these plans vary among insurers, some observations can be made:

- The employer may pay a portion of the premium, and some insurers require such contributions. However, some plans are designed as voluntary benefits with the employee paying the full cost of coverage.
- Many insurers offer several options with varying levels of benefits.

- Benefits are typically paid on a first-dollar basis, but subject to low dollar maximums.
- Benefits are subject to annual maximums based on number of visits or days or on a flat dollar limit, such as $10,000 or $25,000.
- Benefits may be paid directly to the insured, or the plan may use a preferred-provided network. In the later case, the insured will typically receive a discount on charges that plan benefits do not cover.
- Some offer vision, dental, and prescription drug benefits for an additional premium; other plans provide the insured with discount cards for services.

EXAMPLE

One insurer offers a limited-benefit plan with four options. The benefits provided include

- $40 to $100 for up to five office visits to physicians per year
- $40 to $100 for up to three diagnostic tests and X rays per year
- $200 to $1,000 per day for hospitalizations for up to 30 days per year
- $100 to $250 for one emergency room visit per year
- optional benefits for dental and prescription drug coverage for an additional premium

---

In 2014, under the Affordable Care Act, most Americans will have access to affordable health insurance policies that provide a minimum standard of coverage that includes preventive care with no copays or deductibles and no yearly or lifetime limits on medical charges. Mini-med plans will be banned because they will not meet any of these standards. But that's only if the legislation isn't watered down, starved of funding or otherwise prevented from being fully enacted.

DENTAL INSURANCE

Over the last 25 years, dental insurance has increased significantly as an employee benefit. Dental benefits may be offered by insurance companies, dental service plans (often called Delta Dental plans), the Blues, and managed care plans, such as dental HMOs (called DHMOs). Like medical expense coverage, a significant portion of dental coverage is also self-funded by employers.

Although group dental insurance contracts have been patterned after group medical expense contracts, some of their provisions are different, while others are unique to dental coverage. These provisions pertain to benefits, exclusions, and benefit limitations. In contrast to medical expense plans, for which an employer usually pays a substantial share of the premium cost, a large percentage of dental plans are provided as voluntary benefits. This requires an employee to pay 100 percent of the premium cost.

Benefits

Most dental insurance plans pay for almost all types of dental expenses, but a particular plan may provide more limited coverage. One characteristic of dental insurance is the inclusion of benefits for both routine diagnostic procedures (including oral examinations and X rays) and preventive care (including teeth cleaning and fluoride treatment). In fact, a few dental plans actually require periodic oral examinations as a condition for continuing eligibility. There is clear evidence that the cost of providing these benefits will be more than offset by the prevention of the expensive dental procedures required when a condition is not discovered early or when a preventive treatment has not been given.

In addition to benefits for diagnostic and preventive treatment, benefits for dental expenses may be provided for the following categories of dental treatment:

- restoration (including fillings, crowns, and other procedures used to restore the functional use of natural teeth)
- oral surgery (including the extraction of teeth, surgical treatment of diseases, injuries, and defects of the jaw)
- endodontics (treatment for diseases of the dental pulp within teeth, such as root canals)
- periodontics (treatment of diseases of the surrounding and supporting tissues of the teeth)
- prosthodontics (replacement of missing teeth and structures by artificial devices, such as bridgework and dentures)
- orthodontics (prevention and correction of dental and oral anomalies through the use of corrective devices, such as braces and retainers)

For benefit plan design purposes, these treatments are usually divided into the following categories of dental services. The following is a typical example:

- service level I—preventive and diagnostic services
- service level II—minor restorative procedures, including fillings, inlays, onlays, and veneers
- service level III—major restorations, including crowns, bridges, dentures, and implants as well as other major services involving periodontics, and oral surgeries
- service level IV—orthodontic services

Most dental plans provide benefits for the first three service levels; some plans provide benefits for service level IV. These service levels are key to designing plans in which members have focused financial incentives to seek routine services for prevention of future expenses and have a greater stake in more costly major services decisions. Thus, for example, a typical dental plan will aim to provide its most complete payment for level I services and somewhat less complete payment for level II services, while providing the least complete benefit for level III and level IV services (if covered).

Benefit Payment Methods

Dental plans have several types of benefit payment methods. Plans that pay benefits on an indemnity basis usually make payments on the basis of reasonable-and-customary charges. Most plans have annual deductibles in the neighborhood of $50 to $100. However, the deductible typically does not apply to level I services. The use of coinsurance is also common. It is typically 80 percent or higher for level I services, with 100 percent being the most common. Level II services are usually subject to coinsurance in the range of 70 to 85 percent. Level III and level IV services typically have coinsurance of between 50 and 60 percent.

Very few indemnity plans have scheduled maximum benefits. These benefits are provided on a first-dollar basis with no deductibles or specified coinsurance percentage. Benefit maximums, however, are usually lower than reasonable-and-customary charges, thereby forcing employees to bear a portion of the costs of their dental services.

Dental plans that are structured as PPOs usually have deductibles and coinsurance similar to indemnity plans except that higher coinsurance percentages are used when services are received from network providers.

In-network benefits are also paid on the basis of negotiated charges with providers.

Deductibles and coinsurance are usually not used for most service levels in DHMO plans as long as network providers are used. However, the member may be responsible for a copayment for level II and level III services. Level IV services are usually subject to coinsurance, often 50 or 60 percent.

Exclusions

All dental plans contain exclusions, but the number and type vary. Some of the more common exclusions are charges for the following:

- services that are purely cosmetic, unless necessitated by an accidental bodily injury while a person is covered under the plan. (Orthodontics, although they are often used for cosmetic reasons, can usually also be justified as necessary to correct abnormal dental conditions.)
- replacement of lost, missing, or stolen dentures or other prosthetic devices
- duplicate dentures or other prosthetic devices
- services that do not have uniform professional endorsement

Limitations

Dental insurance plans also contain numerous limitations that are designed to control claim costs and to eliminate unnecessary dental care. In addition to deductibles and coinsurance, virtually all dental plans have overall benefit maximums. Except for DHMOs, which usually do not have a calendar-year limit, most plans contain a calendar-year maximum (typically varying from $500 to $2,500) but no lifetime maximum. However, some plans have only a lifetime maximum (such as $5,000), and a few plans contain both a calendar-year maximum and a larger lifetime maximum. These maximums may apply to all dental expenses, or they may be limited to all expenses except those that arise from orthodontics (and occasionally periodontics). In the latter case, benefits for orthodontics will be subject to a separate, lower lifetime maximum, which is typically between $500 and $2,000.

Most dental plans limit the frequency with which some benefits will be paid. Routine oral examinations and teeth cleaning are usually limited to once every 6 months, and full-mouth X rays to once every 24 or 36 months. The replacement of dentures may also be limited to once in some specified period (such as 5 years).

The typical dental plan also limits benefits to the least expensive type of accepted dental treatment for a given dental condition. For example, if either a gold or a silver filling can be used, benefit payments will be limited to the cost of a silver filling, even if a gold filling is inserted.

ADDITIONAL BENEFITS FOR EXECUTIVES

Some employers have plans that provide additional medical and dental benefits for executives. Although this group of employees is most likely able to afford the expenses such plans cover, these supplemental benefits are frequently viewed as a way to attract and retain key employees.

From a purely administrative standpoint, it would be relatively easy to self-fund these benefits, but the benefits would most likely represent taxable income to employees. As a result, these additional executive benefits are usually insured as either separate coverage or as a rider to the plan that covers other employees.

This type of plan usually covers the executives and their dependents. Benefits almost always include coverage to provide reimbursement for deductibles and coinsurance under the employer's plan that apply to all covered employees. It is also common to find coverage for annual physicals and the extra cost of private hospital rooms. In addition, there frequently is extra coverage, although possibly limited to an annual maximum, such as $10,000, for such expenses as mental or emotional treatment, hearing care, vision care, and dental work.

FEDERAL TAX TREATMENT

Contributions by the employer for an employee's coverage or the coverage of the employee's dependents are tax deductible to the employer as long as the employee's overall compensation is reasonable. As a general rule, employer contributions do not create any income tax liability for an employee. Moreover, benefits are usually not taxable to an employee.

There are, however, some aspects of the tax treatment of medical expense coverage that are unique to this type of employee benefit and need further explanation. These include tax liability from employer contributions, taxation of benefits, deductible employee contributions, special rules for self-funded medical expense plans, and a credit for certain individuals. Effective for 2011 under PPACA, employers must disclose the value of the benefits they provide for each employee's health insurance coverage on the employee's W-2 form. This is for informational purposes only, and will not effect the employee's taxable income.

Tax Liability from Employer Contributions

Under IRS rules, an employee has no tax liability from employer contributions to the cost of medical expense coverage for an employee, the employee's spouse, or the employee's dependents. For purposes of these rules a dependent includes two categories of persons—a qualifying child and a qualifying relative.

A qualifying relative is a person who has a relationship to the employee, such as a parent, a sibling, or a child. The person must receive more than one-half of his or her support from the employee.

The rule for defining a dependent child changes under health care reform. Under PPACA, if a group health plan or individual plan provides dependent coverage of children, the plan must make coverage available until the child turns age 26, effective on or after September 23, 2010. The IRS, DOL and HHS have jointly issued interim final regulations to implement the age 26 mandate. For "grandfathered" health plans, a transitional rule applies prior to January 1, 2014. The mandate only applies if the child under age 26 is not eligible to enroll in some other eligible employer-sponsored group health plan.

It is important to make two points. First, the definition of dependent and of a child for purposes of medical expense coverage is different than the definition that applies for most income tax purposes. Second, the definition is worded in such a way that an employee's domestic partner would not likely qualify as a dependent. Therefore, the value of any employer-provided coverage for the employee's domestic partner, minus any employee contributions, represents taxable income to the employee for federal income taxes. The federal government does not recognize any domestic partner relationships.

Taxation of Benefits

Except in very rare situations, medical expense plans are designed so that benefits received do not create any income tax liability for an employee. There are two situations in which taxable income could occur, however. The first is if benefits exceed actual medical expenses. Should this occur, the excess is taxable to the extent it is attributable to employer contributions.

Second, tax-free benefits must be for "medical expenses" as determined by the IRS. For example, such procedures as routine cosmetic surgery and teeth whitening are not considered medical expenses and would create taxable income if benefits were paid.

Limitations and exclusions in medical expense plans typically prevent either of these two situations from occurring.

Deductible Employee Contributions

One major difference between group medical expense coverage and other forms of group insurance is that a portion of an employee's contribution for coverage may be tax deductible as a medical expense if that individual itemizes his or her income tax deductions. Under the Internal Revenue Code, individuals are allowed to deduct certain medical care expenses (including dental expenses) for which no reimbursement is received. This deduction is limited to expenses (including amounts paid for insurance) that exceed 7.5 percent of the person's adjusted gross income. In 2013 under PPACA, the threshold for the itemized deduction for unreimbursed medical expenses will increase from 7.5 percent to 10 percent of adjusted gross income. This increase will be waived for individuals age 65 and older for tax years 2013 through 2016.

However, employees may receive even more favorable tax benefits if they elect salary reductions through a cafeteria plan for medical (and dental) premiums and expenses that would otherwise be unreimbursable by insurance. If an employer's cafeteria plan has a premium-conversion plan, an employee may elect a salary reduction to pay his or her premium contribution. If the cafeteria plan includes a health flexible spending account (FSA), an employee can elect an additional salary reduction to fund medical expenses that are not covered by the employer's plan because of deductibles, coinsurance, exclusions, and limitations. The employee must elect the reduction prior to the beginning of the plan year and forfeit amounts not used for benefits during the year, or up to 2½ months thereafter if the plan incorporates such an extension.

Salary reductions also reduce income for purposes of Social Security and Medicare taxes and therefore may reduce future Social Security benefits. In most states, they lower income for purposes of state income taxes. As the following example shows, the use of salary reductions can have a significant effect on an employee's spendable income by lowering taxes paid.

EXAMPLE

Charlie is a single employee with an annual income of $75,000. He pays $1,000 per year toward the cost of his employer-provided medical expense coverage. He expects to have $2,000 in unreimbursed medical and dental expenses for the year. Charlie's marginal federal income tax bracket is 25 percent. This percentage is increased to 28 because of state income taxes. Charlie's standard deduction and exemptions for income tax purposes are $15,000.

Without a cafeteria plan, Charlie's federal and state taxes are calculated as follows:

Annual income	$75,000
Minus standard deduction and exemptions	-15,000
Taxable income	$60,000
Income taxes (.28 x $60,000)	$16,800
Social Security and Medicare taxes (.0765 × $75,000)	5,738
Total taxes	$22,538

If Charlie participates in his employer's premium-conversion plan and health FSA, Charlie's taxes are calculated as follows:

Annual income	$75,000
Minus contribution for premium-conversion plan	–1,000
Minus health FSA contribution	–2,000
Minus standard deduction and exemptions	– 15,000
Taxable income	$57,000
Income taxes (.28 × $57,000)	$15,960
Social Security and Medicare taxes [.0765 × ($75,000 – $3,000)]	5,508
Total taxes	$21,468

Effect of Self-Funded Plans

The tax situation may be different if an employer provides medical expense benefits through a self-funded plan (referred to in the Internal Revenue Code as a self-insured medical reimbursement plan), under which employers either (1) pay the providers of medical care directly or (2) reimburse employees for their medical expenses. If a self-funded plan meets certain nondiscrimination requirements for highly compensated employees, the employer can deduct benefit payments as they are made, and the employee will have no taxable income. If a plan is discriminatory, the employer will still receive an income tax deduction. However, all or a portion of the benefits received by highly compensated employees, but not by other employees, will be treated as taxable income.

Self-Employed Persons

Self-employed persons (for example, sole proprietors), partners, and persons who own more than 2 percent of the stock of an S corporation are not considered employees. If a sole proprietorship, partnership, or S corporation pays the cost of medical expense coverage for those persons or their family members, this amount constitutes taxable income to the proprietor, partner, or 2 percent owner. However, the proprietor, partner, or S corporation stockholder may be entitled to an income tax deduction for this amount. The deduction cannot exceed the individual's earned income from the proprietorship, partnership, or S corporation that provides the medical expense plan. In addition, the deduction is available only if the person is not eligible to participate in any subsidized medical expense plan of another employer for whom the person or his or her spouse works.

CHAPTER REVIEW

Key Terms and Concepts

health insurance
medical expense insurance
major medical insurance
preexisting-conditions provision
deductible
common accident provision
coinsurance (medical expense insurance)
stop-loss limit
preadmission certification
second surgical opinions
extended care facilities
home health care
hospice care
birthing centers
managed care

health maintenance organizations (HMOs)
capitation
preferred-provider organization (PPO)
point-of-service (POS) plan
consumer-directed medical expense plan
defined-contribution medical expense plan
high-deductible health plan
health reimbursement arrangement
carve-out (medical expense insurance)
coordination-of-benefits (COB) provision
Medicare carve-out
Medicare supplement

limited-benefit plan

Review Questions

Review questions are based on the learning objectives in this chapter. Thus, a [3] at the end of a question means that the question is based on learning objective 3. If there are multiple objectives, they are all listed

1. What observations can be made about the future of the health care system? [1]

2. Your client, Sue, is covered by an employer-provided major medical policy. Which of the following medical expenditures that Sue incurred are covered under a typical policy?
   a. She required hospitalization in a semiprivate room for a period of 20 days following an operation on her heart. [2]
   b. She had cosmetic surgery on her nose to improve her looks. [2]
   c. She required care as an inpatient at an extended care facility after release from a 4-day stay in the hospital following a serious operation. [2]
   d. She received custodial or rest care for 5 days at her home after release from an overnight stay in the hospital following minor surgery. [2]
   e. She required a prescription drug for her arthritis that costs $500 per month. [2]

3. Most major medical plans contain an exclusion for preexisting conditions. How does this exclusion differ from the other exclusions found in major medical plans? [2]

4. Your client is concerned about the types of deductibles that apply to her medical expense plan. Explain to her how the following deductibles operate:
   a. initial deductible [2]
   b. family deductible [2]

5. Peggy is covered under a comprehensive major medical plan that has a $250 calendar-year deductible and an 80 percent coinsurance provision. If Peggy incurs $2,000 of covered medical expenses during the year (assuming no limitations), how much of this will she have to pay out of pocket? [2]

6. What are the basic characteristics of a managed care plan? [3]

7. What are the characteristics of HMOs that distinguish them from insurance companies and/or the Blues? [3]

8. How do preferred-provider organizations (PPOs) differ from HMOs? [3]

9. How is a point-of-service (POS) plan a modification of a traditional HMO arrangement? [3]

10. What are the two general approaches to consumer-directed medical expense plans? [4]

11.   What is the value of benefit carve-outs to medical expense plans? [5]

12.   Briefly describe the following types of benefit carve-outs:
       a. prescription drugs [5]
       b. vision benefits [5]
       c. behavioral health [5]

13.   What persons may be eligible for coverage under an employee's medical expense plan? [6]

14.   How does the Health Insurance Portability and Accountability Act (HIPAA) affect eligibility under medical expense plans? [6]

15.   A child in the custody of her mother is covered as a dependent under the major medical coverage of both her father and her stepfather. Which coverage is primary if both coverages are subject to the usual coordination-of-benefits provision? [6]

16.   When is Medicare the primary payer and when is it the secondary payer of benefits for individuals who are also covered under an employer medical expense plan? [6]

17.   How do limited-benefit plans differ from more comprehensive medical expense plans? [7]

18.   Explain whether a group dental plan typically covers each of the following dental expenses:
       a. X rays [8]
       b. root canals [8]
       c. replacement of lost dentures [8]
       d. teeth whitening [8]
       e. braces [8]

19.   What types of additional medical expense benefits may be available to executives? [9]

20.   To what extent are employee contributions for medical expense coverage deductible for federal income tax purposes? [10]

21.   How do premium-conversion plans and health flexible spending accounts (FSAs) result in tax savings for employees? [10]

Learning Objectives

An understanding of the material in this chapter should enable the student to

1. Explain COBRA and the various other alternatives for continuing employer-provided medical expense coverage.

2. Describe the various types of medical expense coverage available in the individual marketplace.

3. Explain how the market has evolved to make it easier for unhealthy individuals to obtain medical expense insurance.

4. Describe health saving accounts.

5. Describe the premium and renewability provisions found in medical expense contracts.

6. Explain the federal income tax rules that apply to individual medical expense insurance.

Private insurance protection is available to the one-third of Americans under age 65 who do not qualify for employer-provided coverage. Less than 10 percent of the population under age 65 obtains private individual medical insurance for themselves and their families. An estimated 15 percent of the population has no medical expense insurance, and almost as many are covered by Medicaid. One reason for this lack of individual coverage is its significant cost. Although legislation has made coverage potentially available for more persons in recent years, there is still a severe cost problem. For example, the premium for a person in his or her late fifties can be several thousand dollars per year. Although we use the word *individual,* some of the insurance available is a continuation of prior employer-provided coverage. Health savings accounts may also be used within an employment relationship.

Numerous circumstances account for the need for individual medical expense insurance. These include

- the lack of employer-provided coverage for some employees, usually those who work for small employers
- the termination of employment for such reasons as voluntarily quitting, being fired or laid off, becoming disabled, or retiring
- the termination of dependent coverage, even when employee coverage continues. This can occur because of divorce, separation, or a child becoming too old.
- not being in the labor market. Some people have the resources to forgo employment. Others, for many reasons, are unable to find or hold jobs.
- self-employment

Another segment of the population that often obtains individual coverage consists of those persons eligible for Medicare. Medicare often provides benefits that are more limited than enrollees had prior to age 65. As a result, more than 60 percent of individuals aged 65 and older have some type of coverage to supplement Medicare.

CONTINUATION OF EMPLOYER-PROVIDED COVERAGE

In the absence of any provisions for continuation or conversion, there generally is a termination of employer-provided coverage for an employee on the earliest of the following:

- the date on which employment terminates. In some plans, coverage ceases on the last day of the month in which employment terminates.
- the date on which the employee ceases to be eligible
- the date on which the master contract for the employer-provided coverage terminates
- the date on which the overall maximum benefit of major medical coverage is received, as unlimited benefits are phased in under PPACA
- the end of the last period for which the employee has made any required contribution

Coverage on any dependent usually ceases on the earliest of the following:

- the date on which he or she ceases to meet the definition of dependent

- the date on which the coverage of the employee ceases for any reason except the employee's receipt of the overall maximum benefit
- the date on which the dependent receives the overall maximum benefit of major medical coverage, as unlimited benefits are phased in under PPACA
- the end of the last period for which the employee has made any required contribution for dependent coverage

However, insurance coverage often is available past these dates because of federal legislation or employer practices. In some cases, the former coverage can be continued, at least for a period of time; in other cases, the prior employment results in the availability of individual coverage without evidence of insurability.

Continuation of Coverage under COBRA

COBRA   A federal law known as *COBRA* (Consolidated Omnibus Budget Reconciliation Act of 1985) requires that group health plans allow employees and certain beneficiaries to elect to have their current health insurance coverage extended at group rates for up to 36 months following a "qualifying event" that results in the loss of coverage for a "qualified beneficiary." The term *group health plan* as used in the act is broad enough to include medical expense plans, dental plans, vision care plans, and prescription drug plans, regardless of whether benefits are self-funded by the employer or provided through other entities, such as insurance companies or managed care organizations. COBRA applies to group health plans even if employees pay the full cost of coverage as long as the plan would not be available at the same cost to an individual if he or she were not employed. However, there is one exception to this rule: Voluntary benefit plans are not subject to COBRA if they have portability provisions whereby a former employee can continue coverage on an individual basis at no increase in cost.

The act applies only to employers who had the equivalent of 20 or more full-time employees on a typical business day during the preceding calendar year; certain church-related plans and plans of the federal government, however, are exempt from the act. Failure to comply with the act will result in an excise tax of up to $100 per day for each person denied coverage. The tax can be levied on the employer as well as on the entity (such as an insurer or HMO) that provides or administers the benefits.

qualified beneficiary

qualifying event

A *qualified beneficiary* is defined as any employee, or the spouse or dependent child of the employee, who on the day before a qualifying event was covered under the employee's group health plan. In addition, the definition includes any child who is born to or placed for adoption with the employee during the period of COBRA coverage. This change gives automatic eligibility for COBRA coverage to the child. Each qualified beneficiary has his or own election rights.

Under the act, each of the following is a *qualifying event* if it results in the loss of coverage by a qualified beneficiary:

- the death of the covered employee
- the termination of the employee for any reason except gross misconduct. This includes quitting, retiring, or being fired for something other than gross misconduct.
- a reduction of the employee's hours so that the employee or dependent is ineligible for coverage
- the divorce or legal separation of the covered employee and his or her spouse
- for spouses and children, the employee's eligibility for Medicare
- a child's ceasing to be an eligible dependent under the plan

The act specifies that a qualified beneficiary is entitled to elect continued coverage without providing evidence of insurability. The beneficiary must be allowed to continue coverage identical to that available to employees and dependents to whom a qualifying event has not occurred. Coverage for persons who elect COBRA continuation can be changed when changes are made to the plan that covers active employees and their dependents.

Each qualified beneficiary must be allowed to continue coverage from the qualifying event until the earliest of the following:

- 18 months for employees and dependents when the employee's employment has terminated or coverage has been terminated because of a reduction in hours. This period is extended to 29 months for a qualified beneficiary if the Social Security Administration determines that the beneficiary was or became totally disabled at any time during the first 60 days of COBRA coverage.
- 36 months for other qualifying events
- the date the plan terminates for all employees

- the date the coverage ceases because of a failure to make a timely payment of premium for the qualified beneficiary's coverage
- the date the qualified beneficiary subsequently becomes entitled to Medicare or becomes covered (as either an employee or dependent) under another group health plan, provided the group health plan does not contain an exclusion or limitation with respect to any preexisting condition. If the new plan does not cover a preexisting condition, the COBRA coverage can be continued until the earlier of (1) the remainder of the 18- or 36-month period or (2) the time when the preexisting-conditions provision no longer applies.

If a second qualifying event (such as the death or divorce of a terminated employee) occurs during the period of continued coverage, the maximum period of continuation is 36 months.

EXAMPLE

When Peter Gonzalez terminated employment, he and his family were eligible for 18 months of COBRA coverage. When he died 15 months after electing the coverage, a second qualifying event occurred for his spouse and dependent children. The normal period of COBRA continuation resulting from an employee's death is 36 months. Because the spouse and children had already had COBRA coverage for 15 months, the second qualifying event extended the potential period of coverage for an additional 21 months.

At the termination of the COBRA period, a qualified beneficiary must be offered the right to convert to an individual insurance policy if a conversion privilege is available to employees under the employer's plan.

When a qualifying event occurs, the employer must notify the benefit plan administrator, who then must notify all qualified beneficiaries within 14 days. In general, the employer has 30 days to notify the plan administrator. However, an employer may not know of a qualifying event if it involves divorce, legal separation, or a child's ceasing to be eligible for coverage. In these circumstances, the employee or family member must notify the employer within 60 days of the event, or the right to elect COBRA coverage will be lost. The time period for the employer to notify the plan administrator begins when the employer is informed of the qualifying event, as long as this occurs within the 60-day period.

The continuation of coverage is not automatic; a qualified beneficiary must elect it. The election period starts on the date of the qualifying event and may end not earlier than 60 days after actual notice of the event to the qualified beneficiary by the plan administrator. Once coverage is elected, the beneficiary has 45 days to pay the premium for the period of coverage prior to the election.

Under COBRA, the cost of the continued coverage may be passed on to the qualified beneficiary, but the cost cannot exceed 102 percent of the cost to the plan for the period of coverage for a similarly situated active employee to whom a qualifying event has not occurred. The extra 2 percent is supposed to cover the employer's extra administrative costs. The one exception to this rule occurs for months 19 through 29 if an employee is disabled, in which case the premium can be as high as 150 percent. Qualified beneficiaries must have the option of paying the premium in monthly installments. In addition, there must be a grace period of at least 30 days for each installment.

Premiums under employer-provided plans tend to be the same for all employees, regardless of age. Therefore, continuation of coverage under COBRA is often the most cost-effective way for an older former employee to obtain medical expense coverage for as long as the COBRA period lasts. However, circumstances vary, and other alternatives need to be explored as well. Younger employees may have little difficulty finding less expensive coverage in the individual marketplace, particularly if they are healthy.

Continuation of Coverage in Addition to COBRA

Even before the passage of COBRA, it was becoming increasingly common for employers (particularly large employers) to continue group insurance coverage for certain employees—and sometimes their dependents—beyond the usual termination dates. Obviously, when coverage is continued now, at a minimum an employer must comply with COBRA. However, an employer can be more liberal than COBRA by paying all or a portion of the cost, providing continued coverage for additional categories of persons, or continuing coverage for a longer period of time. Some states have continuation laws for insured medical expense plans that might require coverage to be made available in situations that COBRA does not cover. One example is coverage for employees of firms with fewer than 20 employees; another is coverage for periods longer than those COBRA requires.

Retired Employees

Some employers continue coverage on retired employees. Although coverage can also be continued for retirees' other dependents, it is often limited only to spouses. Retired employees under age 65 usually have the same coverage that active employees have. However, coverage for employees aged 65 or older (if included under the same plan) may be provided under a Medicare carve-out or a Medicare supplement.

Because of changes in accounting rules for retiree medical expense coverage and increasing benefit costs, many employers have lowered or eliminated retiree benefits or are considering such a change. Some employers do not alter plans for current retirees or active employees who are eligible to retire. Rather, the changes apply to future retirees only. These changes, which run the gamut, include the following:

- the elimination of benefits for future retirees
- the shifting of more of the cost burden to future retirees by reducing benefits. Such a reduction may be accomplished by providing lower benefit maximums, covering fewer types of expenses, or increasing copayments.
- adding or increasing retiree sharing of premium costs after retirement
- shifting to a defined-contribution approach to funding retiree benefits. For example, an employer might agree to pay $5 per month toward the cost of coverage after retirement for each year of an employee's service. Many plans of this nature have been designed so that the employer's contribution increases with changes in the consumer price index, subject to maximum increases, such as five percent per year.
- encouraging retirees to elect benefits from managed care plans if they are not already doing so. With this approach, retirees are required to pay a significant portion of the cost if coverage is continued through a traditional major medical plan.

Surviving Dependents

Coverage may also continue for the survivors of deceased active employees and/or deceased retired employees. Coverage for the survivors of active employees does not commonly continue beyond the period COBRA requires, and coverage for the survivors of retired employees may be limited to surviving spouses. In both instances, the continued coverage is usually identical to what was provided prior to the employee's death. It is also common for the employer to continue the same premium contribution level.

Laid-off Employees

Medical expense coverage can be continued for laid-off workers, and large employers frequently provide such coverage for a limited period. Few employers provide coverage beyond the period COBRA requires, but some employers continue to make the same premium contribution, at least for a limited period of time.

Disabled Employees

Medical expense coverage can be continued for an employee (and dependents) when he or she has a temporary interruption of employment, including one arising from illness or injury. Many employers also cover employees who have long-term disabilities or have retired because of a disability. In most cases, this continuation of coverage is contingent on satisfaction of some definition of total (and possibly permanent) disability. When coverage is continued for disabled employees, an employer must determine the extent of employer contributions. For example, the employer may continue the same premium contribution as for active employees. There is nothing, however, to prevent a different contribution rate—either lower or higher.

Extension of Benefits

extension of benefits

When coverage is terminated rather than continued, most employer-purchased medical expense contracts have an *extension of benefits* for any covered employee or dependent who is totally disabled at the time of termination. The disability must have resulted from an illness or injury that occurred while the person was covered under the contract. Generally, the same level of benefits is available as before termination. Although some contracts cover only expenses associated with the same cause of disability, other contracts cover any expenses that would have been paid under the terminated coverage, regardless of cause. The extension of benefits generally ceases after 12 months or when the individual is no longer totally or continuously disabled, whichever comes first.

Conversion

Except when termination results from the failure to pay any required premiums, medical expense contracts usually contain (and are often required to contain) a conversion provision, whereby most covered persons whose group coverage terminates are allowed to purchase individual medical expense coverage without evidence of insurability and without any limitations because of a preexisting-conditions provision. Conversion provisions are rare in dental insurance contracts.

Covered persons commonly have 31 days from the date of the group coverage's termination to exercise this conversion privilege, and coverage is then effective retroactively to the date of termination. This conversion privilege is typically given to any employee who has been insured for at least 3 months, and it permits the employee to convert his or her own coverage as well as any dependent coverage. In addition, a spouse or child whose dependent coverage ceases for any other reason may also be eligible for conversion (for example, a spouse who divorces or separates, and children who reach age 26).

State laws and insurance company practices vary with respect to the conversion provision and COBRA. In some cases, conversion is contingent upon an individual electing COBRA coverage and maintaining it for the maximum election period. At that time, a conversion policy is available. In other cases, a person who is eligible for both the conversion privilege and the right to continue the group insurance coverage under COBRA has two choices when eligibility for coverage terminates. He or she can either elect to convert under the provisions of the policy or elect to continue the group coverage under COBRA. If the latter choice is made, the COBRA rules specify that the person must again be eligible to convert to an individual policy within the usual conversion period (31 days) after the maximum continuation-of-coverage period ceases. In either situation, policy provisions may also make the conversion privilege available to persons whose coverage terminates prior to the end of the maximum continuation period. If the conversion option is elected, there are no COBRA rights if the conversion policy terminates.

The insurance company or other provider of the medical expense coverage has the right to refuse to issue a conversion policy to anyone (1) who is covered by Medicare or (2) whose benefits under the converted policy, together with similar benefits from other sources, would result in overinsurance according to the insurance company's standards. These similar benefits may be found in other coverages that the individual has (either group or individual coverage) or for which the individual is eligible under any group arrangement.

Conversion Privilege

- Requires no evidence of insurability
- Provides full coverage of preexisting conditions
- Allows 31 days for conversion
- Coverage retroactive to start of 31-day period
- Includes right to convert dependents' coverage
- May not be available to anyone covered by Medicare
- May not be available if conversion would result in overinsurance

---

The use of the word *conversion* is often a misnomer. In actuality, a person whose coverage terminates is given only the right to purchase a contract on an individual basis at individual rates. Most Blue Cross and Blue Shield plans and some HMO plans offer a conversion policy that is similar or identical to the terminated group coverage. Insurance companies may, however, offer a conversion policy (or a choice of policies) that contains a lower level of benefits than existed under the former employer-provided coverage.

Some plans offer a conversion policy that is written by another entity. For example, an HMO might enter into a contractual arrangement with an insurance company. In some cases, the HMO and insurance company are commonly owned or have a parent-subsidiary relationship.

Self-funded plans, which are exempt from state laws that mandate a conversion policy, may still provide such a benefit. Rather than providing coverage directly to the terminated employee, an agreement is made with an insurance company or other provider of medical expense coverage to make a policy available.

Group-to-Individual Portability

The Health Insurance Portability and Accountability Act (HIPAA) makes it easier for individuals who lose employer-provided medical expense coverage to find alternative coverage in the individual marketplace. The purpose of the federal portability legislation is to encourage states to adopt their own mechanisms to achieve this goal, and most states have complied. The federal rules apply in a state only if the state does not have its own plan. The state alternative must do all the following:

- provide a choice of health insurance coverage to all eligible individuals

- impose no preexisting-conditions restrictions
- include at least one policy form of coverage that is either comparable to comprehensive health coverage offered in the individual marketplace or comparable to, or a standard option of, coverage available under the group or individual laws of the state

If a state fails to adopt an alternative to federal regulation, then insurance companies, HMOs, and other health plan providers in the individual marketplace are required to make coverage available on a guaranteed-issue basis to individuals with 18 or more months of creditable coverage, whose most recent coverage was under a group health plan. However, coverage does not have to be provided to an individual who has other health insurance or who is eligible for COBRA coverage, Medicare, or Medicaid. No preexisting-conditions exclusions can be imposed. Health insurers have three options for providing coverage to eligible individuals:

- They may offer every health insurance policy they offer in the state.
- They may offer their two most popular policies in the state, based on premium volume.
- They may offer a low-level and a high-level coverage, as long as they contain benefits that are similar to other coverage the insurer offers in the state.

TYPES OF POLICIES AVAILABLE

A variety of medical expense policies are available in the individual marketplace. These can be purchased from insurance companies, Blue Cross and Blue Shield plans and managed care organizations. Some of these policies provide broad coverage; other policies provide limited coverage. Many associations, such as AARP and professional societies, have programs through which their members can obtain coverage.

Individual Major Medical Policies

Many insurance companies offer major medical insurance in the individual marketplace. In the majority of cases, the policies are actually individual PPO coverage, with a lower level of benefits if services are received from providers outside the PPO network. In other cases, they are traditional indemnity policies; covered persons have complete freedom to choose any medical provider and have the same level of benefits paid. With a few exceptions, the coverage available is very similar to what is found under employer-provided medical expense plans.

Unlike employer-provided coverage, for which an employee must accept the plan limits as determined by the employer, the purchaser of individual coverage has some choices to make. The most frequent choice is the selection of the annual deductible. The number and dollar amount of options vary by company, but a set of choices ranging from $250 to $10,000 is quite common. The average deductible purchased today is about $2,000. A few insurers offer major medical contracts with very high deductibles, ranging from a low of $10,000 or $20,000 to a high of $1 million.

A similar choice might exist with respect to a policy's coinsurance percentage. Some companies' policies have the same coinsurance percentage for all contracts; other companies allow a choice. For example, one company lets the purchaser of a policy select whether the policy will pay 50, 80, 90, or 100 percent of covered expenses. The last option is available only if the purchaser also selects a high deductible.

Some major medical policies cover prescription drugs like any other medical expenses; most policies, however, impose limitations, such as separate copayments, maximum annual benefits, or different coinsurance percentages. Still other policies make prescription drug coverage an optional benefit that must be added by the purchase of a policy rider.

Maternity coverage frequently requires the purchase of a separate rider for coverage. Benefits are often subject to a waiting period of 10 or 12 months. Benefits may also be paid at something less than their full level during the first year or two of coverage.

Individual policies are likely to have slightly less generous benefits than employer-provided coverage. For example, there may be more limited coverage for mental and nervous disorders. Because of state-mandated benefits, however, individual policies might provide broader coverage than major medical coverage that would exist under a self-funded, employer-provided plan. Examples in some states are coverage for acupuncture treatment or mammograms. Such state mandates encourage many employers to self-fund benefits because ERISA exempts non-insured plans from state insurance mandates.

HMO Coverage

Many health maintenance organizations sell individual coverage, which usually is identical to coverage offered to employers for their benefit plans. However, the emphasis on comprehensive coverage with modest copayments and preventive medicine often makes the HMO coverage more expensive than the coverage available under major medical policies. Some HMOs offer coverage only to persons who have lost employer-provided coverage from the same HMO. Other HMOs market their coverage to everyone; the premium is sometimes lower for persons who converted from employer-provided coverage. Although the situation is changing somewhat, HMOs have historically emphasized the marketing of coverage through employer plans and have marketed individual coverage less aggressively than insurance companies.

Medicare Supplement (Medigap) Policies

Although Medicare provides significant benefits to many Americans, the program has several limitations that can lead to large out-of-pocket costs for some beneficiaries. The reasons for these costs include the following:

- a significant Part A deductible for each spell of illness
- no stop-loss limit for Part B expenses
- very limited coverage for treatment outside the United States

Estimates indicate that about two-thirds of Medicare recipients have some type of coverage to supplement Medicare; this group is split between those with coverage provided by a former employer, those who purchase coverage in the individual marketplace, and those who elect Medicare Advantage plans. Employer-provided coverage for retirees may take the form of either a Medicare carve-out or a Medicare supplement.

medigap insurance　　In the individual marketplace, a Medicare supplement is frequently referred to as *medigap insurance*. As the name implies, the objective is to fill some of the gaps left after Medicare benefits have been paid. When originally developed, medigap plans were as diverse as the companies that sold them. This led to confusion in the marketplace and to questionable sales practices and duplications of coverage. As a result, the federal government enacted legislation to deal with the structure and marketing of medigap plans.

In 1990, the medigap market became directly subject to federal regulation when Congress directed the National Association of Insurance Commissioners (NAIC) to develop a group of standardized medigap policies. Congress mandated several other features, including a 6-month open enrollment period, limited preexisting-conditions exclusions, prohibition of the sale of duplicate coverage, increased individual loss ratios, and guaranteed renewability.

Basic Benefits

The NAIC originally adopted ten standard medigap plans; all ten required the inclusion of a core of specified basic benefits. States may approve, and insurers may offer, fewer than the ten standard plans. Most states now permit the sale of all ten plans, but some limit the types sold, and a few states are not affected by the mandate because alternative standardized programs were already in place prior to the federal legislation. Three states—Massachusetts, Minnesota, and Wisconsin—had medigap programs prior to the NAIC standards. These programs were allowed to continue, and the policies issued are somewhat different from the standardized federal programs. However, they are required to contain the basic medigap benefits available in all other states. There are now two additional plans that contain consumer-directed health plan features and differ somewhat from the original ten plans. The rules for standardized policies apply to the individual marketplace. Group Medicare supplements that employers offer to their retirees are not considered medigap policies and may differ.

The basic benefits that all ten original plans must include consist of the following:

- hospitalization—the copayment or cost sharing of Part A benefits for the 61st through the 90th day of hospitalization and the 60-day lifetime reserve. In addition, coverage is extended for 365 additional days after Medicare benefits end.
- medical expenses—the Part B percentage participation for Medicare-approved charges for physicians and medical services after a beneficiary has satisfied the Part B deductible
- blood—the payment for the first 3 pints of blood each year

Additional Benefits of Medigap Plans

The ten currently available medigap plans that can be sold include, in addition to the basic benefits, an array of benefits for services that Medicare covers in part or that Medicare does not cover at all. These benefits include paying

- the Part A copayment for the 21st through the 100th day of skilled-nursing facility care
- the hospital inpatient Part A deductible for each benefit period
- the Part B deductible
- charges for physicians' and medical services that exceed the Medicare-approved amount (100 percent of these charges)
- charges for emergency care in a foreign country (with several limitations)
- an at-home provider to give assistance with activities of daily living (ADLs) while a beneficiary qualifies for Medicare home health care benefits (with certain limitations)
- limited annual amounts for preventive care (annual physicals, screening tests, and so forth)

The ten currently available medigap plans are shown in the following table. The policies available in the individual marketplace must be identified by the letters A through N. Insurers can offer plan F as high-deductible policies with a deductible that is set annually by the federal government. The 2011 deductible is $2,000.

Insurance companies selling Medicare Supplement policies must make Plan A available. If they make any other plan available, they must offer either Plan C or Plan F. The most widely available Medicare supplement plans are A, C, D, and F. Plan A generally represents less than 5 percent of Medicare supplement sales, however. Plan F represents more than half, while plans C and D make up approximately a third of total sales. Plans K and L and Medicare SELECT policies (described later), which are generally less available, represent no more than 10 percent of total Medicare supplement sales.

Benefits	A	B	C	D	F*	G	K	L	M	N
Table 13-1 Medicare Supplement (Medigap) Policies										
Basic	X includ. 100% Part B coinsurance	X includ. 100% Part B coinsurance	X includ. 100% Part B coinsurance	X includ. 100% Part B coinsurance	X includ. 100% Part B coinsurance	X includ. 100% Part B coinsurance	Hospitalization and preventative care paid at 100%, other basic benefits at 50%	Hospitalization and preventative care paid at 100%, other basic benefits at 75%	X includ. 100% Part B coinsurance	X includ. 100% Part B coinsurance except**
Skilled-nursing facility (days 21–100)			X	X	X	X	50% skilled nursing facility co-insurance	X 75% skilled nursing facility co-insurance	X	X
Part A deductible		X	X	X	X	X	50% Part A deductible	75% Part A deductible	50% of Part A deductible	X
Part B deductible			X		X					
Part B excess charges					100%	100%				
Foreign travel emergency			X	X	X	X	Out-of-pocket limit $4,640, then 100%	Out-of-pocket limit $2,320, then 100%	X	X

*Plan F also offers a high deductible plan. It pays after one has paid a $2,000 calendar year deductible

**Plan N includes Basic, including 100% of Part B coinsurance, except for up to $20 copayment for office visits, and up to $50 copayment for emergency room visits that do not result in an inpatient admission.

In exchange for a lower premium, Plan L covers less of the copayments and coinsurance than other Medicare Supplement plans, but has an out-of-pocket maximum, which limits the amount the policyowner will pay annually. Medicare Supplement Plan K offers a lower monthly premium than Plan L, but offers higher copayments and a higher annual out-of-pocket limit. Medicare Supplement Plan M became available for purchase in 2010. As one of several new plans, these new plans offer attractive coverage for those willing to exchange higher out-of-pocket expenses for lower monthly premiums. Medicare Supplement Plan N consists of a $20 copayment for doctor visits and a $50 copayment for emergency room visits, which is applied once the deductible is paid.

Plans E, H, I and J are no longer available to buy. If a consumer has one of these plans, he or she can continue the plan. Plans H, I, and J were originally designed to pay 50 percent of outpatient prescription drug charges after a $250 deductible, up to an annual $1,250 or $3,000 calendar limit. Insurance companies may no longer issue these policies to new insureds with a drug benefit included. Persons already insured under these policies have several options. They may continue to renew them with drug benefits included as long as they do not enroll in the Medicare prescription drug program. However, they will then probably be subject to the penalty for late enrollment if they later enroll in the program because the benefits under the Medicare supplement policy will likely not qualify as creditable coverage. If they enroll in the Medicare prescription drug program, they may keep in force their existing Medicare supplement policies but with the drug benefit eliminated and the premium adjusted accordingly. Alternatively, they can switch to another available Medicare supplement policy that has no drug benefit. Such a switch is allowed without evidence of insurability or a penalty for preexisting conditions as long as it occurs during the initial enrollment period for Medicare prescription drug coverage.

Other Plans

With two exceptions, insurance companies cannot offer policies that provide benefits that differ from those under the approved NAIC plans . The first exception is that the companies can now offer two plans with consumer-directed features. Called plans K and L, these plans include the same basic core benefits and in addition, include benefits for the following:

- the Part A deductible
- the daily copayment for days 21 through 100 of skilled-nursing facility care
- the first 3 pints of blood
- the percentage participation for Part B services
- hospice and respite care cost sharing

Under plan K, the insured must pay 50 percent of these amounts except for Part B preventive services, which are covered at 100 percent. When the insured's out-of-pocket payments for these services plus the Part B deductible equal $4,640 (in 2011 and subject to indexing), plan K will pay

100 percent of the self-responsible amounts (any required copayments and percentage participation) for Medicare services (other than prescription drugs) for the rest of the calendar year. However, provider charges that exceed Medicare-approved amounts (excess charges) do not count toward the annual out-of-pocket limit.

Plan L is identical to plan K except that the percentage the insured must pay is 25 percent rather than 50 percent. In addition, the out-of-pocket limit is $2,320 (in 2011).

Because of the relatively limited benefits and cost sharing, plans K and L are significantly less expensive than the other plans.

Medicare SELECT policy
The second exception is for policies issued under the Medicare SELECT program. A *Medicare SELECT policy* is one of the standard medigap policies, but it can exclude or limit benefits (except in emergencies) for medical services if they are not received from network providers. Medicare SELECT policies are issued by insurance companies as PPO products and by some HMOs. As a general rule, the cost of a Medicare SELECT policy is 15 to 25 percent less than the cost of a comparable medigap policy that does not use such preferred-provider networks. An insured who has a Medicare SELECT policy has the right to switch to a regular medigap policy the same company sells, as long as the new policy has equal or less coverage than the Medicare SELECT policy.

Eligibility

Persons aged 65 or older may buy any available Medicare supplement policy, regardless of health status, at any time during the 6-month period after initial enrollment for Medicare Part B benefits. Insurance companies are allowed to exclude benefits for no more than 6 months because of preexisting conditions, but this period is reduced or eliminated if the insured had medical expense coverage immediately prior to Medicare eligibility. Some policies, however, immediately provide benefits for preexisting conditions or have an exclusion period shorter than 6 months. If a person initially elects a Medicare Advantage option in lieu of original Medicare benefits, the person will be eligible to purchase a Medicare supplement policy, without evidence of insurability, if he or she leaves the Medicare Advantage plan during the first 12 months of coverage and returns to original Medicare. Similarly, a person who drops Medicare supplement coverage and elects a Medicare Advantage plan can regain Medicare supplement coverage if he or she decides to drop the plan during the first 12 months of coverage.

In addition, a person can obtain a medigap policy without evidence of insurability because of the termination of an employer-provided plan that supplements Medicare, or because a Medicare Advantage plan no longer provides coverage or the person loses eligibility by moving out of the plan's service area.

Policies are guaranteed renewable.

Other Individual Health Insurance Coverages

Several other forms of health insurance coverage are relevant to the discussion of individual medical expense insurance. This section focuses on dental, temporary medical, international travel medical, limited-benefit, hospital confinement indemnity, and specified disease policies available in the individual insurance market.

Dental Insurance

Most dental coverages are offered through group contracts under employer-provided plans. Individual dental insurance policies are available, but they are not widely purchased because of their relatively high cost in relation to the maximum benefits available. Individual dental coverages are similar in most aspects to other employer-provided benefits. However, they are more likely to provide the following:

- lower maximum benefits per calendar year for all services with lower internal benefit limits for specified services, such as orthodontia, if offered
- higher patient copayments
- longer waiting periods for specified basic and major dental services

Coverage is sometimes made available for an additional premium under individual medical expense policies.

Temporary Medical Insurance

temporary medical insurance
Temporary medical insurance (sometimes called short-term medical insurance) generally provides coverage for periods between 30 days and 1 year to under-age-65 individuals and their dependents who are between permanent medical plans. This market includes people who lack coverage because they are

- losing employer-provided coverage and will not be eligible for Medicare for a year or two
- between jobs
- recent college graduates
- part-time and temporary employees
- newly divorced
- employees during temporary interruptions of employment
- foreigners temporarily residing in the United States

Policies that provide temporary medical expense insurance are quite similar to individual major medical policies; applicants usually have a choice of deductibles and coinsurance percentages. These plans are nonrenewable, but an individual may purchase an additional policy beyond the original policy period if he or she is insurable, and any condition that occurred during prior coverage will be considered a preexisting condition under subsequent coverage periods. Some companies do not limit the number of additional periods for which coverage is available; other companies impose a maximum period of total coverage, such as 1 year.

International Travel Medical Insurance

international travel medical insurance

International travel medical insurance is available for international travelers. U.S. citizens traveling abroad, foreign nationals traveling anywhere internationally, and recent immigrants to the United States may purchase some form of this coverage. In addition to vacation travelers, this market includes employees of domestic, international, and multinational corporations that require their employees to travel abroad, missionary groups, and intercultural and student exchange programs.

The period of coverage for international travel medical insurance can range from a minimum of 15 days to a maximum of 1 year; optional renewal of some policies is up to 5 years. Benefits cover the expenses of inpatient and outpatient hospitalizations as well as medical and related services. The insured may select a deductible, usually in a range of $100 to $2,500. Levels of coinsurance are frequently available at 80 percent up to a specific dollar amount—$5,000, for example—with a benefit payment of 100 percent thereafter to the policy maximum. Such maximums may range from $10,000 to as high as $2 million or more. The expense of repatriating mortal remains in the event of death and medical evacuation to a person's home country for more suitable treatment or after an extended hospitalization are usually covered. Coverage typically ceases when a person returns to his or her home country.

Generally, the health-related benefits are folded into a broader policy covering many non-health-related travel contingencies, and they may also provide assistance in making arrangements to obtain covered services.

Limited-Benefit Policies

Some insurers provide limited-benefit policies in the individual marketplace that are similar to those in the employer-provided market. Such policies are typically inadequate for prolonged sicknesses, serious accidents, or the significant medical expenses that can arise outside a hospital setting. Although this type of medical policy is obviously better than no medical expense coverage, it is no substitute for broader coverage. Purchasers of limited-benefit policies are generally lower-income individuals and families who are unlikely to be financial planning clients. These plans are also referred to as "mini-med" plans.

Mini-med health plans are health insurance plans with very low total payout amounts and bare bones coverage. These plans are often offered by employers with a high number of part-time employees or nontraditional employees. These employees generally cannot afford a full insurance policy and the employer cannot cover the number of employees with an affordable plan. For example, McDonalds provides a mini-med plan to an estimated 30,000 employees in more than 10,000 locations.

Health care reform legislation passed last year and going into full effect by 2014, sought to eliminate mini-med plans. The plans are viewed by consumer groups and employee groups as the worst form of health insurance. They claim the premiums pay for little, if any, coverage and employees do not understand what coverage is provided.

However, under the law, some employers could apply for waivers allowing their plans to remain even if it did not conform to the reform act's requirements. Over 1,000 employers have been granted such waivers as of March, 2011, so many mini-med plans remain in place. This has led critics to charge the law is unworkable.

The waivers are needed because most, if not all, mini-med plans run afoul of federal rules in the reform law that set a minimum annual dollar coverage limit on essential benefits that health care plans must provide in 2011, 2012 and 2013. The minimum limit is $750,000 in 2011, $1.25 million in 2012 and

$2 million in 2013. Under the health care reform law, low-wage employees might qualify for government-subsidized coverage that will be available from insurers offering coverage through new state insurance exchanges starting in 2014, reducing the need for mini-med plans.

Hospital Confinement Indemnity, Specific Disease, and Critical Illness Insurance

Three types of medical expense insurance are designed to supplement the benefits available under principal policies of medical expense insurance. These policies—hospital confinement indemnity insurance, specified disease insurance, and critical illness insurance—share certain characteristics. They help the insured face the significant additional financial consequences of a serious illness or injury by providing direct cash payments, usually made without regard to other coverages. These payments may be used for

- out-of-pocket expenses of medical treatment left uncovered by even a comprehensive medical plan
- associated nonmedical expenses, such as travel, lodging, meals, child care, and loss of income

Hospital confinement indemnity insurance, specified disease insurance, and critical illness insurance are no substitute for adequate medical expense and disability income insurance. If medical expense and disability income coverages are adequate, there are many financial planners who question whether such supplemental policies are necessary, particularly if a person has appropriate financial reserves for emergencies.

hospital
confinement
indemnity
insurance

Hospital Confinement Indemnity Insurance. *Hospital confinement indemnity insurance* gives the insured a fixed daily cash benefit during a covered hospitalization. A spouse or dependent child is usually eligible for coverage, although benefits may be reduced.

The policy provides daily benefits in the event of hospital confinement in a specified dollar amount (such as $250 per day) for a defined period (such as 90 days). These additional benefits are available as a standard feature or as a rider:

- a lump-sum payment on the first day of hospital confinement
- an intensive care benefit, such as $400, for a specified number of days in addition to the standard daily payment

- a surgical and anesthesia benefit, with scheduled limits and a yearly maximum
- payment for emergency room and related physician services due to an illness or accident, with limitations on duration or expense per event or per year
- an outpatient sickness benefit, with limits per treatment and per year
- daily payment for recovery after a qualified hospital stay
- an accidental death benefit

specified disease insurance

Specified Disease Insurance. *Specified disease insurance* (also referred to as dread disease insurance) provides benefits to insured individuals and covered family members upon the diagnosis of or medical events related to the treatment of a disease named in the policy. It does not cover accidents or injuries. Specified disease insurance for cancer only was once the most prevalent form of this insurance. Today, however, most policies cover cancer in addition to other diseases, which might include many or all of the following:

· Addison's disease	· poliomyelitis
· amyotrophic lateral sclerosis	· Q fever
· botulism	· rabies
· Budd-Chiari syndrome	· Reye's syndrome
· cystic fibrosis	· rheumatic fever
· diphtheria	· Rocky Mountain spotted fever
· encephalitis	· sickle-cell anemia
· Legionnaires' disease	· Tay-Sachs disease
· lupus erythematosus	· tetanus
· malaria	· toxic shock syndrome
· meningitis	· trichinosis
· multiple sclerosis	· tuberculosis
· muscular dystrophy	· typhoid fever
· myasthenia gravis	· undulant fever
· osteomyelitis	· whooping cough

Specified disease policy benefits vary widely. Benefit provisions may utilize a combination of three payment structures: per-day or per-service, expense-incurred, or a lump-sum payment. Benefits are contingent on a diagnosis of the specified disease, but payments will cover the first day of care or confinement even though the diagnosis is made at some later date. This retroactive application of benefits usually applies to relevant services received within 90 days prior to the diagnosis. The following table presents a summary of illustrative benefits.

Table 13-2 Specified Disease Insurance: Summary of Selected Benefits	
Service	**Benefit**
Hospital confinement	$300 daily for up to 90 days; $600 daily in coronary or intensive care unit up to 30 days
Surgery	Up to $7,500 per fee schedule
Anesthesia	Up to 25 percent of the surgical benefit
Physician's attendance	Actual charges up to $35 per day for in-hospital visits
Chemotherapy, radiation, immunotherapy, or radioactive isotopes therapy	50 percent of the first $50,000 of charges and 100 percent of the next $100,000, limited to $125,000 per calendar year
Experimental treatment	Up to $25,000 for experimental bone marrow transplant and $2,500 for donor-related expenses plus transportation
Transportation and lodging	Up to $50 per day for lodging, mileage, or coach airfare for travel for insured and companion (each)
Ambulance	Actual charges for an ambulance to the hospital and up to $5,000 for air ambulance
Artificial limbs and prostheses	Actual charges with lifetime maximum of $2,000 per insured person
Equipment	Up to $1,000 per calendar year for rental or purchase

Specified disease policies frequently offer a first-occurrence benefit that pays a one-time amount for each covered person who receives a diagnosis of internal cancer. The amount may range from $1,000 to as high as $50,000 or more.

critical illness insurance

Critical Illness Insurance. *Critical illness insurance is a supplemental medical insurance that provides a substantial one-time lump-sum cash benefit for a listed* critical illness. These "illnesses" result from injury as well as disease and include specified major surgeries.

The applicant selects a maximum benefit amount, which can range from $10,000 to several hundred thousand dollars. The maximum benefit is payable only once—upon the first diagnosis of a condition or specified surgical treatment that is covered. Each covered condition and surgical treatment is explicitly defined in the policy. Typically, the maximum benefit is payable for the following medical conditions or major surgery:

- Alzheimer's disease
- blindness
- life-threatening cancer
- deafness
- heart attack
- major organ transplant
- multiple sclerosis
- paralysis
- renal failure
- stroke

The policy may also provide a lesser benefit, such as 25 percent of the maximum benefit, for each of the following:

- initial coronary angioplasty (surgical treatment)
- initial coronary artery bypass (surgical treatment)
- initial diagnosis of cancer in its original site (other than skin cancer)

The percentage payment of the maximum benefits for the above conditions is payable only once; the maximum benefit is reduced by the amount paid, and the premium is also reduced accordingly. The policyowner is notified of the new maximum amount and the new premium. The policy terminates on the date the maximum benefit amount is paid under the terms of the policy.

INSURING THE UNHEALTHY

Historically, persons with a preexisting medical condition had a difficult time obtaining individual medical expense coverage. If the medical condition was severe, insurers would often decline coverage. If the medical condition was less severe, insurers might write substandard coverage by doing one or more of the following: charging an additional premium, excluding the condition, or imposing a waiting period before benefits would be payable for the condition.

Over time, the ability of the unhealthy to obtain coverage has improved significantly. If there is prior employer-provided coverage, federal legislation like COBRA and HIPAA eliminates the availability, but not necessarily the affordability, problem for many persons. States have also increasingly addressed the issue of access to individual medical expense coverage. Some of these state actions, such as the mandate of a conversion provision in group medical expense contracts, date back many years. In addition, some Blue Cross and Blue Shield plans, in return for preferential regulatory and tax status, offer periodic enrollment periods when normal medical underwriting requirements are reduced or waived.

In more recent years, more than half of the states have established some type of high-risk pool, whereby anyone turned down for medical expense coverage in the normal marketplace can obtain coverage through the pool. Although these pools vary among the states, basic major medical coverage is usually available, but benefits for preexisting conditions are often subject to waiting periods. Premiums tend to be higher than regular medical expense insurance, but state subsidies keep premiums below the level needed to fully cover expenses and claims costs. The best way to find out about the options for insuring an unhealthy person is to contact the insurance department of the state where that person resides.

Federal health care reform has added a new option, effective in 2010. People without insurance because of a pre-existing condition will be eligible for subsidized, temporary coverage through a new, high-risk insurance program. U.S. citizens and legal immigrants who have been uninsured for at least six months will be eligible. Premiums are set for a standard population instead of a higher risk group. Maximum out-of-pocket limits will be the same as HSA (health savings account) limits ($5,950/individual and $11,900/family). This program is expected to be replaced by the insurance exchanges to be introduced in 2014.

Another program with similar goals is designed for early retirees, age 55–64. The Early Retiree Reinsurance Program (ERRP) provides reimbursement to participating employment-based plans for a portion of the costs of health benefits for early retirees and early retirees' spouses, surviving spouses, and dependents. The program was authorized in the Affordable Care Act. Effective in 2010, this program also limits out-of-pocket spending to $5,950 for individuals and $11,900 for families, excluding premiums.

CONSUMER-DIRECTED MEDICAL EXPENSE PLANS

One approach to consumer-directed medical expense plans is the use of savings accounts. Two techniques that take this approach are health savings accounts (HSAs) and Archer medical savings accounts (Archer MSAs). Individuals can establish HSAs or employers can establish them for the benefit of the individual employees. The ability to establish new Archer MSAs has been phased out, but a few people still have them.

Health Savings Accounts

health savings accounts (HSAs)

In addition to providing prescription drug coverage for older Americans, the Medicare Prescription Drug, Improvement, and Modernization Act established *health savings accounts (HSAs)*. HSAs are designed to be successors to Archer MSAs, which are briefly discussed later, and the two have many features in common. However, they also have some notable differences that make HSAs more attractive than Archer MSAs and available to a much larger pool of consumers.

In some cases, employers set up HSAs for their employees and contribute to the accounts. In other cases, employers merely provide the underlying medical expense coverage, and employees must establish and fund their own accounts. By 2010, over 10 million people were covered by medical expense policies that would allow them to establish HSAs, and about half had done so.

General Nature

An HSA is a personal savings account from which unreimbursed medical expenses, including deductibles, percentage participation, and copayments, can be paid. The HSA must be in the form of a tax-exempt trust or custodial account established in conjunction with a high-deductible health (medical expense) plan. An HSA is established with a qualified trustee or custodian in much the same way that an IRA is established. Any insurance company or bank (as well as certain other financial institutions) can be a trustee or custodian, as can any other person or entity already approved by the IRS as a trustee or custodian for IRAs.

HSAs are individual trusts. This prohibits a husband and wife from having a joint HSA. But as long as both are eligible, each may have a separate HSA.

Some insurers that sell high-deductible health plans for use with HSAs also market HSAs; other insurers leave it to the purchasers of a high-deductible health plan to establish their HSAs with other institutions.

Even though employers can sponsor HSAs, these accounts are established for the benefit of individuals and are portable. If an employee changes employers or leaves the workforce, the HSA, including the balance in the account, remains with the individual. However, the prior underlying insurance does not continue unless the former employee elects COBRA or purchases a conversion policy.

Eligibility

HSAs can be established by employees, the self-employed, and anyone else who meets the following rules for qualification:

- The individual must be covered by a high-deductible health plan. That plan may be insured or self-insured if offered by an employer as long as it meets the criteria for a qualifying high-deductible plan.
- The individual is not eligible to be claimed as a dependent on another person's federal income tax return.
- With some exceptions, a person who is covered under an high-deductible health plan is denied eligibility for an HSA if he or she is covered under another health plan that does not meet the definition of a high-deductible plan but provides any benefits which are covered under the high-deductible health plan. The exceptions include coverage for accident, disability, dental care, vision care, and long-term care as well as liability insurance, insurance for a specified disease or illness, and insurance paying a fixed amount per period of hospitalization. Participation in a typical health flexible spending account (FSA) would make an individual ineligible to participate in an HSA unless the health FSA only provided reimbursement for types of expenses not covered under the high-deductible health plan.

An employer can establish HSAs for its employees, or an individual (whether employed or not) may establish his or her own HSA.

High-Deductible Health Plan

For purposes of HSA participation, a high-deductible health plan is defined as having the following deductibles and annual out-of-pocket limitations for covered services. These figures are for 2011 and subject to annual inflation adjustments:

- In the case of self-only coverage, the deductible must be at least $1,200, and annual out-of-pocket expenses cannot exceed $5,950.
- In the case of family coverage, the deductible must be at least $2,400, and annual out-of-pocket expenses cannot exceed $11,900.

If these high-deductible plans use preferred-provider networks, they can have higher out-of-pocket limits for services provided outside the network, and any deductibles for nonnetwork services are not taken into account when determining the out-of-pocket limits specified above.

One point should be emphasized about the deductible for family coverage. It is not a family deductible as was described in the discussion on major medical insurance. In that situation, there is an individual deductible that applies to each family member as well as a separate deductible for the family. This is sometimes referred to as an embedded or stacked deductible, and policy benefits are paid for any family member once his or her deductible is satisfied, even if the family deductible has not been met.

In the case of a high-deductible policy used with an HSA, there will usually not be an individual deductible if a policy is written for a family. Rather, there will be a single deductible—referred to as a common deductible—that must be satisfied before any benefits are payable, even if all claims are for one family member. It is permissible, however, to use an individual deductible, but only if the individual deductible is equal to at least the required HSA family deductible of $2,400. For example, a policy with an individual deductible of $2,500 and a family deductible of $5,000 would be acceptable.

The following incurred expenses do not count toward the plan's required deductible and out-of-pocket limit:

- payments for services not covered by the high-deductible health plan
- payments for services received from nonnetwork health care providers, if the plan uses a preferred-provider network
- amounts above a plan's reasonable specific service or lifetime maximums
- amounts in excess of reasonable and customary fees
- penalties for failure to obtain a plan-required certification

Nevertheless, copayments count toward the out-of-pocket limit, even if the plan does not consider copayments as contributing toward the satisfaction of the deductible. In addition, the deductible amount counts towards the out-of-pocket limit.

Preventive Care

Generally, a high-deductible health plan established in conjunction with an HSA cannot provide benefits before the deductible is satisfied, but there is an exception for benefits for preventive care. A high-deductible health plan may provide benefits for the following preventive care services before the insured satisfies the plan's required high deductible:

- annual physicals, immunizations, and screening services
- routine prenatal and well-child care
- tobacco cessation programs and obesity weight-loss programs
- employee assistance, disease management, or wellness programs
- treatment of a related condition that is incidental or ancillary to a preventive care service or screening, such as removal of polyps during a diagnostic colonoscopy
- drugs or medications taken by a person who has developed risk factors for a disease before the disease manifests itself or to prevent the reoccurrence of a disease from which the person has recovered. An example is the drug treatment of high cholesterol to prevent heart disease, or the treatment of recovered heart attack or stroke victims with medications to prevent a recurrence. Other prescription drugs that do not qualify under this exception remain subject to the plan's high deductible.

Preventive care generally does not include treatment of existing conditions.

Contributions

Contributions must be in the form of cash, typically in the form of a check or salary deduction. Contributions to an HSA for a self-employed or unemployed individual are made directly by that person. For an employed person, contributions can be made by the employer, the employee, or a combination of the two. Family members may also make contributions to an HSA on behalf of other family members. Contributions to the HSA can also be made under a cafeteria plan.

Contributions by an individual are deductible for federal income tax purposes even if the individual does not itemize deductions. Contributions by an employer are tax deductible to the employer and are not included in an employee's gross income or subject to Social Security, Medicare, and other employment taxes.

With one exception, an employer that makes contributions to HSAs is subject to a nondiscrimination rule that requires the employer to make comparable contributions for all employees who have HSAs. However, full-time employees and part-time employees (those working fewer than 30 hours per week) are treated separately. The comparability rule requires that the employer contribute either the same dollar amount for each employee or the same percentage of each employee's deductible under the health plan. The exception to the comparability rule is that an employer can make larger contributions for non-highly compensated employees than for highly compensated employees. For example, an employer could contribute $1,000 to the accounts of each non-highly compensated employee while making no contribution or a lesser contribution to the accounts of highly compensated employees. The definition of highly compensated employee for purposes of this rule generally includes (1) those owning more than 5 percent of the business and (2) those earning more than $100,000 and ranking in the top 20 percent of employees based on compensation. Failure to comply with this rule subjects the employer to an excise tax equal to 35 percent of the aggregate amount contributed to HSAs during the period when the comparability rule was not satisfied.

Employer contributions as well as an employee's contributions belong to the employee and are nonforfeitable.

General Contribution Limits. The maximum annual contribution to an HSA in 2011 is $3,050 if the account holder has self-only coverage and $6,150 if the account holder has family coverage. As a result of the Tax Relief and Health Care Act of 2006, the full maximum contribution is allowed even if it exceeds the policy deductible under the high-deductible health plan. If both a husband and wife establish an HSA and have family coverage (that is, a single policy covering both of them), they can allocate the maximum contribution in any way they determine. If they have separate individual policies, each is subject to the limits that apply to single coverage.

Individuals aged 55 or older are also permitted an additional annual catch-up contribution of $1,000. If both a husband and wife are aged 55 or older, the catch-up contribution is available to each of them only if they have separate HSAs.

Annual contributions can be made in a lump sum or spread out over time. However, the contributions for a specific tax year cannot be made before the tax year begins or after the taxpayer's original filing date (without extensions) for that tax year. For most individuals, this is the earlier of April 15 of the following year or the date a return is filed. This is similar to the rules for IRA contributions.

EXAMPLE

Jack and Eva are each age 56. They have a family medical expense policy with a $5,000 deductible through Jack's employer, and Jack established an HSA. The maximum contribution to the HSA for 2011 is $7,150, which consists of the $6,150 regular limit and an additional catch-up amount of $1,000 for Jack.

However, if they each established an HSA, they each would be eligible to make the $1,000 catch-up contribution to their own accounts. Any portion of the $6,150 contribution not put into Jack's account by his employer could be allocated among the two accounts as they agreed upon. The net effect is that the total HSA contributions would increase to $8,150.

These contributions can be made in one or more payments between January 1, 2011, and the date they file their 2011 tax return.

If an individual quits participating in an HSA during a tax year, the actual HSA contribution that can be deducted for the tax year is limited to 1/12 of the annual amount times the number of months that an individual is eligible for HSA participation.

An excess contribution occurs to the extent that contributions to an HSA exceed the tax-deductible limits or are made for an ineligible person. Any excess contribution made by the employer is included in the employee's gross income. Whether the excess contribution was made by an employer or an account holder, the account holder is subject to a 6 percent excise tax on excess contributions for each year these contributions are in an account. This excise tax can be avoided if the excess amount and any net income attributable to the excess amount are removed from the HSA prior to the last day prescribed by law, including extensions, for filing the account holder's income tax return. The net income attributable to the excess contributions is included in the account holder's gross income for the tax year in which the distribution is made.

Roll-Over Contributions. An account balance from an Archer MSA can be rolled over to an HSA on a tax-free basis. Similarly, account balances from an existing HSA can be rolled over to a new HSA.

The Tax Relief and Health Care Act of 2006 also allows certain other types of tax-free rollovers in specific circumstances. For example, an account holder who establishes an HSA is allowed a one-time rollover of funds from an HRA or health FSA. The amount of the rollover, which is in addition to any regular contribution for the year, is limited to the lesser of the balance in such an account on (1) September 21, 2006, or (2) the date of the rollover. If the account holder does not remain eligible to participate in an HSA for at least 1 year after the rollover, the amount of the rollover is included in income for tax purposes and subject to a 10 percent penalty tax. Finally, an account holder may make a one-time-only rollover from an IRA. The amount of the rollover is limited to the tax-deductible amount for the year and reduces any regular contribution allowed.

Account Growth and Investment Options

Unused amounts in an HSA accumulate on a tax-free basis and carry over to subsequent years without limit. The size of an HSA balance carried over from prior years has no effect on a current year's contribution.

Account holders can invest HSA funds in essentially the same manner as IRA funds. Allowable investments include bank accounts, annuities, certificates of deposit, stocks, mutual funds, and bonds. They cannot be invested in life insurance policies or most types of collectibles. In addition, an HSA trust or custodial agreement may limit the investment options available.

HSA funds can decrease in value if the underlying investments also decrease in value. Therefore, an account holder must be prudent in how HSA funds are invested.

Distributions

An individual can take distributions from an HSA at any time. The amount of the distribution can be any part or all of the account balance. Subject to some exceptions, distributions of both contributions and earnings are excludible from an account holder's gross income if used to pay medical expenses of the account holder and the account holder's legal spouse and tax dependents as long as these expenses are not paid by other sources of insurance. There is no requirement that these family members be covered by a high-deductible health insurance plan. If both a husband and wife have

HSAs, the reimbursement for any family can come from either or both HSAs but together cannot exceed the amount of the unreimbursed expense.

For the most part, the eligible medical expenses are the same ones that would be deductible, ignoring the 7.5 percent of adjusted gross income limitation, if the account holder itemized his or her tax deductions. Tax-free withdrawals are permitted for the purchase of COBRA continuation coverage, or for the purchase of health coverage while an individual receives unemployment compensation. They are also permitted for the purchase of long-term care insurance up to certain deductible limits. However, tax-free withdrawals are not otherwise permitted for the purchase of health insurance by persons under age 65.

Even though contributions cannot be made after an individual reaches age 65 and becomes a Medicare beneficiary, tax-free distributions can still be used for any future qualified medical expenses, which include premiums for original Medicare, Medicare prescription drug coverage, Medicare Advantage plans, and medical expense coverage under employer-sponsored plans. However, tax-free distributions cannot be used to pay premiums for individual Medicare supplement policies.

From a financial planning standpoint, account holders may want to wait until after retirement or age 65 to take HSA distributions as long as they have the resources to pay for unreimbursed medical expenses prior to that time. This will allow their HSA balances to grow on a tax-favored basis for use in their older years when unreimbursed medical expenses may be higher and/or income may be lower.

Distributions are permitted for other reasons, but they are subject to income taxation and possibly to a 10 percent penalty tax. However, the penalty tax does not apply in the case of distributions after an individual's death, disability, or the attainment of age 65.

EXAMPLE
Kirby has a balance of $7,000 in his HSA. At age 67, he rediscovered his childhood sweetheart and fell madly in love. She agreed to marry him, and he wants to give her a big diamond ring. Because she told Kirby that she would take care of him for life, he decided to cash in his HSA and apply the proceeds to the purchase of the ring. His tax accountant informed Kirby that this arrangement would not be a qualified medical expense. He can withdraw the funds without penalty because he is at least age 65, but the $7,000 must be included in his gross income for federal income tax purposes.

Termination of Employment

Former employees, including retirees, may continue HSAs that were established prior to termination of employment, and the rules for contributions and distributions are as previously described.

As long as they are not Medicare eligible, retirees who did not have an HSA prior to retirement can establish one at that time as long as all the proper rules are satisfied. Such an HSA may present an opportunity for a retiree to reduce income taxes. However, the requirement of having a high-deductible plan will probably negate this advantage if an individual has substantial medical expenses.

EXAMPLE
Kathleen, a widow, retired at age 60 from her job as an attorney. She likes the concept of consumer-directed health plans and has decided to establish an HSA. In order to be eligible for the HSA, she purchased a major medical policy with an annual deductible of $2,500. She plans on making the maximum allowable contribution to the HSA until she is eligible for Medicare. She will then use her HSA balance to pay her Medicare premiums.

Estate Tax Treatment

Upon death, the remaining balance in an HSA is includible in the account holder's gross estate for estate tax purposes. If the beneficiary of the account is a surviving spouse, the HSA belongs to the spouse and he or she can deduct the account balance in determining the account holder's taxable estate. The surviving spouse can then use the HSA for his or her medical expenses. If the beneficiary is someone other than the spouse, the HSA ceases to exist, and the beneficiary must include the fair market value of the account in his or her gross income for tax purposes. If no beneficiary is named, the tax is payable by the estate or the beneficiary of the estate.

Archer Medical Savings Accounts

Archer MSAs
Archer medical savings accounts, commonly referred to as *Archer MSAs*, were the predecessors to HSAs. Fewer than 100,000 were ever established. Many account holders have terminated Archer MSAs or rolled them over to HSAs. Although new Archer MSAs can no longer be established, persons who have them can still make contributions if they continue to meet the eligibility requirements.

Archer MSAs are similar to HSAs in many respects. However, they have a few notable differences that include the following:

- Eligibility to make contributions is limited to the self-employed and employees of small employers with 50 or fewer employees.
- The required high-deductible policy has somewhat different deductible amounts and out-of- pocket limits. The deductible must apply to all covered expenses, including preventive care.
- Contributions are limited to 65 percent of the policy deductible for the high-deductible health plan.
- The account holder or the employer, but not both, can make contributions.
- Distributions for medical expenses of a family member is not allowed in any year that contributions are made unless the family member is covered under a high-deductible health plan.

POLICY PROVISIONS

Premiums

Premiums for individual health insurance policies can be paid annually, semiannually, quarterly, or possibly monthly. The total premiums for a year will be higher than the annual premium if paid in installments. Several factors may affect the level of premiums. These include age, gender, occupation, and whether the insured has certain avocations or is a smoker.

Most policies have a 31-day grace period. If the premium is paid during this period, the policy will continue in force with no lapse in coverage. If a premium is not paid within the grace period, the policy will lapse as of the beginning of the grace period.

Most policies contain a provision whereby a lapsed policy can be reinstated for some period of time after it lapses. Some insurers will automatically reinstate a policy if a premium is received within a short period of time following the grace period. Otherwise, the insurer may wish to reunderwrite the policy. No benefits are paid for losses that occur between the date of lapse and a policy's reinstatement. Accidental injuries sustained after the date of reinstatement are covered from the date of reinstatement. However, there is usually a 10-day waiting period before losses from sickness are covered.

Renewability

It is important to look at the provision in a medical expense policy regarding renewability. Because of the uncertain nature and cost of future medical claims, it is rare to find noncancelable policies, unless they provide very limited benefits. Many policies are guaranteed renewable to at least age 65, when a person qualifies for Medicare. Many policies, however, limit their obligation to continue coverage if the insurer decides to stop writing that particular type of insurance contract. Insurers that issue optionally renewable policies are required to give the policyowner advance notice of any intention not to renew, usually at least 30 days.

FEDERAL TAX TREATMENT

The tax situation for self-employed individuals is discussed in the previous chapter. Other individuals who itemize deductions are allowed to deduct most unreimbursed medical care expenses (including dental expenses) to the extent the total of these expenses exceeds 7.5 percent of adjusted gross income. Premiums paid for medical expense and dental insurance are included as an expense for purposes of this deduction. However, premiums for policies that pay a stated periodic payment to a person while hospitalized, regardless of benefits from other sources, are considered premiums for disability income insurance and are not deductible.

As a result of trade legislation passed in 2002, a tax credit is available to certain taxpayers. These include (1) individuals who are certified as having lost their jobs because of trade-related reasons, such as competition from foreign imports, and (2) individuals who are at least age 55 and receiving benefits from the Pension Benefit Guaranty Corporation. The credit is equal to 65 percent of the cost of the premium for continuing coverage under COBRA (and possibly for the purchase of certain other medical expense coverage) for an individual and his or her eligible family members. The credit, however, is not available to a taxpayer who has medical expense coverage under Medicare, Medicaid, or an employer-sponsored plan for which the employer pays at least 50 percent of the cost of the coverage.

As a general rule, benefits received from individually paid medical expense and dental insurance are not subject to income tax, even if they exceed expenses actually incurred. One exception includes benefits received for expenses that were deducted in prior years.

CHECKLIST FOR EVALUATING AND COMPARING MEDICAL EXPENSE INSURANCE

- What is the type of coverage?

  ___ Major medical
  ___ HMO
  ___ PPO
  ___ Point of service
  ___ HSA
  ___ Other

- What is the annual policy premium?
- Are there any discounts for good health or healthy behaviors, such as not smoking?
- Are there any preexisting conditions that are not covered? If so, for how long?
- To what extent is each of the following services covered? Identify any exclusions or limitations that apply to each service that will affect the client or family.

  ___ Inpatient hospital services
  ___ Outpatient surgery
  ___ Physician visits (in the hospital)
  ___ Office visits
  ___ Skilled-nursing care
  ___ Medical tests and X rays
  ___ Prescription drugs
  ___ Mental health care
  ___ Drug and alcohol abuse treatment
  ___ Home health care visits
  ___ Rehabilitation facility care
  ___ Physical therapy
  ___ Speech therapy
  ___ Hospice care
  ___ Maternity care
  ___ Chiropractic visits
  ___ Preventive care and checkups
  ___ Well-baby care
  ___ Dental care

___ Vision care

- Are there any annual or lifetime maximum limits? If so, what are they?
- What is the annual deductible?

    ___ Per person
    ___ Per family

- What coinsurance or copayments apply?

    ___ After meeting deductible
    ___ Per office visit
    ___ For inpatient hospital care

- What is the stop-loss or out-of-pocket limit?
- What preauthorization or certification procedures must be met?
- If coverage is individually purchased, what are the provisions for renewal?

CHAPTER REVIEW

Key Terms and Concepts

COBRA
qualified beneficiary
qualifying event
extension of benefits
medigap insurance
Medicare SELECT policy
temporary medical insurance

international travel medical insurance
hospital confinement indemnity
  insurance
specified disease insurance
critical illness insurance
health savings accounts (HSAs)
Archer MSAs

Review Questions

Review questions are based on the learning objectives in this chapter. Thus, a [3] at the end of a question means that the question is based on learning objective 3. If there are multiple objectives, they are all listed.

1. COBRA requires that group health plans allow employees and certain beneficiaries to elect to have their current health coverage extended following a "qualifying event."
    a. What types of plans does COBRA cover? [1]
    b. What are the various qualifying events? [1]
    c. What are the categories of qualified beneficiaries? [1]

2. How does the Health Insurance Portability and Accountability Act make it easier for individuals who lose employer-provided medical expense coverage to find alternative coverage in the individual marketplace? [1]

3. a. What are the basic benefits all ten original Medicare supplement policies must include? [2]
   b. What are the eligibility criteria for Medicare supplement insurance? [2]

4. Describe the following types of individual health insurance coverages:
   a. temporary medical insurance [2]
   b. international travel medical insurance [2]
   c. hospital confinement indemnity insurance [2]
   d. specified disease insurance [2]
   e. critical illness insurance [2]

5. What developments have made it easier for unhealthy individuals to fund medical expense coverage? [3]

6. Who is eligible to establish a health savings account (HSA)? [4]

7. What are the rules that apply to HSAs with respect to each of the following?
   a. contributions [4]
   b. distributions [4]

8. What is the estate tax treatment of HSAs? [4]

9. Why do insurers rarely issue medical expense policies on a noncancelable basis? [5]

10. What is the federal tax treatment of premiums and benefits for medical expense insurance purchased by an individual? [6]

Learning Objectives

An understanding of the material in this chapter should enable the student to

1. Explain the need for and sources of disability income protection.
2. Briefly describe how sick-leave plans work.
3. Describe the characteristics of insured group disability income plans.
4. Explain the income tax treatment of employer-provided disability income benefits.
5. Describe the characteristics of individual disability income policies.
6. Describe the business uses of disability income insurance.

In terms of its financial effect on the family, the long-term disability of a breadwinner is more severe than death. In both cases, income ceases. In the case of long-term disability, family expenses—instead of decreasing because the family has one less member—may actually increase due to the cost of providing care for the disabled person. Financial planners need to understand the disability risk and the methods for managing this risk.

The purpose of disability income insurance is to partially (and sometimes totally) replace the income of persons who are unable to work because of sickness or accident. Any employee may miss a few days of work from time to time; however, there is a tendency to underestimate both the probability and the potential severity of disabilities that last for longer periods. At all working ages, the probability of becoming disabled for at least 90 consecutive days is much greater than the chance of dying. About half of all employees will have a disability that lasts at least 90 days sometime during their working years, and one out of every ten persons can expect to be permanently disabled before reaching age 65.

SOURCES OF COVERAGE

Disability income protection can come from several sources: social insurance programs, employer-provided benefits, and individually purchased policies. These sources are discussed in this chapter. Not discussed are liability settlements—an additional source of recovery often available to individuals who become temporarily or permanently disabled as the result of an auto accident or some nonoccupational occurrence caused by the negligence of another party. The disabled person may recover damages from the negligent party or his or her insurance company as the result of a settlement or court judgment. This recovery may involve a lump-sum payment, a structured settlement, or both.

Possible Sources of Disability Income Coverage

- Workers' compensation programs
- State temporary disability laws
- Social Security
- Employer-provided sick-leave plans
- Employer-provided short-term disability income insurance plans
- Employer-provided long-term disability income insurance plans
- Individual disability income insurance policies

Social Insurance Programs

Several types of disability coverage are available under social insurance programs. For example, persons suffering injury or illness in the workplace are covered under workers' compensation programs. Although benefits may be payable for life for total disabilities and may be as high as two-thirds of predisability income, benefits are subject to maximum dollar amounts that make them inadequate for all but lower-paid workers. Benefits of limited duration are also available in a few states under temporary disability laws.

Most employed persons are potentially eligible for disability benefits under the Social Security program if they are disabled longer than 5 months. However, the Social Security definition of disability is more restrictive than that in most individual or group insurance policies. In addition, benefits are likely to be inadequate for many workers, particularly those with annual earnings over $30,000. In spite of these limitations, the Social Security program is the major source of disability income, with about 9 million disabled workers and their dependents annually collecting in excess of $100 billion in benefits.

Employer-Provided Benefits

short-term disability income plan

long-term disability income insurance

Employer-provided income protection consists of two distinct types of plans. *Short-term disability income plans* provide benefits for a limited period of time, usually 6 months or less. Benefits may be available under sick-leave plans, which are often uninsured, or underinsured short-term disability income plans. *Long-term disability income insurance* provides extended benefits (possibly for life) after an employee has been disabled for a period of time, frequently 6 months.

Employers are less likely to provide employees with disability income benefits than with life insurance or medical expense benefits. Still, it is estimated that nearly three-quarters of all full-time employees have some form of employer-provided short-term protection, either in the form of self-funded plans or insured short-term disability income insurance plans. However, only about one-third of full-time employees have any type of employer-provided long-term disability income insurance other than Social Security.

Individual Disability Income Insurance

Many individuals have a need for disability income insurance that social insurance and employer-provided benefits do not meet. However, insurance companies that offer disability income policies are very concerned about overinsurance and the accompanying moral hazard and, consequently, limit the amount of benefits relative to the individual's income. As a result, many individuals with coverage through their employers or other sources are ineligible for additional disability income protection.

Individual coverage is often not available to persons with an income below a specified amount, such as $18,000 or $25,000. Anyone who earns more than $25,000 or $30,000 per year from gainful employment and is not already covered by private individual disability income insurance has a significant need for disability income protection. This includes the self-employed, business owners and partners, individual workers, and anyone who would have inadequate financial resources if he or she were to become disabled and unable to continue working for compensation.

Disability income insurance is not available for every occupation from every insurance company. Therefore, it is important for persons in many occupations and their financial planners to be aware of variations in the marketplace. For example, some companies do not insure persons in certain hazardous or unstable occupations for disability income; other insurers offer a special disability policy for these occupations; still other insurers offer their regular policy at higher-than-standard premium rates.

Furthermore, many corporate events can alter employer-provided disability income protection and therefore increase the need for individual protection. First, corporate mergers or acquisitions may result in a change in management and management philosophy, which may result in the termination of previously provided benefits. Second, bankruptcy or severe financial problems may prompt management to cut back on such employee benefits as disability income insurance. Third, the insurance company that provides disability income protection through the employer could terminate the policy; if the employer is unable to find another insurance company willing to write the coverage, disability protection ceases. Even if coverage could be obtained from another insurer, management may decide not to seek replacement coverage.

Because most employers do not provide long-term disability income insurance, it is quite possible that an employee who leaves a job in which he or she had disability income protection may not be provided with that protection by a new employer. Such job changes create a definite need for individual disability income protection. One advantage of relying on individual protection rather than on employer-provided group protection is that the individual is not subject to termination of coverage at the whim of the employer's decision makers. Also, individual coverage is portable and can go with the insured to new geographic locations and down new career paths.

Disability income coverages are also important for partnerships and closely held corporations. Such coverages can provide the financial means for healthy partners or stockholders to purchase the ownership interest of the disabled partner or stockholder. Business enterprises can also use disability income to pay business overhead and to replace lost income or revenue that results from a key person's disability.

SICK-LEAVE PLANS

sick-leave plan

Employers provide short-term disability benefits to employees through two approaches: sick-leave plans and short-term disability income insurance plans. *Sick-leave plans* (often called salary continuation plans) are usually uninsured and generally fully replace lost income for a limited period of time, starting on the first day of disability. In contrast, short-term disability income insurance plans usually provide benefits that replace only a portion of an employee's lost income and often contain a waiting period before benefits start, particularly for sickness.

paid time off (PTO) program

In recent years, a few employers have combined their sick-leave plans with other types of payments for time not worked, such as vacations, holidays, and personal leave into a single *paid time off (PTO) program*. One rationale for such programs is that many employees view sick days as a right and will take the maximum number of days available, whether sick or not. With a paid time off program, an employee is given a specified bank of days off with full pay and can take this paid time off for any reason. The bank of days is usually slightly less than the total number of days under the prior programs, but within the range of the number of days that most employees took off.

PTO programs have generally had the effect of lowering the number of days that employees call in sick, because these days can be used for other purposes. This lowers an employer's benefit costs and minimizes other problems associated with unscheduled absences.

However, there may be a negative side of a PTO program for the employer. Some employees who should stay home may come to work when they are sick. Their productivity may be impaired, and the may sicken other employees by spreading germs.

Eligibility

Almost all sick-leave plans are limited to permanent full-time employees. Most plans also require an employee to satisfy a short probationary period (commonly 1 to 3 months) before being eligible for benefits. Sick-leave plans may also be limited to certain classes of employees such as top management or nonunion employees.

Benefits

Most sick-leave plans are designed to initially provide benefits equal to 100 percent of an employee's regular pay. Most plans, however, provide a reduced level of benefits after an initial period of full pay.

Several approaches are used to determine the duration of benefits. The most traditional approach credits eligible employees with a certain amount of sick leave, such as 10 days each year. Most plans with this approach allow employees to accumulate unused sick leave up to a maximum amount, which rarely exceeds 6 months (sometimes specified as 180 days or 26 weeks).

Another approach bases the duration of benefits on an employee's length of service. For example, an employee with less than 3 months of service may get no sick days. After this limited period, the employee may get 5 days during the next year, with the number of days increasing to 30 with 10 years of service.

An alternative to this approach provides benefits for a uniform length of time (such as 26 weeks) to all employees, except possibly those with short periods of service. However, benefits are reduced to less than full pay after some period of time that is related to an employee's length of service. For example, an employee with 2 years of service might get 4 weeks of sick leave at full pay and 22 additional weeks at half pay. After each additional year of service, the number of weeks at full pay increases by 4, until all 26 weeks would be available at full pay after 6 years of service.

Most sick-leave plans are coordinated with social insurance programs. For example, if an employee is entitled to 100 percent of pay and receives 60 percent of pay as a workers' compensation benefit, the sick-leave plan pays the remaining 40 percent.

INSURED GROUP DISABILITY INCOME PLANS

Insured group disability income plans consist of two distinct products: short-term coverage and long-term coverage. In many respects, the contractual provisions of both short-term and long-term disability income contracts are the same or very similar. In other respects—notably, the eligibility requirements, the definition of disability, and the amount and duration of benefits—they differ significantly.

Eligibility

Many of the eligibility requirements in group disability income insurance plans are similar to those in other types of group insurance contracts. In addition to being in a covered classification, an employee must usually work full-time and be actively at work before coverage commences. Any requirements concerning probationary periods, insurability, and premium contributions must also be satisfied.

Disability income insurance plans frequently differ in both the classes of employees who are eligible for coverage and the length of the probationary period. Employers are more likely to provide short-term benefits to a wider range of employees, and it is not unusual for short-term plans to cover all full-time employees.

Long-term disability plans often limit benefits to salaried employees, because claims experience has traditionally been less favorable for hourly paid employees. Some long-term plans also exclude employees below a certain salary level, because this category of employees, like hourly paid employees, is considered to have a reasonable level of benefits under Social Security.

Common Eligibility Requirements for Group Disability Income Insurance

- Be a member of a covered class of employees.
- Work full-time.
- Be actively at work.
- Satisfy any probationary period.
- Show any required evidence of insurability.
- Authorize withholding of any required employee contributions.

Long-term disability income plans tend to have longer probationary periods than short-term disability income plans. While the majority of short-term disability plans either have no probationary period or have a probationary period of 3 months or less, it is common for long-term disability plans to have probationary periods ranging from 3 months to 1 year. Whereas short-term plans require only that an employee be actively at work on the date he or she is otherwise eligible for coverage, long-term plans sometimes require that the employee be on the job for an extended period (such as 30 days) without illness or injury before coverage becomes effective.

Definition of Disability

Benefits are paid under disability income insurance contracts only if the employee meets the disability definition as specified in the contract. Virtually all short-term disability income insurance contracts define disability as *the total inability of the employee to perform each and every duty of his or her regular occupation.* A small minority of contracts use a more restrictive definition, requiring that an employee be unable to engage in any occupation for compensation. Partial disabilities are usually not covered, but a few newer plans do provide such benefits. In addition, the majority of short-term contracts limit coverage to nonoccupational disabilities because employees have workers' compensation benefits for occupational disabilities.

own-occupation definition of disability

dual (or split) definition of disability

A few long-term disability income contracts use the same liberal definition of disability that is commonly used in short-term contracts, but the term *material duties* often replaces the term *each and every duty.* This is referred to as an *own-occupation definition of disability.* The majority of long-term disability contracts use a *dual (or split) definition of disability* under which benefits are paid for some period of time (usually 24 or 36 months) as long as an employee is unable to perform his or her regular occupation. After that time, benefits are paid only if the employee is unable to engage in any occupation for which he or she is qualified by reason of training, education, or experience. The purpose of using a dual definition of disability rather than an own-occupation definition of disability is to require and encourage a disabled employee after a period of time to adjust his or her lifestyle and earn a livelihood in another occupation.

A more recent definition of disability in some long-term contracts contains both an occupation test and an earnings test. Under the occupation test, a person is totally disabled if he or she meets the definition of disability as described in the previous paragraph. However, if a person does not satisfy the occupation test, he or she is still considered disabled as long as the person satisfies an earnings test—that is, his or her income has dropped by a stated percentage, such as 20 percent, because of injury or sickness. This newer definition makes a group insurance contract similar to an individual disability income policy that provides residual benefits.

The definition of disability in long-term contracts may differ from that in short-term contracts in several other respects. Long-term contracts are somewhat more likely to provide benefits for partial disabilities. However, the amount and duration of such benefits may be limited when compared with those for total disabilities, and the receipt of benefits is usually contingent on a previous period of total disability. In addition, most long-term contracts provide coverage for both occupational and nonoccupational disabilities. Finally, short-term contracts usually have the same definition of disability for all classes of employees. Some long-term contracts use different definitions for different classes of employees—one definition for most employees and a more liberal definition for executives or salaried employees.

Exclusions

Under certain circumstances, disability income benefits are not paid even if an employee satisfies the definition of disability. Common exclusions under both short-term and long-term disability income contracts specify that no benefits will be paid

- for any period during which the employee is not under the care of a physician
- for any disability caused by an intentionally self-inflicted injury
- unless the period of disability commenced while the employee was covered under the contract
- if (or to the extent that) benefits are payable under workers' compensation or similar laws

It was once common for disabilities resulting from pregnancy to be excluded. Such an exclusion is now illegal under federal law if an employer has 15 or more employees. Employers with fewer than 15 employees may still exclude pregnancy disabilities unless they are subject to state laws to the contrary.

Additional exclusions are often found in long-term contracts. These commonly deny benefits for disabilities resulting from

- war, whether declared or undeclared
- participation in an assault or felony. Some insurers have recently expanded this exclusion to include the commission of any crime.
- mental illness, alcoholism, or drug addiction. However, most contracts provide benefits for an employee who is confined in a hospital or institution that specializes in the care and treatment of such disorders; other contracts provide employees with benefits but limit their duration (such as for 24 months per disability).
- preexisting conditions

The exclusion for preexisting conditions is designed to counter the adverse selection and potentially large claims that could occur if an employer established a group disability income plan or if an employee elected to participate in a plan because of some known condition that is likely to result in disability. Although variations exist, a preexisting-conditions provision commonly excludes coverage for any disability that commences during the first 12 months an employee is covered under the contract if the employee received treatment or medical advice for the disabling condition both (1) prior to the date the employee became eligible for coverage and (2) within 90 consecutive days prior to the commencement of the disability.

When coverage is transferred from one insurance company to another, it is not unusual, particularly in the case of large employers, for the new insurance company to waive the limitation for preexisting conditions for employees who were insured under the previous contract.

Benefits

Group disability income contracts contain benefit schedules that classify employees and specify the amount of disability income to be provided. They also include provisions pertaining to the length of time that benefits are paid and the coordination of benefits with other available sources of disability income.

Benefit Schedules

There are a variety of benefit schedules in group disability income contracts. Benefits may be available to all employees or limited to specific groups of employees. In addition, benefits may be expressed as either flat-dollar amounts, varying dollar amounts by classification, or a percentage of earnings.

Giving a disabled employee a level of income that is comparable to his or her regular earnings encourages absenteeism and diminishes the incentive to return to work. In general, disability income plans are designed to provide a level of benefits that replaces between 50 and 70 percent of an employee's gross income. Although this may appear to represent a substantial reduction of regular earnings, remember that a disabled employee does not have the usual expenses associated with working, such as transportation costs. In addition, disability income benefits financed with after-tax employee contributions are not subject to Social Security and Medicare taxes, and employer-financed benefits are subject to Social Security and Medicare taxes only during the last calendar month in which an employee worked and during the 6 months that follow.

Reasons for Limited Benefits
• Return to work is encouraged. • Work-related expenses are reduced. • Benefits may not be subject to Social Security taxation.

Many short-term disability income plans and the majority of long-term plans base benefits on a single percentage of regular earnings (excluding bonuses, commissions, overtime, and incentive-based income). This percentage varies widely for short-term plans, and benefits as low as 50 percent or as high as 100 percent are not unusual. Many insurers are reluctant to underwrite plans that provide benefits higher than 70 percent of earnings. In some instances, short-term plans may use different percentages, such as 100 percent of earnings for 4 weeks and 70 percent of earnings for the remaining benefit period. The length of time for which the higher level of benefits is provided may also be a function of the length of an employee's service.

Long-term plans typically provide benefits that range from 50 to 70 percent of earnings; 60 and 66 2/3 are the most prevalent percentages. Some plans also use a sliding scale, such as 66 2/3 percent of the first $5,000 of monthly earnings and 50 percent of earnings in excess of $5,000.

Plans that determine benefits as a percentage of earnings also commonly place a maximum dollar amount on the benefit that will be provided, regardless of earnings. For example, a long-term plan might be subject to a monthly maximum that varies from $1,000 for some small groups to $6,000 to $10,000 (and sometimes higher) for groups with a large number of well-paid executives. The purpose of the maximum is to prevent the absolute benefit from being so high that an employee, by adjusting his or her lifestyle, could live comfortably on the disability income benefit and thus have no financial incentive to return to work.

Period of Benefits

To determine the period for which benefits are paid, it is necessary to determine when benefits begin and how long they are paid. In both respects, there are differences between short-term and long-term plans.

waiting
(elimination)
period

Short-Term Plans. Short-term disability income contracts commonly contain a *waiting period* (often referred to in such contracts as an elimination period). The waiting period is the length of time for which an employee must be disabled before benefits begin. The typical short-term contract has no waiting period for disabilities resulting from accidents, but a waiting period of 1 to 7 days is used for disabilities resulting from sicknesses. Some plans have a single waiting period that applies to disabilities from either accidents or sicknesses; a few plans have no waiting periods for either. Waiting periods longer than 7 days are occasionally used, particularly when there is a sick-leave plan to provide benefits during the initial portion of a disability. In a few cases, benefits are paid retroactively to the date of disability if the disability lasts for a predetermined period of time, but it is generally felt that retroactive benefits cause employees to prolong their return to work in order to receive benefits for the full period of their disability.

Once an employee begins to receive benefit payments under a short-term disability contract, the benefits continue until the end of the benefit period the contract specifies, if the employee remains disabled for that long. Although short-term contracts may provide benefits up to 2 years (with long-term contracts providing benefits for periods over 2 years), benefits rarely continue for more than 1 year. In fact, the majority of short-term contracts stipulate that benefits are paid for either 13 or 26 weeks; the latter period is more prevalent.

In a few cases, the maximum period of benefits applies to a specified duration of time (such as any consecutive 12 months), regardless of the number of separate disabilities. In most plans, both the maximum benefit period and the elimination period apply to each separate disability. Successive periods of disability caused by the same accident or the same or related sickness are generally considered to be a single disability, unless they are separated by a period of continuous resumption of active employment.

Long-Term Plans. Long-term disability income plans have waiting periods of 3 to 6 months; 6 months is more common. The length of the waiting period often corresponds to the length of time benefits are paid under a firm's short-term disability income plan or salary continuation plan. Unlike short-term plans, the waiting periods for sicknesses and accidents are the same.

Typical Benefit Periods
• Short-term plans—13 weeks or 26 weeks subject to a 1- to 7-day waiting period for sickness • Long-term plans—2 years to life, subject to a 3-month or 6-month waiting period

Long-term disability income benefits may be paid for as short a period as 2 years or as long as the lifetime of the disabled employee. At one time, it was common for long-term disability income benefits to stop at age 65, but this is no longer permissible under the Age Discrimination in Employment Act. Several different approaches are now used for older employees. In a few cases, benefits are paid until age 70 for any disability that occurred before that age. For disabilities occurring at age 70 or later, benefits are paid for a reduced duration. A more common approach is to use a graded benefit period and give benefits to age 65 for employees who are disabled before a specified age. Employees disabled after the specified age receive benefits for a limited duration, as shown in the following table.

Table 14-1 Duration of Disability Income Benefits	
Age at Commencement of Disability	**Benefit Duration**
59 and younger	To age 65
60–64	5 years
65–69	To age 70
70–74	1 year
75 and older	6 months

As in short-term disability income plans, provisions are made in long-term plans for successive disabilities. The majority of contracts stipulate that successive periods of disability that are separated by less than some period (usually varying from 3 to 6 months) of continuous, active full-time employment are considered a single disability unless the subsequent disability (1) arises from an unrelated cause and (2) begins after the employee has returned to work.

Coordination with Other Benefits

To minimize the possibility of an employee's receiving total benefits higher than his or her predisability earnings, disability income plans commonly stipulate that benefits are coordinated (often referred to as integration) with other sources of disability income. In general, the insurance laws or regulations of most states allow reductions to be made as a result of benefits from social insurance programs and group insurance or retirement plans the employer provides, but not as a result of benefits from individual disability income contracts unless they were purchased by the employer.

Benefits under short-term plans are generally coordinated with (1) workers' compensation benefits, if the plan covers occupational disabilities, (2) temporary disability laws, if they are applicable, and (3) Social Security benefits, if the maximum benefit period is longer than 5 months.

Long-term disability income benefits are usually coordinated with benefits provided under the following:

- Social Security
- workers' compensation laws
- temporary disability laws
- other insurance plans for which the employer makes a contribution or payroll deduction
- pension plans for which the employer has made a contribution or payroll deduction to the extent that the employee elects to receive retirement benefits because of disability
- sick-leave plans
- earnings from employment, either with the employer or from other sources

It is possible for the coordination with other benefits to totally eliminate a long-term disability benefit. To prevent this from happening, many plans provide (and some states require) payment of a minimum benefit, such as $50 or $100 per month. Most plans also contain a provision freezing the amount of any Social Security reduction at the initial level that was established when the claim began.

As a general rule, both the insured and the insurer profit if the insured is able to collect Social Security benefits for a disability; the insured has an increased overall benefit, and the insurer has a substantially lower claim to pay. Consequently, insurers are often willing to provide assistance to claimants by helping them file Social Security claims and appeal decisions to deny claims.

Supplemental Benefits

buy-up plan

It is becoming increasingly common to find group long-term disability income plans that provide employees with a base of employer-paid benefits and that allow each covered employee to purchase additional coverage at his or her own expense under a *buy-up (or supplemental) plan*. For example, a plan may provide basic benefits of 50 percent of earnings and an option for an employee to increase this amount to 55, 66⅔, or 70 percent of earnings. These buy-up plans are becoming more popular, because employers feel the need to control the costs of benefits by shifting a greater burden of the cost to employees.

carve-out (benefit plan)

Some plans are also designed as *carve-out* plans to provide benefits for certain employees, typically key executives. For example, an employer might design one plan to cover most of its employees, but it might cover top executives with another group plan that provides enhanced benefits in the form of a larger percentage of earnings and a more liberal definition of disability. Another variation of a carve-out plan would provide executives with a lower benefit percentage than other employees would receive, but it could include supplemental benefits in the form of individual disability income policies. In addition to more favorable policy provisions, a carve-out plan might offer better rate guarantees and an overall higher benefit than a group plan could offer. Furthermore, the portability of the individual policy might be attractive to executives but might not necessarily appeal to the employer.

Catastrophic Benefits Rider

A few disability insurers that also sell long-term care insurance have recently started to offer a catastrophic benefit rider. These make additional benefits available if the insured suffers a severe disability that includes cognitive impairment or the inability to perform two or more of six activities of daily living (ADLs). These are the same criteria that trigger benefits in long-term care policies.

The employer can typically purchase benefits that range from an additional 10 to 40 percent of earnings, as long as total-disability benefits do not exceed a specified limit that may be as high as 100 percent of earnings. The employer also selects the length of time the catastrophic benefits are paid, which can vary from 1 year to the duration of the regular disability benefits the policy provides. (Note that at least one insurer offers a 10 percent benefit for 1 year as part of its standard disability income policies, with the employer having the option to select larger benefits or a longer benefit duration.) In addition, an employer may have the option to add a flat monthly benefit payable if an employee's spouse suffers a cognitive impairment or is unable to perform two or more ADLs.

Other Contract Provisions

Many provisions in group disability income contracts are similar to those in other types of insurance contracts. These provisions pertain to incontestability, a grace period, the entire contract, and the payment of premiums. The provisions discussed here either are unique to group disability income benefit contracts or differ in certain respects from similar provisions in other types of group insurance contracts.

Claims

The provisions concerning claims under both short-term and long-term disability income contracts are essentially the same. The insurance company must be notified within a relatively short time period—20 or 30 days or as soon as is reasonably possible—after the disability for which benefits are being claimed begins. A formal proof of loss must then be filed with the insurance company, usually within 90 days after the commencement of the disability or after the end of the week, month, or other time period for which benefits are payable. The proof of loss normally consists of a statement by the employee concerning the disability, a statement by the attending physician, and a statement by the employer that indicates the date and reason that active employment ceased. Provisions also require periodic reports from the attending physician or permit the insurance company to request these reports at reasonable intervals. The insurance company also has the right to have the employee examined by a physician of its own choice (and at its own expense) at reasonable time periods during the duration of the claim.

Rehabilitation

As an incentive to encourage disabled employees to return to active employment as soon as possible, but perhaps at a lower-paying job, most insurance companies include a provision for rehabilitation benefits in their long-term disability income contracts. This provision permits the employee to enter a trial work period of 1 or 2 years in rehabilitative employment. During this time, disability benefits continue but are reduced by some percentage (varying from 50 to 80 percent) of the earnings from rehabilitative employment. If the trial work period indicates that the employee is unable to perform the rehabilitative employment, the original long-term benefit is continued and the employee is not required to satisfy a new waiting period.

Although there are seldom other provisions in long-term disability income contracts that require the insurance company to aid in the rehabilitation of disabled employees, it has become increasingly common for insurance companies to provide benefits for rehabilitation when it is felt that the cost of these benefits will be offset by shortening an employee's disability period. These benefits may be in the form of physical therapy, job training, or adaptive aids to enable a disabled person to perform job functions.

In the past, the decision to seek rehabilitation was left to the disabled person. Some insurers now require the person to undertake rehabilitation or have benefits reduced or stopped.

The rehabilitation of disabled persons is continuing to grow in importance among companies. More and more companies are taking a proactive role in managing disability claims by employing more skilled professionals and by intervening earlier in the claims process. Because early intervention is undoubtedly a key factor in getting disabled employees back to work sooner, many benefit consultants think it advantageous for an employer to use the same insurance company for its short-term and long-term disability income plans. This approach enables the insurer's rehabilitation staff to become involved when a claim is filed under the short-term plan rather than waiting until the waiting period for long-term benefits has been met.

Termination

For the most part, the provisions in disability income contracts concerning the termination of either the master contract or an employee's coverage are the same as those in other types of group insurance. There is one notable exception: A conversion privilege is rarely included.

Additional Benefits

Several types of additional benefits are occasionally found in long-term disability income contracts. The most common are a cost-of-living adjustment (COLA), a pension supplement, and a survivors' benefit.

Some disability income plans have COLAs to prevent inflation from eroding the purchasing power of disability income benefits being received. Under the typical COLA formula, benefits increase annually during the period of disability, along with changes in the consumer price index.

Many firms make provisions in their pension plan for treating disabled employees as if they were still working and accruing pension benefits. Such a provision requires that contributions on behalf of disabled employees be made to the pension plan, usually from the employer's current revenues. However, some disability income contracts stipulate that the contributions necessary to fund a disabled employee's accruing pension benefits be paid by the disability income contract.

Additional Benefits Sometimes Provided
• Cost-of-living adjustments
• Continued growth of pension benefits
• Income benefit to survivors
• Payments for child care
• Benefits for disability of employee's spouse
• Payment of medical expense insurance premiums

Note also that some pension plans provide disability income benefits by allowing disabled employees to begin receiving retirement benefits when they are totally and permanently disabled. It is common to limit these early retirement benefits to employees who have satisfied some minimum period of service or reached some minimum age. However, employee benefit consultants generally seem to feel that separate retirement and disability income plans are preferable.

Some long-term contracts provide a benefit to survivors in the form of continued payments after the death of a disabled employee. In effect, the disability income payments are continued, possibly at a reduced amount, for periods ranging up to 24 months; 3 to 6 months is more common. Payments are generally made only to eligible survivors, who typically are the spouse and unmarried children under age 21.

Other types of additional benefits are even less common. Examples include child-care payments for disabled employees who can work on a part-time basis, spousal disability benefits payable to the employee, and benefits to pay premiums for medical expense coverage.

FEDERAL INCOME TAX TREATMENT OF EMPLOYER-PROVIDED BENEFITS

Deductibility of Contributions

Employer contributions for an employee's disability income insurance are fully deductible to the employer as an ordinary and necessary business expense. Contributions by an individual employee are considered payments for personal disability income insurance and are not tax deductible.

Federal Income Tax Liability of Employees

Employer contributions for disability income insurance result in no taxable income to an employee. Receipt of benefits under an insured plan or sick-leave plan may or may not result in the receipt of taxable income. To make this determination, it is necessary to look at whether the plan is fully contributory, noncontributory, or partially contributory.

Fully Contributory Plan

Under a fully contributory plan, the entire cost of an employee's coverage is paid by after-tax employee contributions, and benefits are received free of income taxation.

Noncontributory Plan

Under the usual noncontributory plan, the employer pays the entire cost, and benefits are included in an employee's gross income. Some persons who are permanently and totally disabled may be eligible for a tax credit, but this credit is relatively modest. For example, the maximum credit for a married person filing jointly is $1,125, and this figure is reduced if adjusted gross income (including the disability benefit) exceeds $10,000. For purposes of this tax credit, the IRS uses the stringent Social Security definition of disability.

A 2004 IRS Revenue Ruling allows an employer to design a disability income plan so that an employee can receive tax-free benefits from a noncontributory plan. In order to receive these benefits, however, the employee must elect to have the employer-paid premium for his or her coverage reported as taxable income. Such an election, which applies separately to each employee covered under a plan, must be made prior to the beginning of a plan year and is irrevocable during that period. The election must also apply to the full cost of the employer-provided coverage. Few plans have incorporated such an election. It creates administrative burdens for the employer, and most employees prefer to minimize their income-tax burden on a current basis. If this option is available, an employee should discuss its implications with a tax advisor before making such an election.

Partially Contributory Plan

Under a partially contributory plan, benefits attributable to employee contributions are received free of income taxation. Benefits attributable to employer contributions are includible in gross income, but employees may be eligible for the tax credit described previously.

The portion of the benefits attributable to employer contributions (and thus subject to income taxation) is based on the ratio of the employer's contributions to the total employer-employee contributions for an employee who has been under the plan for some period of time. For example, if the employer paid 75 percent of the cost of the plan, 75 percent of the benefits would be considered attributable to employer contributions and 25 percent to employee contributions.

EXAMPLE

Harry is covered under a long-term disability income insurance plan of his employer. Harry and the employer pay 25 percent and 75 percent of the premium cost, respectively. The income tax treatment is as follows:

- The employer's contributions are deductible as a normal business expense and are not taxable as income to Harry.

- Harry's contributions are not tax deductible.

- Twenty-five percent of any disability income benefit payments are tax free to Harry; 75 percent of such payments are taxable as income, but Harry may be eligible for a tax credit if his adjusted gross income is low enough.

INDIVIDUAL DISABILITY INCOME INSURANCE POLICIES

Individual disability income coverages and related disability policies vary widely. This makes disability income planning a challenge for financial services professionals. Many variations involve such factors as the disability definition itself, how recurring disability is handled, the duration of benefits, the waiting period, waiver-of-premium protection, and COLAs.

Definition of Disability

Disability can mean different things to different people and is not defined the same way in every disability income policy. However, an insured will receive benefits only if he or she satisfies the precise definition that is contained in a disability income policy. There are definitions for total disability as well as less-than-total disability

Total Disability

Early disability income contracts focused solely on the concept of total disability. The insured was either disabled totally or not disabled at all. All contracts still cover total disability, but as explained later they may also provide benefits when a disability is not total. Definitions of total disability fall into two broad categories: any occupation and own occupation. However, there are variations in each of these categories.

Any Occupation. The narrowest and most strict definition of total disability is the inability to perform the duties of any occupation because of injury or sickness. Fortunately, private disability income policies no longer use such a definition.

any-occupation definition of disability

In an effort to match coverage more closely with an individual's needs, a more liberal definition was developed. This definition is commonly referred to as an *any-occupation or any-occ definition of disability*. With an any-occupation definition of disability, total disability is defined as a condition that prevents a person from performing the duties of any occupation for which that person is reasonably suited by education, training, and experience.

EXAMPLE

Charlie, a successful traveling salesman, was severely injured in an automobile accident and began receiving disability income benefits. After several months of recovery and rehabilitation, he was able to return to an office job in the marketing department of one of the firms whose products he formerly sold. Even though his salary is less than what he earned as a traveling salesman, Charlie will no longer be considered disabled because he is suited for the job by his education (a degree in marketing), training, and experience.

Own Occupation. Some insurers issue policies with an own-occupation definition of disability as was defined for group disability income policies.

With such a definition, an insured is considered totally disabled if he or she is unable to perform the substantial and material duties of his or her regular occupation at the time of disability. Even if the person returns to work in another occupation, the insurer will still pay the full disability income benefits as long as the insured can no longer perform the duties of the former regular occupation.

EXAMPLE
Fiona was a successful architect who was severely disabled by a neurological disorder. She is no longer able to draw the plans and blueprints required of her former occupation. However, she has been able to secure a job as lecturer at a local university. With an own-occupation definition of disability, she will also be able to collect her full disability income benefits.

The own-occupation definition of disability as previously described was once more commonly available than it is currently. Today, insurers are more likely to use variations that are more restrictive.

**modified
own-occupation**

One variation is to terminate benefits at any time that the insured returns to work in any gainful employment position for which he or she is suited by education, training or experience. However, partial or residual disability income benefits may become payable at this time. This variation is sometimes referred to as a *modified own-occupation* definition of disability.

Another variation is to use a dual definition of disability as is common in group insurance. An own-occupation definition is used for a limited period of time that might range from 2 to 5 years. After that time, an any-occupation definition is used.

What Insurers Use. Many insurers will use several of the definitions of total disability previously described. In their most preferred occupational classes, they may be willing to issue a policy with an own-occupation or modified own-occupation definition of disability as long as certain underwriting criteria are met. For other occupational classes, they may use a dual definition of disability. For the least preferred occupational classes, they will use an any-occupation definition.

Less-Than-Total Disability

As disability income contracts evolved and became more competitive, there were complaints that the definition of disability did not take into account disabilities that were not totally disabling, but resulted in lost income because the insured was unable to perform some of the duties of his or her regular occupation. As a result, insurers developed several approaches to pay benefits when the insured is less than totally disabled. These approaches, which are usually in the form of a rider to a basic disability income policy for total disability, include

- partial disability benefits
- residual disability benefits

The availability of benefits for less-than-total disability is often an incentive for an insured to return to work.

partial disability ***Partial Disability Benefits.*** The earliest form of coverage for less-than-total disability was benefits for *partial disability*. This is defined as the inability to do some of the specific duties relating to a job. Its purpose is to pay limited benefits to an insured who is attempting to return to work after a minimum specified period of total disability. Typically, the benefit is equal to 50 percent of the basic total disability benefit and is only paid for a limited period, such as 3, 6, or 12 months. The benefit is a fixed amount and has no relationship to the income earned upon return to employment. In fact, the insured may return to a job that pays the same wages as prior to disability.

EXAMPLE
Rose is a consultant and used to travel frequently for her job. She was totally disabled for several months and received a monthly indemnity of $4,000 from her disability income policy. After recovering from the total disability, she was able to return to work, but unable to travel. Her former employer gave her a job that utilized her skills, but it paid less than her previous position. Rose is eligible for a partial disability payment if such a benefit is in her policy. Even if the new position had the same salary as her old position, she would also be eligible for the partial disability benefits because she could not fully perform her old job.

---

residual disability ***Residual Disability Benefits.*** Partial disability benefits are not as common as they once were and have largely been replaced by residual disability benefits. A *residual disability* is defined as a disability that results in the insured's inability to perform some of the duties of his or her own occupation, resulting in a loss of income. It is typically coupled with an own-occupation definition of total disability.

Residual benefits focus on the loss of income rather than on the physical limitations of the disability. The benefits can be paid if the insured returns to either full-time or part-time employment. Residual benefits continue until the end of the benefit period specified in the policy as long the insured continues to meet the definition of disability.

EXAMPLE

Herb is an attorney who previously earned $240,000 per year, or $20,000 per month. For several months, he was totally disabled because of a serious heart attack. Eventually, he was able to return to work on a part-time basis, at an annual salary of $150,000, or $12,500 per month. Herb suffered a residual loss of income of $90,000 on an annual basis, or $7,500 on a monthly basis.

The actual mechanics of understanding residual disability benefits are somewhat more complicated than this example indicates. First, there may be a qualification period before an individual is eligible for residual disability benefits. This is the period that the insured must be totally disabled before qualifying for such benefits. Common periods are 30, 60, and 90 days.

Second, the insurer starts the benefit calculation by comparing income before and after the disability to determine the percentage loss of income. This percentage is then multiplied by the benefit for total disability to determine the residual disability benefit.

EXAMPLE

Let's return to the example of Herb. Assume that his monthly disability income benefit for total disability is $12,000. His $7,500 monthly loss of income is 37.5 percent of his pre-disability income of $20,000. Therefore, his residual disability benefit will be 37.5 percent of his $12,000 total disability benefit, or $4,500.

Third, residual benefits often cease (or are not paid initially) if the income loss is below a certain percentage (usually 20 percent) of pre-disability earnings. Conversely, policies are likely to continue paying the total disability income benefit if earnings fall significantly. This figure used for this calculation is usually 75 or 80 percent. In addition, there may be a minimum residual disability benefit, such as 50 percent of the total disability benefit, during the first few months that residual disability benefits are paid. This period is commonly 6 months, after which benefits are based on the actual reduction in income.

EXAMPLE

Let's return again to Herb and assume that his insurer uses the percentages previously mentioned. Let's further assume that Herb returns to work and finds that he is able to work almost full time and his salary increases to $16,000 per month. The decrease in his income is now $4,000 per month, or 20 percent of his pre-disability income. Therefore, his insurer would stop his disability income benefits. On the other hand, assume he is only able to work one day per week at a monthly income of $4,000. This represents a drop in income of 80 percent, and the insurer would continue to pay the total disability income benefit of $12,000 per month.

Fourth, it is important to look at how pre-disability earnings are calculated. There are several possible variations. For example, an insurer may calculate an average monthly income based on the last 3 years of earnings. Another insurer might use only the prior 6 or 12 months, or the highest 12 months in the prior 3 years. For insureds whose incomes fluctuate, the calculation used can make a significant difference in the benefit received. Some insurers also index prior earnings for inflation, often based on the consumer price index. Without such indexing, the residual disability benefit will decrease as the insured receives future pay increases during disability.

Finally, there are variations in what types of work result in the receipt of residual benefits. Under some definitions of residual disability, loss of income is measured as the difference between pre-disability income and post-disability income from the same occupation. If the insured takes a job in another occupation, the full total disability benefits are still paid as long as the insured cannot perform all the duties of his or own occupation. This can sometimes result in an insured having a larger income than prior to disability. Several insurers now issue what is called a loss-of-earnings policy. With this approach, loss of income is measured as the difference between pre-disability income and post-disability income from any occupation. In this case, total disability benefits are not paid if the insured returns to work. However, the insured is then eligible for residual disability benefits.

Presumptive Disability

presumptive-disability provision

Many disability income policies include provisions setting forth specific losses that qualify for permanent total-disability status. They are referred to as *presumptive-disability provisions,* because the individual is presumed to be totally disabled even if he or she is able to return to work or gain employment in a new occupation.

A presumptive-disability provision generally includes loss of sight, loss of speech, loss of hearing, or the total loss of use of or the severance of both hands, both feet, or one hand and one foot. As with other disability coverages, the presumptive-disability benefits cease if the insured individual recovers to an extent that he or she no longer qualifies for the presumptive disability. For example, an individual may lose the use of both hands because of paralysis from a stroke or other causes. If the individual gradually recovers use of one or both hands, he or she no longer qualifies for presumptive-disability benefits.

Recurring Disability

Most disability policies have provisions setting forth a specified period of recovery (usually measured by return to work) that automatically separates one disability from another. This period is typically either 6 or 12 months.

EXAMPLE

Suppose Jen became disabled as a result of an auto accident and was totally disabled for 6 months. She then returned to work for 8 months before having a relapse and becoming totally disabled again from causes associated with the auto accident. The new disability is treated as a separate disability because Jen's recovery and return to work exceeded 6 months, which is the specified period separating recurring disabilities in her policy. If Jen's return to work lasted fewer than 6 months, her second period of disability would be treated as a continuation of the initial disability, and no new waiting period would apply.

For disability policies with a limited benefit period, it can be advantageous to have each relapse classified as a new disability— which then starts with a new benefit period—rather than a recurring disability.

Ability to Keep the Coverage in Force

Virtually all disability income policies are guaranteed renewable until the earlier of the end of the benefit period selected or a stated age, such as 65 or 67. All the insured has to do to keep the policy in force is pay the required periodic premium.

After the insured reaches age 65 or 67, the insurer may allow further renewability on a conditionally renewable basis. Generally, the insurer allows the insured to renew the policy on an annual basis without evidence of insurability as long as the insured is gainfully employed for at least 30 hours per week. The right to renew ends on the first policy anniversary on which the insured is not so employed. Benefits are often provided only for total disability. The premium for each year of such a renewal is based on the insured's age and the insurer's rates in use at the time of renewal.

If a policy is only guaranteed renewable, the insurer can change the premium on a class basis. This usually occurs because of adverse claims experience for a block of business. However, many policies are also noncancelable. This means that the premium, with certain exceptions, cannot change during the renewability period beyond what is specified in the policy declarations. These exceptions include additional premiums that result from increased benefit levels because of automatic benefit increases or the insured's exercising an option to purchase additional benefits.

Although noncancelable policies are common, insurers are more restrictive in who can purchase a policy with this provision than they were a few years ago. In many cases, insurers offer policy forms with the provision only to the most favorable occupation classifications.

When Benefits Start

Disability income policies generally have a waiting period before benefit payments begin. Most insurance companies give the purchaser an option to select the duration of this period. Because benefits are paid on a monthly basis at the end of the month, the first benefit payment is made as much a 30 days after the end of the waiting period. Common waiting periods are 30, 60, 90, 180, and 365 days. A few policies are available with a 0-day waiting period but only for disability due to accident. The premium increase for shorter waiting periods is significant, because benefits are payable for many short-term disabilities. For example, the annual premium for a policy with a 180-day waiting period is less than half the cost of a policy with a 30-day waiting period.

Many factors should be considered when selecting the waiting period for a disability income policy; perhaps the most important is cost. The ability of the insured to pay living costs and other expenses during the waiting period is also of importance. Another pertinent factor is whether the insured has other sources of funds available during short-term disabilities.

Insurance companies differ as to whether they require consecutive days or allow the accumulation of nonconsecutive disability days to satisfy the waiting period. Some policies explicitly spell out that nonconsecutive days will satisfy the waiting period. In other policies, the language is silent on this point, and the company's claims-handling philosophy determines the answer.

Residual-disability benefits that many policies provide have what is commonly known as a qualification period, which specifies the number of days of total disability the insured must sustain before residual-disability benefits are payable. The most generous residual-disability policies have a 0-day qualification period and therefore require no total-disability period prior to eligibility for residual- or partial-disability benefits. Under that type of contract, residual benefits could begin at the end of the waiting period to replace lost income, such as the income lost by a surgeon suffering from severe arthritis. A policy that has residual benefits with a qualifying period equal to the waiting period could also start paying residual benefits at the end of the waiting period if the individual had been totally disabled for the entire waiting period and recovered enough to return to work with a reduced income immediately after the end of the waiting period. It is quite common for the qualification period associated with residual benefits actually to exceed the waiting period, but there is not necessarily a connection between the waiting period and the qualification period.

Duration of Benefit Period

Just as disability income policies differ according to definitions of disability and length of waiting period, they also differ according to the duration of benefits that they provide once the individual becomes disabled. Possible benefit periods include one year, 2 years, 3 years, 5 years, 10 years, to age 65 or age 67, or even the insured's lifetime. However, an insurer usually makes only a few of these options available to an applicant, and the possible choices commonly vary by underwriting class. For example, one insurer allows persons in its least favorable underwriting classes a choice of 2 years or 5 years. Persons in its most favorable underwriting classes also may elect benefits until age 65. Some insurers that previously offered benefits to age 65 have changed the benefit duration to age 67. This reflects the increase in the age that a person must attain to receive full Social Security retirement benefits. There are a few insurers that specialize in writing policies only for short durations, usually 5 years or less.

The effect of the length of the benefit period on cost is significant. The premium for a policy with a 2-year benefit period may be as low as 40 to 50 percent of the premium required to extend benefits to age 65 or 67. However, policies with short benefit durations do not provide comprehensive protection against the financial consequences of long-term disabilities.

Many insurers do not offer lifetime benefits and, if they do, this option is available only to their most favorable underwriting classes. When a policy provides lifetime benefits, the insurer typically pays such benefits only if the disability commences before a specified age, such as 50, 55, or 60. Disabilities that commence after that age are often limited to benefit periods of 2 or 5 years or may terminate at a specified age, such as 65, 68, or 70. In other words, lifetime benefit payments are available only for disabilities that initially occur before a specified age and remain continuous and uninterrupted for the remainder of the insured's life.

In most cases, the same benefit period applies to all disabilities, regardless of whether they arise from injury or sickness. However, some policies do make a distinction. These policies often provide lifetime benefits if a disability results from injury but limit benefits to age 65 or 67 if the disability stems from sickness. Although a few insurers allow an applicant to select different benefit periods for injury and sickness, the benefit period for sickness cannot exceed the benefit period for injury.

Disability benefits continue for as long as the insured individual is disabled according to the contract provisions. Insurance companies often require repeated verification that the disability still satisfies the qualifications for benefit eligibility. Benefits for total disability cease when the individual has recovered enough that the disability no longer satisfies the criteria of total disability. In policies providing residual benefits, benefit payments may continue at a reduced amount when the individual has recovered enough to return to work but still sustains more than a 20 percent reduction in income.

Level of Benefits Payable

Disability income policies specify the dollar amount of monthly benefits payable during periods of total disability after the insured satisfies the waiting period. At the time of policy issuance, the stated monthly benefit amount should be in line with the insured's income and provide fairly complete protection. Over time, however, the stated benefit amount is likely to become inadequate as the insured's income increases because of both inflation and job promotions. Disability income policies are available with provisions to counteract such erosion in benefit levels. These provisions fall into two different categories. The first category consists of provisions that provide increases in the benefit payments during periods of disability when benefits are being distributed. The second consists of provisions aimed at increasing the benefit level while the coverage is in force but the insured is not disabled.

Cost-of-Living (COLA) Riders

cost-of-living-adjustment (COLA) rider Provisions dealing with increasing benefits during periods of disability are often referred to as either *cost-of-living-adjustment (COLA) riders* or provisions for inflation protection. They tend to have either a fixed-percentage increase per year or a floating-percentage increase, where the floating amount is determined by some external index, such as a consumer price index. These benefits are almost always provided as an optional rider for an additional premium over and above the premium for the base policy. Many companies with COLA riders offer purchasers a choice about the percentage increase ceilings on the rider; increases of up to 7 percent are often allowed. However, the higher the percentage, the higher the cost of the rider.

In addition to these annual increase limitations, a cost-of-living adjustment rider usually contains an aggregate limit on benefit increases, such as two times the original monthly benefit amount. For example, an insured may purchase a fixed 5 percent COLA rider to a policy originally providing $2,000 per month in benefits and may subsequently become disabled for a continuous period of 20 years. After the individual has been disabled for 1 year, the benefit amount increases to $2,100 per month, reflecting the 5 percent increase. After 2 years, the benefit increases to $2,205 if the increases are based on a compound-interest adjustment, or to $2,200 if the increases are based on a simple-interest adjustment. If the COLA rider contains an aggregate limit of twice the original benefit amount, no additional increases are allowed once the benefit amount reaches $4,000.

Increased Predisability Coverage

There are basically three approaches to keeping individual disability income benefits in step with increased income for insured individuals who are not disabled. The oldest and least attractive method is to purchase new policies to supplement the in-force policies incrementally as income increases. The drawback to this approach is that it requires evidence of insurability every time the individual obtains incremental amounts of coverage. If his or her health deteriorates, additional coverage may not be available at any price.

The second approach to adjusting disability benefit levels is through a rider that guarantees the right to purchase additional coverage at specified future intervals up to some specified maximum age, such as 45, 50, or 55. This approach is similar to the first one in that the individual must purchase additional coverage every time an adjustment is needed, but he or she can acquire the additional amounts at the specified intervals, regardless of the insured's health. However, these incremental purchases are subject to underwriting requirements regarding the individual's current income. In other words, the insurance company will not issue new coverage if the incremental addition increases aggregate disability income benefits above the underwriting guidelines for that individual's current income on the option date.

Ways to Keep Up with Inflation Before Becoming Disabled

- Purchase new policies periodically (requires evidence of insurability).
- Purchase a guaranteed insurability (guaranteed purchase) option.
- Purchase a rider that automatically increases the benefit amount periodically.

The third and most attractive way to adjust benefits upward for inflation while the insured is not disabled is to use riders that automatically increase the base benefit amount on a formula basis, such as a stated flat-percentage amount at each policy anniversary. Even this approach requires purchasing additional coverage, and the premium will be increased appropriately. As with the second approach, the additional increment of coverage is purchased at premium rates based on the insured's attained age at the time it is added to the policy. The real advantage to this approach is that the changes are automatic unless the policyowner refuses them.

Insurance companies are not required to provide any inflation adjustments, and some insurance companies that sell disability income policies choose not to make such riders available. Insurance companies that offer both options—purchasing additional coverage in the future and automatic percentage increases in benefits—limit future incremental additions and make sure that they are in line with the insured's earnings. These companies often refuse to issue the options if the insured has another policy that already contains such riders or if the base policy was issued on an extra-premium basis due to health problems.

Exclusions and Limitations

Although most disability income policies contain relatively few exclusions and limitations, there tends to be very little uniformity among policies regarding which exclusions and limitations are included.

Exclusions

Most, if not all policies exclude disabilities resulting from war. In addition, they have an exclusion relating to disabilities arising from any preexisting condition that was not disclosed or was misrepresented in the application. However, policies are not consistent in how they define a preexisting condition. For example, one insurer considers a condition preexisting if it resulted from an accident or sickness that occurred within 5 years before a policy's issue date. No benefits will ever be paid for such a condition. Another insurer is much more liberal and only excludes benefits for a disability that arises from a preexisting condition if the disability commences during the first 2 policy years. Policies may also exclude benefits for disabilities in one or more of the following situations:

- occurring while the insured is a member of the armed services
- during the period an insured is incarcerated
- arising from intentional self-inflicted injury
- arising from attempted suicide
- arising from the use of drugs or alcohol
- sustained during the commission of a felony
- caused by, contributed to, or which results from the suspension, revocation, or surrender of the insured's professional license or certification

Limitations

Policies may also contain limitations that either delay the start of benefit payments or restrict their duration.

Most policies apply a 90-day waiting period to disabilities arising from a normal pregnancy if the specified policy waiting period is of a shorter duration. If the disability arises from complications of pregnancy, the normal waiting period applies.

A few policies limit the duration of benefits if the insured resides in a country other than the United States or Canada. The period of benefits under such a limitation is normally 12 or 24 months.

Some policies limit the duration of benefits for disabilities resulting from mental or nervous disorders. Typically, the insurer pays a benefit for only 24 months unless the insured is continually confined in a mental hospital or institution. In that case, the regular benefit period applies.

Premium Payments

Premiums for disability income policies are similar to life insurance policy premiums in that they are based on the policyowner's age at the time of policy issuance and remain level for the duration of the coverage. Consequently, an individual can lock in lower premiums by buying a policy at a younger age and keeping it in force. Premiums also vary by such factors as health, gender, occupation, geographic location, and the type and level of benefits.

Premiums are usually level during the duration of a disability income policy. However, some insurers have step-rate plans so that young professional employees can pay lower premiums for the early years of their careers. The premium is level, but lower than normal until the insured reaches a specified age, such as 35 or 40. At that time, the premium increases to a higher amount that remains level thereafter. Some insurers also offer annually renewable premiums as an alternative to level premiums. This premium structure is much like that found in an annually renewable term life insurance policy. For example, at age 35 an annually renewable premium may be about half the cost of a level premium. However, within about 15 years, the premiums will be comparable. After that point, the annual premium will exceed the level premium by increasing amounts.

Premiums can be paid on an annual, semiannual, quarterly, or monthly basis and can be set up on a payroll-deduction basis or an automatic bank draft plan. Premiums must be paid on a timely basis to keep the coverage in force, but the policies do contain a 31-day grace period for late premium payments. Most insurance companies also allow lapsed policies to be reinstated automatically if the premium is paid within a few days (varying from 15 to 45 among insurers) after the end of the grace period.

Most disability income policies automatically include a waiver-of-premium provision. Some companies waive premiums after 90 days of disability, while other companies waive premiums after 60 days of disability. The shorter the waiting period, the higher the premium for the waiver-of-premium provision if it is charged separately. Disability policies differ as to whether the waiver of premium requires consecutive days or allows aggregate nonconsecutive days from short disability periods to satisfy the waiting period.

Some policies waive only future premiums after the waiver-of-premium waiting period has been satisfied; other policies retroactively waive prior premium payments made after the onset of disability but before the waiver-of-premium eligibility requirements have been met. Once the insured individual recovers and no additional disability benefits are payable, premiums will no longer be waived and premium payments must be resumed. Premium waivers generally do not continue beyond age 65 or age 67 even in policies providing lifetime benefits.

Rehabilitation and Other Additional Benefits

Disability income contracts often contain some additional benefits as standard contract provisions. The following discussion looks at a few of these provisions, but readers should not view this as a complete discussion of every such provision that might be found or introduced in the future.

rehabilitation
benefit

Perhaps the most common provision is a *rehabilitation benefit*. This provision is often rather general and states that the insurer, at the insured's request, will consider joining in a program of rehabilitation. The insurer's role is determined by a written agreement with the insured, and the insurer pays benefits in accordance with this agreement. Even if a policy does not have a rehabilitation provision, the insurer may pay for rehabilitation benefits if it feels these benefits will lower the amount of a claim because the insured will return to work sooner. This benefit is paid in addition to any income benefits otherwise payable because of disability.

A disability may occur if an individual donates an organ for transplant to another person. In the absence of a provision to the contrary, an insurer would not pay a disability income benefit because the disability did not arise from the insured's injury or sickness. However, the majority of policies now treat a disability resulting from such a circumstance as a sickness, without any special limitations. A few policies also treat disabilities from cosmetic surgery in the same way. Because of a policy's elimination period, it is very unlikely that such claims will occur unless the insured has complications from the surgery. Some policies that have such provisions require that the policy has been in force for a minimum of 6 or 12 months before the benefit becomes available.

transition benefit   Some policies contain what is often referred to as a *transition benefit*. With such a provision, benefits continue to survivors for a short period after an insured's death. The insured must have been receiving disability benefits at the time of death for a minimum period, often 24 months. The duration of the transition benefit is usually in the range of 3 to 6 months.

capital sum   Some policies pay what is usually called a *capital sum*. This is a lump sum payable if the insured suffers a serious injury, such as the loss of sight in one eye with no possibility of recovery or the severance of a hand or foot above the wrist or ankle. It is payable if the insured survives the loss for a certain period, such as 30 days. The amount of the capital sum is typically either 6 or 12 times the policy's basic monthly disability benefit.

A few insurers build small annual benefit increases into their policies as a standard benefit. Other insurers provide this benefit as one type of rider for inflation protection.

A small number of insurers have classes of disability income policies that allow the insured to convert the policy to a long-term care insurance policy. The conversion is allowed at certain ages, even if an insured is disabled, with no medical evidence of insurability required. The insurer builds the cost of the conversion privilege into the policy's basic premium. However, the premium for the new long-term care policy is based on the insured's attained age and benefits selected at the time of conversion. The insured usually has a more limited choice of benefit provisions than is available to most persons who are eligible for long-term care insurance in the regular marketplace.

Incontestability

The laws of all states require that disability income policies contain incontestability provisions. Generally, the incontestable clause specifies that the policy will remain contestable for 2 years after the date of issue during the lifetime of the individual insured. Some insurance companies, however, include a provision that extends the contestable period for any disabilities that occur during the first 2 years of coverage. Under such a policy, if an individual is disabled for 13 months out of the first 2 years of the policy, the policy does not count the 13 months toward satisfying the 24-month period. This type of extension provision is not included in the better disability income policies available in the marketplace.

Social Security Offset Rider

Social Security offset rider

Many insurance companies offer an optional provision in the form of a *Social Security offset rider* that requires a separate extra premium to cover additional benefits payable when the individual is disabled under the base policy but does not qualify for Social Security disability benefits. The supplemental benefit is paid over and above the base disability benefit of the underlying policy. When claiming benefits under this option, the insured is generally required to apply for the Social Security benefits, then supply the insurance company with evidence that the benefits have been denied by the Social Security Administration or other governmental agency (which often use a more stringent definition of disability than the insurance company). Some policies also require that the insured must appeal the government's benefit denial before benefits will be paid under this rider. Under a typical Social Security offset rider, the benefit payments are not retroactive, and the first benefit payment is not dispensed until the insurance company has accepted the denial of government benefits. Therefore, in most cases, the first benefit payment will be 13 or more months after the onset of disability.

The reason for this type of rider is, that to avoid overinsurance, underwriting guidelines limit the amount of coverage that an individual can purchase. In setting these guidelines, the insurance companies usually take into consideration the level of benefits that might be payable under Social Security for disability purposes. An individual can purchase this rider to supplement the maximum benefit available in the base policy so that total benefits the insured collects from the insurance company are essentially the same as he or she would have collected if the individual qualified for Social Security disability benefits.

Benefits under the Social Security rider terminate for any period that the insured does receive benefits from Social Security. Benefits also terminate at the full Social Security retirement age even if the individual continues to be totally disabled. Election to take early retirement benefits under Social Security also terminates benefits.

Other Riders

There are numerous other riders that may be available to an applicant for disability income insurance. There is little consistency among insurers as to which riders they offer, and new riders are often introduced. Some of the riders found in the marketplace include the following:

- **return-of-premium rider.** It refunds all or a portion of the premium paid if the insured's claim experience is favorable. This is appealing to persons who are reluctant to purchase disability income policies because they feel they will get nothing if they pay significant premiums for many years and have no claims. However, its purchase may increase the cost of a policy by anywhere from 25 to 100 percent.

- **pension supplement completion rider.** It provides an additional benefit to fund retirement income for the applicant. Many persons allocate a part of their income to retirement funding. When they are disabled, this income may no longer be available and can be replaced by the rider.

- **catastrophic benefit rider.** It provides an additional benefit in certain situations in which in insured is so severely disabled that he or she is likely to incur significant extra expenses because of the disability. The events that trigger such a benefit vary among insurers but often include the insured having a significant cognitive impairment (such as Alzheimer's disease) or a presumptive disability, or being a paraplegic or quadriplegic.

- **mental and nervous disorder riders.** Some disability income policies limit the duration of disability benefits for mental or nervous disorders unless the insured is in a mental hospital or institution. Insurers who issue such polices may offer a rider that deletes the exclusion and treats such disabilities like any other disability. Most insurers, however, do treat disabilities from all causes in the same way. Some of these insurers may offer a rider that allows the insured to elect a shorter benefit duration for disabilities resulting from mental and nervous disorders. This rider often results in a premium savings of about 10 percent.

- **long-term care purchase option rider.** A few insurers have a rider that permits the insured to purchase long-term care insurance at specified future dates without evidence of insurability. There is an additional premium for the rider, but it is modest because the rider is usually made available only to relatively young applicants. Unlike a conversion provision, however, the insured is not exchanging the disability income policy for a long-term care policy. Rather, he or she is purchasing a long-term care insurance policy in addition to the disability income policy.

Insurance Company Limitations on Amount of Coverage

Insurance company statistics have shown that the higher the percentage of a person's predisability income that is replaced by disability income benefits, the higher the likelihood that claims experience will exceed claims expected. In other words, high levels of disability benefits tend to stimulate higher aggregate claims. This is especially true if the benefits exceed the cash income available prior to disability. There have been a surprising number of fraudulent claims in disability income insurance where the insured intentionally maimed himself or herself with the express intent of ceasing work and collecting disability income benefits. Some of the more notorious cases have involved medical practitioners who injected painkillers before severing fingers or other extremities of the body. In cases where fraud was detected, the individuals were unable to collect disability income benefits even though they were permanently disabled.

To minimize the motivation for fraudulent claims as well as padding legitimate claims by malingering, insurance companies limit the amount of coverage they will issue to any individual in relation to that individual's income. For most individuals, this is the income generated from his or her efforts in a profession or trade. It includes wages, salary, bonuses, fees, commissions, and any other fees for services rendered. Some insurers will also include deferred compensation amounts and retirement plan contributions paid to or on behalf of an applicant. Insurers are also very concerned about the stability of income. For example, if an applicant received an unusually large bonus just before applying for coverage, the insurer would want to be certain that such a bonus would continue in the future. If not, they would be unwilling to consider the entire bonus in calculating earned income. For a sole proprietor and a general partner in a partnership, earned income is often defined as the individual's share of the business's gross revenue minus his or her pro rata share of the normal business operating expenses. For an owner of a closely held corporation, earned income may include a share of the profits generated from his or her involvement in the business.

Generally speaking, disability income coverage is not available for benefit amounts that exceed 60 to 70 percent of the individual's gross earned income. In fact, as the level of income increases, the percentage of income replacement that insurance companies will issue decreases. High-income professionals are often limited to less than 50 percent of their earned income level in setting the maximum benefit level for their disability policies.

These issue limits are reduced to the extent that an applicant already has disability income protection from such sources as employer provided benefits and other individual policies. In addition, insurers look at other resources the applicant can use if he or she is disabled. These include the applicant's unearned income (such as investment income, pension income, and any other income not derived from a person's job activities) and net worth. As unearned income increases as a percentage of earned income, the frequency of disability claims increases and the motivation to return to work decreases after a disability commences. Most insurers reduce their issue limits if unearned income exceeds a percentage of earned income or a specified dollar amount. For example, one insurer reduces its issue limits if an applicant's annual unearned income exceeds earned income (before taxes) by the lesser of 10 percent of income or $30,000. The reduction is equal to one-half the amount of the unearned income in excess of the threshold.

An individual can often liquidate net worth to generate unearned income. As a result, some insurers will not issue a disability income policy to anyone with a net worth in excess of some amount, such $5 million. Other insurers reduce their issue limits for high net worth persons. However, it should be pointed out that some insurers look at each case individually and use discretion. For example, a person who is actively involved in a business and has been responsible for its net worth may be properly motivated to return to work. On the other hand, an individual who has inherited significant net worth may be a poor risk for disability income coverage.

Insurers also have minimum amounts of coverage that they will issue. These are often in the range of a monthly benefit of $300 to $500. Insurers may also have special-issue limits for some young professionals without earnings records because they are just starting their careers. For example, one insurer will offer a monthly benefit of $4,500 to first-year physicians, $3,000 to medical residents, $2,500 to medical interns, and $3,000 to first-year attorneys, CPAs, engineers, and architects.

Underwriting

The underwriting process for disability income insurance is much more complex than that for life insurance. Although underwriting for life insurance and for disability income insurance coverages has many similarities, disability coverages entail more refined classifications and, therefore, a more involved evaluation process. The evaluation process is more complicated because disability can be, and often is, a recurrent condition throughout an individual's lifetime. For example, an individual with a bad back may require repeated hospitalization and rehabilitation therapy even though he or she may have a long life. Joint problems associated with knees and elbows often start with injuries at a young age and get progressively worse with wear and the onset of arthritis.

The job of underwriting for disability income insurance is to correctly classify individuals as to how costly their medical maintenance will be over their lifetime. The individual must be classified appropriately on the basis of existing information so that the premium for that individual and similar individuals adequately covers the cost of claims for that group over the duration of their coverage.

Modifying the Standard Issue

Depending on the insurer, 25 percent to 40 percent of issued policies may require some sort of modification or adjustment from the standard issue. As in life insurance, disability premiums can be increased for individuals who present a higher level of risk to the insurance company. Another modification in disability income insurance is to insist on a longer waiting period for some high-risk insureds, which eliminates more of the short-term problems and disabilities. In some cases, a longer waiting period may be applicable to specified causes or conditions, or the insurance company may insist on a relatively long waiting period that applies to all causes of disability. This approach does not preclude coverage for a particular condition, but it limits claim payments to the longer durations. The most limiting modification is an outright exclusion of any benefits associated with disabilities stemming from specified causes or conditions. Although this approach may seem drastic, it at least allows individuals to obtain disability coverage for causes other than the major problem that is preventing them from getting full disability protection.

The disability underwriting process commonly includes one or more requests from the home office for additional information. Although this does delay the issuance of coverage, it does not necessarily indicate that the coverage will not be issued. Disability insurers use many resources in an attempt to insure all applicants who fall within their acceptable risk classifications. Obviously, some risks will not meet the minimum company standards and will be rejected outright. Individual applicants who are rejected by one company may not necessarily be uninsurable; another company may classify risks in a different manner and apply different cutoff standards. Individuals who experience difficulty in obtaining disability income insurance should shop for coverage from other insurers on a sequential basis and should not apply for coverage with many insurers concurrently. Certain brokers who specialize in substandard coverage can be helpful in obtaining disability coverage for individuals with serious health problems.

Federal Income Taxation

Premiums a person pays for individually owned disability income insurance are not deductible for federal income tax purposes; benefits a person receives are tax free.

BUSINESS USES OF DISABILITY INCOME INSURANCE

The disability of business owners or key employees poses a serious risk to a business's financial health. Just as a family suffers from the loss of the income of its breadwinners, a business suffers from the loss of its productive resources. The problems are particularly acute for small enterprises in which the workforce may not be large enough to have a backup for critical tasks that could be interrupted because of disabilities. Good examples of business owners in need of disability income insurance are self-employed attorneys, accountants, physicians, and dentists who operate solo practices and employ a support staff of one or more persons. When these business owners become totally disabled, the primary business activities are often halted. However, it is necessary to maintain the business premises and at least a skeletal support staff so that business can be resumed when the business owner recovers from the disability. For example, accounts receivable must still be collected, and ongoing expenses must still be paid.

Business Overhead Expense Insurance

Business overhead expense policies are available to cover many of the ongoing costs of operating a business while the business owner is totally disabled. These policies tend to be limited to benefit durations of 1 or 2 years and have relatively short waiting periods. The intent is to keep the necessary staff and premises available for the resumption of business if the business owner recovers from the disability. Such policies are not designed to provide disability income to the business owner for the loss of his or her own income.

Insurance companies are extremely cautious in writing business overhead expense insurance and in keeping the benefit amount in line with established stable costs for previous periods. Consequently, supporting financial statements to verify the stability of the business and to establish the appropriate level of insurable expenses must accompany the application for this coverage. Insurable expenses include such things as salaries for secretaries, nurses, and other staff necessary to resume business upon the business owner's recovery, as well as the ongoing expenses for rent, utilities, taxes, accounting services, and so forth. Actual expenses are reimbursed at time of disability up to a maximum monthly indemnity selected at the time of policy issue.

Key Person Insurance

Business entities are dependent on their personnel to carry out business activities and generate revenues and profits. Very often, the unique talents and experiences of a few key individuals are crucial to the success of the business entity. The loss of an individual's contributions by reason of disability or death could deal a devastating blow to the financial well-being of the enterprise. In fact, sometimes the dependence is so critical that losing the individual's participation could lead to the bankruptcy or termination of the business. This is particularly true of professionals who operate as sole practitioners.

Many business enterprises have recognized the importance of key individuals who make the most critical contributions and have therefore obtained disability income insurance to cover these key individuals. Benefits from key employee disability policies are payable to the business entity when the insured key employee is disabled. The justification for this coverage is similar to that for key person life insurance policies. Proceeds from key person disability policies can be used to replace lost revenue directly attributable to the key person's disability. They can also be used to fund the search for individuals to replace the insured person, the extra cost of hiring specialized individuals to replace the multiple talents of the insured, and the training costs that may be incurred to prepare replacements to carry out the duties the insured performed. The costs of training, hiring, and compensating are usually rather easy to ascertain, whereas estimating lost revenue is a very difficult and complex task. These policies are not designed to provide continuance of salary for the key employee.

Even though a business entity may determine a desired amount of disability income protection for each key individual, it may not be able to obtain that amount of coverage. The underwriting processes of insurance companies limit the maximum amount of coverage available on any one individual. Companies utilize a wide range of guidelines to set these limitations, and getting an insurer to waive any of these limitations is usually difficult. Sometimes a business entity is able to make a strong enough argument on both financial and economic grounds to justify an exception and obtain the desired amount even though it exceeds underwriting guideline limitations.

Premiums for a business-owned disability income policy are not deductible for federal income tax purposes if benefits are payable to the business; the receipt of these proceeds by the business is free of any federal income tax liability. Payment of those premiums does not create any taxable income for the insured employee.

Salary Continuation for Owners and Key Employees

A business entity can purchase individual disability income policies to fund formal plans to continue salary for disabled owners or key employees. Formal plans can be set up in two different ways. The corporation can own the policy and be the beneficiary under the policy, or the corporation can pay the premiums on a policy owned by the employee to whom benefits will be paid. When the corporation is both the owner and the beneficiary of the policy, premium payments are nondeductible by the corporation, and the corporation receives the insurance proceeds free of any federal income tax liability. Premium payments for such coverage are not considered taxable income to the employee. However, any income paid to the disabled employee is taxable.

When the corporation merely pays the premiums on a policy owned by the employee, the premiums are deductible expenses of the corporation as long as they meet reasonable expense criteria. The premium payments are not considered taxable income to the employee; however, benefits paid under the policy are taxable income to the employee.

In some informal plans to continue salary, the corporation pays a large enough bonus to the employee for the employee to buy an individual disability income policy. If the bonus payments are reasonable compensation, they are deductible by the corporation. The bonus is taxable income to the employee. The premium payments made by the employee are not deductible. Any benefit payments the employee receives have no effect on the corporation, and the employee receives them free of any federal income tax liability.

Disability Buy-Sell Funding

A business owner's disability often threatens the viability of that enterprise. Preserving the value of the business often necessitates shifting the business owner's ownership interest to one or more other individuals who can continue to conduct the affairs of the business. In cases that involve multiple ownership of the business, the most likely parties to purchase the ownership interest of a disabled owner are the nondisabled co-owners. Unfortunately, few business owners have adequate amounts of liquid assets to make an outright purchase of the ownership interest from the disabled co-owner.

Just as buy-sell agreements triggered by the death of an owner can be funded with life insurance, a buy-sell agreement triggered by the disability of an owner can be funded with disability income insurance. Special disability policies have been designed specifically for the purpose of funding buy-sell agreements. These policies can fund either an installment purchase or a lump-sum buyout.

The types of buy-sell arrangements are similar to those discussed earlier in this book for situations arising from death. However, some extra care is necessary in drafting the agreement. The definition used in the disability policy should be the same definition as that specified in the buy-sell agreement. The waiting period for a buy-sell policy is typically 1 year or longer in order to avoid triggering the buyout for disabilities that last less than 1 year. Most buy-sell policies pay the benefit in one lump sum.

Although a discussion is beyond the scope of this book, readers should also be aware that different approaches to buy-sell agreements can have significantly different tax implications.

CHECKLIST FOR EVALUATING AND COMPARING DISABILITY INCOME POLICIES

- What is the definition of total disability? If the definition of total disability is a two-step definition, how many years apply to the own-occupation definition?
- What are the amount and frequency of total-disability benefits?
- What waiting (elimination) period applies to total-disability benefits?
- What is the duration of total-disability benefits?
- Are partial-disability benefits covered? If yes,

    ___ What is the definition of partial disability?

    ___ What period of total disability is required before benefits are payable?

- Are residual-disability benefits covered? If yes,

    ___ What is the benefit amount?

    ___ How long are they payable?

    ___ Is a prior period of total disability required?

- What is the annual policy premium?
- Is there a presumptive-disability provision?
- Is there coverage for disabilities arising from organ donations?
- What cost-of-living increases are available for benefits being paid and coverage in force, and what is the basis on which such increases are made?
- Does the policy contain any modifications from standard issue?
- What is the renewability provision?
- What is the waiver-of-premium provision?
- Is there a return-of-premium option?
- What are the rehabilitation benefits?
- Does the policy contain riders? If yes,

    ___ What do they cover?

    ___ Is there an additional premium for their use?

CHAPTER REVIEW

Key Terms and Concepts

short-term disability income plan
long-term disability income insurance
sick-leave plan
paid time off (PTO) program
own-occupation definition of disability
dual (or split) definition of disability
waiting (elimination) period
buy-up plan
carve-out (benefit plan)
any-occupation definition of disability

modified own-occupation
partial disability
residual disability
presumptive-disability provision
cost-of-living-adjustment (COLA) rider
rehabilitation benefit
transition benefit
capital sum
Social Security offset rider

Review Questions

Review questions are based on the learning objectives in this chapter. Thus, a [3] at the end of a question means that the question is based on learning objective 3. If there are multiple objectives, they are all listed.

1. Why is there a need for disability income insurance protection? [1]

2. What are the sources of coverage that may protect your client against financial trouble in case of disability? [1]

3. What is the nature of sick-leave plans? [2]

4. What are the typical eligibility requirements in an insured group disability income plan? [3]

5. How does the definition of total disability in group long-term contracts differ from that in group short-term contracts? [3]

6. What types of exclusions are in group disability income contracts? [3]

7. What types of benefit schedules are in group disability income plans? [3]

8. How are group disability income benefits coordinated with other benefits? [3]

9. Describe the following additional benefits that are occasionally in group long-term disability income contracts:
    a. cost-of-living (COLA) rides [3]
    b. pension supplements [3]
    c. survivors' benefits [3]

10. What are the income tax consequences for each of the following clients who receive disability income benefits from an employer plan?
    a. Kevin receives disability benefits under a fully contributory plan. [4]
    b. Patty receives disability benefits under a noncontributory plan. [4]
    c. Julie receives disability benefits under a partially contributory plan. [4]

11. How might the definition of total disability differ among individual disability income policies? [5]

12. What are residual disability benefits, and how are they calculated? [5]

13. What advice might a planner give a client regarding each of the following aspects of individual disability income insurance policies?
    a. recurring disabilities [5]
    b. ability to keep the coverage in force [5]
    c. when benefits start [5]
    d. duration of benefit period [5]
    e. level of benefits payable [5]
    f. premium payments [5]

14. What are the three approaches an individual who is not disabled can use to keep individual disability income policy benefits in step with the individual's increasing income? [5]

15. How does a return-of-premium option work? [5]

16. What are some of the additional benefits that might be found in an individual disability income policy? [5]

17. Why may it be a good idea to add a Social Security offset rider to an individual disability income policy? [5]

18. Identify some of the riders that might be added to a disability income policy. [5]

19. What are insurance company limits on the amount of coverage that an individual income disability policy can provide? [5]

20. How can individual disability income policies be used by a business for each of the following purposes? [6]
    a. paying business overhead expenses [6]
    b. key person protection [6]
    c. salary continuation for owners and key employees [6]
    d. disability buy-sell funding [6]

Learning Objectives

An understanding of the material in this chapter should enable you to

1. Explain the need for long-term care and the sources of long-term care financing.

2. Describe the development of long-term care insurance, including the National Association of Insurance Commissioners (NAIC) model legislation.

3. Explain the effect of the Health Insurance Portability and Accountability Act (HIPAA) on long-term care insurance.

4. Describe the characteristics of individual long-term care insurance policies.

5. Describe the characteristics of partnership programs for long-term care.

6. Describe how group long-term care insurance policies differ from individual policies.

Since the early 1980s, long-term care insurance has evolved from being virtually nonexistent to being an important form of insurance carried by almost 8 million persons.[48] About 45 insurers market individual long-term care insurance products, but 10 insurers write over 80 percent of the coverage. The major providers of employee benefits now make group products available and account for about one-third of the persons insured. Financial planners need to understand this important product in order to advise their clients.

During its relatively short life, long-term care coverage has been hailed as a major source of financial security and criticized as a coverage that fails to meet consumers' real long-term care needs. State and federal legislation affecting coverage has also been common. In this environment, long-term care

---

48. *Individual LTC Insurance, Annual Review 2010*, LIMRA International, Inc., 2010.

products have continued to evolve, with frequent introduction of newer and more comprehensive products. Long-term care coverage can probably best be described as having grown from infancy to somewhere between the childhood and teenage years. Coverage will change to meet consumer demands and expectations and to reflect insurers' experience with the product. The largely untapped market for coverage will continue to grow as the number of older Americans increases.

The discussion first looks at the need for long-term care. This is followed by a brief description of sources of long-term care financing other than insurance. We continue with a discussion of how and why insurance policies have evolved into the products now being offered. It then presents an analysis of the more common products in the marketplace today—both individual and group—and concludes with a checklist for evaluating and comparing policies.

IMPORTANCE OF LONG-TERM CARE PLANNING

An Aging Population

Long-term care has traditionally been thought of as a problem primarily for the older population. The population aged 65 or over is the fastest-growing age group; today it represents about 13 percent of the population, a figure that is expected to increase to between 20 percent and about 25 percent over the next 50 years. The segment of the population aged 85 and over is growing at an even faster rate. While less than 10 percent of the over-65 group is over 85 today, this percentage is expected to double over the next two generations.

An aging society presents changing problems. Those who needed long-term care in the past were most likely to have suffered from strokes or other acute diseases. With longer life spans today and in the future, a larger portion of the elderly are incapacitated by such chronic conditions as Alzheimer's disease, arthritis, diabetes, osteoporosis, and lung and heart disease—conditions that often require continuing assistance with day-to-day needs. The likelihood that a person will need to enter a nursing home increases dramatically with age. One percent of persons between the ages of 65 and 74 reside in nursing homes, and the percentage increases to 6 percent between the ages of 75 and 84. At age 85 and over, the figure rises to approximately 25 percent. Statistics of the Department of Health and Human Services indicate that persons aged 65 or older face a 40 percent chance of entering a nursing home at some time during the remainder of their lives. Nearly half of the persons who enter nursing homes remain longer than 1 year, and the average nursing home stay of current residents is about 2½ years.

Nursing home statistics tell only part of the story. An even greater percentage of the elderly have age-related conditions that require varying degrees of assistance to enable them to perform normal daily activities. In some cases, this assistance is provided in other types of supportive-living arrangements, such as assisted-living facilities and adult foster homes. In many cases, however, the elderly remain in their own homes or the homes of relatives and receive their care from relatives, home health agencies, and community-based programs. The latter programs include Meals on Wheels and adult day care centers.

The elderly are not the only group of persons who need long-term care. Many younger persons are unable to care for themselves because of handicaps resulting from birth defects, mental conditions, illnesses, or accidents.

Increasing Costs

The Congressional Budget Office estimated the year 2004 national expenditures for care for the elderly in institutional settings at over $92 billion; home health care exceeded $42 billion. These costs, about 11 percent of national health care expenditures, are increasing faster than inflation because of the growing demand for nursing home beds and the shortage of skilled medical personnel. By 2020, these annual amounts are expected to rise to approximately $139 billion for nursing home care and $69 billion for home care.[49]

The out-of-pocket payments for long-term care by individuals who must use personal resources can be astronomical. Currently, average annual nursing home costs are almost $80,000 for private accommodations and can be much higher. Although the average nursing home stay is 2½ years, some stays exceed the average by many years. Two visits a day by a home health aid to help with bathing and dressing and household chores can cost $2,500

---

49. *Projections of Expenditure for Long-Term Care Services for the Elderly*, Congressional Budget Office, March 1999, pp. 3–4; and *Financing Long-Term Care for the Elderly*, Congressional Budget Office , April 2004, p. 5.

a month.[50] By 2030, the annual cost of nursing home care is expected to approximate $207,000 with comparable increases in home care charges.[51]

Inability of Families to Provide Full Care

Traditionally, family members have provided long-term care, often at considerable personal sacrifice and stress. However, it is becoming more difficult for families to provide long-term care for these reasons:

- geographic dispersion of family members
- increased participation in the paid workforce by women and children
- fewer children in the family
- more childless families
- higher divorce rates
- inability of family members to provide care because they, too, are growing old

Inadequacy of Insurance Protection

Private medical expense insurance policies (both group and individual) almost always have an exclusion for convalescent, custodial, or rest care. Some policies do provide coverage for extended care facilities and for home health care. In both cases, the purpose is to provide care in a manner that is less expensive than care in a hospital. However, coverage is provided only if a person also needs medical care; benefits are not provided if a person is merely "old" and needs someone to care for him or her.

Medicare is also inadequate because it does not cover custodial care unless this care is needed along with the medical or rehabilitative treatment provided in skilled-nursing facilities or under home health care benefits.

SOURCES OF LONG-TERM CARE FINANCING

Several sources other than insurance are available for financing long-term care; however, there are drawbacks associated with each.

---

50. *The MetLife Survey of Nursing Home & Assisted Living Costs*, October 2008, The MetLife Mature Market Institute, p. 5.

51. *Long-Term Care Insurance: Protection for the Future*, American Council of Life Insurance from its web site at acli.org.

One source is to rely on personal financial resources. In addition to income, these resources may include savings, investments, and home equity that is accessed by loans and reverse mortgages. Few individuals have sufficient retirement income to fully meet their potential long-term care expenses. Unless a person has substantial assets on which to draw, this approach may force an individual and his or her dependents into poverty. It may also mean that the person will not meet the financial objective of leaving assets to heirs.

An often overlooked source of providing or financing long-term care is relatives, or even friends. In some cases, family members may act as caregivers themselves; in other cases, they may give financial support to provide care or pay for long-term care insurance premiums. The support of relatives, however, may not last forever. For example, a spouse may no longer be able to provide care because of his or her own physical condition. And aging children may not have the financial resources to continue the same level of support because of their own long-term care needs.

Another source is to rely on public assistance. The Medicaid program in most states provides benefits, which usually include nursing home care (and possibly home health care) to the "medically needy." However, a person is not eligible unless he or she either is poor or has a low income and has exhausted most other assets (including those of a spouse). There is also often a social stigma associated with accepting public assistance. In addition, the facilities that accept Medicaid recipients may be located away from family members and/or provide a lower quality of care than a person with adequate resources can purchase.

look-back period   One strategy that is sometimes used is to give a person's assets away at the time nursing home care is needed and ultimately rely on Medicaid. (This will work only if income, including pensions and Social Security, is below specified limits.) However, Medicaid benefits are postponed if assets were disposed of at less than their fair market value within a specific time period (called the *look-back period*) prior to Medicaid eligibility rather than the date of asset transfer. The Deficit Reduction Act of 2005 lengthens the look-back period from 3 years to 5 years for most transfers. The act also changes the start of the ineligibility period to the date the applicant would otherwise be Medicaid eligible. The effect of the act is to make artificial impoverishment for the purpose of Medicaid eligibility more difficult. One solution is to purchase long-term care insurance in an amount sufficient to provide protection for the length of the look-back period. If care is needed, a person can rely on the insurance coverage and transfer assets to heirs. When the insurance coverage runs out and the look-back period is over, the person can apply for Medicaid.

partnership program
Several states have attempted to encourage better coverage for long-term care by waiving or modifying certain Medicaid requirements if a person carries a state-approved long-term care policy. Such a policy is part of a state *partnership program* under which insurers issue long-term care insurance policies that meet requirements established by the state. These programs are covered later in this chapter.

continuing care retirement communities (CCRCs)
Continuing care retirement communities (CCRCs), also referred to as life care facilities, are growing in popularity as a source to meet long-term care needs. Residents in a CCRC pay an "entrance fee" that allows them to occupy a dwelling unit but usually does not give them actual ownership rights. The entrance fee may or may not be refundable if the resident leaves the facility voluntarily or dies. As a general rule, the higher the refund is, the higher the entrance fee is. Residents pay a monthly fee that includes meals, some housecleaning services, and varying degrees of health care. If a person needs long-term care, he or she must give up the independent living unit and move to the assisted-living or nursing home portion of the CCRC, but the monthly fee usually remains the same.

The disadvantages of this option are that the cost of a continuing care retirement community is beyond the reach of many persons, and a resident must be in reasonably good health and able to live independently at the time he or she enters the facility. Therefore, the decision to use a CCRC must be made in advance of the need for long-term care. Once such care is needed or is imminent, this approach is no longer viable.

A few insurers now include long-term care benefits in some cash value life insurance policies. Essentially, an insured can begin to use these accelerated benefits while he or she is still living. For example, if the insured is in a nursing home, he or she might be able to elect a benefit up to 25 percent or 50 percent of the policy face amount. However, any benefits received reduce the future death benefit payable to heirs. One potential problem with this approach is that the acceleration of benefits may result in the reduction of the death benefit to a level that is inadequate to accomplish the purpose of life insurance-the protection of family members after a wage earner's death. If benefits are accelerated, there is less left for the surviving family. In addition, the availability of an accelerated benefit may give the insured a false sense of security that long-term care needs are being met when, in fact, the potential benefit may be inadequate to cover extended nursing home stays.

Some Ways to Pay for Long-Term Care
• Personal income and assets
• Family support
• Medicaid/public assistance programs
• Continuing care retirement communities
• Accelerated benefits in life insurance policies
• Long-term care insurance

long-term care insurance

Finally, there is *long-term care insurance*, which is a form of health insurance that usually provides coverage for custodial care and skilled-nursing care. Benefits may be provided for care received in many different settings, including nursing homes, hospice facilities, assisted-living residences, at home, and in adult day care centers.

DEVELOPMENT OF INSURANCE COVERAGE

It is common for insurance coverages to evolve over time. However, the evolution of long-term care products has been dramatic—both the magnitude of the changes and the speed with which these changes have occurred.

Early Policies

The long-term care policies in existence in the early 1980s were primarily designed to provide care during the recovery period following an acute illness. They seldom met the needs of persons who required long-term care for chronic conditions. In addition, the sale of early long-term care policies was often accompanied by improper sales practices. Consumers were led to believe that policies were much more comprehensive than they actually were. In effect, policyowners felt that they were purchasing "nursing home" insurance that would cover them anytime nursing home care was needed. Only when such care was needed did many of these policyowners realize that their coverage had severe restrictions and was very limited.

Finally, for many years, no favorable tax treatment was given to long-term care insurance. Premiums for coverage were not deductible, and benefits and employer-paid premiums under group plans resulted in taxation to employees.

Evolution of Coverage

Criticism of the early long-term care policies created considerable pressure for change. Consumer groups argued for more government regulation. The federal government conducted studies and held hearings, with the results painting a less-than-flattering picture of long-term care policies. Change itself, however, resulted primarily from the actions of insurance companies themselves and from state insurance regulators. But the threat of federal regulation was always present. The negative publicity about early policies had a dampening effect on the public's perception of long-term care insurance. This led many insurance companies to modify their policies and companies entering the business to offer more comprehensive policies. At the same time, the National Association of Insurance Commissioners (NAIC) began to take a very active interest in long-term care insurance. This culminated in the adoption of the Long-Term Care Insurance Model Act in 1987. In 1988, model regulations were issued to enable the states to implement the model act. The act and the regulations have been amended many times since. Sometimes these amendments changed previous act provisions; at other times, they addressed new issues. The majority of states have adopted the model act. However, the version in force in a given state is not always the latest NAIC version. A few states still have little regulation of long-term care policies, and other states have adopted legislation different from the model act, although it may be similar to what the NAIC recommended.

Considerable changes also took place at the federal level with passage of the Health Insurance Portability and Accountability Act in 1996. This law, referred to as HIPAA, provides favorable tax treatment to long-term care insurance contracts that meet certain standards. These contracts are referred to as *tax-qualified* policies.

The long-term care policies of most insurance companies have gone through many revisions. Although coverage is still not always complete, there is little comparison between the early policies and most of what is marketed today. Not only have policies become more comprehensive over the last few years, but premiums decreased for several years as a result of intensified competition. More recently, however, several insurers have increased premiums on existing policies. In addition, the newly introduced policies of recent years have all been priced higher due to such factors as very low lapse rates, lower-than-anticipated investment returns on reserves, new statistics on claims, and insurance departments notifying the carriers that future rate increases will be ever more difficult to obtain.

Existing policyowners are sometimes able to obtain the enhancements in newer policies, but frequently at an increased premium. Some companies allow the policyowner to add the enhanced benefits by paying the new premium based on the policyowner's original age of issue. Other companies require evidence of insurability, and they use attained-age rates.

Most companies that write individual policies now issue only the tax-qualified long-term care insurance contract prescribed by HIPAA. Some companies issue both qualified contracts and non-tax-qualified long-term care insurance contracts, and a few companies issue only *non-tax-qualified* contracts. Although purchasers of these contracts do not receive the tax advantages that qualified contracts provide, the nonqualified contracts often include provisions that make it easier to qualify for benefits.

Insurers are also increasingly offering partnership policies.

NAIC MODEL LEGISLATION

Because of its widespread adoption by the states, it is appropriate to discuss the NAIC model legislation regarding long-term care. The legislation consists of a model act that is designed to be incorporated into a state's insurance law and model regulations that are designed to be adopted for use in implementing the law. This discussion is based on the latest version of the model legislation, which seems to be amended almost annually. Even though most states have adopted the NAIC legislation, some states may not have adopted the latest version. However, the importance of the model legislation should not be overlooked. With most insurers writing coverage in more than one state, it is likely that the latest provisions have been adopted by one or more states where an insurer's coverage is sold. Because most insurance companies sell essentially the same long-term care product everywhere they do business, the NAIC guidelines are often, in effect, being adhered to in states that have not adopted the legislation.

Before proceeding with a summary of the major provisions of the NAIC model legislation, it is important to make two points. First, the model legislation establishes guidelines. Insurance companies still have significant latitude in many aspects of product design. Second, many older policies are still in existence that were written prior to the adoption of the model legislation or under one of its earlier versions.

The model legislation focuses on two major areas—policy provisions and marketing. Highlights of the criteria for policy provisions include the following:

- Certain words or terms cannot be used in a policy unless they are specifically defined in accordance with the legislation. Examples include adult day care, home health care services, personal care, and skilled-nursing care.

- No policy can contain renewal provisions other than guaranteed renewable or noncancelable.

- Limitations and exclusions are prohibited except in the following cases:

    - preexisting conditions

    - mental or nervous disorders (but this does not permit the exclusion of Alzheimer's disease)

    - alcoholism and drug addiction

    - illness, treatment, or medical condition arising out of war, service in the armed forces, participation in a felony, suicide, and aviation if a person is a non-fare-paying passenger

    - treatment in a government facility and services available under Medicare and other social insurance programs

- No policy can provide coverage for skilled-nursing care only or provide significantly more coverage for skilled care in a facility than for lower levels of care.

- The definition of preexisting condition can be no more restrictive than to exclude a condition for which treatment was recommended or received within 6 months prior to the effective date of coverage. In addition, coverage can be excluded for a confinement for this condition only if it begins within 6 months of the effective date of coverage.

- Eligibility for benefits cannot be based on a prior hospital requirement or higher level of care.

- Insurance companies must offer the applicant the right to purchase coverage that allows for an increase in the amount of benefits based on reasonable anticipated increases in the cost of services the policy covers. The applicant must specifically reject this inflation protection if he or she does not want it.

- Insurance companies must offer the applicant the right to purchase a nonforfeiture benefit.

- A policy must contain an incontestable clause that makes a policy incontestable after 2 years on the grounds of misrepresentation alone. The policy, however, can be contested after that time on the basis that the applicant knowingly and intentionally misrepresented relevant facts pertaining to the insured's health.

The following provisions of the model legislation pertain to marketing:

- An outline of coverage must be delivered to a prospective applicant at the time of initial solicitation. Among the information this outline must contain is (1) a description of the coverage, (2) a statement of the principal exclusions, reductions, and limitations in the policy, (3) a statement of the terms under which the policy can be continued in force or terminated, (4) a description of the terms under which the policy may be returned and the premium refunded, (5) a brief description of the relationship between cost of care and benefits, and (6) a statement whether the policy is intended to be tax qualified.

- A shopper's guide must be delivered to all prospective applicants. Most insurers use one prepared by the NAIC.

- The policy must contain a 30-day free-look provision after a policy's delivery. Any premium paid is refunded if the insured decides to cancel the policy before the free-look period ends.

- An insurance company must establish procedures to ensure that any comparisons of policies by its agents or other producers are fair and accurate and to prohibit excessive insurance from being sold or issued.

- Applications for insurance must be clear and unambiguous so that an applicant's health condition can be properly ascertained. The application must also contain a conspicuous statement near the place for the applicant's signature that says the following: "If your answers to this application are incorrect or untrue, the company has the right to deny benefits or rescind your policy." The purpose of these requirements is to control postclaim underwriting—the practice of rescinding a policy or denying a claim based on information obtained at the time a claim is filed that could have been obtained at the time of the application.

- No policy can be issued until the applicant has been given the option to elect a third party to be notified of any pending policy lapse because of nonpayment of premium. The purpose of this provision is to eliminate the problem of policy lapse because a senile or otherwise mentally impaired person fails to pay the premium.

NAIC Model Legislation Concerning Marketing of Long-Term Care Insurance

- Prospective purchasers must be given an outline of the coverage, a shopper's guide, and a 30-day free look at the policy.
- Procedures for fair and accurate policy comparisons must be established.
- Applications must be clear and unambiguous.
- Applicants must have option to name a third party to be notified of pending lapse due to nonpayment of premium.

EFFECT OF HEALTH INSURANCE PORTABILITY AND ACCOUNTABILITY ACT (HIPAA)

The Health Insurance Portability and Accountability Act (HIPAA) made the tax treatment of long-term care insurance more favorable. However, this favorable tax treatment is given only to long-term care insurance policies that meet prescribed standards. The long-term care provisions in the act are primarily changes in the income tax code. States still have the authority to regulate long-term care insurance contracts.

Eligibility for Favorable Tax Treatment

qualified long-term care insurance contract

The act provides favorable tax treatment to a *qualified long-term care insurance contract*. This is defined as any insurance contract that meets all the following requirements:

- The only insurance protection provided under the qualified long-term care insurance contract is for qualified long-term care services.
- The contract cannot pay for expenses that are reimbursable under Medicare. However, this requirement does not apply to expenses that are reimbursable if (1) Medicare is a secondary payer of benefits or (2) benefits are payable on a per diem basis.
- The contract must be guaranteed renewable.

- The contract does not provide for a cash surrender value or other money that can be borrowed or paid, assigned, or pledged as collateral for a loan.
- All refunds of premiums and policyowner dividends must be applied as future reductions in premiums or to increase future benefits.
- The policy must comply with various consumer protection provisions. For the most part, these are the same provisions contained in the NAIC model legislation and already adopted by most states.

qualified long-term care services

The act defines *qualified long-term care services* as necessary diagnostic, preventive, therapeutic, curing, treating, and rehabilitative services, and maintenance or personal care services that are required by a chronically ill individual and provided by a plan of care prescribed by a licensed health care practitioner.

chronically ill individual

A *chronically ill individual* is one who has been certified as meeting one of the following requirements, often referred to as benefit triggers:

activities of daily living (ADLs)

- The person is expected to be unable to perform, without substantial assistance from another person, at least two *activities of daily living (ADLs)* for a period of at least 90 days due to a loss of functional capacity. The act allows six activities of daily living: eating, bathing, dressing, using the toilet, maintaining continence, and transferring in and out of a bed, chair, or wheelchair. A qualified long-term care insurance contract must contain at least five of the six ADLs.
- Substantial supervision is required to protect the individual from threats to health and safety because of severe cognitive impairment.

The act also specifies that any contract issued before January 1, 1997, that met the long-term care requirements in the state where the policy was issued will be considered a tax-qualified long-term care contract. If such a contract undergoes a material change, however, the policy must then conform to the HIPAA requirements to retain this status.

Federal Income Tax Provisions

A tax-qualified long-term care insurance contract is treated as accident and health insurance. With some exceptions, expenses for long-term care services, including insurance premiums, are treated like other medical expenses. That is, self-employed persons may deduct the premiums paid, and persons who itemize deductions can include the cost of long-term care services, including insurance premiums, for purposes of deducting medical expenses in excess of 7.5 percent of adjusted gross income. However, there is a cap on the amount of personally paid long-term care insurance premiums that a person can claim as medical expenses. These limits, which are based upon a covered individual's age and subject to cost-of-living adjustments, are shown below. There are no deductions for payments made to a spouse or relative who is not a licensed professional with respect to such services.

Table 15-1 Long-Term Care Deductible Limits, 2011	
Age	**Annual Deductible Limit per Covered Individual**
40 or younger	$ 340
41–50	640
51–60	1,270
61–70	3,390
Older than 70	4,240

Any employer contributions for group contracts are deductible to the employer and do not result in any taxable income to a person considered an employee for tax purposes. Coverage cannot be offered through a cafeteria plan on a tax-favored basis. In addition, if an employee has a flexible spending account for unreimbursed medical expenses, any reimbursements for long-term care services must be included in the employee's income. However, long-term care insurance premiums may be paid from a health savings account (HSA) up to the deductible limits in the table above.

An employee receives benefits under a qualified long-term care insurance contract tax free, with one possible exception. Under contracts written on a per diem basis, proceeds are excludible from income up to $300 per day in 2011. (This figure is indexed annually.) Amounts in excess of $300 are also excludible to the extent that they represent actual costs for long-term care services.

CHARACTERISTICS OF INDIVIDUAL POLICIES

For many types of insurance, policies are relatively standardized. For long-term care insurance, the opposite is true. Significant variations (and therefore differences in cost) exist from one insurance company to another. An applicant also has numerous options with respect to policy provisions.

The discussion in this section of the chapter focuses on issue age, types of care covered, benefit variations, benefit amounts, benefit duration, the ability to restore benefits, the degree of inflation protection, renewability, and cost. The provisions and practices described represent the norm in that most policies fit within the extremes that are described. However, the norm covers a wide spectrum.

Issue Age

Significant variations exist among insurance companies with respect to the age at which they will issue policies. At a minimum, a healthy person between the ages of 40 and 79 is eligible for coverage from most insurance companies. Some companies also have an upper age in the range of 84 to 89, beyond which coverage is not issued. Restrictive policy choices and very high premiums often accompany coverage written at age 80 or older, when available.

Considerably more variation exists with respect to the youngest age at which coverage is written. Some companies have no minimum age. Most companies sell policies to persons as young as age 18. Still other companies have a higher minimum age, often age 40.

Types of Care Covered

There are many types of care for which a long-term care policy may provide benefits. By broad categories, these can be categorized as nursing home care, assisted-living care, hospice care, care in an Alzheimer's facility, home health care, care at an adult day care center, care coordination, alternative plans of care, and other benefits. A long-term care policy may provide benefits for one, several, or all of these types of care.

Nursing Home Care

nursing home
care

custodial care

Nursing home care encompasses skilled-nursing care and custodial care in a licensed facility. Skilled-nursing care consists of nursing and rehabilitative care that can be performed only by, or under the supervision of, skilled medical personnel and must be based on a doctor's orders. Such care may be provided on a daily basis or at less frequent intervals. *Custodial care*, sometimes referred to as personal care, is provided primarily to handle personal needs, such as walking, bathing, dressing, eating, or managing medication, and can usually be provided by someone without professional medical skills or training.

bed reservation
benefit

Policies that provide nursing home care often also provide a *bed reservation benefit*, which continues payments to a long-term care facility) if a patient temporarily leaves because of hospitalization or any other reason. Without a continuation of payments, the bed may be assigned to someone else and unavailable upon the patient's return to the facility. The duration of the bed reservation benefit is for a limited period, such as 20 or 60 days.

Assisted-Living Facility Care

assisted-living
care

Assisted-living care is provided in facilities that care for the frail elderly who are no longer able to care for themselves but do not need as high a level of care as a nursing home provides.

Hospice Care

Hospice care does not attempt to cure medical conditions but rather is devoted to easing the physical and psychological pain associated with dying. In addition to providing services for the dying patient, a hospice may offer counseling to family members. A hospice may be a separate facility, but this type of care can also be provided on an outpatient basis in the dying person's home. Most long-term care insurance policies that provide benefits for hospice care make no distinction in the setting.

Alzheimer's Facilities

The states require long-term care insurance policies to cover Alzheimer's disease and related forms of degenerative diseases and dementia under the same terms as they cover other conditions that qualify an individual as chronically ill. Therefore, coverage is provided if an individual receives services in a nursing home, in an assisted-living facility, or at home—as long as the policy covers the specific type of care. Most policies, however, have some specific reference to Alzheimer's facilities. In some cases, they are included as part of the definition for assisted-living facilities. In other cases, they are referred to separately but defined as facilities that must meet the policy's definition of either a nursing home or an assisted-living facility.

Home Health Care

Home health care includes part-time skilled-nursing care, therapy, and part-time services from home health aides. It also often includes help from a homemaker companion who is an employee of a state-licensed home health care agency. The companion may assist with such tasks as cooking, shopping, cleaning, bill paying, or other household chores.

Adult Day Care Centers

adult day care center

The *adult day care center* is a relatively new care setting that provides social, medical, and rehabilitative services to people with physical and mental limitations. These centers are designed for the elderly, who may be severely impaired but live at home and whose family caregiver is unavailable to stay at home during the day. Without the services these centers provide, many people could not remain at home.

Adult day care centers are usually open 5 days a week from 6 to 12 hours per day and typically offer a full range of long-term care services. The centers also provide meals under the direction of a dietitian and meet social needs through recreational and educational activities. Many programs offer transportation between home and the center. Medical services in the form of physical, speech, and occupational therapy may also be provided.

Insurance industry representatives often use the terms "adult day center" and "adult day services" to describe this form of long-term care, thereby avoiding the words "day care," which seniors may find offensive.

Care Coordination

care coordinator

Many policies will either reimburse for or directly provide the services of a *care coordinator* who works with an insured, his or her family, and licensed health care practitioners to assess a person's condition, evaluate care options, and develop an individualized plan of care coordination that provides the most appropriate services. The care coordinator may also periodically reevaluate ongoing plans of care and act as an advocate for the insured. Some long-term care policies mandate that the insured use the services of the care coordinator in order to receive full benefits.

Alternative Plans of Care

Many policies provide benefits for alternative plans of care, even though the policy might not cover the types of care. For example, a policy covering only nursing home care might provide benefits for care in an assisted-living facility if these benefits are an appropriate and cost-effective alternative to care in a nursing home. It is, however, not intended to make a facility-only policy one that pays for home health care. As a general rule, the alternative plan must be acceptable to the insurance company, the insured, and the insured's physician.

Other Benefits

Most long-term care policies contain at least some other benefits. In most cases, these benefits focus on enabling a person to continue living at home. Sometimes they are included as a part of the home health care benefit, but more often they are separate benefits with their own limits of coverage. They include

respite care

- the purchase or rental of needed medical equipment and emergency alert systems
- modifications to the home, such as a ramp for a wheelchair or bathroom modifications
- *respite care*, which allows occasional full-time care for a person who is receiving informal home health care. These persons are usually receiving care from a family member or friend. This benefit gives these caregivers needed time off. Respite care can be provided in a person's home or by moving the person to a nursing facility or an assisted-living facility for a short stay.
- caregiver training, which is the training of a family member or friend to provide care so that a person can remain at home

Benefit Variations

There are almost as many variations among long-term care policies as there are among insurance companies writing the product. Much of this variation is related to the types of care for which benefits are provided. These benefit variations fall into three broad categories: facility-only policies, home-health-care-only policies, and comprehensive policies.

Facility-Only Policies

facility-only policy Many early long-term care policies were designed to provide benefits only if the insured was in a nursing home. This type of policy was frequently referred to as a nursing home policy. These policies still exist, but they frequently also provide benefits for care in other settings, such as assisted-living facilities and hospices. The term *facility-only policy* is often used to describe this broader type of policy, and a facility-only policy, in its most generic sense, also includes nursing home policies.

Home-Health-Care-Only Policies

home-health-care-only policies Home-health-care-only policies were originally developed to be used either as an alternative to nursing home policies or to complement such policies if more comprehensive coverage was desired. A *home-health-care-only policy* is designed to provide benefits for care outside an institutional setting. A home-health-care-only policy may also provide benefits for care in assisted-living facilities, and this is one area in which they often overlap with facility-only policies.

Although some insurers still write stand-alone home health care policies, many other insurers have exited this market and now write the coverage as part of a broader comprehensive long-term care insurance policy.

Comprehensive Policies

comprehensive long-term care insurance policy Most long-term care policies written today can be described as comprehensive policies. A *comprehensive long-term care insurance policy*, sometimes referred to as an integrated policy, combines benefits for facility care and home health care into a single contract. However, variations exist within this type of policy with respect to what is covered as part of the standard policy and what is an optional benefit that the applicant may select. For example, some policies cover almost all care settings as part of their standard benefits; other policies provide facility-only coverage as a standard benefit with home health care covered as an option for an additional premium.

Some Examples

The following examples of actual long-term care policies in the marketplace illustrate some of the wide variations in benefits.

EXAMPLE
1. This policy is advertised as a nursing home policy. The policy provides coverage for • nursing home care • hospice facility care • a bed reservation benefit • an alternative plan of care

EXAMPLE
2. The policy is advertised as a long-term care insurance policy providing facility benefits only. The policy provides coverage for • nursing home care • assisted-living facility care • hospice facility care • a bed reservation benefit • an alternative plan of care

EXAMPLE
3. The policy is advertised as a home health care policy and provides coverage for • home health care • adult day care • a care coordinator • caregiver training • a homemaker companion • respite care

EXAMPLE

4. The policy is advertised as a home health care policy and provides benefits for

- home health care
- adult day care
- a care coordinator
- an alternative plan of care
- caregiver training
- respite care

EXAMPLE

5. The policy is a comprehensive policy with standard benefits for facility care and optional benefits for home and community-based care. The standard benefits are for

- nursing home care
- assisted-living facility care
- hospice care
- a bed reservation benefit
- a care coordinator
- an alternative plan of care

Optional coverage includes a rider that provides benefits for

- home health care
- adult day care
- caregiver training
- a homemaker companion

EXAMPLE
6. The policy is a comprehensive policy that provides benefits for • nursing home care • assisted-living facility care • hospice care • a bed reservation benefit • home health care • adult day care • respite care • an alternative plan of care • caregiver training • a home health care coordinator

Benefit Amounts

When purchasing long-term care insurance, the applicant selects the level of benefit he or she desires up to the maximum level the insurance company will provide. Benefits are often sold in increments of $10 per day up to frequently found limits of $400 to $500. Most insurance companies will not offer a daily benefit below $40 or $50. Some policies base benefits on a monthly (rather than daily) amount that can vary from $1,000 to $12,000 or more.

The same level of benefits is usually provided for all types of institutional care. Most comprehensive policies that provide home health care benefits once limited the daily benefit to one-half the amount payable for institutional stays. However, many insurers now allow applicants to select home health care limits that are as high as 75 percent to 100 percent of the benefit for institutional care; a few insurers even offer limits as high as 125 percent or 150 percent. If a policy provides home health care benefits only, the daily amount of that benefit is what the applicant selected.

Policies pay benefits in one of two basic ways: reimbursement or per diem.

Reimbursement Policies

reimbursement basis   The majority of newer policies pay benefits on a *reimbursement basis*. These contracts reimburse the insured for actual expenses up to the specified policy limit. For example, a policy with a daily benefit amount of $200 will pay only

$150 if that was the insured's actual charge for care. Tax-qualified policies that provide benefits on a reimbursement basis must be coordinated with Medicare.

Per Diem Policies

per diem basis   Some policies provide benefits on a *per diem basis*. This means that the benefits selected are paid regardless of the actual cost of care. In this case, a policy with a daily benefit of $200 will pay $200 even if actual long-term care charges for the day are only $150. Per diem contracts are seldom coordinated with any benefits that are payable under Medicare. If home health care benefits are provided, most per diem policies pay benefits regardless of the service provider. In such cases, benefits are paid even if a family member provides care at no charge. Some policies, however, define the type of service provider from whom care must be received.

EXAMPLE

Teresa, aged 70, recently entered a nursing home following a lengthy hospitalization. The cost of her care is $200 per day. Because she will need skilled-nursing care for many months, Medicare will pay the cost of the first 20 days of care in full and provide an additional 80 days of benefits with a daily copayment. Teresa also has a tax-qualified long-term care insurance policy that will provide benefits of $150 per day after a 30-day elimination period.

If Teresa's policy provides benefits on a reimbursement basis, no benefits will be payable as long as Teresa is collecting any benefits from Medicare. When Medicare payments cease after 100 days, Teresa will collect $150 per day as long as her policy counts the days she was receiving Medicare benefits toward the elimination period.

If Teresa's policy provides benefits on a per diem basis and if the policy is not integrated with Medicare, Teresa will collect a daily benefit of $150 beginning on the 31st day, regardless of any Medicare reimbursement.

Note that per diem policies are sometimes referred to as indemnity policies even though the usual insurance meaning of indemnity implies payment of benefits for actual expenses up to policy limits. In this sense, reimbursement policies, not per diem policies, are actually contracts of indemnity. Per diem policies are valued contracts.

disability-based policy   A few insurers offer a variation of the per diem policy that pays benefits as long as the insured satisfies a policy's benefit trigger, even if no long-term care is being received. Such a policy is referred to as a disability-based policy.

Period of Benefits

To determine the period of benefits under a long-term care insurance policy, it is necessary to look at the elimination period and the maximum duration of benefits.

Elimination Period

The applicant is required to select a period of time that must pass after long-term care commences but before benefit payments begin. The majority of long-term care insurers refer to this period as an elimination period. Some insurers, however, call it a waiting period or a deductible period. Most insurers allow an applicant to select from three to five optional elimination periods. For example, one insurer allows the choice of 20, 60, 100, or 180 days. Choices may be as low as 0 days or as high as 365 days.

In a comprehensive policy, there is generally a single elimination period that can be met by any combination of days during which the insured is in a long-term care facility or receiving home health care services.

There are several ways that home health care services can be counted toward the elimination period. Some policies count only those days when actual services are received for which charges are made and will be covered after the elimination period is satisfied. If an insured receives services 3 days during the week, this counts as 3 days. If the insured's policy has a 60-day elimination period, benefit payments will not begin until the insured has been receiving services for 20 weeks (or 140 calendar days). Some policies count each week as 7 days toward the satisfaction of the elimination period if services were received on any number of days in the week, even 1 day. In this case, the insured will start receiving benefit payments after 60 days have elapsed from the first service.

Another variation in reimbursement policies is for the insurer to start counting days toward satisfaction of the elimination period as soon as long-term care is certified as being necessary, even if services are received from someone who does not make a charge. Therefore, family members or friends could provide the services until the elimination period is satisfied, and the insurer will then start paying benefits for the services of a paid caregiver.

Despite what some people think, there is no relationship between the elimination period and the requirement that tax-qualified policies cannot pay benefits for the inability to perform ADLs unless this inability is expected to last at least 90 days. If an insured is certified as being anticipated to be unable to perform the requisite number of ADLs for at least 90 days, benefit payments will start after the satisfaction of the elimination period, be it 0, 20, 60, or any other specified number of days. If the insured makes a recovery after the elimination period is satisfied but before the end of the 90-day period, the insured is fully entitled to any benefits received because the period was expected to be at least 90 days.

Maximum Duration of Benefits

The applicant is also given a choice as to the maximum period for which benefits are paid, often referred to as the benefit period. This period begins from the time benefit payments start after satisfaction of the elimination period. In addition, the benefit period does not necessarily apply to each separate period for which long-term care services are received. Rather, it is a period that applies to the aggregate time benefits are paid under the policy. When the maximum benefits are paid, the policy will terminate. However, if benefits are only partially exhausted during a course of long-term care, they may be restored under certain circumstances, as explained later. Also as explained later, the length of the benefit period may actually differ from the period chosen if a policy uses a pool-of-money concept.

Most insurers require the applicant to select the benefit period, and they make several options available. For example, one insurer offers durations of 1, 2, 3, and 5 years as well as lifetime benefits. In some states, the minimum benefit period allowed is one year; in others it is 2 years. Typically, a single benefit period applies to long-term care, no matter where it is received. A few policies, however, have separate benefit periods for facility care and home health care. There are also a few policies, usually the per diem type, that specify the maximum benefits as a stated dollar amount, such as $100,000.

pool of money   There are actually two ways that the benefit period is applied in the payment of benefits. Under one approach, benefit payments are made for exactly the benefit period chosen. If the applicant selects a benefit period of 4 years and collects benefits for 4 years, the benefit payments cease. This approach is found mostly in older policies. Today, the predominate approach uses a *pool of money*. Under this concept, there is an amount of money that can be used to make benefit payments as long as the pool of money lasts. The applicant does not select the amount in the pool of money; it is determined by multiplying the daily benefit by the benefit period selected. For example, if the daily benefit is $200 and the benefit period is 1,460 days (or 4 years), then the initial pool of money is $292,000 ($200 × 1,460). Several important points about this pool of money should be mentioned:

- Daily benefit payments from the pool of money cannot exceed the daily policy benefits.
- Under comprehensive policies, the pool of money is typically determined by using the daily benefit amount for institutional care.
- Adjustments are made to the pool of money during periods of benefit payments to reflect any inflation protection that applies to the policy benefits.

EXAMPLE

Renee has a comprehensive long-term care insurance policy that provides benefits on a reimbursement basis for a benefit period of 4 years. Her daily benefit is $200 for care in a long-term care facility and $100 per day for home health care. The policy makes benefit payments using the pool-of-money concept. Assume that Renee is chronically ill and receives home health care for 2 years at a cost of $80 per day for 5 days each week after she satisfies her elimination period. At that time, her condition deteriorates and she enters a nursing home that has a daily cost of $230.

Under a pool-of-money concept, the amount available for Renee's benefit payments is $292,000, as previously calculated. During the 2 years (104 weeks) that Renee receives home health care, the policy will make benefit payments equal to the full cost of her care because it is less than $100 per day. This totals $41,600 ($80 × 104 × 5). Therefore, the pool of money is reduced by this amount to $250,400 by the time she enters the nursing home. The policy will then pay a daily benefit but only up to the policy limit of $200 per day. (The extra $30 per day is her responsibility.) Consequently, Renee can receive benefits for an additional 1,252 days ($250,400 ÷ $200). The net effect is that Renee will actually receive benefit payments over a period that is equal to almost 5½ years. This period would be somewhat longer if an inflation increase had been assumed for the pool of money.

---

shared benefit　　　　A few insurers use the concept of a *shared benefit* when a husband and wife are insured under the same policy or with separate policies that are linked with shared benefit riders. Under this concept, each spouse can access the other spouse's benefits. There are variations as to how this is accomplished. Under one variation, for example, if each spouse has a 4-year benefit period and one spouse has exhausted his or her benefits, benefit payments can continue by drawing on any unused benefits under the other spouse's policy. In effect, one spouse could have a benefit period of up to 8 years as long as the other spouse receives no benefit payments. Under another variation, an insurer might use a single pool-of-money design. A single pool combines benefits for both spouse, and either or both spouses simultaneously can draw benefit payments from the pool. At the death of one spouse, whatever is in the pool remains for the survivor.

Restoration

Many policies written with less than a lifetime benefit period provide for restoration of full benefits if the insured received less-than-full policy benefits and has not required long-term care for a certain time period, often 180 days. If a policy does not have a restoration-of-benefits provision, maximum benefits for a subsequent claim are reduced by the benefits previously paid. In some cases, this benefit is a standard part of the policy; in other cases, it may be added with a rider.

Inflation Protection

Most states require a long-term care policy to offer some type of automatic inflation protection. (Such protection must be included in certain partnership policies.) The applicant is given the choice to select this option, decline the option, or possibly select an alternative option. If the applicant selects the automatic-increase option, the cost of the option is built into the initial premium, and no additional premium is levied at the time of an annual increase. As a result of the NAIC model act and HIPAA, the standard provision found in almost all policies is a 5 percent benefit increase that is compounded annually over the life of the policy. Under such a provision, the amount of a policy's benefits increases by 5 percent each year over the amount of benefits available in the prior year. The increase affects both the daily or monthly maximum, as well as the lifetime benefit amount in policies with finite lengths. The lifetime benefit maximum is usually increased by the same percentage as the daily/monthly amount. Some policies, however, have two stated inflation rates—one for the daily/monthly maximum and another for the lifetime maximum.

A common alternative that many insurers make available is based on simple interest, whereby each annual automatic increase is 5 percent of the original benefit amount. Other options that are occasionally found are increases (either simple or compound) based on different fixed percentage amounts, such as 3 or 4 percent, or on the consumer price index.

The effect of an automatic increase in daily benefits can be dramatic, as the following table indicates. However, such an increase is also accompanied by a significant premium increase in the policy from its inception.

Table 15-2 Effect of Automatic Increase on $100 Per Day Benefit			
End of Policy Year	No Increase	5% Simple Interest	5% Compound Interest
5	$100	$125	$128
10	100	150	163
15	100	175	208
20	100	200	265
25	100	225	339
30	100	250	432

If an automatic-increase option is not selected, some insurers allow a policyowner to increase benefits without evidence of insurability on a pay-as-you-go basis at specified intervals, such as every 1, 2, or 3 years. Each benefit increase is accompanied by a premium increase that is based on attained-age rates for the additional coverage. This type of inflation protection is rarely appropriate for younger applicants since the cost of coverage can become prohibitive in their old age, just when they might need it the most.

The amount of the periodic benefit increase under a pay-as-you-go option may be a fixed dollar amount, such as a daily benefit increase of $20 every third year, or based on a specified percentage or an index, such as the CPI. Some insurers have an aggregate limit on the total amount of benefit increases or an age beyond which they are no longer available. Failure to exercise a periodic increase or a series of increases over a specified period typically terminates the right to purchase additional benefits in the future.

It is important to note that increases in benefits might be inadequate to offset actual inflation in the annual cost of long-term care, which has been higher than the general inflation rate over the last decade.

Eligibility for Benefits

Almost all tax-qualified contracts use the same two criteria for determining benefit eligibility; the insured is required to meet only one of the two. The first criterion is that the insured is expected to be unable, without substantial assistance from another person, to perform at least two of the six ADLs that are acceptable under HIPAA for a period of at least 90 days due to loss of functional capacity. The second criterion is that substantial supervision is required to protect the individual from threats to health and safety because of severe cognitive impairment.

Non-tax-qualified contracts, on the other hand, have more liberal eligibility requirements. Many of these contracts use the same criteria that are in tax-qualified contracts, except there is no 90-day expectation of need that applies to the inability to perform the ADLs. A small number of non-tax-qualified contracts use more than the six ADLs allowed by HIPAA and/or require only that the insured be unable to perform one ADL. Finally, some non-tax-qualified contracts make benefits available if a third criterion—medical necessity—is satisfied. This generally means that a physician has certified that long-term care is needed, even if neither of the other criteria is satisfied.

Exclusions

Most long-term care policies contain the exclusions permitted under the NAIC model act. One source of controversy is the exclusion for mental and nervous disorders. This is an area that insurers have frequently avoided in the past because of the possibility of fraudulent claims and the controversies that often arise over claim settlements. The exclusion states as follows: "We will not pay benefits for any long-term care which is due to mental, psychoneurotic, or personality disorders without demonstrable organic disease." Many of these policies specifically state that Alzheimer's disease and senile dementia, as diagnosed by a physician, are considered to have a demonstrable organic cause, even though state laws often require insurers to cover these disorders.

The mental or nervous disorder exclusion has been removed from most currently issued policies. This does not mean that the policy will pay for treatment in a mental facility or for treatment of a mental disease. It only means that long-term care benefits will not be withheld if an insured otherwise meets the criteria for benefits.

Underwriting

The underwriting of long-term care policies, like the underwriting of medical expense policies, is based on the health of the insured. However, underwriting for long-term care insurance focuses on situations that will cause claims far into the future. Most underwriting is done on the basis of questionnaires and copies of physician's records rather than on the use of actual physical examinations. At older ages (usually 72 and older) or for those with questionable health history, applicants may be asked to have a face-to-face assessment by a nurse. The assessment usually includes height, weight, blood pressure, review of health history, and a cognitive test. More and more companies are now requiring at least a phone interview of the applicant by a nurse to review health history, ask additional questions, and perhaps perform a cognitive test. In addition, numerous questions are now asked on the application about the health of relatives. For example, if a parent or grandparent had Alzheimer's disease, there is an increased likelihood that the applicant will get this disease in the future. In addition, the insurance company is very interested in medical events, such as temporary numbness in a limb or fainting spells, that might be an indication of future incapacity.

Underwriting tends to become more restrictive as the age of an applicant increases. Not only is a future claim more likely to occur much sooner, but adverse selection can also be more severe.

Many insurers have a single classification for all acceptable applicants for long-term care insurance, but other insurers have three or four categories of insurable classifications, each with a different rate structure.

Some long-term care policies have a preexisting-conditions provision; it specifies that benefits are not paid within the first 6 months for a condition for which treatment was recommended or received within 6 months prior to policy purchase. Other policies, however, have no such provision or state that the provision does not apply to preexisting conditions that are listed on the policy application. There is little need for such a provision because insurers are required in most states to underwrite at the time coverage is written and are not allowed to use postclaims underwriting. If properly underwritten at the time of application, claims within the usual preexisting-conditions period are unlikely. Elimination periods for benefits often serve a similar purpose.

Renewability

From a renewability standpoint, long-term care policies currently being sold are guaranteed renewable, which means that an individual's coverage cannot be canceled except for nonpayment of premium. Although premiums cannot be raised on the basis of a particular applicant's claim, they can (and sometimes are) raised by class.

Nonforfeiture Options

Most companies give an applicant for long-term care insurance the right to elect a nonforfeiture benefit, and some states require that such a benefit be offered. With a nonforfeiture benefit, the policyowner will receive some value from a policy if the policy lapses because the required premium is not paid in the future. Few applicants, however, elect this option because of its cost.

The most common type of nonforfeiture option, and the one almost always available in tax-qualified policies, is a shortened benefit period. With this option, coverage is continued as a paid-up policy, but the length of the benefit period (or the amount of the benefit if stated as a maximum dollar amount) is reduced. Under the typical provision, the reduced coverage is available only if the lapse is on or after the policy's third anniversary. The amount of the benefit is equal to the greater of the total premiums paid for the policy prior to lapse or 30 times the policy's daily nursing home benefit.

Some non-tax-qualified policies offer a return-of-premium rider, under which a portion of the premium is returned if a policy lapses after a specified number of years. For example, the policy of one insurer pays nothing if a policy lapses before it has been in force for 5 full years. It returns 15 percent of the total premiums paid if the policy was in force for 6 years, 30 percent for 7 years, 45 percent for 8 years, 60 percent for 9 years, and 80 percent for 10 or more years.

In some states that require an insurer to offer a nonforfeiture benefit, a policy must contain a contingent nonforfeiture benefit upon lapse if the policyowner does not purchase the nonforfeiture benefit. This provision gives the policyowner the right to elect certain options if the premium has increased by a specified percentage since the time of policy issue. The percentage is a sliding scale that is determined by the issue age. For example, the percentage is 110 if the policy was issued when the insured was 50 to 54. The figure drops to 70 percent for an issue age of 60, 40 percent for an issue age of 70, and 20 percent for an issue age of 80. The options are a reduction in benefits to a level sustainable by the current premium or the conversion of the policy to a paid-up status with a shorter benefit period. The policyowner is not required to select either of these options and can continue to pay the higher premium and maintain the current policy benefits.

Premiums

Premium Payment Period

The majority of long-term care policies have premiums that are payable for life and determined by the age of the insured at the time of application. A few insurers, however, offer other modes of payment. Lifetime coverage can sometimes be purchased with a single premium. Some insurers offer policies that have premium payment periods of 10 or 20 years or to age 65, after which time the premium is paid up. These policies are particularly attractive to applicants who do not want continuing premium payments after retirement.

Most long-term care policies have a waiver-of-premium provision that waives premiums if the insured has been receiving benefits under the policy for a specified period of time, often 60 or 90 days, or upon payment of benefits under the policy. Most policies also have a 31-day grace period for the payment of premiums.

Factors Affecting Premiums

Numerous factors affect the premium that a policyowner will pay for a long-term care policy. Even if the provisions of several policies are virtually identical, premiums will vary among companies. For example, the annual premiums for three similar policies from three different companies are shown in the table below. Each policy has a daily benefit of $100 per day, a 90-day elimination period, a lifetime benefit period, and a 5 percent annual compound inflation increase. Unlike the situation for other types of insurance, long-term care insurance rates do not vary by gender.

Table 15-3 Comparison of Annual Long-Term Care Premiums for Similar Policies			
Age	Company A	Company B	Company C
40	$1,231	$1,678	$2,151
50	1,955	1,942	2,506
60	3,052	2,661	3,473
70	5,113	4,387	6,031

The first four factors mentioned below are givens for an applicant with a particular company. The effect of the remaining factors depends to varying degrees on choices made by an applicant.

Age. Age plays a significant role in the cost of long-term care coverage, as shown in the table above. These figures demonstrate that long-term care coverage can be obtained at a reasonable annual cost if it is purchased at a younger age.

Underwriting Class. Each insurer has one or more underwriting classes for long-term care insurance. Some insurers have a single class; all applicants are either accepted and charged the rate for that class or declined for coverage. Other insurers have a series of underwriting classes that have different rate structures. The insured's medical condition determines the class into which he or she falls. Even with several underwriting classes, there are still applicants who will be unacceptable to the insurer.

Marital Status. Most insurers offer a spousal discount. Experience has shown that long-term care claims from married persons are less frequent and of shorter duration than claims from single or widowed persons. This favorable claim experience results because many married couples take care of each other for as long as possible before professional long-term care providers are called upon. Some insurers give a spousal discount, which may be 20 to 40 percent or more, only if they insure both spouses; other insurers may also give a discount (10 percent, for example) to anyone who lives with his or her spouse.

Insurers may also apply these discounts to siblings who live together and/or to unmarried couples who have committed relationships.

Tobacco Use versus Nonuse. The use of tobacco is a significant health hazard. Not only does it affect medical expense claims, but it also results in an increased need for long-term care. Therefore, tobacco use may disqualify a person for an insurer's preferred rate class or require placement in a higher rate class.

Types of Benefits. The benefits a policy provides have a significant bearing on the cost. Most policies cover care in a long-term care facility. Many policies also cover home health care and other benefits provided to persons who are still able to reside in their own homes. This broader coverage increases premiums by 60 to 70 percent.

Duration of Benefits. The longer the maximum benefit period, the higher the premium. The longer the elimination period, the lower the premium. With many insurers, a policy with an unlimited benefit period and no elimination period will have a premium about double that of a policy with a 2-year benefit period and a 90-day elimination period.

Inflation Protection. Policies may be written with or without automatic benefit increases for inflation. All other factors being equal, the addition of a 5 percent compound annual increase in benefits can raise premiums by 50 to 100 percent over a policy with no automatic inflation protection.

Nonforfeiture Benefits. Except for some partnership policies, a policy may be written with or without a nonforfeiture benefit. The inclusion of such a benefit can increase a premium by anywhere from 20 to 50 percent or more, depending on the type of nonforfeiture benefit and other policy features.

An Example

As the following example shows, an applicant for long-term care insurance must often make several decisions before the final selection of a long-term care insurance policy.

EXAMPLE

Fred, aged 65, has decided that he needs long-term care insurance. Five years ago, he and his wife sold their small jewelry store and were able to retire comfortably. Their plans of a leisurely life during retirement years were soon shattered when Fred's wife had a serious stroke. For 3 years, Fred was able to care for her at home with the assistance of professional caregivers. After she was totally paralyzed 2 years ago by a second stroke, Fred found it necessary to put her in the nursing home where she recently died.

Having spent almost $250,000 to provide his wife with the best care possible, Fred is fully aware of the effect that long-term care can have on a family's assets. He wants to make sure that any long-term care expenses he might incur will not further deplete the $500,000 in remaining assets that he and his wife spent a lifetime accumulating and intended to leave to their children and grandchildren.

Fred has contacted a well-respected insurance agent whom he has known for several years and asked her to help him find a long-term care insurance policy that meets his objectives. Fred has indicated that he would like a policy that provides these benefits:

- a daily facility benefit of $150. A top-quality nursing home in Fred's town will cost about $250 per day, but Fred feels he can afford to pay $100 from his Social Security and retirement income.

- a home health care benefit of $150 per day

- a lifetime benefit period

- a 20-day elimination period

- 5 percent annual compound inflation protection

Fred's agent calculates that such a policy will have an annual premium of $5,060. Fred feels that this is somewhat more than he can pay without withdrawing funds from his assets and asks her what can be done to reduce the premium to about $4,000 per year. She comes up with the following alternatives:

- If Fred lowers the daily benefit to $130 per day, the premium will drop to $4,380. A further decrease to $120 per day will result in a premium of $4,050. Fred decides to consider this option.

- If Fred decreases the home health care benefit to 50 percent of the facility benefit, the premium will drop to $4,130. Fred realizes how costly home health care can be and doesn't like this option.

- If Fred elects a 5-year benefit period, the premium will drop to $4,135. For a 4-year benefit period, the premium will be $3,800. Fred is aware of some patients in his wife's nursing home who had been there for as long as 10 years and doesn't like this option either.

- If he increases the elimination period to 90 days, the premium will drop to $4,150. The premium for a 180-day elimination period will further decrease the premium to $3,750. Fred is willing to think about a 90-day elimination period, but he feels that 180 days is too long.

- If Fred changes the inflation protection from compound interest to simple interest, the premium will drop to $4,260. Fred hopes to live for many more years and realizes the effect that inflation will have on long-term care costs. This option doesn't appeal to him.

Fred decides to take a day or two to think about his options. He calculates that the longer elimination period will increase his out-of-pocket costs by $10,500 (70 days times $150) over what they would otherwise be if he needs long-term care. He also calculates that the lower benefit amount of $120 will increase his annual out-of-pocket costs by $10,950 (365 days times $30). Fred realizes that these out-of-pocket costs will come from his accumulated assets. He also understands that he could afford the benefits he originally desired if he were willing to reduce his assets by about $1,000 per year to pay the $5,060 premium.

Fred finally decides that the policy with the $5,060 premium is the most appropriate choice. Its benefits will make it more likely that his family will provide the level of care he wants if he is unable to make decisions for himself.

PARTNERSHIP PROGRAMS FOR LONG-TERM CARE

The partnership programs for long-term care are alliances between certain state governments and insurance companies to encourage the sale of approved long-term care policies. The goals of these programs are to protect people from being impoverished by long-term care expenses and to avoid their immediate dependence on Medicaid.

Many middle-class people in nursing homes qualify for Medicaid by spending virtually all of their assets on long-term care or by transferring the assets to put themselves in a state of poverty. The result has been a staggering financial burden on Medicaid that endangers its mission to care for the poor in many states. The cycle of spending down to Medicaid dependence can be broken if more middle-class Americans—especially those of more modest means who are likely to spend down to qualify for Medicaid—could be broadly encouraged to purchase long-term care insurance.

The potential savings to the Medicaid program are obvious. If the policy's benefits prove sufficient to meet the cost of care, a person with long-term care insurance may not have to rely on Medicaid at all. Moreover, a comprehensive policy provides resources to care for someone at home. For most persons, this is the preferred site for receiving care, and many Medicaid programs only cover institutional care.

In return for the potential cost savings generated by reducing Medicaid dependence, states are willing to offer an incentive for the purchase of long-term care insurance by allowing people who purchase such coverage to qualify for Medicaid while maintaining a higher-than-usual personal asset level. States are generally able to recover assets from the estates of deceased Medicaid recipients to the extent they received Medicaid benefits. Partnership programs also protect a certain amount of assets from such estate recovery.

However, it is important to emphasize that partnership programs do not guarantee future Medicaid eligibility. They do not waive income requirements that apply to Medicaid eligibility. Program beneficiaries, therefore, must spend essentially all their income on long-term care expenses before they are eligible for Medicaid benefits. This standard Medicaid requirement effectively eliminates the value of the program with respect to Medicaid eligibility for many high-income persons. In addition, Medicaid programs also require that a recipient meet certain functionality standards with regard to the need for care, and these may be more stringent than the benefit triggers in a partnership policy.

Program Development

Starting in the late 1980s, the Robert Wood Johnson Foundation awarded program development grants to four states: California, Connecticut, Indiana, and New York. The resulting and continuing programs in these four states, known as partnership programs, became operational in the early 1990s. Because Medicaid programs are established under federal guidelines, approval for these programs was needed from the federal government. The Department of Health and Human Services granted such approval, or waivers, that permitted these states to implement their programs. Purchasers of long-term care insurance policies under these programs could then maintain some or all of their assets and still qualify for Medicaid without having to spend down their assets to levels typically required for Medicaid eligibility.

The Omnibus Budget Reconciliation Act of 1993 eliminated an important feature of state partnership programs approved by the Department of Health and Human Services after May 14, 1993. Any partnership program approved after that date was no longer able to exempt amounts from Medicaid's estate recovery requirements for individuals who applied to Medicaid after exhausting their private long-term care insurance benefits. Even though a new partnership program could continue to allow a participant to retain greater asset amounts upon application for Medicaid, the state was required to recover Medicaid's long-term care expenditures from the participant's estate, including the previously protected assets. Thus, the asset-protection component of any new partnership program would be in effect only while the participant was alive. This requirement effectively removed the asset-protection incentive that was essential for consumer interest in any long-term care insurance policy that a new state partnership program might offer.

However, the Deficit Reduction Act of 2005 restored the ability of states to obtain a Medicaid plan amendment that allows exemption from the estate recovery requirement for qualified partnership programs. But these partnership programs may exempt only the amounts of the insurance benefits made to or on behalf of an individual under a partnership policy that meets the requirements specified in the law. These standards are largely consistent with the practices of the four original programs and conform to NAIC and HIPAA provisions.

Nature

Although the newer programs have many similarities and are subject to certain federal rules, each state's program also has its own unique features. In addition, the federal rules implemented by the Deficit Reduction Act do not apply to the four original partnership programs. However, in many respects they have similar provisions. As a result, financial advisors need to be aware of the specific program that exists in the state where a client resides. Detailed information may be available on the web site of the state insurance department.

The following discussion looks at partnership programs with respect to their relationship with Medicaid and the nature of the policies available.

Relationship with Medicaid

The new partnership programs allowed by the Deficit Reduction Act must use a dollar-for-dollar asset protection model. This means that, when private long-term insurance benefits are used, an amount equal to the long-term benefits that were paid up to the time of Medicaid application is disregarded for purposes of determining Medicare eligibility. Policy benefits paid are also sheltered from a state's estate recovery program after the insured's death.

The original four partnership states can continue to use the rules that originally were adopted. All four use the dollar-for-dollar asset protection model. However, New York and Indiana also use a total assets model if the insured purchases a policy that has a level of benefits beyond a specified threshold. In such cases, all assets are protected, even if they exceed the policy benefits.

One limitation to the original partnership programs was that, although an insured could receive insurance benefits while living in any state, assets were protected only in the state where the policy was purchased. Connecticut and Indiana later entered into a reciprocity agreement. Under the Deficit Reduction Act, the new programs must have reciprocity with each other unless a state specifically rejects such a provision. To date, none has. This means that, if the insured purchases a policy in one of the new partnership states, he or she will have Medicaid asset protection under the Medicaid program of another new partnership state to which he or she moves. Over time, these states may also enter into reciprocity agreements with the four original partnership states.

It is important to point out that Medicaid rules can change. For example, a state could eliminate or significantly alter its rules for asset protection or reciprocity.

Policy Characteristics

For, the most part, the nature of policies in the new partnership states differ very little from the policies being sold prior to the partnership legislation. However, there are a few specific requirements:

- A partnership policy must be designed as a tax-qualified policy.
- The policy must be issued after the effective date of the partnership program. There is no automatic grandfathering of existing policies. However, most states allow the insured either to exchange an existing policy for a partnership policy or to obtain an endorsement that converts an existing policy to a partnership policy as long as the original policy would otherwise qualify as a partnership policy.
- The insured must be a resident of the state sponsoring the partnership program at the time insurance coverage first goes into effect.
- The policy must provide for inflation protection. If the insured is aged 60 or younger, the policy must have some form of annual compound inflation protection. However, the precise nature of the compounding is up to the individual states. If the insured is over age 60 and under age 76, there must be some form of inflation protection, but it can take any of the forms discussed earlier in the chapter. Finally, insureds aged 76 or older must be offered inflation protection but are not required to purchase it.
- Agents who sell, solicit, or negotiate partnership policies must receive training and understand the role partnership policies play in the financing of long-term care. Some states require training programs only for agents selling partnership programs, but most partnership states extend this training to agents selling any long-term care insurance policies. In most states, this training is based on an 8-hour NAIC model course.

THE CLASS ACT

CLASS Act   The CLASS Act, or Community Living Assistance Services and Supports Act, is a long-term care program created through the Affordable Care Act. The program is expected to have complete regulations issued by October 1, 2012. Currently, there are several questions about the program, and many doubt that the program can remain solvent. The purpose of this section is to describe the basic framework of the CLASS program as established by the Affordable Care Act.

The law requires the Secretary of the Department of Health and Human Services, in consultation with experts and actuaries, to develop three actuarially sound plans to implement as the *CLASS program.* The CLASS program will pay benefits for long-term care services to qualifying participants who have paid in premiums. The funding for the program will be through premiums paid by working participants. Within these three potential CLASS plans, key elements of the program include:

- premiums
- vesting periods
- benefit triggers
- cash benefits

The premiums charged for the CLASS program are supposed to ensure the programs solvency for a rolling 75-year period. However, some participants will not be required to make full premium payments. Nominal premiums, of no more than $5 per month adjusted by the consumer price index, will be paid by individuals whose income is below the federal poverty line and by full-time students under 22 years of age.

CLASS vesting period

Each of the three plans must also include a vesting period of 5 years before an enrollee can be eligible for benefits. Enrollees will pay premiums into the fund, and will establish eligibility much like Social Security, by being credited for quarters they paid into the CLASS program. An important feature of the CLASS program is that no medical underwriting can be used to qualify participants, so even employees with significant medical problems can be enrolled and receive benefits after 5 years in the program. This lack of medical underwriting is a major source of skepticism over the CLASS program.

CLASS benefit triggers

Each plan is also to establish benefit triggers. An eligible beneficiary who meets these benefits triggers can collect their benefits from the program. Benefits must be payable when an individual has a functional limitation, as certified by a licensed health care practitioner, that is expected to last for a continuous 90 days, and meets one of the following criteria:

- The individual is determined to be unable to perform at least the minimum number of activities of daily living without substantial assistance from another individual;
- The individual requires substantial supervision to protect the individual from threats to health and safety due to substantial cognitive impairment (such as Alzheimer's disease); or
- The individual has a level of functional limitation similar to the level of functional limitation described by the first two triggers, which will be established by the Department of Health and Human Services.

eligibility assessments

Under the Affordable Care Act, the Secretary of HHS is also required to establish procedures for eligibility assessments. These are essentially screening processes to make sure enrollees are eligible for benefits under the vesting requirements and the functional impairment rules.

CLASS cash benefit

Each plan developed under the CLASS Act must provide a cash benefit to eligible beneficiaries when one of the benefit triggers is satisfied along with the other eligibility requirements. The cash benefit is to be no less than $50 a day, and will be determined on a sliding scale. This means that theoretically, the sicker you were, the greater the benefit you would receive. Also, note that the cash benefit is not subject to any aggregate or lifetime limit, which means that benefits could be paid for a very long period.

CLASS enrollment

Enrollment into the program is a major concern. As the law stands now, employers can automatically enroll employees into the program, unless the employee opts out. Employers will have the option to automatically enroll their employees, make payroll deductions for enrollees to pay premiums, do both of these things, or do nothing at all. The Secretary of the Department of Health and Human Services is required to establish other ways for potential participants to enroll in the program.

Life Independence Accounts

The final issue under the CLASS Program is dealing with distributing the cash benefits to qualifying eligible beneficiaries. The law establishes what is known as a "Life Independence Account", which would act as a bank account that could be accessed by debit cards. This final issue will be addressed in the three plans that are developed by HHS.

Overall, there is much concern over the CLASS Program. This is still a very controversial topic in Congress, and we must wait to see what will happen with the program. If the program survives the political process and is implemented, it could be a great opportunity for some. Individual clients could gain access to some long-term care benefits, employers could offer a minimal long-term care benefit to employees, and the CLASS Program could be a great segue into a conversation with your clients about their long-term care needs.

GROUP COVERAGE

Success in the individual marketplace led to interest in group long-term care insurance as an employee benefit. The first group long-term plan was written in 1987, and a growing number of employers, mostly large ones, now make coverage available. The number of insurance companies writing coverage has also grown, but it still remains relatively small and is primarily limited to the largest group insurance carriers. However, over 2 million employees and their family members now have group coverage. In most cases, coverage is voluntary with the employee paying the full cost.

For the most part, group long-term care policies are comparable to the better policies that are being sold in the individual marketplace. There are a few differences, however, mostly because of the characteristics of group coverage:

- Eligibility for coverage generally requires that an employee be full-time and actively at work. At a minimum, coverage can be purchased for an active employee and/or the spouse. Some policies also make coverage available to retirees and to other family members of eligible persons, such as minor children, parents, parents-in-law, grandparents, and possibly adult children.
- The cost of group coverage is usually slightly less than the cost of individual coverage. To some extent, this is a result of the administrative services, such as payroll deduction, being performed by the employer.
- An employee typically has fewer choices with respect to benefit amounts, benefit duration, inflation protection, and the length of the elimination period.
- If a participant leaves employment, the group coverage can usually be continued on a direct-payment basis, under either the group contract or an individual contract.

CHECKLIST FOR EVALUATING AND COMPARING LONG-TERM CARE POLICIES

- What is the annual policy premium?
- Is the policy qualified to receive favorable tax treatment?
- Does the policy qualify as a partnership policy?
- What is the length of the free-look period?
- What services are covered?

  ___ Nursing home care

  ___ Assisted-living care

  ___ Custodial care

  ___ Home health care

  ___ Adult day care

  ___ Other

- Is the policy a reimbursement policy or a per diem policy?
- How much does the policy pay per day for the following?

  ___ Facility care

  ___ Home health care

  ___ Other

- How long will benefits last?

  ___ For facility care

  ___ At home

- Does the policy have a maximum lifetime benefit? If yes, what is it?
- Does the policy have a maximum length of coverage for each period of confinement? If yes, what is it?

  ___ For facility care

  ___ For home health care

- What is the length of time before preexisting conditions are covered?
- How long is the elimination period before benefits begin?

  ___ For facility care

  ___ For home health care

- What is the age range for enrollment?
- Is there a waiver-of-premium provision?

___ For facility care

___ For home health care

- What is the period that an insured must receive benefits before premiums are waived?

- Does the policy offer an inflation adjustment feature? If yes,

   ___ What type of option is it?

   ___ What is the rate of increase?

   ___ How often is it applied?

   ___ To what benefits is it applied?

   ___ For how long?

   ___ Is there an additional cost? If so, how much?

- What nonforfeiture options are available?

CHAPTER REVIEW

Key Terms and Concepts

look-back period
partnership program
continuing care retirement
  communities (CCRCs)
long-term care insurance
qualified long-term care insurance
  contract
qualified long-term care services
chronically ill individual
activities of daily living (ADLs)
nursing home care
custodial care
bed reservation benefit
assisted-living care
adult day care center
care coordinator
respite care

facility-only policy
home-health-care-only policies
comprehensive long-term care
  insurance policy
reimbursement basis
per diem basis
disability-based policy
pool of money
shared benefit
CLASS Act
CLASS vesting period
CLASS benefit triggers
eligibility assessments
CLASS cash benefit
CLASS enrollment
Life Independence Accounts

Review Questions

Review questions are based on the learning objectives in this chapter. Thus, a [3] at the end of a question means that the question is based on learning objective 3. If there are multiple objectives, they are all listed.

1. Why is there a need for long-term care insurance? [1]

2. What are the sources for providing long-term care other than insurance? [1]

3. Summarize the criteria for policy provisions in the NAIC model legislation for long-term care insurance. [2]

4. What are the requirements that a long-term care insurance contract must meet to be "qualified" under the Health Insurance Portability and Accountability Act (HIPAA)? [3]

5. Describe the federal income tax treatment of a qualified long-term care insurance contract. [3]

6. What are the usual issue ages for long-term care insurance contracts? [4]

7. What are the types of care a long-term care insurance policy might cover? [4]

8. Describe the amounts and duration of long-term care benefits. [4]

9. Explain how insurance companies determine whether a long-term care policyowner is eligible for benefits. [4]

10. What factors affect the amount of the premium for a long-term care insurance contract? [4]

11. What is the nature of the partnership programs for long-term care? [5].

12. Compare group long-term care insurance with the coverage being sold in the individual marketplace. What differences exist between the two types of coverage? [6]

> ## Learning Objectives
> *An understanding of the material in this chapter should enable the student to*
>
> 1. Describe the types of property and liability loss exposures that families and businesses face.
>
> 2. Explain the policy provisions typically found in property and liability insurance policies.
>
> 3. Briefly explain the tax treatment of property and liability insurance premiums and loss settlements for individuals and businesses, and explain why there is a need for property and liability insurance planning.

Property and liability insurance is an area of financial planning that is often overlooked or given less than thorough attention. Financial planners should be equipped to help their clients assess their property and liability risks.

According to a survey by the Chubb Group of insurance companies, "57 percent of the 102 financial planners surveyed indicated that they evaluate their clients' asset protection through property/casualty insurance. An even higher number, 72 percent, said they determine if their clients have an appropriate level of liability insurance." A Chubb officer commented, "A financial plan that does not include property/casualty insurance and risk management potentially leaves a client's entire asset base at risk."[52] Failure to carry appropriate and adequate property and liability insurance can result in a severe uninsured loss that scuttles a client's otherwise sound plan for capital accumulation and preservation.

---

52. Chubb Insurance Companies Press Release: "Financial Planners Pay More Attention to P/C Insurance and Risk Management," March 21, 2006, Warren, NJ (http://www.chubb.com/corporate/chubb4930.html, accessed 12/15/06). In this context, "property/casualty insurance" means the same thing as "property and liability insurance."

Property and liability insurance is important for many additional reasons, including but not limited to these:

- Many individuals, especially those with good employee benefits, spend more on property and liability insurance than they spend on all other types of insurance combined.
- Property and liability insurance is complicated, and exposures and policies must be thoroughly analyzed to determine whether a client is adequately protected.
- Many policy endorsements and other coverage options are available.

A number of financial planning issues involve property and liability exposures and insurance. For example, higher deductibles, or a decision to forgo certain insurance coverages, can reduce insurance costs but increase the need for a sizable emergency fund. The converse is also true. An individual with a substantial emergency fund can often make more efficient use of property and liability insurance by choosing higher deductibles and forgoing some nonessential fringe coverages.

The high premium costs associated with property and liability insurance raise other financial planning issues. For example, because insurance is highly competitive, wise shopping for price and service is advisable. Last but not least, any financial planning that involves property and liability loss financing should recognize the tax implications.

The discussion begins by describing property and liability loss exposures. In connection with property exposures, the chapter explains how the insurable value of property is established and how losses are settled. The liability discussion explains the types of damages covered by liability insurance, how the value of any claim is determined, and how claims are settled. The basic types of policies and their income tax implications are also discussed.

PROPERTY AND LIABILITY LOSS EXPOSURES

A loss exposure is the possibility that a loss could occur. Although property insurance and liability insurance are often provided in the same insurance policy, a clear distinction exists between the loss exposures addressed by each type of coverage.

- A property loss exposure is the possibility that a person or organization will sustain a property loss resulting from the damaging, destruction, taking, or loss of use of property in which that person or organization has a financial interest.

- A liability loss exposure is the possibility of a claim alleging a person's or organization's legal responsibility for injury or damage suffered by another party. Notice the emphasis on the possibility of a claim rather than on the payment of damages. Many liability claims result in no payment to the claimant because they are successfully defended. However, even then, the defense costs, adverse publicity, and other matters can create a distinct financial loss. Therefore, a liability loss occurs when a responsibility to pay damages is alleged, whether or not damages are ultimately paid to the party making the claim.

PROPERTY INSURANCE

Property insurance deals with property in two broad categories, real property and personal property. However, property insurance does not protect property. It protects property owners and other parties that meet two qualifications. First, they must have an insurable interest in the property at the time of the loss, and second, their interest must be insured under a contract of insurance. The amount any insured party may be entitled to recover from property insurance proceeds depends not only on the extent of that party's insurable interest but also on the method used to determine the value of the property as well as any financial loss resulting from the fact that the property cannot be used. For example, a driver may need to rent a car while his or her own car is being repaired following an accident. Likewise, a family may incur expenses to live in a hotel while its house is being repaired, and a business may suffer a loss of income if the place of business has been damaged or destroyed.

Property insurance covers only losses that result from a covered cause, also known as a covered peril. When damage to property by a covered peril occurs, the insurance contract specifies certain duties that the insured party and the insurer must meet. The amount payable under a property insurance policy depends on various provisions in the insurance contract, especially limits, deductibles, and insurance-to-value provisions.

Types of Property

From a legal perspective, all property falls into one of two categories:

- real property

- personal property

real property
Real property, a term closely related to the more familiar term real estate, is defined as land and anything that is growing on it, or affixed to it, and the bundle of rights inherent in the ownership. It includes such items as crops, mineral rights, air rights, buildings, items that are permanently attached to buildings, fences, in-ground swimming pools, driveways, and retaining walls.

The antonym of real property is not imaginary property, but rather personal property. In the context of financial planning, "personal" often means "nonbusiness." The term "personal property," however, has nothing to do with individuals and families. Personal property is owned and used by individuals, families, and businesses.

personal property
Personal property is defined to include anything that is subject to ownership other than real property. This includes such items as clothes, furniture, dishes, artwork, musical instruments, money, securities, airline tickets, office equipment, business inventory, vehicles, and boats. It also includes intangible property, such as copyrights and patents.

Rather than use these broad legal categories, insurance policies often use more specific terms, such as building, structure, private passenger auto, or trailer.

Insurable Interests and Insured Parties

Property insurance policies pay only when policyowners or other insured parties have an insurable interest in the property that has suffered a loss. Two or more persons who jointly own property are likely to be listed as policyowners and entitled to the policy's protection. In any case, the insurer will not reimburse an insured party for more than that party has lost. Coverage applies to the extent of each insured party's insurable interest in the property at the time of the loss, subject to policy limits and any other relevant provisions.

Lenders have an insurable interest in specific property pledged as collateral for a loan. Therefore, a mortgagee, who has lent money to the purchaser of a home or another building, has an insurable interest in the building, and a bank has an insurable interest in an auto pledged as security for an auto loan. The interest of a mortgagee named in the policy's declarations can be protected by a property insurance policy's mortgage clause, and a lender's interest in personal property can be protected by a loss payable clause. In either case, the lender's insurable interest in the property is equal to the unpaid balance on the loan.

Mortgage Clause

mortgage clause

A *mortgage clause* is a standard part of a homeowners policy and many other property insurance policies covering real property. The mortgage clause applies when a mortgagee (lender, mortgage holder) is listed in the policy declarations. The policy gives the mortgagee some rights and imposes on the mortgagee some obligations. The mortgagee has a right to

- receive any loss payments from the insurer to the extent of its insurable interest in the property. The mortgagee has a right to this payment even if the policyowner's claim is denied, so long as the mortgagee:
    - notifies the insurer of any change in ownership or occupancy or any increase in hazard of which the mortgagee is aware
    - pays any premium due if the policyowner fails to do so
    - surrenders any claim it might have against the policyowner to the extent the insurer pays the mortgagee
- receive separate advance notice if the insurer decides to cancel or nonrenew the policy

The requirement that the mortgagee notify the insurer of any increase in hazard is especially relevant in light of the recent increase in mortgage foreclosures. In one recent case, the insured fell behind on her payments and the bank did not notify the insurer that it had begun foreclosure proceedings. A fire destroyed the house soon after the insured filed for bankruptcy. The insurer denied coverage for the lender, and the courts agreed. By increasing the moral hazard, the foreclosure proceedings constituted an increase in risk, and the bank failed in its obligation to report this increase in hazard to the insurer.[53]

A property insurance claim check is issued jointly to the policyowner and the mortgagee. It is up to these parties to determine how the proceeds are split. In most cases, the mortgagee endorses the check to the policyowner so the property can be repaired or replaced. However, in the absence of any

---

53. *U.S., Bank v. Tennessee Farmers Mut. Ins. Co.* 2007 WL 4463959 (Tenn Ct. App. Dec. 21, 2007).

provision in the mortgage loan agreement to the contrary, the mortgagee can apply its share of the loss settlement to the loan principal.

Loss Payable Clause

loss payable
clause

A *loss payable clause* is added to a policy as an endorsement and is used for autos and other types of personal property that have been financed. A loss payable clause gives the lender more limited rights than those found in the mortgage clause. For example, under the clause that is used for autos, the lender will still be paid if the policyowner is denied coverage but only if coverage was denied because of certain fraudulent acts or omissions. The lender receives notification if the policy is canceled so other provisions can be made to protect its insurable interest. However, the lender cannot pay the premium to keep the coverage in force.

Property Valuation

Property insurance policies invariably include valuation provisions that specify the approach to use to determine the value of covered property. That approach should be used when determining how much insurance to purchase, and it will be used when determining how much the insurer will pay in the event of a property loss.

Traditionally, most property insurance policies provided coverage on an actual cash value basis. Replacement cost valuation, the other dominant approach, is increasingly common, especially for insurance on houses and other buildings. Other variations include coverage on the basis of agreed value, often used with antiques and collectibles; the stated amount approach; and the valued policy laws found in some states.

Actual Cash Value

The concept of actual cash value is based on the principle of indemnity, which means that an insured should not profit from a loss but should be put into approximately the same financial position that existed before a loss.

Policies written on an actual cash value basis (such as auto physical damage and personal property under many homeowners policies) state that losses will be settled at actual cash value at the time of loss but not in an amount greater than the amount required to repair or replace the property.

actual cash value   AAIS homeowners policies define actual cash value as "the cost to repair or replace property using material of like kind and quality, to the extent practical, less a deduction for depreciation, however caused." However, most property insurance policies do not include a specific definition of actual cash value. As a result, there are varying court interpretations, statutes, and regulations concerning its precise meaning. Generally, it is defined as replacement cost minus physical depreciation. As an illustration, assume a 10-year-old refrigerator is destroyed in a fire. It cost $900 when new, but a similar new model now sells for $1,200. The $1,200 amount is the replacement cost. However, according to the principle of indemnity, the insured is not entitled to a new refrigerator, because the one that was destroyed was several years old. The issue then becomes the amount of the deduction for physical depreciation. Insurance companies tend to have depreciation schedules for various items, and refrigerators typically last about 15 years. Therefore, the insurer would probably assume the refrigerator was two-thirds depreciated and offer the insured one-third of $1,200, or $400.

In some cases, market value is used to establish the insurable value of property. The fair market value of property is the amount for which a knowledgeable seller, under no unusual pressure, would sell the property and a knowledgeable buyer, under no unusual pressure, would purchase it. The actual cash value of an auto is usually considered to be its fair market value. It is relatively easy to establish the actual cash value of any auto, because there is an active market for autos, and the price at which comparable used cars have recently sold is readily available

Replacement Cost

replacement cost   When property is valued on a *replacement cost* basis (as the dwelling building is in most homeowners policies), no deduction is made for depreciation. In the past, it was argued that this method of settlement violated the principle of indemnity because the insured was put into a better position after the loss. In many cases, however, there is no way to put the insured into exactly the same position that existed before the loss. For example, if a windstorm blows the shingles off a roof, the insured clearly needs new shingles. However, if the old shingles had already served a portion of their life expectancy, an actual cash value settlement would require the insured to use additional resources to fully repair the roof. Such a result, obviously, would leave the insured feeling less than fully indemnified. To alleviate this situation, replacement cost coverage is commonly written on homes and commercial buildings.

Replacement cost coverage is also increasingly common with both commercial and residential personal property. If the refrigerator in the previous example had been insured on a replacement cost basis rather than an actual cash value basis, the insurer would pay the $1,200 cost of a similar new model, even though the customer had originally purchased the refrigerator for only $900.

Replacement cost is based on replacement with materials or items of like kind and quality as that lost. For example, if a kitchen were destroyed, the value of the loss would be determined by characteristics of the old kitchen. The insurance company would pay the cost to replace an old laminated counter top with a new counter top of something similar. The insured would have to assume the extra cost if he or she wanted a new granite counter top. Similarly, the insurance company would not pay to replace standard low-cost kitchen cabinets with expensive custom-made cabinets.

Agreed Value

agreed value   With some types of property, it is extremely hard to determine values after an item has been totally destroyed or lost through theft. Examples include fine art and antiques. To avoid this dilemma, the insurer and the insured may agree upon a value at the time a policy is written. In the event of a total loss to the property, the insurer pays the *agreed value*. The insurance company will probably want detailed appraisals before issuing a policy with an agreed value.

Stated Amount

stated amount   The *stated amount* approach is often used in insurance policies on antique autos or other unusual vehicles. The policy lists a stated value for the item. At the time of the loss, the insurer will pay the stated amount, the actual cash value, or the cost to repair or replace the property—whichever is least. In many cases, the insurer therefore pays less than the stated value.

EXAMPLE

"Smoky" Blaze is a retired fireman. Smoky owns a few cherished memorabilia, including an original painting of The Great Chicago Fire and an old fire truck he purchased when his fire company upgraded its equipment. Smoky displays the painting in his living room. He keeps the fire truck next to his Cadillac in the garage attached to his house and occasionally drives it in a parade.

Smoky's house, which has a replacement cost value of $300,000, is insured for that amount on a homeowners policy, which provides replacement cost coverage on the dwelling building and attached structures and actual cash value coverage on personal property with a $150,000 limit. The painting is insured for $40,000 on a fine arts floater that provides agreed value coverage. The fire truck, which has a great deal of sentimental value for Smoky, is insured for $40,000 on an antique auto policy that provides stated amount coverage. The Cadillac is insured on a personal auto policy that provides actual cash value coverage but does not state a dollar limit.

An electrical fire starts in Smoky's garage and destroys the garage, the fire truck, and the Cadillac. The fire also spreads to the house and does damage to Smoky's personal property, including the painting. At the time of the loss, the old fire truck has an actual cash value of $30,000, based on its market value. It will cost $100,000 to repair the house and another $50,000 to replace Smoky's other personal property with equivalent new property.

Smoky's insurer will pay (ignoring deductibles):

- the $100,000 cost of repairing the house

- the $40,000 agreed value of the painting

- the $30,000 actual cash value of the fire truck

- the actual cash value of the Cadillac, which will be established by determining the current market value of similar vehicles

- the actual cash value of Smoky's other personal property, which will be based on its $50,000 replacement cost minus deductions for physical depreciation

Valued Policy Laws

valued policy laws   A few states have *valued policy laws* that can apply to certain types of property losses and/or certain perils. As a rule, this type of law applies to real property only. Under such a law, the full amount of insurance coverage is paid if a total loss occurs. For example, $500,000 is paid for a total loss to a building insured for $500,000 even if the actual cash value or replacement cost of the building is lower. Valued policy laws were introduced to prevent agents and insurance companies from benefiting from premiums and commissions that are too high because a building is insured for an amount greater than what the insurer will pay in the event of a loss. The burden is on the insurance company to either prevent overinsurance or to be bound by the amount of coverage it has sold if a loss occurs.

Today, underinsurance is more often a problem than overinsurance. Insurers and their agents face the challenge, especially during inflationary periods, of adequately increasing insurance limits at every renewal in order to keep policy limits in line with insurable property values so that the insurer is able to pay for a major property loss. Adequate insurance to value benefits policyowners, and it enables insurers to collect premiums consistent with the values they insure, which, in turn, helps avoid a need for rate increases.

Covered Perils

A peril is a cause of loss. Many different perils can cause a loss to real and personal property. However few, if any, property insurance policies cover losses from every peril that could occur. Insurance policies take two distinct approaches in describing the causes of loss covered under a given policy:

- named perils, also known as "specified perils"
- open perils, also referred to as "special form" or "all risks"

Named-Perils Coverages

named-perils coverages *Named-perils coverages* (also referred to as specified-perils coverages) list the covered perils. If a peril is not listed, losses that result from that peril are not covered by that policy.

Some policies are designed for very specific types of losses and cover few perils. As one might expect, a flood insurance policy, for example, covers only flood-related losses. On the other hand, named-perils policies can be extremely broad. An example is the personal property coverage under a homeowners 3 (HO-3) policy. The HO-3 policy contains a list of many covered perils for household property, ranging from fire to theft to volcanic eruption.

A mere listing of the covered perils in a named-perils policy can be somewhat misleading because the precise meaning of the terms is often established by either legal precedent or specific policy language. For example, the term *fire* is not usually defined in insurance policies because its meaning has long been established by the courts. A fire consists of a rapid oxidation or combustion that causes a flame or glow. Therefore, an item scorched because it was too close to the heating element on an electric range would not be covered under the peril of fire. In addition, courts have determined that the peril of fire covers only hostile fires, which are those that are outside normal confines. For example, a fire in a fireplace is a friendly rather than a hostile fire. As a result, damage to an item accidentally thrown into a fireplace would not be covered under a named-perils policy covering fire. Note that a fire that spreads beyond the fireplace has turned from a friendly fire into a hostile fire.

An interesting—and false—urban legend has been in circulation for the past 40 years about the man who submitted a fire insurance claim on the cigars he had smoked. Various versions of this story call it arson and give several differing reasons why the claim was not covered, but we think the best reason of all lies in the fact that the cigars were not burned by a hostile fire.[54]

Unlike the peril of fire, the meanings of most covered perils are clarified to varying degrees in insurance policies. For example, the peril of volcanic eruption in the previously mentioned HO-3 policy is defined to cover volcanic eruptions other than those arising from earthquakes, land shock waves, or tremors.

Open-Perils Coverages

open-perils coverages

Open-perils coverages (sometimes called all-risks coverages) cover all causes of loss to covered property unless a given type of loss is specifically excluded. The dwelling building coverage under the HO-3 policy is an example of a typical open-perils policy in that some potentially significant losses are not covered. The policy has exclusions for earth movement and water damage that eliminate coverage for earthquakes and floods. In most cases, such perils can be insured for an extra premium under an HO-3 policy or a separate policy. The policy also contains exclusions for perils that are generally uninsurable, such as war and nuclear accidents. Other perils are modified by policy language. For example, although vandalism and malicious mischief to the building are generally covered, this peril is not covered if a building has been vacant for more than 60 days preceding a loss. Similarly, smoke is not a covered peril if it arises from agricultural smudging or industrial operations.

Settling Claims

Settling property insurance claims is usually somewhat more complicated than settling life insurance claims. Property insurance policies therefore need

---

54. For details on this urban legend and its critics, see snopes.com/crime/clever/cigarperson.asp.

to spell out the post-loss duties of both the insured and the insurer in some detail. Most of these duties are fairly obvious.

Duties of the Insured

A typical property insurance policy requires, for example, that the insured must promptly tell the insurer there has been a property loss, and the insured must cooperate with the insurer in showing that a covered loss occurred within the policy period. If property coverage is on a named-perils basis, the insured also needs to establish that the loss was caused by one of the named perils.

The insured also needs to cooperate with the insurer in establishing the value of covered property that has been lost or damaged. It is much easier to do this when an insured has maintained receipts of major purchases and has a current inventory of personal property supplemented by photographs or videotapes. Of course, the insured should keep this information at a separate location so that the information itself is not among the property that is destroyed.

Duties of the Insurer

The insurance company has a duty to pay losses fairly and promptly once the coverage and the value of the property loss have been established. The insurance policy and/or state law might specify that losses are payable within a stated period, such as 60 days.

The insurer will usually settle property insurance claims by paying the policyowner unless some other person with an insurable interest is also covered by the policy. A mortgage holder or a lender named as a loss payee is also entitled to be paid to the extent of the lender's interest in the property.

Insurers typically settle property insurance claims by issuing a check or draft to the policyowner and/or other insured parties. However, many policies give the insurer the right to repair or replace the damaged property rather than making a monetary settlement. Thus, for example, an insurer might have a glass shop replace a broken windshield on a car rather than giving the policyowner cash and having the policyowner deal with a repair shop. Auto insurers often do this because they have arrangements with glass shops to provide prompt quality service at a discount that enhances policyowner service and helps keep premiums down.

Other Insurance

other insurance clause

Most property and liability insurance policies contain detailed *other insurance clauses* that explain how an insurer's obligations are affected or coordinated when other insurance covers the same loss. Three approaches are common in property insurance policies:

- pro rata coverage. If two similar policies provide coverage on the same property, loss payments will be prorated based on the limits of insurance. For example, if one policy provides $200,000 of insurance on a building and another similar policy provides $300,000 of coverage, the first insurer will pay two-fifths of any loss, and the second will pay three-fifths.

- primary and excess coverage. A common approach with auto insurance is that one policy provides primary coverage and the other covers any losses within the scope of its coverage that have not been covered by the primary policy. For example, Karen, who has a personal auto policy that provides collision coverage on her car with a $1,000 deductible, lends her car to Bob, who has collision coverage under his own policy with a $500 deductible that applies to his use of a nonowned auto. If Bob is involved in an accident, Karen's insurance will pay for the damage to her car after subtracting a $1,000 deductible. Bob's insurance will pay $500—the difference between the coverage provided by the two policies.

- exclusion for property covered by other insurance. Some property insurance policies contain a provision relieving the insurer of liability for property that is specifically insured in another policy. For example, homeowners policies generally do not cover losses to personal property that is separately described and specifically covered in a separate policy or an endorsement to the homeowners policy. If, for example, an amateur photographer has a camera worth $1,000 that is specifically insured for $500 in a scheduled personal property endorsement to the homeowners policy, the insurer will pay $500 under the endorsement and nothing additional under the personal property coverage of the homeowners policy. Likewise, if an auto owner purchases a second auto insurance policy while the current policy is still in force, the new policy will replace the old policy; it does not provide duplicate or additional coverage.

Limits, Deductibles, and Insurance-to-Value Provisions

The amount payable under a policy that provides property insurance coverage is also affected by the policy's limits, deductibles, and insurance-to-value provisions.

Limits

Without adequate policy limits, a client might not be indemnified for a loss that insurance otherwise covers. *Policy limits*, or *limits of insurance*, are a dollar amount, stated in the policy, that applies to a specific item, a specific category of property, or a specific type of coverage. Policy limits state the maximum amount payable for most claims covered by the policy. Some property insurance policies do not contain an explicit dollar limit but instead cover the actual cash value of an auto or other property, or cover income lost during a specified period of time.

Policy limits are sometimes called limits of liability. This terminology recognizes the fact that the insurer's obligation or "liability" to provide benefits is limited by the face amount of the policy. It can be confusing, however, to refer to limits of *liability* when dealing with *property* insurance.

A property insurance limit may apply to a specific listed or "scheduled" item, such as a building or a diamond ring. In another policy or coverage, a dollar limit may apply to a broad class of unscheduled property, such as personal property belonging to a family. Sublimits may apply to specific types of property.

EXAMPLE
A typical homeowners policy might provide $200,000 in personal property coverage with a $1,500 sublimit that applies to watercraft. Suppose Samantha has a homeowners policy with these limits, and a boat with an actual cash value of $5,000 is stolen from her carport. Although the limit of insurance on Samantha's personal property is $200,000, she cannot collect more than $1,500 for theft of her boat.

Deductibles

Many property insurance policies have deductibles that apply to each loss. In most cases, the deductible is a set dollar amount. Although insurance policies and companies tend to have standard deductibles, such as $250 for collision losses to an auto, deductibles can usually be increased with an accompanying premium reduction. Deductibles can sometimes be decreased for an additional premium.

A few policies—earthquake coverage is a common example—have percentage deductibles. Under such a policy, the deductible is equal to a percentage, such as 5 percent, of the amount of insurance.

While deductibles minimize attitudinal hazard by making the insured bear a portion of any loss, they also lower premium costs by eliminating the relatively high administrative costs of adjusting small claims. Significant discounts are often available for selecting higher deductibles, and an evaluation of this savings should be part of a financial planning analysis.

Insurance-to-Value Provisions

The vast majority of property insurance losses are partial losses. Exceptions occur when property is totally destroyed or stolen. Anyone who expects to be fully indemnified if a total loss occurs ought to carry property insurance in an amount equal to the full insurable value of the property. The insurable value of the property is usually its replacement cost or its actual cash value.

Property insurance rates are based on an assumption that covered property is insured to value. Insurance-to-value provisions create a win-win situation for both the insurer and the insured. If most property an insurer covers is substantially underinsured rather than insured to value, the insurer would not collect enough premium to cover its exposures without raising its rates per $100 of coverage. Insurance buyers would end up paying higher rates and still have inadequate coverage.

To promote and maintain this win-win scenario in which insurance buyers carry an amount of insurance that reflects the property's insurable value and pay a fair rate for their coverage, many insurance policies contain provisions designed to encourage insurance to value. This encouragement is in the form of a penalty for underinsurance. Simply stated, a policyowner who is underinsured at the time of a loss will also be underpaid, even for a partial loss.

coinsurance

property insurance

Coinsurance Provision. A *coinsurance provision* in many commercial property insurance policies serves this purpose. Although the same term is used, it is important to remember that coinsurance in property insurance is not the same as coinsurance in medical expense insurance.

A coinsurance provision requires the policyowner to carry insurance at least equal to a percentage of the property's insurable value in order to receive full payment for losses. The percentage is usually either 80, 90, or 100, and the policy will specify whether this is a percentage of actual cash value, replacement cost, or some other value.

The best way to explain coinsurance is to use an example—in this case, the replacement cost provision that applies to many commercial buildings. It states that if the amount of insurance is at least 80 percent (or 90 or 100 percent) or more of replacement cost at the time of loss, the loss will be paid on a replacement cost basis up to the limit of coverage. Of course, the insurer will never pay more than the limit of insurance or the insurable value of the loss. If the amount of insurance is less than 80 percent of replacement cost, the insurer will pay the portion of the cost to repair or replace the damage that the limit of insurance bears to 80 percent (or other selected percentage) of the replacement cost at the time of loss. This is explained by the following formula:

$$\text{Loss payment} = \frac{\text{Limit of insurance}}{80\,\%\text{ of replacementcost}} \times \text{Replacementcost of the loss}$$

EXAMPLE

Assume a building has a replacement cost of $200,000 but the policyowner carries only $140,000 of coverage on a replacement cost basis on a policy with an 80 percent coinsurance clause. Also assume a windstorm destroys a roof that would cost $8,000 to replace. Using the above formula:

$$\text{Loss payment} = \frac{\$\,140,000}{80\,\% \times \$\,200,000} \times \$\,8,000$$

$$= \frac{\$\,140,000}{\$\,160,000} \times \$\,8,000 = \$\,7,000$$

Therefore, the insurer will pay $7,000 (ignoring any deductible).

The same formula is used if losses are settled in an actual cash value basis except that the replacement cost is replaced by the actual cash value, both in determining the insurable value and in determining the amount of the loss.

Homeowners Loss Settlement Provision. Homeowners insurance policies—and also some businessowners policies—include a different type of insurance-to-value provision that bears a slight resemblance to coinsurance. This provision applies only to the dwelling building and other structures; it does not apply to personal property for which it is usually more difficult to establish a value when the policy is written. In essence, the homeowners loss settlement provision works like this:

- If the amount of insurance on the dwelling building equals at least 80 percent of the replacement cost value of the building, the insurer will pay the replacement cost of the loss.
- If the building is slightly underinsured, the insurer will pay an amount somewhere between the actual cash value of the loss and the replacement cost value of the loss. The amount is determined by applying a formula that is essentially the same as the coinsurance clause previously discussed.
- But—and here's the added feature—if the building is more than slightly underinsured, the insurer will still pay at least the actual cash value of the loss.

In any case, the insurer will not pay more than the applicable amount of insurance or the insurable value of the loss, and a deductible will also apply. The example illustrates more specifically how the homeowners loss-settlement provision operates.

EXAMPLE

Alex and Sandra own a home with a replacement value of $200,000. A kitchen fire causes a loss to the building with a replacement cost of $10,000 and an actual cash value of $8,000.

If Alex and Sandra's homeowners policy has a policy limit of $160,000 or more that applies to the dwelling building, they will recover the $10,000 replacement cost.

If they are only slightly underinsured and their homeowners policy has a policy limit of $150,000, Alex and Sandra will recover $9,375, determined by applying the coinsurance formula:

$150,000/$160,000 x $10,000 = $9,375

Because $9,375 is more than the actual cash value of the property, the insurer will pay the amount determined by the formula, which is between the actual cash value and the replacement cost value of the loss.

Suppose, instead, that the policy limit is $120,000. Even though they are rather substantially underinsured, Alex and Sandra will still receive the $8,000 actual cash value of the loss.

LIABILITY INSURANCE

The United States' legal climate encourages lawsuits. A client whose momentary carelessness or negligence causes injury or damage to another party can be sued for an amount that equals or exceeds his or her entire life's savings and perhaps future earnings. Even clients with limited assets can face a large liability judgment.

A client who has not been negligent can also be sued by a claimant who *alleges* that the client is responsible for the claimant's injury or damage. In many cases, a strong defense leads to the conclusion that the client is not legally responsible to pay damages, and the suit is dismissed. In other cases, a sound defense reduces the amount of damages the courts award. A sound defense can be expensive, but its importance cannot be understated.

Fortunately, liability insurance is available both to cover defense costs and to pay damages awards for many types of claims. The following discussion looks at the types of liability claims that are commonly insured and briefly examines the bases of legal liability.

Types of Liability Losses

Liability claims involve an alleged responsibility to pay damages. Damages can be categorized as compensatory damages or punitive damages:

compensatory damages

punitive damages

- *compensatory damages*, designed to financially compensate or reimburse a claimant who has suffered a loss

- *punitive damages*, designed to punish a wrongdoer, or tortfeasor, whose outrageous conduct has caused another party to suffer a loss

Liability insurance policies are designed primarily to cover compensatory damages. Some policies exclude punitive damages, and some state laws prohibit insurers from paying punitive damages. The thinking here is that a wrongdoer is not really punished when the "punishment" is absorbed by his or her insurance.

The types of liability losses typically covered by property and liability insurance fall into the following categories:

- bodily injury

- property damage
- personal injury
- contractual liability
- wrongful acts

These categories are briefly described below. Other liability insurance coverages might apply to advertising injury; professional liability, such as medical malpractice or attorney's errors and omissions; or other consequences.

Bodily Injury

bodily injury

Bodily injury occurs when a person suffers bodily harm, sickness, or disease, and it includes required care, loss of services, and death that results.[55] The injured party may incur such tangible losses as medical bills, lost income, or the need to hire someone to perform services, such as cleaning the house or mowing the lawn.

Bodily injury can also result in an award of damages for pain and suffering. In many cases, pain and suffering payments far exceed those paid for medical bills and lost income.

Bodily injury can also result in claims by parties other than the person actively suffering the injury. For example, relatives can sue for wrongful death or loss of companionship.

Property Damage

personal property

Allegedly causing destruction or damage to someone else's real or personal property can also result in a liability claim. The *property damage* can consist of actual damage to the property, but it can also arise because of lost income or extra expenses that result from the inability to use the property.

Personal Injury

personal injury

Attorneys often consider "personal injury" and "bodily injury" to be synonymous. In the language of liability insurance, however, *personal injury* refers to a group of offenses that

---

55.   This is typical of the definitions found in insurance policies.

generally include libel, slander, invasion of privacy, and other offenses named in the policy, such as defamation or malicious prosecution.

Contractual Liability

contractual liability
Legal liability can also arise from the failure of a person or business to meet contractual obligations. This *contractual liability* may result from breach of contract, responsibility for damage to the property of others in one's possession, and implied warranties.

Wrongful Acts

Coverage known as directors and officers liability insurance provides coverage for wrongful acts, defined broadly to include a wide range of acts or omissions, such as "any error, misstatement, misleading statement, act, omission, neglect, or breach of duty committed, attempted, or allegedly committed or attempted by an insured." Coverage applies only to acts or omissions the insured might commit in his or her capacity as a corporate director or officer. A claim by a corporation's stockholders might allege, for example, that a director's or officer's wrongful acts led to a decline in value of the claimants' common stock.

Bases of Legal Liability

A liability claim develops as the result of the alleged invasion of the rights of others. A legal right is more than a mere moral obligation of one person to another; it has the backing of the law to enforce the right. Legal rights impose many specific responsibilities and obligations, such as not invading privacy or property, as well as not harming others.

The invasion of such legal rights is a legal wrong. The wrong can be criminal or civil. A criminal wrong is an injury that involves the public at large and is punishable by the government, typically by imposing a fine or a jail term.

Civil wrongs are based upon torts and contracts. Contracts can involve legal wrong when implied warranties are violated, bailee responsibilities are not fulfilled, or contractual obligations are breached. *Torts* are wrongs independent of contract (for example, false imprisonment, assault, fraud, libel, slander, and negligence). Although the government takes action with respect to crime, civil injuries are remedied by court action instituted by the injured party in a civil action. The remedy sought is usually the award of monetary damages. The consequences of a crime are not usually insurable, but the liability for damages growing out of a civil wrong can—and often should be—insured.

Figure 16-1
Legal Basis for Liability

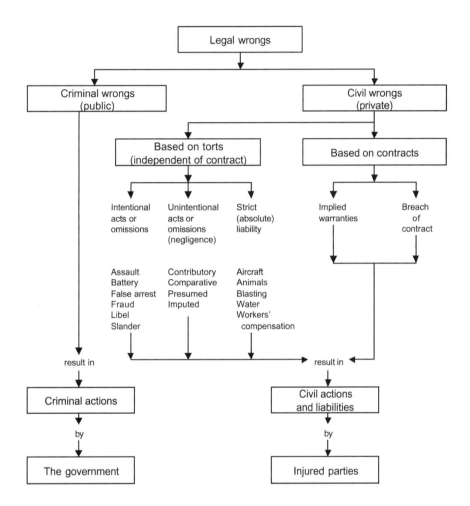

Figure 16-1 illustrates the legal basis for liability. Although liabilities include criminal wrongs, the emphasis for liability insurance is on civil wrongs and particularly on the many legal wrongs based upon torts. Of greatest importance are torts that result from *negligence* (unintentional acts or omissions), which are said to encompass more than nine out of ten claims for bodily injury or property damage to others.

Liability under Contract Law

Liability under contract law is based on the invasion of another's rights under a contract. It occurs only as a result of a contract between one party and another. In contrast, liability under tort law is based on the breach of one's duty to respect the rights of the general public. It can result from either common law or statute.

Breach of Contract. The nonfulfillment of promises that are made in an agreement, or breach of contract, is the most obvious type of civil wrong based on contracts. The failure to honor a warranty expressly contained in a contract is an example of such a breach.

Implied Warranties. One of the most common extensions of liability under contract law concerns manufacturers and distributors of products. In connection with sales or a contract to sell, the law imposes certain obligations termed implied warranties. When a buyer reasonably relies on the skill or judgment of the seller, there is an implied warranty that the goods are reasonably fit for the purpose for which they were sold. A seller can also be held liable if products are supplied to a user without giving proper notice of their dangerous qualities.

Liability under Tort Law

Torts include all civil wrongs not based on contracts. As such, they are a broad residual classification of many private wrongs against another person or organization. They occur independently of contractual obligations and can result from (1) intentional acts or omissions, (2) strict liability imposed by law, or (3) negligence.

Intentional Acts or Omissions. Lawsuits sometimes occur because of injuries or damage caused by intentional acts or omissions. One example is battery, which is the offensive or harmful touching of another without his or her express or implied consent. Assault is a second example, and this involves threatened battery. Other examples include fraud, trespass (entry on land of another without permission), and false arrest or detention, which results from the unprivileged restriction of another's freedom of movement. In addition, libel (written) and slander (oral) involve false statements made about someone else. All of these acts are based on planned or premeditated acts or omissions, although the harmful results may not have been anticipated.

strict liability

Strict or Absolute Liability. The law in particular situations holds persons responsible for injuries or damage no matter how careful they may have been in trying to avoid losses to others. Under what is called *strict liability* or *absolute liability*, certain persons are held liable for damages, regardless of whether or not fault or negligence can be proved against them. Examples include injury from blasting operations by contractors, injury caused by any type of wild animal kept in captivity, and damage resulting from a release of pressure or weight of water, such as a weak dam bursting. Other illustrations of this trend include the absolute liability (up to certain amounts) that airlines have for the safety of their passengers and workers' compensation laws, which hold the employer liable for most employee work-related injuries and diseases.

negligence

Negligence Liability. Negligence is a tort, and most of the liability imposed by law stems from accidents attributable to negligence. If negligence can be shown to be the proximate cause of an injury to another, the negligent party is liable to the injured party for damages. *Negligence* is the failure to exercise the proper degree of care required by circumstances. It can consist of not doing what was required under the circumstances, or of doing something that should not have been done. Behavior in any circumstances that fails to measure up to that expected of a careful, prudent person in like circumstances constitutes negligence. Faulty judgment can result in liability for negligence, even if the motive behind the act was the best.

Negligence requires the existence of four specific elements:

- a legal duty
- a wrong
- injury or damage
- proximate cause

Legal Duty. A *legal duty* to act, or not to act, depends on the circumstances and the persons involved. A bystander has no legal duty to try to prevent a mugging, but a police officer does. Lifeguards have a legal duty to attempt to save a drowning victim, but others usually do not. Whether or not a legal duty is owed to someone else is decided by the courts, and many factors can determine the degree of care required.

Elements of a Negligent Act

- A certain standard of care is owed to others.
- That standard of care is not met.
- There is injury or damage.
- Failure to meet the standard of care is the proximate cause of the injury or damage.

Wrong. A *wrong* is a breach of legal duty, based on a standard of conduct that is determined by what a prudent person would have done or not done in similar circumstances. To do a wrong, the act or omission must be voluntary. Thus, if a person in the course of avoiding great danger injures another person without intent, there is held to be no voluntary act and hence no liability. Negligence usually involves injury that is unintentional. On the other hand, it is no defense if the act that injures a party was committed without intent to do an injury or if the motive behind the act was good and praiseworthy.

Injury or Damage. The third requirement for negligence liability is that there is *injury* or *damage*. The guilty person must pay an amount that reasonably compensates the injured party for any losses for which the negligence is the proximate cause.

Proximate Cause. A fourth requisite for fixing liability is found in the rule that the wrongdoer's voluntary act must have been the proximate cause of the injury or damage. For the act to be held a proximate cause, there must have been a continuous succession of events from the act to the final event that caused the injury. If there was an independent and intervening cause, the continuous succession of events is broken. Thus, a fire ignited negligently and spread by the winds is one continuous succession of events. If, however, a third party was deliberately pushed into the flames by someone else and injured, there would not have been a continuous sequence. No liability for the injury would attach to the party responsible for the fire.

Several modifications, by court cases or statutes, sometimes change the usual rules pertaining to negligence liability. These include *contributory* and *comparative* negligence laws and the doctrines of *presumed* and *imputed* negligence.

Contributory and Comparative Negligence. *Contributory negligence* is the legal principle whereby an injured person cannot recover damages for injuries from another negligent person if the injured party was also negligent. Such a person is said to be contributorily negligent and is barred from recovery, no matter how slight the negligence.

contributory negligence

last clear chance doctrine

The harsh effects of the contributory negligence doctrine are sometimes mitigated by applying the *last clear chance doctrine*. According to the last clear chance doctrine, a negligent party, despite his or her negligence, can recover damages from another party who failed to exercise a last clear chance to avoid the accident. For example, a jaywalker who was struck while illegally crossing the street might recover damages upon showing that the driver could easily have avoided striking her. The concept is sometimes used successfully in defense proceedings in contributory negligence states. However, most states now employ a comparative negligence rule.

comparative negligence

Most states have enacted statutes providing that contributory negligence does not bar recovery for damages. Such statutes apply the idea of *comparative negligence*, which provides that damages be diminished in proportion to the amount of negligence attributable to the person injured or to the owner or person in control of the damaged property.

At first glance, there seems to be substantial merit to have each person share the cost of an accident in proportion to his or her share of negligence. For example, 80 percent of the damages to others is paid if a person has been held 80 percent negligent. In some states, however, under complete comparative negligence, the person who was primarily responsible for the accident would also receive 20 percent of his or her damages if the other party was deemed 20 percent negligent. The critics of the comparative negligence law used in these states point out this drawback. Other states have partial comparative negligence statutes, under which a plaintiff can recover only if the degree of his or her negligence is less than (or in some states not greater than) the defendant's negligence. In the preceding example, the person who was 20 percent negligent would receive 80 percent of his or her damages, and the other party would receive nothing. In actual practice, slight negligence tends to be disregarded, and suit against the party primarily responsible is permitted. Settlements out of court also frequently ignore slight negligence or take it into consideration in making partial payments.

Presumed Negligence. To establish a case, the claimant in ordinary circumstances must show a failure to exercise reasonable care on the part of the defendant. The burden of proof, therefore, is on the claimant. In certain cases, however, presumed negligence can be assumed from the facts. Negligence is presumed without the need for the injured person to prove it. The burden of proof is shifted to the defendant, an exception to the common-law rule that a plaintiff must prove the defendant's fault.

The doctrine operates when an accident causes an injury (1) if the instrumentality would not normally cause injury without negligence, (2) if inspection and use of the instrumentality is within exclusive control of the party to be held liable, and (3) if the party to be held liable has superior knowledge of the cause of the accident and the injured party is unable to prove negligence. There must be no contributory negligence, and the accident must be of such nature that injury would not ordinarily occur without negligence.

Modern situations to which this doctrine has been applied include auto injuries in cases where no witnesses are available, railroad or aviation injuries, medical malpractice claims (such as an operation on the wrong part of the body or on the wrong person), and damage caused by defective products.

imputed negligence

Imputed Negligence. Not only is a negligent person liable for his or her acts or omissions that cause injuries or damage to others, but sometimes the responsibility also extends to the negligence of other persons under the concept of *imputed negligence.* Courts and statutes have extended the rules of negligence to apply to employers, landlords, parents, auto owners, and many other parties.

If the negligent party acts in the capacity of employee or agent of another, the wrongdoer and the owner or operator of a property can be held liable because of imputed negligence. For example, employers can be personally liable for the torts of their employees. Imputed liability is also important in property rentals, where landlords can be held responsible for the actions of their tenants.

Parents, too, although generally not liable for the negligent actions of their children, can be held liable by some state statutes. These statutes usually impose limited liability up to several thousand dollars on the parents for damage caused by their children, but they can extend further for specific types of dangerous instruments (guns, for example) used by minors. A child can also be legally liable for his or her own wrongful acts but is seldom able to pay substantial damages.

Under statutes called vicarious liability laws, liability in most states is imputed to auto owners even if they are not driving or riding in their cars when the injuries or damage occurs. In addition, under the family purpose doctrine, such liability applies particularly to the car owner whose family members negligently use the car, either under the idea of agency (when the car is used for family purposes) or on the basis of using a dangerous instrumentality.

Several dozen states have passed dram shop or liquor liability laws that make taverns, other businesses, and individuals dispensing liquor liable for injuries that may be caused by their intoxicated patrons, such as in an auto accident.

Some states impose liability if children are injured on a premises because they were attracted there by such items as swimming pools, ladders, gasoline, unlocked autos, or other attractive nuisances. Other states impose liability for injuries from domestic animals even if it would otherwise be difficult or impossible to prove negligence.

Settling Liability Claims

Liability policies specify the duties of the insured following losses and the obligations of the insurance company for settling claims.

Duties of the Insured

Most liability insurance policies require the insured to perform duties similar to the following in the case of a covered accident or occurrence:

- Give written notice as soon as practical to the company or its agent. The written notice should include (1) the identity of the policy and the insured, (2) reasonable information on the time, place, and circumstances of the accident or occurrence, and (3) names and addresses of any claimants or witnesses.
- Forward promptly to the insurance company every notice, demand, summons, or other process relating to the accident or occurrence.
- Assist the insurance company, at its request, to do the following:
  - Make settlement.
  - Enforce any of the insured's rights against others who may be liable to the insured.
  - Help with the conduct of suits, and attend hearings and trials.
  - Secure and give evidence, and obtain the evidence of witnesses.

Duties of the Insurer. If a claim is made or a suit brought against an insured because of an occurrence to which coverage applies, the insurance company has two primary obligations.

First, the insurer will provide a defense at its expense by a counsel of its choice, even if a suit is groundless, false, or fraudulent. The company typically has the right to settle any claim or suit as it deems appropriate. The choice of whether a settlement is made is at the insurer's option. In some cases, settlements are made because they are less expensive than going to trial. Even though some insureds may view this as admitting their liability when they are convinced they are not liable, there is usually nothing they can do to prevent a settlement. It once was common to let the insured veto a settlement under professional liability policies, but this right has largely disappeared.

Second, the insurer will pay up to the limit of liability for the damages for which the insured is legally liable. Damages include any prejudgment interest awarded against the insured.

TAX TREATMENT

The tax implications of premium payments for, and loss settlements from, property and liability policies vary by type of loss and type of taxpayer.

Deductibility of Premiums

Premiums paid by individual taxpayers for nonbusiness property and liability insurance are not tax deductible. However, premiums paid for business coverage by individuals, partnerships, or corporations are deductible business expenses.

Tax Treatment of Premiums for Employees

Group property and liability insurance as an employee benefit is not widespread, but some group plans exist. These plans typically require an employee to pay the full cost of his or her coverage, and the tax implications are the same as if the employee had purchased an individual policy. If the employer pays any part of an employee's premium, the employer can deduct this cost as a business expense. However, the employer must then report this amount as taxable income to the employee.

Tax Treatment of Benefits

Benefits the insurer pays on behalf of the insured under liability insurance policies do not result in taxable income to the policyowner or insured.

Under property insurance policies, benefits paid for direct loss to real or personal property result in a capital gain to the extent that a taxpayer receives reimbursement in excess of his or her basis in the property. However, the situation is treated as an involuntary conversion, and the gain can be postponed to the extent that a taxpayer uses the proceeds to purchase replacement property and the purchase amount exceeds the taxpayer's basis in the lost or damaged property.

EXAMPLE

Erin purchased a diamond ring for $10,000 many years ago. The ring was stolen, and she recovered $25,000, which was the current value of the ring, from her insurer. If she does not purchase a replacement ring, she will have a capital gain of $15,000, just as if she sold the ring for $25,000. If she purchases a replacement ring at a cost of $25,000 or more, she can postpone the entire gain until the future sale of the ring. If she purchases a $22,000 replacement ring, $3,000 of the settlement is taxable as a gain in the year the theft was discovered. The ring will continue to have a tax basis of $10,000, and the remaining $12,000 of the gain is taxable if Erin later sells the ring for $22,000 or more.

The situation for certain consequential losses is less clear. To the extent that benefits are paid for actual expenses incurred, there is no taxable income. Business income coverage, however, will result in ordinary income because it insures the policyowner against loss of net profits. Policy proceeds merely replace the net profits that would have been fully taxable if no loss had occurred.

Deductibility of Uninsured Losses

The Internal Revenue Code allows a deduction for certain losses to the extent they are not compensated for by insurance. This involves losses when there is no insurance and losses when the insurance provides less than full protection because there are inadequate limits or deductibles. Those losses must arise from fire, storm, shipwreck, or other casualty, or from theft.

Interestingly, the term *casualty* is not defined by the Internal Revenue Code, but IRS and legal interpretations generally consider casualty to be a sudden, unexpected, or unusual event that results in damage, destruction, or loss of property. This definition is very broad and clearly includes losses from such perils as floods, earthquakes, weather-related events, vandalism, fire, motor vehicle accidents, and the like.

Theft is also broadly interpreted to mean loss of money or property resulting from, for example, embezzlement, extortion, larceny, or robbery. Losses from situations caused intentionally by a taxpayer or involving normal wear and tear do not meet the definition.

The maximum amount of the losses for tax purposes is the lesser of (1) the decrease in the fair market value of the property as a result of the casualty or theft or (2) the taxpayer's adjusted basis in the property. Therefore, the amount of the deductible loss for the ring previously discussed would be $10,000 if there were no insurance.

Businesses and individual taxpayers can deduct losses in full if the loss is incurred in a trade or business or any transaction entered into for profit. Other losses of individual taxpayers are deductible only if they itemize income tax deductions and then only to the extent that (1) each separate loss exceeds $100, and (2) the total of all casualty and theft losses for the year exceeds 10 percent of adjusted gross income.

NEED FOR PROPERTY AND LIABILITY INSURANCE PLANNING

Many insurance policies include a variety of approaches and coverage options that require choices by the client. Property and liability insurance is no exception. If anything, the range of choices, coverage options, and endorsements is even wider with property and liability insurance than with other lines of insurance.

Property insurance policies can cover buildings and their contents, as well as autos and other personal property. A client should be concerned not only with the possibility that the property itself suffers a loss of value but also with the likelihood of lost income or additional expenses resulting from the fact that lost or damaged property can no longer be used. Property can be valued on the basis of its depreciated actual cash value, its replacement cost, its agreed value, a stated amount, or some other basis. Covered causes of loss may be listed, or the open-perils approach may be used, covering losses by all causes not otherwise excluded. Clients need to consider the potential causes of loss to their specific property, as well as the value of covered property, and they also must select an appropriate limit of insurance. They must also choose deductibles; here, tax effects can be relevant.

Important sources of liability losses involve the ownership, maintenance, or use of the client's auto and other autos, as well as other personal and business exposures. Liability insurance may cover a client's potential liability resulting from bodily injury, property damage, personal injury (definitions vary), contractual liability, wrongful acts, advertising injury, professional liability, errors and omissions, or other sources depending on the policy. Liability losses can be very large, and it is important to ensure that all significant insurable exposures are covered and that limits are set high enough to provide reasonable protection for the client's assets. Many clients purchase liability insurance in layers, as explained in a later chapter, by combining primary insurance coverage with an umbrella policy.

Some clients believe that if they have an auto insurance policy and a homeowners insurance policy, their property and liability exposures are adequately protected. The financial planning process should determine not only whether such policies have been purchased but also where and how they may fall short of providing adequate protection. In many situations, policy endorsements or additional separate policies are available to compensate for shortcomings in the standard unendorsed policies or to accommodate special needs.

Coverage in standard policies is limited for various reasons. Certain perils, such as war, wear and tear, and intentional destruction of covered property by the insured, are considered uninsurable. Other perils are excluded because the cost of coverage tends to be relatively high or because not everyone has a need for the coverage, but those who want coverage can obtain it at a cost. For example, not all policyowners are susceptible to floods and earthquakes, but property insurance coverage is usually available for those who need and want it. Not every policyowner has expensive jewelry or valuable works of art, but those who do may need specialized coverage on those items through a homeowners policy endorsement. Likewise, most policyowners do not have domestic employees or own a large yacht or a motor home, but those who do may need workers' compensation insurance, a yacht policy, or endorsements to their personal auto policy. Standard policies generally limit the dollar amount of coverage for certain property items or for certain liability exposures. Again, those who need higher amounts of coverage can often obtain it for an additional premium.

In property and liability insurance, particular attention should be paid to policy limitations and coverage options, so that a client can be properly advised of the need to tailor coverage to specific circumstances.

CHAPTER REVIEW

Key Terms and Concepts

real property	property insurance
personal property	compensatory damages
mortgage clause	punitive damages
loss payable clause	bodily injury
actual cash value	personal property
replacement cost	personal injury
agreed value	contractual liability
stated amount	strict liability
valued policy laws	negligence
named-perils coverages	contributory negligence
open-perils coverages	last clear chance doctrine
other insurance clause	comparative negligence
coinsurance	imputed negligence

Review Questions

Review questions are based on the learning objectives in this chapter. Thus, a [3] at the end of a question means that the question is based on learning objective 3. If there are multiple objectives, they are all listed.

1. What property and liability loss exposures do families and businesses face? [1]

2. Explain to your client the difference between a policy providing specified-perils (named-perils) coverage and an open-perils (all-risks) policy. [2]

3. When a property loss occurs,
   a. what duties are typically imposed on the insured? [2]
   b. what obligations does the insurer typically have? [2]

4. Jim Smith has a homeowners policy with replacement cost coverage. After a fire at his home, the damage is estimated at $50,000 on an actual cash value basis and $60,000, ignoring depreciation (that is, on a replacement cost basis). The replacement cost of his home at the time of the loss is $300,000. Ignoring the deductible, how much would Jim recover in each of the following situations?
   a. if Coverage A in his policy is $250,000 [2]
   b. if Coverage A in his policy is $220,000 [2]
   c. if Coverage A in his policy is $180,000 [2]

5. Bill has a property loss of $90,000 and finds that it is covered by two policies—Policy A for $100,000 and Policy B for $80,000. Ignoring deductibles, how much of the loss would be paid by each policy in each of the following situations?
   a. Policy A and Policy B both have pro rata other insurance provisions. [2]
   b. Policy A is written on a primary basis, and Policy B is written on an excess basis. [2]
   c. Policy A excludes property covered by other insurance. [2]

6. Billy, a summer employee at Jones Dry Cleaners, was driving the company truck to pick up dry cleaning in the neighborhood when he failed to see a stop sign, bounced off a car that had the right of way, and hit a phone pole. Indicate the type of liability loss if each of the following resulted from the accident:
   a. the cost of surgery, loss of income, and pain and suffering for the driver of the car that Billy hit [2]
   b. the cost to the phone company to repair its pole [2]
   c. the suit by the driver of the other car that resulted from Billy's slandering her with foul language in front of witnesses at the accident scene [2]

7. What are the four requirements that technically must exist before negligence can be proven? [1]

8. Using the situation in question 6, indicate under what rule of law each of the following can happen:
   a. Billy's employer is found liable for the injuries suffered by others that were caused by Billy. [1]
   b. Neither Billy nor his employer is required to pay the injured driver of the other car because a police officer at a radar trap indicated that the other driver had entered the intersection at an excessive rate of speed and the court held that the other driver was 20 percent at fault. [1]
   c. Billy's employer is required to pay the injured driver of the other car only 80 percent of her damages because a police officer at a radar trap indicated that the other driver had entered the intersection at an excessive rate of speed and the court held that the other driver was 20 percent at fault. [1]

9. When a liability loss occurs, what are
   a. the typical duties of the insured? [2]
   b. the obligations of the insurance company? [2]

10. With property and liability insurance, what basic tax rules apply to each of the following? Point out where differences exist by type of taxpayer and/or type of loss.
    a. deductibility of premium [3]
    b. taxation of premiums for employees [3]
    c. taxation of benefits [3]
    d. deductibility of uninsured losses [3]

11. Why is property and liability insurance an important element of any financial plan? [3]

Learning Objectives

An understanding of the material in this chapter should enable the student to

1. Briefly describe the nature of the standard homeowners policy forms; explain the coverages provided by the HO-2, HO-4, HO-5, HO-6, and HO-8 and the key ways they differ from the HO-3.

2. Describe the definitions, coverages, and exclusions contained in Sections I and II of the HO-3 homeowners policy form.

3. Describe the coverage provided by the various endorsements available to tailor a homeowners policy to individual needs.

4. Explain why property and liability policies other than a homeowners policy may be required to meet the needs of individuals and families, and describe the key policies available.

Most clients purchase a homeowners policy not only to obtain property insurance coverage against loss or damage to their home but also to obtain insurance protection against the many sources of liability that can arise out of a family's activities. Homeowners insurance is not a single policy, but rather a family of similar policies that provide different degrees of coverage. Two policy forms in the homeowners family are for people who do not literally own homes but rent an apartment or purchase a condominium unit.

Homeowners policies are relatively complex policies. Various exclusions in the policy deal with uninsurable loss exposures. Other limitations and exclusions deal with exposures that can best be handled with a separate policy or an endorsement; these often give the informed financial advisor an opportunity to help a client improve his or her property/liability coverage program.

Without analyzing every detail, this discussion on property and liability insurance summarizes the coverage of standard homeowners policies and also discusses some coverage options, including flood insurance and title insurance. Questions regarding a specific policy can often be resolved by reading the policy itself.

Financial planners should be able to alert their clients to potential property and liability risk exposures. Specific recommendations and implementations are usually handled by a property/liability insurance agent or broker, with one exception: Title insurance is usually arranged by a real estate firm or a mortgage company.

HOMEOWNERS POLICIES

homeowners policy

Insurance Services Office (ISO)

There is not only one *homeowners policy*, but rather a series of policy forms for different types of situations and with differing degrees of coverages for real and personal property, as well as personal liability. In this book, the discussion centers around the forms of *ISO (Insurance Services Office)*. ISO is an advisory organization that provides a wide range of services for insurance companies, including the development and filing of standardized insurance policies. Many property and liability companies purchase the services of ISO, and its policy forms are commonly used. A smaller advisory organization—the American Association of Insurance Services (AAIS)—also has a series of homeowners forms for its affiliates. In addition, some insurance companies develop and file their own independent forms. Although the AAIS forms and the independent forms are arranged differently and often use different wording, their coverage is very similar to the ISO forms.

ISO Forms

There are six standard ISO homeowners forms:

- Homeowners 2—Broad Form
- Homeowners 3—Special Form
- Homeowners 4—Contents Broad Form
- Homeowners 5—Comprehensive Form
- Homeowners 6—Unit-Owners Form
- Homeowners 8—Modified Coverage Form

In making reference to these forms, it is common to call them Form 2, Form 3, and so on, or HO-2, HO-3, HO-4, HO-5, HO-6, and HO-8. The latter terminology is used in this book.

The HO-2, HO-3, HO-5, and HO-8 are designed for owner-occupants of one- to four-family dwelling units. Each unit may contain no more than two families or one family and two roomers or boarders. The HO-4 is designed for tenants of residential property and also for the owner of an apartment building who occupies one of its units. The HO-6 is designed for the owners of condominium units.

Each homeowners form has two major sections. Section I provides property coverage, and it is in this section that the forms differ. The liability coverage of Section II is identical in all six forms.

The HO-3 is the most common of the forms and appropriate for most owners of homes. It is analyzed in some detail. Following this analysis, the other forms and their use are briefly discussed.

Sections of a Homeowners Policy
• Section I—Property Coverage (different in each homeowners form)   • Section II—Liability Coverage (same in all homeowners forms)

Definitions

Like many property and liability insurance policies, homeowners policies begin by defining many terms used throughout the policy. When a defined term is used elsewhere in the policy, it usually appears in quotation marks or in boldface type. Terms are used differently in different policies, and to understand their meaning in a specific policy, one must refer to the definitions in that policy.

The homeowners policy includes two especially important defined terms—"insured" and "insured location"—that also demonstrate the broad scope of coverage these policies provide.

Insured

An insured is a party entitled to protection under the policy. Persons who fall within the definition of "you," as defined in the policy, have somewhat more protection than other insureds.

Many persons qualify as insureds under both Section I (property) and Section II (liability) of a homeowners policy. These include

- "you." As defined in the homeowners policy, "you" and "your" refer to the person named in the policy declarations and the spouse of

that named insured, if not also listed, as long as he or she is a
resident of the same household.

- residents of the named insured's household who are relatives
- residents of the named insured's household who are under the age
  of 21 and in the care of any of the persons previously mentioned
- a full-time student (as defined by the school) who was a resident
  of the insured's household before moving out to attend school, as
  long as the student is either

  - under 24 and a relative of an insured
  - under 21 and in the care of an insured

Two other categories of persons are considered insureds for the purposes of
the Section II (liability) coverage. These categories include

- any person or organization responsible for animals or watercraft
  owned by anyone on the previous list. However, they are insureds
  only with respect to animals or watercraft to which the policy applies
  and only if this possession is with the owner's permission and not in
  the course of any business. For example, a neighbor while caring
  for a pet because the named insured is on vacation is an insured,
  but a veterinary hospital where the pet is boarded is not.
- any person employed by any one of the insureds in the earlier list
  with respect to any vehicles insured under the policy and other
  persons using the vehicles on an insured location with the consent
  of the named insured

Insured Location

This term is used only in Section II of the policy, the liability section. As
defined, an insured location includes the following:

- the residence premises. This includes the one- to four-family
  dwelling, other structures, and grounds where the policyowner
  resides as shown in the declaration.
- that part of other premises, other structures, and grounds used
  by the named insured or spouse as a residence (for example, a
  vacation home) if it is shown in the declarations or if it is acquired
  during the policy year as a residence by the named insured
- other premises not owned by an insured but where an insured is
  temporarily residing
- vacant land, other than farm land, owned by or rented to an insured
- individual or family cemetery plots or burial vaults of an insured

- any part of a premises occasionally rented to an insured for other than business use

HO-3 Property Coverages

Section I of the HO-3 contains five categories of property coverage:

- Coverage A for the dwelling building
- Coverage B for other structures, such as a garage not attached to the house
- Coverage C for household contents and other personal property
- Coverage D for loss of use
- Additional Coverages that provide protection for assorted situations

The insurance buyer determines the limit of insurance he or she wishes to purchase for Coverage A (the dwelling itself). In choosing a limit of insurance, it is important to recognize that the insurable value of the house is not directly related to either its purchase price or its market value. Because the HO-3 provides dwelling coverage on a replacement cost basis, the insurable value of the house is the cost to reconstruct the house new, using material of like kind and quality. Also, the value of the land is not relevant in determining the replacement cost of the building, but the land's value has a major effect on the market value of the house. Sometimes the mortgage holder requires an amount of insurance at least equal to the outstanding amount of the mortgage, even though the mortgaged property includes both the building (which is covered property) and the land (which is not covered property). Clients with several acres of valuable land or land at an especially high-priced location, such as oceanfront property, might want to pay special attention to these factors and attempt to convince the lender that there is no point in insuring the property for more than the insurance could possibly pay.

It is, however, sound advice to purchase dwelling insurance in an amount that equals the full replacement cost value of the building itself, for at least two reasons. First, a penalty will be imposed if, at the time of the loss, the house is not insured to at least 80 percent of its replacement cost value. In many cases, the penalty is that the insured receives only the actual cash value of the damaged property, not its full replacement cost. Second, although total losses happen much less frequently than partial losses, they do occur. Moreover, replacement cost values tend to increase as a result of inflation, and a limit of insurance that was adequate last year might be inadequate this year when the policy is renewed.

The standard limits for Coverages B, C, and D are 10, 50, and 30 percent, respectively, of the Coverage A limit, as shown in the following example.

EXAMPLE
Suppose Henry purchases an HO-3 with a Coverage A limit of $500,000 on the dwelling. Standard limits for his other coverage would then be as follows: •   Coverage B limit: $50,000 (10% of Coverage A) •   Coverage C limit: $250,000 (50% of Coverage A) •   Coverage D limit: $150,000 (30% of Coverage A)

These limits are generally adequate for a typical client. However, they can be increased for an additional premium, and a client who has, for example, an expensive outbuilding or personal property of above-average value should consider additional coverage. The Coverage C limit can also be reduced to as little as 40 percent of the Coverage A limit.

The limits on coverages B, C, and D are not part of the Coverage A limit, but rather additional amounts of insurance. So, in the example just given, Henry could collect up to $950,000 if his home is destroyed by a covered peril.

Coverage A for the Dwelling Building

Coverage A provides property insurance for the dwelling building at the address listed in the declarations page of the policy. The land itself is specifically excluded from coverage. Coverage A also applies to structures attached to the dwelling, such as a garage, decks, or fences, and to materials and supplies located on or next to the residence premises for construction, repair, or alteration of the dwelling or other structures on the residence premises.

Excluded Perils and Losses. Coverages A and B of the HO-3 use the open-perils approach, which provides coverage for all losses to covered property unless the cause or circumstances of the loss are excluded. The HO-3 contains a number of exclusions that preclude coverage for certain types of building damage that are somewhat expectable or can be prevented with reasonable care. For example:

•   Wear and tear, marring, smog, rust or other corrosion, dry rot, deterioration, and inherent vice (the tendency of something like fabric to deteriorate) are not covered. These types of things normally happen as property ages.

- Mold, fungus, or wet rot is not covered unless it is hidden within or by walls, floors, or ceilings and results from accidental discharge of water or steam from plumbing or appliances. Mold grows where damp conditions are allowed to exist, and serious mold growth can usually be constrained with proper maintenance. In some cases, however, hidden damage occurs, and that hidden damage is covered.

- Pollution damage is not covered unless the pollution results from certain perils.

- Bird, vermin, rodent, or insect damage is not covered.

- Damage by pets or other animals kept by an insured is not covered.

- Loss due to frozen pipes is not covered unless the insured took reasonable care to maintain heat in the building or to drain the pipes. If an insured has taken such precautions and the freezing results from a power outage or a furnace malfunction, then the water damage is covered.

- Theft of construction materials from an uncompleted dwelling is not covered in the basic policy, but may be available through an optional endorsement. The insured is expected to safeguard these materials.

- Vandalism and malicious mischief to a dwelling that has been vacant for more than a stated time period, such as 90 days, is not covered.

- Freezing, thawing, ice, and water damage to fences, swimming pools, foundations, retaining walls, and so forth is not covered.

A second set of exclusions in the HO-3 is designed, in effect, to plug a loophole that results from the open-perils approach to coverage. The following example illustrates this point. The standard HO-3 excludes flood coverage because of its catastrophic nature. (Because one flood can simultaneously affect many insureds, flood insurance is best handled by a government insurance program. Some private insurers also offer flood coverage.) However, under the open-perils approach, any peril that is not excluded is covered. So if a policyowner were to say, for example, that the flood was caused by defective planning or zoning, and if defective planning or zoning is not excluded, this claim might be covered under a different, nonexcluded peril. To plug this loophole, a set of exclusions precludes coverage for losses resulting from

- weather conditions
- acts or decisions, including the failure to act or decide by any person, group organization, or government body
- inadequate or defective planning, zoning, development, surveying, siting, design, specifications, workmanship, repair, construction, renovation, grading, or compaction, or defective materials used in repair, construction, renovation, or remodeling, as well as defective maintenance

However, even if one of the excluded perils can be considered the cause of the loss, any "ensuing loss" to covered property is covered if it is not otherwise excluded. Although this seems somewhat involved, a simple example should clarify the intent. As noted, insurers intend to exclude flood coverage but to provide fire coverage. If a flood occurs in a particular area because poor planning did not provide adequate drainage, it is still an excluded flood loss—not covered. But if the same flood causes an electrical short circuit that leads to a fire, the ensuing fire damage is covered.

Another set of exclusions affects not only Coverages A and B but also all other coverages. The standard HO-3, like most property insurance policies covering real property at a fixed location, excludes coverage for war, nuclear reaction, flood, and earthquake losses. The first two are uninsurable. Flood and earthquake coverage are available using separate policies or endorsements.

Also excluded are intentional losses committed by an insured, as well as neglect by the insured to use all reasonable means to protect property at and after the time of loss. The destruction or confiscation of property by a government agency is not a covered cause of loss; however, this exclusion does not apply to acts ordered to prevent the spread of fire. Therefore, if firefighters set a backfire while attempting to contain a brush fire or a forest fire, a house burned by that backfire would be covered.

One of the more noteworthy exclusions, especially from a financial planning perspective, is the ordinance or law exclusion. After a loss, it might not be possible to rebuild a home that is in a historical area, a home in a recently rezoned neighborhood, or simply an old home unless it is modified to comply with current building codes. The extra expenses can be substantial. An Additional Coverage automatically included in the HO-3 provides an additional limit of 10 percent of Coverage A to cover ordinance or law expenses. However, clients who have a recognized exposure might well be advised to purchase additional coverage through an endorsement.

EXAMPLE
Here are two clients who should probably carry ordinance or law coverage: • Holly Wood lives in a California community where, because of brush fires, homeowners who are rebuilding are required to use tile or aggregate roofs, rather than shingles. Tile or aggregate roofs are more likely to resist fire, and they are also more expensive. • Sandy Shores lives in a coastal community where houses are currently required to be 8 feet above the ground to prevent flooding problems. Sandy's house, which is 4 feet above the ground, met the requirements in effect in 1988 when her house was constructed.

Many situations more subtle than the two in the example above also create significant ordinance or law exposures.

Basis of Loss Settlement. Losses under Coverage A are settled on a replacement cost basis, with no deduction for physical depreciation.

Coverage B for Other Structures

Coverage B provides insurance on a replacement cost basis for other structures on the residence premises that are set apart from the dwelling by a clear space. Examples of other structures include swimming pools, detached garages, and garden sheds. If a garage is attached to the house and not separated by a clear space, it is covered as part of the dwelling, and the policy limit for Coverage A—Dwelling should be set high enough to cover both the residence and the garage.

The HO-3 does not cover another structure rented to somebody who is not a tenant of the dwelling, unless it is used only as a private garage. Likewise, a structure is not covered if it is used to store business property unless it is business property an insured or a tenant of the dwelling owns. However, if the business property stored in the garage includes gaseous or liquid fuel (other than fuel in a vehicle's fuel tank), the structure is not covered.

Coverage C for Personal Property

Coverage C provides insurance for personal property owned or used by any insured while it is located anywhere in the world. In addition, if the named insured or spouse so requests it after a loss, coverage is also provided for the property of a guest.

Some people have more than one residence. A client might, for example, have a winter home in the South or a summer home near the ocean. A $1,000 sublimit applies to coverage for personal property usually located at another residence. Clients who keep personal property in more than one residence should purchase specific insurance for each location rather than rely on the small amount of coverage available under the homeowners policy for the primary residence. Another reason to recommend specific insurance is that the homeowners policy does not cover theft of personal property from another residence of the insured—not even for $1,000—unless the insured is temporarily living there.

This limitation is not intended to limit coverage for homeowners who are in the process of moving from one primary residence to another and have not yet arranged insurance at the new location. Therefore, property in a newly acquired principal residence is not subject to the $1,000 sublimit for 30 days after the move begins.

Perils Covered. Coverage for personal property is written on a named-perils basis in the HO-3. These perils include

- fire or lightning. Neither term is defined in the policy, but as explained in the previous chapter, it is a well-established principle that coverage is limited to damage by hostile fires. Although fire and lightning are separate perils, property insurance policies traditionally cover them together. If only one of these perils were covered, it would often be impossible to determine where the lightning damage stopped and the fire damage began.
- windstorm or hail. However, losses from rain, snow, sleet, sand, or dust are not covered unless they are a result of direct wind or hail damage to a building. In addition, damage to watercraft is not covered unless the watercraft is in a fully enclosed building.
- explosion
- riot or civil commotion
- aircraft
- vehicles
- smoke other than that from agricultural smudging or industrial operations. Agricultural smudging intentionally creates a dense smoke to prevent plants from frost, and the consequences are both expected and predictable.
- vandalism or malicious mischief

- theft. This also includes mysterious disappearance, which is the loss of property from a known place when it is likely that it has been stolen. However, several exclusions apply to theft, including the following:

  - theft committed by an insured
  - theft in or to a dwelling under construction, including material and supplies, unless the dwelling is finished or occupied
  - theft from the part of a residence premises rented by an insured to someone other than an insured
  - theft of property from another residence of the insured (such as a vacation home) unless the insured is temporarily living there
  - theft of property belonging to an insured who is a student when the property is at a residence away from home if the student has not been there at any time during the 60 days immediately preceding the loss
  - theft of watercraft, including furnishings and equipment
  - theft of trailers and campers

- falling objects
- weight of ice, snow, or sleet
- accidental discharge or overflow of water or steam
- sudden and accidental tearing apart, cracking, burning, or bulging of a steam, hot water, air conditioning, or automatic fire protective sprinkler system, or appliance for heating water
- freezing of a plumbing, heating, air conditioning, or automatic fire protective sprinkler system, or household appliance
- sudden and accidental damage from artificially generated electrical current
- volcanic eruption

Sublimits. Coverage C limits the amount of insurance available to certain classes of property. In some cases, this limitation is for all perils; in other cases, it is for theft losses only. Several endorsements are available to increase many of these limits.

Sublimits apply to the total amount of loss by any covered peril of property from any single category. The dollar amounts listed below appear in the policy edition used at the time of this writing:

- $200 for money, bank notes, bullion, coins, medals, scrip, stored value cards, smart cards, and gold, silver, and platinum other than goldware, silverware, and platinumware
- $1,500 for securities, accounts, deeds, evidences of debt, letters of credit, notes other than bank notes, manuscripts, personal records, passports, tickets, and stamps
- $1,500 for watercraft, including trailers, furnishings, equipment, and motors
- $1,500 for trailers not used with watercraft
- $2,500 for property on the residence premises (and $500 away from the residence premises) used primarily for business purposes
- $1,500 for certain electronic apparatus and accessories while away from the insured premises
- $500 for other property away from the residence premises used primarily for business purposes

The following limitations apply to loss by theft but not other perils:

- $1,500 for jewelry, watches, furs, and precious and semiprecious stones
- $2,500 for firearms and related equipment
- $2,500 for silverware, goldware, platinumware, and pewterware

Excluded Property. Some categories and types of property are excluded from coverage under Coverage C:

- articles insured elsewhere
- animals, birds, and fish
- most motor vehicles
- aircraft
- hovercraft
- property of roomers or boarders other than those related to an insured
- property in an apartment rented to others. However, there is some coverage under Additional Coverages.
- property rented or held for rental to others off the residence premises
- business data
- credit cards, electronic fund transfer cards, or access devices used solely for deposit, transfer, or withdrawal of funds. However, there is limited coverage under Additional Coverages.

- water or steam

In a few cases, some limited coverage is provided as an Additional Coverage or under other parts of the policy. In most cases, coverage can also be obtained under separate insurance policies.

EXAMPLE

Burglars entered Martine's home and stole $500 in cash and a ring worth $2,000. Martine has an HO-3. Martine will recover $200 for the cash and $1,500 for the jewelry for a total of $1,700.

A fire in Janelle's home destroyed $500 in cash and a ring worth $2,000. Janelle has an HO-3. Janelle will recover $200 for the cash and $2,000 for the jewelry for a total of $2,200. Janelle recovers more than Martine because the $1,500 sublimit on jewelry applies only to loss by theft.

A fire in Donna's home destroyed $500 in cash and a ring worth $2,000. Donna has an HO-3 and a separate jewelry policy covering the ring for $1,000. Donna will recover $200 for the cash under her homeowners policy. She will also recover $1,000 for the ring under her jewelry policy. Donna's homeowners policy does not cover her ring at all, because it is specifically insured elsewhere.

Basis of Loss Settlement. Under a standard homeowners policy, Coverage C losses are settled on an actual cash value basis, which contemplates a deduction for physical depreciation. However, replacement cost coverage is frequently added through the use of an available endorsement. The replacement cost option is usually a wise choice, because it substantially increases the amount a client will recover for an insured loss and covers the extra costs of buying new property to replace existing household property that is several years old or more. The insurance recovery is greater because the replacement cost value of personal property is invariably higher than the actual cash value of the same property. Therefore, most clients who purchase the replacement cost coverage option should also consider purchasing a higher limit of insurance for Coverage C. Many insurers require a limit higher than 50 percent of Coverage A—the usual limit—when the replacement cost endorsement is used.

Coverage D for Loss of Use

Coverage D covers certain exposures a client is likely to incur when his or her residence cannot be occupied as a result of a covered property loss.

additional living expenses   If the named insured and family must live elsewhere while the portion of the residence that they normally occupy is being repaired or rebuilt, the named insured is entitled to benefits for *additional living expenses*. These additional living expenses result from the increased costs necessary to maintain the family's normal standard of living.

Coverage is also provided for the fair rental value, minus noncontinuing expenses, of the portion of the residence premises that is rented to others. Finally, up to 2 weeks' coverage is provided for the expenses of living elsewhere when civil authorities prohibit the named insured from using the residence premises because neighboring property is damaged by an insured peril. For example, expenses resulting from an evacuation because of a nearby brush fire are covered, but not the same expenses resulting from a flood threat.

There is no coverage under Coverage D for losses arising out of the cancellation of leases or other agreements.

Additional Coverages for Section I (Property)

Section I contains several Additional Coverages that fill in some of the gaps of the other four property coverages. In most cases, these provide amounts of insurance in addition to the limits under Coverages A, B, and C. Some of the more significant additional coverages include

- *ordinance or law*. Ten percent of the Coverage A limit, an additional amount of insurance, may be used to meet the increased costs of complying with an ordinance or law, such as a building code, that increases the expense of restoring property after a covered loss. A higher amount of coverage is available by endorsement, and many clients should consider it.
- *debris removal*. Before property can be repaired or replaced, the damaged property (debris) must be removed. Subject to limitations detailed in the policy, coverage is provided for the expense of removing debris of covered property that has been damaged by a covered peril.
- *fallen trees*. The HO-3 will pay up to $500 per tree or $1,000 per loss for the cost of removing a tree felled by windstorm, hail, ice, snow, or sleet that has damaged a covered structure, blocks a driveway, or blocks a handicap access ramp.

- *trees, shrubs, plants, and lawns.* As detailed in the policy, a limited amount of coverage is available for trees, shrubs, and other plants damaged by certain perils. Weather-related losses are not covered.

- *landlord's furnishings.* Furniture in a furnished apartment that is rented to a tenant is covered for up to $2,500 for other named perils, but not for theft.

- *credit cards, ATM cards, forged checks, and counterfeit money.* The HO-3 provides up to $500 in coverage for losses in this category but does not cover business use or the dishonesty of an insured. This limit can be increased by endorsement. Although identity theft is a growing concern, the extent of anyone's financial exposure involving any given credit card is usually limited to $500 or less by law and by the policies of the issuing company.

- *grave markers and mausoleums.* Property in this category does not fit neatly among the types of property covered by homeowners policies. Because they are affixed to the land, grave markers and mausoleums are real property usually located in a cemetery away from the residence premises. Stone monuments do not burn. However, many families have a loss exposure, primarily involving the possibility of vandalism. The homeowners policy covers these real property items for the same named perils as personal property. The policy does not mention whose grave markers are covered; presumably, coverage would apply to those in which the policyowner has an insurable interest.

- *loss assessments.* Many clients today live in housing developments with an association that owns and maintains the common property. For example, homeowners in an over-55 active adult community might belong to an association through which all residents collectively own the clubhouse, the pool, the tennis courts, and the fences and signs at the entrance. If damage occurs to any of this community property, the association may assess association members to recover the loss to the extent it is not covered by the association's property insurance. The loss assessment coverage in the basic HO-3 provides $1,000 to cover such assessments, charged during the policy period, that are made because association property has been damaged by a peril covered under Coverage A of the policy.

Unfortunately, many associations are poorly managed by volunteers, have inadequate property insurance, and maintain inadequate cash reserves to handle an emergency without assessing association members. The $1,000 limit can be increased by endorsement. Many clients who live in a condominium or who are members of a homeowners association should seriously consider increasing this limit.

HO-3 Liability Coverages

Section II is the same in all ISO homeowners forms. Like Section I, it contains more than one coverage. These are

- Coverage E for personal liability
- Coverage F for medical payments to others
- Additional Coverages that provide some miscellaneous liability and related benefits

Section II provides broad liability coverage against many of the claims that a typical homeowner might face. It is subject to a number of exclusions, however, many of which eliminate homeowners coverage for losses that can be covered by other policies or endorsements.

Coverage E—Personal Liability

In Coverage E, the insurer agrees to defend the insured against any claim alleging that an insured is responsible to pay damages for bodily injury or property damage that would be covered by the policy. The insurer also agrees to pay any covered damages for bodily injury and property damage, up to the policy limit, for which the insured is found to be liable. The insurer pays defense costs in addition to the stated policy limit, and it provides a defense even if a claim is groundless, false, or fraudulent.

Although it covers claims for liability arising out of bodily injury liability, an unendorsed homeowners policy does not cover personal injury claims. Personal injury refers to a group of offenses that generally include libel, slander, and invasion of privacy. Personal injury liability coverage can be added to a homeowners policy by endorsement or obtained under an umbrella policy.

The basic limit of liability is typically $100,000, but it can be increased for a relatively small additional premium. A personal umbrella policy is often purchased to provide an additional layer of $1 million or more in addition to the protection provided by the homeowners policy, an auto policy, and possibly other liability policies. In selecting liability limits for a homeowners policy, the usual approach is to purchase homeowners insurance with the minimum limit required to qualify for an umbrella (typically $300,000 or $500,000) and then to purchase an umbrella that adds at least $1 million of additional coverage.

Section II of a homeowners policy provides broad coverage that is more specifically defined by the policy's exclusions. Some exclusions apply only to Coverage E, while others also apply to Coverage F.

Table 17-1 Motor Vehicle Exposures Covered by Section II of the HO-3 Policy	
Covered Motor Vehicle Liability Exposures	**Examples**
Motor vehicle in dead storage on an insured location	An unlicensed antique auto is stored in the insured's garage.
Motor vehicle used to service an insured's residence	A riding lawn mower is used to maintain the insured's yard.
Motor vehicle designed for assisting people who are handicapped	A motorized wheelchair, or a three- or four-wheeled power scooter, is used by a handicapped person.
Motorized vehicle designed for recreational use off public roads, and *not owned* by an insured	An insured borrows an unlicensed dune buggy for a ride through the sand dunes.
Motorized vehicle designed for recreational use off public roads, and *owned* by an insured and *on an insured location*	An insured owns an unlicensed dirt bike used by the insured's grandchild on the insured's property.
Motorized golf cart, not capable of exceeding 25 miles per hour, owned by an insured and used to play golf on a golf course, or legally used within a private residential association	The insured lives in a gated retirement community and owns a golf cart used for playing golf on the community's golf course, and also for visiting and running errands within the community.
Trailer not towed by, hitched to, or carried on a motor vehicle	An insured has parked the family's travel trailer at campsite for use on a 2-week vacation. Once the trailer is unhitched, the liability exposure is covered under the homeowners policy because it is no longer a "motor vehicle," as defined, and therefore is not subject to the motor vehicle exclusion.
Source: *Personal Insurance*, American Institute for CPCU/Insurance Institute of America, © 2002. Reprinted with permission of the Institutes.	

Motor Vehicle Exclusions and Coverage. Homeowners policies include a rather involved motor vehicle liability exclusion. As one might expect, the homeowners policy does not cover vehicles registered for use on public roads. Auto owners are expected to have auto insurance. However, not all motor vehicle-related claims are excluded. Table 17-1 describes various motor vehicle liability exposures that the homeowners policy covers.

Watercraft Exclusions and Coverage. Another detailed exclusion precludes liability coverage for some, but not all watercraft exposures. The following table summarizes the exposures that *are* covered. Coverage for excluded exposures is generally available under a policy specifically designed to cover boats or other watercraft. In addition to the motor vehicle and watercraft exclusions, Section II of the homeowners policy contains exclusions for both bodily injury and property damage that

Table 17-2 Watercraft Exposures Covered by Section II of the HO-3 Policy	
Covered Watercraft Liability Exposures	**Examples**
Watercraft that are stored	A 30-foot sailboat stored out of the water at a marina for the winter
Sailboats (with or without auxiliary power) shorter than 26 feet	A 17-foot catamaran owned by the insured
Sailboats (with or without auxiliary power) longer than 26 feet *not owned by or rented to* an insured	A 32-foot sailboat the insured borrowed from her brother for a vacation
Inboard or inboard-outdrive watercraft with engines of 50 horsepower or less *not owned by* an insured	A 50-horsepower jet ski rented by an insured
Inboard or inboard-outdrive watercraft of more than 50 horsepower *not owned by or rented to* an insured	A 150-horsepower inboard motor boat borrowed from a neighbor
Watercraft with one or more outboard engines or motors with 25 total horsepower or less	A fishing boat with a 15-horsepower motor, owned by the insured
Watercraft with one or more outboard engines or motors with more than 25 total horsepower *not owned by* an insured	A boat with a 75-horsepower outboard motor, borrowed from a friend
Watercraft with outboard engines or motors of more than 25 total horsepower owned by an insured if acquired during the policy period. If the insured acquires such watercraft before the policy period, they are covered only if the insured declares them at the policy inception, or reports the intention to insure them within 45 days of acquiring them.	A new boat with a 100-horsepower outboard motor purchased by the insured after the effective date of the policy
Source: *Personal Insurance*, American Institute for CPCU/Insurance Institute of America, © 2002. Reprinted with permission of the Institutes.	

- arises out of aircraft or hovercraft. Most families do not have these exposures.

- arises out of or in connection with a business engaged in by an insured. There are some exceptions to this exclusion, however, and Coverage E applies if

    – a house is occasionally rented to others and used only as a residence

    – part of the residence is rented to others

    – part of the residence is rented and used as an office, school, study, or private garage

    – an insured is under age 21 and involved in part-time or occasional self-employed business (for example, lawn mowing) with no employees

    Several endorsements are available to provide limited coverage for businesses on the residence premises, but in many cases, commercial coverage is needed.

- arises out of the rendering or failure to render professional services. An accountant, a nurse, or another professional should purchase professional liability insurance to address these significant liability exposures.

- arises out of a location owned or rented by an insured that does not meet the policy definition of an insured location. This exclusion precludes coverage for premises claims, such as a claim that somebody was injured by a condition on the property. It does not preclude coverage for claims based on the insured's activities away from home.

- is caused by transmission of a communicable disease. Claims alleging that the insured transmitted to someone else the HIV virus that causes AIDS, or transmitted herpes, or even passed along the common cold are not covered.

- arises out of sexual molestation, corporal punishment, or physical or mental abuse. Providing insurance coverage against some of these claims is considered to be against public policy. Although it is not defined, corporal punishment generally refers to hitting, slapping, spanking, and similar disciplinary actions. Teachers, elder-care workers, or persons providing day care for children can sometimes obtain separate coverage that helps defend against allegations of the types excluded here, which sometimes are false or groundless.

- arises from the use, sale, manufacture, delivery, transfer, or possession of a controlled substance. It is obviously against public policy to provide products liability coverage for a dope dealer.

Another set of exclusions apply only to Coverage E. These preclude coverage for liability arising from

- any contract or agreement other than written contracts (1) relating to the ownership, maintenance, or use of an insured location—liability assumed in a lease, for example, is covered—and (2) for liability of others assumed by the insured before an occurrence takes place. People often are asked to sign construction contracts, purchase agreements, tool-rental agreements, and other documents that involve some transfer of liability. Although many people routinely sign contracts without reading them, clients would well be advised to pay attention to any legal obligations of other parties that they agree to assume, whether or not they have contractual liability insurance protection.

EXAMPLE

Ned hires a contractor to replace the siding on his house. Ned signs a contract that includes wording to the effect that Ned will be responsible if the contractor is sued for negligence in connection with the work on Ned's home. While the contractor is doing the work, a gust of wind blows a siding panel into the street in front of Ned's house and causes an auto accident. The drivers sue the contractor, but the contractor turns the claim over to Ned because of the contract. Ned's homeowners policy will protect him against this contractual liability claim, up to Ned's policy limit. Because of the liability he assumed in the contract, Ned will be personally responsible for any damages that exceed policy limits.

Suppose, instead, that Ned and the contractor had no written agreement before the accident, but after the accident occurred, Ned wrote a letter to the contractor stating that Ned would assume responsibility and would file a claim under his homeowners policy. Under these circumstances, Ned's homeowners policy would provide no protection because he assumed liability after the occurrence had already taken place.

- property damage to property owned by an insured
- damage to property that is rented to, occupied by, or in the care of the insured except for property damage caused by fire, smoke, or explosion
- bodily injury to any person who is eligible to receive benefits or who is provided benefits under a state workers' compensation law, nonoccupational disability law, or occupational disease law.

Workers' compensation coverage is needed if this loss exposure exists.

- bodily injury arising out of nuclear energy
- bodily injury to any insured. The policy does not provide coverage if one insured injures another insured.

Coverage F—Medical Payments to Others

Coverage F provides up to $1,000 per person of coverage (or more if the basic limit is increased) for the necessary medical expenses of persons other than an insured who are injured while on an insured location with the permission of an insured. Benefits are paid regardless of fault even though this coverage is in the liability section of the policy. Injuries that occur off an insured location are also covered on the same basis if they

- arise out of a condition in an insured location
- are caused by the activities of an insured
- are caused by a resident employee of an insured in the course of employment for an insured

To a degree, the medical payments to others coverage overlaps with the bodily injury liability coverage. The key distinction is this:

- Liability coverage applies only when an insured is legally responsible for damages.
- Medical payments claims are often paid because the insured feels a *moral* obligation to another person, even when the insured is not negligent and has no legal responsibility for that person's injuries.

Often, a bodily injury liability claim involves a relatively small amount of money, and the insurer will pay it as a medical payments claim to eliminate any need to determine whether the insured was legally responsible for the other party's injuries.

EXAMPLE

Walter Booth held a birthday party at his home for his 6-year-old son. During the festivities, a deck collapsed, and Walter, his son, and six guests were treated for minor injuries. Another guest broke his leg and was unable to work on his job as a bricklayer for the 8 weeks it took to recover.

Walter has a homeowners policy with a $100,000 Coverage E—Liability limit and a $1,000 Coverage F—Medical Payments to Others limit.

The homeowners policy provides no coverage for Walter and his son's medical expenses, because they are insureds under the policy.

The Coverage F—Medical Payments to Others coverage will pay up to $1,000 for each of the six injured guests' injuries. Coverage applies even if the Booths are not legally responsible for the injuries as might, for example, be the case if the deck collapsed because a guest's car had rolled into a pole supporting the deck. In either case, for small claims like this there is no need to determine whether the Booths were liable for this incident, and their insurance addresses the moral obligation they might feel toward their injured guests, even if they have no legal obligation to pay the guests' expenses.

Coverage E—Liability of the homeowners policy addresses the bricklayer's bodily injury claim against the Booths for medical expenses, lost wages, and pain and suffering. The bricklayer may recover damages up to the policy limit of $100,000, provided it is clear that the Booths are legally responsible to pay damages to this guest as a result of the collapse. The insurer will also investigate the claim and defend the Booths if there is reason to believe the deck collapse did not result from their negligence. Any other guest whose damages exceeded $1,000 could also make a bodily injury liability claim against the Booths and attempt to demonstrate that the loss was caused by their negligence.

The liability coverage of the Booths' homeowners policy thus provides protection against sizable claims that involve a legal obligation to pay damages, as well as paying defense costs and other legal expenses associated with the claim. The Medical Payments to Others coverage pays relatively small claims without the need to demonstrate liability or the expense of determining liability; it therefore helps preserve the goodwill of the insureds.

Additional Coverages for Section II

Section II—Liability of homeowners policies includes several Additional Coverages, including an agreement to pay claims expenses and first aid expenses. Two additional coverages are especially noteworthy:

- damage to property of others
- loss assessment

Damage to Property of Others. This coverage is roughly comparable to the medical payments to others coverage discussed earlier except, of course, that it deals with property damage rather than bodily injury. The homeowners policy covers up to $1,000 per occurrence for property damage to the property of others caused by an insured. However, this additional coverage does not apply to losses when

- the loss is caused intentionally by an insured who is aged 13 or older
- the damaged property is owned by another insured

- the damaged property is owned by or rented to a tenant of an insured or a resident of the named insured's household
- the damage arises out of a business engaged in by an insured
- the damage arises out of any act or omission in connection with premises owned, rented, or controlled by an insured other than the insured location
- the damage arises out of ownership or use of aircraft, hovercraft, watercraft, or motor vehicles other than recreational vehicles that are

  (1) designed for off-road use

  (2) not owned by an insured, and

  (3) not subject to motor vehicle registration

In addition, there is an offset for any duplicate benefits paid under Section I.

EXAMPLE
Liz borrows a neighbor's self-propelled lawn mower because her own push mower is in the shop. While mowing the lawn in her back yard, Liz loses control of the mower, and it self-propels itself into Liz's swimming pool. Liz's homeowners policy covers damage to the mower for up to $1,000 without having to prove that Liz was actually responsible for the loss. Maybe it really wasn't Liz's fault. Perhaps the mower was defective, or maybe the neighbor failed to instruct Liz in its use. Regardless, Liz's homeowners coverage for damage to property of others applies, because she did not intentionally damage the mower.   In another incident, Liz's 4-year-old son, Aiden, found a can of spray paint and "decorated" the neighbor's shed. Although the damage was intentional, because Aiden is less than 13 years old, the damage to property of others will provide coverage up to $1,000.

Loss Assessment Coverage. Section I of the homeowners policy provides $1,000 loss assessment coverage when a condominium association or homeowners association assesses its members on account of a property loss. A similar provision in Section II of a standard homeowners policy likewise provides up to $1,000 for the insured's share of a loss assessment resulting from a liability claim against a property owners' association. Coverage applies to assessments made as the result of claims alleging (1) liability for bodily injury or property damage or (2) liability of an association's director, officer, or trustee.

Liability claims can be large even when shared with other association members. Suppose, for example, a child drowns in the association's swimming pool while the lifeguard is flirting with another guest, and survivors bring a wrongful death claim against the association and are awarded $5 million in damages. Suppose the association has liability insurance with a limit of $1 million, leaving the association responsible to pay $4 million in damages that it cannot recover from the insurer. The association must assess its members to recover the additional $4 million. If the homeowners association has 80 members, each will be assessed $50,000. Most members will recover only $1,000 under their homeowners policies because they have not purchased additional coverage. Most also will not have an emergency fund that can take a $49,000 hit.

The standard $1,000 limit in homeowners policies can be increased by endorsement, and the additional coverage is relatively inexpensive. Clients who belong to a condominium or homeowners association should seriously consider purchasing additional coverage. Clients in these situations would also be well advised to ensure that their association maintains adequate property and liability insurance. The need seems obvious, but many associations are run by board members who are not well versed in these areas or whose primary goal is to minimize expenses by purchasing minimal insurance coverage.

OTHER HOMEOWNERS FORMS

There are other homeowners forms. Unless modified by endorsement, the liability coverage of all homeowners forms is the same. The ways in which property coverages differ from the HO-3 are discussed below, followed by *Table 17-3*, which provides a side-by-side comparison.

HO-2 Broad Form

The HO-2 is sometimes used when the cost of insurance is the overriding concern. The difference between the HO-2 and the HO-3 is that the HO-2 costs a little less and provides a little less property coverage. Rather than providing open-perils coverage on the dwelling building and other structures, the HO-2 covers both buildings and personal property against the specific causes of loss named in the policy. The covered causes of loss were previously discussed in connection with the personal property coverage of the HO-3. Although the list of covered perils is long, it does not include every possible cause of accidental loss to a house.

A subtle difference between open-perils coverage and named-perils coverage involves the burden of proof. When a policy covers loss by named perils, the burden is on the insured to demonstrate that the loss was caused by one of the perils for which coverage is provided. Open-perils coverage, on the other hand, is based on the presumption that any property loss that has occurred is covered unless the insurer can demonstrate that one of the exclusions applies. This subtle distinction is sometimes important when property was obviously damaged, but it is difficult to determine how the damage occurred. Where proof is not readily available, the HO-3, in effect, gives the insured the benefit of the doubt.

HO-4 Contents Broad Form

The HO-4 is called a homeowners policy even though it is intended primarily for people who live in rented quarters and do not own a home. The HO-4 is part of the homeowners policy family, and it is essentially the same thing as an HO-3 without coverage on the building or other structures. The policyowner selects a limit for Coverage C—Personal Property, and Coverage D is set at 30 percent of that amount.

Although the HO-4 is usually written for tenants of an apartment building or a one-or-more-family dwelling, an HO-4 may also be purchased by the owner of a multi-unit apartment building—too large to be eligible for an HO-3—who also occupies one of the apartment units and wishes to protect his or her personal possessions and personal liability.

A client who owns a home or a condominium unit is usually forced to buy homeowners insurance because he or she is required to do so by the lender that provides the mortgage. Tenants often overlook their insurance needs because nobody requires homeowners insurance, they believe their personal property is not worth insuring, or they fail to recognize the importance of liability insurance. Many have not even checked into the cost of an HO-4 and do not realize that the coverage is relatively inexpensive, which is also why insurers do not aggressively market HO-4 coverage. In light of these factors, a financial advisor whose client is a tenant must often take the initiative to ensure that the client has protected his or her assets with this important coverage.

HO-5 Comprehensive Form

The HO-5 differs from the HO-3 in that Coverage C—Personal Property is written on an open-perils basis. The HO-5 therefore provides the broadest coverage of any standard homeowners policy and, of course, coverage can be expanded even further by endorsement. However, the HO-5 is not as popular as the HO-3, largely because of the added cost.

Both the HO-4 and the HO-6, discussed next, can be endorsed to provide comparable open-perils coverage on personal property.

HO-6 Unit-Owners Form

An increasing number of clients have insurance needs that require special attention because they live in condominium or cooperative units. People who own condominium or cooperative units jointly own a building with other co-owners and individually are responsible for their own specific unit. A condominium's ownership deed, also called the "master deed" or "condominium declarations," is a document that establishes unit owners' rights and responsibilities. These documents usually include a section describing insurance requirements. Property not insured by the condominium association is usually the responsibility of the individual unit owner.

Because insurance requirements vary, clients should examine these documents carefully, consulting a legal advisor if necessary to determine the extent of their responsibilities. The association's insurance might provide only "bare walls" coverage for the building structure and the walls that support the structure, leaving the unit owner responsible for other walls and fixtures inside the unit. Or the association's insurance might include coverage for the fixtures, plumbing, wiring, or partitions inside the individual unit.

The HO-6 is designed to cover the unique loss exposures of a condominium or cooperative unit owner. In general, the HO-6 resembles an HO-4 for tenants that, as mentioned, is like an HO-3 without coverage on buildings or other structures. Because unit owners may have an insurable interest in the building, the HO-6 provides $5,000 in named-perils coverage under Coverage A; this amount can be increased when necessary.

The policyowner selects a limit for Coverage C—Personal Property. The Coverage D limit is automatically set at 50 percent of the Coverage C limit. Although the standard HO-6 provides named-perils coverage, Coverages A and C can both be changed by endorsement to apply on an open-perils basis.

HO-8 Modified Coverage Form

The HO-8, not a widely used homeowners form, has been mostly written on older homes where the replacement cost of a dwelling significantly exceeds its market value. Typically, these are somewhat run-down, older homes. Providing replacement coverage in these cases might create a moral hazard because the policyowner could collect substantially more under an insurance settlement than by selling the house. In addition, the premium for replacement cost coverage might be beyond the means of many persons who own such homes.

The perils insured against for all coverages are limited to fire, lightning, windstorm or hail, explosion, riot or civil commotion, aircraft, vehicles, smoke, vandalism and malicious mischief, and volcanic eruption. Theft is covered only from the residence premises and up to a limit of $1,000. This limitation reflects the fact that HO-8s are often written in areas where the crime rate is higher.

There are also other limitations. Only 10 percent of Coverage C is provided on property off the insured premises. Additional Coverages are more limited and, for example, do not include collapse or extra expenses because of ordinances or laws.

Loss settlements under Coverages A and B are based on common construction materials and methods that are functionally equivalent to the original construction. Settlements are limited to market value if repairs are not made. (Note, however, that some states require loss settlements to be on an actual cash value basis.)

The issue of functional equivalency is discussed later with respect to the Functional Replacement Cost endorsement.

Comparison of Homeowners Forms

The following table compares the homeowners forms.

Table 17-3 Homeowners Forms						
	HO-2 Broad	HO-3 Special	HO-4 Tenants	HO-5 Comprehensive	HO-6 Unit-owners	HO-8 Modified
Perils insured against	Broad named perils	Open perils for dwelling; broad named perils for personal property	Broad named perils for personal property	Open perils	Broad named perils	Limited named perils
Coverage A—Dwelling	Amount selected	Amount selected	—	Amount selected	$5,000	Amount selected
Coverage B—Other Structures	10% of A	10% of A	—	10% of A	—	10% of A
Coverage C—Unscheduled Personal Property	50% of A	50% of A	Amount selected	50% of A	Amount selected	50% of A
Coverage D-Loss of Use	30% of A	30% of A	30% of C	30% of A	50% of C	10% of A
Coverage E—Personal Liability	$100,000	$100,000	$100,000	$100,000	$100,000	$100,000
Coverage F—Medical Payments to Others	$1,000 per person	$1,000 per person	$1,000 per person	$1,000 per person	$1,000 per person	$1,000 per person

HOMEOWNERS ENDORSEMENTS—TAILORING THE POLICY TO INDIVIDUAL NEEDS

Homeowners policies are designed for the typical needs of a broad range of homeowners. An individual homeowner may need to tailor the policy to meet his or her own special needs. These needs can be met in many instances through the use of appropriate policy endorsements that can add or delete coverage, change definitions, or clarify the intent of the insurance company.

Although an individual company can design almost any type of endorsement, nearly 60 standard homeowners endorsements have been prepared by ISO for use with its homeowners forms. Several of these endorsements are briefly described below. The name used is the actual name of the ISO endorsement, and they are listed in alphabetical order. Some endorsements apply to the entire policy; others modify only Section I or Section II.

Note that it is not generally necessary to add an endorsement to increase the limits of insurance for Coverages C, D, E, or F. This is accomplished by listing the higher amount in the policy declarations and paying the necessary additional premium.

Endorsements That Modify Section I and Section II

Additional Insured—Residence Premises

In some cases, persons other than the named insured have an interest in residential property. For example, a sister might occupy a house that she and her brother jointly inherited from their parents. This endorsement adds others (such as the brother) as insureds. However, the additional insured's coverage under Section II is only for liability with respect to the residence premises.

Assisted-Living Care Coverage

As the population ages, an increasing number of people live in assisted-living facilities. Many are no longer able to perform the activities of daily living necessary to live on their own. Some are liquidating their life savings in order to meet expenses; others have had the foresight to purchase long-term care insurance that pays for all or part of their care and helps preserve their assets. Still others have spent down their assets and rely on Medicaid for their support. In any case, people whose parents or relatives live in assisted-living facilities often overlook their need for property and liability insurance.

The assisted-living care coverage endorsement provides limited personal property, additional living expenses, and liability coverage for a named relative of a homeowner-insured who lives in these facilities but is not a member of the insured's household. Additional expense coverage is provided for up to $500 per month, and sublimits apply for hearing aids, eyeglasses, contact lenses, false teeth, medical-alert devices, walkers or canes, and wheelchairs.

Home Business Insurance Coverage

This endorsement provides both business property and liability coverage for certain home businesses owned solely by the named insured or jointly by the named insured and resident relatives. Coverage is provided for the following:

- business property, property of others in the insured's care because of the business, and business property leased by the insured if there is a contractual responsibility to insure it
- accounts receivable and valuable papers and records
- business income and extra expense losses
- liability coverage for bodily injury, property damage, personal and advertising injury, products, and completed operations

There is no coverage for liability for the rendering or failure to render professional services.

Home Day-Care Coverage Endorsement

This endorsement is for persons who conduct day-care businesses in their homes for either children or older adults. It provides coverage for personal property used in the day-care business and extends Section II liability coverage to home day-care services. However, liability is excluded for injuries arising out of motor vehicles, watercraft, and saddle animals. Note that Section II excludes liability arising out of sexual molestation and physical or mental abuse inflicted by an insured or an employee. These are obvious liability loss exposures for a day-care center.

Loss Assessment Coverage

The purpose of this endorsement is to increase the $1,000 limits for loss assessments by a homeowners association. Although it can be added to any homeowners form, it is especially common with an HO-6.

Permitted Incidental Occupancies (Residence Premises)

This endorsement deletes many of the homeowners exclusions that pertain to a business conducted on the residence premises. If business is conducted in a separate structure on the premises, it is necessary to list that structure under Coverage B and select a limit of property coverage for the building. The $2,500 limit for business property under Coverage C is deleted, and the full limit of Coverage C applies to business and personal property. Liability coverage is still excluded for bodily injury to an employee or to a pupil if the injury is a result of corporal punishment.

This endorsement merely extends the existing homeowners coverage. It does not pick up many of the unique business situations covered by the Home Business Insurance Coverage endorsement.

Residence Held in Trust

For various reasons, clients are sometimes advised to establish a trust that holds the title to their home. When this is done, the residence held in trust endorsement should be used to modify various provisions in Section I and Section II of a homeowners policy to deal with the parties whose interests are insured in a trust situation.

Structures Rented to Others

This endorsement provides both property and liability coverage for structures on an insured premises that are rented to others.

Endorsements That Modify Section I (Property)

Additional Limits of Liability—Coverages A, B, C, and D

This endorsement amends the policy to provide coverage for the full replacement cost of the dwelling at the time of loss if the loss exceeds the stated policy limit. Limits for other property coverages are also increased in the same proportion. As a condition for this protection, the policyowner agrees to maintain insurance at full replacement value as determined by the insurer and to report any alterations that increase the dwelling's value by 5 percent or more.

In effect, the endorsement merely guarantees that the insurer has required an adequate amount of coverage. This might seem like a trivial matter, but it can make an important difference, even when a house has been properly appraised. The cost of repairing or replacing houses sometimes increases dramatically following a hurricane, forest fire, or earthquake that damages many homes in the same area and creates a high demand for building materials and contractors' services. This endorsement ensures that enough insurance is available to replace the dwelling even in these situations.

Coverage C—Increased Special Limits of Liability

This endorsement can be used to increase coverage for some of the items where limited amounts of protection are available under Coverage C. The limits can be increased for

- money, bank notes, bullion, coins, medals, scrip, stored value cards, smart cards, and gold, silver, and platinum other than goldware, silverware, or platinumware
- securities, accounts, deeds, evidences of debt, letters of credit, and other valuable papers
- jewelry and watches
- firearms
- electronic apparatus for use in a motor vehicle

An increased amount of coverage is selected for each category. Although this endorsement increases the sublimits that apply to certain types of property, it does not expand coverage to include additional perils, nor does it modify the policy's deductible. When high jewelry values are to be protected, the scheduled personal property endorsement, discussed later, is often a better choice.

Credit Card, Electronic Fund Transfer Card or Access Device, Forgery, and Counterfeit Money Coverage

This endorsement increases the $500 limit for these types of losses.

Earthquake

In most states, this endorsement can be used to add coverage for the peril of earthquake as well as tremors that accompany volcanic eruption. In place of the regular deductible, there is an earthquake deductible equal to 5 percent of the limit of insurance that applies to Coverage A or Coverage C, whichever is greater. The deductible percentage can be increased for a premium credit. Coverage for masonry veneer is optional for an extra premium.

The situation is different in the largest market for earthquake insurance—California. The state requires insurers that sell homeowners policies to offer earthquake coverage. However, because of adverse claims experience and the financial inability of insurers to withstand catastrophic claims from future earthquakes, the market for homeowners policies virtually disappeared in the mid-1990s. At that time, many insurers ceased to write new policies or withdrew from the market altogether. As a result, a state agency was formed to make earthquake coverage available. This coverage is now sold by many insurers along with their homeowners policies, but the insurer of the earthquake coverage is the state agency. Although there is coverage available for the residence, there is no coverage for other structures and a limited amount of coverage for personal property, debris removal, and additional living expenses. A standard deductible of 15 percent of a home's insured value may be reduced to 10 percent.

Some insurers still make earthquake coverage available in California as part of their homeowners policies, and other types of insurers specialize in this market with separate policies. In most cases, more comprehensive coverage and lower deductibles are available from these sources.

Functional Replacement Cost Loss Settlement

Older homes often have replacement values far in excess of their market values. An example would be a 100-year-old Victorian house that might sell for several hundred thousand dollars but that would cost several million dollars to reproduce. The HO-8 Modified Coverage Form, mentioned earlier, is one approach to dealing with older homes, especially those in a depressed area. The functional replacement cost endorsement to an HO-2, HO-3, or HO-5 provides an alternative that appeals to homeowners who want the broader coverage of these policies without purchasing a limit of insurance equal to the property's full replacement cost value. Some insurance companies are unwilling to insure such dwellings for replacement cost because of the potential moral hazard. In addition, property owners may not want to pay the premium for replacement cost coverage.

functional replacement cost   This endorsement replaces the replacement cost provision of an HO-2, HO-3, or HO-5 policy with a provision for *functional replacement cost*. This is defined to mean the cost to repair or replace the damaged dwelling with less costly construction materials and methods that are functionally equivalent to obsolete, antique, or custom construction materials and methods used in the original construction of the dwelling. For example, dry wall would replace plaster walls, composition shingles would replace slate, hollow core doors might replace solid wood interior doors, and wall-to-wall carpeting over plywood might replace hardwood floors. All of this, unfortunately, might result in the loss of a dwelling's unique character.

Some states prohibit loss settlements that are less than the actual cash value of a loss. In these states, a modified endorsement is used so that the insured receives the actual cash value when it exceeds the functional replacement cost.

This endorsement has an 80 percent coinsurance provision based on functional replacement cost, which may be as difficult to determine as regular replacement cost.

Identity Fraud Expense Coverage

Introduced recently, this endorsement provides protection against many of the expenses that can result from identity theft, one of America's fastest-growing white collar crimes. Coverage applies in the event of identity fraud, the unauthorized use of an insured's identity to commit an unlawful activity. The endorsement itself does not cover money or property that might be wrongfully appropriated by an identity thief, but it covers certain expenses a victim might incur. Subject to a $250 deductible, up to $15,000 in coverage is provided in each of the following types of expenses:

- costs of notarizing affidavits or related documents to verify the fraud
- costs for certified mail to financial institutions and law enforcement agencies
- lost income (up to $5,000) due to the insured's time off work to complete fraud affidavits and to meet with law enforcement agencies, credit agencies, and attorneys
- loan application fees required to reapply for loans that had been rejected due to inaccurate credit information
- reasonable attorney fees incurred as a result of identity fraud
- long distance phone charges required to report or discuss identity fraud

Clients can also be advised of various measures that can reduce the probability of an identity theft. For example, they should shred documents that contain financial data, including credit card bills, bank statements, mutual fund statements, and so forth. Periodically checking their credit records can reveal inaccurate or unauthorized credit activities. Likewise, clients should minimize the use of their Social Security number or drivers license number and avoid placing important mail in an unlocked mailbox.

Increased Limits on Business Property

The endorsement allows a policyowner to increase the $2,500 limit that applies to business property on the premises. The endorsement is of value to a person who has an office at home but does not conduct a business on the premises.

Increased Limits on Personal Property in Other Residences

Coverage under the homeowners forms for the insured's property usually located at a secondary residence is limited to $1,000. The endorsement can be used to provide increased coverage. The endorsement might, for example, be suitable to protect the property of a college student living in a dormitory, whose computer, stereo, and photographic equipment alone are worth more than $1,000.

Inflation Guard

This endorsement, which has been very popular during periods when home values are steadily increasing, provides inflation protection in the form of automatic increases for all Section I coverages by the annual percentage selected. The increase is effective on a pro rata basis during the annual policy period.

Multiple Company Insurance

When an affluent client requires very large amounts of property insurance, the Section I coverage can be divided between two or more insurers if they all agree to such an arrangement. This endorsement specifies the percentage of the total amount of property insurance each insurer will pay. Only one of the insurance policies will provide the Section II coverage.

Ordinance or Law—Increased Amount of Coverage

This endorsement can be used to increase the Additional Coverage limit of 10 percent of Coverage A for increased costs of construction because of enforcement of an ordinance or law. These additional costs can be significant when major changes have occurred in building codes, such as provisions aimed at minimizing losses due to floods or earthquakes when a structure is rebuilt or undergoes significant repairs.

Other Structures—Increased Limits

When the standard amount of insurance for Coverage B is inadequate, this endorsement is used to provide additional insurance on structures that are described in the endorsement. For example, an insured with $200,000 of coverage on a dwelling would automatically have $20,000 of insurance for

Coverage B. If the insured had a separate structure used as an art studio that had a replacement cost of $35,000, this endorsement could provide the additional $15,000 of protection.

Personal Property Replacement Cost Loss Settlement

Most clients should probably consider this popular endorsement, which changes the loss settlement basis for personal property from actual cash value to replacement cost. Some property, such as antiques, fine art, and collectibles, is not eligible for replacement cost coverage.

If the replacement value of a loss is more than $500, repair or replacement must be made before the replacement cost provision is applicable. The insured can make a claim for the actual cash value at the time of loss and amend it to replacement cost within 180 days.

Premises Alarm or Fire Protection System

This endorsement acknowledges that an insurer-acceptable alarm system or automatic sprinkler system is in place. The policyowner agrees to maintain the system in working order and to let the insurer know promptly if any changes are made to the system or if it is removed. In exchange, the policyowner receives a premium reduction.

Refrigerated Property Coverage

This endorsement adds up to $500 coverage (with a $100 deductible) for losses to property in refrigerators or freezers caused by interruption of electrical services (either on or off the premises) or the mechanical failure of the refrigerator or freezer. Some insurers that do not use ISO forms automatically include refrigerated property coverage in their basic homeowners policy forms.

Scheduled Personal Property Endorsement

Clients who have possessions of high value that are subject to the sublimits of the standard homeowners policy commonly use this popular endorsement. It broadens coverage on specific categories of valuable personal property, such as jewelry, furs, cameras, musical instruments, silverware, golfer's equipment, fine arts, and stamp and coin collections. Each item is usually listed separately and insured for a specified value, but some coverage can be written on a blanket basis for certain classes of property.

Coverage is open-perils with few exceptions and applies worldwide. There is also coverage for up to 30 days for newly acquired property in a category insured under the endorsement. It is limited, however, to 25 percent of the amount of insurance for that category.

Once property is insured under this endorsement, there is no coverage for it under Coverage C. The Section I deductible does not apply to scheduled items.

Losses are generally settled on an actual cash value basis. However, fine art is written on an agreed value basis, and another available endorsement can provide coverage for other personal property on an agreed value basis.

Sinkhole Collapse

Property is sometimes damaged or destroyed when earth collapses because of voids created under limestone or similar rock formations. This endorsement provides coverage for losses to covered property (not land) from such collapses.

Special Computer Coverage

Designed for homeowners or unit owners who do not have open-perils coverage on their other personal property, this endorsement provides open-perils coverage on computer equipment.

Special Loss Settlement

The loss settlement provision of homeowners policies was discussed in chapter 16. This endorsement lowers the 80 percent insurance-to-value requirement to either 50, 60, or 70 percent. It is used when the replacement cost of a dwelling far exceeds its market value and the insurer is unwilling to write a policy for as much as 80 percent of replacement cost.

Special Personal Property Coverage—HO-4

This endorsement allows tenants to change the named-perils coverage for personal property under an HO-4 to open-perils coverage like the coverage provided by an HO-5.

Unit-Owners Coverage A and Unit-Owners Coverage C

These endorsements change the named-perils coverage of an HO-6 to open-perils coverage. If both endorsements are purchased, the condominium owner has a policy much like an HO-5.

Endorsements That Modify Section II (Liability)

Additional Residence Rented to Others

Sometimes a policyowner owns a separate rental property. This endorsement can be used to extend the Section II coverages to liability that arises out of such property as long as it is listed in the endorsement and contains no more than four living units.

Business Pursuits

The business pursuits endorsement provides coverage for liability that arises out of or in connection with a business in which an insured engages. An example is a suit against a salesperson who accidentally injured a customer. The endorsement is most commonly used by persons in sales, clerical, and teaching occupations.

Coverage does not apply with respect to a business owned or financially controlled by an insured or in which an insured is a partner. (A commercial policy is needed for this.) In addition, there is no coverage for liability that arises out of professional services, with the exception of teaching. Bodily injury to fellow employees is also excluded.

Farmers Personal Liability

People whose principal business or occupation is not farming sometimes own some land where farming operations take place. This endorsement provides Section II coverage for this activity at those locations listed in the endorsement. Several exclusions in the endorsement apply to unique farming activities.

Personal Injury

Attorneys and others often use "personal injury" as a synonym for "bodily injury." In the language of liability insurance, the two terms have different meanings. In liability insurance policies, personal injury refers to a group of offenses—such as libel, slander, and invasion of privacy—that are listed in the policy. The homeowners personal injury endorsement modifies the definition of bodily injury to include personal injury, which is defined in this endorsement to include the following offenses:

- false arrest, detention, or imprisonment, or malicious prosecution
- libel, slander, or defamation of character
- invasion of privacy, wrongful eviction, or wrongful entry

The coverage does not apply to an insured's violation of criminal law, employment-related injuries, business-related and professional injuries, civic or public activities performed for pay, injury to another insured, or contractual liability other than that relating to the insured's home.

Although the personal injury endorsement can protect against these offenses under a homeowners policy, many clients would best be advised to forgo the homeowners endorsement and instead obtain this protection under a personal umbrella policy.

Snowmobiles

The snowmobile endorsement provides coverage for listed snowmobiles when they are used off the insured premises. However, coverage does not apply if the snowmobiles are (1) subject to motor vehicle registration, (2) used to carry paying passengers, (3) used for a business purpose, (4) rented to others, or (5) operated in organized competitions.

Watercraft

The watercraft endorsement provides coverage for boats that are longer or more powerful than those covered by the standard homeowners coverage. It does not cover liability arising out of (1) racing or speed competitions except for sailboats, (2) injuries to employees who maintain or use the boats, (3) watercraft used to carry persons for a fee, or (4) watercraft rented to others.

OTHER RESIDENTIAL FORMS

Homeowners policies do not cover all types of residential loss exposures. The following discussion briefly describes three other types of residential coverage:

- dwelling policies
- mobile home insurance
- insurance for farms and ranches

As with homeowners policies, insurance companies may have their own forms or use those developed by ISO or AAIS. The following discussion is based primarily on the ISO forms.

Dwelling Policies

dwelling policy

A *dwelling policy* is designed primarily for a residence that is ineligible for a homeowners policy for one or more of the following reasons:

- The dwelling is rented to others.
- The dwelling does not meet the insurer's eligibility requirements for homeowners coverage. This may be because of low value, too many living units, the old age of the dwelling, or the poorer-than-average physical condition of the dwelling.

In addition, a few insureds may elect a more restrictive and less expensive dwelling policy because they do not want all the homeowners coverages or are unwilling or unable to pay the price of a homeowners policy. Under the ISO program, a dwelling policy can also be written for houseboats in some states and for mobile homes, subject to certain restrictions.

Like the homeowners form, ISO has several dwelling forms:

- Dwelling Property 1—Basic Form (DP-1)
- Dwelling Property 2—Broad Form (DP-2)
- Dwelling Property 3—Special Form (DP-3)

The DP-2 and DP-3 are similar to the Section I coverages of the HO-2 and HO-3, respectively. The DP-1 is a more limited policy, and the coverage is slightly less comprehensive. For example, the standard dwelling forms have no coverage for the peril of theft, and off-premises coverage for personal property is limited to 10 percent of Coverage C.

There are five coverages under the forms:

- Coverage A—Dwelling
- Coverage B—Other Structures
- Coverage C—Personal Property
- Coverage D—Fair Rental Value
- Coverage E—Additional Living Expenses (not included with DP-1)

The applicant selects the coverages to purchase and the limits of coverage. Tenants can purchase a policy without Coverages A and B, and landlords can purchase a policy without Coverage C.

The peril of theft can be endorsed to the dwelling forms and, for owner-occupied dwellings, the coverage is then similar to that under the homeowners forms. Tenants are eligible only for more limited coverage.

The dwelling forms do not automatically provide liability coverages as the homeowners forms do. However, these important coverages can be added by endorsement.

Mobile home Insurance

mobile home insurance

Insurance on an owner-occupied mobile home, known as *mobile home insurance*, is very similar to insurance on a conventional dwelling. An endorsement, added to an HO-2 or HO-3, alters a few definitions and amends a few policy provisions to adapt coverage for this type of living unit. For example, because furniture is often built in and part of a mobile home, the mobile home insurance Coverage C limit is lowered to 40 percent of the Coverage A limit. Because these homes are mobile, an extra coverage provides up to $500 to cover the cost of moving a mobile home out of harm's way when it is endangered by an insured peril. The $500 limit can be increased by endorsement.

The homeowners forms may be modified to cover a mobile home on an actual cash value basis. The insurer sometimes requires this modification on an older mobile home, because mobile homes depreciate in value as they age.

The owner of a mobile home who does not occupy it can insure the mobile home under a dwelling form. The tenant of a mobile home is eligible for an HO-4 policy.

Farm and Ranch Policies

Many people earn their livelihood by owning farms and ranches, and numerous policies are available to provide them with the necessary property and liability protection. Coverage tends to be written by insurers that use their own forms and often specialize in writing coverage for the persons engaged in this type of occupation.

In addition to coverages for the farm or ranch dwelling and household personal property, coverage is needed for farm structures and farm personal property. Other property loss exposures include food spoilage, damage to private power and light poles, and loss to animals from numerous perils other than sickness or disease. There are also unique liability loss exposures, such as animal boarding, injury or sickness from chemicals, and injury to the public if they are allowed to pick fruits or vegetables.

The available farm and ranch policies tend to look much like homeowners policies with additional coverage for many of these and other farming and ranching loss exposures.

FLOOD INSURANCE

When discussing property insurance with a client, it is all too easy to overlook flood insurance. Many clients do not even consider flood coverage, because they do not think they live in an area susceptible to flooding. Many people in that category lived in North Carolina in 1999 when 55,000 homes were flooded, 15,000 homes became uninhabitable, and 8,000 homes were completely destroyed. More than 80 percent of the flooded properties were outside high-risk flood hazard areas.[56] In 2005, Gulf Coast hurricanes Katrina and Rita again caused flood damage to thousands of homeowners who had not purchased flood insurance.

National Flood Insurance Program (NFIP)

Roughly 25 percent of all claims paid by the National Flood Insurance Program are for policies in low- to moderate-risk communities.[57] Flood is an excluded peril in almost all insurance policies that cover real property and many that cover personal property. At one time, coverage was virtually impossible to obtain, but this changed in the late 1960s when Congress passed legislation that enacted the *National Flood Insurance Program (NFIP)*. This program is currently administered by the Federal Insurance and Mitigation Administration (FIMA). Under the NFIP, the federal government provides limited amounts of flood insurance coverage—often at subsidized rates—for the owners of dwellings commercial buildings, and the contents of both.

Although coverage was once purchased directly from the National Flood Insurance Program, most policies are now written through private insurance

---

56. NBC17.com, Flooding Fact Sheet based on information provided by the National Flood Insurance Program, http://wncn.nbcweatherplus.com/weathernews/2932395/detail.html, accessed 1/11/07.

57. "Flood Statistics," Federal Emergency Management Agency, floodsmart.gov/floodsmart/pages/statistics.jsp, accessed 1/11/07.

companies under the *write-your-own-program*. Under this program, the NFIP reimburses the insurance company for any losses that exceed the sum of premiums collected and any investment income earned on these premiums. Consumers obtain their policies through private insurance agents.

On September 30, 2010, President Obama signed the National Flood Insurance Program Reextension Act of 2010, which Congress passed on September 24, 2010. This extends the National Flood Insurance Program until September 30, 2011. For the most current information on the NFIP, see floodsmart.gov or fema.gov.

The NFIP is not the only source of flood insurance. Some private insurers are also willing to write flood insurance on residential property, and one reportedly offers limits as high as $15 million.[58]

Eligibility

For property owners to be eligible for the national flood insurance program, they must live in a community that participates in the program. These communities must agree to establish and enforce certain land use restrictions to minimize the community's exposure to flood losses. These, for example, might include a prohibition against new construction in flood-prone areas.

Unfortunately, even when flood insurance is available, many consumers do not purchase it, particularly if they live in an area where floods seem unlikely. To minimize uninsured flood losses, the government prohibits the issuance of federal loans or federally assisted or insured loans to persons in highly flood-prone areas (called special hazard flood areas) unless they purchase coverage.

The maximum dollar amount of coverage available for residential property through the flood insurance program is limited to $250,000 on the building and $100,000 on the contents for communities eligible for the "regular program." These limits might be less than the value of the dwelling and personal property in it. However, as explained below, not all types of property are covered, and flood damage often does not result in a total loss. To avoid insuring property when a flood is imminent, the program includes a 30-day waiting period before a flood insurance policy can become effective.

---

58. "New Flood Insurance Policy Provides up to $15 Million in Limits," *PR Newswire*, Monday April 3, 2006. Web site address prnewswire.com, accessed 2/15/2007.

Detailed and current information on the national flood insurance program is available online at floodsmart.gov. The following coverage summary is adapted from information there.

Property Covered

The Standard Flood Insurance Policy (SFIP) Forms contain complete definitions of the coverages they provide. Direct physical losses caused by "floods" are covered. Also covered are losses resulting from flood-related erosion caused by waves or currents of water activity exceeding anticipated cyclical levels, or caused by a severe storm, flash flood, abnormal tidal surge, or the like, which result in flooding, as defined. Damage caused by mud flows, as specifically defined in the policy forms, is covered. A mud flow is a flooding condition where a river of liquid and flowing mud moves on the surface of normally dry land areas. Mud flows differ from mud slides, in which a dry or wet mass of rock or earth moves downhill. Mud flows are covered by flood insurance; mud slides are not.

The NFIP defines a basement as any area of a building with a floor that is below ground level on all sides. Although flood insurance does not cover basement improvements, such as finished walls, floors or ceilings, or personal belongings that may be kept in a basement, such as furniture and other contents, it does cover structural elements, essential equipment, and other basic items generally located in a basement. Many of these items are covered under building coverage, and some are covered under contents coverage. The NFIP encourages people to purchase both building and contents coverage for the broadest protection.

The following items are covered under building coverage, as long as they are connected to a power source and installed in their functioning location:

- sump pumps
- well water tanks and pumps; cisterns and the water in them
- oil tanks and the oil in them; natural gas tanks and the gas in them
- pumps and/or tanks used in conjunction with solar energy
- furnaces, hot water heaters, air conditioners, and heat pumps
- electrical junction and circuit breaker boxes, and required utility connections

Also covered under building coverage are the following:

- foundation elements

- stairways, staircases, elevators, and dumbwaiters
- unpainted drywall and sheet rock walls and ceilings, including fiberglass insulation
- cleanup

The following items are covered under contents coverage:

- clothes washers
- clothes dryers
- food freezers and the food in them

Increased Cost of Compliance Coverage

Increased Cost of Compliance (ICC) under the NFIP provides for the payment of a claim to help meet the cost to comply with state or community floodplain management laws or ordinances from a flood event in which a building has been declared substantially damaged or repetitively damaged. When an insured building is damaged by a flood and the state or community declares the building to be substantially damaged or repetitively damaged, ICC will help pay for the cost to elevate, floodproof, demolish, or relocate the building up to $30,000. This coverage is in addition to the building coverage for the repair of actual physical damage from flood under the Standard Flood Insurance Policy (SFIP).

HARD-TO-INSURE RESIDENTIAL PROPERTY

Even though most residential property is eligible for coverage in the standard insurance market, some residential property fails to meet most insurers' underwriting guidelines. This can occur for a variety of reasons, including the

- high replacement cost of the property relative to its market value
- physical condition of the property
- environment of the property. For example, the neighborhood is one of high crime or susceptibility to brush fires or severe coastal storms.
- poor reputation of the owner or occupants
- excessiveness of past claims of the applicant
- use of the property. For example, it may be a remote cabin that is seldom occupied and in an area without fire protection.

Policies that are available on these properties can be more limited than policies written in the general marketplace. Some companies specialize in substandard coverage and write policies for a variety of properties but at higher-than-normal premiums.

FAIR (Fair Access to Insurance Requirements) plans

Many states have taken actions to make coverage available, often at subsidized rates. More than 30 states have *FAIR (Fair Access to Insurance Requirements) plans*. These plans originally began as a result of urban riots in the 1960s, which made property insurance very difficult to obtain in many major cities. The current plans are state-run programs to provide insurance for buildings and their contents if the property owner is unable to obtain coverage in the standard insurance market, for whatever reason. In most cases, coverage is written by a pool or syndicate of private insurers that are assessed for any losses of the plan if premiums are inadequate.

Each state has its own FAIR plan, and they do differ. Nevertheless, a few generalizations can be made. Some types of property are still largely uninsurable. These may include property that is vacant, poorly maintained, subject to unacceptable hazards (such as the manufacture of fireworks), or not built in accordance with safety and building codes. Coverage is usually written under forms that are more limited than homeowners policies. Often the perils insured against are only fire and a limited number of other perils. Coverage is also subject to maximum limits and mandatory deductibles.

Some states, primarily in the Southeast and on the Gulf Coast, have beachfront and windstorm plans to provide protection that insurers are unwilling to write because of the loss exposure to hurricanes. Some of these plans cover only the perils of windstorm and hail, and property owners obtain protection for other perils in the general insurance market.

HIGH-VALUE RESIDENTIAL PROPERTY

Insurance on expensive homes can present unique and interesting challenges for the financial planner. These challenges result from high property values and unique types of property and liability exposures. They also arise from the demanding nature of people who are accustomed to receiving personal attention and a high level of service tailored to their special needs. Because large values are involved, wealthy clients have a great deal to lose, both in terms of property losses and as the result of high-profile liability suits that may be made against them. Challenges a financial planner might face include

- property values higher than an insurer is willing to write under a standard homeowners program designed for the more typical situation
- old or historic homes
- unique construction that can be difficult or costly to rebuild
- gardens, swimming pools, tennis courts, or stables
- high-risk locations, such as oceanfront or mountainside property
- property in several locations, several states, or several countries with no coordination of insurance
- multiple insurance agents, brokers, or insurance companies
- policies with different, nonconcurrent expiration dates
- high-value jewelry, furs, silver, or fine arts items
- antique or collector cars
- boats, yachts, or aircraft
- collections or other valuable belongings (a wine cellar, for example)
- high-value property outside the home—in transit, on loan to a museum, aboard a yacht, or elsewhere
- full-time or part-time nannies or other domestic employees who may reside on the premises
- frequent use of contractors
- a high-profile lifestyle
- frequent parties and many guests
- potential kidnap and ransom exposure
- lack of personal interest in insurance matters

Insurance programs designed for the typical client cannot properly service clients with significant and unusual exposures. Some insurers, and some insurance agents and brokers, specialize in this market and have developed policies specially designed to address the needs of the well-to-do. Standard HO-3 or HO-5 homeowners policies can also be used in many cases, provided they have been tailored with the endorsements necessary to meet any unique exposures. High deductibles are often advisable both to keep premiums down and to avoid a high frequency of insurance claims for normal maintenance and repair. High liability limits are especially important, and they are generally provided through a personal umbrella policy. Once established, an affluent client's property and liability insurance program should be regularly monitored and reviewed to keep pace with frequently changing property and liability exposures. Of course, the client's business exposures must also be properly insured to protect his or her assets against loss.

FLOATER POLICIES

floater

Several policies are available to provide broad insurance protection on a wide variety of personal property. These policies are commonly referred to as *floaters* because the insured property is often subject to being moved or is "floating around" rather than remaining at a fixed location.

With the broadening of the homeowners forms over the years and the development of endorsements to meet specialized needs, the use of personal floater policies has diminished. However, they are still written for persons who are not eligible for homeowners policies or who, for some reason, prefer to have the property insured separately.

Personal Articles Floater

personal articles floater

A *personal articles floater* is used to provide open-perils coverage for certain scheduled and valuable items of personal property. A personal articles floater is essentially the same as the scheduled personal property endorsement to the homeowners policy.

Personal Property Floater

personal property floater

A *personal property floater* is designed primarily to provide open-perils coverage for unscheduled personal property on a worldwide basis. The personal property floater essentially provides the same coverage on personal property that is available under an HO-5 policy or under an HO-4 or HO-6 policy that has an endorsement for open-perils coverage on personal property. The floater may be appropriate for persons who are not eligible for a homeowners policy. For example, the floater could be used by a couple who sold their home and stored their personal property with a friend while taking an around-the-world trip for a year. It may also be appropriate for an itinerant person, such as an actor, who does not maintain a permanent home.

Personal Effects Floater

personal effects floater

A *personal effects floater* provides open-perils worldwide coverage on such property as baggage, clothes, cameras, and sports equipment typically worn or carried by tourists. However, a personal effects floater does not provide coverage for such items as money, passports, and tickets. Without any endorsements, most homeowners policies cover this property only on a named-perils basis.

TITLE INSURANCE

title insurance

Title insurance is a unique type of insurance not generally handled by property liability insurers but rather by title insurance companies that specialize in this area. It is designed to protect the purchaser of real estate against defects in title that can result in the loss of ownership or that can be corrected only after certain costs are incurred. These defects can arise from many sources, including forged titles, invalid wills, inaccurate property descriptions, and undisclosed liens and easements. To provide protection against loan defaults, lenders of funds for the purchase of real property usually require that a borrower purchase title insurance.

One method to protect against a defective title is to have an abstract of title prepared (often by an attorney) prior to the purchase of the property. This abstract, based on public records, lists all liens, mortgage loans, easements, and the like. If any previously unknown condition is found, the potential purchaser can have the situation rectified, renegotiate, or withdraw from the transaction. Property is often purchased subject to existing mortgage loans, liens, or easements, and the real purpose of the abstract is to find circumstances about which the purchaser had no knowledge.

Although an abstract of title provides a great deal of protection, there are still sometimes situations in which an existing circumstance that was unknown when the title was prepared arises in the future, such as the appearance of a long-lost heir with a legitimate claim to the property. An abstract of title does not provide any indemnification to the property owner, and suits against the attorney or other person preparing the abstract are usually not a recourse unless negligence can be shown. Title insurance, however, is designed to protect against this loss. It is almost always required by lenders who finance property purchases and also frequently obtained when cash purchases are made.

The title insurance company conducts a title search and then issues a policy to provide protection against losses that arise from circumstances other than the items already found in the title search and listed in the policy.

Some characteristics of title insurance include the following:

- The policy provides protection only against unknown title defects that have occurred prior to the effective date of the policy but are discovered after the effective date.
- The policy is written on the assumption that losses will not occur, because most title defects are known and listed in the policy.
- The policy term is indefinite and continues until title to the property is again transferred. At that time, the new owner will need to purchase a new title insurance policy because the existing policy is not assignable.
- The premium is paid only once—when the policy is issued—and neither party can cancel the policy.
- The insured is indemnified up to the policy limits if a loss occurs. However, there is no guarantee that possession of the property will be retained.
- The amount of insurance is usually the initial purchase price of the property, and a potential loss in the future can be much higher than the policy limit because of inflation.

CHECKLIST FOR EVALUATING AND COMPARING HOMEOWNERS POLICIES

- What is the homeowners form?

    __ HO-2

    __ HO-3

    __ HO-4

    __ HO-5

    __ HO-6

    __ HO-8

- If the policy is not an ISO form, how does it differ?
- What is the annual policy premium?
- What is the Section I deductible?

- Does the policy automatically contain coverages that are optional with other insurers?
- What are the limits for the various coverages?

  ___ Coverage A—Dwelling
  ___ Coverage B—Other Structures
  ___ Coverage C—Personal Property
  ___ Coverage D—Loss of Use
  ___ Coverage E—Personal Liability
  ___ Coverage F—Medical Payments to Others

- Are the coverage limits adequate?
- What provisions, if any, are there for increasing policy limits?
- Does the insured own personal property subject to sublimits?
- Is personal property covered for replacement cost?
- Are there, or is there any need for, any of the following endorsements?

  ___ Additional insureds
  ___ Open-perils computer coverage
  ___ Open-perils personal property coverage
  ___ Business pursuits
  ___ Credit card, electronic fund transfer card, forgery, and counterfeit money
  ___ Earthquake
  ___ Higher limits for certain types of personal property
  ___ Home business insurance coverage
  ___ Home day-care coverage
  ___ Identity fraud
  ___ Increased ordinance or law coverage
  ___ Increased loss assessment coverage
  ___ Increased property limits on business property
  ___ Personal injury
  ___ Premises alarm or fire protection system credits
  ___ Scheduled personal property coverage
  ___ Sinkhole collapse
  ___ Snowmobile
  ___ Watercraft
  ___ Other property loss exposures

___ Other liability loss exposures

- Is the flood peril adequately covered in another policy?

CHAPTER REVIEW

Key Terms and Concepts

homeowners policy
Insurance Services Office (ISO)
additional living expenses
functional replacement cost
dwelling policy
mobile home insurance
National Flood Insurance Program (NFIP)

FAIR (Fair Access to Insurance Requirements) plans
floater
personal articles floater
personal property floater
personal effects floater
title insurance

Review Questions

Review questions are based on the learning objectives in this chapter. Thus, a [3] at the end of a question means that the question is based on learning objective 3. If there are multiple objectives, they are all listed.

1. Frank and his wife, Ellen, own a home. Also living in the house is their oldest daughter, Elaine, who returned home after finishing college 8 years ago. Their 21-year-old daughter, Destiny, is currently at college, living in an on-campus dorm room. What members of the family are covered as insureds under Frank's homeowners policy? [1]

2. What locations are included as insured locations in a homeowners policy? [1]

3.   Nathan's home is covered for $250,000 (Coverage A) under an HO-3 policy. Which of the following losses are covered under Nathan's HO-3 policy?
a. vandalism to Nathan's home [2]
b. damage to the inside walls and hardwood floors of Nathan's home caused by rain water that blew in when he accidentally left the window open during a storm [2]
c. damage to the family room couch and end tables inside Nathan's home caused by rain water that blew in when he accidentally left the window open during a storm [2]
d. earthquake damage to the walls of Nathan's home [2]
e. stains on the wall-to-wall carpet inside Nathan's home due to housebreaking the new family pet, plus the hole in the outside of Nathan's home cut by a woodpecker [2]
f. theft of the $2,000 cast aluminum porch furniture from the back deck of Nathan's home [2]
g. $1,500 in cash burned in a fire in Nathan's home [2]
h. $2,000 of damage to Nathan's wife's furs as a result of a fire [2]
i. $2,000 of Nathan's wife's jewelry stolen by a burglar [2]
j. $1,000 of additional expense incurred while Nathan's family has to live elsewhere for 1 1/2 days after a small fire loss [2]
k. $2,000 of windstorm damage to the detached garage at Nathan's home [2]

4.   Which of the following losses are covered under Sarah's HO-3 policy?
a. Sarah's guests received bodily injuries and the side of her neighbor's house received property damage when a gas grill exploded during a cookout at her house. [2]
b. While running a meeting at work, Sarah accidentally injured a coworker by shining a laser pointer into the coworker's eye. [2]
c. While at the local mall, Sarah carelessly backed out of a parking space and damaged another shopper's car. [2]
d. Sarah's 3-year-old son Matthew ripped out some of the neighbor's flowers for a Mother's Day gift. [2]
e. Sarah's daughter injured a team member when she tossed a bat into the bat rack and it bounced off and hit the teammate, cutting her head. [2]

5.   Doug convinced his friend Denise to smoke marijuana, after which the couple engaged in unprotected sex. Denise later discovered that she had contracted AIDS, and she sued Doug, alleging that his delivery of a controlled substance had impaired her judgment. She further alleged that he knew he had AIDS at the time of the incident and that her illness was a result of his negligence. Does the liability coverage of Doug's homeowners policy protect him against either or both of these allegations? [1]

6.   How does each of the following homeowners property coverages differ from
     the HO-3 property coverages?
     a. HO-2 [1]
     b. HO-4 [1]
     c. HO-5 [1]
     d. HO-6 [1]
     e. HO-8 [1]

7.   What coverage does each of these commonly used endorsements add to the
     homeowners policy?
     a. home day-care coverage [3]
     b. increased special limits [3]
     c. earthquake [3]
     d. inflation guard [3]
     e. personal property replacement cost loss settlement [3]
     f. scheduled personal property [3]
     g. business pursuits [3]

8.   What coverage does the National Flood Insurance Program (NFIP) provide,
     and how can a client obtain such coverage? [4]

9.   What alternatives are available for obtaining property coverage for clients
     who fail to meet the underwriting guidelines of most insurers? [4]

10. Describe the characteristics of title insurance. [4]

Learning Objectives

An understanding of the material in this chapter should enable the student to

1. Describe the problems associated with auto accidents and the methods of compensating accident victims.

2. Describe the basic components of the Personal Auto Policy, and explain the coverages parts A, B, C, and D of the Personal Auto Policy provide.

3. Describe the key endorsements available to tailor the Personal Auto Policy to common client needs.

4. Describe the potential sources of auto insurance coverage for hard-to-insure drivers.

5. Explain the key factors for a client to consider when shopping for auto insurance.

6. Briefly describe the policies available for insuring watercraft and aircraft.

7. Describe the need for and general features of personal umbrella liability insurance.

This discussion of property and liability insurance looks at personal auto and umbrella liability insurance.

Every client—even one who does not own a car—faces the possibility of serious injury and disability and major financial loss resulting from his or her ownership, maintenance, or use of an auto. A significant potential for financial loss exists when a client owns an auto worth $10,000, $30,000, $50,000, or more that could be damaged in an auto accident or by another cause. Even more significant loss exposures lie in the fact that a client could become legally responsible to pay damages to another person who is injured in an auto accident the client causes. Careful drivers are not immune. Although a few statistics are cited in this chapter, they are not necessary to prove that many auto accidents happen every day, and many of them are caused by careful drivers who had a momentary attention lapse or an unfortunate error in judgment. Few would deny the importance of auto insurance in preserving a client's personal assets. Therefore, a financial planner must have at least a basic understanding of the important coverage personal auto policies provide. The section also briefly discusses insurance relating to two other modes of transportation: watercraft and aircraft.

Homeowners insurance is usually required by a mortgagee, and auto liability insurance is invariably required by law, as well as by the bank or finance company that helps finance the purchase or lease of an auto. On the other hand, personal umbrella insurance is rarely, if ever, mandatory. Yet as this discussion demonstrates, umbrella coverage should be recommended to virtually every client with assets to protect, and it is therefore a type of coverage with which every financial planner should be familiar.

AUTO INSURANCE

The discussion of auto insurance begins with a look at some of the problems associated with auto accidents and auto insurance, and it continues with a history of the methods of compensating auto accident victims. A description of the personal auto policy (PAP) and insurance for high-risk drivers follows.

Problems Associated with Auto Accidents and Auto Insurance

Given the severe financial consequences that can arise from auto accidents, most Americans view auto insurance as a necessity for themselves and for the other drivers who might injure them. Yet there are many problems in providing auto insurance to everyone at an affordable price. These problems center around the

- large number of auto accidents
- high cost of auto accidents
- uninsured and underinsured drivers
- difficulty that some individuals have in obtaining auto insurance

Large Number of Auto Accidents

Auto accidents occur frequently (over 6 million are reported to police every year). Young drivers have a disproportionate number of accidents, and regardless of the driver's age, speeding and/or substance abuse are often involved.

High Cost of Auto Accidents

The costs associated with auto accidents each year in the United States are staggering. Increasing medical, legal, and auto-repair costs contribute to the steady increase in auto accident costs. Insurance covers many losses related to property damage, medical expenses, lost income, emergency services, and legal fees. Additional costs not covered by insurance include lost productivity, public assistance programs, and the costs of providing and administering insurance protection.

Uninsured and Underinsured Drivers

Although variations exist from state to state, the number of persons without auto insurance is estimated at between 5 and 30 percent. Even in states with compulsory insurance laws, no perfect mechanism prevents an uninsured, or even unlicensed, driver from getting behind the wheel.

When uninsured drivers are involved in accidents, they can rarely pay for the property damage and bodily injury they cause themselves or others. Another problem is the underinsured driver. The minimum amount of auto liability insurance needed in most states (usually no more than $25,000 for any injured person) is often below the amount necessary to adequately compensate an innocent victim for his or her injuries.

Because of uninsured and underinsured drivers, innocent victims of auto accidents may be inadequately compensated for their injuries, and society must often bear some of the burden. As a result, states have undertaken various actions to minimize these problems.

Difficulty of Some Persons in Obtaining Auto Insurance

Auto insurance can be difficult to obtain. Overregulation of insurance rates in some states has, at times, made it difficult for insurers to collect an adequate premium, forcing them, instead, to withdraw from the market or to limit the number of auto insurance applications they accept. In any state, high-risk drivers (for example, younger persons or drivers with serious or multiple traffic violations) are often unable to find coverage in the standard insurance market. An increasing number of insurers are willing to write these substandard applicants, and all states have established residual market programs, commonly known as assigned risk[59] plans, to ensure the availability of auto insurance.

Affordability is also a problem. High premiums are a direct result of both high loss frequency and high claims severity. Some of the auto insurance legislation mentioned later in this chapter attempts to control auto insurance costs and therefore make the insurance more affordable.

Controlling Accidents and Compensating Auto Accident Victims

Since the early days of the motor car, society has been concerned about the number and severity of auto accidents and the methods of compensating auto accident victims.

Numerous laws and regulations have been passed—often with strong support from the insurance industry—to control the number of auto accidents and to lessen the number of injuries and deaths. Among these are

- federal auto design and safety standards
- highway design standards
- seat belt laws
- drunk-driving laws
- tightening of licensing standards for young drivers
- license retesting for older drivers

Appropriate compensation for auto accident victims presents another concern, focused especially on the victims who were not at fault. Historically, accident victims were compensated under the traditional tort liability system discussed in an earlier chapter. Because contributory negligence laws made it difficult for many accident victims to collect damages, most states adopted one of the variations of comparative negligence that were previously discussed. In addition, various other methods of ensuring compensation have been developed over the years. These include

- compulsory insurance
- financial responsibility laws
- unsatisfied judgment funds

---

59. In this context, the word "risk" refers to the policyowner. The phrase "assigned risk" is used generically by insurance practitioners to refer to all auto residual market plans, although only one type, technically known as "automobile insurance plans," literally assigns risks (policyowners) to specific insurers.

- uninsured motorists coverage
- underinsured motorists coverage
- no-fault auto insurance

Not every method exists in every state, and none of these methods is exactly the same in all states where it is used. Most of these methods do not alter the concept of tort liability but are aimed at increasing the likelihood that a source of monetary recovery exists for innocent victims.

Compulsory Insurance

All states and the District of Columbia have some type of compulsory auto insurance law that requires auto owners to have liability insurance before they can legally drive. Unfortunately, such laws are far from perfect for several reasons:

- Victim compensation must come through traditional legal channels and can be delayed by an overburdened legal system.
- Compulsory insurance laws do not guarantee that an innocent victim will be compensated. Some drivers may not license their vehicles; others may drop insurance after a vehicle is licensed. A person may be injured by a hit-and-run driver, an out-of-state driver without insurance, a driver of a stolen car, or a driver of a fraudulently registered auto.
- Required liability limits are relatively low, typically $20,000 or $25,000 for bodily injury to any one person, $40,000 or $50,000 in the aggregate for all bodily injury claims in an accident, and $10,000 or $15,000 for property damage claims.

The "no pay, no play" concept has been considered by lawmakers in many states as a means of encouraging compliance with compulsory insurance laws. No pay, no play statutes limit the rights of uninsured drivers to collect damages from insured drivers. A few states have recently enacted such laws.

Financial Responsibility Laws

financial responsibility law

All states have some type of *financial responsibility law*. Failure to comply with financial responsibility laws results in the revocation or suspension of a person's driving privileges. These laws require proof of future financial responsibility, generally proof that liability insurance is in force after

- an auto accident involving bodily injury or property damage that exceeds a specified limit

- conviction of a serious offense, such as drunk driving or reckless driving
- loss of a driver's license because of repeated motor vehicle violations
- failure to pay a legal judgment that arose from an auto accident

The major criticism of financial responsibility laws is that they become effective only after an accident or serious offense and do not provide any compensation to the innocent victims of that accident. In addition, the same limitations that apply to compulsory auto insurance also apply to financial responsibility laws.

Unsatisfied Judgment Funds

unsatisfied judgment funds
A few states (all of which also have compulsory insurance requirements) have *unsatisfied judgment funds*, which the states established to compensate persons who are unable to collect legal judgments that result from auto accidents. The injured person—in addition to obtaining a legal judgment against the negligent party—must show that the judgment cannot be collected. The maximum amount that can be collected from the fund is usually limited to the state's minimum compulsory insurance requirement and is reduced by collateral sources of recovery, such as workers' compensation benefits or insurance.

The negligent driver must repay the fund for payments made to the injured person or lose his or her driver's license until repayment is made.

Collecting from unsatisfied judgment funds involves a slow and cumbersome process. Some funds have had financial problems as a result of inadequate funding, which usually comes from fees levied on insured drivers or insurance companies that write auto insurance in the state.

Uninsured Motorists Coverage

uninsured motorists coverage
Under *uninsured motorists coverage*, the injured insured is able to collect the amount he or she would have collected from the insurer of an insured driver if that driver had been carrying insurance. In effect, the insured's own company acts as the insurer of the uninsured driver. In most states, insurers that write auto insurance are required to offer uninsured motorists coverage. However, the policyowner can voluntarily waive the coverage in writing. In a few states, uninsured motorists coverage must be included in any auto insurance policy.

The term *uninsured motorists* is broadly defined to include not only uninsured drivers, but also the drivers of hit-and-run vehicles and persons whose insurer cannot pay because it has become insolvent. Uninsured motorists coverage, however, does not apply if the negligent party carries insurance that has inadequate limits to fully indemnify the innocent party. Uninsured motorists coverage is analyzed in more detail when the personal auto policy is discussed.

Limitations to uninsured motorists coverage include the following:

- The limits of coverage are equal only to a state's compulsory insurance or financial responsibility limits unless the policyowner has purchased higher limits.
- The insured must establish that the other party was legally liable.
- The coverage usually applies to bodily injury only. States vary as to whether the coverage applies to property damage.
- The innocent victim, not the uninsured driver, bears the cost of the coverage.

Underinsured Motorists Coverage

underinsured
motorists
coverage

Underinsured motorists coverage provides protection to auto accident victims when a negligent driver has liability insurance but the limits are insufficient to pay the damages for which he or she is responsible. For example, assume a negligent driver causes bodily injury of $30,000 to another person but carries only $25,000 of insurance, which is the minimum requirement in his state. If the innocent victim has $100,000 of underinsured motorists coverage, he or she can collect the additional $5,000 from his or her own insurance company.

Underinsured motorists coverage is provided through a policy endorsement available in about half the states. It can be purchased only if the policyowner also carries uninsured motorists coverage with the same limit. In most other states, underinsured motorists coverage must be included along with uninsured motorists coverage and for the same limits.

No-Fault Auto Insurance

The traditional insurance and tort systems for compensating auto accident victims have long been subject to criticism, centering around the following issues:

- Many innocent persons are unable to collect anything for their injuries under the traditional tort system because injuries are caused by uninsured and hit-and-run drivers.

- Injuries from auto accidents are a societal problem for all insured parties whether they are negligent or not.

- It is often difficult or impossible to determine who is at fault in an accident.

- The traditional tort system has resulted in many serious claims being underpaid because of inadequate insurance limits. There is also evidence that many small claims are overpaid for the sake of a quick settlement.

- Under the traditional insurance and tort systems, a large portion of premium dollars is used to pay claims costs and attorneys' fees.

- The traditional tort system is slow. In some states, delays of 3 to 5 years between an accident and a resulting trial are common.

The result of these shortcomings to the traditional systems of compensating auto accident victims led to the passage of some type of no-fault law in many states. The concept of no-fault auto insurance is not new, having been originally proposed in the 1930s. However, the first such law was enacted in Massachusetts in 1971, and most existing laws date to the 1970s. A few additional states passed laws in the 1980s and early 1990s, but a few others also terminated existing laws. Today 12 states, in addition to Puerto Rico, have no-fault laws.

Despite the appeal of no-fault laws, many arguments against them have been raised, such as the following:

- They have not resulted in lower premiums, probably because the right to sue is modified only for relatively minor injuries.

- The traditional systems of compensating auto accident victims work well, with most cases being settled relatively quickly and out of court.

- The inability in some states to sue for pain and suffering has not been popular with plaintiffs' attorneys and many drivers, who feel such suits are their right.

- There are ways to modify the current tort systems, such as limiting attorneys' fees and increasing the use of arbitration rather than trials.

- Some of the costs of auto accidents tend to be shifted from negligent parties to innocent victims.

- Widespread fraud exists.

Types of No-Fault Laws

pure no-fault   The original proposals for no-fault auto insurance were based on the premise that the tort liability system would be abolished for auto accidents. Under such a *pure no-fault* system, each owner of an auto would be required to carry first-party insurance that compensated all persons injured in auto accidents involving that vehicle. The right to sue a negligent party, even for pain and suffering, would not exist. No state has adopted a pure no-fault law. The types of laws that do exist fall into three broad categories—modified no-fault laws, add-on plans, and choice no-fault laws.

Modified No-Fault Laws

modified no-fault   The most common form of no-fault legislation limits the right of an injured party to recover damages from a negligent party but does not eliminate it. States with *modified no-fault* laws have taken two approaches in allowing suits. Some states have a *dollar threshold*, also referred to as a *monetary threshold*, anywhere from $400 to $5,000 dollars. If a person's injuries are below this amount, he or she must collect from first-party no-fault benefits and cannot sue. However, suits are allowed once the amount reaches the threshold. The injured party can still receive no-fault benefits, but his or her insurer is reimbursed to the extent any amount from a legal judgment duplicates any no-fault benefits received. Other states have a *verbal threshold* and allow suits when there is a fatal injury, serious injury, or serious disfigurement. What constitutes a serious injury or disfigurement varies among these states.

Add-On Plans

add-on plan   An *add-on plan* has no restriction on the right to sue a negligent party, but first-party no-fault type benefits are available. The insurer that pays these benefits has subrogation rights against the negligent party. Some argue that add-on plans should not be referred to as a type of no-fault because the traditional tort system has not been altered.

In some add-on states, both liability insurance and no-fault benefits are compulsory; in other states, liability insurance is compulsory, but the no-fault benefits are optional. In still other states, both liability insurance and no-fault benefits are optional.

Choice No-Fault Laws

choice no-fault   A *choice no-fault* law, used in only a few states, gives
the insurance buyer two choices: coverage under the
traditional tort liability system or coverage under a modified no-fault law at
a reduced premium. Depending on the jurisdiction, a person who elects to
retain the right to seek damages under the traditional liability system may or
may not be able to purchase no-fault-type benefits similar to those in an
add-on plan.

Types of No-Fault Laws

• Pure no-fault: right to sue negligent party would be eliminated

• Modified no-fault: right to sue negligent party only if injuries exceed a dollar
  or verbal threshold

• Add-on no-fault: right to sue negligent party in addition to right to collect
  first-party no-fault benefits

• Choice no-fault: right to sue negligent party as an alternative to collecting
  under a modified no-fault plan

Types of No-Fault Benefits

**personal injury
protection (PIP)
endorsement**   No-fault benefits are provided by adding an endorsement
to an auto insurance policy. This endorsement varies
from state to state to conform to each state's no-fault law.
Usually, the endorsement is referred to as a *personal injury protection (PIP)
endorsement*.

Benefits are normally subject to dollar or time limits, and some states require
insurers to make optional higher benefits available. Some states also require
insurers to offer optional deductibles to reduce or eliminate certain no-fault
benefits. The use of these deductibles can make sense to the extent that
the no-fault benefits duplicate other medical expense or disability income
insurance. No-fault benefits in most states include

- medical expenses
- rehabilitation expenses
- loss of earnings (or some proportion thereof)
- expenses for essential services, such as house or yard work that
  an injured person can no longer perform
- funeral expenses
- survivors' benefits arising from death in an auto accident

No-fault benefits are typically available to the policyowner and relative members of his or her household riding in any vehicle, as well as to other persons riding in the policyowner's vehicle. State law varies as to which policy pays when a person is eligible for benefits as an injured passenger in someone else's auto and also under his or her own auto insurance policy.

The personal injury protection endorsement does not change the liability coverage available under an auto insurance policy. However, no-fault insurance does result in fewer liability claims.

Coordination of Benefits

No-fault benefits apply to injuries that medical expense insurance, disability insurance, and workers' compensation might also cover. It is therefore logical to consider how benefits are coordinated among these various sources of recovery. The answer depends on what other source of recovery is involved and on the applicable statute.

Federal regulations prohibit Medicare payments to persons injured in auto accidents who have recovered, or are expected to recover, under no-fault coverage. Most state laws require that workers' compensation provides primary coverage and that workers' compensation benefits should be subtracted from the amount due as no-fault benefits. State laws sometimes indicate which coverage is primary in other situations when more than one might apply. Many states make no-fault auto insurance primary over various forms of health insurance.

PERSONAL AUTO POLICY

The discussion of auto insurance focuses on the most common auto policy—ISO's personal auto policy, often referred to as the PAP. Like the homeowners policy, it is a package policy that provides both property and liability insurance for family members. As with homeowners insurance, some insurers use their own auto policy forms. These forms tend to be similar to the PAP.

The following discussion looks at the basic format of the PAP, eligibility, some definitions that apply throughout the policy, and the policy territory. This is followed by an analysis of the various coverages in the policy. Like homeowners policies, the basic PAP does not meet everyone's needs and often must be modified. Finally, some of the more common endorsements are briefly described.

Format of the PAP

Following a declarations and definitions section, the PAP provides four types of insurance coverage:

- Part A—Liability Coverage
- Part B—Medical Payments Coverage
- Part C—Uninsured Motorists Coverage
- Part D—Coverage for Damage to Your Auto

In states with no-fault laws, an endorsement that provides the required no-fault benefits replaces Part B.

The policy also contains two other sections—Part E and Part F—that spell out the duties of an insured following a loss and that contain other policy provisions.

Eligibility

A PAP can be written on eligible vehicles owned or leased by an individual or by a husband or wife residing in the same household. Vehicles with other forms of ownership (such as a father and a son) can also be insured with an endorsement. A vehicle rented to others or used as a public or livery conveyance is not eligible and must be insured under a commercial policy.

Eligible vehicles include private passenger autos, such as cars, vans, and sport utility vehicles, owned by the policyowner or leased under a written contract of 6 continuous months or longer. Pickups are also eligible vehicles if their gross vehicle weight rating is 10,000 pounds or less. However, vans and pickups are ineligible for coverage if they are used for the transportation or delivery of goods and materials except when (1) they are used for farming or ranching, or (2) their use is incidental to the named insured's business of installing, maintaining, or repairing furnishings or equipment. An example of the latter is an electrician's or an appliance repair person's van.

Other vehicles, such as motor homes, motorcycles, golf carts, and snowmobiles, can also be insured by endorsement in most states.

Finally, the policy can be endorsed to provide auto insurance to a person who does not own any vehicles eligible for coverage under a PAP. Examples include a person who frequently rents a car or has use of a company car on a regular basis.

Definitions

Like a homeowners policy, the PAP contains numerous definitions. One important definition—*insured*—is different for different parts of the policy and is discussed later. However, some definitions are used throughout the policy. These definitions include *covered auto, you, family member*, and *occupying*.

Covered Auto

covered auto   A *covered auto* (referred to in the PAP as "your covered auto") is any vehicle listed in the policy declarations. In addition, it includes three other categories of vehicles: newly acquired autos, trailers, and temporary substitute vehicles.

Newly Acquired Autos

newly acquired auto   A *newly acquired auto* is one that meets the eligibility requirements previously described but is acquired after the effective date of the policy.

If the newly acquired auto replaces an existing vehicle, it is automatically insured for the broadest Parts A, B, and C coverages that apply to any vehicle listed in the declarations. There is no need to notify the insurance company, although it is a good idea to do so. If the new auto is an additional vehicle, the same automatic coverage applies only if the policyowner asks the insurance company to insure the vehicle within 14 days of purchase.

The situation is different for damage to the auto (Part D). The PAP provides automatic insurance for the broadest Part D benefits provided to any vehicle in the declarations only if the insurance company is notified within 14 days of purchase. There is also coverage for newly acquired autos even if Part D is not in effect on any vehicles listed in the declarations, but only if the insurance company is notified within 4 days of purchase that such coverage is wanted. If the 4-day notification is satisfied, any loss prior to insurance company notification is subject to a $500 deductible.

EXAMPLE

Tom Howard's car is insured under a PAP for Coverages A, B, C, and D. Tom trades his car in for a new one. Tom's Coverages A, B, and C apply to the new car automatically, with no necessity to notify the insurer.

Tom's Coverage D also applies to the new car automatically but only if Tom notifies the insurer within 14 days.

Trailers

A *trailer* is a vehicle designed to be pulled by a private passenger auto or van. It also includes a farm wagon or farm implement while it is being towed.

Temporary Substitute Vehicles

temporary substitute vehicle

A temporary substitute vehicle is one the insured does not own but is using temporarily in place of a vehicle listed in the policy declarations if that vehicle is out of normal use because of breakdown, repair, servicing, loss, or destruction.

You

The terms *you* and *yours* are used throughout the PAP. They refer to the named insured shown in the policy declaration and the spouse of the named insured if a resident of the same household.

If the spouse ceases to be a resident of the same household, the spouse is still a "you" or "your" until the earliest of the following:

- the end of 90 days following the spouse's change of residency
- the effective date of another policy that lists the spouse as a named insured
- the end of the policy period

Family Member

A *family member* is any person related to "you" by blood, marriage, or adoption who is a resident of the same household. This includes a ward or foster child.

Occupying

Occupying means in, upon, or getting in, on, out, or off. Therefore, a person who is injured while getting into or out of an auto is, by definition, occupying that auto.

Policy Territory

The PAP applies only to accidents and losses that occur in the United States, its territories or possessions, Puerto Rico, or Canada. Coverage also applies if a covered auto is being transported between these locations.

PART A—LIABILITY COVERAGE

The discussion of Parts A, B, and C of the PAP focuses on answering four questions:

- What is covered?
- Who are the insureds?
- What exclusions apply?
- What happens when other insurance also covers a claim?

What Is Covered?

Part A of the PAP provides bodily injury and property damage liability protection to any insured who is legally responsible for an auto accident. As with other liability policies, the insurer agrees to pay defense costs until the limit of liability has been exhausted by payment of judgments or settlements.

split limits   The applicant selects the liability limits when he or she purchases insurance, and they apply to each covered accident. The current version of the PAP is written with split limits, but it can be endorsed to provide single limit coverage. With *split limits*, three separate dollar amounts, such as $25,000/$50,000/$10,000, apply to each accident. The first limit is the maximum amount that will be paid to any one person for bodily injury; the second limit is the maximum that will be paid for all bodily injury claims in one accident; the third limit applies to total property damage claims. With a single limit, there is just one limit that applies in the aggregate to all bodily injury and liability claims arising from an accident. The limits available often range from $50,000 to $500,000 or more.

EXAMPLE

Gary Rock's PAP provides split limits under Part A of $500,000/$1,000,000/$50,000. In an auto accident, Gary injures two people in another car. One is awarded damages of $750,000 and the other is awarded damages of $300,000. Their car, worth $60,000, is totally demolished.

The insurer will pay only $500,000 of the $750,000 award because that is the per person policy limit for bodily injury. The policy will pay the full $300,000 to the other person. The policy will pay only $50,000 for the damage to the car because that is the policy's property damage limit.

Most clients carry the minimum amount of liability insurance needed to satisfy the required underlying limits of an umbrella liability policy (usually in the range of $250,000/$500,000/$50,000). Umbrella liability policies are discussed later in this chapter.

The PAP specifies that the insurer's limit of liability shown in the declarations is the most the company will pay, regardless of the number of insureds, claims made, vehicles or premiums shown in the declarations, or vehicles involved in any accident. For example, if a son has an accident while driving a family car, the son and both parents might be sued. Even though three insureds are sued, the policy limits apply only once to all three claims. An identical provision applies to Part B and Part C of the PAP. In addition, the policy specifies that no one is entitled to receive duplicate payments for the same elements of loss under more than one of Part A, Part B, and Part C of the policy. For example, an injured passenger who sued an insured could not receive a liability payment under Part A for specific medical expenses and medical payments under Part B for the same medical expenses.

The PAP also contains a provision that raises the limits of liability, if necessary, to those required in a state where an accident occurs if the state is not where the insured vehicle is principally garaged. Any other mandatory coverage, such as no-fault benefits, is also provided automatically for out-of-state accidents.

The PAP also provides certain supplementary payments for expenses arising from an accident the policy covers. These payments, like defense costs, are in addition to the stated liability limits. They are

- up to $250 for bail bonds
- premiums on appeal bonds and bonds to release attachments
- interest occurring after a judgment
- up to $200 per day for loss of earnings because of attendance at hearings or trials
- other reasonable expenses incurred at the insurer's request

Who Are the Insureds?

The insureds under Part A include several categories of persons. From the policyowner's standpoint, the most important category is probably the named insured, spouse, and family members for legal liability arising out of the ownership, maintenance, or use of any auto or trailer. There is also coverage for any other person using a covered auto.

In addition, other persons or organizations may have coverage because of their legal liability arising from the actions of any of the parties previously mentioned. For example, if the named insured is driving a vehicle as part of his or her job or while doing work for a charity, it is possible that the employer or charity could also become a party to a legal action. The employer or charity is insured under the policy as long as it does not own or hire the vehicle.

What Exclusions Apply?

The PAP does not provide liability coverage in every situation. One exclusion denies coverage for anyone who intentionally causes an auto accident. However, other insureds still have coverage if they are sued because of that person's actions. Another exclusion denies coverage to any insured, other than a family member using the covered auto, who uses a vehicle without a reasonable belief that he or she is entitled to do so.

Several exclusions pertain to business situations. Certain types of exposures should be covered under a commercial auto policy rather than the PAP. One of these exclusions denies coverage for the ownership or operation of a vehicle if it is used as a public or livery conveyance, such as a taxicab or limousine hired out to carry persons or property. This exclusion does not preclude coverage where expenses of carpooling or a vacation are shared.

Another exclusion pertains to persons engaged in the business of selling, repairing, servicing, storing, or parking vehicles designed for use mainly on public highways. For example, a named insured who is an auto mechanic would not have coverage when driving customers' cars, nor would the customer's personal auto policy cover the mechanic's liability. A similar exclusion denies liability coverage when the named insured is using certain other vehicles in the course of any business (other than farming or ranching). However, this exclusion does not apply to a private passenger auto, pickup, or van, or to a trailer used with any of the three types of vehicles.

A final business situation exclusion applies to bodily injury to employees of any insured. This exclusion applies to domestic employees, however, only if they either are or should be covered under a workers' compensation policy.

Some exclusions apply to property damage to property being transported by an insured or to property (other than a residence or private garage) rented to, used by, or in the care of any insured. There may be some coverage for these loss exposures under a homeowners policy.

The PAP provides no liability coverage for vehicles with fewer than four wheels or vehicles designed mainly for off-road use except trailers, nonowned golf carts, and vehicles used in a medical emergency. If a policyowner needs to insure such vehicles as motorcycles or mopeds, coverage can be added by an endorsement.

A significant exclusion for many insureds precludes coverage for any vehicle other than a covered auto that is either owned by the named insured or spouse or furnished for his or her regular use. If the vehicle is owned, it should be listed and insured along with other owned vehicles. If a vehicle is furnished for regular use, such as an employer-provided car, it should either be insured by the employer or this exclusion should be modified by endorsement. A similar exclusion applies to vehicles owned by or furnished for the regular use of family members. However, this exclusion does not apply to the named insured or spouse. For example, assume a 22-year-old son living at home owns an uninsured car. He would be insured under his parents' policy for driving other cars, but as a family member, he would not have "free" coverage for driving his own vehicle. However, his parents would have coverage if they drove his car on an occasional basis, as long as it was not available to them for regular use.

Finally, there is no liability coverage for vehicles at a race track competing in, practicing for, or preparing for any type of organized race or speed contest.

Other Insurance

In some cases, more than one PAP might provide coverage. The most common example occurs when a person drives a friend's car. A person remains covered as a named insured under his or her own PAP while driving another auto. He or she is also an insured under the friend's PAP as a person using the covered auto. In situations like these, it is said that the insurance "follows the car." More specifically, the insurance the car owner purchased is primary and the driver's insurance is secondary. The driver's insurance applies, but only after the limits of the insurance policy on the car have been exhausted.

EXAMPLE

Sheila, who has a PAP with a single limit of $500,000, borrows a car owned by George, whose PAP has a $50,000 limit. Sheila causes an auto accident in which a pedestrian is injured, and a judgment for $60,000 in damages is awarded against Sheila. Because insurance follows the car, George's PAP provides primary coverage up to its $50,000 limit, and Sheila's insurance provides excess coverage, paying the remaining $10,000.

If George had no auto liability insurance, Sheila's policy would pay the entire $60,000 judgment on her behalf.

PART B—MEDICAL PAYMENTS COVERAGE

What Is Covered?

Part B of the PAP provides payment for the reasonable and necessary medical expenses of a covered auto's occupants who are accidentally injured. Only those expenses that result from medical services rendered within 3 years of the date of an accident are covered. Benefits are paid under medical payments coverage regardless of fault.

The benefit limit, typically in the range of $1,000 to $10,000, is selected by the applicant and applies separately to each person injured in an accident. No one can collect for the same expenses more than once under Part A, Part B, and Part C. If an insured incurred $10,000 of medical expenses when struck by a hit-and-run driver, duplicate payments for the same expenses would not be paid under medical payments coverage and uninsured motorists coverage. For example, if the medical payments coverage paid its limit of $5,000, the insured could collect only $5,000 more under Part C for the actual medical expenses.

In most states with no-fault laws, an endorsement that provides the no-fault benefits replaces Part B.

Who Are the Insureds?

The medical payments coverage of the PAP protects the occupants of a covered auto who are accidentally injured, regardless of fault. In that sense, it resembles the Medical Payments to Others coverage of homeowners policies. A major difference between these two coverages lies in the fact that the injured persons entitled to PAP medical payments coverage include the named insured, spouse, and other family members. Coverage applies even when a named insured or family member is not occupying a covered auto, so long as he or she is either occupying a motor vehicle designed for use on public roads or a trailer, or is a pedestrian struck by one of these vehicles. For example, a young couple who are injured while riding to their high school prom in a rented limousine are covered under their parents' personal auto policies.

What Exclusions Apply?

With a few minor exceptions, the exclusions that apply to Part B are the same as those for Part A. That is, if liability coverage does not apply to an accident, medical payments coverage is likewise not available.

Other Insurance

The other insurance provision that applies to medical payments coverage is similar to the one for liability coverage. Coverage is excess over other collectible auto insurance on a nonowned auto that provides payments for medical or funeral expenses. Therefore, although the couple on their way to a prom are indeed covered by their parents' PAP, it is excess over any medical payments coverage on the limousine.

PART C—UNINSURED MOTORISTS COVERAGE

What Is Covered?

Part C of the PAP provides uninsured motorists coverage (and underinsured motorists coverage in many states). Under Part C, the insurer agrees to pay compensatory damages that an insured is legally entitled to recover from the owner or operator of an uninsured motor vehicle because of bodily injury (and property damage in a few states) sustained by an insured and caused by an accident. The coverage applies to claims for medical expenses, lost wages, and pain and suffering, but it does not include punitive or exemplary damages.

Typically, an applicant must purchase a minimum amount of uninsured motorists coverage in accordance with a state's financial responsibility law. Above that, the applicant can purchase an amount of coverage as high as the liability limits that apply under Part A.

The insurance company has no obligation to pay an uninsured motorists claim unless the owner or operator of the uninsured vehicle is legally responsible to pay damages to the insured. The insured must file a claim against his or her own insurer and, in the ideal situation, the insured and the insurer will reach a satisfactory settlement. If not, the matter is subject to an arbitration provision. The results of a suit against the uninsured party are not binding on the insurer if it is brought without the insurer's written consent.

For purposes of Part C, an uninsured vehicle is not only one without insurance. The term also includes

- a vehicle that is insured for less than the limits of the financial responsibility laws of the state where the covered auto is principally garaged
- a hit-and-run vehicle whose operator cannot be identified and that hits
  - the named insured, spouse, or family member
  - a vehicle that any of these insureds are occupying
  - a covered auto
- a vehicle to which insurance applies at the time of the accident but the insurance company is insolvent, becomes insolvent, or denies coverage. For example, the insurer of the other driver who caused a collision might have a PAP, but that driver's insurer denies coverage because the other driver-insured intentionally caused the collision to occur.

Uninsured Motor Vehicle
• One with no insurance
• One with liability limits lower than the applicable state law requires
• One driven by a hit-and-run driver
• One whose insurer denies coverage or becomes insolvent

Part C, however, specifically excludes certain vehicles from the definition of an uninsured vehicle. These are vehicles that are

- owned by or furnished for the regular use of any family member
- owned or operated by a self-insurer under an applicable motor vehicle law unless the self-insurer is or becomes insolvent
- owned by any government agency unit
- operated on rails or crawler treads
- designed mainly for use off public roads
- located for use as a residence or premises

Who Are the Insureds?

The insureds under Part C include the named insured, his or her spouse, and any family members. They also include any other persons who occupy a covered auto. In addition, anyone else who is entitled to recover damages because of bodily injury to any of the previously mentioned persons is an insured. This includes, for example, the spouse of a passenger injured while riding in the covered auto if a claim is brought for loss of consortium.

What Exclusions Apply?

The PAP excludes uninsured motorists coverage if an insured is injured while occupying or struck by an auto that is owned by the insured but is not covered under the policy. However, a few state courts have said this exclusion is not enforceable because the intent of the law was to protect injured persons, and an uninsured motorist claim must be paid as long as one auto is insured under the policy.

There are also exclusions similar to those previously discussed for use of the covered auto without permission or as a public or livery conveyance.

Other Insurance

As with Part A and Part B, losses are settled on a pro rata basis except that coverage on a nonowned vehicle is primary to coverage on a vehicle that an insured owns. Under Part A and Part B, the insured, in effect, has insurance equal to the combined limit of all policies covering a loss. This is not true under Part C. If more than one policy provides coverage, the recovery for damages under all policies may not exceed the highest limit for any one vehicle under any of the policies.

EXAMPLE
Assume Policy A provides $25,000 of uninsured motorists coverage and Policy B provides $50,000 of coverage. The maximum amount of coverage is then $50,000. Policy B will pay the entire claim if it is the primary policy. If Policy A is primary, it will pay the first $25,000 of a claim, and Policy B would pay the next $25,000.

PART D—COVERAGE FOR DAMAGE TO YOUR AUTO

Part D is the portion of the PAP that provides coverage for physical damage to the covered auto and to certain other nonowned autos. Part D provides first-party property coverage rather than third-party liability coverage. Coverage is on damage to autos rather than on injuries to people.

What Is Covered?

There are actually two major coverages: (1) *collision* and (2) *other than collision*. "Other than collision" was formerly called "comprehensive," and this terminology is still frequently used colloquially and in commercial policies. The term is no longer used in personal auto policies because of a concern that some consumers might assume anything referred to as "comprehensive" is all-encompassing and covers losses of all kinds. As with virtually every other type of coverage, other-than-collision coverage is subject to some exclusions.

An insurance applicant can elect both other-than-collision and collision coverage, or only other-than-collision coverage; he or she cannot purchase collision coverage alone. A client may also choose not to purchase any Part D coverage; this is often a wise decision when purchasing coverage on older vehicles with diminished values small enough to be handled with emergency funds.

The policyowner can select deductibles that apply to each coverage. Frequently, the policyowner purchases a lower deductible for other-than-collision coverage than for collision coverage because of the significant cost savings by selecting a larger collision deductible.

Part D also provides an additional coverage, referred to as *transportation expenses*.

Collision

collision   *Collision* is defined as the upset of the covered auto or any nonowned auto or its impact with another vehicle or object.

Other than Collision

other than collision   The PAP never specifically defines the term *other than collision*. Technically, if a loss is not caused by a collision, it must be a result of other than collision. Together, these two coverages give an insured open-perils coverage on an insured auto, subject to the various policy exclusions. The PAP has a specific list of sources of loss that are considered other than collision. These are

- missiles and falling objects
- fire
- theft or larceny
- explosion or earthquake
- windstorm
- hail, water, or flood
- malicious mischief or vandalism
- riot or civil commotion
- contact with a bird or animal
- breakage of glass. However, the policyowner may choose to consider this part of the collision loss if it is caused by collision.

In some cases, it is difficult to determine when a loss results from collision or other than collision. For example, a car damaged in a collision by a thief who stole it is a theft loss covered under other than collision. In many cases, this is the most advantageous place for coverage because policyowners sometimes purchase it without collision coverage, and the deductible is often lower. Similarly, if a flood sweeps a car into a tree, the damage is covered as a flood loss under the other-than-collision coverage.

Transportation Expenses

The PAP also pays up to $600, without application of the policy deductible, for the costs of renting a car or other temporary transportation expenses because of a loss to a covered auto or because of a loss to a nonowned auto for which the named insured or spouse is legally responsible. However, this benefit is paid for a collision loss only if the policyowner has purchased collision coverage. Similarly, it is paid for an other-than-collision loss only if other-than-collision coverage is in effect.

The amount of the benefit is limited to $20 per day and is payable beginning 48 hours after a theft loss and ending when the vehicle is returned to use or the insurer pays for its loss. For other types of losses, the benefit begins when the vehicle is withdrawn from use for more than 24 hours and is limited to the period of time reasonably required to repair or replace the vehicle.

What Vehicles Are Covered?

Part D applies to both covered autos and nonowned autos. The term *covered auto* was previously defined and applies throughout the PAP. The term *nonowned auto* for purposes of Part D, however, is defined differently and includes either of the following:

- any private passenger auto, pickup, van, or trailer not owned by, furnished to, or available for the regular use of the named insured, spouse or any family member while in the custody of or being operated by the named insured, spouse, or any family member
- any auto or trailer not owned by the named insured or spouse that is used as a temporary substitute for a covered auto that is out of normal use because of breakdown, repair, servicing, loss, or destruction

---

EXAMPLE

Assume that a son lives with his parents and owns a car without collision coverage. If one of his parents borrows his car, their collision coverage does not apply to an accident they might have as a result of using the car merely because it was at the end of the driveway. Under Part D of their PAP, it does not fit the definition of either a covered auto or a nonowned auto. If, on the other hand, one of the parents borrows the son's car because their car is in the shop for service, the parents' collision coverage applies, because the car now qualifies as a temporary substitute auto.

The coverage for nonowned autos applies to vehicles that are rented on a temporary basis, such as when an insured is on a trip, but the policy deductible applies. If the insured purchases the loss damage waiver from the car rental company, however, the rental company will impose no deductible. In addition, the administrative hassle of resolving the matter might be minimized. These potential advantages of purchasing the rental company's loss damage waiver must be weighed against its relatively high cost—possibly $15 or $20 per day. Note that some credit cards provide a degree of physical damage coverage for certain vehicles if the card is used to pay for the rental.

Coverage for a nonowned auto is the broadest coverage applicable to any covered auto under the policyowner's PAP.

What Exclusions Apply?

Numerous exclusions apply to Part D. Some of these are similar to the exclusions previously discussed in connection with other parts of the PAP. For example, losses to any vehicle are excluded if it was used as a public or livery conveyance or in a racing competition. Losses to nonowned autos are excluded when used without a reasonable belief that an insured is entitled to use them or when the vehicle is used by anyone in the business of selling, repairing, servicing, storing, or parking vehicles designed for use on public highways.

Several exclusions apply to various types of property under certain circumstances. For example, there is no coverage for loss to

- electronic equipment that reproduces, receives, or transmits audio, visual, or data signals unless it is permanently installed in the vehicle. Coverage on permanently installed electronic equipment is limited to $1,000 unless the equipment is in a location used by the auto manufacturer for equipment of that type. For example, after-market speakers mounted in the vehicle's door cutouts to replace OEM speakers are covered in full, but an auxiliary amplifier and subwoofer the owner installs in the trunk of his car are covered for no more than $1,000. Tapes, CDs, and data disks or other media are not covered by the PAP.
- more than $1,500 of nonelectronic custom equipment not otherwise excluded, such as special carpeting, height-extending roofs, a pickup truck bed liner, and custom wheels. A 2009 custom equipment exclusion endorsement is to be added to all policies reflecting the increasing popularity of such custom auto equipment. Although higher values are excluded, $1,500 in coverage is now provided to address the needs of those who have customized their vehicles with temperance. Policyowners whose vehicles are extensively customized may pay an additional premium and request a companion excess custom equipment coverage endorsement that replaces the $1,500 sublimit with a specified higher limit.
- radar detectors and similar equipment
- a trailer, camper body, or motor home (including facilities or accessories used with them) not shown in the policy declarations. This exclusion does not apply, however, to nonowned trailers or trailers acquired during the policy period as long as the insurer is asked to insure them within 14 days of acquisition.

How Are Losses Settled?

The insurer's limit of liability is generally the lesser of (1) the actual cash value of stolen or damaged property or (2) the amount necessary to repair or replace the property with other property of like kind and quality. However, $1,500 is the maximum payment for loss to a nonowned trailer. And, as mentioned, $1,000 is the maximum payment for electronic equipment that is installed in locations not used by the auto manufacturer for the installation of such equipment, and $1,500 is the sublimit on other custom equipment.

The insurance company has the right to pay losses in money or to repair or replace damaged or stolen property. It also has the option of returning stolen property to the named insured and paying for any damage that results from the theft, or of keeping all or part of the property and paying the insured an agreed or appraised value. Loss payments in the form of money include applicable sales tax.

The policy contains an appraisal provision that applies to situations when the insurer and insured cannot agree on the amount of a loss.

If there is other insurance, losses are settled on a pro rata basis except that coverage on a nonowned auto is excess over other collectible insurance. In other words, the insurance "follows the car."

PAP ENDORSEMENTS

As with homeowners policies, various ISO endorsements can be added to personal auto policies to better meet the needs of certain individuals. Some personal auto endorsements apply to more than one of the four coverages previously discussed; others apply to one specific coverage only. Several of these endorsements are briefly described.

Extended Nonowned Coverage

Two endorsements may be used to "buy back" certain excluded coverage in the PAP by extending the coverage applicable to nonowned autos. By eliminating exclusions in the standard PAP, both endorsements expand or "extend" the types of vehicles that qualify as nonowned autos for which coverage may apply. Neither extended nonowned coverage endorsement modifies the other-insurance provision of the PAP. As with other nonowned autos, insurance follows the car, and the auto liability and medical payments insurance purchased by the vehicle owner is primary.

The *extended nonowned coverage—vehicles furnished or available for regular use* endorsement provides liability and medical payments coverage for vehicles not owned by the named insured or a family member that are furnished or available for the regular use of the individual named in the endorsement. An option is available to provide coverage for family members as well, but only for a vehicle regularly furnished to the named individual. A client, for example, who regularly drives a vehicle owned by an employer that carries minimum limits of liability insurance might select this endorsement.

The *extended nonowned coverage—vehicles furnished or available for use as public or livery conveyances* endorsement provides liability and medical payments coverages for an individual who frequently operates a vehicle as a public or livery conveyance. As with the preceding endorsement, an option is available to extend coverage to include family members. For example, a retired individual with substantial assets to protect, who sometimes helps out as a substitute driver for his son-in-law's limousine service, might purchase this endorsement.

Named Nonowner Coverage

Many clients who do not own an auto do not know that they can purchase an auto insurance policy designed to address their needs.

EXAMPLE

Bob's only vehicle is a company car. He has absolutely no protection of his own if he borrows or rents another vehicle. Carol lives in New York City where parking costs and public transportation make it impractical to own a car, but she frequently rents a car while on vacation or to make trips outside the city.

The *named nonowner coverage* endorsement is for use by people like Bob and Carol, who do not own an auto but want to have protection when they drive nonowned vehicles. Parts A, B, and C of the PAP are available.

If the named insured acquires an auto, there is coverage for 14 days to give the insured time to specifically insure the vehicle. Optional coverages for family members and for regularly furnished autos are also available through the named nonowner coverage endorsement.

Miscellaneous Type Vehicle Endorsement

The miscellaneous type vehicle endorsement is used to cover miscellaneous types of owned vehicles, such as motor homes, motorcycles and similar-type vehicles, all-terrain vehicles, dune buggies, and golf carts. Each vehicle is listed in a schedule, and the policyowner can purchase the same coverages that apply to other autos in the PAP.

Snowmobile Endorsement

An endorsement similar to the *miscellaneous type vehicle endorsement* can be used to insure snowmobiles.

Limited Mexico Coverage

Without an endorsement, the PAP does not provide coverage when an insured is driving in Mexico. It is necessary that acceptable coverage be obtained through a licensed Mexican insurance company before driving into Mexico. To drive in Mexico without such coverage is a criminal offense. Coverage can be purchased at the border. Alternatively, it may be possible to add this protection to an existing PAP if an insurance company is a member of a foreign insurance association.

However, this is not the purpose of the *limited Mexico coverage* endorsement. The endorsement is effective only if the insured has also purchased liability insurance through a Mexican insurer, and coverage is excess over that policy. The main advantage of the endorsement is the ability to have higher liability limits than the Mexican insurance provides, as well as other policy coverages. The endorsement is primarily used by people who live near the border and occasionally take brief trips into Mexico. All policy coverages can be purchased for losses that occur in Mexico within 25 miles of the United States' border, and the coverage applies only while the insured is in Mexico for 10 days or less. The insurer will defend the insured under the liability coverage only if the original suit is brought in the United States and if the suit does not involve a Mexican citizen or resident. Repairs to a covered auto are not covered if they are made in Mexico unless the vehicle cannot be driven in its damaged condition.

Coverage for Damage to Your Auto (Maximum Limit of Liability)

Insurers are often reluctant to write Part D coverage on antique or restored vehicles because of the difficulty in determining value when a loss occurs. This endorsement lists a stated amount, which becomes the maximum that the insurer will pay for a loss. This does not mean, however, that the stated amount is automatically paid if a total loss occurs. The insurer's maximum limit of liability is the smallest of the following three amounts (minus the applicable deductible):

- the stated amount selected
- the actual cash value of the stolen or damaged property
- the amount necessary to repair or replace the property with property of like kind and quality

Joint Ownership Coverage

This endorsement is used to modify the definition of "insured" when individuals are not married, reside together, and jointly own one or more vehicles. It can also be used when related persons jointly own a vehicle but do not live together.

Trust Endorsement

Financial planners should be aware of the insurance ramifications when a client's property is retitled in the name of a trust. Many autos are legally owned by a trust, typically a revocable living trust the policyowner establishes for estate planning reasons. Too often, the insurer is not even informed that the vehicle has been retitled in the name of the trust. Traditionally, when the insurer was aware of the situation, a certificate of insurance was used to serve as proof of insurance on vehicles the named insured and a trust owned jointly. However, this approach was not suitable for the most common situations in which the vehicle is titled solely in the name of the trust.

In 2005, ISO introduced a *trust endorsement* that lists the name of the trust and the trustee, if other than the named insured. The endorsement also adds a statement to the definitions section of the policy to the effect that a vehicle is deemed to be owned by a person if title is transferred to the trust named in the schedule or in the declarations. This is similar to the provision that treats autos under a long-term lease as though they were owned autos.

Auto Loan/Lease Coverage

In some cases, the total loss to a leased vehicle or a financed auto results in the insured's being required to pay the lessor or lending company an amount that exceeds the actual cash value of an insured vehicle. The purpose of this endorsement is to fill the gap between what the insurer pays the policyowner and the amount the policyowner must pay to the lender. The coverage is commonly referred to as gap coverage.

The endorsement provides indemnification for any unpaid lease or finance amounts other than overdue payments at the time of loss, financial penalties under a lease for excessive use or abnormal wear and tear, security deposits not refunded by a lessor, costs for extended warranties or life and health insurance purchased, and carryover balances from previous leases or loans.

Towing and Labor Costs Coverage

This endorsement pays for towing and labor if a covered auto or nonowned auto is disabled for any reason. The limit of towing and labor costs coverage is a stated amount, such as $25, $50, or $100 per disablement. The labor costs of repair work (such as changing a flat tire) are covered only at the place of disablement.

The endorsement can be used only for autos that are already covered under Part D of the PAP. It is not unusual for the towing and labor coverage to be a standard part of an insurance company's PAP if collision coverage is purchased.

Towing and labor costs protection originated as a fringe benefit of auto insurance the auto clubs provided, and other insurers began to offer the coverage to remain competitive. It is a popular coverage addition, partly because it is a low-cost option and partly because it provides a sense of security in the event of an auto breakdown. However, many clients should consider bypassing the towing and labor costs coverage option for at least two reasons. First, the maximum benefit, as mentioned, is usually a nominal amount, such as $25, $50, or $100. Most clients could easily handle a cost of this magnitude as a current expense. Second, towing and labor coverage duplicates a benefit available to clients who are members of an auto club. Third, many auto manufacturers provide towing coverage on vehicles that are under warranty; in this situation, towing and labor coverage is redundant at best.

Trip Interruption Coverage

In 2005, ISO introduced a trip interruption coverage endorsement that is somewhat related to towing and labor costs coverage. The endorsement provides coverage up to $600 for reasonable transportation expenses, lodging, and meals when a vehicle is withdrawn from use for 24 hours or more because it is in an accident or breaks down more than 100 miles from home. Coverage is excess over benefits that vehicle warranties, auto clubs, or other sources provide.

Other Endorsements

There are several other endorsements that provide coverage either for property that is excluded under the PAP or where the amount of coverage is limited. These endorsements are very briefly described below:

- *Optional limits transportation expense coverage.* The $20 per day and $600 maximums that apply to transportation expenses are increased to $30 and $900, respectively, under this endorsement.
- *Electronic equipment coverage.* This endorsement can be used to provide coverage in excess of $1,000 on electronic equipment that is permanently installed in locations not used by the auto manufacturer for such equipment.
- *Excess customizing equipment coverage.* This endorsement can be used to increase the sublimit on custom equipment other than electronic equipment.
- *Covered property coverage.* This endorsement provides coverage for awnings, cabanas, and other similar equipment designed for use with insured vehicles, such as vans, camping trailers, or motor homes.

HARD-TO-INSURE DRIVERS

Not everybody can readily obtain auto insurance in the standard marketplace. Hard-to-insure drivers who must obtain substandard coverage include persons with poor driving records and, often, those who are young or who have little driving experience. Statistics clearly show that these groups have a high probability of being involved in future accidents.

Another category of hard-to-insure drivers consists of persons with very high-powered and/or expensive autos. Some insurers specialize in this market, particularly for individuals who have good driving records.

The number of hard-to-insure drivers varies significantly from state to state; the number is much higher in states where insurance companies lose money on auto insurance because the state insurance departments are unwilling to grant necessary rate increases.

residual market   Hard-to-insure drivers can usually find some coverage in what is referred to as the *residual market* (sometimes referred to as the *shared market* or *substandard market*). The residual market consists of specialty insurers and state programs to make insurance available, though not necessarily affordable. A small number of drivers with very poor driving records (for example, several drunk driving convictions) may still be unable to obtain insurance from either of these sources in some states.

Specialty Insurers

A number of insurers specialize in writing coverage for high-risk drivers. They charge substantially higher premiums than in the standard marketplace and often provide more limited coverage. For example, the limits for liability coverage are sometimes only those specified in a state's financial responsibility or compulsory insurance law. However, it is not unusual to have optional higher limits available.

Medical payments coverage can also be limited, and collision coverage, if written, is often subject to a high deductible.

State Programs

State programs for hard-to-insure drivers are commonly referred to as assigned risk plans. This term is no longer formally used, however, because of its negative connotations. State programs for hard-to-insure drivers tend to have higher-than-normal premiums (often much higher) and more limited coverage than in the standard marketplace, but significant variations exist among the states. The state programs usually follow one of three models:

- automobile insurance plans
- joint underwriting associations
- reinsurance facilities

Automobile Insurance Plans

automobile insurance plan   An *automobile insurance plan* is the type of program that exists in most states. To be eligible, an applicant must show that he or she has been unable to obtain coverage within a recent specified period of time. Each auto insurer in the state is assigned its proportionate share of the drivers in the automobile insurance plan based on the total volume of auto insurance written in the state. The company to which the policy is assigned issues and services it. It also receives any profits or absorbs any losses from the policies it writes.

Joint Underwriting Associations

This arrangement involves an association of auto insurers, and all business of the association is placed in a pool. The insurance companies share any underwriting losses in proportion to the auto insurance premiums each company writes in the state. A limited number of companies are designated to issue and service policies on behalf of the joint underwriting association.

Reinsurance Facilities

With reinsurance facilities, insurers must accept all applicants who have a valid driver's license, and they issue and service policies for these applicants. However, if an applicant is considered high-risk, the insurer has the option of assigning the premiums for the applicant to the reinsurance facility. All auto insurance companies in the state share underwriting losses from this type of business in proportion to auto insurance premiums written.

Insuring Hard-to-Insure Drivers

- Specialty high-risk auto insurers
- State automobile insurance (assigned risk) plans
- Joint underwriting associations
- Reinsurance facilities

SHOPPING FOR AUTO INSURANCE

The cost of auto insurance varies significantly among insurers in a highly competitive market. In fact, studies by some state insurance departments show that the premium for a hypothetical insured can be two to four times higher if purchased from certain insurance companies rather than others. Therefore, it pays to shop around. Of course, as previously stated, such factors as the financial strength of the insurer and the service from the company and its agents also need to be evaluated.

Many factors affect auto insurance rates, and some of them are not readily within the control of the insured at the time he or she purchases auto insurance. These factors include the age, gender, and marital status of drivers; the use of the insured vehicles (that is, driving to work, pleasure, or business); and the geographic territory where vehicles are normally used and garaged.

Other factors are subject to some control by the insured but not necessarily at the moment he or she purchases a policy. These include driving record and the type and age of vehicles owned. The latter is particularly significant for physical damage coverage because the Part D premium can be several times higher for a new luxury auto than for a van that is several years old.

Even though most companies commonly use these previously mentioned factors to determine premiums, companies can apply them differently. For example, premiums are higher if a family has a teenager who drives. If the teenager primarily or solely drives the old family van, many companies will rate this vehicle for the teenager. However, other companies will assign the teenage driver to the highest-rated vehicle even if he or she does not use it.

Other factors can also affect auto insurance premiums for one or more policy coverages. Many companies give discounts for at least some of the following:

- a driver education course for young drivers
- students with good grades
- a defensive driving course
- senior citizens, but the discount may require the periodic attendance of a classroom program on driver education
- nonsmokers
- anti-theft devices in a vehicle
- air bags or automatic seat belts in a vehicle
- reduced use of a vehicle by a student who is away at school over a specified distance from home, provided the student does not have an insured vehicle at school
- no accidents for some period of time, such as 3 years
- other policies with the same company. For example, some insurers give a discount if they write both auto insurance and homeowners insurance for a policyowner.

Other important factors in the cost of auto insurance are the coverages selected, their limits, and deductibles. For policyowners with an umbrella liability policy, the limits for liability insurance need only to be those the umbrella policy requires. If a policyowner and family have an adequate medical expense insurance plan, it is probably unnecessary to carry any more Part B coverage for medical payments than a state might require. However, note that this coverage applies to more than just family members and also covers funeral expenses. Similarly, if a policyowner and family members have adequate medical expense and disability income insurance, the need to carry other than minimally required no-fault benefits should be evaluated.

Financial planners often disagree over the appropriate limit of uninsured/underinsured motorists coverage. Some argue that it should be the same as a policy's liability limits. Others argue that this is unnecessary if other insurance exists that will pay for a family's medical expenses and lost wages. However, higher limits do give an insured the right to collect damages for pain and suffering.

Finally, there are ways to lower Part D premiums. Higher deductibles, particularly on collision coverage, can result in significant savings over a period of years. In addition, a policyowner must evaluate the need for coverage on an older vehicle. For example, there are those who argue that it is probably not cost effective to carry physical damage coverage on a vehicle that is worth as little as $3,000 or $4,000. Obviously, this threshold amount varies by such factors as the net worth and risk tolerance of an individual.

INSURING WATERCRAFT AND AIRPLANES

Many people own watercraft. For some watercraft, liability coverage is available under a homeowners policy, but that policy provides no protection for larger boats and little physical damage protection for any boat. As a result, many insurers market various types of watercraft policies to meet the insurance needs of boat owners. There is no single common policy like the ISO forms for homeowners and auto insurance.

Some individuals own private aircraft for their personal or business use. Coverage for aircraft is very specialized and is usually obtained from a small number of aviation pools that underwrite and manage such insurance for their member companies.

Watercraft Policies

There are several types of watercraft policies. Some insurers have policies designed primarily for small boats, such as those no longer than 20 or 22 feet. These policies typically provide physical damage coverage on the boat, motor, equipment, and trailer and contain a deductible. They can also be used to provide liability and medical payments coverage.

There are two common types of package policies for boats—boatowners policies and yacht policies. A boatowners policy is typically used for boats under a particular length, such as 26 or 30 feet, whereas the yacht policy is used for larger boats. A boatowners policy is generally written by an insurer's personal lines department, while a yacht policy is often written by the insurer's ocean marine department. As a result, the policies tend to use different wording, but the coverage is largely the same.

Boatowners and yacht policies are similar to auto policies in that they contain

- liability coverage, sometimes referred to as protection and indemnity insurance
- medical payments coverage
- uninsured boaters coverage
- physical damage coverage, often referred to as hull insurance. This provides protection not only for the boat but also for equipment, accessories, motors, and trailers. Coverage can usually be written on either a named-perils or an open-perils basis.

As a general rule, the exclusions that apply to these coverages also parallel those found in auto insurance policies.

Other coverages are also available in boatowners and yacht policies. These include coverage for the

- legal obligation of the policyowner to remove a wrecked or sunken vessel
- liability arising out of transportation of the boat on land
- costs of towing and assistance if the boat is disabled
- liability to crew members and other maritime workers covered under various federal acts

Boatowners and yacht policies frequently contain warranties. Failure to comply with these warranties can result in the denial of coverage or higher premiums, depending on the precise policy provision. Common warranties are that the boat will

- be used for pleasure
- not be used during specified seasonal periods unless the policyowner obtains permission from the insurance company and pays any additional premium
- be operated only in the navigational area described in the policy

It is also common to find a warranty that requires at least two occupants in a boat when it is used for waterskiing.

Aviation Policies

Aviation policies for private aircraft are similar to auto insurance with respect to liability insurance in that coverage pays for bodily injury that arises out of the insured's ownership, maintenance, or use of insured aircraft. Coverage also applies to bodily injury liability arising out of the location where the insured aircraft is stored. Exclusions similar to those in auto insurance policies apply to aviation policies. In addition, there are exclusions for damage or injury from noise and pollution.

Medical payments coverage is available to cover passengers. Crew members can also be covered for an additional premium.

The physical damage coverage, also referred to as *hull coverage*, is open-perils and can be written to apply to the following: (1) all losses, (2) only losses that occur while the plane is not in flight, or (3) only losses that occur while the plane is not in motion.

PERSONAL UMBRELLA LIABILITY INSURANCE

umbrella liability policy

Virtually every financial planning client has assets to protect, and virtually every client with assets should be advised to protect those assets with a personal *umbrella liability policy*. Without this coverage, individuals and families face the possibility of losing a lifetime's accumulation of capital and other assets because they are seized to pay a legal judgment. At one time, umbrella liability insurance was viewed as a policy for wealthy people with a large asset base or a high income. In view of the magnitude of today's legal awards, umbrella liability insurance is appropriate for most middle-income individuals as well.

An umbrella policy protects clients in two ways:

- *high limits over underlying insurance.* Umbrella policies provide high limits of "excess" liability coverage, over and above the "underlying" primary liability coverage that basic auto and homeowners policies provide. For example, a person whose personal auto policy has a single Coverage A liability limit of $500,000 could buy a $1 million umbrella policy to be protected against future auto liability claims up to $1.5 million, the sum of the two policies. If the person also had a homeowners policy with a Coverage E liability limit of $300,000, that policy and the umbrella combined would provide protection up to $1.3 million for liability losses covered by the homeowners policy.

- *broadened drop-down coverage over a self-insured retention.* Many umbrella policies provide not only additional limits but also broader coverage by covering some kinds of claims—such as claims for slander and other personal injury offenses—that an auto policy or a homeowners policy does not cover. The self-insured retention, which works like a deductible, is discussed in the next section of this chapter.

Unlike homeowners insurance and auto insurance, there was historically no standard personal umbrella liability policy, and each insurer that offered this type of insurance developed its own policy. The situation changed somewhat with the development of an ISO policy. Although insurers can now adopt the ISO policy, most continue to use their own policy forms. This results in significant variations among policies. Therefore, the following discussion is general. The appropriate policy for a particular individual is the one that best covers his or her specific loss exposures, and a thorough evaluation of alternative policies is often appropriate.

The following discussion looks at the general nature of personal umbrella liability policies, the underlying coverage requirements, the persons insured, and the exclusions that often exist.

General Nature

A personal umbrella policy is designed primarily to provide liability coverage for catastrophic legal claims or judgments. The smallest limit of coverage available from most insurers is $1 million, and limits up to $5 or $10 million are often available. The policy covers not only bodily injury and property damage liability but also personal injury liability.

A personal umbrella policy requires the policyowner to carry certain underlying liability coverages of specified minimum amounts. These generally include auto liability insurance, watercraft liability insurance if the policyowner owns any watercraft, and personal liability insurance under a homeowners or other policy. If a claim is made under an underlying policy, the umbrella policy will pay only after the limits of the underlying policy are exhausted. The umbrella policy is excess and will pay up to its limits so that the insured effectively has an amount of coverage equal to the sum of the limits of the umbrella policy and the underlying coverage.

EXAMPLE

Charlene Smith has a $1 million umbrella policy and an auto liability policy of the required underlying limit of $250,000 per person. If an injured party obtains a legal judgment of $700,000 against her, the underlying auto policy will pay $250,000 and the umbrella policy will pay the remaining $450,000.

---

self-insured retention   If an underlying policy does not cover a loss that is not excluded from a personal umbrella policy, the umbrella policy is the primary insurer and will cover the loss subject to a *self-insured retention* (SIR). The SIR is like a deductible and requires the policyowner to pay the first portion of the loss—typically $250. However, SIR amounts vary by company and can be $500 or $1,000 or even higher. The self-insured retention is not applicable to losses that underlying policies cover. Note that the term *drop-down coverage* is often used to describe a situation in which an umbrella policy covers a loss that underlying insurance does not cover. In effect, the umbrella drops down to cover the entire loss, other than the SIR, rather than act as excess coverage.

The following figure shows the relationship of a typical personal umbrella policy to the underlying policies.

Figure 18-1
Relationship of Personal Umbrella Policy to Underlying Policies

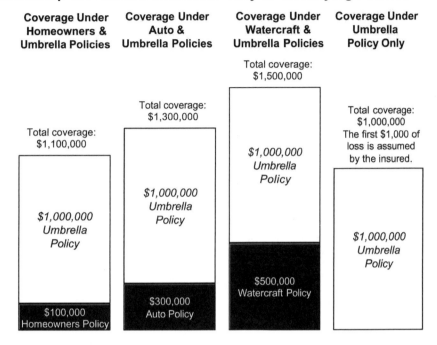

In addition to paying liability claims, most personal umbrella policies pay defense costs that are not payable by underlying policies and provide various other supplementary coverages similar to those in the homeowners and PAP policies (premiums on appeal bonds, expenses incurred at the company's request, and so on).

Finally, some states require that the policyowner be given the right to extend coverage under a personal umbrella policy to uninsured and underinsured motorists coverage.

Underlying Coverage Requirements

A requirement of the personal umbrella policy is that the policyowner maintain certain underlying coverages of specified minimum amounts. Some insurers also require that these underlying coverages be purchased from them.

At a minimum, the following underlying coverages are required, and the amounts shown, although they vary from company to company, are not unusual:

- auto liability insurance: $250,000/$500,000/$50,000 or $300,000 to $500,000 single limit
- homeowners liability insurance: $100,000 or $300,000
- watercraft liability insurance if the policyowner owns a boat: $300,000 or $500,000

Other underlying coverages for recreational vehicles, aircraft, and employers liability may also be required, particularly if liability from these vehicles or situations is covered under the personal umbrella liability policy.

If the policyowner fails to maintain the required underlying coverages, the insurer will pay only the amount it would have been required to pay if the underlying policies had been in force. In the previous example, if the insured's liability limits had been $50,000, rather than the required $250,000 limit, the umbrella policy would still pay only $450,000 of the $700,000 award. The auto policy would pay $50,000, and the insured would have an uninsured loss of $200,000.

A premium reduction may apply if the actual underlying limits are greater than those the personal umbrella policy requires.

What Exclusions Apply to Umbrella Coverage?

At one time, personal umbrella policies were relatively inexpensive and contained few of the exclusions found in homeowners and auto policies. Claims experience over the years, however, has led to increased premiums and more numerous exclusions. In fact, some umbrella liability policies now have almost the same exclusions that are in homeowners and auto policies. However, the number and nature of the exclusions vary significantly among companies, and exclusions should be evaluated carefully when selecting a personal umbrella policy.

For example, an individual who is actively involved in recreational boating might frequently operate watercraft that other persons own. Some policies cover damage to such watercraft when an insured is liable; other policies exclude coverage for nonowned watercraft that are in the insured's care, custody, or control.

Some of the exclusions often found in personal umbrella policies preclude coverage for liability that arises from the following:

- intentional injury unless it results from actions to prevent or eliminate danger or to protect persons or property

- government programs, such as workers' compensation
- damage to property owned by an insured
- damage to certain types of nonowned property in an insured's care, custody, or control. There is seldom a blanket exclusion for all property of this type, but damage to certain classes of property (for example, autos, watercraft, and aircraft) is often excluded. In addition, damage to property for which an insured has assumed contractual liability is often excluded. The insured should have some type of property insurance in such situations.
- the use of watercraft, and possibly other recreational vehicles, unless underlying coverage applies
- the use of aircraft
- business pursuits, other than those arising out of the use of a personal auto or other circumstances when underlying coverage exists
- the rendering or failure to render professional services. A few insurance companies will cover this loss exposure for an additional premium
- directors' and officers' activities, other than those performed for a not-for-profit organization but only if the insured receives no compensation other than reimbursement of expenses
- transmission of communicable diseases
- sexual molestation, corporal punishment, and physical or mental abuse

As noted earlier, umbrella policies are not all alike. Far from it. Various umbrella policies are available, and it behooves a financial advisor not only to recommend the client have an umbrella policy but also to ensure that the policy in question addresses the client's specific exposures.

Who Are the Insureds?

Personal umbrella policies usually provide coverage for the named insured, spouse, and family members living in the household. Other residents of the household who are under the age of 21 and in the care of an insured are usually covered.

Other persons or organizations whose people are driving a named insured's or spouse's auto or are liable because of actions of an insured with respect to an auto are also usually covered in a manner similar to coverage under the PAP. Coverage for these persons or organizations may or may not exist with respect to watercraft and recreational vehicles.

Most policies also extend coverage to persons or organizations who have custody of an insured's animals other than such businesses as kennels, veterinary hospitals, and stables.

CHECKLIST FOR EVALUATING AND COMPARING PERSONAL AUTO INSURANCE POLICIES

- What are the limits for each of the following coverages?

    ___ Part A—Liability
    ___ Part B—Medical Payments Coverage or no-fault benefits
    ___ Part C—Uninsured Motorists Coverage
    ___ Part D—Coverage for Damage to Your Auto

- Are the coverage limits adequate?
- If the policy is not an ISO form, how does it differ?
- Does the policy automatically contain coverages or endorsements that are optional with other insurers?
- What is the annual policy premium?
- Is the policyowner taking advantage of all possible discounts?
- What deductible applies to Part D?
- Are low-valued vehicles unnecessarily insured under Part D?
- Are there, or is there any need for, any endorsements for the following?

    ___ Extended nonowned coverage
    ___ Miscellaneous type vehicles
    ___ Snowmobiles
    ___ Underinsured motorists
    ___ Limited Mexico coverage
    ___ Joint owners
    ___ Trusts
    ___ Antique or restored vehicles
    ___ Auto loan/lease coverage
    ___ Towing and labor costs
    ___ Custom equipment
    ___ Trip interruption coverage

_____ Awnings, cabanas, and the like

CHECKLIST FOR EVALUATING AND COMPARING PERSONAL UMBRELLA LIABILITY INSURANCE POLICIES

- What are the policy limits?
- What is the self-insured retention?
- Does the policy provide uninsured or underinsured motorists coverage?
- What is the annual policy premium?
- What are the underlying coverage requirements and are they satisfied?

  _____ Auto liability insurance
  _____ Homeowners liability insurance
  _____ Watercraft liability insurance
  _____ Other

- What persons are insured?
- What types of exclusions apply?

CHAPTER REVIEW

Key Terms and Concepts

financial responsibility law
unsatisfied judgment funds
uninsured motorists coverage
underinsured motorists coverage
pure no-fault
modified no-fault
add-on plan
choice no-fault
personal injury protection (PIP)
  endorsement

covered auto
newly acquired auto
temporary substitute vehicle
split limits
collision
other than collision
residual market
automobile insurance plan
umbrella liability policy
self-insured retention

Review Questions

Review questions are based on the learning objectives in this chapter. Thus, a [3] at the end of a question means that the question is based on learning objective 3. If there are multiple objectives, they are all listed.

1. What key problems are associated with auto accidents and auto insurance? [1]

2. Why should a client consider purchasing uninsured and underinsured motorists coverage even though the state has a compulsory liability insurance law? [1]

3. What methods are used to compensate auto accident victims? Describe the shortcomings of those methods. [1]

4. While driving his car, Jack sustained medical expenses and lost wages due to bodily injury when a drunk teenager driving his own car ran a red light and hit him. Jack in no way contributed to the accident through his own fault. How would the settlement be handled in each of the following situations?
   a. if Jack's bodily injuries equaled $40,000 and the accident occurred in a state with compulsory liability insurance [1]
   b. if Jack's bodily injuries equaled $40,000 and the accident occurred in a state with a modified no-fault law containing a $5,000 threshold [1]

5. What vehicles are typically eligible for coverage under a personal auto policy? [2]

6. Determine the coverage applicable to the following situations.
   a. Pete pays cash for a new car, and when he drives it off the dealer's lot, he hits another car driving along the street in front of the dealership. The accident is Pete's fault. He injures the driver of the other car and damages both his car and the other driver's car. Pete had $100,000 of liability coverage for bodily injury and property damage (Part A) and collision coverage (Part D) with a $250 deductible on the old car he just traded in as part of the purchase of his new car. What coverage, if any, does Pete have for this accident? [2]
   b. Suppose instead that Pete kept his old car, did not notify his insurer that he also had a new car, and the accident to his new car occurred when he returned it to the dealer for a 3,000 mile checkup two months after he bought it. What coverage, if any, does Pete have for this accident? [2]

7. Tom falls asleep at the wheel of his car while driving on the interstate, runs across the median, and causes a tractor trailer truck to flip over while trying to avoid a head-on collision with Tom. The truck driver has a claim for $5,000 of bodily injury; damage to his truck and its contents is $150,000. How much will Tom's Personal Auto Policy pay under Part A—Liability coverage with each of the following limits?
   a. $100,000/$300,000/$50,000 [2]
   b. $300,000 [2]

8.   Your client Betty mentions that she frequently uses cars in connection with her business. Does her Personal Auto Policy provide liability coverage in the following situations?
a. when she drives her family car for business purposes [2]
b. when she drives the company car furnished to her for her regular use [2]
c. when she helps to drive her friend's car to a business meeting in another state [2]

9.   A client with a PAP who frequently borrows her friend's car asks, "Whose liability insurance would cover a liability claim that results from an accident while I'm driving my friend's car?" [2]

10.   A client whose wife frequently gives rides to several other children attending their daughter's nursery school asks, "Is any coverage available under our Personal Auto Policy in case the children are injured in an accident that is not my wife's fault?" [2]

11.   On a family vacation, you rent a car and turn down the loss damage waiver the rental company offers. Which coverage in your Personal Auto Policy would provide you with coverage for damage to the rental car (minus any deductible) in the following situations?
a. The rental car is damaged when you hit a phone pole while swerving to avoid another vehicle. [2]
b. The rental car is scratched by vandals while it is parked in the hotel parking lot. [2]
c. The rental car is badly dented when you hit a deer while you are driving at night. [2]

12.   How can a client get liability coverage for his use of his motorcycle, dune buggy, and snowmobile? [3]

13.   During a meeting to review her financial plan, your client Celeste mentions that she and her family plan a vacation driving around Mexico this year. What should you explain to her about auto insurance coverage for the trip? [3]

14.   How might auto coverage be obtained for clients who are hard-to-insure drivers? [4]

15.   What factors should clients consider when shopping for auto insurance? [5]

16.   What coverages are available to meet the needs of clients who own watercraft and/or airplanes? [6]

17.   Why should a client who has rather high limits of liability in her personal auto and homeowners policies consider also purchasing a personal umbrella liability policy? [7]

Learning Objectives

An understanding of the material in this chapter should enable the student to

1. Briefly explain the key types of commercial property and liability insurance available to meet the protection needs of businesses.
2. Describe the general features of businessowners policies.

This discussion is devoted to business insurance. A financial planner may be asked to make specific recommendations about property and liability coverages for a business owner, but the task of implementing this coverage is usually left to a property and liability insurance agent or broker who works in the business market.

A financial planner still needs a general understanding of the types of business insurance for several reasons. Individual clients sometimes need some of the coverages discussed here. For example, anyone with domestic employees may need workers' compensation coverage for household employees. A semiretired client with a part-time business venture, or a person with a hobby, may also engage in an activity that requires some type of commercial insurance policy to cover his or her business property or liability exposures.

It is especially important for a financial planner to determine whether a client has appropriate liability insurance on his or her business activities to adequately protect personal assets against a claim or judgment. For example, when a client serves on the board of a corporation or a nonprofit organization, it is important to consider the extent to which he or she is protected by the organization's directors and officers liability insurance.

This discussion begins by summarizing the more common types of commercial property and liability insurance. It concludes by describing businessowners policies that provide a package of coverages suitable for many small- and medium-sized businesses.

TYPES OF COMMERCIAL PROPERTY AND LIABILITY INSURANCE

Numerous policy forms and endorsements for commercial property and liability insurance are available. Terminology and insurance company practices are not uniform. The discussion is categorized as follows:

- commercial property insurance
- business income insurance
- crime insurance
- inland marine insurance
- boiler and machinery insurance
- farm insurance
- commercial general liability insurance
- business auto insurance
- workers' compensation and employers liability insurance
- professional liability insurance
- excess and umbrella liability insurance
- surety bonds

Many commercial coverages, such as coverage on ships and commercial aircraft (ocean marine and aviation insurance, respectively), are beyond the scope of this book and are not discussed here.

The focus in most of the following discussion is on the forms used by ISO. Each of these forms can be used as a freestanding "monoline" policy when combined with another form that contains general policy provisions. Often, two or more separate coverage forms are combined into a commercial package policy.

Commercial Property Insurance

commercial property insurance
Broadly speaking, the term commercial property includes business property of all types. ISO has developed a series of so-called *commercial property insurance* policies that deal with property specifically related to buildings and their contents, using those terms rather loosely. The ISO commercial property series of coverages and forms are discussed under this heading.

Covered Property

Commercial property insurance can be used to cover one or more of the following classes of property:

- buildings
- business personal property of the named insured
- personal property of others in the care, custody, or control of the named insured

Each of these classes is specifically defined and subject to various exclusions, some of which can be deleted, or "bought back," by using an endorsement. Other exclusions eliminate coverage for losses that can be covered by other policies.

Various additional coverages and extensions of coverage automatically provide limited coverage for debris removal, pollution cleanup after a loss, newly acquired property, and the cost of research to reconstruct valuable papers and records that have been damaged or destroyed.

Covered Perils

Commercial property can be insured against various perils on either a named-perils basis or a more comprehensive open-perils basis. In all cases, these forms can be expanded with endorsements to cover losses that might arise, for example, from earthquake or the enforcement of ordinances or laws.

Forms for Specific Types of Property

Some commercial property insurance forms have been developed for use in specific situations. These include the following types of builders risk insurance and condominium insurance.

- *Builders Risk Coverage Form.* This form provides protection for buildings under construction and covers the unique loss exposures and valuation issues associated with these structures.
- *Condominium Association Coverage Form.* This form covers property for which a residential or commercial condominium association is responsible. It covers not only property owned by the association but also furniture, fixtures, alterations, and appliances of unit-owners if the association agreement requires the association to insure them.
- *Condominium Commercial Unit-Owners Coverage Form.* This form covers the interest of the owner of a commercial condominium unit.

Note that an owner of a residential condominium unit can protect his or her interest under an HO-6 policy.

Loss Settlement

Losses under commercial property forms are settled on an actual cash value basis. However, a replacement cost coverage option is often elected. Losses are subject to a deductible that, depending upon available options, the policyowner can select.

The settlement of claims is subject to a coinsurance provision that is often 80 percent but can also be 90 or 100 percent. To avoid a possible coinsurance penalty, the policyowner has the option to elect an agreed amount of coverage.

For many businesses, property values, particularly inventory, are subject to wide fluctuations. Various policy forms can be used to address this problem so that premiums charged reflect the varying loss exposures and, at the time of loss, there is adequate insurance to properly indemnify the policyowner and avoid a coinsurance penalty. These forms include value reporting forms, which require periodic reporting of values, and peak season endorsements, which modify policy limits during certain specified periods of the year.

Business Income Insurance

Although business income insurance policy forms are part of ISO's commercial property series, we will discuss them separately. Many businesses will suffer a significant loss of income if direct physical loss or damage to property forces a suspension of business operations. Others will not be able to suspend operations but will instead incur extra expenses to remain in operation. Policy forms are available to cover these loss exposures, and the protection they provide can make the difference between business success and failure.

EXAMPLE 1
Josef Beckmann owns a neighborhood bakery. An overheated oven started a fire that damaged several mixers and a portion of the bakery building. Beckmann's commercial property insurance will pay for the damage to the building, as well as the mixers and other personal property in the bakery. Beckmann will also face a serious cash flow problem, because the bakery will generate no income until the fire damage has been repaired. Business income insurance, if he has purchased the coverage, can provide the needed dough during the period of reconstruction.

EXAMPLE 2
Andrea Beckmann is the only veterinarian in a small community. Unlike her father, Josef, Andrea cannot suspend business if her clinic is damaged or destroyed, because the community's pets will continue to get sick or injured and need her services. Andrea would instead rent temporary quarters and equipment so she could set up a temporary clinic to treat sick animals and perform emergency surgery. Extra expense insurance can cover this operation. If Andrea should temporarily suspend routine services until her clinic could be restored, she would also suffer a loss of business income that business income insurance can cover.

business income insurance

Business income insurance, once known as business interruption insurance, may be purchased not only for profit-seeking commercial businesses but also for nonprofit organizations and governmental entities. Business income coverage applies when property has been damaged by an insured peril. Most policyowners buy business income insurance against the same set of perils as their building and/or personal property, either on a named-perils basis or on an open-perils basis.

Business income insurance covers the following types of losses:

- reduction in net income—the difference between the net income the business would have earned had no loss occurred and the net income the business did earn while recovering from a loss.

- extra expenses to minimize or avoid the suspension of operations—rent at a temporary location, for example, and the cost of obtaining services, such as data processing, that can no longer be handled in house

Policy Forms

ISO forms include two types of business income coverage and an extra expense-only form with these names:

- Business Income (and Extra Expense) Coverage Form
- Business Income (without Extra Expense) Coverage Form
- Extra Expense Coverage Form

Both business income forms cover the sum of (1) net profit or loss that would have been earned or incurred during a period of business suspension and (2) normal continuing business expenses, including payroll, during the suspension. Both forms also cover extra expenses to the extent they reduce the loss that would otherwise be payable by the insurer. In addition, the Business Income (and Extra Expense) Coverage Form covers extra expenses to avoid or minimize the suspension of operations even if they do not otherwise reduce the business income loss.

Several endorsements are designed to adapt these forms to policyowners' particular needs. Some of these are

- *Ordinary Payroll Limitation or Exclusion Endorsement.* By laying off certain noncritical employees, organizations can minimize expenses during prolonged periods of business suspension. This endorsement deletes coverage on the amount of the payroll for these employees and results in a premium reduction.

- *Ordinance or Law—Increased Period of Restoration Endorsement.* The business income forms cover losses only for the period of time needed to repair damaged property with reasonable speed and like-quality materials. Ordinances or laws can effectively extend this period, for example, if a damaged frame building must be torn down and replaced with a masonry fire-resistive building. The endorsement provides coverage during this additional period of time.

- *Business Income from Dependent Properties Endorsement.* Some firms are so dependent on a single supplier or customer that a loss at the supplier's or customer's location would result in the suspension of the firm's operations. This endorsement covers the loss of income that results from direct damage at these other locations.

- *Utilities Services—Time Element Endorsement.* This endorsement extends coverage to loss of earnings that results from off-premises interruptions of utilities and communications services.

extra expense insurance　　　　The Extra Expense Coverage Form is designed to provide *extra expense insurance* for organizations that must remain in operation after a property loss. Businesses that might purchase only extra expense insurance include banks, hospitals, newspapers, insurance agencies, and financial planning firms. In most cases, these businesses also have a business income loss exposure, and in such cases the Business Income (and Extra Expense) Coverage Form is the better way to obtain extra expense coverage.

Loss Settlement

Loss settlements for business income insurance are often more complex than settlements for direct property losses, because it is impossible to know precisely what business income might have been. The policy form provides that the amount of the loss is determined based on the following:

- ' the net income of the business before the loss occurred
- the probable net income of the business if no loss had occurred
- the operating expenses that must continue during the period of restoration so the policyowner can resume operations with the quality of service that existed prior to the loss
- other relevant sources of information

As a general rule, the business income forms pay for losses continuing up to 30 days after business is resumed. The revenue of many businesses will not return to normal for longer periods of time, however, and coverage can be extended by endorsement beyond this 30-day period.

Loss payments are subject to a coinsurance provision. However, the variation in length of business suspensions and the difficulty in estimating future net income and expenses make it difficult to select the proper amount of insurance and the coinsurance percentage. Various options can eliminate or suspend the coinsurance provision.

Crime Insurance

Various commercial insurance coverages, especially those that provide coverage on an open-perils basis, cover theft losses to property other than money, securities, and similar financial instruments so long as the person who commits the theft is not an employee of the insured. An ISO commercial crime policy can also be used to cover the theft of personal property, as well as the theft of money, securities, and other property and also various causes of loss that other forms of insurance do not usually cover.

Of the various crime insurance coverages available, one of the most important—employee theft—is all too often overlooked. Perhaps this is because employee theft deals with a cause of loss rather than a specific type of asset. Often, the need for this coverage is overlooked by businessowners who see no need to question the trusted employees who handle cash and accounting records or control the business inventory. Experience demonstrates, however, that the most trusted employees often steal rather large sums of money over a period of several years before the loss is detected. Even religious organizations, civic organizations, and charitable institutions are victims of employee theft. For example, a clergyman in New York City was charged with stealing well over a million dollars from a church.

Covered Property

Commercial crime forms typically cover one or more of three broad classes of property:

- money, which includes currency, coins, bank notes, travelers checks, and money orders
- securities, which include both negotiable and nonnegotiable instruments, contracts that represent money or other property, tokens, tickets, and stamps
- tangible property other than money or securities, which includes inventory and office equipment. Intangible property, such as a copyright, is not included in this class of property for purposes of crime insurance. In addition, there are exclusions for certain types of property such as electronic data which may be covered under other types of insurance.

Causes of Loss

Crime coverages are written to provide protection from various causes of loss. Crime coverage forms include many terms, which are not necessarily the same as legal definition. These terms include employee theft, burglary, robbery, safe burglary, theft, computer fraud, disappearance and destruction, extortion, forgery, and alteration.

burglary

robbery

theft

computer fraud

- *employee theft*—the unlawful taking of money, securities, or other property by an employee

- *burglary*—the taking of property from inside an insured premises by a person who enters or leaves the premises unlawfully as evidenced by marks of forcible entry or exit
- *robbery*—the taking of property from one person by someone else who has either caused harm or threatened to cause harm to the person. It also includes situations in which property is taken in an unlawful act that a person has witnessed.
- *safe burglary*—burglary from a locked safe or vault or the removal of a safe or vault from inside a building
- *theft*—the unlawful taking of property, a broad term that includes robbery, burglary, shoplifting, and any other act of stealing

- *computer fraud*—a type of theft of property relating to the use of a computer to fraudulently transfer property from its rightful owner to someone else
- *forgery and alteration*—the creation of a document or signature that is not genuine (forgery); changes to a document in a manner that is neither authorized nor intended (alteration)

Policy Forms

ISO currently provides two crime coverage forms; one is written on a loss-sustained basis and the other on a discovery basis. When written on a loss-sustained basis, the only losses covered are those that occur during the policy period and are discovered during that time or within one year after the coverage expires. Subsequent policies will respond to losses if the specified discovery period has expired as long as there has been continuous coverage.

When written on a discovery basis, the current coverage pays all losses discovered while the coverage is in force or within a 60-day extended reporting period, whether or not there was previous coverage. Insurers may use an endorsement to eliminate coverage for losses that occurred prior to a specified retroactive date.

The new forms contain eight optional insuring agreements. None of the insuring agreements is mandatory, and the insured may select one or more. Coverages that apply are indicated by a limit for each one selected that appears on the declarations page:

- employee theft of money, securities, and other property
- forgery or alteration of an organization's checks (including drafts and promissory notes) by parties other than the organization's owners, employees, directors, or representatives
- theft of money and securities from inside the insured's premises or banking premises. There is also coverage for damage to the premises during the actual or attempted theft and to items on the premises, such as locked safes and cash registers.
- robbery and safe burglary of other property inside the insured's premises
- theft, disappearance, or destruction of money outside the insured's premises when in the custody of a messenger, and robbery of other property in the possession of a messenger
- computer fraud to transfer money, securities, or other property from the insured's premises or bank to somewhere else

- funds-transfer fraud for losses resulting from fraudulent instructions to a financial institution to transfer money from the insured's account to someone else
- the acceptance of bogus money orders or counterfeit currency. The acceptance must be in the United States or Canada, but the currency can be that of any country.

Numerous endorsements can be added to the primary forms to provide additional types of crime coverage.

Common Policy Provisions

Some provisions are common to many crime forms, For example:

- There is no coverage for losses caused by the named insured or any of its directors, trustees, or authorized representatives. In addition, there is no coverage for losses caused by employees except under the forms that specifically cover employee theft.
- Loss resulting from the unauthorized disclosure of confidential information is excluded.
- Coverage is for direct losses only. There is no coverage available for loss of business incurred or other consequential losses that might result from criminal acts.
- Most of the forms require the policyowner to notify the police if there is reason to believe that the loss resulted from a violation of law.
- The forms specify how settlements are valued. Money is valued at its face value. If the money is foreign, the insurer can pay the face value in the foreign currency or at its equivalent value in United States currency. Securities are valued as of the close of the business day a loss is discovered. The insurer can pay the value of the securities or replace them in kind. The insurer also has the option of paying the cost of a bond that is required for the issuance of replacement securities. Provided it is repaired or replaced, other property is valued at its replacement cost, and any disputes over value are settled by arbitration.

Inland Marine Insurance

inland marine insurance
Historically, marine insurers wrote insurance on ships and their cargoes, and fire insurance companies wrote insurance on property at fixed locations. As other types of transportation became more common, a hybrid type of insurance—*inland marine insurance*—evolved.

Today, inland marine policies and forms are used to write coverage for the following:

- goods in domestic transit
- property held by bailees
- mobile equipment and property
- property of certain dealers
- instrumentalities of transportation and communication
- difference in conditions (explained later)

Inland marine insurance is largely characterized by coverage for specific situations. It is often written on an open-perils basis but can also be written on a named-perils basis. Commercial property insurance forms often provide some coverage for loss exposures that can also be covered under inland marine forms, usually as additional coverages.

Goods in Transit

Inland marine policies are used to cover domestic goods in transit by mail, rail, truck, or aircraft. It is common for these policies to cover shipments only within and between the continental United States, Alaska, and Canada, but coverage can be endorsed—for example, for shipments to Mexico. Shipments to overseas locations (including Puerto Rico and Hawaii) by either ship or plane are typically insured under ocean marine policies.

Depending on the terms of sale, the responsibility for goods being shipped can fall on the shipper of the goods, the carrier of the goods, or the recipient of the goods. Any of these parties can buy insurance as needed.

The owners of property can purchase transit policies to provide property damage to their goods while in the course of transit by common carriers, contract carriers, or their own vehicles. A trip transit policy covers only the particular shipment specified in the policy. An annual transit policy covers all shipments during an annual period.

There are also policies, called motor truck cargo insurance, that common carriers or contract carriers can use to cover customers' goods when the carrier is legally liable for the damage. These policies do not cover damage for which the carrier is not liable, such as losses arising from acts of God, war, or neglect of the cargo owner.

Mobile Equipment and Property

Several inland marine forms are designed to insure property that is often moved from one location to another. Floater policies are examples of personal forms for this purpose. Examples of property that can be insured under commercial floater forms include the following:

- contractors' mobile equipment
- agricultural equipment
- cameras
- computer equipment
- farm animals
- fine art
- musical instruments
- physicians' and surgeons' equipment
- property on exhibition
- sales samples
- signs
- theatrical property

Property Held by Bailees

Bailees, such as dry cleaners, repair shops, and public warehouses, often have possession of significant amounts of customers' goods. A bailee liability policy can be purchased to cover damage to these goods when the bailee is legally liable. However, many bailees, for the sake of goodwill, purchase a bailees customers policy, which provides coverage whether or not the bailee is legally liable.

Property of Certain Dealers

Certain types of dealers in property have a significant amount of inventory that is likely to be transported. Special policies have been developed for these businesses that pick up not only the transportation loss exposure, but also provide coverage for merchandise in a store, furniture and fixtures of the dealer, and property of others in the dealer's care, custody, or control. These policies are often written for dealers in jewelry, furs, fine art, cameras, musical equipment, stamps, coins, and mobile and agricultural equipment.

Difference in Conditions

difference in conditions (DIC) insurance

A *difference in conditions (DIC) insurance* policy provides open-perils coverage to fill the gaps left by a policyowner's other commercial insurance policies. Traditionally, it was used to provide open-perils coverage to policyowners whose basic policies provided named-perils protection. Even though open-perils coverage is now relatively common, a difference in conditions policy is still used to provide earthquake and flood coverage. It is also used to cover loss exposures not addressed in basic policies, such as property in transit and the consequential losses that result from its damage or destruction. Another use is to provide coverage on overseas property that is broader than is available under the policies that can be purchased in many other countries. A DIC policy can be tailored to meet most of a policyowner's specific property insurance needs.

Instrumentalities of Transportation and Communication

Inland marine forms are used to insure instrumentalities of transportation and communication on either a named-perils or an open-perils basis. These types of property include bridges, tunnels, pipelines, television towers, satellite dishes, and power lines.

Equipment Breakdown (Boiler and Machinery) Insurance

Commercial property and business income insurance forms exclude damage caused by steam boiler explosion, electrical breakdown, or mechanical breakdown. The Equipment Breakdown Protection Coverage Form provides insurance for these types of losses. Insurers that write this type of coverage provide extensive inspection and loss control services to prevent losses, and these insurance company inspections are often accepted by governmental organizations that require periodic inspections of boilers and certain types of machinery.

Equipment breakdown coverage (referred to as boiler and machinery coverage by some insurers) agrees to pay for direct damage to covered property as a result of a breakdown to covered equipment. *Covered equipment* includes (1) equipment built to operate under internal pressure or vacuum other than weight of contents, (2) electrical or mechanical equipment that is used in the generation, transmission, or utilization of energy, (3) communication equipment, (4) computer equipment, and (5) equipment of the types previously mentioned that is owned by a utility and used solely to provide utility services to the insured's premises. *Covered property* is not just the covered equipment but also includes any real or personal property that is (1) owned by the named insured or (2) in the named insured's care, custody, or control and for which the named insured is legally liable. A *breakdown* is a direct physical loss to covered equipment that necessitates its repair or replacement and arises from one of the following causes: (1) failure of pressure or vacuum equipment, (2) mechanical failure, including rupture or bursting caused by centrifugal force, or (3) electrical failure, including arcing.

The insurer also agrees to pay the reasonable costs of temporary repairs and expediting repairs or the cost of permanent replacement of damaged property. Equipment breakdown insurance can also provide business income and extra expense coverage as well as coverage for spoilage to raw materials, property in process, or finished products if the spoilage is caused by the lack or excess of power, light, heat, steam, or refrigeration that results from a breakdown to covered equipment.

Farm Insurance

Homeowners-type policies are available for small- and medium-sized farm operations. Large farms and commercially owned farms are more likely to be insured under commercial forms. In many ways, these farm insurance forms are similar to other commercial insurance forms except that they are modified to meet farmers' unique loss exposures. Property forms can be written on either a named-perils or open-perils basis for various types of farm property, including livestock. An endorsement is available to cover loss of farm income if real or personal farm property is damaged or destroyed by an insured peril. A farm owner's home and personal property can also be insured under these forms.

A form to cover farmers' liability loss exposures essentially combines commercial general liability insurance, homeowners liability insurance for the farm owner's personal needs, and other insurance coverages unique to farming operations.

A special need of many farm owners is insurance on crops. Insurers offer crop hail insurance, which covers losses due to hail and can sometimes be endorsed to cover additional perils, such as windstorm or damage by livestock. These policies may also cover crops while being transported to places of storage. Broader crop insurance is written through the Federal Crop Insurance Corporation, and the federal government subsidizes the cost of this coverage. It provides insurance if a farmer's production of a crop is substantially less than expected for almost any reason, including drought, excessive moisture, and bad weather.

Another special need for some farmers is animal mortality insurance. This is essentially term life insurance and is used for such animals as valuable horses, registered cattle, or breeding stock. This type of coverage can also be purchased on racehorses, circus animals, show cats and dogs, and laboratory animals. These animals are generally covered for death from almost any cause as well as theft.

Commercial General Liability Insurance

commercial general liability (CGL) insurance

Commercial general liability (CGL) insurance is designed to cover a wide variety of liability loss exposures that can face an organization, including

- premises liability. An owner or tenant can be liable if someone is injured or property is damaged because of a condition in or arising out of premises that are owned or occupied.
- business operations liability. A business can be liable if bodily injury, personal injury, or property damage results from the activities of the business owner or an employee. These activities can take place on or away from the business location.
- products liability. Legal liability often arises from bodily injury or property damage caused by a defective product that is manufactured or sold by a business.
- completed operations liability. Similarly, legal liability can arise out of work that has been performed by an insured. For example, a fire can start as a result of an improperly installed gas line.
- contractual liability. In many cases, a business, through written or oral contracts, assumes liability for the acts of others.
- contingent liability. A business can face liability because of work performed by independent contractors, such as a subcontractor hired by a firm.

Forms for commercial general liability insurance do not cover all types of business liability. Because of exclusions, there is little or no coverage for (1) liability for injury to employees, (2) liability that arises from the rendering or failure to render professional services, or (3) liability that arises from aircraft, auto, or watercraft. Coverage that is available for several of these loss exposures is discussed later in this chapter.

The CGL Coverage Form has three coverages:

- Coverage A—Bodily Injury and Property Damage Liability
- Coverage B—Personal and Advertising Injury Liability
- Coverage C—Medical Payments

Coverage A—Bodily Injury and Property Damage Liability

Coverage A applies to legal liability and defense costs that arise from bodily injury and property damage.

This coverage does not apply to claims for damages based on libel, slander, or other personal injury offenses; errors; omissions; or wrongful acts that do not result in bodily injury or property damage, as these terms are defined in the policy. Coverage A of the CGL does not specifically exclude such losses, because it does not cover them in the first place. Personal injury is covered by Coverage B, and directors and officers liability insurance and other professional liability policies can provide for other liability coverage needs not met by a CGL.

Exclusions in the policy preclude coverage for losses that can be covered by workers' compensation and employers liability, aircraft, auto, and watercraft insurance. Policyowners must also be aware of other significant exclusions, including those briefly summarized as follows:

- bodily injury or property damage that is expected or intended from the insured's standpoint except when it results from reasonable force to protect persons or property
- certain contractual assumptions of liability. These include contractual assumptions made after bodily injury or property damage has occurred; some contracts with railroads; and some contracts with architects, engineers, and surveyors that involve their errors and omissions in performing professional duties.
- liquor liability of insureds who are in the business of manufacturing, distributing, selling, serving, or furnishing alcoholic beverages. Liquor liability arises from (1) causing or contributing to the intoxication of a person, (2) furnishing alcoholic beverages to underage persons, and (3) statutes pertaining to the sale, gift, distribution, or use of alcoholic beverages. Because this exclusion applies to those in the beverage business, it does not preclude so-called host liability coverage for other businesses that occasionally host a party or event where beverages are served. Firms in the beverage business need liquor liability coverage to protect against this significant loss exposure.

- pollution. The CGL Coverage Form excludes coverage for most pollution liability, including clean-up costs that arise from pollution. Endorsements and other forms can sometimes be used to cover this loss exposure.

- property damage to certain classes of property, including

  - property owned, rented, or occupied by the named insured

  - property loaned to the named insured

  - personal property in the care, custody, or control of the insured

  - premises that have been sold, given away, or abandoned, except property built by the named insured for sale and never occupied, rented, or held for rental

  - the part of real property being worked on by the named insured or a subcontractor if the damage arises from the work

  - the part of any property that must be restored, repaired, or replaced because the named insured's work was incorrectly performed on it

- damage to the insured's product that arises out of the product. For example, if a generator that the insured sold explodes, the cost to replace it would not be covered, but any resulting damage to other property is covered.

- damage to the insured's work. For example, if the named insured repaired a generator, there would be no coverage for damage to the insured's work if the completed work led to an explosion. However, liability coverage would exist for damage to other property as a result of the explosion.

- damage to impaired property or property not physically injured. This exclusion eliminates coverage to property that has not been physically damaged because of the insured's defective product, poor workmanship, or failure to perform a contractual agreement. For example, if a building cannot be occupied because the electrical work the named insured performed does not meet building code specifications, there is no physical damage to the building, but its owner can suffer a significant loss before the faulty work is corrected.

- product recall. Products are sometimes recalled voluntarily or because of government action. Claims for damages that arise from such actions are excluded. In addition, the manufacturer or distributor of the product can incur significant recall expenses. These loss exposures can be insured through specialty insurers.

- employment-related practices. Most insurers now exclude employment-related practices from CGL coverage. These practices include wrongful termination, discrimination, and sexual harassment. Because coverage is also often limited under other types of liability policies, many employers purchase separate employment practices liability insurance for these loss exposures.

- professional liability. The CGL Coverage Form does not provide coverage for employees for liability that arises out of their providing or failing to provide professional health care services. In addition, insurers frequently exclude the professional liability of certain classes of business by adding an endorsement. Professional liability is discussed in a later section of this chapter.

- liability for damages realized from the loss, or loss of use, of electronic data

Coverage B—Personal and Advertising Injury Liability

Coverage B provides protection for personal injury liability, which is discussed in earlier chapters. However, the CGL also covers advertising injury liability. Advertising injury can arise out of the following:

- oral or written publication of material that slanders or libels a person or organization or disparages its goods, products, or services

- oral or written publication of material that violates a person's right of privacy

- the use of another's advertising idea in an advertisement

- infringement upon another's copyright, trade dress, or slogan in an advertisement

Among the Coverage B exclusions are liability that arises out of (1) publication of material if the insured knows it is false, (2) willful violation of a penal statute or ordinance, (3) the failure of goods, products, or services to conform with advertised quality or performance, and (4) the wrongful description of the price of goods, products, or services.

Coverage C—Medical Payments

Coverage C is similar to the medical payments coverage of a homeowners policy. It pays medical expenses for bodily injury to persons injured on premises that the named insured owns or rents and because of the named insured's operations.

The coverage does not apply to the following persons:

- any insured other than a volunteer worker
- anyone hired to do work for or on behalf of any insured or a tenant of any insured
- a person injured on that part of a premises that the person normally occupies
- a person entitled to collect workers' compensation or disability benefits for the injury
- a person injured during physical exercises or athletic contests

Who Is an Insured?

Several categories of persons are insureds under the CGL Coverage Form: (1) the named insured and others with a family or business relationship to the named insured, (2) employees of the named insured, and (3) certain other persons or organizations.

Policy Provisions

Three specific policy provisions will be mentioned. These pertain to coverage territory, the events that trigger coverage, and policy limits.

Coverage Territory. Claims under the CGL Coverage Form are covered only if they take place in the coverage territory. For most claims, this includes the United States, its territories or possessions, Puerto Rico, and Canada. There is also coverage in international waters or airspace as long as travel is between the above locations. In addition, coverage is worldwide for products made or sold in the previously mentioned locations, for activities of persons who are away from these locations for short periods of time on business trips, and for personal and advertising injury offenses that take place through the Internet or similar electronic means of communication. Firms with broader business territories need to arrange appropriate coverage.

occurrence policy   **Events That Trigger Coverage.** The more commonly used CGL coverage form is written on an occurrence basis. In an *occurrence policy*, a liability claim is covered only for injury or property damage that occurs during the policy period. The policy that responds to a claim is the one that is in effect when the injury or property damage occurs, even if a claim is made years later.

claims-made policy   The other CGL coverage form is written on a claims-made basis. The *claims-made policy* that responds to a claim is the one in force when a claim is made, not the policy in force when the injury or property damage occurred.

The distinction between these two types of triggering events is discussed further in the section on professional liability insurance, for which claims-made coverage is more common.

CGL Coverage Forms

- Occurrence basis: Coverage applies to bodily injury or property damage that occurs during the policy period, regardless of when claims for damages are made.
- Claims-made basis: Coverage applies to claims made while the policy is in force, even when the loss-causing events occur earlier.

Limits of Liability. The CGL Coverage Form has several different limits of liability. Note that defense costs are payable in addition to these limits.

There are two aggregate limits that apply for an annual policy period. Once they are exceeded, the insurer has no further obligations to pay or defend claims. However, the limits are reinstated when a policy is renewed. One of these limits applies to claims that arise out of products or completed operations. The other is a general aggregate limit that applies to all other amounts paid under Coverages A, B, and C.

There are several sublimits. One of these applies to each occurrence for the sum of amounts paid under Coverage A and Coverage B. Another limit applies to personal and advertising liability claims by any one person or organization.

Finally, a Coverage C limit applies to medical payments for any one person during a year, and another limit applies to any damage to a premises that a business rents or temporarily occupies.

Commercial Auto Insurance

Three types of commercial auto insurance policies are as follows:

- Business Auto Coverage Form
- Garage Coverage Form
- Motor Carrier Coverage Form

Business Auto Coverage Form

The Business Auto Coverage (BAC) Form provides the most common type of commercial auto insurance and is similar to the Personal Auto Policy with respect to the coverages that can be purchased.

Coverages. Available coverages include liability, medical payments, no-fault benefits, uninsured motorists, underinsured motorists, collision, comprehensive, specified causes of loss, and towing and labor. Comprehensive is equivalent to the Personal Auto Policy's other-than-collision coverage. Specified-causes-of-loss coverage is a more limited named-perils alternative to comprehensive coverage.

The definition of *auto* is very broad and includes any land motor vehicle, trailer, or semitrailer—except mobile equipment—designed for use on public roads or subject to a compulsory insurance or financial responsibility law.

Covered Autos. Ten classifications of autos can be insured under the BAC Form, and different classifications of autos can be insured for each type of coverage. For example, one classification of autos might be insured for liability, while a different classification might be insured for collision. The ten classifications each have a symbol (a number) that is entered in the declarations section of the form by the appropriate coverage. The ten covered auto classifications are

- symbol 1—any auto
- symbol 2—owned autos only
- symbol 3—owned private passenger autos only
- symbol 4—owned autos other than private passenger autos
- symbol 5—owned autos subject to no-fault
- symbol 6—owned autos subject to compulsory uninsured motorists law
- symbol 7—specifically designated autos
- symbol 8—hired autos only
- symbol 9—nonowned autos only
- symbol 10—equipment subject to compulsory or financial responsibility or other motor vehicle insurance law

A *nonowned auto* is an auto owned by a named insured's employee or a member of his or her household but only while used in the named insured's business or personal affairs. A *hired auto* is an auto, other than a nonowned auto, that is leased, hired, rented, or borrowed by the named insured. Many businesses own no auto but have a loss exposure from accidents that involve nonowned and hired autos.

Temporary substitute autos, other than ones owned by the named insured, are also covered for liability coverage if the autos are used in place of a covered auto because of its breakdown, repair, servicing, loss, or destruction.

Who Is an Insured. The definition of insured includes the named insured, most other persons driving owned autos, and persons or organizations liable because of the acts or omissions of any of the previously mentioned persons. Although the business would have coverage, partners of a partnership, member of a limited liability company, and employees are not insured with respect to an auto they or a member of their household own.

Exclusions. Several exclusions in the BAC Form exclude situations that are covered under workers' compensation and employers liability insurance and the CGL Coverage Form. There is no coverage for property that is owned by or is in the care, custody, or control of an insured. However, this property can be insured under the appropriate property and inland marine forms. Claims that arise from pollutants carried by covered autos are also excluded, but separate coverage is available.

Limit of Liability. Liability coverage under the BAC Form is subject to a single limit of insurance that applies to all bodily injury, property damage, and covered pollution costs or expenses that arise from a single accident, and there is no aggregate annual limit. Defense costs are paid in addition to this limit. Split liability limits can be added by endorsement.

Losses for physical damage are limited to the lesser of (1) the actual cash value of the property at the time of loss or (2) the cost of repairing the property with other property of like kind and quality.

Other Commercial Auto Forms

Other commercial auto forms are designed for specific types of businesses.

Garage Coverage Form. The Garage Coverage Form is designed to meet the special needs of auto dealers. It is more than just an auto policy because it also provides liability coverage comparable to what is available under the CGL. It also provides an option for insuring the dealer's autos.

Motor Carrier Coverage Form. The Motor Carrier Coverage Form is designed for businesses that provide transportation by vehicles in the furtherance of commercial enterprise. These include common carriers, contract carriers, and private carriers who transport their own property. The coverage is similar to the BAC Form with modification for motor carriers' unique needs.

Workers' Compensation and Employers Liability Insurance

An employer faces a significant loss exposure for liability that arises from employees' injuries or deaths—either under tort law or because of government statutes. Coverage for this loss exposure is largely excluded under other liability policies and is usually insured under a Workers Compensation and Employers Liability (WC&EL) Insurance Policy. The National Council on Compensation Insurance developed the policy form used in a majority of states.

Some employers operate in states where a monopolistic state fund is the only insurer providing workers' compensation benefits. These employers may still need employers liability insurance, and a variation known as stopgap coverage is available to address this need. Other employers do not purchase workers' compensation insurance because they are large enough to self-fund workers' compensation benefits.

The WC&EL Policy contains three insuring agreements:

- Part One—Workers Compensation Insurance
- Part Two—Employers Liability Insurance
- Part Three—Other States Insurance

Each part is discussed below. The order of the discussion switches the last two parts because Part Three pertains to workers' compensation insurance. Some common endorsements are also described.

Part One—Workers Compensation Insurance

workers' compensation insurance

The states to which Part One applies are listed in the policy declarations. The *workers' compensation insurance* coverage states that the insurer agrees to pay all compensation and benefits required of the insured by the workers' compensation law of any state listed. These benefits vary from state to state. The insurer also agrees to pay any defense costs that arise out of a workers' compensation claim and certain other expenses the insured might incur as part of a claim.

The policy explains that the insured is responsible for any penalties under a workers' compensation law because of (1) willful misconduct, (2) illegal employment, (3) failure to comply with health and safety laws and regulations, and (4) discrimination against employees who file claims. If the insurer pays any of these penalties, the policyowner must reimburse the insurer.

The policy does not specify the benefits to be paid except by stating that it will pay what the workers' compensation law requires. If the policy and the law conflict, the policy agrees to conform to the law.

There is no specified dollar limit of liability for Part One. The policy will pay the state-mandated benefits to employees who are injured and to the survivors of any who die.

Part Three—Other States Insurance

This part of the WC&EL Policy provides coverage when an employer expands operations to include other states listed in the policy declarations for which Part Three applies. In many cases, the declarations list all states except those with monopolistic state funds or in which the insurer is not licensed to do business. The policyowner must notify the insurer when operations begin in these states.

Part Two—Employers Liability Insurance

employers liability insurance
Part Two of the WC&EL Policy—*employers liability insurance*—is a traditional form of liability insurance that protects an employer when it is sued because of injuries to employees. These suits occasionally arise for various reasons, including the following:

- An injured employee is not covered under a workers' compensation law.
- A spouse or family member sues for loss of services because of an employee's injury or death.
- An employee sues the employer in a capacity other than as an employer. For example, an employee injured by a faulty product of the employer may be able to bring suit against the employer as a manufacturer rather than as an employer.

- A spouse or family member sues because of bodily injury as a consequence of the injury or death of an employee. For example, a husband may have a heart attack after learning that an enraged coworker has killed his wife.
- The manufacturer of a product that injures one of the employer's workers can be sued by the worker and, in turn, sue the employer for improper maintenance of the product. This is referred to as a *third-party-over suit*.

In the insuring agreement under Part Two, the employers liability insurance agrees to pay damages and defend the insured because of bodily injury by accident or disease to an employee. For bodily injury by accident, the policy that covers an injury is the one in effect when the injury occurs. For bodily injury by disease, it is the policy that is in effect on the employee's last day of last exposure to the conditions causing or aggravating the injury.

The Part Two coverage contains three limits of liability, all of which the policyowner can select. One limit of liability applies to bodily injury by accident and is the maximum amount that will be paid for any one accident, regardless of how many employees are injured. There is no annual limit for bodily injury by accident. Two limits of liability apply to bodily injury by disease. One is per employee, and the other is an aggregate limit for the policy period.

Part Two contains several exclusions. Some exclusions eliminate coverage under Part Two for claims that arise out of state workers' compensation laws and various federal acts. Workers' compensation claims are covered under Part One, and endorsements, as described later, can be used to cover liability imposed by federal acts.

There is no coverage outside the United States, its territories or possessions, and Canada except for employees temporarily working in these locations.

Other exclusions eliminate coverage for

- most contractual liability. However, contractual liability is largely covered under the CGL Coverage Form.
- punitive damages for injury or death of illegally employed persons
- bodily injury to employees employed in violation of the law and with the knowledge of the insured or any executive officer
- damages that arise out of employment practices. As discussed later, this can be insured elsewhere.
- fines or penalties imposed for violation of federal or state law

Endorsements

Several endorsements are available to broaden the coverage of the WC&EL Policy.

The Voluntary Compensation and Employers Liability Coverage Endorsement obligates the insurance company to pay an amount equal to what is available under a state's workers' compensation law to employees who are not covered under the law. If an injured employee who is entitled to benefits brings suit, the coverage the endorsement provides reverts to the employer's liability coverage. A few insurers sell an additional endorsement to provide benefits for United States citizens hired to work abroad for indefinite periods. The benefits paid are those of the specific act or state listed in the endorsement.

Several federal acts either require the payment of workers' compensation benefits to certain groups of employees or allow certain groups of employees to sue employers, regardless of state limitations on employee suits. Endorsements are available for employees with loss exposures that might arise out of the following acts:

- United States Longshore and Harbor Workers Compensation Act (for most maritime workers other than crew members of vessels)
- Jones Act (for crew members of vessels)
- Defense Base Act (for civilian employees working at foreign military bases or working abroad for agencies of the United States government)
- Outer Continental Shelf Lands Act (for workers engaged in exploration of natural resources)
- Nonappropriated Fund Instrumentalities Act (for civilian employees of certain operations on military facilities)
- Migrant and Seasonal Agricultural Worker Protection Act
- Federal Employers' Liability Act (for employees of interstate railroads)

Professional Liability Insurance

professional liability insurance

Professional liability insurance can best be defined as insurance to protect against liability for the failure to use the degree of skill expected of a person in a particular occupation. Although the terms tend to be used interchangeably, professional liability insurance is often referred to as malpractice insurance for those occupations in which professional liability is likely to result from bodily injury and errors and omissions insurance for other occupations.

Several other types of insurance **are also** categorized as professional liability insurance. These are directors **and officers** liability insurance, employment practices liability insurance, employee benefits liability insurance, and fiduciary liability insurance.

Policies for Various Occupations

Professional liability policies have been developed for many occupations. For some occupations, several insurers write coverage; for other occupations, the number of insurers in the market may be only one or a small number. Businesses and employees both need protection against liability claims; in some cases, the business policy also covers employees. For example, a stockbrokerage firm might have a policy that covers it as well as the representatives it employs. In other cases, however, the employee may need to obtain his or her own coverage. Although coverage is often obtained directly through an insurance agent, professional associations are frequently a source of group coverage or plans of mass-marketed individual insurance.

Although ISO has developed standard policies for some occupations, individual insurers develop many professional liability policies. Policy variations exist among professions and insurers and should be evaluated with respect to limits, covered acts, defense coverage, coverage triggers, exclusions, and coverage territory.

Covered Acts. Professional liability policies differ in the exact wording of their insuring agreements. At a minimum, they cover acts, errors, or omissions that arise out of the rendering of professional services. For many professions, they also cover claims that result from the failure to render appropriate services.

Professional liability policies are not designed to cover routine business activities, such as the maintenance of an office premises, and they do not eliminate the need for a CGL or auto policy to cover the many business activities that do not involve professional services.

Defense Coverage. Professional liability policies cover defense costs. Some policies provide this benefit in addition to the stated policy limits, but most policies include these costs as part of the policy limits. In most policies, the insurer agrees to conduct the defense and has the right to appoint the defense attorney.

Most insurers now reserve the right to defend and settle claims as they see fit, but some policies still require the insurer to obtain the insured's consent before a claim is settled. If the insured does not consent to a settlement that has been recommended by the insurance company, many of these insurers limit policy benefits to the amount for which the claim could have been settled.

Coverage Triggers. Most professional liability policies are written on a claims-made basis. This means that the policy in force when a claim is made is the policy that covers the claim, not the policy in force when the event that caused the claim occurred. As long as a series of policies remains in force, the professional continues to have coverage for prior acts.

A series of claims-made professional liability policies typically ceases to pay claims if coverage is no longer carried unless the last policy contains an extended reporting period. In most policies, the extended reporting period is not automatic but must be requested and paid for. Some insurers make extended periods of only 1 to 3 years available, but others offer an unlimited extended period. The latter is of particular importance to someone, such as a retired obstetrician, who might be sued for a birth defect many years after a child is delivered.

Some insurers make extended reporting periods available if either the insurer or the policyowner terminates a policy. Other insurers make coverage available only if the insurer terminates the policy by cancellation or nonrenewal.

A few professional liability policies consider claims to have been made during the policy period as long as the insured, during the policy period, reports any circumstances of an event that might result in a future claim.

Significant gaps in coverage can occur if a policyowner switches from a policy written on a claims-made basis to one written on an occurrence basis or vice versa. Policyowners should make these changes with care and should obtain proper endorsements to eliminate any gaps.

Exclusions. Professional liability policies commonly exclude dishonest, criminal, or malicious acts; contractual liability; and punitive damages. Policies that cover errors and omissions also typically exclude bodily injury and damage to tangible property—which usually are, or should be, covered by a CGL.

Other exclusions may apply to a particular occupation's professional liability insurance.

Coverage Territory. Some professional liability policies cover claims that occur from activities anywhere in the world. Suits may or may not have to be brought in the United States or Canada. Other policies are written for a more restrictive territory, such as the United States and Canada.

Directors and Officers Liability Insurance

Clients who sit on a corporation's board of directors or a nonprofit organization's board of trustees sometimes do not realize that they face serious liability exposures. In recent years, especially in light of various corporate scandals, individual board members have increasingly been held accountable for their actions or inactions. Stockholders frequently bring suits alleging that they have been financially harmed by the corporation's negligent management. Other suits are brought against directors and officers by a corporation's employees, customers, and clients. Clients who are aware of these exposures—and their financial planners can help make them aware—are usually unwilling to take the risk of serving on corporate boards unless the corporation protects them against such suits.

Recognizing that corporate directors and officers face a severe liability exposure directly resulting from their service to the corporation, these corporations usually agree to indemnify their directors and officers for any costs that result from suits against them. Some state laws even require such indemnification.

directors and officers (D&O) liability insurance

Directors and officers (D&O) liability insurance is purchased by a corporation, but the corporation (unless it is a nonprofit organization) is often only the policyowner and not an insured; the insureds are the directors and officers.

D&O policies contain at least two insuring agreements. The first agreement covers the directors and officers for their personal liability as directors and officers that results from alleged wrongful acts, such as any breach of duty, neglect, errors, misstatements, misleading statements, omissions, and other acts. However, benefits provided under this coverage are usually not paid to the extent that the corporation has indemnified an officer or director.

The second insuring agreement reimburses the policyowner for any sum that it is required or permitted by law to pay to the directors and officers as indemnification.

Some directors and officers liability insurance policies have a third insuring agreement that covers the corporation for its liability arising from the acts of officers and directors.

D&O policies commonly exclude coverage for situations that are covered under a firm's other liability policies, such as bodily injury or damage to tangible property. Other exclusions often preclude coverage for claims that arise because of

- fraudulent acts
- acts that result in personal gain to which a director or officer is not entitled
- violations of certain securities laws
- failure to maintain adequate insurance for the corporation
- suits that involve one director or officer against another (with some exceptions)
- service on boards not affiliated with the corporation, but this coverage can be obtained if the corporation wants to encourage such service

Because of the high cost of D&O suits, defense costs are often subject to policy limits. In addition, D&O policies may have both an initial deductible and a percentage of participation above the deductible amount. For example, the insured (or the corporation) may be responsible for the first $25,000 of any claim and 5 percent of any remaining amount.

Employment Practices Liability Insurance

employment practices liability insurance

Coverage for employment-related claims is often excluded under CGL policies. *Employment practices liability insurance* can cover these claims.

An employment practices liability policy covers only those employment practices specified in the policy. These can include discrimination, sexual harassment, wrongful termination, breach of employment contract, failure to employ or promote, and wrongful discipline.

The parties insured usually include the business, its officers and directors, and some or all of its employees and former employees. Like the D&O policy, there may be both a deductible and percentage participation above the deductible.

Employee Benefits Liability Insurance

employee benefits liability insurance

Employee benefits liability insurance covers claims that arise out of improper advice or other errors or omissions in the administration of employee benefit plans. The parties insured usually include the business, its directors and stockholders, and officers and directors who are authorized to administer a plan. There is usually a per-employee policy limit as well as an aggregate limit for the policy period. Most policies have a deductible. The coverage is typically provided as an endorsement to the CGL policy for an extra premium.

Fiduciary Liability Insurance

fiduciary liability insurance

Fiduciary liability insurance also involves employee benefit plans, but it involves claims that result from the breach of fiduciary duties, such as pension plan losses because of improper investments. In some cases, employee benefits liability coverage is incorporated into a fiduciary liability insurance policy. Some policies cover all breaches of duties; other policies cover only breaches of duties imposed by ERISA. The insureds usually consist of the employer that sponsors a benefit plan; the plan itself; and past, present, and future directors, officers, and employees in their plan capacities as fiduciaries, administrators, or trustees.

Excess and Umbrella Liability Insurance

Many individuals obtain additional liability insurance coverage, over and above basic liability policies, under a personal umbrella policy. This same need exists for businesses. Careful analysis is necessary to determine the appropriate policy in order to avoid unintentional gaps in coverage. The following discussion briefly describes excess liability insurance and then goes into more detail on commercial umbrella liability policies.

Excess Liability Insurance

excess liability insurance

An *excess liability insurance* policy is written to provide additional liability limits for claims that are covered under specified underlying coverages. There is no drop-down coverage for claims excluded by the underlying coverages. Excess liability insurance is often used to obtain larger limits for such loss exposures as directors and officers liability when a firm's umbrella policy does not cover that particular loss exposure.

There are two basic types of excess liability insurance policies, and a policy can combine these two approaches. Under the first approach—referred to as a *follow form*—the excess policy incorporates the policy provisions and conditions of the underlying policies. Therefore, there are always additional limits available if a claim is covered by the underlying insurance. Under the second approach—referred to as a *self-contained policy*—the excess policy is subject to its own provisions and conditions. This can result in coverage gaps because a claim is paid by the excess policy only if it is covered under the provisions of both an underlying policy *and* the excess policy.

Some excess policies combine these two approaches by incorporating the provisions and conditions of the underlying policies and then making modifications for certain situations.

Commercial Umbrella Liability Insurance

Commercial umbrella policies operate much like the personal umbrella policies discussed in chapter 18. Unlike follow form excess policies, there is often coverage for claims that are excluded by the underlying policies. However, each insurer that sells commercial umbrella liability insurance usually uses its own form, and differences exist. Therefore, it is important to look at relevant policy provisions, including required underlying limits, insuring agreements, policy limits, events that trigger coverage, exclusions, and coverage territory. Adding to the complexity that can result from analyzing these variations is the terminology insurers use. For example, some insurers that sell commercial umbrella liability insurance policies refer to them as excess policies.

   Required Underlying Limits. The following are typical of required underlying limits:

- CGL

    - $1 million each occurrence
    - $2 million general aggregate
    - $2 million products-completed operations aggregate

- business auto liability—$1 million single limit

- employers liability
  - $100,000 bodily injury each accident
  - $100,000 bodily injury by disease each employee
  - $500,000 disease aggregate

Depending on the insurer, the type of policyowner, and the breadth of the umbrella policy, other underlying limits may be required for such loss exposures as liquor liability, watercraft, and aircraft.

The self-insured retention for claims the underlying policies do not cover may be as low as $500 for small businesses or as high as $25,000 or more for large businesses.

Insuring Agreements. Umbrella policies often have a single insuring agreement that applies to all covered losses. For example, an insurer can agree to pay up to $10 million for any claim in excess of the underlying limits for which the insured is liable for bodily injury, property damage, personal injury, or advertising injury. A policy can have a broader insuring agreement or separate insuring agreements to pick up other specialized loss exposures, such as professional liability, if the insurer is willing to cover them.

Policy Limits. Policy limits are selected by the insured, subject to insurer standards, and can be many millions of dollars. Most policies now have an aggregate limit that applies for the policy period. Defense costs can be included in the policy limit or in addition to it.

Events That Trigger Coverage. Umbrella policies are usually written on an occurrence basis, but some underlying policies can have a claims-made trigger. This can result in coverage gaps. Some insurers write umbrella policies with both types of triggers in the same policy and use the same trigger that applies to a claim under the underlying coverages.

Exclusions. Although commercial umbrella policies provide broader coverage than the underlying policies, they do contain exclusions, and it is important to evaluate these exclusions when obtaining coverage. In some cases, the exclusions are like those in the underlying policies, such as intentional injury and damage to the insured's product and work. In other cases, exclusions in the underlying policies are omitted from the umbrella policy or made less restrictive. However, the exclusions in an umbrella policy can be more restrictive. For example, it is not unusual to see an exclusion for punitive damages even though they may be covered by the underlying policies.

Coverage Territory. Most umbrella policies provide worldwide coverage. However, some policies require that suits be brought in the United States, its territories or possessions, or Canada.

Surety Bonds

surety bond

A *surety bond* is an agreement in which a surety provides a guarantee of indemnity if a second party, the principal, fails to perform a specified act or fulfill an obligation to a third party, the obligee. Surety bonds are not insurance contracts. However, they are often discussed within the context of insurance. Surety bonds are marketed by insurance agents and brokers, and many insurance companies also function as sureties.

Parties to a Surety Bond

There are three parties to a surety bond:

- The principal is the party who buys the bond and agrees to perform certain acts or fulfill certain obligations.

- The obligee is the party who is reimbursed if the principal fails to uphold the agreement.

- The surety is the party who agrees to indemnify the obligee because of the principal's failure to uphold the agreement. This indemnity can be in the form of cash or the fulfillment of the principal's obligation. The surety can be any person or organization but is usually an insurance company.

Characteristics of Surety Bonds

Surety bonds have several unique characteristics. These pertain to the liability of the principal, the expected losses, the coverage period, the bond limit, and the statutory nature of some bonds.

Liability of the Principal. Unlike an insured under an insurance contract, a principal who defaults on a bond is liable to the surety to the extent of any expenditure the surety incurs. The surety can require the principal to post collateral to repay the surety if the principal defaults.

Expected Losses. A surety generally expects to pay few losses and underwrites in a strict manner to determine whether the principal is capable of meeting its obligations. The surety will carefully scrutinize the principal's financial resources, character, and ability to perform.

Coverage Period. The coverage period under most surety bonds is indefinite, and the premium for the bond is paid only once. In most cases, neither the surety nor the principal can cancel a bond.

Bond Limit. A surety bond is written for a dollar limit, and that is the maximum amount of the surety's obligation to the obligee. Some bonds, however, pay court costs and interest on judgments in addition to the bond.

Most surety bonds pay only the obligee's actual loss if it is less than the bond limit, but some bonds are written on a basis that requires the forfeiture of the entire bond limit if the principal defaults.

Statutory versus Nonstatutory Bonds. Governmental ordinances, regulations, or statutes require many bonds, and the provisions of these statutory bonds and the obligations of the parties are established by law. The obligations of the parties under nonstatutory bonds are established by contract between the obligee and the principal.

Types of Surety Bonds

Several categories of surety bonds exist, and each is briefly described below. These include contract bonds, license and permit bonds, public official bonds, judicial bonds, federal surety bonds, and credit enhancement insurance.

Contract Bonds. Contract bonds guarantee that the principal will fulfill a commitment according to the provision of a contract. They are most often required of contractors and suppliers.

License and Permit Bonds. State and local governments often require persons who engage in many types of occupations to obtain licenses. They also frequently require permits for various types of activities. Various bonds are often required in connection with these licenses and permits. For example, a license or permit bond might guarantee that the principal will pay required taxes, including remittance of sales taxes collected, or that the principal will provide a means of indemnity for persons injured by its activities.

Public Official Bonds. Statutes often require that persons who are elected or appointed to certain positions be bonded. These bonds guarantee that the principal will uphold the promise made to faithfully and honestly perform the official duties of his or her office. These bonds terminate when a successor takes office.

Judicial Bonds. Numerous bonds are required by courts, and these can be divided into three broad categories—fiduciary bonds, litigation bonds, and bail bonds.

Fiduciary bonds are often required of persons who act as administrators, trustees, and guardians. They guarantee that a person who is responsible for the property of another will faithfully exercise his or her duties, give proper accounting of any property received, and make proper indemnification if the court determines that the principal is responsible for any financial loss that relates to the property.

The purpose of litigation bonds, also referred to as court bonds, is to require a person or organization that is seeking a court remedy to protect other parties from damages if the party seeking the remedy does not prevail.

Bonds are also required in many other legal activities, some of which are garnishment of wages, seizure of a tenant's personal property for back rent, suits to recover property, and removal of mechanic's liens and injunctions.

Finally, a bail bond guarantees that the bonded person will appear in court at the appointed time. Failure to do so can result in the forfeiture of the entire bail amount.

Federal Surety Bonds. Many federal agencies require businesses they regulate to carry bonds. These bonds guarantee that the business will comply with federal standards, including the payment of taxes and duties.

Credit Enhancement Insurance. Also referred to as financial guarantee insurance, this coverage is actually a form of surety bond that guarantees that principal and interest will be paid to the purchasers of debt instruments. The issuer of the debt, such as a municipality or a corporation, purchases the bond to enhance its audit rating.

Miscellaneous Bonds. Numerous other types of bonds do not fit into the previous categories. For example, an employer that self-insures its workers' compensation exposure will need to post a bond to guarantee that statutory benefits will be paid to employees.

Issuers of securities are often required to post a lost instrument bond to replace securities or other valuable papers that have been lost or stolen. The bond guarantees that the principal will reimburse the issuer if the original securities turn up and their holder is able to collect on them.

BUSINESSOWNERS POLICIES

businessowners policy (BOP)

A *businessowners policy (BOP)* is designed to provide property and liability coverage for small- to medium-sized businesses and organizations that meet certain eligibility requirements. A BOP resembles a homeowners policy in the sense that it includes a package of coverages designed to meet most of a typical policyowner's needs. Because it presents a prepackaged set of coverages, a BOP often includes some coverages that might otherwise be overlooked. Where it meets a client's needs, a BOP is usually more convenient and less expensive than purchasing each coverage individually in a commercial package policy.

Despite its breadth, a businessowners policy usually is not the only insurance policy a small business needs. A business with employees generally also needs workers' compensation insurance. A business that owns one or more motor vehicles requires a business auto insurance policy.

ISO has developed a BOP form, but the ISO form does not dominate the market. Many insurers use their own forms, which may be broader or more restrictive than the ISO form. Therefore, rather than specifically examining the ISO form, the discussion here deals with BOPs in general.

Eligibility

BOPs are intended for small- to-medium-sized standard main-street businesses with no unusual features. Every insurer has its own BOP eligibility rules, which typically permit a BOP to be written on the following businesses:

- *retail, wholesale, service, or processing buildings and personal property.* This category includes shoe stores, furniture clothing stores, and so forth subject to a maximum square foot area, typically 15,000 to 25,000 square feet. Not only owner-occupants but also landlords and tenants are typically eligible for a BOP.
- *office buildings.* Eligibility is usually restricted to buildings of a certain height, such as six stories, or a certain total floor area. Tenants occupying offices in a larger building may also be eligible.
- *apartment buildings.* Size restrictions limit eligibility to a certain height, such as six stories, or a certain number of apartments.

- *contractors*. Some insurers will write a BOP on smaller construction contractors that present no unusual risks.
- *restaurants*. BOPs are often available for fast-food restaurants.

Although many types of businesses can be eligible for coverage under a BOP, several are specifically ineligible. Typically ineligible are such businesses as garages, auto dealers, parking lots, bars, restaurants with extensive cooking operations, places of amusement, and banks.

Policy Coverages

The liability coverage of a BOP is essentially the same as that of the commercial general liability (CGL) policy discussed earlier in this chapter.

Most insurers offer a BOP policy that provides property coverage on an open-perils basis, and many also provide a named-perils version. The open-perils version, often referred to as a special-form policy, is by far the more popular. A typical BOP includes several standard features, described below, that differentiate it from the standard coverage a commercial property form provides.

Standard Replacement Cost Coverage

BOPs typically value both buildings and personal property on a replacement cost basis, often with an actual cash value option. In contrast, standard commercial property policies provide actual cash value coverage with a replacement cost option.

Insurance-to-Value Provision

In contrast to commercial property policies that generally include a coinsurance provision, BOPs were traditionally written with neither a coinsurance provision nor any other insurance-to-value provision. Many insurers still have no insurance-to-value provision, but ISO forms and others include a provision similar to the loss clause of the homeowners policy. A policyowner who carries insurance to at least 80 percent of the replacement cost value of the property is entitled to have losses settled on a replacement cost basis. Recovery for those who are underinsured is limited to the actual cash value of the lost or damaged property or, for those who are only slightly underinsured, an amount somewhere between the actual cash value and the replacement cost value of the property as determined by applying the coinsurance formula.

Automatic Seasonal Increase Provision on Personal Property

Some BOPs include a provision that automatically adjusts the personal property coverage limit to allow for seasonal changes in inventory values that affect some businesses. If the policyowner carries insurance in an amount equal to at least 100 percent of the monthly average value of the property during the 12 months preceding the loss, the limit is automatically increased by 25 percent.

EXAMPLE

Bullina China Shop increases its dinnerware inventory twice a year in preparation for Christmas shopping and June weddings. Bullina's average inventory value over the past 12 months was $60,000, and other store contents are valued at $20,000. When a windstorm swept through the area on June 1 and destroyed the entire shop, Bullina's inventory was valued at $80,000. Bullina currently carries personal property coverage under a BOP with a $80,000 limit.

Bullina will recover $100,000—$80,000 for stock and $20,000 for other personal property—under its BOP, which includes the automatic seasonal increase provision.

Business Income and Extra Expense Coverage Automatically Included

Most BOPs automatically include business income and extra expense coverage subject to neither a dollar limit nor a coinsurance requirement. Most do impose a 1-year time limit, agreeing to pay lost income and extra expenses during a period of interruption not exceeding 12 months.

Property Coverage Options

Many insurers offer some of the following coverage options under their BOP program, often with relatively low limits or with coverage more restrictive than that available under a commercial property form or in a separate policy. The following coverages may either be included automatically or available by endorsement:

- employee dishonesty
- money and securities
- forgery
- glass breakage
- outdoor signs
- mechanical breakdown

- money orders and counterfeit paper currency
- computer coverage
- accounts receivable coverage
- valuable papers and records coverage

Nonowned and Hired Auto Liability Coverage

Insurance on owned autos is not available in a BOP. However, a business whose only auto liability exposure involves the use of employee-owned autos or borrowed or rented vehicles can often protect itself against these incidental exposures by endorsing nonowned and hired cars liability coverage to a BOP.

CHAPTER REVIEW

Key Terms and Concepts

commercial property insurance
business income insurance
extra expense insurance
burglary
robbery
theft
computer fraud
inland marine insurance
difference in conditions (DIC)
  insurance
commercial general liability (CGL)
  insurance
occurrence policy

claims-made policy
workers' compensation insurance
employers liability insurance
professional liability insurance
directors and officers (D&O) liability
  insurance
employment practices liability
  insurance
employee benefits liability insurance
fiduciary liability insurance
excess liability insurance
surety bond
businessowners policy (BOP)

Review Questions

Review questions are based on the learning objectives in this chapter. Thus, a [3] at the end of a question means that the question is based on learning objective 3. If there are multiple objectives, they are all listed.

1. A client has just purchased a building and started a small parts manufacturing business. Without getting into too much detail about the specifics of his business, you recommend that he see an insurance agent who specializes in commercial property and liability coverages. He replies, "I know I need insurance on the building, the equipment, and my inventory, but what other coverages do I need to see an agent about?" What important coverages might he need? [1]

2. What are the three common types of business income insurance forms, and what coverage does each provide? [1]

3. What are the three broad classes of property covered alone or in various combinations by commercial crime insurance forms? [1]

4. What policy provisions are common to many crime insurance forms? [1]

5. In which situations are inland marine policies and forms currently used to provide coverage? [1]

6. What type of commercial liability coverage should you recommend to a client in each of the following situations?
    a. a client who may be sued if a defective product is manufactured or sold [1]
    b. a client who is concerned about being sued by a person who is injured or whose property is damaged by the client's ongoing business activities at the person's home [1]
    c. a client who is concerned about being sued by a customer who is injured or whose property is damaged because of a condition in the client's store (such as a wet floor) [1]
    d. a client who is concerned about being sued by a person who is injured or whose property is damaged by work the client already performed [1]
    e. a general contractor who is concerned about being sued for poor work done by a subcontractor [1]
    f. a client who is concerned with having to pay a judgment against the railroad if the railroad is sued by the parents of a child who is injured while playing on the side track on the client's business property [1]
    g. a client who is concerned about being held liable for the employees who drive her company's delivery trucks [1]
    h. a client who is concerned about being sued by an injured employee not covered by the workers' compensation law, or by an employee's spouse or family member because of the employee's injury or death [1]
    i. a dentist who is concerned about being sued by one of his patients [1]
    j. an insurance agent who is concerned about being sued by a client for bad advice about the appropriate coverages to purchase [1]
    k. a client who is concerned about members of the board of directors of her corporation being sued for breaches of corporate duty [1]
    l. a client who is concerned about his business being sued for discrimination or sexual harassment [1]

7. What are the similarities and differences between excess liability insurance and commercial umbrella liability insurance? [1]

8. What are the unique characteristics of surety bonds? [1]

9. What are the key features of the businessowners policies commonly available? [2]

10.   After his retirement, Edwin agreed to serve on the boards of directors of a bank and a for-profit hospital. He also agreed to serve on the board of trustees of a local not-for-profit charity. As an afterthought, he asks you, as his financial planner, whether this service involves any special risks to consider in his planning. How would you respond? [1]

a priori reasoning • reasoning with conclusions that are based on self-evident propositions (also known as *deductive reasoning*). As an example, one can reason deductively, or *a priori*, that the probability of a result of tails in the flip of a balanced coin is one chance in two. *Compare* inductive reasoning.

AAIS (American Association of Insurance Services) • an advisory organization that provides various services to its member companies, including the development and filing of standardized property and liability insurance forms

absolute liability • *See* strict liability

accelerated benefits provision • a provision in a life insurance policy that allows death benefits to be paid to the policyowner prior to the insured's death under certain circumstances such as if the insured is terminally ill

accidental death • a death that is caused by an unintentional event that is sudden and unexpected

accidental death benefit rider • a life insurance rider that increases the death benefit, usually doubling it, if the insured dies accidentally

accumulation period • the period of time in a deferred annuity during which the purchase price is deposited with the insurer and accumulated at interest

accumulation unit • a unit of a variable annuity that is purchased during the annuity's accumulation stage. Units are revalued each month.

actively-at-work requirement • a provision in a group insurance master contract specifying that the employee is not eligible for coverage if he or she is not actively on the job on the otherwise effective date of coverage. Coverage commences when the employee returns to work.

activities of daily living (ADLs) • activities such as eating, bathing, and dressing. The inability to perform a specified number of these activities triggers eligibility for benefits in a long-term care insurance contract.

actual cash value • a method of valuing property. Usually, it is defined as replacement cost minus physical depreciation but in some cases is defined as fair market value.

add-on plan • a no-fault type of auto insurance system that makes first-party benefits available but does not restrict the right to sue for damages

additional living expenses • the extra costs of maintaining a family's standard of living while the family's residence is being repaired or rebuilt following a covered loss. Covered by homeowners policies.

adult day care • day care at centers specifically designed for the elderly who live at home but whose spouses or families cannot stay home to care for them during the day

advance-premium mutual • a mutual insurance company that establishes the full premium for coverage at the start of the policy period

adverse selection • selection against the insurance company. It is the tendency for those who know that they are highly vulnerable to specific pure risks to be most likely to acquire and to retain insurance to cover related losses.

advertising injury liability • liability that can arise out of (1) oral or written publication of slanderous or libelous material or (2) material that violates a person's rights of privacy. It also includes liability that arises through the misappropriation of advertising ideas or styles of doing business and infringement of copyright, title, or slogan.

advisory organization • an organization that assists insurance companies in such areas as gathering and analyzing statistical information for rate-making purposes and drafting recommended policy language

age setback • an assumption for rating purposes that an annuitant is some years younger than his or her actual age

agent (insurance) • a legal representative of an insurance company with authority to act on behalf of the insurer

agreed value • a method of valuing property in which value is determined before loss and the agreed value is paid in the event of a total loss

alien insurer • an insurer that is formed in a country other than the United States but that writes business in the United States

all-risks policy • *See* open-perils policy

alteration • the act of making changes to a document in a manner that is neither authorized nor originally intended

Alzheimer's facility • a facility with a high level of staffing and other capabilities to provide the personal assistance individuals with Alzheimer's disease need. It may be a stand-alone facility or part of a nursing home or assisted-living facility.

American Agency System • *See* independent agency system

annual exclusion • the dollar amount of a gift exempt from federal transfer taxation. This amount can be doubled if the donor is married and the donor's spouse elects to split the gift on a timely filed gift tax return.

Annual Statement • a document that insurance companies are required to file with state insurance commissioners to report the company's current financial conditions and changes that have occurred during the year

annual transit policy • a type of inland marine insurance policy that covers all shipments during an annual period

annuitant • the person whose life governs the duration of benefit payments under a life annuity; usually also the person who receives periodic annuity payments

annuity • a periodic payment to begin at a specified or contingent date and to continue for a fixed period or for the duration of a designated life or lives

annuity certain • an annuity with benefit payments that continue for a definite period of time without being linked to the duration of a specified human life

annuity principle • the concept of many persons pooling their funds to provide annuities to all while they live or for some period certain. Each person receives annuity payments consisting of the annuitants' principal, the unliquidated principal of other annuitants who die early, and investment income on these funds.

annuity unit • a variable annuity's accumulation units are converted to a fixed number of annuity units at the beginning of the liquidation period. The dollar value of each unit fluctuates with the investment performance of the separate account underlying the annuity.

antigag clause rules • legislation that prevents managed care organizations from including provisions in contracts with doctors that prevent them from discussing with patients treatment options that may not be covered under their plans or from referring extremely ill patients for specialized care outside of their plans

any-occupation • a strict definition of disability that requires a person to be so severely disabled that he or she cannot engage in any occupation

apparent authority • authority that, in the absence of contrary action by the principal, appears to a reasonable person to be possessed by the principal's agent **applicant** the person or organization that applies for insurance

Archer MSA • a type of personal savings account from which unreimbursed medical expenses can be paid. It can be used for employees of small employers or the self-employed and is established in conjunction with a high-deductible health plan. New Archer MSAs can no longer be established.

assessment mutual • a mutual insurance company that reserves the right to levy assessments on its policyowners to cover adverse underwriting experience

assigned risk • *See* automobile insurance plan

assignment provision • a clause that specifies the conditions under which a policyowner can transfer some or all of his or her ownership rights in the policy to another

assisted-living care • care provided in facilities that provide care for the frail elderly who are no longer able to care for themselves but who do not need the level of care provided in a nursing home

assumption-of-risk doctrine • a common-law defense formerly available to employers under which a worker could not recover damages for an injury if he or she knowingly assumed the risks inherent in the job

attained age rate • the insurance rate at the insured's present age, used for attained age term conversions and sometimes for long-term care insurance upgrades

attitudinal hazard • a condition of carelessness or indifference on the part of an individual as to whether a loss occurs and/or the size of a loss if one does occur

attorney-in-fact • the person or entity that directs a reciprocal exchange

auto insurance • a property and liability insurance policy that provides (1) liability coverage for losses that arise out of the use, operation, or maintenance of an auto, (2) medical payments benefits, (3) uninsured motorists benefits, and (4) physical damage coverage

automatic premium loan option • life insurance policy provision by which a delinquent premium is automatically paid by a policy loan

automatic reinsurance • *See* treaty reinsurance

automobile insurance plan • a state plan that assigns drivers who have been unable to obtain auto insurance to insurance companies in proportion to their volume of business in a state. Formerly called *assigned risk*.

aviation insurance • insurance policies to provide liability, physical damage, and medical payments coverage for the owners of aircraft

backdating • issuance of a life insurance policy as if it had been purchased when the insured was younger in order to obtain a lower periodic premium

bail bond • a bond that guarantees that the bonded person will appear in court at the appointed time

bailee • a person or organization in temporary custody of the property of another for some reason, such as for service or repair of the property

bailees customers policy • an insurance policy that covers customers' goods whether or not a bailee is liable for their loss or destruction

bailment • the situation in which a person or business has temporary custody of the property of others

bail-out provision • a clause in an annuity contract that allows the purchaser to surrender the contract without a surrender charge if the interest rate being credited falls below a specified but nonguaranteed minimum

bed reservation benefit • a benefit under a long-term care insurance policy that continues to pay a long-term care facility for a limited time if a patient must temporarily leave because of hospitalization or another reason. Without a continuation of benefits, the bed might be rented to someone else and unavailable upon the patient's release from the hospital.

beneficiary • the person or entity designated to receive the death proceeds of a life insurance policy

binder • a temporary written or oral agreement between an agent and an applicant for insurance whereby the principal-insurer is committed to provide the desired insurance

birthing center • a facility, separate from a hospital, designed to provide a homelike atmosphere for the delivery of babies. Deliveries are performed by nurse-midwives, and mothers and babies are released shortly after birth.

Blue Cross and Blue Shield plans • organizations formed for the purpose of prepaying subscribers' medical care expenses. Blue Cross plans provide coverage primarily for hospital expenses, and Blue Shield plans provide coverage primarily for physicians' services.

boatowners policy • a package policy that provides liability and physical damage coverage for small- and medium-sized boats

bodily injury • bodily harm, sickness, or disease. It includes required care, loss of services, and death that results.

boiler and machinery insurance • *See* equipment breakdown insurance

branch manager • an insurance company employee who heads up a branch office for marketing the insurer's products in a given geographic area

branch office system • in life insurance, a marketing system whereby insurers establish branch offices in the areas where they write business. The offices are headed by branch managers.

broker • a marketing intermediary between the insurer and policyowner who represents the policyowner

builders risk insurance • commercial property insurance that provides protection for buildings and construction and the unique exposures associated with these types of structures

burglary • the removal of property from inside a premises by a person who enters or leaves the premises unlawfully as evidenced by marks of forcible entry or exit

business income insurance • insurance that covers business losses after the occurrence of a direct physical damage loss that results in the suspension of business operations. The three basic types of losses covered include net income, normal ongoing business expenses, and extra expenses. Formerly called *business interruption insurance*.

business insurance • the category of insurance used by businesses and other organizations

business interruption insurance • *See* business income insurance

business operations liability • bodily injury, personal injury, or property damage liability that results from the activities of a business owner or employee

business overhead expense insurance • a policy available to cover many of the ongoing costs of operating a business while the business owner is totally disabled

businessowners policy (BOP) • a common type of policy designed to meet most property and liability needs of certain small- and medium-size businesses

buy-sell agreement • a contract binding the owner of a business interest to sell the business interest for a specified or determinable price at his or her death or disability and binding a designated purchaser to buy at that time

buy-up plan • an employee benefit plan under which a covered person can purchase additional coverage (for example, life insurance or disability income insurance) at his or her own expense. Also referred to as a *supplemental plan*.

cafeteria plan • an employee benefit plan under which an employee can use a specified amount of employer funds and/or salary reductions to design his or her own benefit package from an array of available benefits

calendar-year deductible • a deductible that applies to medical expenses incurred within a calendar year. A new deductible must be satisfied in a subsequent calendar year.

cancelable • a contract feature that allows the insurance company to terminate the coverage at any time (and perhaps for any reason) during the term of coverage by notifying the insured

capital needs analysis • a system for determining how much life insurance a client needs if the principal sum is to be preserved in the process of meeting the financial objectives for his or her survivors

capital sum • a lump sum payable under a disability income policy if the insured suffers a serious injury, such as the loss of sight or severance of a hand or a foot

captive agent system • *See* exclusive agency system

captive insurer • an insurance company owned by a parent corporation and formed primarily to insure the loss exposures of the parent corporation

care coordinator • a licensed health care practitioner who assesses a person's condition, evaluates care options, and develops an individualized plan of care that provides the most appropriate services

carryover provision • a provision in a medical expense plan that allows any expenses applied to the deductible and incurred during the last 3 months of the year to also be applied to the deductible for the following year

carve-out (benefit plan) • the practice of excluding certain classes of employees from a benefit plan and providing benefits to them under an alternative arrangement. Carve-outs are generally used to contain employee costs or provide broader or tax-favored benefits to key employees and executives.

carve-out (medical expense insurance) • coverage under a medical expense plan that has been singled out for individual management by a party other than the employer or the employee's primary health plan provider

cash option • an option that allows an annuitant, at the start of the liquidation period, to withdraw the funds in cash, rather than as an annuity

cash refund annuity • a refund annuity that specifies if the annuitant dies before receiving total benefit payments equal to the purchase price of the annuity, all or a stated percentage of the difference will be refunded in cash

cash value • the savings element that builds up in a permanent life insurance policy, an endowment policy, or an annuity contract

cash value accumulation test • a test to determine whether an insurance policy meets the definition of a life insurance policy for federal income tax purposes. To qualify under this test, the cash value must not exceed the net single premium that would be needed to fund the policy's death benefit.

cash value life insurance • a type of life insurance under which premiums are sufficient not only to pay the insurer's death claims and expenses but also to build up a savings fund within the policy

casualty loss • usually considered a loss that is sudden, unexpected, or unusual and which results in damage, destruction, or loss of property

catastrophic benefits rider • a disability income insurance rider that makes additional benefits available if the insured suffers a severe disability that includes cognitive impairment or the inability to perform two or more of six activities of daily living

cede • transfer a portion of the amount of insurance written by a primary or original insurer to a reinsurer

certificate of insurance • a description of the group insurance coverage provided to employees. It is given to the employees, but it is not part of the master contract.

choice no-fault • a modified no-fault law that allows an insurance applicant either to elect traditional tort coverage or to elect no-fault coverage at a reduced premium

chronically ill individual • a person who, for purposes of long-term care insurance, is expected to be unable to perform at least two activities of daily living (ADLs) for at least 90 days or who needs substantial services to protect the individual from threats to health and safety due to substantial cognitive impairment

civil wrong • a legal wrong other than a criminal wrong. It is based upon torts or contracts.

claims adjusting • the basic insurance function of paying covered claims

claims-made policy • a liability insurance policy that covers only claims that are first reported during the policy period as long as the event that caused the claims occurred after a specified retroactive date in the policy

class rate • an average price per unit of insurance that applies to a category or classification of similar insureds

closed-panel plan • a benefit plan under which covered persons must obtain services from practitioners selected by the provider of benefits

COBRA • a provision of the Consolidated Omnibus Budget Reconciliation Act of 1985 that requires group health plans to allow employees and certain beneficiaries to extend their current health insurance coverage at group rates for up to 36 months following a qualifying event that results in the loss of coverage

coinsurance (medical expense insurance) • the percentage of covered expenses under a medical insurance plan that is paid by the insurance company once a deductible is satisfied. Eighty percent is common.

coinsurance (property insurance) • a provision whereby a property owner must share in a loss if the amount of insurance carried is less than a specified percentage of the property's insurable value

COLA rider • *See* cost of living adjustment rider

collateral assignment method • the technique used with split-dollar life insurance whereby the employee owns the policy and has the responsibility for paying the premium. The employer's share of the policy proceeds is secured by an assignment.

collision • in auto insurance, the upset of an auto or its impact with another vehicle or object

commercial general liability (CGL) insurance • commercial liability insurance designed to cover a wide variety of liability loss exposures that can face an organization, including premises, business operations, products, completed operations, contractual, and contingent liability

commercial insurance • as contrasted with personal insurance, a category of insurance—particularly of property and liability insurance—that is purchased by businesses and other organizations

commercial package policy • a policy that covers many of the property and liability loss exposures of a business and contains two or more separate coverage forms

commercial property insurance • coverage for losses to real and personal business property. As commonly used, the term applies to policies that cover losses from most perils other than those that relate to crime, transportation, and equipment breakdown. Numerous forms cover various classifications of property from specified perils or on an open-perils basis.

commingling of funds • an unfair trade practice that occurs when an agent mixes the insured's or insurer's funds with the agent's personal funds

common accident provision • a provision in a major medical expense contract whereby if two or more members of the same family are injured in the same accident, the covered medical expenses for all family members will, at most, be subject to a single deductible, usually equal to the individual deductible amount

comparative negligence • the legal principle whereby an injured party can recover a portion of the damages for his or her injuries if he or she was also negligent. In some jurisdictions, a plaintiff can recover only if his or her negligence is less (or not more) than the defendant's negligence.

compensatory damages • damages designed to financially compensate, or reimburse, a claimant who has suffered a loss for which another party is legally responsible

completed operations liability • bodily injury or property damage liability caused by work that has been performed by an insured

comprehensive coverage • *See* other than collision

comprehensive dental plan • *See* nonscheduled dental plan

comprehensive long-term care insurance policy • a long-term care insurance policy that combines benefits for facility care and benefits for home health care services into a single contract. *Also known as* an integrated policy.

compulsory insurance law • a law in most states that requires the owners of autos to carry liability insurance before a vehicle can be registered

computer fraud • the use of a computer to fraudulently transfer property from its rightful owner to someone else

concealment • failure by one party to a contract to affirmatively disclose to the other party all of the important facts that are the exclusive knowledge of the first party. Even if it is not intentional or fraudulent, concealment can make an insurance contract voidable.

condition precedent • a condition in an insurance contract that must be fulfilled by the policyowner before the insurer can be held liable for a loss

condition subsequent • a condition in an insurance contract that must be fulfilled by the policyowner after the insurer has become liable in order to avoid the insurer's release from liability

conditional contract • an agreement in which one party has an obligation to perform only if the other party meets certain conditions specified in the agreement

conditional receipt • a receipt given to an applicant for life insurance in exchange for the payment of the first premium in which the insurer, through its agent, specifies that the coverage will be effective as of the date of the receipt, subject to the condition that the proposed insured later be found to have been insurable as of the date the receipt was issued

condominium commercial unit-owners coverage • commercial property insurance that covers the interest of the owner of a commercial condominium unit

consideration • a right or something of value (such as money) given to another party in exchange for the assumption of an obligation by the other party. Consideration is a requirement for a valid contract.

consumer-directed medical expense care • an approach to medical expense insurance that gives employees increased choices and responsibilities involving their health care

contingent beneficiary • the person or entity designated to receive the death proceeds of a life insurance policy if the primary beneficiary predeceases the insured

contingent liability • legal liability that arises because of work performed by an independent contractor, such as a subcontractor of a business

contingent payee • in life insurance, the person or entity designated to receive the remaining death proceeds if the beneficiary dies after the insured but before the beneficiary has received the full amount of the proceeds payable

continuing care retirement community (CCRC) • a facility that provides lifetime care for older adults. Initial occupancy is in an independent living unit, but a resident must move to an assisted-living or nursing home unit if health deteriorates.

contract of adhesion • a contract that is prepared in all of its details by one party, rather than having its terms bargained over between the parties to the contract. Because insurance policies are generally contracts of adhesion, if ambiguity exists in the terms, the courts are likely to rule in favor of the insured and against the insurer (the party that drew up the contract).

contract of indemnity • a policy in which the insurer agrees, if a covered loss occurs, to pay an amount directly related to the amount of the loss

contractual liability • the assumption of legal liability of others through a written or oral contract

contributory negligence • the legal principle whereby an injured person cannot recover damages for injuries from another negligent party if the injured party was also negligent

contributory plan • a type of employee benefit plan in which the insured pays a portion of the premium cost

conversion • a provision in a group benefit plan that gives an employee whose coverage ceases the right to convert to an individual insurance policy without providing evidence of insurability. The conversion policy may or may not be identical to the prior group coverage.

convertibility • a feature in term life insurance that allows the policyowner to replace the term coverage with permanent individual life insurance without having to show evidence of insurability. In group insurance, the right is available only at certain times, including termination of the insured from the group or from an eligible class within the group.

coordination-of-benefits provision • a provision in most group medical expense plans under which priorities are established for the payment of benefits if an individual is covered under more than one plan. Coverage as an employee is generally primary to coverage as a dependent. When parents are divorced, the plan of the parent with custody is primary, the plan of the current spouse of the parent with custody is secondary, and the plan of the parent without custody pays last. Other rules apply to other situations.

copayment • a fixed dollar amount that an insured must pay for a covered medical service

cost-of-living adjustment (COLA) rider • increases in benefit levels because of changes in some index, such as the CPI. These increases apply to Social Security income benefits and sometimes to benefits under private insurance and retirement programs.

cost shifting • the attempt by employers to control benefit costs by shifting these costs to employees. Examples include the requirement of larger employee contributions and increased deductibles.

counteroffer • an offer made by an offeree to the original offeror in lieu of acceptance of the original offer

coverage gap • under Medicare prescription drug plans, the range in which the beneficiary must pay the full cost of prescription drugs. Under a standard benefit structure, the gap begins after a beneficiary has incurred a specified dollar amount of expenses and continues until the plan begins paying again after total drug costs reach a second specified dollar amount. *Also called* doughnut hole.

covered auto • a vehicle specifically listed in the policy declarations of an auto insurance policy. In the Personal Auto Policy, "your covered auto" also includes newly acquired autos, trailers, and temporary substitute vehicles.

credibility • the degree of reliability one can place on past results as an indicator of likely future results

credit, Social Security • the basis on which eligibility for benefits under Social Security is determined. Up to four credits may be earned in any calendar year. *Also referred to as* quarter of coverage.

credit enhancement insurance • creditable prescription drug coverage a prescription drug coverage under other plans that is deemed to be equivalent to or better than the standard benefit plan for Medicare prescription drug coverage

credit enhancement insurance • a form of surety bond that guarantees that the principal and interest will be paid to the purchasers of a debt instrument. Also known as *financial guarantee insurance*.

creditable prescription drug coverage • prescription drug coverage under other plans that is deemed to be equivalent to or better than the standard benefit plan for Medicare prescription drug coverage

crime insurance • various insurance coverages for losses that arise from illegal activities, such as burglary, robbery, extortion, forgery, employee dishonesty, and theft

criminal wrong • an injury, including to the public at large, that is punishable by the government

critical illness insurance • a form of supplemental medical expense insurance that provides a substantial one-time lump-sum cash benefit for listed critical illnesses

cross-purchase agreement • a business buy-sell agreement for partnerships and corporations in which the surviving co-owners will be the purchasers of the business interest of a deceased owner

current assumption whole life insurance • a nonparticipating whole life insurance policy in which premium rates are redetermined by the insurer periodically, based on its then-current assumptions as to mortality, interest, and expenses

currently insured • an insured status under Social Security that requires a person to have at least six credits during the thirteen calendar quarters ending with the quarter in which death occurs

custodial care • nursing home care given to help with personal needs, such as walking, bathing, dressing, eating, or taking medicine. Such care can usually be provided by someone without professional medical skills or training. *Sometimes called* personal care.

declarations • factual statements that are a part of an insurance policy and that identify the specific person, property, or activity being insured; the parties to the insurance transaction; and other descriptive information about the insurance being provided

decreasing term insurance • a form of term life insurance in which the amount of insurance systematically decreases from year to year

deductible • the initial amount or portion of covered losses that is borne by the insured, rather than by the insurance company

deductive reasoning • *See* a priori reasoning

deferred annuity • an annuity for which benefit payments begin more than one payment interval after the date of purchase

defined-contribution medical expense plan • a plan under which the employer makes a fixed-dollar contribution that an employee can use toward paying the cost of medical expense coverage, regardless of the premium

definitions • explanations of the meaning of key terms in an insurance policy to clarify the coverage

Delta Plans • service plans sponsored by state dental associations for the purpose of providing dental benefits. Also called *Delta Dental Plans*.

demutualization • the process of converting a mutual insurance company into a stock company

dental health maintenance organization (DHMO) • an HMO that provides dental care only

dependent • most commonly defined under a group medical expense plan to include an employee's spouse who is not legally separated from the employee and any other unmarried dependent children (including stepchildren and adopted children) under age 19 or, if full-time students, usually age 23 or 26

difference in conditions (DIC) insurance • a separate insurance policy that provides open-perils coverage to fill in the gaps left by the insured's other commercial property insurance policies

direct loss • the first loss or losses that arise immediately from the occurrence of a peril. For example, the cost to repair a dented fender is a direct loss following an auto accident.

direct recognition • in life insurance, the practice of paying smaller dividends on policies that have outstanding policy loans than on other policies

direct-response marketing • a method of marketing insurance without the intermediary of an agent or broker

directors and officers DO liability insurance • insurance that covers directors and officers of a corporation and that is purchased by a corporation. The policy covers directors and officers for their personal liability as directors and officers that results from wrongful acts, and it also covers reimbursement to the policyowner for any sum that it is required or permitted by law to pay to the directors and officers as indemnification.

disability-based policy • a long-term care insurance policy with a per diem basis of payment that provides benefits even if no care is being received as long as the insured satisfies the policy's benefit trigger

disability income insurance • insurance to partially replace income of persons unable to work because of sickness or accident

disability insured • the insured status under Social Security necessary to receive disability benefits. It requires that a worker (1) be fully insured and (2) have had a minimum amount of work under Social Security within a recent period.

discount plan • a plan that provides discounts to members for products or services. Used for prescription drug, vision, and dental expenses.

dividend options • a set of provisions in a participating life insurance policy that describe how the policyowner can use the dividends, usually to reduce the premium payment, to buy additional paid-up permanent insurance, to accumulate at interest, to buy term insurance, or to make the policy a paid-up policy at an earlier age than originally planned

divisible surplus • that portion of an insurer's surplus that is declared as a dividend to be distributed to policyowners and/or stockholders of the insurer

domestic insurer • an insurer incorporated in the state where it does business

double indemnity provision • *See* accidental death benefit

doughnut hole • *See* coverage gap

dram shop laws • laws that impute liability to taverns and other businesses that serve liquor for injuries that may be caused by intoxicated patrons

dread disease insurance • *See* specific disease insurance

dwelling policy • one of a series of policies for the insurance of dwellings. The forms are somewhat less comprehensive than homeowners policies and can be used for dwellings that do not meet certain homeowners standards.

dynamic risk • a possibility of loss that results from changes in society or in the economy. An example of a dynamic risk is the possibility that a retailer's inventory will become obsolete because of a sudden change in consumer tastes.

earnings test • the process for determining whether income benefits of Social Security beneficiaries under the full retirement age should be reduced because of earned income that exceeds a specified amount that is subject to annual indexing

earthquake insurance • a homeowners endorsement or separate policy that covers property for earthquake as well as tremors that accompany volcanic eruption. The coverage has a large deductible, such as 5 percent of the limit of insurance.

elimination period • the term usually applied to a waiting period in long-term care insurance. *See* waiting period.

employee benefits liability insurance • insurance that covers claims arising out of improper advice or other errors or omissions in the administration of employee benefit plans

employee theft • the unlawful taking of money, securities, or other property by an employee

employers liability insurance • a type of liability insurance that protects an employer when it can be sued because of injuries to employees. Usually accompanies workers' compensation coverage.

employment practices liability insurance • a liability policy that covers against specified employment practices, such as discrimination, sexual harassment, and wrongful termination

endorsement • a provision added to a property or liability insurance policy, sometimes for an extra or reduced premium charge, by which the scope of the policy's coverage is clarified, restricted, or enlarged

endowment life insurance • a type of life insurance policy that pays the face amount if the insured dies during a specified period of time and also pays the face amount if he or she lives to the end of that period

enterprise risk management • an approach to managing all an organization's risks and opportunities, involving not only pure hazard risks but also speculative business risks.

entire contract provision • in life and health insurance, a provision that specifies that the policy and the attached application constitute the entire agreement between the parties

entity agreement • a business buy-sell agreement for partnerships and corporations in which the business itself is the designated purchaser of the deceased's business interest

equipment breakdown insurance • commercial property and liability insurance that provides coverage for damage caused by steam boiler explosion and electrical or mechanical breakdown; referred to as boiler and machinery coverage by some insurers

errors and omissions insurance • a type of professional liability insurance for those in such occupations as insurance sales, real estate appraising, and accounting, where the professional's acts or omissions are unlikely to result in bodily injury

estate tax • a tax imposed upon the transfer of property at a person's death. The federal government and many states levy such taxes.

evidence of insurability • documentation or other evidence submitted to the insurance company regarding the physical condition or other attributes of the applicant for insurance coverage, which is taken into account when the insurer determines whether to accept the risk

excess liability insurance • a policy written to provide additional liability limits for claims that are covered by specified underlying coverage

excess lines broker • *See* surplus lines broker

exclusion ratio • the ratio used to determine the portion of the benefit payment from an annuity that is tax free as a return of the investment in the contract. It is the ratio of the total amount invested to the total amount expected to be received.

exclusions • provisions in an insurance contract that indicate what the insurer does not cover. Exclusions can apply to perils, types of losses, types of property, or types of activities.

exclusive agency system • a marketing system in property and liability insurance in which the agent represents only one insurer (or group of affiliated insurers), and the insurer has ownership rights over the business written by the agents

exclusive-provider organization (EPO) • a variation of a preferred-provider organization in which coverage is not provided outside the preferred-provider network except in those infrequent cases where the network does not have an appropriate specialist

exposure unit • the unit of measurement for which an insurance rate is developed. Examples are each $1,000 of life insurance protection or each $100 of property value.

express authority • authority specifically granted by a principal to an agent by means of an agency agreement

extended care facility • a health care facility for a person who no longer requires the full level of medical care provided by a hospital but does need a period of convalescence under supervised medical care. Also known as a *skilled-nursing facility*.

extended nonowned coverage • an auto insurance endorsement for persons who have a vehicle that is made available for their regular use

extended term insurance • paid-up term life insurance purchased through the use of a life insurance policy's cash value as a single premium

extension of benefits • a provision in a medical expense plan under which benefits are extended for any covered employee or dependent who is totally disabled at the time coverage would otherwise terminate. The disability must have resulted from an injury or illness that occurred while the person was covered under the group contract. The length of the extension generally ranges from 3 to 12 months.

extortion • the loss of money, securities, or other property surrendered away from the insured premises as a result of the threat of bodily harm to someone who is, or is allegedly, being held captive

extra expense insurance • commercial insurance that provides coverage for expenses to avoid or minimize the suspension of operations following damage to property

extra percentage tables • tables used in treating substandard applicants for life insurance in which separate, higher-than-normal mortality rates are used in calculating the premium for the coverage

facility-only policy • a long-term care insurance policy that provides benefits for care in a nursing home and other settings, such as an assisted-living facility and hospice

facultative reinsurance • reinsurance that is optional for both the primary insurer and the reinsurer

FAIR (Fair Access to Insurance Requirements) plan • a state-run program to provide property insurance, within limits, if a property owner is unable to obtain coverage in the standard marketplace. The actual coverage is usually written by a pool or syndicate of private insurers.

family deductible • a provision in a major medical plan that waives future deductibles for all family members once a specified aggregate dollar amount of medical expenses has been incurred or after a specified number of family members have satisfied their individual deductibles

family purpose doctrine • a legal principle that imputes liability to motor vehicle owners for the negligence of family members who use the motor vehicle

federal surety bond • a bond that guarantees that a business will comply with federal standards, including the payment of taxes and duties

fee schedule • a list of covered benefits and the maximum fee that will be paid to the provider of benefits. Such a schedule is found in many surgical expense policies, dental policies, vision care plans, and group legal expense plans.

fellow-servant doctrine • a common-law defense that was available to employers, under which a worker could not collect if an injury resulted from a fellow worker's negligence

fiduciary bond • a bond that guarantees that a person who is responsible for the property of another faithfully exercises his or her duties, gives proper accounting of any property received, and makes proper indemnification if the court determines that the principal is responsible for any financial loss that relates to the property. It is often required of persons who act as administrators, trustees, or guardians.

fiduciary liability insurance • insurance that covers claims that result from the breach of fiduciary duties, such as pension plan losses because of improper investments

field underwriting • the initial screening of applicants for insurance performed by the agent or broker

fifth dividend option • a provision in cash value life insurance whereby dividends can be used to purchase term insurance

50 percent refund annuity • a refund annuity that pays a benefit to a beneficiary if the annuitant dies before receiving benefits equal to half the cost of the annuity. Installments continue until the total benefits paid equal half the cost of the annuity.

file-and-use law • a law regulating insurance rates that allows insurers to file their rates with the regulatory authority and immediately begin to use those rates unless/until the regulatory authority disapproves the rates

financial guarantee insurance • *See* credit enhancement insurance

financial needs analysis • a system for determining how much life insurance a client needs if the principal sum is to be liquidated in the process of meeting the client's financial objectives for his or her survivors

financial responsibility law • a law in all states that requires proof of future auto insurance after certain circumstances occur. These can include an auto accident, conviction for certain traffic offenses, or failure to pay a legal judgment that arises from an auto accident.

financial risk • a category of risk for which the possibility of loss involves a decrease or a disappearance of monetary value, usually in an unexpected or relatively unpredictable manner

fire • rapid oxidation or combustion accompanied by a flame or glow

first-to-die policy • a joint-life insurance policy on the lives of two or more persons and payable upon the death of the first person to die

fixed-amount option • a life insurance settlement option under which the death proceeds are distributed in level installments consisting of principal and interest for as long as the proceeds last

fixed annuity • an annuity that provides a stated periodic dollar benefit, regardless of the insurer's investment return

fixed-period option • a life insurance settlement option under which the death proceeds are distributed in installments consisting of principal and interest over a specified period of time

flat extra premium • a method of treating substandard life insurance applicants by charging a specified extra premium per $1,000 of insurance, regardless of age

flexible benefit plan • *See* cafeteria plan

flexible premium life insurance • various types of life insurance in which the premium is flexible, at the option of either the insurer or the policyowner

flexible spending account (FSA) • a cafeteria plan provision that allows an employee to fund certain types of expenses on a before-tax basis. Called a health FSA if used for unreimbursed medical expenses

flex-rating law • a law regulating insurance rates that requires regulatory approval of new rates only if they differ from the existing rates by at least some specified percentage, such as 5 or 10 percent

floater • a property insurance policy to provide broad insurance protection on property that is subject to being moved

follow form • a basic form of an excess liability policy that incorporates the policy provisions and conditions of an underlying policy, thus providing additional limits of coverage only if a claim is covered by the underlying insurance

foreign insurer • an insurer that writes business in a state but is incorporated in another state

forgery • the creation of a document or signature that is not genuine

formulary • a list of preferred medications that a prescription drug plan will cover

fraternal insurer • a not-for-profit insuring organization that writes mainly life insurance on members of a fraternal society

fraud • intentional deception or intentional misleading of another person. In order to constitute fraud, intent must be shown, and the information concealed or misrepresented must be relied upon by and injure the other party.

free-look provision • a clause found in some lines of insurance contracts that gives the policyowner a specified period of time, such as 10 days, to return the policy and receive a full refund of the premium paid

FSA • *See* flexible spending account (FSA)

full advance funding • a funding method for insurance by which taxes or premiums are set at a level to fund all promised benefits from current service for those making current contributions

full retirement age • the age at which a worker can retire under Social Security and receive nonreduced benefits equal to his or her primary insurance amount (PIA). Also referred to as *normal retirement age.*

fully insured • an insured status under Social Security. This status requires either (1) 40 credits or (2) at least as many credits (but a minimum of six) as there are years elapsing after 1950 (or after the year in which age 21 is reached, if later) and before the year in which a person dies, becomes disabled, or reaches age 62, whichever occurs first.

functional replacement cost • the cost to repair or replace damaged real property with less costly construction materials and methods that are functionally equivalent to the old construction

fundamental risk • a loss possibility that can affect a large segment of society at the same time. An example is the possibility of widespread unemployment during an economic downturn.

gambling • the deliberate creation of a speculative risk by betting on an uncertain outcome. Playing poker for money is an example of gambling.

gatekeeper PPO • a preferred-provider organization that requires a participant to select a primary care physician in the manner of an HMO subscriber. However, at the time medical service is needed, the participant can elect to go outside the PPO network.

general agency system • in life insurance marketing, the term used to describe a marketing system whereby a general agent is granted a franchise by an insurer to build an agency force for marketing the insurer's products in a given geographic area

gift • for federal gift tax purposes, a completed transfer and acceptance of property for less than full and adequate consideration

gift tax • a tax imposed on transfers of property by gift during the donor's lifetime

government insurance • various types of insurance operated by state or federal governments. Includes both social insurance programs and other programs.

grace period • an additional period of time, usually 30 or 31 days, granted in some types of insurance for the policyowner to pay the premium after it has become due. During the grace period, the coverage remains in force.

gross estate • for federal estate tax purposes, the property of a decedent that passes by will and by other means

gross rate • an insurance rate that includes loading for profits and contingencies as well as a provision for expected future loss costs

group insurance • in contrast with individual insurance, all types of private insurance that cover many people under one master contract issued to a sponsoring organization, such as an employer

group-model HMO • a closed-panel HMO under which physicians and other medical personnel are employees of another legal entity that has a contractual relationship with the HMO to provide medical services for its subscribers

guaranteed purchase (insurability) option • a rider to a life insurance policy that gives the insured the right to buy additional insurance in specified amounts at specified times or ages without having to provide evidence of insurability

guaranteed renewable • a characteristic of an insurance contract in which the insured retains the right to renew the coverage at each policy anniversary date, usually up to a stated age. Also, the insurer is not allowed to cancel the coverage during the period of protection. However, the insurer does retain the right to raise the rates for the coverage for broad classes of insureds.

guaranty fund • a state fund that at least partially protects consumers against the insolvency of insurers. The typical fund assesses solvent insurers to pay the unpaid claims of insolvent companies.

guideline premium and corridor test • a two-pronged test to determine whether an insurance policy meets the definition of a life insurance policy for federal income tax purposes. The test relates to both the size of the total premium paid and the size of the death benefit relative to the cash value.

hazard • an act or condition that increases the likelihood of the occurrence of a loss and/or increases the severity of a loss. The three types of hazards are physical hazards, moral hazards, and attitudinal hazards.

health association • an organization that provides medical expense coverage to members. Examples include HMOs and Blue Cross and Blue Shield plans.

health FSA • *See* flexible spending account (FSA)

health insurance • protection against the financial consequences of poor health

Health Insurance Portability and Accountability Act (HIPAA) • federal legislation, passed in 1996, that reforms the health care system through numerous provisions. One of the act's purposes is to make insurance more available, particularly when an employed person changes jobs or becomes unemployed.

health maintenance organization (HMO) • a managed system of health care that provides a comprehensive array of medical services on a prepaid basis to voluntarily enrolled persons living within a specific geographic region. HMOs both finance health care and deliver health services. There is an emphasis on preventive care as well as cost control.

Health Maintenance Organization Act • a federal act in 1973 that encouraged the growth of HMOs

health reimbursement arrangement (HRA) • an account funded with employer dollars from which an employee can withdraw amounts to pay medical expenses that are not covered under a high-deductible medical expense plan

health savings account (HSA) • a tax-favored savings account for use with a high-deductible medical expense plan and from which certain unreimbursed medical expenses can be paid. Successors to and more attractive than Archer MSAs.

high-deductible health plan • medical expense plan with a deductible as high as $5,000 or more. When used in an employment setting, the employer may contribute a lower or equal amount to a savings account from which employees can pay medical expenses not covered because of the deductible.

high-risk pool • a state-run insurance pool to provide medical expense coverage for persons who have been rejected in the normal marketplace

HIPAA • *See* Health Insurance Portability and Accountability Act

hired auto • in commercial auto insurance, an auto, other than a nonowned auto, that is leased, hired, rented, or borrowed by the named insured

HMO • *See* health maintenance organization

hold-harmless agreement • an agreement in which one party, such as a tenant, accepts the responsibility of another party, such as a landlord, for losses that would otherwise fall on that other party

home health care • medical care that is received at home. Care is usually part-time and performed under a plan prescribed by a physician.

home-health-care-only policy • a long-term care insurance policy designed to provide benefits only for care outside an institutional setting, although some policies may provide benefits for care in assisted-living facilities

homeowners policy • a policy that provides coverage for a family's home, personal possessions, and liability that arises out of the many activities of family members. Several homeowners forms provide varying degrees of coverage for different types of homeowners and tenants.

homogeneity • the quality or state of being of the same or a similar kind or nature

hospice care • a health care facility or service that provides benefits to terminally ill persons. The emphasis is on easing the physical and psychological pain associated with dying rather than on curing a medical condition.

hospital confinement indemnity insurance • a medical expense policy that pays a fixed dollar amount for each day a person is hospitalized, regardless of other insurance

HRA • *See* health reimbursement arrangement

hull insurance • the term often applied to physical damage coverage in watercraft and aviation policies

human life value • the present value of that portion of a person's estimated future earnings that will be used to support dependents

illustration • a presentation or depiction that includes nonguaranteed elements of a life insurance policy over a period of years

immediate annuity • an annuity with benefit payments that begin one payment interval (for example, 1 month) after the date of purchase

impaired risk annuity • an annuity that considers the annuitant's reduced life expectancy in the underwriting process and increases the annuity payments (or lowers the premium) accordingly

implied authority • the authority that an agent has as necessary to carry out acts needed to exercise his or her express authority

implied warranty • an obligation imposed by law on the manufacturer or distributor of products

imputed negligence • legal responsibility extended by the courts to persons other than those who cause injury directly

incident of ownership • an element of ownership or degree of control over a policy, such as a life insurance policy

incontestable clause • a provision in life and health insurance that specifies that, except for nonpayment of the premium, the insurer will not contest the policy after it has been in force for a specified period (usually 2 years) during the insured's lifetime

increasing term insurance • a form of term life insurance in which the amount of insurance systematically increases from year to year

indemnity • *See* principle of indemnity

independence • a requirement of the law of large numbers that the occurrence of a loss to one exposure unit should not affect the likelihood of loss to another exposure unit.

independent adjuster • a claims adjuster or claims adjusting firm that is not an employee of an insurance company

independent agency system • a marketing system in property and liability insurance in which an agent represents several insurers or groups of insurers and has ownership rights over the business written by the agency

indeterminate premium whole life insurance • *See* interest-sensitive whole life insurance

indexed annuity • an annuity that guarantees a minimum fixed rate of interest credits but also provides higher credits if a specified stock index rises sufficiently

indexed universal life insurance • a type of universal life insurance in which interest is credited based on an external index, such as Standard and Poor's 500

indirect loss • a loss that occurs only as a secondary result following the occurrence of a peril. An example is the additional living expenses a family might incur to pay for substitute living accommodations following fire damage to their home.

individual equity • the principle that each individual's insurance premium payments are based on an actuarial analysis that reflects the insurer's cost of providing benefits for the risks faced by that individual

individual insurance • in contrast with group insurance, insurance purchased and owned by individuals and families

individual practice association • an HMO under which participating physicians practice individually or in small groups in their own offices. In many cases, these physicians also accept non-HMO patients on a traditional fee-for-service basis.

inductive reasoning • reasoning in which a generalized conclusion is derived from particular instances. Inductive reasoning is based on statistical analysis. *Compare* a priori reasoning.

inflation guard endorsement • a homeowners endorsement that provides an automatic increase for property coverages. The policyowner selects the annual percentage increase.

initial deductible • a deductible that must be satisfied before any benefits are paid under a medical expense plan

inland marine insurance • a specialized type of insurance used for goods in transit, property held by bailees, mobile equipment and property, property of certain dealers, and instrumentalities of transportation and communication

inside buildup • the increase in the cash value of a permanent life insurance policy

installment refund annuity • a refund annuity specifying that if the annuitant dies before receiving total benefit payments equal to the purchase price of the annuity, the difference will be refunded in the form of continuing benefit payments

insurable interest • a right or relationship with regard to the subject matter of an insurance contract such that the insured will suffer financial loss from damage, loss, or destruction to that subject matter

insurable risk • a risk that substantially meets the following requirements: (1) the amount of the loss must be important, (2) the loss must be of an accidental nature, (3) future loss must be calculable, (4) the loss must be definite, and (5) the risk cannot be excessively catastrophic

insurance • an economic system that reduces financial risks when policyowners transfer risks to an insurer that combines their potential losses

insurance agent • *See* agent

insurance commissioner • the state official responsible for the regulation of the business of insurance

insurance contract • the agreement that transfers financial risk from a policyowner to an insurer. It may begin with an oral agreement but then is usually converted to written form.

insurance equation • an equation that shows that an insurance company's sources of income (premiums, investment earnings, and other income) equal its cost factors (covered losses, cost of doing business, and profit)

insurance policy • *see* insurance contract

Insurance Services Office • *See* ISO

insured (noun) • a party to whom or on whose behalf insurance benefits may be payable

insuring agreement • a provision in an insurance contract that spells out the basic promise of the insurance company to pay benefits according to the terms of the policy

interest option • a life insurance settlement option under which the death proceeds are retained by the insurer temporarily, with only the interest earnings thereon distributed to the beneficiary

interest-sensitive whole life insurance • a current assumption whole life insurance policy under which a low initial premium is guaranteed for a period of time, often 3 or 5 years. After that time, the premium is recalculated on the basis of current mortality, interest, and expense assumptions.

international travel medical insurance • interim medical insurance for international travelers. It is usually folded into a broader policy to cover many non-health-related travel contingencies.

irrevocable beneficiary • a beneficiary that cannot be changed by the policyowner without the beneficiary's permission

ISO (Insurance Services Office) • an advisory organization that provides various services to insurance companies, including the development and filing of standardized insurance forms

joint (joint-life) annuity • an annuity with benefit payments that continue only until the first death among specified lives

joint-and-last-survivor annuity • an annuity with benefit payments that continue until the last death among specified lives

joint-and-one-half annuity • a joint-and-last-survivor annuity with periodic benefit payments that drop to one-half the former amount following the first death among the annuitants

joint-and-two-thirds annuity • a joint-and-last-survivor annuity with periodic benefit payments that drop to two-thirds of the former amount following the first death among the annuitants

joint-life policy • a type of life insurance policy covering the lives of two or more persons

joint underwriting association • an association, or pool, of auto insurers that writes hard-to-place drivers in some states

judicial bond • a bond required by courts, including fiduciary bonds and litigation bonds

key employee • a person in an organization whose capital, technical knowledge, skills, experience, business connections, or other attributes make him or her highly valuable to the organization's financial success

key employee life insurance • insurance on the life of a key employee to cover the possibility of an income loss and/or an increase in expenses resulting from the key employee's death

last clear chance doctrine • the legal principle that holds that although a claimant is negligent, the defendant is liable if he or she had the last clear chance to avoid an accident and failed to take advantage of that chance

late remittance offer • an offer made by an insurer to the owner of a lapsed life insurance policy that invites him or her to pay the premium and reinstate the coverage without having to provide evidence of insurability

law of large numbers • a mathematical principle stating that as the number of independent trials or events is increased, the actual results from those trials or events will come closer and closer to the results that one would expect to occur based on the underlying probability

legal reserve • the minimum amount of the reserve, as specified by state law, that a life insurer must maintain to meet its assumed future claim costs under a block of policies. It is discounted for future premium and investment income under those policies.

legal wrong • the invasion of a legal right. It can be either criminal or civil.

less value statute • a state law that prohibits a life insurer from promising something on the face of the policy while taking it away in the fine print, such as by offering a settlement option of less value than the policy's death proceeds

liability risk • a possibility of loss as a result of being held legally responsible for an injury to another, usually for bodily injury or damage to his or her property

license bond • a surety bond that is often required by state and local governments for persons in many types of occupations that need licensing

lien • a method of treating substandard applicants for life insurance in which the policy is issued as standard except that the death proceeds are reduced if death occurs within the first few years of coverage

life annuity (whole life annuity) • an annuity whose benefit payments continue for the duration of a designated life

life annuity certain • a life annuity that provides a guaranteed minimum number of benefit payments whether the annuitant lives or dies. It is a combination of an annuity certain and a pure deferred life annuity.

life-care facility • *See* continuing care retirement community

life income option • a life insurance settlement option, and in some insurance policies a nonforfeiture option, under which the proceeds are distributed over the lifetime of the recipient, perhaps subject to some type of minimum guarantee as to the aggregate amount to be paid

life insurance • insurance that provides for payment of a specified amount at the insured's death or, possibly, at a specified date if the insured is still living

life settlement • an arrangement that involves transferring the ownership of a life insurance policy to a third-party investor, much like a viatical settlement, but in cases where the insured is not chronically or terminally ill. Life settlements provide a relatively new way for seniors to convert their life insurance policies to cash.

limited-benefit plan • a medical expense plan that generally provides first-dollar coverage for certain medical expenses but has significantly lower benefits for catastrophic expenses than do other types of medical expense plans

limited-payment life insurance • a form of whole life insurance for which premiums are payable for only a specified number of years or until a specified age of the insured

line of insurance • a type of insurance, such as life, medical expense, disability income, homeowners, or auto liability

liquidation • the process, overseen by an insurance commissioner, of dissolving a financially troubled insurance company

liquidation period • the period of time during which annuity benefit payments are made

liquidity • an asset characteristic that describes the extent to which the asset can be converted into cash quickly without loss of value

litigation bond • a bond whose purpose is to require a person or organization who is seeking a court remedy to protect other parties from damages if the party seeking the remedy does not prevail

Lloyd's association • an association of individual insurers in which insurance is underwritten by its members rather than by the association itself

Lloyd's of London • a British organization made up of and regulating the activities of members, both individual and corporate, who act as insurers. The organization itself does not write insurance.

loading • that portion of an insurance rate or premium that covers the insurer's expected operating expenses and provides a margin for profits and contingencies

longevity insurance • a class of pure deferred annuities that provide a future income stream during the distribution period, which typically begins at a relatively advanced age such as 85. Survivors receive no benefit if the annuitant dies before the distribution period begins.

long-term care insurance • a form of health insurance that usually provides coverage for custodial care, intermediate care, and skilled-nursing care. Benefits may also be available for home health care, adult day care, and assisted living.

long-term care rider • a provision in some annuities by which the periodic annuity payment increases when the annuitant is determined to meet long-term care by satisfying the same criteria that trigger benefits under a long-term care insurance policy.

long-term disability income insurance • disability income coverage that provides extended benefits after a person has been disabled for 6 months or longer

look-back period • a specific time period prior to Medicaid eligibility during which Medicaid benefits are reduced (or their onset postponed) if the individual's assets were disposed of at less than their fair market value

loss • a decline in value, usually in an unexpected or relatively unpredictable manner

loss assessment coverage • a coverage in many property and liability insurance policies that pays the insured's share of losses levied against members of a homeowners or condominium association

loss-of-earnings policy • a disability income policy that measures lost income as the difference between pre-disability income and post-disability income from any occupation

loss exposure • a loss that might occur

loss frequency • the number of losses that occur within a given time period among a given number of units exposed to that loss possibility

loss payable clause • a provision in a property insurance policy that protects a lender's insurable interest in personal property. If a covered loss occurs, the lender receives payment to the extent of its insurable interest.

loss prevention • risk control measures intended to lower the probability of loss or the frequency with which a given type of loss occurs. Loss prevention measures must obviously be put in place before loss occurs.

loss ratio • most commonly, the ratio of incurred losses and loss adjustment expenses to premiums earned

loss ratio method of rate making • a method in which the actual loss ratio is compared to the desired or expected loss ratio to determine the change needed in an existing insurance rate

loss reduction • risk control measures that aim to reduce the severity of loss. Loss reduction measures may be taken either before or after the loss occurs.

loss reserve • in property and liability insurance, an insurer's liability for losses that have already occurred but have not yet been paid or otherwise settled

loss severity • the size of a loss or the average size of a group of losses

lost instrument bond • a bond which guarantees that the principal will reimburse the insurer of lost securities if the original securities turn up and their holder is able to collect on them

major medical insurance • a medical insurance plan designed to provide substantial protection against catastrophic medical expenses. There are few exclusions and limitations, but deductibles and coinsurance are common.

malpractice insurance • a type of professional liability insurance for those in occupations where an act or omission is likely to result in bodily injury

managed care • a process to deliver cost-effective health care without sacrificing quality or access. Common characteristics include controlled access to providers, comprehensive case management, preventive care, risk sharing, and high-quality care.

marital deduction • an unlimited amount that can be taken as a deduction against the federal gift and estate tax for transfers to the donor's spouse

mass • as a characteristic of a statistical group or an insured group, sufficient size within such a group as to allow the true underlying probability to emerge

master contract • a contract issued to someone other than the persons insured that provides benefits to a group of individuals who have a specific relationship to the policyowner

material • so important as to affect whether an insurer will accept an applicant or the terms under which it will accept the applicant

maximum possible loss • the worst loss that could happen

maximum probable loss • the worst loss that is likely to happen

Medicaid • a joint federal and state program to provide medical expense benefits for certain classes of individuals and families with low income and assets

medical expense insurance • protection against financial losses that result from medical bills because of an accident or illness

medical payments coverage • a coverage in many liability policies that pays the medical expenses of persons injured on an insured premises or because of the actions of an insured. Payments are made, regardless of fault, in the hope of reducing liability claims. • in auto insurance, a coverage that pays medical and funeral expenses incurred by a covered person in an auto accident

Medicare • the health insurance portion of the Social Security program that is available to persons aged 65 or older and limited categories of persons under age 65

Medicare Advantage • Part C of Medicare program, previously known as Medicare+Choice, that allows beneficiaries to select HMOs and other alternatives to the traditional Medicare program

Medicare carve-out • an employer-provided medical expense plan for persons over age 65 under which benefits are reduced to the extent that they are payable under Medicare for the same expense

Medicare Part A • part of Medicare program that provides benefits for expenses incurred in hospitals, skilled-nursing facilities, and hospices

Medicare Part B • part of Medicare program that provides benefits for most medical expenses not covered under Part A, except for prescription drugs

Medicare Part C • *See* Medicare Advantage

Medicare Part D • part of Medicare program that provides for prescription drug coverage

Medicare+Choice • See Medicare Advantage

Medicare secondary rules • regulations that specify when Medicare will be secondary to an employer's medical expense plan for disabled employees and active employees aged 65 or older

Medicare SELECT policy • a medigap policy that pays benefits for nonemergency services only if care is received from network providers

Medicare supplement • an individual or employer-provided medical expense plan for persons aged 65 or older under which benefits are provided for certain specific expenses not covered under Medicare. These can include a portion of expenses not paid by Medicare because of deductibles, coinsurance, or copayments, and certain expenses excluded by Medicare. In individual insurance, also referred to as a *medigap policy.*

medigap insurance • *See* Medicare supplement

Mental Health Parity Act • federal legislation that requires mental health benefits to be on par with limits that apply to other medical conditions. The act applies to employers with more than 50 employees.

MIB Group, Inc. (MIB) • an organization sponsored by its member life insurance companies to gather and maintain principally medical information disclosed by applicants for life insurance

misappropriation • the unlawful retention of funds that belong to someone else

miscellaneous type vehicle endorsement • an auto insurance endorsement to insure such vehicles as all-terrain vehicles, dune buggies, golf carts, motor homes, and motorcycles

misleading advertising • an unfair trade practice involving confusing, deceptive, false, or otherwise misleading advertising or promotional practices

misrepresentation • a false and material statement made by an applicant for insurance. It is the basis for the insurer to make the contract voidable.

misstatement of age or gender clause • a life insurance policy provision that specifies that if the insured's age or gender has been misstated, the benefits payable under the policy will be adjusted to what the premium paid would have purchased at the correct age or gender

mixed-model HMO • an HMO that has characteristics of two or more of the basic HMO forms. It occurs most often when one HMO purchases a different type of HMO or when an HMO expands its capacity or geographic region by adding other medical care providers under a different type of arrangement.

mobile home insurance • insurance coverage, similar to homeowners insurance, that provides coverage to owner-occupants of mobile homes

model law • a draft bill—the suggested wording of a new law—for consideration by state legislators. Any state may choose to adopt a model bill or to adopt it with modifications.

model regulation • a draft regulation that may be implemented by a state insurance department if a model law is passed

modified endowment contract (MEC) • a life insurance policy that fails to meet the Internal Revenue Code's 7-pay test. Distributions, therefore, receive less favorable tax treatment than other life insurance contracts receive.

modified no-fault • a no-fault system with the right to sue another party once certain monetary or verbal thresholds are exceeded

modified own-occupation • a definition of disability under which total disability benefits are not paid if the insured is able to be gainfully employed in a position for which he or she is suited by education, training, or experience

modified whole life insurance • a form of whole life insurance in which a level premium lower than that for conventional whole life insurance is charged for the first few policy years and a higher level premium is charged thereafter

moral hazard • a dishonest tendency that is likely to increase loss frequency and/or severity

morbidity • the relative incidence of disease

morbidity table • a table showing the rate at which individuals suffer illness and disease at each age

mortality • the relative incidence of death

mortality table • a table showing the rate at which individuals alive at different ages are expected to die during the coming year

mortgage clause • a provision in property insurance policies that protects a lender's insurable interest in real property. If a covered loss occurs, the lender can receive payments to the extent of its insurable interest, even if a policyowner's claim is denied.

motor carrier insurance • insurance designed for businesses that provide transportation by vehicles in the furtherance of a commercial enterprise

motor truck cargo insurance • a type of inland marine insurance policy used by common carriers or contract carriers to cover customers' goods when the carrier is legally liable for damage

mutual holding company • a holding company controlled by policyowners that owns a controlling interest in a new stock insurance company that takes over a mutual insurer's business

mutual insurance company • a not-for-profit insurance company owned by its policyowners, who elect its board of directors

NAIC • *See* National Association of Insurance Commissioners

name • a member of Lloyd's of London

named insured • the term often applied to the owner of an insurance policy named in the policy declarations, particularly in property and liability insurance

named nonowner coverage • an auto insurance endorsement for persons who want coverage when using a nonowned auto but do not own an auto

named-perils coverage • an insurance contract that covers only losses that arise from one of a series of listed perils. If the peril is not listed, it is not covered by the policy.

National Association of Insurance Commissioners (NAIC) • a voluntary association of state insurance regulatory officials that is involved in financial examinations of insurers and develops model insurance laws and regulations

National Conference of Insurance Legislators (NCOIL) • an association of state insurance legislators

National Flood Insurance Program (NFIP) • a federal program that provides property insurance for the peril of flood

NCOIL • *See* National Conference of Insurance Legislators

negligence • failure to exercise the proper degree of care required by the circumstances

net amount at risk • in a life insurance policy, the difference between the policy's face amount and the reserve at any point in time

net level annual premium • in life insurance, the actuarial spreading of the net single premium on a level basis over a policy's premium-paying period

net payment cost index • a method of estimating the net cost of life insurance on a time-value-adjusted basis, assuming that the policy's death benefit will be paid at the end of a specified time period

net single premium • in life insurance, the amount needed today for all insureds in a classification, together with future investment earnings, to pay all claims within that class of insureds

network-model HMO • an HMO that contracts with two or more independent groups of physicians to provide medical services to its subscribers

newly acquired auto • in personal auto insurance, an auto that meets a policy's eligibility requirements but is acquired after the effective date of the policy

no-fault auto insurance • a modification of the traditional tort liability system that provides first-party benefits to injured persons and imposes some restrictions on their rights to sue negligent parties

nonadmitted asset • an asset of an insurer that is not permitted by regulatory authorities to be counted as an asset for Annual Statement purposes

nonadmitted insurer • an insurer that does not have a license to conduct insurance business in a particular state. Nonadmitted insurers typically provide surplus lines insurance.

nonassessable policy • a policy where the initial premium is the final premium (other than reductions for dividends). There can be no assessment of the policyowner if the premium is inadequate.

noncancelable • in an insurance contract, the right of the insured to renew the coverage at each policy anniversary date, usually up to some stated age. The coverage may not be terminated by the insurer during the term of coverage. Also, the rates for the coverage are guaranteed in the contract, although they are not necessarily level.

nonfinancial risk • a category of risk for which the possibility of loss does not represent a reduction in monetary value, although sometimes such losses are compensated by the award of money. An example is pain and suffering.

nonforfeiture options • a set of choices available regarding how a life insurance policyowner can use the policy's cash value. These choices include the options to surrender for cash, buy a reduced amount of paid-up whole life insurance, or buy extended term insurance. • For long-term care insurance, an optional benefit provides extended benefits or a cash refund if a policy lapses after it has been in force for a specified number of years.

noninsurance transfer • the contractual transfer of risk by a contract other than an insurance contract. Subcontracting is an example.

nonoccupational disability laws • *See* temporary disability laws

nonowned auto • In personal auto insurance, a vehicle not owned by or furnished for the regular use of the insured or any family member • in commercial auto insurance, an auto owned by a named insured's employee or a member of his or her household, but only while used in the named insured's business

nonparticipating policy • a type of life insurance policy that pays no dividends to the policyowner

non-tax-qualified policy • a type of long-term care insurance contract that fails to meet certain standards of the Health Insurance Portability and Accountability Act for favorable tax treatment

normal retirement age • *See* full retirement age

notice of loss • the process by which the insurer is notified that a loss has occurred. This begins the loss adjustment process. The actual process of notification is spelled out in a policy and varies by line of insurance.

nursing home care • a term that encompasses skilled-nursing care, intermediate care, and custodial care in a licensed facility

OASDHI • the old age, survivors, disability, and heath insurance program of the federal government. This program consists of Social Security and Medicare.

OASDI • the old-age, survivors, and disability insurance portion of the OASDHI program, commonly referred to as Social Security

obligee • the party to a surety bond who is reimbursed because of the failure of the principal to uphold an agreement

occurrence policy • a liability insurance policy that covers claims that arise out of occurrences that take place during the policy period, regardless of when claims are made

open competition • the reliance mainly on competitive forces in the insurance marketplace to produce acceptable insurance rates

open-ended HMO • an HMO that allows a subscriber to go outside the HMO network of medical care providers

open-panel plan • a benefit plan under which covered persons can obtain services from any practitioner or may have to select one from a limited list of practitioners who have agreed to the plan's terms and conditions

open-perils coverage • an insurance coverage that covers all types of losses except those that are specifically excluded by the policy's terms

opportunity cost • the benefit given up by taking one course of action rather than another—for example, the investment income that is lost when funds are kept as cash rather than invested

optionally renewable • the insurer reserves the right to refuse to renew the coverage at each policy anniversary date, either for specified reasons or for any and all reasons

ordinance or law coverage • insurance for the extra costs to bring damaged property into conformity with current building codes or ordinances

ordinary life insurance • a form of whole life insurance for which premiums are based on the assumption that they will be paid until the insured's death and that provides a guaranteed cash value

original Medicare • the term used to describe the traditional Medicare Parts A and B

other insurance clause • a provision in property and liability insurance policies that specifies how losses are shared if more than one policy covers a loss

other than collision • the term used in auto insurance to refer to physical damage to a vehicle that is not caused by collision. Formerly referred to as *comprehensive*.

ownership provision • in life insurance, a clause that specifies that the insured is the owner of the policy (unless the application states otherwise) and that the owner can change the beneficiary (unless named irrevocably), assign the policy, and exercise other ownership rights

own-occupation • a definition of total disability that requires a disabled person to be unable to perform each and every duty (or material duties) of his or her regular occupation

package policy • an insurance policy that combines two or more types of insurance, often property and liability insurance, in a single contract

paid time off (PTO) program • a benefit program that combines sick leave and other types of payments for time not worked into a single program

paid-up additions • additional amounts of permanent life insurance purchased on a single-premium basis through the use of the policy's dividends

pain and suffering • intangible losses arising from bodily injury

parol evidence rule • a legal principle that specifies that oral contemporaneous evidence may not be used to contradict or to vary the terms of a valid written contract

partial advance funding • the funding method used by Social Security and Medicare whereby taxes are more than sufficient to pay current benefits and thus provide some accumulation of assets for the payment of future benefits

partial disability • the inability to perform some stated percentage of job duties or taking a longer-than-normal amount of time in which to complete job duties

participating policy • a type of life insurance policy that can pay dividends to the policyowner

participation rate • in an indexed annuity, the percentage of the increase in the stock index that is used to credit the account of the annuity contract owner

particular risk • a loss possibility that affects only individuals or small groups of individuals at the same time, rather than a large segment of society. An example is the possibility of loss due to the theft of one's wallet.

partnership policy • a long-term care insurance policy issued under the rules of a state partnership program

partnership program • a state program under which Medicaid requirements are modified for persons who maintain approved long-term care insurance policies

pay-as-you-go financing • a funding method for government insurance programs whereby taxes are set at a level to provide just enough income to pay future benefits

per diem basis • a method of paying under long-term care insurance policies in which the insured receives a specified daily or weekly benefit amount, regardless of the actual cost of care

percentage participation • the percentage of covered medical expenses that must be paid by a person receiving benefits and that will not be paid by a medical expense plan

peril • a cause of loss. Fire, earthquake, and flood are examples.

permanent life insurance • *See* cash value life insurance

permit bond • a surety bond often required by state and local governments for persons engaged in various types of activities for which a permit is needed. It guarantees, for example, that the principal is in compliance with laws or payment of taxes.

personal articles floater • an open-perils policy for certain scheduled and valuable items of personal property owned by an individual or a family

personal auto policy (PAP) • the most common auto insurance policy for individuals. It is a package policy that can provide liability, medical, no-fault, uninsured motorists, and physical damage coverages.

personal care • *See* custodial care

personal effects floater • a policy to provide open-perils worldwide coverage for baggage, clothes, cameras, and other items commonly worn or carried by tourists

personal injury • a group of legal liability offenses that typically include libel, slander, invasion of privacy, false arrest, and defamation of character

personal injury protection (PIP) endorsement • the usual name for an endorsement that provides a state's no-fault auto insurance benefits

personal insurance • insurance purchased by individuals and families rather than by businesses and other organizations

personal producing general agent (PPGA) • an agent of a life insurance company who is the insurer's general agent in a given territory but whose primary task is to sell the insurer's products, rather than to build an agency force for the insurer. A PPGA may also be allowed to represent other insurers.

personal property • an asset, other than real property, that is subject to ownership

personal property floater • a policy to provide open-perils coverage for unscheduled personal property worldwide

personal risk • a loss possibility associated with death, injury, illness, old age, or unemployment

physical hazard • a physical condition relating to location, structure, occupancy, exposure, and the like

plan change provision • an insurance policy provision that states the parties may agree to change the terms of the contract

point-of-service (POS) plan • a hybrid arrangement that combines aspects of a traditional medical expense plan with an HMO or a PPO. At the time of medical treatment, a participant can elect whether to receive treatment within the plan's network or outside the network.

policy loan • an advance of money available to a life insurance policyowner from the policy's cash value

policyholder • *See* policyowner

policyowner • the person or entity that owns an insurance policy. The policyowner generally has the right to change, renew, or cancel the policy and the obligation to comply with policy conditions, such as premium payments.

pool of money • long-term care insurance approach to benefits in which a sum, based on the daily benefit amount times days in the benefit period, can be used to make benefit payments as long as the pool of money lasts, subject to the daily benefit limit

portability • the ability to continue employer-provided or employer-sponsored benefits after termination of employment • the concept of allowing an employee to use evidence of prior medical expense coverage to eliminate or reduce the length of any preexisting-conditions provision when the employee moves to another medical expense plan

POS plan • *See* point-of-service plan

possibility • something could occur. A possibility either exists or does not exist; it cannot be measured.

PPO • *See* preferred-provider organization

preadmission certification • a requirement under many medical expense plans that a covered person or his or her physician obtain prior authorization for any nonemergency hospitalization

preexisting-conditions provision • a provision that excludes coverage for a limited period of time for a physical or mental condition for which a covered person in a benefit plan received treatment or medical advice within a specified time period before becoming eligible for coverage

preferred-provider organization (PPO) • benefit plan that contracts with preferred providers to obtain lower-cost care for plan members. Also refers to health care providers that contract with employers or others to provide medical care services at a reduced fee.

premises liability • bodily injury or property damage liability of an owner or tenant because of a condition in or arising out of premises that are owned or occupied

premium • the price charged for a period of coverage provided by an insurance policy and found by multiplying the rate by the number of units of coverage

premium-conversion plan • a cafeteria plan provision that allows employees to elect a before-tax salary reduction to pay for their contributions to an employee-sponsored health plan or certain other types of employee benefits

premium tax • a tax levied by a state on an insurer's gross insurance premiums

prescription drug expense benefits • medical expense benefits for the cost of prescription drugs. These benefits are often separate from other medical expense coverage because of techniques that can be used to contain costs.

presumed negligence • negligence that can be assumed from the facts of certain situations. It can occur if (1) the action would not normally cause injury without negligence, (2) the action is within the control of the party to be held liable, and (3) the party to be held liable has superior knowledge of the cause of the accident or the injured party is unable to prove negligence.

presumptive-disability provision • a provision in a disability income contract by which an individual is presumed to be totally disabled as long as certain circumstances exist. Examples include loss of sight or of one hand. A person with a presumed disability may in fact be able to return to work.

primary beneficiary • the person or organization that is to receive the proceeds of a life insurance policy if he, she, or it survives the insured

primary insurance amount (PIA) • the amount a worker will receive under Social Security if he or she retires at full retirement age or becomes disabled. It is also the amount on which all other Social Security income benefits are based.

principal • the entity for whom an agent acts, such as an insurance company • the party to a surety bond who buys the bond and agrees to perform certain acts or to fulfill certain obligations

principle of indemnity • legal principle that the purpose of insurance is to indemnify (financially compensate) people entitled to insurance benefits in an attempt to make them financially whole; however, people should not profit from an insured loss

prior approval law • a law regulating insurance rates that requires proposed rates be approved by the regulatory authority before they may be used by the insurer

private insurance • all forms of insurance that privately owned insurers provide. *Contrast with* government insurance.

probability • the proportion of times that events will occur in the long run. The probability of some occurrence can be expressed numerically as a number between 0 and 1 or as a percentage from 0.0 percent to 100 percent.

probate estate • all property interests possessed by a decedent that pass to others by will or under a law of intestacy

probationary period • in group insurance, a period at the start of a person's employment during which the person is not eligible to participate in the group insurance plan

products liability • bodily injury or property damage liability caused by a defective product that is manufactured or sold by a business

professional liability insurance • insurance that protects against liability for the failure to use the degree of skill expected of a person in a particular occupation

prohibited provisions • certain provisions that states do not allow insurers to include in their contracts

proof of loss • a statement that details the specifics of a loss. It can be a sworn written statement or, in life insurance, a death certificate. The specifics are spelled out in policies and vary by line of insurance.

property damage • destruction or damage to real or personal property, including loss of use

property risk • a loss possibility associated with the loss or destruction of property

prospectus • a highly detailed document accompanying the sale of securities, including variable life insurance, variable universal life insurance, and variable annuity contracts, providing full disclosure of all of the provisions of the contract

protection and indemnity insurance • the term often applied to liability coverage in watercraft policies

proximate cause • one requirement for proving negligence. There must be a continuous succession of events from the negligent act to the final event causing injury.

PTO program • *See* paid time off (PTO) program

public adjuster • a person who represents a claimant for a fee in negotiating the settlement of a claim against an insurance company

public official bond • a bond often required of persons who are elected or appointed to certain public positions and that guarantees that the principal will uphold the promise made to faithfully and honestly perform the official duties of his or her office

punitive damages • damages awarded in addition to compensatory damages when a defendant's behavior is so severe that the legal system feels an example should be made of the behavior

pure annuity • *See* straight life annuity

pure (net) rate • that portion of an insurance rate that is designed to cover future loss costs

pure no-fault • a no-fault system with no right to sue a negligent party. No state has a pure no-fault law.

pure premium method of rate making • a method in which a pure or net rate is calculated, after which a loading is calculated and added to the pure or net rate

pure risk • a possibility of loss that involves only two outcomes, loss or no loss

qualified beneficiary • any employee, spouse, or dependent child who, on the day before a qualifying COBRA event, was covered under the employer's group health plan

qualified long-term care insurance contract • a long-term care contract that meets specified standards and qualifies for favorable tax treatment under the Health Insurance Portability and Accountability Act (HIPAA). *Also called* tax-qualified policy.

qualified long-term care services • services that must be provided by a qualified long-term care insurance contract. These include necessary diagnostic, preventive, therapeutic, curative, treatment, and rehabilitative services and maintenance or personal care services that are required by a chronically ill individual and provided by a plan of care prescribed by a licensed health care practitioner.

qualifying event • in life insurance, a condition or event that triggers the payment of accelerated benefits, such as an illness that is expected to reduce the insured's life expectancy to 24 months or less • under COBRA, one of the following events that results in loss coverage by a qualified beneficiary: employee's death or termination; reduction of hours making employee ineligible for coverage; legal separation of employee and eligible dependent or spouse; eligibility for Medicare; or child's ceasing to be a dependent

quarters of coverage • *See* credit, Social Security

rate • the price charged for each unit of insurance coverage

rate making • the process of determining the price to be charged for insurance. It involves the determination of future loss costs and adding the necessary margins for expenses and profit.

rate-up age method • a method of treating a substandard applicant for life insurance that bases the premium rate and policy values on an age older than the actual age

real property • land and anything that is growing on it, erected on it, or affixed to it, and the bundle of rights inherent in the ownership

reasonable-and-customary charge • a charge that falls within the range of fees normally charged for a given procedure by physicians with similar training and experience in a geographic region. It is usually based on some percentile of the range of charges for specific medical procedures.

rebating • the usually illegal practice of returning a part of the premium to the policyowner (except as a dividend) as a price-cutting sales inducement

reciprocal exchange • a type of insurer organized as an unincorporated pool of funds owned by policyowners and managed by an attorney-in-fact. The insured/insurer relationship is governed by a Subscribers Agreement or Power of Attorney in which policyholders assume liability as individuals and grant the attorney-in-fact the right to manage, for a fee, as an insurer, the funds contributed by policyholders and others to the unincorporated association.

reentry term insurance • a form of renewable term life insurance under which one renewal rate schedule is used if the insured can prove continuing insurability, and a higher schedule is used if the insured cannot prove continuing insurability.

refund annuity • a life annuity that promises to return in some manner a portion or all of the purchase price

rehabilitation • the process, overseen by an insurance commissioner, of restoring an insurance company to financial stability

rehabilitation benefit • a benefit under workers' compensation laws or disability income plans that provides rehabilitative services for disabled workers. Benefits may be given for medical rehabilitation and for vocational rehabilitation, including training, counseling, and job placement.

rehabilitation provision • a provision in a disability income contract that allows a person to receive reduced benefits during trial work periods in rehabilitative employment. The original benefit is resumed if the person is unable to perform the rehabilitative employment.

reimbursement basis • the method of paying long-term care insurance benefits that reimburses the insured for actual expenses incurred up to the specified policy limit

reinstatement provision • in life insurance, a clause giving the owner of a lapsed policy the right to reacquire the coverage under certain conditions

reinsurance • an arrangement in which an insurance company transfers to another insurance company some or all of the risks it has taken on by writing primary insurance

reinsurance facility • a system of providing auto insurance to high-risk drivers. Insurers write coverage but assign premiums to a statewide reinsurance pool. All insurers in the state share the pool's losses and expenses.

renewability • a feature frequently found in individual term life insurance that allows the policyowner to renew the policy for another period of protection, up to a stated point in time, without having to show evidence of insurability

replacement • replacing one life insurance policy with another. To prevent financial harm to the policyowner, agents and insurers must follow prescribed procedures.

replacement cost • the cost to repair or replace damaged or destroyed property with new property of like kind and quality, with no deduction for depreciation

representation • a statement in an insurance application that is substantially true to the best of the applicant's knowledge and belief. A false representation of a material fact is a misrepresentation.

reserve • an amount that must be maintained by an insurance company to meet definite future obligations. *See also* legal reserve, loss reserve, unearned premium reserve

residual-disability benefits • a provision for the replacement of lost earnings due to less-than-total disability. The benefit is based on a person's reduction in earnings rather than his or her physical condition.

residual market • specialty insurers and government programs that provide insurance for hard-to-insure drivers or property

respite care • occasional full-time care at home for a person who is receiving home health care. Coverage for such care under a long-term care insurance policy enables family members (or other persons) who are providing much of the home care to take a needed break.

restoration of benefits • a provision in long-term care insurance that provides for a restoration of used benefits after a period without claims

return-of-premium term insurance • a variation on traditional term life insurance that returns all premiums if the insured is still alive at the end of the policy term. A portion of the premium may also be returned if the policy is surrendered during the policy term after some minimum time period has elapsed.

return-of-premium option • a provision in disability insurance that provides for the return of some portion of premiums at specified intervals, such as 5 years or 10 years, if no claims have been made during that period

revocable beneficiary • a beneficiary that can be changed by the policyowner without the beneficiary's permission

rider • the term used in life insurance in place of the term endorsement

risk • the possibility of loss

risk and insurance survey form • a questionnaire or checklist used to identify the risks that confront a family or organization

risk avoidance • a risk control method that involves not incurring certain types of risks or eliminating existing risks

risk control • risk management techniques used to minimize losses through such activities as avoidance, loss prevention, loss reduction, and noninsurance transfers

risk financing • risk management techniques used to pay for losses through such means as risk retention in various ways and risk transfer, including insurance

risk identification • the first step in the risk management process, involving the careful and systematic discovery of all the risks that confront a household or organization

risk management • a systematic process for treating risks based on risk identification, risk measurement, choice and use of methods of treatment, and administration

risk retention • the risk financing method used when a person or organization keeps, or retains, the financial burden of any losses that occur rather than transfers them to an insurer or some other party

risk-tolerance level • the degree to which an individual is attracted to or averse to the possibility of loss

risk transfer • the loss financing method that shifts as much as possible of the financial consequences of a risk to some other party through insurance or a noninsurance transfer, such as a credit arrangement

robbery • the removal of property from one person by someone else who has either caused harm or threatened to cause harm to the person. It also includes situations in which property is taken in an unlawful act that a person has witnessed.

salary continuation plan • *See* sick-leave plan

savings bank life insurance • life insurance allowed to be written by mutual savings banks in Connecticut, Massachusetts, and New York on residents of, and persons regularly employed in, those three states

second surgical opinion • a cost-containment strategy under which covered persons are encouraged or required to obtain the opinion of another physician after certain categories of surgery have been recommended. If a second opinion is mandatory, benefits are reduced if the second opinion is not obtained. Benefits are usually provided for the cost of a third opinion if the opinions of the first two physicians are in disagreement.

second-to-die policy • *See* survivorship life policy

Sec. 79 plan • a group term life insurance plan that qualifies for favorable federal income tax treatment under Sec. 79 of the Internal Revenue Code

self-insurance • a formal program of risk retention usually characterized by factors necessary for a sound insurance enterprise, including funding based on actuarial calculations

self-insured retention • the initial portion of a loss under an umbrella policy that must be assumed by the policyowner when there is no underlying policy to cover the loss

settlement options • ways in which a life insurance policy's death proceeds can be taken, typically in cash, under an interest option, under a fixed-period or fixed-amount option, or under a life-income option

7-pay test • a test to determine if a particular life insurance contract is or is not a modified endowment contract. If the total premium paid into the policy in the first 7 years or in the 7 years following a material change in it exceeds the sum of the net level premiums that would be needed to pay up the policy in 7 years, the policy is a MEC.

shared benefit • long-term care insurance approach to benefits in which a husband and wife are insured under the same policy or with the same insurer and can access each other's unused benefits

shared market • *See* residual market

SHIP • *See* State Health Insurance Assistance Plan

shopper's guide • a state-approved booklet that must be provided to potential purchasers of certain types of insurance to enable them to better evaluate the benefits and costs of the insurance

short-term disability income plans • insured or uninsured disability income benefit with a typical duration of 6 months or less

sick-leave plan • an uninsured arrangement for an employer to replace lost income for a limited time period, often starting on the first day of disability

single-premium annuity • an annuity paid with a single premium rather than with installment payments

single-premium whole life policy • a form of whole life insurance that is fully paid-up upon the payment of a single premium

skilled-nursing care • daily nursing and rehabilitative care that can be performed only by or under the supervision of skilled medical personnel and that must be based on doctors' orders

skilled-nursing facility • *See* extended care facility

social adequacy • a principle emphasized by social insurance programs in which benefits are designed to provide a minimum floor of benefits to all beneficiaries, regardless of their economic status. Social adequacy also is reflected in the provision of disproportionately large benefits relative to contributions for some groups of beneficiaries, particularly lower-income groups.

social insurance • government-run or government-regulated insurance programs designed primarily to solve major social problems that affect a large portion of society. Distinguishing characteristics are compulsory employment-related coverage, partial or total employer financing, benefits prescribed by law, benefits as a matter of right, and emphasis on social adequacy.

Social Security • the term commonly used to identify the old-age, survivors, and disability (OASDI) program of the federal government

Social Security offset rider • a disability income policy amendment to provide additional disability income benefits payable when an individual is disabled but does not qualify for Social Security disability benefits

Social Security Statement • an annual statement automatically issued by the Social Security Administration that enables an employee to verify his or her contributions to the Social Security and Medicare programs. The statement also contains an estimate of benefits that will be available because of retirement, disability, or death.

specific rate • property rates for a particular building developed by applying a schedule that measures the relative quantity of fire hazard to the particular loss exposure

specific (schedule) rate • a rate that is created for one particular insured based on that insured's own risk characteristics

specified disease insurance • a type of medical expense coverage that provides benefits for persons who have certain specified diseases or medical events, such as cancer or heart attacks. The policy may pay for actual medical expenses or, more likely, pay a specified dollar amount, regardless of actual medical expenses and without regard to other coverages.

specified-perils policy • *See* named-perils policy

speculative risk • a risk with three possible outcomes: loss, no loss/no gain, or gain

split-dollar carve-out arrangement • a plan whereby life insurance is provided to selected employees under a split-dollar arrangement that is superimposed on a group life insurance plan for employees in general

split-dollar life insurance • a plan under which two parties, usually an employer and an insured employee, share the premium costs, death proceeds, and perhaps the cash value of a life insurance policy pursuant to a prearranged agreement

split limits • in auto liability insurance, separate limits that apply to any one person for bodily injury, to the aggregate for all bodily injury claims in an accident, and to property damage liability claims

staff adjuster • an employee of an insurance company whose full-time job is adjusting claims for that insurer

staff-model HMO • an HMO that owns its own facilities and hires its own physicians. It may also own hospitals, laboratories, or pharmacies, or it may contract for these services.

standard policy provisions laws • state laws that require life and health insurance policies to include certain provisions but allow insurers to select the actual wording as long as it is at least as favorable to the policyowner as the statutory language

State Health Insurance Assistance Plan (SHIP) • a state program that gets money from the federal government to give free health insurance counseling and assistance to people with Medicare

stated amount • an approach to valuing property in some property insurance policies. At the time of the loss, the insurer will pay the least of the stated amount, the actual cash value, or the cost to repair or replace the property.

static risk • in contrast with dynamic risk, a possibility of loss that exists even in the absence of changes in society. Hurricanes are an example.

step-rate annuity • an annuity for which future benefits increase, possibly at a compound annual rate. Step-rate annuities are often used in structured settlements.

stock insurance company • an insurance company owned by stockholders

STOLI • *See* stranger-originated life insurance

stop-loss limit • the maximum amount of out-of-pocket medical expenses that a covered person must pay in a given period (usually 1 year). After this limit is reached, future copayments and deductibles are waived for the remainder of the period.

straight life annuity • a life annuity that provides no guaranteed minimum number of benefit payments or refund of the purchase price. *Also known as* pure annuity.

stranger-originated life insurance (STOLI) • a life insurance purchasing in which speculators with no insurable interest in the insured's life initiate coverage on older persons and fund the premium payments with intentions of profiting upon the death of the insured

strict compliance rule • a legal principle that specifies that a written contract will normally be enforced on the basis of strict conformity with the terms contained in that contract

strict liability • liability under law, regardless of whether fault or negligence can be proved

structured settlement • an agreement to pay a specified set of periodic benefits in lieu of (or in addition to) a single lump-sum amount

subrogation • a process by which an insurer that has paid a claim takes over the legal rights of recovery its insured might have against a responsible third party

substandard annuity • an annuity whose benefit payments are larger per dollar of purchase price than those of a standard annuity because of the annuitant's impaired health

substandard market • *See* residual market

suicide provision • an optional life insurance policy provision that specifies that if the insured, whether sane or insane, commits suicide during the first 1 or 2 years of the policy, the insurer will be liable only for a return of the premium

supplemental plan • *See* buy-up plan

surety • the party to a surety bond who agrees to indemnify the obligee for damages because of the principal's failure to uphold an agreement

surety bond • an agreement in which a surety provides a guarantee of indemnity if a second party, the principal, fails to perform a specified act or fulfill an obligation to the obligee

surplus lines broker • a broker who is authorized to place insurance with nonadmitted insurers in certain circumstances. *Also known as* an excess lines broker.

surrender charge • a fee imposed on the owners of certain types of life insurance policies and annuities at the time they surrender their contracts

surrender cost index • a method of estimating the net cost of life insurance on a time-value-adjusted basis, assuming the policy will be surrendered at the end of a specified time period

survivorship (second-to-die) life policy • a type of life insurance policy that covers two or more persons in which the proceeds are payable on the death of the last person to die

target premium • the level renewal premium that the insurer suggests be paid for a universal life insurance policy

tax-qualified policy • a long-term care insurance contract that meets the requirements of the Health Insurance Portability and Accountability Act for favorable income tax treatment

temporary disability law • a law in a few states that requires employers to provide short-term disability income benefits to employees for non-work-related disabilities. Often referred to as a *nonoccupational disability law*.

temporary life annuity • an annuity whose benefit payments continue until the earlier of the death of a designated person or the end of a specified period of time

temporary medical insurance • short-term medical insurance that generally provides coverage for periods between 30 days and 1 year while a person is between medical expense plans

temporary substitute vehicle • in personal auto insurance, a vehicle not owned by the insured while it is used temporarily in place of a covered auto that is out of normal use because of breakdown, repair, servicing, loss, or destruction

term life insurance • a form of life insurance in which the death proceeds are payable in the event of the insured's death during a specified period and nothing is paid if the insured survives to the end of that period

theft • a broad term that encompasses robbery, burglary, shoplifting, and any other act of stealing

third-party administrator (TPA) • a firm that administers self-insurance programs for a fee

third-party-over suit • a suit that can result when the manufacturer of a product that injures one of the employer's workers is sued by the worker who, in turn, sues the employer for improper maintenance of the product

title insurance • protection for the purchaser of real estate against defects in title that occurred prior to the effective date of coverage but are discovered after the effective date

tort • a civil wrong other than breach of contract

transfer-for-value rule • a rule that specifies that, subject to certain exceptions, if a life insurance policy is transferred from one owner to another for valuable consideration, the death proceeds will be subject to federal income taxation

transfer tax • a tax on gifts, estates, or generation-skipping transfers

transition benefit • a disability income policy provision that continues benefits to survivors for a short period of time after the insured's death

treaty (automatic) reinsurance • reinsurance that is obligatory for the original or primary insurer and the reinsurer with respect to every loss exposure covered by the treaty or agreement

trip transit policy • a type of inland marine insurance policy that covers only the particular shipment specified in the policy

twisting • the illegal practice in life insurance of using misrepresentation to induce a policyowner, to his or her disadvantage, to replace a life insurance policy with a new one

umbrella liability policy • a personal or business liability policy that provides high limits for a broad range of liability situations. The policyowner is required to have underlying liability coverage of specified amounts. Claims not covered by the underlying insurance are subject to a self-insured retention.

unauthorized entity • an insurance company (or other organization, either real or fictitious) that has not gained approval to place insurance business from a department of insurance in the jurisdiction where it or a producer wants to sell insurance

uncertainty • a state of mind that arises from the presence of risk and is characterized by not being sure about something. Uncertainty often is characterized by worry and fear.

underinsured motorists coverage • an auto insurance coverage that enables an insured to collect from his or her own insurance company for bodily injury (and property damage in a few states) that is caused by a legally liable but underinsured driver. Covers the difference between the limit of the underinsured motorists coverage and the amount of the auto liability insurance carried by the underinsured driver.

underlying coverage • the primary policies and limits required by an insurer that provides umbrella liability insurance. If these policies and limits are not carried, the insured must absorb this amount of any claim before the umbrella policy pays.

underwriting • the selection (acceptance or rejection) and pricing of applicants for insurance

unearned premium reserve • in property and liability insurance, an insurer's liability for future claims or premium refunds, as measured by the proportion of the written premiums for those policies that the insurer has not yet earned by providing protection for the full policy period

unemployment insurance • joint federal and state programs to provide income benefits to unemployed workers who meet the specific program requirements. In most states, these programs are financed entirely by employer contributions.

unfair trade practices • insurance practices prohibited by a state unfair trade practices act, such as rebating, twisting, misappropriation, commingling of funds, and misleading advertising. Violators are subject to penalties that include suspension or revocation of licenses.

Uniform Premium Table I • an IRS table used to determine the amount of an employee's taxable income from an employer's group term life insurance premium payments

unilateral contract • a contract in which only one of the parties to it makes a binding promise that, if broken, gives rise to an action against that party for breach of contract

uninsured motorists coverage • an auto insurance coverage that enables an insured to collect from his or her own insurance company for bodily injury (and property damage in a few states) that is caused by a legally liable but uninsured driver

universal life insurance • a type of life insurance policy characterized by flexible premiums, a shift of some investment risk to the policyowner even though the policyowner is not allowed to direct the investment portfolio, the ability to withdraw part of the cash value, and a choice of death benefit designs

unsatisfied judgment fund • a fund in some states to compensate victims who are unable to collect a legal judgment that results from an auto accident. The maximum amount that can be received is usually equal to a state's financial responsibility limits.

use-and-file law • a rating law with which rates are filed with the insurance commissioner within a specified time after the rates are first used. The insurance commissioner may, however, disapprove the rates.

utilization review • the process of reviewing the appropriateness and quality of medical care provided to patients. It can be conducted on a prospective, concurrent, or retroactive basis.

valued contract • an insurance contract in which the amount of recovery does not depend on the financial amount of the loss but rather on the limit specified in the contract

valued policy law • a law in a few states that requires insurers to pay the full coverage amount when real property is totally destroyed by certain perils.

vanishing premium • whole life insurance approach designed so that if experience is favorable, the accumulation account eventually equals or exceeds the net single premium necessary to pay up the contract

variable annuity • an annuity with benefit payments that vary depending on the performance of selected blocks of the insurer's invested assets

variable life insurance • a type of life insurance in which the policyowner directs how the cash value will be invested and bears the investment risk, and in which the death benefit is linked to the investment performance of the policy

variable universal life insurance • a type of life insurance that combines the premium flexibility features of universal life insurance with the policyowner-directed investment aspects of variable life insurance

viatical settlement • the sale of a terminally ill insured's life insurance policy in exchange for a percentage of the face amount

viatical settlement provider • the party that purchases a policy from a viator under a viatical settlement purchase agreement

viatical settlement purchase agreement • contract arranging for the sale of a life insurance policy by a viator to a viatical settlement provider

viator • the policyowner who sells a life insurance policy to a third party

vicarious liability • imputed liability to, for example, owners of vehicles

vision care expense benefits • benefits for vision care expenses that are not usually covered under other medical expense plans. Benefits are provided for the cost of eye examinations and eyeglasses or contact lenses.

void contract • a contract that is entirely without legal effect and, therefore, unenforceable by either party. In essence, a void contract never was a contract.

voidable contract • a contract that can be affirmed or rejected at the option of one of the parties but is binding on the other party

voluntary benefits • a plan offered to employees under which they may purchase insurance coverages with premiums paid through payroll deductions. The employer does not share in the premium cost.

voluntary compensation and employers liability coverage endorsement • an insurance policy endorsement that obligates the insurance company to pay an amount equal to what is available under a state's workers' compensation law to employees who are not covered under the law

waiting period (elimination period) • a period of time that an employee must be disabled before benefits commence under an employee benefit plan, such as disability income insurance, Social Security, workers' compensation insurance, and long-term care insurance

waiver-of-premium rider • a rider under which, if the insured becomes totally disabled, the insurer will waive the premiums on the policy during the continuance of the disability. It is commonly used in life and health insurance.

warranty • a statement that becomes a part of an insurance contract and that must be strictly complied with. A warranty, if false, makes the policy voidable, even if the false statement is not material.

watercraft insurance • insurance policies to provide liability, physical damage, and medical payments coverage for boat owners

whole life annuity • *See* life annuity

whole life insurance • a form of life insurance that provides death benefits upon the death of the insured, no matter when that occurs, if the policy is kept in force by the policyowner

withdrawal • the right, in some life insurance policies, to take part of the cash value without its being treated as a loan. It is commonly found in forms of universal life insurance.

workers' compensation insurance • insurance under which the insurer agrees to pay all compensation required by workers' compensation laws

workers' compensation law • a type of law enacted in all states under which employers are required to provide benefits to employees for losses that result from work-related accidents or diseases. Benefits include medical care, disability income, income for survivors, and rehabilitative services.

yacht policy • a package policy that provides liability and physical damage coverage for large boats

yearly renewable term insurance • a plan that provides a level amount of insurance for 1 year, renewable for a stated number of years, with the premium at each renewal date rising at an increasing rate that reflects the rise in the mortality rate over time

C

D